BASEBALLHQ.COM'S **2017**

MINOR LEAGUE
BASEBALL
ANALYST

ROB GORDON AND JEREMY DELONEY | BRENT HERSHEY, EDITOR | 12TH EDITION

TRIUMPH
BOOKS

This book is available in quantity at special discounts for your group or organization. For further information, contact:

Triumph Books LLC
814 North Franklin Street
Chicago, Illinois 60610
(312) 337-0747
www.triumphbooks.com

Printed in U.S.A.
ISBN: 978-1-62937-310-2

Data provided by TheBaseballCube.com and Baseball Info Solutions

Cover design by Brent Hershey
Front cover photograph by Jonathan Dyer/USA TODAY Sports Images

Acknowledgments

Jeremy Deloney:

Now in my eighth year of the *Minor League Baseball Analyst*, I continue to find enjoyment in the subtleties of writing and proofing. I learn so much from my fellow writers with their thoughts and ideas. For this old-timer, I like to be challenged by new ways of looking at baseball.

My wife, Amy, continues to be the main source of my inspiration. Her incredibly selfless nature allows me to spend an inordinate amount of time in the fall and winter on this book. She is an unbelievable wife, mother, and friend. She deserves all of the thanks I could possibly give. Amy makes me a better "me" and she continues to give me confidence and love. She is a true gift from the man upstairs.

My three children—Owen, Ethan, Madeline—continue to make me a proud father. All of them have very appealing attributes and qualities. In fact, I would rate all three of them as 10A, meaning they are projected to become Hall of Famers. They are intelligent, witty, and kind-hearted. What more could a father ask for?

My work ethic was molded by my parents, Bill and Nancy. They modeled the appropriate behaviors and attitudes, of which I've adopted as my own.

My brothers—BJ and Andy—are instrumental as well. Despite our competitive nature, we remain brothers and friends. Of course, for my kind words, they should spring for the beer during our annual minor league sojourn.

I also remain grateful for the outstanding staff at BaseballHQ, especially Brent Hershey. All are great people. All are great writers and analysts. Thank you.

Rob Gordon:

In 2003 Ron Shandler and Deric McKamey gave me the opportunity to do something I always wanted to do—write about baseball. Ron and Deric showed me the ropes, and explained what scouts look for. Deric's total recall of the most obscure minor league players still amazes me. They have both moved on to bigger and better things, but their imprint on the structure of this book lives on.

Jeremy and I are now in our eighth edition of the *Minor League Baseball Analyst* and I continue to be impressed by his comprehensive and astute knowledge of the minor leagues. Over the past couple of years we have gotten invaluable help from the rest of the BaseballHQ minor league team: Brent Hershey, Chris Blessing, and Alec Dopp. I would especially like to thank Brent who has been the glue that holds this project together.

Many other baseball people provided invaluable support and encouragement over the years. They include Jeff Barton, Jim Callis, John Sickels, Ray Murphy, Rick Wilton, Patrick Davitt, Todd Zola, Jason Grey, Joe Sheehan, Jeff Erickson, Kimball Crossley, Steve Moyer, Phil Hertz, Jock Thompson and Doug Dennis among others.

Someday someone will write a story about Baseball Unlimited. Until then I'll just have to thank the boys—Michael Hartman, Kegan Hartman, Steve Hartman, Michael Cooney, Bob Hathaway, Doug Hathaway, Raj Patel, Derald Cook, Dave Dannemiller, Ted Maizes, Randy Jones, Duncan Hathaway, and John Mundelius. Welcome back Stosh!

My oldest son Bobby had a blast playing JV/varsity baseball for Dearborn High and the coaches—Kyle Jenks, Eric Jenks, and Matt McKay did a great job with the boys, as did his travel baseball coaches Rob Stockman, John Schneider, and Rob Septor. Also a big thank you to the guys at Michigan Strategy Baseball—Craig Cotter, Rob Fay, and Ryan Gilbert.

I would especially like to thank my family. My two boys—Bobby and Jimmy—make the sky bluer, the sun brighter, and the crack of the bat all the more sweet. My sister Susan Arntson helped raise me and tried to keep me out of trouble—mostly. Thanks to the Arntson clan—Jeff, Rachel, Josh, Marissa, and Jake. My mother Sandra Gordon took me on an annual birthday trip to see the Cubs play (Cubs Win!) and my father Robert W. Gordon III has shared my passion for the game of baseball. Finally, a huge thank you to my amazing and beautiful wife Paula—stay strong!

TABLE OF CONTENTS

Translation

by Brent Hershey

The task of covering the baseball prospect stratosphere is, at its essence, about translation. Strip away all the detailed scouting terms (two-plane break, arm bar, etc.) and the plethora of statistics on minor leaguers that are now available, and it boils down to one thing: How will Player X perform in the major leagues?

Too simplistic? Maybe. As prospect coverage has exploded over the past decade-plus since the first *Minor League Baseball Analyst* (MLBA) volume appeared in 2006, the details mentioned above have been important pieces of information that have helped us make projections about the future. And make no mistake—you'll find both detailed descriptions and plenty of numbers in this book. They all meld to add color and dimension to a once-flat picture of a prospect. It's our view that this added detail is a good thing.

How do we gain that level of detail? The founding author of the MLBA, Deric McKamey, stressed the importance of seeing prospects in person, doing their thing at the ballpark. Deric has since moved on (he's now a scout for the St. Louis Cardinals), but this tradition of "getting eyes on" as many players as possible throughout the season is a tenet of our MLBA coverage. It's one reason we expanded our staff, from primary authors Rob Gordon and Jeremy Deloney, who took the reins from McKamey seven years ago, to include myself, Chris Blessing, and Alec Dopp. The team, with our different locations around the country—as well as differing opinions, experiences, backgrounds, and contacts—continues to make the MLBA a rich resource for fantasy players and prospect hounds alike.

But all that collected information must aid us in the translation of what each individual player profiled in this book will become, once he dons an MLB uniform. Our guiding principle with the MLBA each year—our Mission Statement, if you will—is to provide readers with our best projection of a player outcome. In the end, we seek an accurate translation more than anything else.

But there is another translation going on in these pages that is perhaps more subtle, but just as—if not more—important. And that's the translation that the MLBA provides for fantasy baseball players.

Undoubtedly, one benefit of the increase in minor-league coverage in the past decade-plus is that prospect information is everywhere. One can find an avalanche of online opinions, observations, in-person scouting reports, player interviews, and player videos with a rudimentary Google search. This ease of accessibility means that one can easily find information on players as diverse as a top prospect in Triple-A, to a Latin American teenager in the Gulf Coast League—and everyone in between. At your fingertips, indeed.

And as the general prospect coverage market has developed (or exploded, depending on your point of view), sites with a minor-league bent have become specialized. There are resources that focus on just one particular minor league, or sites that just hone in on one organization. These forays have been very valuable, since their narrower emphasis allows them to examine prospects at a level of detail that broader services often can't cover. So when looking for information on any particular player, these specialized sites can provide helpful background and context that add depth to a player's stat line.

But often, there's one thing missing for the fantasy player. What so few of these information services provide consistently is an application suited directly to fantasy baseball. The thirst for prospect information is partially—if not wholly—fueled by readers looking to get a leg up on their fantasy competitors. The goal: to acquire information about minor league players to either A) select them as farm-system players in a keeper/dynasty league, betting that these prospects strengthen one's fantasy team, or B) to have all the information necessary (or know where to find it) to inform a decision to claim, or pass on, a player when he gets called up in mid-season. At the risk of overstating the influence of our own industry, fantasy baseball has contributed to the proliferation of MLB prospect information available to the general public. But while the information is easily available, its fantasy application is sometimes non-existent.

In most cases, readers are left to take general prospect reports and translate them into their own fantasy baseball realm. There are intricacies in fantasy—how small or large depends on your own preferred format—that are often unaccounted for when consuming other reports. A defining feature of the book you have in your hands is that the *Minor League Baseball Analyst* (as well as all of our prospect coverage at BaseballHQ.com) provides this translation to fantasy baseball as a part of its coverage. The translation is built in, an integral part of all our presentation of prospect material. We are all fantasy baseball players, and the evaluations herein reflect that point of view.

In a sense, the MLBA cuts out the middleman, and brings the evaluations, rankings, and commentary direct to you, with potential fantasy impact our first—and only—goal.

We've been doing this for a while. In the summer of 2016, BaseballHQ.com celebrated its 20th anniversary. Our sister publication, Ron Shandler's Baseball Forecaster, just published its 31st edition. Given our track record, you can trust the authors and viewpoints in the pages that follow. We know fantasy baseball, and that starting point engulfs our prospect coverage.

Of course, sometimes this translation doesn't vary much from traditional sites. Yoan Moncada? Near the top of general baseball prospect lists due to his explosive bat speed, premium athleticism, and emerging power. He's near the top of our HQ100 prospect list, too, for much of the same reasons. Moncada's impact will be felt statistically, as well as on the field, once he takes that final step into the major leagues for good.

But other times, our rankings and evaluations will look different than other lists. Given the unique qualifications of catchers, for instance, we will likely not be as high on a defense-first catching prospect as others (or, on the flip side, may rank a sure-fire offensive catcher higher due to the impact he could have on a fantasy roster, given the catching pool). You can make similar determinations on other kinds of players—SB sources, for one, given the league-wide decline in thefts.

In addition, given the advantage a fantasy owner receives when a high-impact talent develops and translates well, some of our rankings may skew a bit towards raw tools, especially at the lower levels of the minors (where players are still under development). Sure, these players have risk attached. But dreaming on what players might become stars is a long-standing prospect watchers activity. And with the results when one does "hit" on a player (Gary Sanchez, we're looking at you), it's something that we as fantasy prospect evaluators readily embrace as well.

So if the lists, rankings and evaluations in the MLBA look a bit different—that's because they are. We're attempting to do the translation for you, so that you can build the strongest possible fantasy team. We embrace being slightly different, and it is a good thing. We hope you agree.

Most importantly, these translations (prospect-to-MLB player; MLB prospect-to-fantasy prospect) are continually evolving. What is so exciting about scouting, writing, and evaluating prospects is that each season—even each month, or each game—is but one data point (or one opinion) in a larger story of each individual player.

As such, our process of identifying which prospects will benefit your fantasy team the most is in constant motion. We learn from the past—about which players we were "right" on, and which ones we weren't—and attempt to incorporate these lessons into our future. And thus, we thank you for each of your input (by way of feedback) of our process in the past, and extend the invitation for continued discussions and feedback as we head into the future.

These prospects are still 17- to 24-year-old human beings that are tasked with completing (and repeating) athletic actions in an ever-changing environment, so anything can (and will) happen as they move towards their personal goals. We at the *Minor League Baseball Analyst* will strive to provide the best projection we can of their future, using all the data and information we have at our disposal.

We're glad you're along for the ride.

•

Long-time readers of the *Minor League Baseball Analyst* will no doubt recognize most of the elements of the pages that follow in this 12th Edition. Though in 2017, we have added a couple twists that highlight our strengths, and provide you the reader with the easiest way to access all of what the MLBA has to offer.

The Insights section provides some narrative details and tools you can use as you prepare for getting the most out of your farm system and the rookies that will emerge during the 2017 baseball season. All the essays are designed to help you assemble your teams, as well as give you some food for thought on the prospect landscape, delving into prospect "readiness"; the top international players; reviews of the 2016 Arizona Fall League, the Rule 5 Draft, and the First Year Player Draft; and a preview of the 2017 college baseball season. No doubt many of these players mentioned in the essays will soon be fantasy cornerstones. Time to get on board.

Up next is the HQ100—our signature list of the top 100 fantasy baseball prospects for 2017. The HQ100 is a compilation of six individual lists (Jeremy Deloney, Rob Gordon, Chris Blessing, Alec Dopp, Brent Hershey, as well as BaseballHQ.com callups writer Nick Richards). This list is ranked by overall fantasy value, in an attempt to balance raw skill level, level of polish/refinement, risk in terms of age/level, and overall potential impact value. And if 100 players isn't enough, Dopp suggests 10 more "Sleepers" just outside the HQ100, young players who could make the jump to the list in 2018.

While the HQ100 is a collaborative exercise, the player profiles—including the skills grades, commentaries and player ratings—are the primary work of one analyst. Assignments are divided up by organization, so that our analysts get to know an MLB team's system from top to bottom. The roster is Deloney (all the clubs in the AL East and AL West, along with CHW, KC, MIN, DET, SF); Gordon (MIA, PIT, STL, CHC, LA, COL); Blessing (ATL, NYM, CIN, ARI, SD); Dopp (MIL, CLE); and Hershey (PHI, WAS). Given our emphasis on seeing players in person— and the daunting task when the book covers 1000+ players—we did share information and insights with each other, tapping the strength of our team. In addition, each writer filled in the gaps with the various scouting and front-office contacts.

As noted at the beginning of the Batters and Pitchers sections, our Potential Ratings have two parts. The first is on upside, graded on a 10-1 scale, with 10 being Hall of Fame potential; 1 is minor league roster filler. A "6" (platoon MLBer) is the lowest grade you'll find in the book, as these are the least likely players to have an impact on your fantasy team.

But potential and actualization are two different things, and the A-E letter grades attempt to assess the likelihood of reaching that potential. It's a proxy for risk, which may or may not include age, ability and/or willingness to improve, current grasp of fundamental skills (fastball command, strikezone judgement), experience, and success in the high minors, among other factors.

In the end, these Potential Ratings are carefully considered by the author, and there is no one "correct" grade. One can make the argument that in a sense, an 8B player can at the same time be a 9D—higher ceiling, but much less likely to reach it. It is up to the author to decide which rating will give the clearest picture of this prospect at this point in time. The most valuable information to fantasy players cannot be encapsulated in one rating, but in the combination of skills grades, statistics, biographical information and commentary that the MLBA provides.

Though the player profiles make up the bulk of the book, don't miss the tools that follow: the Major League Equivalencies; the Organization Grades; the Top Prospects by organization, by position, and by specific skills; the Top 75 prospects for 2017 only; an archive of our Top 100 lists; the glossary and a list of minor league affiliates.

Whew … there's a lot of information in these pages. And while we're sure that the *Minor League Baseball Analyst* meets all your fantasy baseball prospect needs, please let us know how we can continue to improve. We can be reached via email at support@baseballhq.com.

But for now, dig in. Afterwards, your fantasy farm system might never be deeper.

The Question of Prospect Readiness

by Chris Blessing

Show of hands: How many fantasy owners relied on a rookie starting pitcher last season? Did it work out?

Hopefully, you pinned your hopes on Michael Fulmer and/or Junior Guerra. Both pitchers performed like veterans. Unlike, say, Aaron Blair and/or Jose Berrios, who each was ranked in the HQ100 coming into the season, but whose lackluster performance hurt plenty of fantasy teams in 2016. While projection services, such as BaseballHQ.com and the *Baseball Forecaster*, are great tools to project veteran performance, no metric can project how a rookie pitcher responds to the challenge of MLB hitters.

Last June, BaseballHQ.com co-General Manager and *Minor League Baseball Analyst* editor Brent Hershey challenged the BHQ staff to ponder prospect "readiness." Specifically, he wanted us to discuss the possiblity of creating a "readiness" metric similar to the grading scale we use here in the *Minor League Baseball Analyst* and in the BHQ Organization Report player bios. The responses were varied. An excerpt from one of my responses:

> *Without our scouting writers putting eyes on guys, we can't do our due diligence to put together an effective measure to a pitcher's readiness. We'd have a better shot at hitters, but it would still be poor. I don't see how we can come up with a measurement without first person quantitative research and extensive qualitative research.*

I believe a readiness metric could be done. My friend Mike Newman and I discussed the validity of creating such a metric at RotoScouting.com several years ago. We concluded that creating a reliable metric would be too staff- and time-intensive for the site to handle. Fast-forward two years, and finding qualified individuals to do the quantitative research is a challenge. As you may know, the prospect media has taken a hit with many qualified evaluators either going to work for organizations or quitting the industry entirely. Without quality researchers, a scouting-based metric is likely to fail.

This doesn't mean there isn't help out there for fantasy owners. Take the Zach Eflin "Callups" blurb published by BaseballHQ.com in June by Nick Richards. The blurb noted Eflin's minor league success—through 11 Triple-A games, Eflin pitched to a 2.90 ERA, with a 5.0 Cmd and .199 opp BA. But Nick also noted his success in the majors would depend on improving his breaking ball. In 11 MLB starts, Eflin never flashed an out pitch, and his K/9 ratio ended up at just over 4. A young MLB starter cannot maintain success without eliciting swing and misses; Nick's comments were spot on. Eflin's secondary pitches need to improve before getting MLB hitters out consistently.

But back to the rookie starter who had the most success this season: AL Rookie of the Year Michael Fulmer. In the "Top 75 Impact Prospects for 2016" ranking in last year's *Forecaster*, we ranked Fulmer 22nd among rookie-qualified pitchers, 54th overall. Hindsight being 20/20, we should have ranked him first. How did we miss so big on Michael Fulmer? Here is my rationale.

Want to quickly enrage a fan base? Call their recently selected first-round pick a future mid-rotation starter. I identified Fulmer as such in a scouting report for Bullpen Banter in 2012. Why is it relevant revisiting Fulmer's 2012 projection today? Because many prospect evaluators labeled his ceiling as such going into the season. This may have caused evaluators and fantasy writers to sleep on Fulmer.

The stigma associated with projecting a prospect as a mid-rotation starter is ridiculous. There are so few top-line pitching available to fantasy owners. Owners, like MLB General Managers, covet mid-rotation starters. They don't dominate hitters like frontline starters, but they do contribute solid returns. Since his debut, Fulmer's performance lines up more with a frontline starter than the mid-rotation starter many projected. This could be an anomaly or the scouting community collectively missed something vital about Fulmer, like the dominance of his changeup and his advanced command.

The 19-year-old Fulmer I scouted lived around the strike zone. Even his command was beyond his level and years. Fulmer is the rare prospect where his stuff needed to catch up to his control and command. By the time he debuted, hitting the catcher's mitt was old habit.

Solid command enabled Fulmer to succeed quickly in the major leagues. A pitcher sporting solid-or-better command in the minors is more likely to succeed initially in the big leagues than a pitcher relying on stuff to get big league hitters out, regardless of minor league success. It's something to keep in mind as you read the pitcher profiles in this book.

But what about the hitters?

Is (insert name) ready to contribute? I'm asked this question almost daily during the baseball season. Whether injuries have devastated a lineup or the product you've drafted is hard to stomach, fantasy owners are always looking for a jolt of electricity to revive their season.

Truthfully, most hitting prospects aren't ready for the big leagues. Fundamentally, most aren't ready to transition to a major league batter's box yet. Some were never given the chance to develop early in their careers. Why? Organizations saw something they craved and wanted to push it. Like a prospect with big power but a two-part swing, or an 80-grade defender at short with no plate discipline. To understand hitter readiness, we must study the development path.

Former Atlanta Braves catching prospect Christian Bethancourt was a mainstay on prospect lists from 2012 through 2015. I scouted Bethancourt as an 18- and 19-year-old with Single-A Rome in the Braves organization. Now 25 and a member of the San Diego Padres organization, he's being groomed for a catcher/pitcher/outfield hybrid utility player (say what?). Still several years away from his prime, Bethancourt faces an uphill battle to reach his full potential. Despite phenomenal hand/eye coordination, Bethancourt doesn't have the plate discipline needed to be an everyday performer. Let's go back to the point in development where things went wrong.

Bethancourt limped through his full season with Rome in 2010. His offensive skills were incredibly raw, but his hand/eye coordination allowed him to slash .251/.276/.331. Unless a pitcher buried a breaking ball in the dirt, Bethancourt would put bat to ball, usually resulting in weak contact. Bethancourt even struggled defensively. He was raw behind home plate, but everyone was consumed with his 80-grade arm.

Bethancourt looked better his second go-around in Rome in 2011. He was taking pitches, laying off pitches he couldn't drive and barreling fastballs up the middle for base hits. His defense even improved. After slashing .303/.323/.385 in 54 games, Atlanta did the unthinkable and promoted Bethancourt to High-A Lynchburg, where his approach reverted back to 2010. He slashed .271/.277/.325 with Lynchburg and .243/.275/.291 the next season with Double-A Mississippi. Repeating Double-A in 2013, Bethancourt fared better, but still struggled to lay off unhittable pitches. Then, the Braves called Bethancourt up. He has struggled mightily with the bat since making his debut in 2013. Remarkably, he has walked only 18 times in 482 plate appearances (4%). Unless his hits find holes, he's never on base enough to factor in fantasy.

One player that didn't have many flaws was Twins outfielder Byron Buxton. When I wrote my Buxton scouting report in 2015, I anticipated his big league debut to come sometime during the 2016 season. He wasn't ready when the Twins called him up in June 2015 and it showed. For starters, Buxton only appeared in 31 games the previous season and was dusting off some rust from the inactivity. He also struggled identifying spins on off-speed pitches. After some injuries to the big league outfielder and a great Double-A series in front of the visiting Twins front office, Buxton packed his bags for the Twin Cities with only 240 AA at-bats under his belt.

His debut was awful. He slashed a miserable .209/.250/.326. MLB struggles continued until a call up in September 2016. In his final 29 games, Buxton slashed .287/.357/.653 and hit 9 HR. Can he keep it going? Skeptics worry the 34% strikeout rate may be a sign for more struggles to come for the Twins outfielder.

A lack of baseball maturity, not a skill deficiency, led to Buxton's struggles. Recently, we've been blessed by the debuts of Kris Bryant, Carlos Correa and Francisco Lindor, who each debuted hitting close to All-Star levels. However, most hitting prospects struggle, even elite guys like Buxton. Hopefully, you didn't sell low on the 23-year-old at his lowest point.

What does this all mean? As a *MLBA* reader, you have this incredible tool of experienced prospect writers compiling player reports for fantasy consumption. Our team has experienced eyes at the ballpark considering the risks of prospect ownership first-hand. J.P. Crawford may be the top all-around SS prospect; but is he the best fantasy option? Maybe it's Dansby Swanson, Brendan Rodgers, Amed Rosario or Gleyber Torres. That's what we're here for.

In sum, be leery of quick minor league promotions. Quick promotions usually lead to unresolved issues. Once a prospect debuts in the major leagues, it is hard to correct swing deficiencies.

One final shortcut: stay clear of players already displaying poor walk rates or high strikeout rates in the minors, especially if organizations won't allow these prospects to correct issues against lesser competition. Your final fantasy standings might depend on it.

Top 20 International Prospects for 2017

by Jeremy Deloney

Over the last few years, MLB has implemented changes (with more to come in the new Collective Bargaining Agreement) to the process of signing of international players. There will not be an international draft for now, but MLB teams have been scouring the globe to help add talent to their clubs. And the astute fantasy owners should be following suit.

Listed below are various international prospects who inked contracts during the international signing period in 2016 or players who could make the jump to the U.S. in the next two seasons. Because of the uncertainty of defections and eligibility, some top Cuban prospects may not be profiled below.

Please note that some players eligible for this list who have already signed contracts with major league organizations have player boxes in this book. For the purposes of space, those players aren't profiled here. Such prospects include: Kevin Maitan (SS, ATL), Lazaro Armenteros (OF, OAK), Yanio Perez (INF, TEX), Adrian Morejon (LHP, SD), Vladimir Gutierrez (RHP, CIN), Alfredo Rodriguez (SS, CIN), and Jorge Ona (OF, SD).

In alphabetical order:

Luis Almanzar (SS, SD)
The 17-year-old has a clean, quick right-handed stroke and likes to use the entire field in his professional and mature approach. Though he doesn't exhibit much over-the-wall pop now, he has natural strength and should develop at least average power. Almanzar has the talent to stick at shortstop, though could slide over to either 2B or 3B given his nimble footwork and range. He also runs quite well.
Signing bonus/status: Signed for $4 million
MLB Debut: 2022

Yasal Antuna (SS, WAS)
The 17-year-old switch-hitter may not be the most athletic infielder in this international class, but he is polished for his age. He brings a mature approach to the plate and uses a clean, short stroke to make easy contact. By spraying the ball to all fields, he should hit for a nice BA, but it may take him a while to reach his power potential, however, as he has a level swing path and current lack of strength. He doesn't run particularly well and may end up at 3B where his strong arm would be an asset.
Signing bonus/status: Signed for $3.9 million
MLB Debut: 2022

Gabriel Arias (SS, SD)
Because of his lean, projectable frame, it wouldn't be a surprise to see the 16-year-old moved to 3B in short order. He has the potential to add significant strength and he could develop into a power hitter in the future. He offers a clean swing and a level bat path while showing the ability to put bat to ball. Arias runs well, though is expected to slow down as he grows. Defensively, he has a cannon for an arm and ranges well to both sides. He could use improvement with his footwork and release, but the tools are there for him to eventually become an above average defender.
Signing bonus/status: Signed for $1.9 million
MLB Debut: 2023

Juan Contreras (RHP, ATL)
The pitching depth was thin in this international class, but the 17-year-old stood out for his pure arm strength and speed. He's more of a thrower than pitcher at this point and he exhibits crude mechanics. However, Contreras could eventually register velocity in the high-90s once he cleans up his delivery and arm action. He currently throws in the 89-94 mph range and he throws downhill from his over-the-top release. He needs to significantly improve his control as well as his raw secondary offerings. Because of his arm speed, his change-up has plus potential.
Signing bonus/status: Signed for $1.2 million
MLB Debut: 2023

Jose Miguel Fernandez (2B, Cuba)
As a 28-year-old, Fernandez has a mature game with a high floor, but lacks the upside and electricity of other international signees. The left-handed hitter certainly knows how to put the bat on the ball as he rarely strikes out and gets on base at a healthy clip. The rest of his game is rather uninspiring. He doesn't hit for much power, his speed is fringe-average at best, and his defense is suspect. Despite the negativity, he is a polished hitter who has—and will—hit for a high BA. He doesn't hit many HR, but he hits hard line drives to the gaps.
Signing bonus/status: Defected from Cuba; declared a free agent
MLB Debut: 2018

David Garcia (C, TEX)
The 16-year-old switch-hitter has the skill set to develop into a solid all-around catcher. Garcia is already a sound defender with fundamental skills. He receives the ball well and has agility and mobility to block balls. His clean footwork helps his quick release and the hope is he adds more strength to his throwing. As a hitter, the power potential is fringy at best, but he understands the strike zone and has a compact stroke to make easy contact.
Signing bonus/status: Signed for $800,000
MLB Debut: 2023

Jose Adolis Garcia (OF, Cuba)
The 24-year-old has an impressive tools arsenal; he is a good hitter, but tends to be a free swinger who rarely walks. His pitch recognition needs improvement, but he has plus bat speed and average power from the right side. He is very fast, with the range and instincts to play CF. His incredible arm strength is a definite asset; he could play RF if needed. Though he may not become a superstar, he has everyday player skills.
Signing bonus/status: Defected from Cuba; declared a free agent
MLB Debut: 2018

Luis Garcia (SS, WAS)
The strength in the July international class was the shortstop position and the 16-year-old is one of the best. He is extremely athletic and has a great chance to stick at the position over the long-term. Garcia has quick, clean hands and above average range to both sides. As a hitter, he makes easy contact with a fast bat and should be able to hit for more power as he grows in his lean frame. His overall skill set is enhanced by his instincts and poise.
Signing bonus/status: Signed for $1.3 million
MLB Debut: 2023

Victor Garcia (OF, STL)
Already blessed with a strong, powerful frame, the 17-year-old may have the best power potential of any international signee. He stands 6-2, 225, and swings a very fast bat. He can hit the ball a long way to all fields and he runs well underway. Contact is the big question—his long stroke leads to high strikeout totals and his uppercut can be exploited. There is also concern about his body as he gets older. Garcia may eventually have to move to 1B, but he should be able to showcase enough power to make it worthwhile.
Signing bonus/status: Signed for $1.5 million
MLB Debut: 2023

Lourdes Gurriel (INF/OF, TOR)
The 23-year-old defected with his brother Yulieski from Cuba, and signed with the Blue Jays in November 2016. Much like other Cubans, his stint in the minors could be a short one. He is a bit of a free-swinger at present, though has the tools to be a middle-of-the-order run producer. He offers above average pop from the right side and has enough athleticism to be an asset on the bases as well as in the middle of the diamond. He could get to the majors in short order.
Signing bonus/status: Signed for 7 years, $22 million
MLB Debut: 2018

Yadiel Hernandez (OF, WAS)
Though the 29-year-old was signed to a meager bonus in September, he has a very good chance to reach the majors at some point in 2017. He doesn't stand out for his power or speed, but is a very good hitter who works counts, gets on base, and makes easy contact with a sweet, compact stroke. Hernandez can play CF with good jumps and routes, but he profiles better in LF or RF due to his strong arm. A relatively unheralded signing, he could be a big asset for the Nationals.
Signing bonus/status: Signed for $200,000
MLB Debut: 2017

Freudis Nova (SS, HOU)
Nova is a natural shortstop who offers significant upside. He brings all five tools and has as much athleticism as any 2016 international signee. The 16-year-old has exceptional bat speed, yet recognizes pitches well and should hit for both BA and power. His hitting instincts are still raw, however, and it will take time to develop his hand-eye coordination. As a defender, he is very quick, owns plus range, and has a strong arm.
Signing bonus/status: Signed for $1.2 million
MLB Debut: 2023

Tirso Ornelas (OF, SD)
The 16-year-old is a pure lefthanded hitter who should be able to hit for BA. He features a clean stroke and average bat speed. Blessed with keen hand-eye coordination, Ornelas puts bat to ball and can use the entire field. Questions remain about his power potential, but he should hit loads of doubles due to his level swing path. He isn't fleet afoot and the lack of speed will likely limit him to an outfield corner. His glovework is below average currently, but he does exhibit average arm strength.
Signing bonus/status: Signed for $1.5 million
MLB Debut: 2023

Shohei Otani (RHP/DH, Japan)

Without question, the 22-year-old is the best player not currently affiliated with MLB. He is a unique talent in that he is a top pitcher and hitter. As a pitcher, Otani fires the ball into the high-90s and can reach triple digits. His secondary offerings are also top-notch, including a splitter and knockout curveball. He throws consistent strikes and is adept at setting hitters up. There isn't much negative to say about any part of his game. As a hitter, he hits for plus power to all fields and he exhibits advanced plate discipline. He will command a huge contract when he is posted by Nippon.
Signing bonus/status: Will likely be posted after 2017 season
MLB Debut: 2018

Johan Oviedo (RHP, STL)

The 18-year-old has already pitched with the Cardinals affiliate in the Dominican Summer League and he was praised for his plus arm strength and control. Oviedo has a large pitcher's frame at 6'5" 230 pounds, and he can touch 98 mph with his fastball. He complements the heater with a swing-and-miss curveball, though his change-up needs plenty of work. There are a lot of moving parts in his delivery, but the Cardinals have a lot to work with in his arm speed. He does throw with maximum effort and he may best profile as a power reliever.
Signing bonus/status: Signed for $1.9 million
MLB Debut: 2023

Cionel Perez (LHP, HOU)

The Astros originally signed Perez for a $5 million bonus in October after he defected from Cuba, but the club voided the deal due to a medical concern. They later agreed to a $2 million bonus in December. The 20-year-old has the potential to become a mid-rotation starter once he reaches his peak and his advanced skills could get him to the majors quickly. He isn't very big (5'10"), but he can fire his fastball into the 90-95 mph range and has the potential to throw harder. He uses two breaking balls in his hard slider and average curveball while his change-up is currently below average.
Signing bonus/status: Signed for $2 million
MLB Debut: 2018

Jeisson Rosario (OF, SD)

Though the 17-year-old may not have one overwhelming tool, he does everything well and exhibits no significant weakness. Rosario thrives on his instincts and feel for the game. He offers a short stroke from the left side and hits the ball hard to all fields. Because of his line drive approach, he may never hit for much power. However, he makes loud contact to the gaps and has the speed to leg out doubles and triples. He is an athletic defender who can play all outfield positions, though a corner position is likely in the cards as his range may be a bit short for CF.
Signing bonus/status: Signed for $1.85 million
MLB Debut: 2022

Norge Ruiz (RHP, OAK)

The durable 22-year-old, signed in December, could make an impact in the majors at some point in 2017 or 2018. Though he's not a flamethrower, his deep arsenal is enhanced by his ability to vary his arm slots and speeds. He establishes the plate with a low-90s sinker and he induces a high amount of groundballs. His other pitches include a slider, plus change-up, splitter, and cutter. Ruiz has been tough to make hard contact against and should become a mid-rotation starter very quickly.
Signing bonus/status: Signed for $2 million
MLB Debut: 2018

Jose Sanchez (SS, WAS)

The 16-year-old is a true shortstop prospect who will likely remain at the position over the long-term. Sanchez is extremely lean presently, but should be able to add good weight to his frame and learn to make more solid contact. His best attributes are on the defensive side where he has exceptional range and quick, clean hands. He offers fluid actions and exhibits sound instincts. Sanchez has sufficient bat speed and possesses plate discipline that allows him to get on base consistently. He makes excellent contact and is a tough out.
Signing bonus/status: Signed for $950,000
MLB Debut: 2023

Yunior Severino (SS, ATL)

One of the more impressive bats in the international class, the 17-year-old would still have value if moved away from shortstop and to 2B or 3B. Severino is a talented hitter with plus bat speed and above average power potential. There is still room to grow, but he takes vicious cuts and has the loft and leverage to reach the seats. As a switch-hitter, he has more power from the right side, but a cleaner swing from the left. His swing mechanics will likely be overhauled to take advantage of his natural bat speed. Though a decent defender, his range is a little short, but his arm is playable anywhere.
Signing bonus/status: Signed for $1.9 million
MLB Debut: 2023

2016 Arizona Fall League Risers/Fallers

by Alec Dopp

The Arizona Fall League (AFL) celebrated its twenty-fifth anniversary this past autumn, welcoming prospects from all 30 big-league clubs to central Arizona for a month's worth of competition. As the premier offseason developmental league of Major League Baseball, the league often serves as a litmus test for players whom fantasy owners will undoubtedly become heavily invested in dynasty-style formats.

Here, we're going to fixate our attention on lesser-touted prospects (both AL and NL) whose fantasy stocks were most improved and depreciated by their AFL performances. This takes into account statistical output, as well as scouting observations from taking in more than 50 AFL games in 2016.

Risers

Greg Allen (OF, CLE): The San Diego State product parlayed his 2016 breakout between High-A and Double-A into an impressive fall showing, pacing the league in SB (12) with 3 HR and a .269/.380/.449 slash. Allen's plus speed gives him a chance to be an SB asset, and his consistently high walk rates as a pro will help his cause. He makes quality contact as a switch-hitter and uses the entire field, tools that will help him provide quality BA return. His power figures to be mostly gap-oriented, with a realistic upside of 10-12 HR atop any order.

Carson Kelly (C, STL): After earning a big-league cup of coffee in 2016, Kelly turned around and led Glendale's roster with 3 HR alongside a handsome .842 OPS against fall league arms. The 22-year-old's calculated, disciplined approach and quality contact ability will lend itself to a favorable BA/OBP upside, and he should have a chance to chip in with double-digit HR totals. Kelly's defensive skill set is not stellar, showing an average arm and blocking skills in Arizona, but the Cardinals are convinced he will stick behind the plate long-term.

Max Schrock (2B, OAK): Schrock scurried his way through three levels of the minors in 2016 before slashing .278/.304/.407 across 13 games with Mesa. While those numbers weren't earth-shattering, Schrock displayed some of the best contact skills of anyone on the fall league circuit via a compact, violent swing through the zone. Short and stocky, Shrock may never be a contributor in the power department, but flashes of plus speed—he stole 22 bases in 129 games in 2016—and keen instincts should make him a future BA/SB asset.

Edgar Santana (RHP, PIT): After harboring a 2.71 ERA/8.0 Dom tandem across three levels in 2016, Santana stifled fall league bats to the tune of no runs allowed across 13.2 innings with 18 strikeouts and two walks. The 25-year-old righty touches 98 mph and sits in the mid-90s with his lively fastball, backing it up with an 86-88 mph slider with hard bite and tilt that misses plenty of bats. After his strong fall showing, Santana could get his shot to contribute to Pittsburgh's bullpen early next season.

Jared Miller (LHP, ARI): The definition of intimidation—he stands 6-foot-7, 240 pounds—Miller capped his standout 2016 campaign across four levels with a dominant one in the AFL, posting a 0.00 ERA with 30 strikeouts and four walks across 18.1 relief frames. While the 23-year-old lacks traditional closer velocity (his fastball sits 91-93 mph), Miller pairs his heater with a late-breaking 83-86 mph slider and curveball to rack up lofty whiff totals, which could propel him to Arizona's bullpen in the near future.

Fallers

Michael Gettys (OF, SD): Following his 2016 breakout in the low minors (.305 BA, 12 HR, 33 SB), the former second-round pick struggled mightily in Arizona, slashing just .157/.224/.329 with a league-high 40% strikeout rate. It is easy to dream on Gettys' plus raw power and speed as it relates to future HR/SB returns, but the 21-year-old possesses an ultra-aggressive approach and poor contact skills that will undoubtedly pose a difficult challenge for him as he progresses up the minor-league ladder.

Jacob Nottingham (C, MIL): Considered one of the more promising offensive backstops in the minors, Nottingham's lackluster 11 HR, .641 OPS showing in Double-A in 2016 gave way to a mere .505 OPS across 19 games in the desert. Strong and thick, the 21-year-old has a chance to post quality HR/RBI returns, though his free-swinging approach and lack of contact project him as a future BA liability. His defensive chops behind the plate remain raw, and a move to first base would reduce his value.

Courtney Hawkins (OF, CHW): Drafted as a promising power-speed prep bat, Hawkins' worst season as a pro (.203 BA/12 HR in Double-A) gave way to more problems in Arizona, as the 23-year-old mustered a .595 OPS with just 1 HR in 73 AB. His plus raw power still remains an intriguing tool, though pitch recognition issues and contact inconsistencies figure to prevent it from manifesting into sustainable HR production. Now lacking any SB ability, Hawkins' fantasy value as a corner OF bat projects to be limited.

Austin Voth (RHP, WAS): After stockpiling lofty strikeout totals early in his pro career, Voth witnessed his K/9 bottom out at 7.6 in Triple-A in 2016, which was followed soon after by a 6.9 Dom (and 5.16 ERA) during his stay in the desert. The 24-year-old sat in the upper-80s with his fastball in the fall league, which was hittable in the zone. Both his changeup and slider lacked much bat-missing ability, as well, which means his impact potential as a back-end fantasy starter could be lower than anticipated.

Tanner Scott (LHP, BAL): The hardest-throwing southpaw in the minors turned in a mixed bag as a late-inning reliever in 2016 (4.76 ERA, 11.3 Dom, 8.0 Ctl), and his fall league campaign was similarly uneven (6.32 ERA, 9.8 Dom, 4.0 Ctl). Scott touched 100 mph on several occasions in Arizona, backing it up with the makings of an average slider that registers 89-92 mph on the gun. His control took steps forward this fall, but his command within the strike zone remains very suspect and will require considerable refinement before he is entrusted with a high-leverage, late-relief role at the next level.

The 2016 Rule 5 Draft Recap

by Jeremy Deloney

The 2016 MLB Winter Meetings concluded, as they do every year, with the annual Rule 5 Draft. The unique aspect of this annual player movement exercise for fantasy purposes is that a handful of minor-league players who just months ago were buried in one organization, now have a shot to make an Opening Day MLB roster with a new club. Of course, some of these players will not secure a roster spot, in which case they will get returned to their original organzation. But given the opportunity for the players below to be fantasy-eligible come March, here's a short primer on players selected, their potential 2017 and long-term impacts. (Note that some of these players were traded during and after the draft; we list only the current and original teams.)

Miguel Diaz (RHP, SD); selected from Milwaukee
Profile: Blessed with pure arm strength and a loose delivery, the 23-year-old can fire an explosive fastball into the strike zone with ease. He also owns a solid slider and rudimentary change-up. Repeating his delivery has been a challenge, though it hasn't prevented him from throwing strikes.
2017 Fantasy Impact: Diaz will be given every opportunity to win a rotation spot in spring training, though it is a lot ask for someone who has never thrown a pitch above Low-A. He could also spend time in the bullpen, but he should stick.
Long-term Impact: Diaz has solid upside and could use more time in the minors to develop his secondary offerings. He profiles as a #3 starter with a moderately high strikeout rate.

Luis Torrens (C, SD); selected from New York Yankees
Profile: Torrens is a solid defender with nimble feet, above average agility, a strong arm and quick release. Though not gifted with the bat, he has potential, particularly in the power department. He works counts to get on base and to find pitches to drive.
2017 Fantasy Impact: Given the Padres don't figure to contend, he could be brought along as a third catcher and play rarely. Don't expect him to contribute much given his age and lack of experience.
Long-term Impact: Torrens is likely the best prospect selected in this Rule 5 draft. He could become a solid all-around talent who contributes with both the bat and glove, though it's a long-term project on offense.

Allen Cordoba (SS, SD); selected from St. Louis
Profile: The 21-year-old has been outstanding the past two seasons in rookie ball, and is an extreme contact hitter with exceptional hand-eye coordination and pitch recognition. He doesn't profile to much over-the-wall pop, but he uses the entire field and has a feel for the bat. Defensively, he'll likely be able to stay at shortstop due to his quickness and very strong arm.
2017 Fantasy Impact: Cordoba shoudn't contribute much in 2017. He is far from polished, though has good present tools. He is very likely to win a reserve infielder spot and hit at the bottom of the order when he does play.

Long-term Impact: Cordoba offers very good tools and could be a solid player in 3-5 years. Of the selected players in this draft, the Padres may try to work out a trade with St. Louis to keep him in the system.

Kevin Gadea (RHP, TAM); selected from Seattle
Profile: The 22-year-old dominated in 69 IP in 2016 with a 12.4 Dom. Though he can still be more of a thrower than a pitcher, his 90-95 mph fastball features heavy, late life. He mixes in an average curveball and developing change-up. Because of his smooth arm and lean frame, there is potential for more velocity down the line.
2017 Fantasy Impact: Gadea will likely be used as a reliever in 2017. From a fantasy perspective, he should only be considered in very deep leagues.
Long-term Impact: If he's able to start down the line, Gadea could register strikeouts if he's able to add strength and stamina. He could also develop into a dynamic, late-innings arm.

Armando Rivero (RHP, ATL); selected from Chicago Cubs
Profile: The 28-year-old has a tall, durable frame and excellent velocity (92-97 mph fastball). His heater tends to be a bit too straight, and his hard slider is average at best. If he can clean up the walks (career 4.4 Ctl), then he could be a solid option in high-leverage situations.
2017 Fantasy Impact: Rivero is a solid bet to stick; he has the arm strength for back-to-back games and his experience should serve him well. Expect a lot of strikeouts regardless of his role.
Long-term Impact: At 28, he doesn't have a high ceiling, but could give the Braves solid innings over the next several years. It is always difficult to project closers, but he does pitch aggressively and could be a deep sleeper for saves.

Tyler Jones (RHP, ARI); selected from New York Yankees
Profile: Jones, 27, has a big frame and big fastball to match. Though he mostly sits in the mid-90s, he can rear back and hit 97-98 on occasion. The trouble has been finding a dependable secondary offering, but his slider flashes solid-average.
2017 Fantasy Impact: Even with an above average fastball and closing experience, Jones would likely only have a low-leverage role in 2017 if he makes the club.
Long-term Impact: He has been a high strikeout pitcher in the minors and that should continue in the majors. He also improved his control which bodes well for his future.

Caleb Smith (LHP, CHC); selected from New York Yankees
Profile: The versatile 25-year-old has been a starter, but pitched almost exclusively as a reliever in 2016 at Double-A. Smith isn't a flashy pitcher, rather a command/control guy who can retire hitters with his impressive change-up, but his strikeout rate did increase dramatically in 2016.
2017 Fantasy Impact: With the Cubs loaded at every position, (including the bullpen), Smith is a long-shot to make the roster and would only likely have minimal impact in 2017.
Long-term Impact: His long-term upside isn't very high. It isn't inconceivable for him to return to a starting rotation some day, but it would be more of a back-end starter at best.

Justin Haley (RHP, MIN); selected from Boston
Profile: None of Haley's offerings will raise eyebrows, but he knows how to pitch and he locates his average, 89-92 mph fastball with precision to both sides of the plate. He mixes in a good slider, average curveball, and fringy change-up with mechanics that give him some deception and good angle to the plate.
2017 Fantasy Impact: Haley is a solid bet to make the Twins, though his role won't be determined until spring training. He's spent most of his career as a starter, though there are more open spots in the bullpen. He will have minimal fantasy impact.
Long-term Impact: A potential of a #4-5 starter because he keeps walks to a minimum, he has a good shot at succeeding. Haley is the prototypical low ceiling/high floor pitcher.

Dylan Covey (RHP, CHW); selected from Oakland
Profile: The 25-year-old Covey hits his spots with a terrific 89-94 mph fastball, and he induces a high amount of groundballs. Also employs a big-breaking curveball for strikeouts. His rigid delivery negatively impacts his command, but it also gives him a hint of deception.
2017 Fantasy Impact: There should be opportunity for Covey to win a bullpen spot. He offers some upside; he's been a starter for his entire career and it would be intriguing to see how his heavy fastball works in short stints.
Long-term Impact: He has the pitch mix to thrive as a starter and it is far too premature to keep him as a reliever full-time.

Tyler Webb (LHP, PIT); selected from New York Yankees
Profile: Webb is not going to blow his 89-93 mph fastball by anyone, and his average slider won't miss many bats. However, the 26-year-old knows how to retire lefties and he could be used as a situational reliever. He's been able to post high strikeout rates despite his fringy stuff and his control has been good.
2017 Fantasy Impact: Situational relievers don't have much fantasy value; Webb's struggles with right-handed hitters is problematic. He has more real-life value than he does in fantasy world.
Long-term Impact: He will likely serve as a match-up reliever for his entire career.

Daniel Stumpf (LHP, DET); selected from Kansas City
Profile: The 25-year-old pitched in three games for PHI after being a 2015 Rule 5 draftee. Stumpf is very tough on left-handed hitters with a sly delivery and an effective pitch mix. He doesn't throw very hard—88-93 mph—but he mixes well and is able to throw his slider for strikes. Erratic control could be his downfall.
2017 Fantasy Impact: It shouldn't be difficult to make the Tigers roster as a situational reliever, but he needs to throw more strikes to win a role. He doesn't have much fantasy upside.
Long-term Impact: Similar to Webb, Stumpf really only projects to a lefty-on-lefty reliever. As such, he doesn't hold much upside.

Aneury Tavarez (OF, BAL); selected from Boston
Profile: Tavarez doesn't offer much size—5'9", 175 pounds—but he is very athletic and exhibits above average speed. He's an average defender with acceptable range and fringy arm strength. He could benefit by being more selective at the plate in order to better utilize his speed.

2017 Fantasy Impact: Tavarez is a solid player who could contribute with BA and SB, but he doesn't own any loud tools and he doesn't have a great chance at making the big league roster.
Long-term Impact: Tavarez projects as a reserve outfielder who can serve as a defensive replacement or provide a bit of offense off the bench.

Glenn Sparkman (RHP, TOR); selected from Kansas City
Profile: The 24-year-old has a solid pitch mix, led by his 90-94 mph fastball and hard slider. The development of his change-up will be the key to his future. The injury history is a concern.
2017 Fantasy Impact: Sparkman should be able to compete for a long relief spot. With improved control, his chances improve. He won't have much fantasy value, however.
Long-term Impact: He still profiles best as a starter because of his ability to maintain velocity and throw consistent strikes. But his high strikeout rate is unlikely to continue.

Josh Rutledge (INF, BOS); selected from Colorado
Profile: With significant MLB experience, Rutledge has shown his ability to play a number of positions, and it should give him a chance to win a utility job.
2017 Fantasy Impact: He won't be a starter, but he can fill in at 2B, 3B or in the OF as needed.
Long-term Impact: As a 27-year-old with nearly 1000 AB in the majors, he will be best served in a reserve capacity. He can provide a little BA, a little power, and a few SB.

Hoby Milner (LHP, CLE); selected from Philadelphia
Profile: An unusual pitcher due to his very lean frame and sidearm delivery, the 25-year-old was terrific against lefthanded hitters in 2016. He also was able to post a 10.5 Dom, which is surprising given his high-80s fastball and rudimentary slider. All of his offerings feature ideal movement and he spots the ball well.
2017 Fantasy Impact: The Indians have pitching depth, but Milner has a chance given his deceptive delivery and ability to retire left-handed hitters. But he wouldn't have much fantasy value.
Long-term Impact: Because of his arm slot, Milner will remain in the bullpen full-time. But it is tough to envision much big league success unless he adds a few ticks to his fastball.

Mike Hauschild (RHP, TEX); selected from Houston
Profile: The 26-year-old Hauschild had success in the upper minors, but he lacks upside, though he could be a solid #4-5 starter. The tall, durable righty has a 89-94 mph fastball with heavy life, and a slider that sometimes misses bats. A groundballer, Hauschild's ability to command the plate gives him value.
2017 Fantasy Impact: He should compete for a starting job in the Rangers rotation, though it's more likely he ends up in the bullpen. He won't be much of a fantasy option in 2017.
Long-term Impact: He has the pitch and command to become a #4 starter down the line. With his durable frame and clean arm action, he has a high floor.

2016 First-Year Player Draft Recap

by Jeremy Deloney (AL) and Rob Gordon (NL)

AMERICAN LEAGUE

BALTIMORE ORIOLES

With a need for an influx of talent, the Orioles selected college pitchers with their first three picks. RHP Cody Sedlock (1st round) is a high-upside arm with a deep repertoire and he could front a rotation some day. Both LHP Keegan Akin (2) and RHP Matthias Dietz (2) have mid-rotation potential. Akin, in particular, could reach the majors quickly as a lefty with quality command. Of the position players, OF Austin Hays (3) has the highest upside. He is a sound athlete who provides a spark with both the bat and his legs. 1B Preston Palmeiro (7) gives the Orioles another smooth-hitting position player. The draft class may not stand out for its star quality, but the pitchers have a solid chance to succeed.

Sleeper: LHP Zach Muckenhirn (11) was stellar in his pro debut. He doesn't have an electric arm, but he commands the plate with precision and can register strikeouts.

Grade: B

BOSTON RED SOX

The Red Sox were thrilled when prep LHP Jason Groome (1) was available at #12. He was under consideration for the first three picks in the draft based upon his electric fastball and dominant curveball. SS C.J. Chatham (2) was the other draftee to get a high bonus and he was the best athlete in the Red Sox class. The best pro debut of any draftee throughout baseball may have been from 3B Bobby Dalbec (4), who many organizations were more interested in as a pitcher. He hit .386/.427/.674 with 7 HR with short-season Lowell. The Red Sox are high on both college righties Mike Shawaryn (5) and Shaun Anderson (3).

Sleeper: RHP Steve Nogosek (6) was a college closer at Oregon and he has the arm strength and two-pitch mix to be very potent in short stints. He could also be tried as a starter.

Grade: B+

CHICAGO WHITE SOX

Blessed with two first round picks, the White Sox went the college route with their first six picks and 25 of their first 26 selections. That doesn't mean there isn't upside with some of the draftees. At the top, Chicago targeted C Zack Collins (1), who immediately becomes one of the top offensive prospects in the system. He has shown improved glovework and should be able to stick behind the plate. He can get on base consistently and exhibits plus power to all fields. RHP Zack Burdi (1) was the second first rounder and he could reach the majors as soon as 2017 out of the bullpen. Adding to the impressive haul is RHP Alec Hansen (2) who was widely considered a top ten pick prior to the college season. He had a phenomenal pro debut.

Sleeper: LHP Bernardo Flores (7) was not particularly strong in college, but he has a deep repertoire and pure arm strength that can pump low-to-mid-90s fastballs into the strike zone.

Grade: A-

CLEVELAND INDIANS

Plain and simple, this was a draft class that focused on position players, with several of them plucked out of high school. The top two picks, OF Will Benson (1) and 3B Nolan Jones (2) give the Indians two high-upside players who could someday hit in the middle of the lineup. Jones is more of a pure hitter while Benson can hit the ball a long, long way. After three college picks, the Indians returned to high school with two more position players. OF Conner Capel (5) and 3B Ulysses Cantu (6) have plenty of development time ahead of them, but are both intriguing. RHP Aaron Civale (3) and RHP Shane Bieber (4) were the highest selected pitchers in this draft class.

Sleeper: OF Andrew Calica (11) has a smooth stroke with a well above average approach at the plate. There isn't much thunder in the bat, but he hit .382/.474/.556 with 15 SB in his pro debut.

Grade: C+

DETROIT TIGERS

This is an organization that has exhibited a strong college slant over the years, and this draft was no different. After selecting a high-upside prep arm in RHP Matt Manning (1), the Tigers opted for college arms with their next four picks (rounds 4 through 7) before adding three college bats in rounds 8 through 10. They didn't have any picks in the 2nd or 3rd round, but did a decent job overall. Manning is the clear stud in the class, though RHP Kyle Funkhouser (4) was the 35th overall pick in 2015. He could be a steal if he continues to highlight his strengths like he did in his pro debut. As usual, there aren't high ceilings associated with most of the picks, but there are a handful who could advance quickly.

Sleeper: RHP Zac Houston (11) was a college reliever who found pro ball much to his liking. He has the strong frame and fastball to wipe out hitters. He posted a 14.9 Dom in 29.2 innings between short-season and Low-A.

Grade: C

HOUSTON ASTROS

After selecting high school RHP Forrest Whitley (1) with the 17th overall pick, the Astros generally played it safe the rest of the way and focused on college performers at key positions. Whitley has a big frame and more polish than most prep pitchers. He was treated cautiously upon signing, but he showed a plus fastball and two quality breaking balls in his debut. Another big-bodied pitcher who could be a sound major leaguer is LHP Brett Adcock (4) who has excellent stuff, but can't find the plate consistently. While the position players don't have high ceilings, several could contribute in the near future. C Jake Rogers (3) was the best defensive catcher in the draft and OF Ronnie Dawson (2) brings a mix of power and speed.

Sleeper: RHP Nick Hernandez (8) has a strong arm and aggressive demeanor that allows him to be a late-innings reliever. He could use some mechanical refinement, but can hit the mid-90s with ease.

Grade: C

KANSAS CITY ROYALS

Without a first round pick, the Royals didn't exactly have a big bonus pool. However, they came away from the draft with a polished college pitcher in RHP A.J. Puckett (2) and a high-ceiling prep bat in OF Khalil Lee (3). They were the only two signees to sign for over $400,000 and only Puckett received over $1 million. Kansas City selected a diverse mix of pitchers and position players and picked a handful of intriguing picks from junior college or very small colleges. All in all, this was one of the weakest hauls of talent in the draft, but the lack of a first round pick really hurt them. If the prep bats such as Lee and OF Cal Jones (6) develop, then some of the hurt will vanquish.

Sleeper: LHP Richard Lovelady (10) was a reliever in college (Kennesaw State), but possesses an above average fastball for a lefty. He served as a closer in the pros, but a return to a starting role isn't out of the question.

Grade: D

LOS ANGELES ANGELS

With arguably the thinnest minor league system in baseball, it was paramount for the Angels to make savvy selections to bolster the ranks. After picking C/1B Matt Thaiss (1) with number 16 overall, many eyebrows were raised. The Angels selected a college backstop in 2015, but they are insistent that Thaiss could evolve into a high OBP/average power-producing 1B in time. He impressed with his 264 AB in pro ball upon signing. The Angels selected seven position players in the first ten rounds and they nabbed two prep stars in rounds 2 and 3. OF Brandon Marsh (2) signed for over $1 million and has fine tools while INF Nonie Williams (3) has as high of a ceiling as any position player in the system. RHP Chris Rodriguez (4), a high school pitcher, has potential plus stuff, but is more thrower than pitcher.

Sleeper: 2B Jordan Zimmerman (7) is a pure hitter who should hit for a solid BA at any level of baseball. There isn't much pop in his game and he's an average runner, but the bat is more than sufficient.

Grade: B-

MINNESOTA TWINS

Youth was in the Twins plan and they secured the services of high school position players with their first four picks in the draft. While a few modest college arms were picked, the prep stars highlight the class. OF Alex Kirilloff (1) was the Appalachian League MVP after he showcased his natural, smooth hitting skills. The Twins are excited about the upside of SS Jose Miranda (2) who could be an impact player with both bat and glove. C Ben Rortvedt (2) gives the Twins a young backstop that has power potential and the ability to stay behind the plate long-term. Of the pitchers, RHP Griffin Jax (3) may have the highest upside, though high school RHP Tyler Benninghoff (11) was signed to a $600,000 bonus and has a prized arm.

Sleeper: OF Shane Carrier (8) provides muscle and thump to the lineup and has the frame and youth to project to more pop down the line. He needs to clean up his approach, but he profiles as a prototypical RF.

Grade: B

NEW YORK YANKEES

The Yankees also did well with drafting in both the early and late rounds. They chose position players with their first two picks, prep performers with two of their first three selections, and then college players with their next ten. The gem of the class is OF Blake Rutherford (1) who has immense power potential from the left side while also exhibiting sound hitting instincts and defensive play in CF. 2B Nick Solak (2) was a college bat who should hit for a high BA due to his professional approach. Prep RHP Nolan Martinez (3) was given a $1.15 million bonus and he has as much upside as any arm in the system. The top three picks took up most of the bonus pool.

Sleeper: RHP Tyler Widener (12) was a nifty pick who feasted on lower level hitters in his pro debut. He fanned 59 batters in 38 innings and only allowed two runs. His fastball sits in the mid-90s despite his lack of size.

Grade: B

OAKLAND ATHLETICS

Under consideration for the #1 overall pick, LHP A.J. Puk (1) fell to pick #6 and the Athletics were beyond ecstatic. They signed him to a $4.1 million bonus and watched him dominate the NY-Penn League. Oakland continued to stockpile arms, selecting college RHPs Daulton Jefferies (supplemental 1st) and Logan Shore (2) with their next two selections. All three of these pitchers have at least one plus offering in their respective arsenals. Add in prep RHP Skylar Szynski (4) and the Athletics have themselves a crop of excellent arms. There is enthusiasm for C Sean Murphy (3) who was among the best defensive catchers in the draft. He is more about the glove than the bat, which is similar to most other position players selected by Oakland.

Sleeper: OF Tyler Ramirez (7) is a relatively polished college outfielder who fits the Athletics mold of working counts and getting on base. He lacks loud tools, but he has value with his contact ability, average speed, and CF defense.

Grade: B+

SEATTLE MARINERS

OF Kyle Lewis (1) was in the mix for the top overall selection in the draft, but fell to the Mariners at #11 after some teams discounted his level of competition at college. Those teams could regret passing on him as he has multiple tools, highlighted by his plus, raw power. He underwent knee surgery in July and will likely start the season late. After him, two more position players were selected, 3B Joe Rizzo (2) and SS Bryson Brigman (3). Rizzo has a short, compact frame, but plenty of wallop in his bat. Brigman stands out for his contact-making ability and defensive skills. Only three pitchers were selected in the top ten rounds and LHP Thomas Burrows (4) could move quickly as an advanced reliever. RHP Brandon Miller (6) is also another name to watch.

Sleeper: INF David Greer (10) is a solid, overall hitter with the ability to make contact and hit for average power to all fields. He can play a variety of positions, which enhances his profile, but he needs to upgrade his range and glovework.

Grade: B-

TAMPA BAY RAYS

The Rays did not stray from their usual approach and selected players who could pay long-term dividends for the organization. They opted for position players with their first three picks, including prep 3B Josh Lowe (1) who could develop into a middle-of-the-order run producer. Both OF Ryan Boldt (2) and OF Jake Fraley (2) were from the college ranks and can impact the game in a variety of ways. The organization needed an injection of young pitching and the Rays tabbed two prep arms, RHP Austin Franklin (3) and RHP Easton McGee (4) with their next two picks. With their "best player available" approach, the Rays had a solid mix of pitchers and position players from both high school and college. Thirteen players received at least six-figure bonuses.

Sleeper: RHP J.D. Busfield (7) operated out of the bullpen in his pro debut, but the Rays haven't ruled out a starting role for him. He stands 6'7" and uses his height well to keep the ball down in the zone. His fastball generally sits between 90-94 mph.

Grade: B+

TEXAS RANGERS

The Rangers selected high school pitchers with their first two selections and both couldn't be more different from one another. LHP Cole Ragans (1) has an excellent assortment of pitches and advanced command for his age. RHP Alex Speas (2) owns unbelievable athleticism and already one of the best fastballs in the organization, but has little feel for pitching. Two high school bats have significant value in C Sam Huff (7) and 3B Kole Enright (3). Both hit over .300 in their pro debuts. SS Charles LeBlanc (4) is a long and lanky college shortstop with no obvious weakness in his game. If the Rangers can get mileage out of RHP Kyle Cody (6) and clean up his mechanics, he could be a deep sleeper in the system.

Sleeper: RHP Tai Tiedemann (8) has a very lean frame, but exhibits plus athleticism and plenty of projection. It will take time to tweak his mechanics and get him to repeat them consistently, but he will be worth the time.

Grade: A-

TORONTO BLUE JAYS

The Blue Jays didn't select until pick #21, but they enjoyed a deep draft class with several potential contributors in the top 15 rounds. Some of the college hitters could advance rather quickly because of their athleticism and bloodlines. In particular, INF Bo Bichette (2) and 2B Cavan Biggio (5) have more famous fathers, but both have potential to be everyday players. RHP T.J. Zeuch (1) highlights the arms and he can dominate with his fastball by itself. RHP Zach Jackson (3) is a college reliever with one of the better breaking balls in the entire draft class. OF Josh Palacios (4) likely would have been a much higher pick if not for a broken wrist early in the season at Auburn.

Sleeper: OF D.J. Daniels (6) is a phenomenal athlete with tools aplenty. He's still a bit raw with the bat in his hands, but few can match his power-speed combination.

Grade: A-

NATIONAL LEAGUE

ARIZONA DIAMONDBACKS

The Diamondbacks had to wait until the supplemental phase of round one before making their first pick. They took Auburn OF Anfernee Grier, who has plus speed and showed the ability to hit in college but struggled in his debut, striking out in 29% of his AB. The Snakes then popped high school backstop Andy Yerzy (2), Rice RHP Jon Duplantier (3), and Canadian hurler Curtis Taylor (4). Taylor had the best debut, going 1-0 with a 2.20 ERA, 5 BB/23 K in 16.1 IP. While the Diamondbacks added to their depth, they failed to land a sure-fire impact prospect, something the system badly needed.

Sleeper: SS Mark Karaviotis (19) missed most of the '16 college season due to injury, but the University of Oregon product had a stellar pro debut, hitting .347/.491/.485 in 167 AB.

Grade: C

ATLANTA BRAVES

The Braves had the third pick in the draft and opted to go with high school hurler Ian Anderson. The 6'3" Anderson was a consensus first round pick, but most had him going in the middle of round one. The Braves signed Anderson for $4 million, well below the $6.5 million allocated for that pick. He has good stuff and had a solid debut, posting a 2.04 ERA in 39.2 IP, but profiles as a mid-rotation starter. The Braves used the money they saved to go above-slot to get high school lefties Joey Wentz (1S) and Kyle Muller (2), both of whom are projectable. The decision to spread their resources over their top three picks looks like a good gamble for now. The Braves also added Cal backstop Brett Cumberland (2S) and Louisville lefty Drew Harrington (3) and overall this was a nice haul for a team in rebuilding mode.

Sleeper: RHP Matt Rowland (11) has good size and some projection left. He already features a good low-90s sinking fastball that tops at 95 mph and mixes in a hard slider that flashes plus, but is inconsistent.

Grade: B+

CHICAGO CUBS

The Cubs forfeited their first and second round picks when they signed John Lackey and Jayson Heyward. To compensate they went heavy on college pitching, taking collegiate hurlers in rounds 3-6. Their first pick was Oklahoma RHP Thomas Hatch (3) who missed his sophomore season due to a sprained elbow ligament, but was impressive in 2016 and signed for an above-slot $573,900. Hatch profiles as a solid mid-rotation starter, but has yet to make his pro debut. The Cubs also added righties Tyson Miller (4), Bailey Clark (5), and Chad Hockin (6) and drafted only one prep player in the first 15 rounds. For now, Hatch is the only draft pick to make the Cubs Top 15 list, though Clark was impressive in a limited pro debut. Overall this was a thin haul.

Sleeper: RHP Dakota Mekkes (10) boasted impressive numbers as junior at Michigan State, and comes after hitters with a solid low-90s FB and a good slider from a low ¾ arm slot and excelled in his debut, going 1-1, with a 1.80 ERA, 4 BB/27 K in 20 IP.

Grade: D

CINCINNATI REDS

The Reds needed a solid draft in 2016 after subpar drafts the past two seasons, and preliminary results are good. They landed the most polished college bat in the draft class, 3B Nick Senzel (1), toolsy high school OF Taylor Trammell (1S), and Clemson backstop Chris Okey (2). Senzel had arguably the most impressive debut of any player in the draft (.305/.398/.514 with 7 HR/18 SB between rookie ball and Low-A), and Trammell hit .303/.374/.421 with 24 SB in the Pioneer League. The Reds added three solid pitching prospects with prep RHP Nick Hanson (3), Florida LHP Scott Moss (4), and Texas A&M RHP Ryan Hendrix (5). Senzel immediately becomes the top prospect in the system and could be in the majors by 2018.

Sleeper: C Cassidy Brown (12) struggled in his first two seasons at Loyola Marymount before having a breakout season in 2016. Lingering concerns about his bat and ability to stick behind the plate caused him to slide, but his debut was impressive (.322/.409/.383).

Grade: A

COLORADO ROCKIES

Despite an abysmal track record with drafting pitchers with their first selection, the Rockies went back to the well again, taking prep hurler Riley Pint with the 4th pick. Pint has an ideal power pitching frame and can blow hitters away with 93-97 mph fastball that hits 102 and plus power curve, but struggled in his debut. The Rockies also added Georgia righty Robert Tyler (1-S), Vanderbilt lefty Ben Bowden (2), Long Beach State SS Garrett Hampson (3), and high school 3B Colton Welker. Long-term, the success of this draft class hinges the development of Pint. Given his command issues and the organization's lack of success in developing pitching prospects, the jury is still out.

Sleeper: RHP Brandon Gold (10) was a two-way player at Georgia Tech. He isn't overpowering but has the ability to keep hitters off balance, and was solid in his pro debut (23 K/2 BB in 24.2 IP).

Grade: B

LOS ANGELES DODGERS

The Dodgers had three first round picks and used them wisely, landing high school shortstop Gavin Lux at #20, Louisville backstop Will Smith at #32, and Vanderbilt righty Jordan Sheffield at #36. All three immediate enter the Dodgers Top 15 and give the organization some of the best depth in the majors. Lux slashed .296/.375/.399 at two different rookie levels and has solid all-around skills. The Dodgers then added RHPs Mitchell White (2) and Dustin May (3). White has a plus fastball that tops out at 96 mph and impressed in his debut, going 1-0 with a 0.00 ERA, and 6 BB/30 K in 22 IP. But the best debut was by Western Nevada CC OF D.J. Peters (5) who torched the Pioneer League to the tune of .351/.437/.615 with 24 double and 13 home runs.

Sleeper: Cody Thomas OF (13) was a two-sport athlete at Oklahoma who left football after failing to win the starting QB job. Thomas has big-time power, hitting .297/.382/.621 with 10 doubles and 19 home runs in his debut, but also struck out 87 times in 232 AB.

Grade: A-

MIAMI MARLINS

The Marlins had the 7th pick and took the top high school lefty Braxton Garrett. Garrett has a solid three-pitch mix and profiles as a durable #2 starter. The Marlins also added prep OFs Thomas Jones (3) and Sean Reynolds (4) and collegiate righties Sam Perez (5) and Remey Reed (6). Jones was a two-sport star in high school and was signed for an over-slot $1 million, but struggled in his debut, hitting .234 with 20 K in 64 AB. The development of Garrett and Jones will be key to salvaging an otherwise uninspired haul.

Sleeper: James Nelson 3B (15) is the younger brother of former Rockies 2B Chris Nelson. He has good speed and athleticism and showed well in his debut, hitting .284/.344/.364.

Grade: C

MILWAUKEE BREWERS

The Brewers have overhauled their farm system as rapidly and effectively as any organization in baseball and now have one of the deepest systems in the NL. With the 5th pick the Brewers added toolsy Louisville OF Corey Ray. Ray profiles as a Rajai Davis-type OF with less speed and more power. The club had two second round picks and snapped up 3B Lucas Erceg (2) and Mario Felciano (2S) before adding pitchers in RHP Braden Webb (3), RHP Corbin Burnes (4), and RHP Zack Brown. Burns and Erceg had the best debuts, with Burns 3-0 with a 2.02 ERA and Erceg hitting .327/.376/.518 with 9 HR at two stops. The addition of Ray and Erceg gives an already deep system two more potential major league regulars.

Sleeper: Trey York 2B (9) was signed for $25,000 as college senior, but has plus speed and impressed in his debut. York hit .348/.431/.648 with 23 doubles, 15 home runs, and 17 SB in his last year at Tennessee State and then .289/.393/.407 with 15 SB between rookie ball and High-A.

Grade: A-

NEW YORK METS

The Mets used their two 1st round picks to add BC RHP Justin Dunn and UConn RHP Anthony Kay. Dunn has three above-average offerings highlighted by a mid-90s fastball and looked good in his debut, going 1-1 with a 1.50 ERA in 30 IP. Kay, who has yet to make his pro debut, has an advanced changeup and a nice low-90s heater. Florida 1B Peter Alonso (2) has above-average power and slashed .321/.382/.587 in the NYPL. Shortstop Michael Paez (4) has plus speed and Chris Viall (6) has a fastball that tops out at 97 mph. Dunn and Kaye are nice, projectable arms, but the Mets needed an impact bat and failed to land one.

Sleeper: Placido Torres LHP (8) was a standout at Division II Tusculum and succeeds without overpowering stuff. The 5'11" lefty has a fastball that sits at 88-91 mph with an average curve and below-average change, but knows how to change speed and keeps hitters off-balance.

Grade: C+

PHILADELPHIA PHILLIES

The Phillies had the top pick in the draft and wasted little time in taking the top position player, high school OF Mickey Moniak. They signed Moniak for $6.1 million, almost $3 million under slot. The 6'2" Moniak has a lean, projectable frame and should add power as he matures. He showed an advanced bat during the summer showcase events with plus speed. Moniak had a solid debut, hitting .284/.340/.409 in the GCL, but lacks the raw power one would expect from the first overall pick. The Phillies used most of their bonus surplus to sign prep right-hander Kevin Gowdy (2) for $3.5 million and then filled in with SS Cole Stobbe (3) and JuCo lefty JoJo Romero (4). If Gowdy and Moniak develop as they should, this will be a nice haul.

Sleeper: Grant Dyer RHP (8) has a plus fastball and blows hitters away despite his relatively small frame - 6'1", 195. Dyer worked in relief in his debut and used a mid-90s fastball and above-average slider to strikeout 57 in 42.1 IP while posting a 2.34 ERA.

Grade: B+

PITTSBURGH PIRATES

The Pirates have some of the better position prospects in the NL and added Wake Forest 3B Will Craig with the 22nd pick. Craig isn't overly athletic, but has a good bat with an advanced understanding of the strike zone, hitting .280/.412/.362 in his debut. They failed to sign first round supplemental pick Nick Lodolo, but landed two workhorse starters Travis MacGregor (2) and Braeden Ogle (4) and defensive wiz SS Stephen Alemais (3). Craig should add power with an ability to get on base as he moves up and could settle in as an above corner infielder. The inability to sign Lodolo undercuts the depth of this group, but Craig should become a solid everyday regular.

Sleeper: Max Kranick RHP (11) was signed for $300,000 and features a good low-90s fastball, solid-average curve, and a seldom used changeup. Kranick held his own in his debut, going 1-2 with a 2.43 ERA, 4 BB/21 K in 33.1 IP.

Grade: B-

SAN DIEGO PADRES

The Padres had three first round picks and used them to land Stanford RHP Cal Quantrill at #8, prep SS Hudson Potts at #24, and Kent State lefty Eric Lauer at #25. Quantrill had Tommy John in 2015 and missed all of his junior season, but was back on the mound after being drafted, posting a 5.11 ERA in 12 starts. Lauer has a good four-pitch mix and profiles as a solid mid-rotation starter and Potts has shown an ability to barrel the ball consistently. The Padres also landed toolsy Florida OF Buddy Reed (2), and high school right-handers Reggie Lawson (2S) and Mason Thompson (3). The switch-hitting Reed has 70-grade speed and was considered a likely 1st round pick until he struggled in his junior season. If Quantrill comes back at 100%, the Padres will have added good depth to a much improved system.

Sleeper: Ethan Skender INF (28) was drafted by the Reds in 2015 but didn't sign, instead playing one year at State JC of Florida. Skender has solid bat-to-ball skills with a good glove and average speed

Grade: B+

ST. LOUIS CARDINALS

The Cardinals found themselves in the familiar position of having to wait until the back-end of round one, but were able to land top 10 talent in Puerto Rican SS Delvin Perez. Perez fell in the draft due to a failed drug test (PED), but was one of the better athletes in the draft, showing plus speed, a strong arm, and the chops to stick at short. Perez had a nice debut, hitting .294/.352/.393 in the GCL. The Cardinals then added prep OF Dylan Carlson (1), Mississippi State RHP Dakota Hudson (1), Virginia RHP Connor Jones (2), North Carolina RHP Zac Gallen (3), and USC C Jeremy Martinez. Martinez slashed .325/.419/.433 with 32 BB/16 K in 194 AB. Another impressive haul for the savvy Cardinals.

Sleeper: Vincent Jackson OF (14) is a tall, athletic OF who played college ball at Tennessee. He struggled during his junior year due to a thumb injury, but had a solid senior season, hitting .333/.426/.507 playing along Nick Senzel.

Grade: A

SAN FRANCISCO GIANTS

The Giants forfeited their first round pick when they signed Jeff Samardzija and so had to wait until pick #59 to land Vanderbilt OF Brian Reynolds (2). The switch-hitting Reynolds has good tools and impressed in his debut, hitting .313/.363/.484 with 17 doubles and 6 home runs. The Giants went college heavy throughout the draft and did not take a high school player until the 13th round. OF Heath Quinn (3) dominated at three levels, slashing .344/.434/.564 and looks to be a steal, while Gio Brusa (6) has plus power and stroked 15 doubles and 10 home runs in 220 AB. Despite not having a first round pick, the Giants did well with this group.

Sleeper: Jacob Heyward OF (18) is the younger brother Cubs OF Jason Heyward and has good bat speed and plus raw power. Heyward struggled in his junior year, but played well as a pro, hitting .330/.483/.560 in 109 AB.

Grade: B

WASHINGTON NATIONALS

The Nationals had to wait until the end of round one to make their first pick, but then had consecutive picks and landed high school shortstop Carter Kieboom and Florida RHP Dane Dunning. Kieboom had a solid pro debut and projects to be an impact player once he reaches the majors. Dunning had a nice debut as well, going 3-2 with a 2.02 ERA and was then traded to the White Sox as part of the Adam Eaton deal. The Nationals then added Sheldon Neuse (2) and Nick Banks (4) and went well over slot ($1.4 million) to land prep lefty Jesus Luzardo (3). Luzardo has good stuff, but has yet to make his pro debut. The loss of Dunning diminishes the overall haul, but the addition of Kieboom and Adam Eaton make the organization stronger.

Sleeper: Armond Upshaw OF (11) is a switch-hitting JuCo OF from Pensacola State with plus speed. He had an impressive pro debut, hitting .325/.391/.400 after hitting .337 with 33 SB at Pensacola State.

Grade: B+

College Players to Watch in 2017

by Chris Lee

Fantasy owners in deep dynasty/keeper formats need to keep a close eye on collegiate talent as a way to stay ahead. Recent cases in point: Alex Bregman and Dansby Swanson, mentioned in this space two years ago, both arrived in the bigs a year after going pro. In addition, this column gave you advance notice on Trea Turner, Kyle Schwarber and Aaron Nola the year before. The 2017 collegiate season starts in mid-February; here are some names from the the college ranks who could get their names called in this June's First Year Player Draft:

1. Jeren Kendall, OF
Vanderbilt, L/R, 6-0, 190

Kendall's quick, compact left-handed swing generates 400-foot blasts, and he added 16 doubles and eight triples to his nine HR in 2016. With 70-grade speed, he should be able to play center. There's a bit too much swing-and-miss (75% ct%) in his game, his baserunning instincts aren't the best, and his route-running and throwing accuracy need work. But he's the top outfielder in the draft, and a tremendous athlete with a 20-HR/20-SB upside.

2. Alex Faedo, RHP
Florida, R/R, 6-5, 225

Faedo possesses a fastball that sits in the low- to mid-90s and a slider that's just as good. Faedo was fantastic against elite collegiate competition in 2016 (11.5 Dom, 1.8 Ctl, 6.3 Cmd), and then followed up with a great summer in 16 IP for Team USA. Arthroscopic surgery to both knees cost him the entire fall, but isn't expected to hamper him further, and he pitches for a program that's cautious with workloads.

3. Kyle Wright, RHP
Vanderbilt, R/R, 6-4, 220

Wright ascended quickly to collegiate stardom, closing part-time for the national runner-up team as a freshman in 2015 before landing a weekend starting role last year. His repertoire includes a low-90s fastball that can touch 97, a sharp-breaking curve, and an adequate slider and change-up. He gets results (10.0 Dom. 3.1 Cmd in 152 career IP), and scouts feel there's projection remaining. Athletic and fearless on the mound, he's a top-five-overall talent.

4. Tanner Houck, RHP
Missouri, R/R, 6-5, 218

Houck was nearly unhittable (9.1 Dom) in long stretches of 2016 while playing on a bad team, thanks to a moving fastball that sits mid-90s, but can touch 98. Scouts would like to see the change-up and fastball improve a bit, but they're serviceable at the present, and good Ctl (2.3) makes him special. Some feel he's the most-talented college arm in the class.

5. J.J. Schwarz, C
Florida, R/R, 6-2, 215

It was a weird 2016 for Schwarz, who almost exactly matched his 2015 numbers in AB (256), doubles (16), triples (three) and on-base percentage (.398) and saw a marked rise in his bb% (10 to 15). But, his ct% dropped from 82% to 79% and his home run output plummeted from 18 to seven. Teammate Mike Rivera caught the majority of the Gators' games; Schwarz mostly was the DH. Though some scouts believe Schwarz will be good enough behind the plate, the positional uncertainty and the power decline has knocked him out of the top half of the first round for many. Teams will be watching Schwarz intently this spring.

6. Brendan McKay, LHP/1B
Louisville, L/L, 6-2, 212

McKay could actually get consideration as a hitter; he won the John Olerud Award his first two years as college baseball's best two-way player. Though the raw numbers (6 HR, 0 SB) won't excite fantasy owners, some regard him as a top-shelf hitting prospect due to his feel for hitting (86% ct%, 0.73 Eye). A quality fastball that sits in the low-90s, complemented by a curve and a change, helped him post great numbers (10.5 Dom, 3.0 Cmd) in 109.2 innings last year, and he'll likely be picked in first round as a pitcher.

7. J.B. Bukauskas, RHP
North Carolina, R/R, 6-0, 195

Bukauskas jumped from relative anonymity as a high school junior when his velocity went from the high-80s to the high-90s; he shunned seven-figure money from the Arizona Diamondbacks (and skipped his senior year of high school) to go to UNC. He put up elite numbers (12.8 Dom, 3.8 Cmd) as Tar Heel sophomore; though he threw just 78.1 IP; then he yielded just one unearned run in 21.2 for Team USA. The slider's great and the change-up is serviceable, though some think he could project as a closer instead of a starter.

8. Alex Lange, RHP
LSU, R/R, 6-4, 260

Lange's ERA (3.79) soared nearly two runs from his freshman season, but his other metrics (10.1 Dom, 4.0 Ctl) were only slightly off his 2015 performance. The junior has shown durability (226 career IP), a mid-90s fastball that maintains velocity, and a terrific 12-to-6 curveball.

9. Jake Burger, 3B
Missouri State, R/R, 6-2, 220

Burger projects as perhaps the top collegiate power-hitting prospect in a draft that's slim on them. He hit .349/.420/.689 as a sophomore, finishing second in the country with 21 HR. An 85% ct% means he may offer some batting average, though he won't run (3-5 SB).

10. Pavin Smith, 1B
Virginia, L/L, 6-2, 210

Smith showed outstanding hitting maturity (.329/.410/.525, 14% bb%, 90% ct%, 1.57 Eye) one year after helping the Cavaliers to a national title. He likely won't run much as a pro, so future fantasy value depends on batting average skills, plus power growth; he mashed eight HR in a moderate pitcher's park, and some scouts think there's more to come.

Others to watch:
K.J. Harrison, C, Oregon St. ; Evan Skoug, C, TCU; Tristan Beck, SP, Stanford (draft-eligible sophomore)

2017's Top Fantasy Prospects

1	Yoan Moncada	2B	CHW		51	Carson Fulmer	RHP	CHW
2	Andrew Benintendi	OF	BOS		52	Vladimir Guerrero, Jr.	3B	TOR
3	Dansby Swanson	SS	ATL		53	David Paulino	RHP	HOU
4	Alex Reyes	RHP	STL		54	Mitch Keller	RHP	PIT
5	Lucas Giolito	RHP	CHW		55	Riley Pint	RHP	COL
6	Victor Robles	OF	WAS		56	Francisco Mejia	C	CLE
7	J.P. Crawford	SS	PHI		57	Brady Aiken	LHP	CLE
8	Tyler Glasnow	RHP	PIT		58	Yulieski Gurriel	3B	HOU
9	Brendan Rodgers	SS	COL		59	Braxton Garrett	LHP	MIA
10	Austin Meadows	OF	PIT		60	Tyler Jay	LHP	MIN
11	Gleyber Torres	SS	NYY		61	A.J. Puk	LHP	OAK
12	Amed Rosario	SS	NYM		62	Kevin Newman	SS	PIT
13	Rafael Devers	3B	BOS		63	Robert Stephenson	RHP	CIN
14	Lewis Brinson	OF	MIL		64	Sean Reid-Foley	RHP	TOR
15	Anderson Espinoza	RHP	SD		65	Matt Manning	RHP	DET
16	Willy Adames	SS	TAM		66	Anthony Alford	OF	TOR
17	Eloy Jimenez	OF	CHC		67	Jesse Winker	OF	CIN
18	Manuel Margot	OF	SD		68	Dominic Smith	1B	NYM
19	Ozzie Albies	2B	ATL		69	Raimel Tapia	OF	COL
20	Clint Frazier	OF	NYY		70	Zack Collins	C	CHW
21	Bradley Zimmer	OF	CLE		71	James Kaprielian	RHP	NYY
22	Franklin Barreto	SS	OAK		72	Erick Fedde	RHP	WAS
23	Brent Honeywell	RHP	TAM		73	Luis Ortiz	RHP	MIL
24	Cody Bellinger	1B	LA		74	Phil Bickford	RHP	MIL
25	Francis Martes	RHP	HOU		75	Jake Bauers	OF	TAM
26	Reynaldo Lopez	RHP	CHW		76	Justus Sheffield	LHP	NYY
27	Jose De Leon	RHP	LA		77	Matt Chapman	3B	OAK
28	Mickey Moniak	OF	PHI		78	Luke Weaver	RHP	STL
29	Ian Happ	2B	CHC		79	Grant Holmes	RHP	OAK
30	Kyle Tucker	OF	HOU		80	Bobby Bradley	1B	CLE
31	Nick Senzel	3B	CIN		81	Ronald Acuna	OF	ATL
32	Michael Kopech	RHP	CHW		82	Derek Fisher	OF	HOU
33	Aaron Judge	OF	NYY		83	Brett Phillips	OF	MIL
34	Josh Bell	1B	PIT		84	Yadier Alvarez	RHP	LA
35	Kyle Lewis	OF	SEA		85	Leody Taveras	OF	TEX
36	Hunter Renfroe	OF	SD		86	Yohander Mendez	LHP	TEX
37	Jorge Mateo	SS	NYY		87	Kevin Maitan	SS	ATL
38	Amir Garrett	LHP	CIN		88	Triston McKenzie	LHP	CLE
39	Corey Ray	OF	MIL		89	Willie Calhoun	2B	LA
40	Jeff Hoffman	RHP	COL		90	Ryan McMahon	3B	COL
41	Tyler O'Neill	OF	SEA		91	Isan Diaz	SS	MIL
42	Josh Hader	LHP	MIL		92	Ian Anderson	RHP	ATL
43	Kolby Allard	LHP	ATL		93	Trent Clark	OF	MIL
44	Jason Groome	LHP	BOS		94	Alex Kirilloff	OF	MIN
45	Jorge Alfaro	C	PHI		95	Harrison Bader	OF	STL
46	Nick Williams	OF	PHI		96	Tyler Beede	RHP	SF
47	Nick Gordon	SS	MIN		97	Richard Urena	SS	TOR
48	Sean Newcomb	LHP	ATL		98	Mike Soroka	RHP	ATL
49	Alex Verdugo	OF	LA		99	Dylan Cease	RHP	CHC
50	Blake Rutherford	OF	NYY		100	Stephen Gonsalves	LHP	MIN

Sleepers Outside the HQ100

by Alec Dopp

Each year the BaseballHQ.com minors team spends precious hours scouting players, evaluating tools, researching advanced metrics and analyzing video before debating which prospects will end up on the annual HQ100 top prospects list. The unfortunate reality of this practice, however, is that many promising youngsters are withheld from inclusion for any number of reasons—age, lack of track record, injuries, physical limitations, draft positioning, and so on. For owners in keeper leagues and dynasty-style formats, though, the HQ100 may not always satisfy one's hankering for prospect valuation.

If that applies to you, we've got you covered. Below are 10 sleeper prospects who didn't make the cut for this year's HQ100, but who could ascend to that level in 2017 and could be available to owners in long-term keeper and dynasty formats. To accommodate owners in non-mixed leagues, five of the below prospects are currently eligible in NL-only formats; the other five in AL-only leagues.

While the Mets' system may lack established high-upside bats outside of Amed Rosario and Dominic Smith, **Desmond Lindsay (OF)** could be in a position to join that stratosphere in the near future. A former Florida prep standout taken in the second round in 2015, Lindsay slashed .297/.418/.450 with a 4 HR/3 SB tandem in 32 games as one of the New York Penn League's (NYPL) youngest hitters in 2016. The 19-year-old employs a compact swing and explosive wrists that lend themselves to high contact, and projects to hit for at least average power. In addition, he displays an advanced knowledge of the strike zone. A quality athlete with plus speed, Lindsay should also offer SB impact as a quality everyday centerfielder long term.

In a Baltimore system bereft of high-upside talent and depth, 2016 first-rounder **Cody Sedlock (RHP)** might have the best shot at fantasy impact. After a standout junior campaign at the University of Illinois (5-3, 2.49 ERA, 10.3 Dom in 14 GS) Sedlock's pro debut culminated in a 1.07 WHIP, 8.3 Dom and .158 OBA across nine NYPL starts. Tall and lean, the 21-year-old comes after hitters with a heavy low-90s fastball that regularly yields ground-ball contact, flashes of an above-average slider and a circle changeup that has potential to be an average third offering. Sedlock will need to fill the zone with greater frequency and prove he can withstand the rigors of 200-plus innings, but he has the look of a future #3 starter.

After missing a chunk of 2015 by way of an 80-game suspension, **Travis Demeritte (2B)** proceeded to mash 25 HR and lead CAL hitters in extra-base hit percentage (54.4%) in 2016. Atlanta then acquired the 22-year-old from Texas via trade last July, after which his production translated seamlessly to the Carolina League and the Arizona Fall League (AFL). Demeritte's raw power is legit, as he employs plus bat speed and a rare ability to clear all fences, which project him to be a HR/RBI asset. An elongated swing and aggressive approach has yielded subpar contact as a pro, though, and will likely make him a BA burden. Still, with consistently high walk rates and flashes of plus speed, Demeritte should offer OBP/SB value as a solid everyday second baseman.

While Brian Cashman hastily replenished New York's pipeline in 2016, **Domingo Acevedo (RHP)**, a 2013 Dominican signee, might have more intriguing upside than any recent trade acquisition. The 22-year-old posted a 1.90 ERA and 10.1 Dom in the SAL to start 2016 and hardly missed a beat against FSL competition after a mid-year bump (3.22 ERA/9.7 Dom in 10 GS). Tall and lanky at 6-foot-7, 190, Acevedo has touched 103 mph in the past and regularly works 95-98 with his fastball. His mid-80s slider is a tick more advanced than his changeup, though both will need refinement. Acevedo has #2 SP upside with Dom value in a best-case scenario, but his velocity could play well as a high-leverage relief arm.

Firmly placed at No. 76 overall in last year's HQ100, **Daz Cameron (OF)** got lost in the prospect shuffle in 2016 after being demoted from the Midwest League (MWL) to the NYPL mid-year. The 19-year-old then suffered a broken left index finger in July, which ended his season with a .212/.287/.321 slash line and 12 SB in 40 games. While the injury raises some red flags, Cameron remains a young, tools-laden bat with versatile potential. He is a plus runner with SB ability and range necessary to stick in centerfield, and his compact, level swing is conducive to solid contact and line-drive trajectories required for above-average BA returns. Even if his HR totals max out near average (15-18), Cameron should be a coveted OF target in dynasty formats.

Criminally overlooked in a stacked Phillies system, **Adonis Medina (RHP)** is an arm who could shoot up prospect lists with a strong start to 2017. Signed from the Dominican in 2014, Medina, 20, pitched 2016 exclusively from the rotation and went 5-3 with a 2.92 ERA and 1.09 WHIP in 13 NYPL starts. The lack of whiffs (4.7 Dom) or control (3.3 Ctl) wasn't particularly sexy, but the 20-year-old flashed some of the league's best stuff, including a lively plus fastball that will touch 96 mph and good feel for a 79-83 mph slider with plus late break and length necessary to miss bats. His changeup requires refinement and he will need to fill out physically, but the tools for a #2/3 starter with quality Dom skills are there.

The Rays have assembled one of the deeper farm systems in baseball over the past few years, and **Garrett Whitley (OF)** remains a coveted piece to their prospect puzzle. After a rough pro debut split between the GCL and short-season A ball, the 19-year-old centerfielder smoothed out his stroke in route to an above-league-average .735 OPS with 21 SB in the NYPL in 2016. Whitley is a plus runner and will have legit SB upside, and his speed should allow him to stay in center. He also possesses good bat speed and has added some loft to his swing, and he should have 15-17 HR impact. With more consistent contact, Whitley should be an above-average contributor in three categories (R, SB, BA) down the road.

The Dodgers have patiently awaited the return of former first-rounder **Walker Buehler (RHP)** after he missed all of 2015 via Tommy John surgery, and his ultra-abbreviated 2016 debut was encouraging (5.0 IP, 0 H, 0 R, 3 BB, 6 K). Despite a delayed start to his career, the 22-year-old still features as exciting a four-pitch mix as you'll find in the low minors, including a lively mid-90s fastball and flashes of three above-average secondary offerings in his slider, curveball and changeup. Buehler displays good control of each, though his command within the zone will require some polish as he fills out his lean 6-foot-2 frame. If everything comes together, there could be a #2 starter hidden here with quality Dom ability.

The Cardinals took a calculated risk when they used the 23rd overall pick last summer on **Devlin Perez (SS)**, who was projected to be a lock for the top-10 before testing positive for performance enhancing drugs just days before the draft. The 17-year-old still turned in a solid pro debut in the rookie GCL, though, slashing .294/.352/.393 in 43 games. Perez may ultimately have more real-life value than fantasy value given his plus range, arm and quality actions and shortstop, but his plus-plus speed should translate into impact SB. Lean and athletic, he has enough wiry strength to pepper the gaps with 10-15 HR once he matures, while also contributing in BA/R/SB categories as a top-of-the-order type bat.

Though Seattle lacks many high-upside arms in the minors, **Luiz Gohara (LHP)** could be on the verge of breaking out as an impact starter worth targeting. After making strides in his second year between the short-season Northwest League and MWL (1.81 ERA, 10.5 Dom, 3.5 Ctl in 13 GS), the 20-year-old southpaw opened eyes in the AFL, garnering a 19:3 K/BB ratio in 11.2 IP as the league's youngest pitcher. Gohara will touch 97 mph with his double-plus fastball and present it from a downhill angle, and show feel for an above-average mid-80s slider that misses bats against both platoons. His changeup is raw, but shows potential as an average third offering. Honing command of his three-pitch mix will be key if he is to reach his #3 SP potential.

POSITIONS: Up to four positions are listed for each batter and represent those for which he appeared (in order) the most games at in 2016. Positions are shown with their numeric designation (2=CA, 3=1B, 7=LF, 0=DH, etc.)

BATS: Shows which side of the plate he bats from—right (R), left (L) or switch-hitter (S).

AGE: Player's age, as of April 1, 2017.

DRAFTED: The year, round, and school that the player performed at as an amateur if drafted, or where the player was signed from, if a free agent.

EXP MLB DEBUT: The year a player is expected to debut in the major leagues.

H/W: The player's height and weight.

FUT: The role that the batter is expected to have for the majority of his major league career, not necessarily his greatest upside.

SKILLS: Each skill a player possesses is graded and designated with a "+", indicating the quality of the skills, taking into context the batter's age and level played. An average skill will receive three "+" marks.

- **PWR:** Measures the player's ability to drive the ball and hit for power.
- **BAVG:** Measures the player's ability to hit for batting average and judge the strike zone.
- **SPD:** Measures the player's raw speed and base-running ability.
- **DEF:** Measures the player's overall defense, which includes arm strength, arm accuracy, range, agility, hands, and defensive instincts.

PLAYER STAT LINES: Player statistics for the last five teams that he played for (if applicable), including college and the major leagues.

TEAM DESIGNATIONS: Each team that the player performed for during a given year is included.

LEVEL DESIGNATIONS: The level for each team a player performed is included. "AAA" means Triple-A, "AA" means Double-A, "A+" means high Class-A, "A-" means low Class-A, and "Rk" means rookie level.

SABERMETRIC CATEGORIES: Descriptions of all the sabermetric categories appear in the glossary.

CAPSULE COMMENTARIES: For each player, a brief analysis of their skills/statistics, and their future potential is provided.

ELIGIBILITY: Eligibility for inclusion is the standard for which Major League Baseball adheres to; 130 at-bats or 45 days on the 25-man roster, not including the month of September.

POTENTIAL RATINGS: The Potential Ratings are a two-part system in which a player is assigned a number rating based on his upside potential (1-10) and a letter rating based on the probability of reaching that potential (A-E).

Potential

10:	Hall of Famer	5:	MLB reserve
9:	Elite player	4:	Top minor leaguer
8:	Solid regular	3:	Average minor leaguer
7:	Average regular	2:	Minor league reserve
6:	Platoon player	1:	Minor league roster filler

Probability Rating

A:	90% probability of reaching potential
B:	70% probability of reaching potential
C:	50% probability of reaching potential
D:	30% probability of reaching potential
E:	10% probability of reaching potential

SKILLS: Scouts usually grade a player's skills on the 20-80 scale, and while most of the grades are subjective, there are grades that can be given to represent a certain hitting statistic or running speed. These are indicated on this chart:

Scout Grade	HR	BA	Speed (L)	Speed (R)
80	39+	.320+	3.9	4.0
70	32-38	.300-.319	4.0	4.1
60	25-31	.286-.299	4.1	4.2
50 (avg)	17-24	.270-.285	4.2	4.3
40	11-16	.250-.269	4.3	4.4
30	6-10	.220-.249	4.4	4.5
20	0-5	.219-	4.5	4.6

CATCHER POP TIMES: Catchers are timed (in seconds) from the moment the pitch reaches the catcher's mitt until the time that the middle infielder receives the baseball at second base. This number assists both teams in assessing whether a base-runner should steal second base or not.

1.85	+
1.95	MLB average
2.05	–

Abreu,Osvaldo — 6 — Washington

EXP MLB DEBUT: 2019 | H/W: 6-0 170 | FUT: Starting SS | 7C

Bats R | Age 22 | 2012 FA (DR)

Skills	Year	Lev	Team	AB	R	H	HR	RBI	Avg	OB	Slg	OPS	bb%	ct%	Eye	SB	CS	x/h%	Iso	RC/G
Pwr + +	2013	Rk	GCL Nationals	147	24	42	0	24	286	367	381	748	11	84	0.79	16	6	31	95	5.12
BAvg + + +	2014	A-	Auburn	210	31	48	1	15	229	260	305	565	4	80	0.22	10	6	23	76	2.35
4.43 Spd + + +	2015	A	Hagerstown	442	74	121	6	47	274	348	412	759	10	80	0.56	30	11	37	138	5.10
Def + + +	2016	A+	Potomac	497	86	123	6	52	247	322	346	669	10	78	0.51	18	10	27	99	3.88

Above-average defender with some present pull-side doubles power, but little HR projection. Inconsistent plate approach may get exploited at higher levels, but overall has an average hit tool. Some speed on the basepaths, but far from a burner. Solid, but no standout tool.

Acuna,Ronald — 789 — Atlanta

EXP MLB DEBUT: 2019 | H/W: 6-0 180 | FUT: Starting OF | 9E

Bats R | Age 19 | 2014 FA (VZ)

Skills	Year	Lev	Team	AB	R	H	HR	RBI	Avg	OB	Slg	OPS	bb%	ct%	Eye	SB	CS	x/h%	Iso	RC/G
Pwr + + + +																				
BAvg + + +																				
Spd + + + +	2016	Rk	GCL Braves	6	1	2	0	1	333	429	333	762	14	83	1.00	0	0	0	0	5.32
Def + + + +	2016	A	Rome	148	27	46	4	18	311	386	432	818	11	81	0.64	14	7	17	122	5.71

Breakout performer in loaded ATL farm system during full-season debut. Showcased average or better tools across the board. Barrels everything at the plate with quick-twitch swing. Has 20 HR raw power potential. 60-grade runner with defensive chops. Only a thumb injury and nagging leg injuries kept him from top prospect consideration.

Adames,Willy — 6 — Tampa Bay

EXP MLB DEBUT: 2017 | H/W: 6-1 180 | FUT: Starting SS | 9B

Bats R | Age 21 | 2012 FA (DR)

Skills	Year	Lev	Team	AB	R	H	HR	RBI	Avg	OB	Slg	OPS	bb%	ct%	Eye	SB	CS	x/h%	Iso	RC/G
	2013	Rk	DSL Tigers	200	48	49	1	21	245	410	370	780	22	78	1.27	9	12	37	125	6.03
Pwr + + +	2014	A	Bowling Green	97	15	27	2	11	278	375	433	808	13	69	0.50	3	0	33	155	6.08
BAvg + + +	2014	A	West Michigan	353	40	95	6	50	269	342	428	770	10	73	0.41	3	6	34	159	5.31
Spd + + +	2015	A+	Charlotte	396	51	102	4	46	258	347	379	725	12	69	0.44	10	1	33	121	4.88
Def + + +	2016	AA	Montgomery	486	89	133	11	57	274	370	430	800	13	75	0.61	13	6	36	156	5.77

Advanced INF with high ceiling predicated on offensive skills. Set highs in HR, 2B, BB, and SB while dominating LHP with plus bat speed. Knows strike zone and willing to draw walks. Can still expand strike zone and sell out for power, but feel for bat is superb. Has arm and hands to stick at SS, though may move to 2B or 3B down the line.

Adams,Caleb — 79 — Los Angeles (A)

EXP MLB DEBUT: 2018 | H/W: 5-10 185 | FUT: Reserve OF | 6B

Bats R | Age 24 | 2014 (10) La-Lafayette

Skills	Year	Lev	Team	AB	R	H	HR	RBI	Avg	OB	Slg	OPS	bb%	ct%	Eye	SB	CS	x/h%	Iso	RC/G
	2014	Rk	Orem	210	37	53	7	28	252	320	414	735	9	67	0.30	7	1	34	162	4.80
Pwr + +	2015	A	Burlington	235	32	71	3	30	302	386	426	811	12	67	0.42	7	5	25	123	6.19
BAvg + +	2015	A+	Inland Empire	181	24	53	4	26	293	369	453	822	11	67	0.37	3	2	34	160	6.30
Spd + + +	2016	A+	Inland Empire	187	21	54	1	25	289	354	406	761	9	71	0.35	5	2	26	118	5.26
Def + + +	2016	AA	Arkansas	246	28	56	4	24	228	280	321	601	7	67	0.22	9	4	21	93	2.78

Short, instinctual OF who was very good in A+, but not so hot in AA upon promotion in late May. Drives ball to gaps with clean, quick stroke, though strikes out too much for few HR. Doesn't project well with pop due to swing path. Runs fairly well, though not a burner, and can play any outfield spot. Lack of arm strength likely to lead to LF.

Adolfo,Micker — 9 — Chicago (A)

EXP MLB DEBUT: 2019 | H/W: 6-3 200 | FUT: Starting OF | 8D

Bats R | Age 20 | 2013 FA (DR)

Skills	Year	Lev	Team	AB	R	H	HR	RBI	Avg	OB	Slg	OPS	bb%	ct%	Eye	SB	CS	x/h%	Iso	RC/G
Pwr + + +	2014	Rk	Azl White Sox	179	27	39	5	21	218	275	380	654	7	53	0.16	0	0	44	162	4.47
BAvg +	2015	Rk	Azl White Sox	83	14	21	0	10	253	303	313	617	7	70	0.24	3	2	19	60	3.07
Spd + +	2016	Rk	Azl White Sox	16	2	4	1	2	250	294	563	857	6	50	0.13	0	0	75	313	8.68
Def + + +	2016	A	Kannapolis	247	30	54	5	21	219	261	340	601	5	64	0.16	0	1	35	121	2.79

Tall, strong OF with loads of potential, but failed to show tools in first full season. Hitting mechanics and pitch recognition need lot of work, though incredible bat speed and leverage should lead to plus power in time. Runs well for size, though won't steal many bases. Arm strength is ideal for RF but will need to improve reads and routes.

Albies,Ozhaino — 46 — Atlanta

EXP MLB DEBUT: 2017 | H/W: 5-9 160 | FUT: Starting 2B | 8B

Bats B | Age 20 | 2013 FA (CC)

Skills	Year	Lev	Team	AB	R	H	HR	RBI	Avg	OB	Slg	OPS	bb%	ct%	Eye	SB	CS	x/h%	Iso	RC/G
	2014	Rk	Danville	135	25	48	1	14	356	428	452	879	11	87	1.00	15	3	17	96	6.60
Pwr + +	2014	Rk	GCL Braves	63	16	24	0	5	381	473	429	902	15	90	1.83	7	2	13	48	7.14
BAvg + + + +	2015	A	Rome	394	64	122	0	37	310	367	404	771	8	86	0.64	29	8	24	94	5.20
Spd + + + +	2016	AA	Mississippi	330	56	106	4	33	321	383	467	850	9	83	0.58	21	9	31	145	6.15
Def + + + +	2016	AAA	Gwinnett	222	27	55	2	20	248	307	351	658	8	82	0.49	9	4	29	104	3.74

Slender switch-hitting middle infielder made it up to Triple-A during his 19-year-old season. Dynamic hit tool; plays pepper with the fielders. Tremendous balance in swing has allowed to tap into some power no one thought was there. Still learning to use plus-plus speed on the base paths. Chance to be good defender at second or short.

Alcantara,Sergio — 6 — Arizona

EXP MLB DEBUT: 2020 | H/W: 5-9 168 | FUT: Starting SS | 7E

Bats B | Age 20 | 2012 FA (DR)

Skills	Year	Lev	Team	AB	R	H	HR	RBI	Avg	OB	Slg	OPS	bb%	ct%	Eye	SB	CS	x/h%	Iso	RC/G
	2015	A	Kane County	71	5	8	0	5	113	160	127	287	5	76	0.24	1	0	13	14	-1.33
Pwr +	2016	Rk	Azl Diamondbacks	29	9	10	0	2	345	424	448	873	12	93	2.00	2	0	20	103	6.71
BAvg + +	2016	A-	Hillsboro	47	12	15	0	8	319	439	362	800	18	79	1.00	4	2	13	43	6.04
Spd + + +	2016	A	Kane County	180	15	48	1	16	267	320	328	647	7	86	0.54	3	2	17	61	3.59
Def + + + +	2016	A+	Visalia	15	2	4	0	0	267	389	333	722	17	87	1.50	0	1	25	67	5.14

Light-hitting, defensive-oriented SS rebounded nicely after disastrous '15. Solid bat-to-ball skills. Swing path leads to lots of ground ball contact. Very impatient at plate with little game plan. Does not have power in frame. Spectacular defender despite average foot speed. Defense could propel into MLB starting role.

Alemais,Stephen — 6 — Pittsburgh

EXP MLB DEBUT: 2020 | H/W: 6-0 190 | FUT: Starting SS | 7C

Bats R | Age 21 | 2016 (3) Tulane

Skills	Year	Lev	Team	AB	R	H	HR	RBI	Avg	OB	Slg	OPS	bb%	ct%	Eye	SB	CS	x/h%	Iso	RC/G
Pwr + +																				
BAvg + + +	2016	NCAA	Tulane	212	37	66	1	28	311	371	401	772	9	86	0.69	19	5	24	90	5.18
Spd + +	2016	A-	West Virginia	156	23	41	1	18	263	286	314	600	3	88	0.28	9	3	15	51	2.85
Def + + + +	2016	A	West Virginia	37	2	7	0	2	189	231	270	501	5	70	0.18	1	3	29	81	1.44

Pirates 3rd round pick is a plus defender with good range, soft hands, and strong arm. Made consistent contact in college with good strike zone awareness and a line-drive approach, but swing can get big despite below-average power. Has the chops to stick at SS, but Bucs have depth at that position so could be forced into a UT role.

Alfaro,Jhoandro — 2 — Chicago (A)

EXP MLB DEBUT: 2020 | H/W: 6-1 180 | FUT: Starting C | 8D

Bats B | Age 20 | 2014 FA (CB)

Skills	Year	Lev	Team	AB	R	H	HR	RBI	Avg	OB	Slg	OPS	bb%	ct%	Eye	SB	CS	x/h%	Iso	RC/G
Pwr + +																				
BAvg + +																				
Spd + +	2015	Rk	AZL White Sox	88	7	16	0	7	182	217	205	422	4	83	0.27	0	0	13	23	0.69
Def + + +	2016	Rk	DSL White Sox	126	17	30	1	8	238	333	294	627	13	85	0.95	1	1	17	56	3.62

Improving receiver who is advanced for age, though is far from majors. Has tools and work ethic to be contributor with both bat and glove. Exhibits solid-average bat speed and handsy swing, though could add strength as he matures. Makes contact with short stroke and power could develop. Strong arm is asset and needs to work on footwork and release.

Alfaro,Jorge — 2 — Philadelphia

EXP MLB DEBUT: 2016 | H/W: 6-2 225 | FUT: Starting C | 8B

Bats R | Age 23 | 2010 FA (CB)

Skills	Year	Lev	Team	AB	R	H	HR	RBI	Avg	OB	Slg	OPS	bb%	ct%	Eye	SB	CS	x/h%	Iso	RC/G
	2014	AA	Frisco	88	12	23	4	14	261	309	443	752	6	74	0.26	0	0	35	182	4.62
Pwr + + + +	2015	Rk	GCL Phillies	4	0	2	0	1	500	500	750	1250	0	100		0	0	50	250	9.68
BAvg + + +	2015	AA	Frisco	190	22	48	5	21	253	286	432	718	5	68	0.15	2	1	46	179	4.45
4.45 Spd + +	2016	AA	Reading	404	68	115	15	67	285	322	458	780	5	74	0.21	3	2	33	173	4.99
Def + + +	2016	MLB	Philadelphia	16	0	2	0	0	125	176	125	301	6	50	0.13	0	0	0	0	-2.23

Stayed healthy in much-needed full year of development at AA. Ball jumps off his bat to all fields; can both shoot the gaps and send it over the fence. Bat speed and raw power is muted some by swing-and-miss and tendency to expand strike zone. Has the arm/release to shut down the running game.

Alford,Anthony — 8 — Toronto

EXP MLB DEBUT: 2017 | H/W: 6-1 215 | FUT: Starting CF | 8B

Bats R | Age 22 | 2012 (3) HS (MS)

Skills	Year	Lev	Team	AB	R	H	HR	RBI	Avg	OB	Slg	OPS	bb%	ct%	Eye	SB	CS	x/h%	Iso	RC/G
	2014	Rk	Bluefield	29	5	6	1	2	207	324	310	634	15	55	0.38	1	0	17	103	3.64
Pwr + + +	2014	A	Lansing	25	3	8	1	3	320	320	480	800	0	68	0.00	4	0	25	160	5.18
BAvg + + +	2015	A	Lansing	188	49	55	1	16	293	414	394	808	17	68	0.65	12	1	29	101	6.36
Spd + + + +	2015	A+	Dunedin	225	42	68	3	19	302	379	444	824	11	78	0.57	15	6	29	142	5.99
Def + + +	2016	A+	Dunedin	339	53	80	9	44	236	339	378	717	14	65	0.45	18	6	35	142	4.75

Explosive athlete who was beset by injuries, but was hot upon return in July and August. Set high in HR and can work counts to find pitches to hit hard. Plate discipline has improved; he profiles as a top-of-the-order hitter. Runs extremely well and is threat whenever on base. Still a bit raw in CF, but arm and range are highlights.

Allen,Austin — 2 — San Diego — EXP MLB DEBUT: 2019 — H/W: 6-4 225 — FUT: Starting C — 8E

	Year	Lev	Team	AB	R	H	HR	RBI	Avg	OB	Slg	OPS	bb%	ct%	Eye	SB	CS	x/h%	Iso	RC/G
Bats L Age 23																				
2015 (4) Florida Tech																				
Pwr + + +																				
BAvg + + +	2015	A-	Tri-City	196	23	47	2	34	240	313	332	645	10	81	0.55	1	2	28	92	3.61
Spd +	2016	A	Fort Wayne	409	52	131	7	61	320	365	425	791	7	83	0.42	0	0	22	105	5.17
Def +	2016	AA	San Antonio	11	1	3	1	1	273	273	545	818	0	100		0	0	33	273	4.93

Big-bodied, offensive-minded catcher with advanced hit and power tools. Impressive bat speed and approach. Could smooth out swing. Identifies pitches well. Loud power tool yet to materialize in-game. 20-grade runner and defender. Footwork behind the plate needs a lot of work, though strides have been made since introduction to pro ball.

Allen,Greg — 89 — Cleveland — EXP MLB DEBUT: 2018 — H/W: 6-0 175 — FUT: Starting OF — 8C

	Year	Lev	Team	AB	R	H	HR	RBI	Avg	OB	Slg	OPS	bb%	ct%	Eye	SB	CS	x/h%	Iso	RC/G
Bats B Age 24	2014	A-	Mahoning Valley	225	46	55	0	19	244	325	298	623	11	88	1.04	30	5	18	53	3.66
2014 (6) San Diego St	2015	A	Lake County	479	83	131	7	45	273	346	382	728	10	88	0.93	43	16	27	109	4.75
Pwr +	2015	A+	Lynchburg	13	2	2	0	0	154	267	231	497	13	77	0.67	3	0	50	77	1.85
BAvg + + +	2016	A+	Lynchburg	346	93	103	4	31	298	399	402	800	14	85	1.14	38	7	23	104	5.85
Spd + + + + / Def + + + +	2016	AA	Akron	145	26	42	3	13	290	372	441	813	12	81	0.70	7	6	31	152	5.81

Shorter, lean OF who impressed with power and speed in AFL. Possesses elite burst out of box and premium speed for future SB impact. Stays compact and short through zone for gap power and plus contact skills. Selective at plate and will draw walks. Reads balls well, has good closing speed and enough arm to stay in CF.

Alonso,Peter — 3 — New York (N) — EXP MLB DEBUT: 2019 — H/W: 6-3 225 — FUT: Starting 1B — 8D

	Year	Lev	Team	AB	R	H	HR	RBI	Avg	OB	Slg	OPS	bb%	ct%	Eye	SB	CS	x/h%	Iso	RC/G
Bats R Age 22																				
2016 (2) Florida																				
Pwr + + + +																				
BAvg + + +																				
Spd +	2016	NCAA	Florida	211	51	79	14	60	374	455	659	1113	13	85	1.00	2	0	41	284	9.25
Def + +	2016	A-	Brooklyn	109	20	35	5	21	321	383	587	970	9	80	0.50	0	1	51	266	7.60

Prototypical 1B profile. Lots of lackluster performances before shortening swing as a college junior and dominating SEC pitchers. Dominance continued in NYPL. Tremendous raw power, starting using it to all fields in '16. Adequate defender at first, could become average. Absolute base clogger.

Alvarez,Eli — 4 — St. Louis — EXP MLB DEBUT: 2020 — H/W: 5-11 165 — FUT: Starting 2B — 8D

	Year	Lev	Team	AB	R	H	HR	RBI	Avg	OB	Slg	OPS	bb%	ct%	Eye	SB	CS	x/h%	Iso	RC/G
Bats L Age 22																				
2011 FA (DR)																				
Pwr + +	2013	Rk	GCL Cardinals	67	12	14	1	7	209	254	373	627	6	79	0.29	6	2	43	164	3.24
BAvg + + +	2014	Rk	GCL Cardinals	68	11	24	1	15	353	405	632	1038	8	90	0.86	3	1	50	279	8.36
Spd + + + +	2015	Rk	Johnson City	204	32	64	2	31	314	349	451	800	5	84	0.34	9	4	36	137	5.30
Def + + +	2016	A	Peoria	433	70	140	6	59	323	397	476	873	11	78	0.55	36	15	34	152	6.63

Athletic INF continues to rake. Does everything well on the diamond. At the plate he has a short, compact LH stroke that allows him to barrel the ball and generate surprising pop. Plus speed gives him above-average range and had career-best 36 SB. Solid defender with good range, nice hands, and a strong arm.

Alvarez,Yordan — 3 — Houston — EXP MLB DEBUT: 2021 — H/W: 6-5 225 — FUT: Starting 1B — 8E

	Year	Lev	Team	AB	R	H	HR	RBI	Avg	OB	Slg	OPS	bb%	ct%	Eye	SB	CS	x/h%	Iso	RC/G
Bats L Age 19																				
2016 FA (CU)																				
Pwr + +																				
BAvg + + +																				
Spd +																				
Def + +	2017		Did not play in the US																	

Tall, angular 1B with immense potential due to swing and power hopes. Should become offensive asset thanks to plus bat speed and feel for contact. Can be tough out as he puts bat to ball with hand-eye coordination. Power is sub-par now, but should grow to solid-average. Relegated to 1B with limited speed and agility.

Anderson,Blake — 2 — Miami — EXP MLB DEBUT: 2019 — H/W: 6-3 180 — FUT: Reserve C — 6C

	Year	Lev	Team	AB	R	H	HR	RBI	Avg	OB	Slg	OPS	bb%	ct%	Eye	SB	CS	x/h%	Iso	RC/G
Bats R Age 21																				
2014 (S-1) HS (MS)																				
Pwr + +																				
BAvg + +	2014	Rk	GCL Marlins	74	6	8	0	5	108	233	135	368	14	55	0.36	0	1	25	27	-0.96
Spd + +	2015	A-	Batavia	118	9	26	2	16	220	240	322	562	2	64	0.07	0	0	31	102	2.10
Def + + +	2016	A-	Batavia	4	0	0	0	0	0	0	0	0	0	25	0.00	0	0		0	-10.45

Tall, athletic catcher missed all but 4 games with a left shoulder sprain. When healthy has a balanced approach at the plate with a line-drive swing, but lacks the bat speed and contact skills to develop power. Slash line as a pro is .173/.274/.245. Has good blocking and receiving skills with a plus arm and should be able to stick behind the dish.

Anderson,Brian — 35 — Miami — EXP MLB DEBUT: 2017 — H/W: 6-3 185 — FUT: Starting 3B — 8C

	Year	Lev	Team	AB	R	H	HR	RBI	Avg	OB	Slg	OPS	bb%	ct%	Eye	SB	CS	x/h%	Iso	RC/G
Bats R Age 23																				
2014 (3) Arkansas	2014	A-	Batavia	77	11	21	3	12	273	325	455	780	7	86	0.55	1	1	33	182	5.04
Pwr + + +	2014	A	Greensboro	153	27	48	8	37	314	367	516	884	8	82	0.46	0	0	31	203	6.23
BAvg + + +	2015	A+	Jupiter	477	50	112	8	62	235	294	340	634	8	77	0.37	2	2	29	105	3.27
Spd + +	2016	A+	Jupiter	182	27	55	3	25	302	377	440	817	11	79	0.58	3	0	31	137	5.84
Def + + + +	2016	AA	Jacksonville	301	38	73	8	40	243	323	359	682	11	80	0.61	0	0	25	116	4.01

Hard working player has good approach at plate and makes consistent contact. Has good power and makes in-game adjustments. He moves well defensively with good range, soft hands, and a strong arm. Has good speed but is not a SB threat. Started red-hot at A+, but struggled when moved up. Played 1B and 3B in the AFL.

Andujar,Miguel — 5 — New York (A) — EXP MLB DEBUT: 2018 — H/W: 6-0 175 — FUT: Starting 3B — 8D

	Year	Lev	Team	AB	R	H	HR	RBI	Avg	OB	Slg	OPS	bb%	ct%	Eye	SB	CS	x/h%	Iso	RC/G
Bats R Age 22																				
2011 FA (DR)	2013	Rk	GCL Yankees 2	133	18	43	4	25	323	357	496	853	5	84	0.33	4	1	35	173	5.80
Pwr + + +	2014	A	Charleston (Sc)	484	75	129	10	70	267	316	397	713	7	83	0.42	5	1	30	130	4.26
BAvg + + +	2015	A+	Tampa	485	54	118	8	57	243	286	363	649	6	81	0.32	12	1	31	120	3.44
Spd + +	2016	A+	Tampa	230	34	65	10	41	283	335	474	809	7	87	0.60	1	3	34	191	5.36
Def + + +	2016	AA	Trenton	282	28	75	2	42	266	317	358	675	7	85	0.50	2	1	27	92	3.92

Emerging prospect who set high in HR and doubles while continuing to make easy contact with simple stroke. Can be free swinger at times and may lunge at breaking balls. Raw power developing and can shoot gaps. Lacks foot speed for SB, though has range and cannon arm to be average defender. Needs to cut down on errors.

Aplin,Andrew — 8 — Houston — EXP MLB DEBUT: 2017 — H/W: 6-0 205 — FUT: Reserve OF — 6A

	Year	Lev	Team	AB	R	H	HR	RBI	Avg	OB	Slg	OPS	bb%	ct%	Eye	SB	CS	x/h%	Iso	RC/G
Bats L Age 26																				
2012 (5) Arizona State	2014	AA	Corpus Christi	356	49	95	6	50	267	380	354	734	15	84	1.16	21	8	19	87	5.03
Pwr + +	2014	AAA	Oklahoma City	96	14	25	0	15	260	360	313	673	14	84	1.00	5	3	16	52	4.28
BAvg + +	2015	AA	Corpus Christi	105	27	36	0	12	343	465	448	913	19	88	1.85	12	3	19	105	7.60
Spd + + +	2015	AAA	Fresno	233	37	64	2	28	275	392	348	740	16	82	1.10	20	7	17	73	5.17
Def + + + +	2016	AAA	Fresno	399	61	89	5	32	223	297	318	615	10	75	0.43	21	9	27	95	3.12

Athletic OF with at least 20 SB each of last 5 seasons. Plays above average CF defense with terrific arm strength and great range. Reads balls off bat and tracks down well. Has regressed as hitter. Walk rate declined while K rate rose. Works counts, but struggles with breaking balls and offers below average pop to pull side.

Aquino,Aristides — 9 — Cincinnati — EXP MLB DEBUT: 2018 — H/W: 6-4 190 — FUT: Starting OF — 8C

	Year	Lev	Team	AB	R	H	HR	RBI	Avg	OB	Slg	OPS	bb%	ct%	Eye	SB	CS	x/h%	Iso	RC/G
Bats R Age 22																				
2011 FA (DR)	2013	Rk	AZL Reds	194	37	54	4	38	278	314	479	793	5	79	0.25	4	3	46	201	5.27
Pwr + + + +	2014	Rk	Billings	284	48	83	16	64	292	328	577	905	5	77	0.23	21	5	53	285	6.57
BAvg + + +	2015	Rk	Billings	52	7	16	2	13	308	333	558	891	4	83	0.22	0	1	38	250	6.24
Spd + + + +	2015	A	Dayton	231	25	54	5	27	234	269	364	632	5	77	0.21	6	1	31	130	3.10
Def + + + +	2016	A+	Daytona	484	69	132	23	79	273	320	519	839	7	79	0.33	11	7	46	246	5.78

Toolsy OF had breakout season in pitcher-friendly FSL. Slashed .273/.327/.519 two years removed from wrist injury that downgraded hit and power tool. Improved overall approach. Can drive ball out to all fields. 30 HR potential in bat. Plus runner. Has utilized run tool in field but may not translate to MLB.

Aracena,Ricky — 6 — Kansas City — EXP MLB DEBUT: 2020 — H/W: 5-8 160 — FUT: Starting SS — 7D

	Year	Lev	Team	AB	R	H	HR	RBI	Avg	OB	Slg	OPS	bb%	ct%	Eye	SB	CS	x/h%	Iso	RC/G
Bats B Age 19																				
2014 FA (DR)																				
Pwr + +																				
BAvg + +																				
Spd + + + +																				
Def + + +	2016	Rk	Idaho Falls	267	44	67	1	33	251	296	322	618	6	80	0.32	17	8	19	71	3.08

Short, lean INF with advanced feel for game. Owns short stroke from both sides and has potential pop despite lack of size and strength. Very fast runner who can steal bases and leg out xbh. Possesses quickness and instincts with glove while arm strength suitable for any infield spot. Can be impact leadoff hitter with selective eye.

Arauz, Jonathan — 46 — Houston

EXP MLB DEBUT: 2020 | H/W: 6-0 150 | FUT: Utility player | **7D**

Bats B Age 18
2014 FA (PN)

Pwr ++
BAvg +++
Spd +++
Def +++

Year	Lev	Team	AB	R	H	HR	RBI	Avg	OB	Slg	OPS	bb%	ct%	Eye	SB	CS	x/h%	Iso	RC/G
2016	Rk	Greeneville	201	26	50	2	18	249	314	338	652	9	78	0.42	1	3	26	90	3.60

Lean, rangy INF who split time between 2B and SS. Plays fundamental game as well as small ball. Makes hard contact and uses entire field in simple approach. Has some pop in small frame due to solid-average bat speed. Could hit for power as he adds loft to swing. Ranges well to both sides and has nice arm, though will likely settle in at 2B.

Armenteros, Lazaro — 89 — Oakland

EXP MLB DEBUT: 2022 | H/W: 6-0 210 | FUT: Starting CF | **9E**

Bats R Age 17
2016 FA (CU)

Pwr +++
BAvg +++
Spd +++
Def +++

Year	Lev	Team	AB	R	H	HR	RBI	Avg	OB	Slg	OPS	bb%	ct%	Eye	SB	CS	x/h%	Iso	RC/G
2016		Did not play in the US																	

Exciting athlete with as much upside as any. Raw with bat as he doesn't make consistent contact due to vicious, uppercut stroke. More of an all-or-nothing approach right now and has big holes in swing. Electric bat speed gives hope for double-plus pop and use of entire field. Can play CF or RF with plus arm and has above average speed.

Arozarena, Randy — 678 — St. Louis

EXP MLB DEBUT: 2018 | H/W: 5-11 170 | FUT: Starting SS/OF | **8D**

Bats R Age 22
2016 FA (CU)

Pwr +++
BAvg +++
Spd ++++
Def +++

Year	Lev	Team	AB	R	H	HR	RBI	Avg	OB	Slg	OPS	bb%	ct%	Eye	SB	CS	x/h%	Iso	RC/G
2016		Did not play in the US																	

Athletic player signed for $1.25 million. Played SS and OF in Cuba, but future position remains to be determined. Short, compact stroke results in line drives to all fields. Good understanding of the strike zone should allow him to hit for average once he makes his state-side debut. Average power with plus speed give him value.

Arraez, Luis — 4 — Minnesota

EXP MLB DEBUT: 2019 | H/W: 5-10 155 | FUT: Starting 2B | **7D**

Bats L Age 19
2013 FA (VZ)

Pwr +
BAvg ++++
Spd ++
Def +++

Year	Lev	Team	AB	R	H	HR	RBI	Avg	OB	Slg	OPS	bb%	ct%	Eye	SB	CS	x/h%	Iso	RC/G
2015	Rk	GCL Twins	206	23	63	0	19	306	367	388	756	9	95	2.00	8	8	25	83	5.24
2016	A	Cedar Rapids	475	67	165	3	66	347	387	444	832	6	89	0.61	3	3	22	97	5.70

Short, slight INF who led MWL in BA after hitting .300+ each month. Makes incredible contact due to hand-eye coordination and ideal bat control. Doesn't hit ball hard, rather uses speed to leg out xbh. No power at all and not expected to grow into any. Lacks speed for SB, though is dependable defender with range and average arm.

Arroyo, Christian — 46 — San Francisco

EXP MLB DEBUT: 2017 | H/W: 6-1 180 | FUT: Starting MIF | **8C**

Bats R Age 21
2013 (1) HS (FL)

Pwr +++
BAvg +++
Spd ++
Def +++

Year	Lev	Team	AB	R	H	HR	RBI	Avg	OB	Slg	OPS	bb%	ct%	Eye	SB	CS	x/h%	Iso	RC/G
2013	Rk	Azl Giants	184	47	60	2	39	326	389	511	900	9	83	0.59	3	2	42	185	6.86
2014	A-	Salem-Keizer	243	39	81	5	48	333	379	469	848	7	87	0.58	6	1	26	136	5.88
2014	A	Augusta	118	10	24	1	14	203	230	271	501	3	81	0.18	1	2	21	68	1.51
2015	A+	San Jose	381	48	116	9	42	304	338	459	797	5	81	0.26	5	3	34	155	5.16
2016	AA	Richmond	474	57	130	3	49	274	316	373	690	6	85	0.40	1	1	31	99	4.03

Multi-talented INF who saw HR drop, but has opportunity to hit for BA and moderate power. Has simple swing and focuses on using entire field. Should hit doubles and has hand-eye coordination and above average bat speed. Not a burner and won't steal bases. Has played multiple INF spots, though could end up in OF. Owns strong arm.

Asuaje, Carlos — 456 — San Diego

EXP MLB DEBUT: 2016 | H/W: 5-9 160 | FUT: Starting 2B | **7C**

Bats L Age 25
2013 (11) Nova Southeastern

Pwr +++
BAvg +++
Spd +++
Def ++

Year	Lev	Team	AB	R	H	HR	RBI	Avg	OB	Slg	OPS	bb%	ct%	Eye	SB	CS	x/h%	Iso	RC/G
2014	A	Greenville	325	59	99	11	73	305	383	542	924	11	83	0.73	7	4	45	237	7.15
2014	A+	Salem	155	27	50	4	28	323	393	516	909	10	78	0.53	1	3	40	194	7.02
2015	AA	Portland	495	60	124	8	61	251	327	374	700	10	82	0.64	9	6	31	123	4.34
2016	AAA	El Paso	535	98	172	9	69	321	378	473	851	8	85	0.60	10	5	30	151	6.08
2016	MLB	San Diego	24	2	5	0	2	208	240	292	532	4	83	0.25	0	0	40	83	2.09

Overachieving 2B continues to max-out average tool shed. Quick, compact swing from LH side. Patient. Avoids swinging at pitches out of hit zone. Gap-to-gap power. Racked up 54 xbh between Triple-A & SD. Below average range at many positions; most likely to stick at 2B.

Austin, Tyler — 379 — New York (A)

EXP MLB DEBUT: 2016 | H/W: 6-2 220 | FUT: Starting 1B | **7C**

Bats R Age 25
2010 (13) HS (GA)

Pwr ++++
BAvg +++
Spd +
Def ++

Year	Lev	Team	AB	R	H	HR	RBI	Avg	OB	Slg	OPS	bb%	ct%	Eye	SB	CS	x/h%	Iso	RC/G
2015	AA	Trenton	77	8	20	2	8	260	329	455	784	9	79	0.50	3	2	45	195	5.35
2015	AAA	Scranton/WB	264	33	62	4	27	235	303	311	614	9	69	0.32	8	1	19	76	2.99
2016	AA	Trenton	177	22	46	4	29	260	367	395	763	14	74	0.65	1	1	33	136	5.31
2016	AAA	Scranton/WB	201	39	65	13	49	323	416	637	1053	14	71	0.54	5	0	57	313	9.37
2016	MLB	NY Yankees	83	7	20	5	12	241	300	458	758	8	57	0.19	1	0	40	217	5.62

Improving hitter who set easy high in HR while drastically increasing walk rate. Reached NYY on basis of bat and defensive versatility. Can play any corner INF/OF spot and may settle in as utility guy. Makes hard contact with strong bat speed and has become a bit too patient. Long swing and inability to hit spin could hurt BA.

Azocar, Jose — 89 — Detroit

EXP MLB DEBUT: 2019 | H/W: 5-11 165 | FUT: Starting CF | **8E**

Bats R Age 20
2012 FA (VZ)

Pwr +
BAvg +++
Spd ++++
Def +++

Year	Lev	Team	AB	R	H	HR	RBI	Avg	OB	Slg	OPS	bb%	ct%	Eye	SB	CS	x/h%	Iso	RC/G
2016	A	West Michigan	501	56	141	0	51	281	316	335	651	5	76	0.21	14	5	13	54	3.39

Short, quick OF who brings exciting talent to game. Struggled down stretch and lack of strength needs to be addressed. Has zero power in arsenal, yet strikes out far too much. Plus speed should lead to more SB down line as he gets on base more. Swings early in count and needs to up OBP as singles hitter. Arm strength suitable for RF.

Baddoo, Akil — 89 — Minnesota

EXP MLB DEBUT: 2021 | H/W: 5-11 185 | FUT: Starting OF | **8E**

Bats L Age 18
2016 (S-2) HS (GA)

Pwr +++
BAvg ++
Spd ++++
Def ++

Year	Lev	Team	AB	R	H	HR	RBI	Avg	OB	Slg	OPS	bb%	ct%	Eye	SB	CS	x/h%	Iso	RC/G
2016	Rk	GCL Twins	107	15	19	2	15	178	296	271	567	14	66	0.50	8	1	21	93	2.45

Exciting OF with high ceiling, but long ways from reaching it. Has potential to hit 20+ HR with 20+ SB and could also bat leadoff. Shows nice approach at plate and owns bat speed. Makes acceptable contact, though can get power hungry and pull happy. Runs well and should stick in CF, though has seen time in RF. Arm strength a bit short.

Bader, Harrison — 8 — St. Louis

EXP MLB DEBUT: 2017 | H/W: 6-0 195 | FUT: Starting CF | **8D**

Bats R Age 22
2015 (3) Florida

Pwr +++
BAvg +++
Spd +++
Def +++

Year	Lev	Team	AB	R	H	HR	RBI	Avg	OB	Slg	OPS	bb%	ct%	Eye	SB	CS	x/h%	Iso	RC/G
2015	NCAA	Florida	256	53	76	17	66	297	377	566	944	11	79	0.61	8	5	45	270	7.23
2015	A-	State College	29	6	11	2	4	379	379	655	1034	0	83	0.00	2	0	36	276	7.41
2015	A	Peoria	206	34	62	9	28	301	348	505	853	7	79	0.34	15	6	35	204	5.92
2016	AA	Springfield	318	48	90	16	41	283	335	497	832	7	71	0.27	11	10	36	214	5.88
2016	AAA	Memphis	147	22	34	3	17	231	285	354	639	7	74	0.29	2	3	32	122	3.28

Started the season well, hitting .283 at AA, but struggled when moved up. Aggressive approach at the plate with surprising power for size and hit 19 HR, but also resulted in below-average contact rate. Runs well with good range and a strong arm and will stick in CF for now. Lacks a true plus tool, but does everything well.

Baldoquin, Roberto — 46 — Los Angeles (A)

EXP MLB DEBUT: 2018 | H/W: 5-11 200 | FUT: Starting MIF | **7E**

Bats R Age 22
2014 FA (CU)

Pwr ++
BAvg ++
Spd ++
Def +++

Year	Lev	Team	AB	R	H	HR	RBI	Avg	OB	Slg	OPS	bb%	ct%	Eye	SB	CS	x/h%	Iso	RC/G
2015	A+	Inland Empire	289	23	68	1	27	235	258	294	553	3	76	0.13	4	5	21	59	2.02
2016	A+	Inland Empire	227	19	45	0	15	198	266	233	500	8	73	0.34	3	3	16	35	1.49

Short, stout INF who was beset by hamstring injury early and never got going. Hasn't lived up to bat expectations as he lacks plate coverage and swing mechanics need adjustment. Has some power in bat, but hasn't realized. Increased walk rate, though still can be aggressive. Possesses range and nice arm for either 2B or SS.

Banks,Nick — 789 — Washington
EXP MLB DEBUT: 2019 | H/W: 6-1 215 | FUT: Starting OF | 8D

Bats L Age 22 — 2016 (4) Texas A&M
Pwr ++ | BAvg +++ | 4.19 Spd ++++ | Def +++

Year	Lev	Team	AB	R	H	HR	RBI	Avg	OB	Slg	OPS	bb%	ct%	Eye	SB	CS	x/h%	Iso	RC/G
2016	NCAA	Texas A&M	239	48	67	9	49	280	346	473	819	9	80	0.51	7	0	37	192	5.65
2016	A-	Auburn	231	18	64	0	19	277	310	320	630	5	84	0.30	7	2	14	43	3.20

Employs confidence in the box with a smooth and simple LH swing. In first pro exposure, whole-field line drives more frequent than over-the-fence power, though showed more pop in college. Good speed an asset in the field and on the bases, and has a RF arm. But needs offensive consistency.

Barnes,Austin — 245 — Los Angeles (N)
EXP MLB DEBUT: 2015 | H/W: 5-10 195 | FUT: Starting C | 7C

Bats R Age 27 — 2011 (9) Arizona State
Pwr ++ | BAvg +++ | Spd +++ | Def +++

Year	Lev	Team	AB	R	H	HR	RBI	Avg	OB	Slg	OPS	bb%	ct%	Eye	SB	CS	x/h%	Iso	RC/G
2014	AA	Jacksonville	284	56	84	12	43	296	401	507	908	15	87	1.39	8	0	40	211	7.06
2015	AAA	Oklahoma City	292	40	92	9	42	315	388	479	868	11	88	0.97	12	2	30	164	6.33
2015	MLB	LA Dodgers	29	4	6	0	1	207	343	276	619	17	79	1.00	1	0	33	69	3.67
2016	AAA	Oklahoma City	336	59	99	6	39	295	375	443	818	11	84	0.81	18	3	33	149	5.87
2016	MLB	LA Dodgers	32	3	5	0	2	156	270	188	458	14	72	0.56	0	0	20	31	1.04

Athletic backstop saw time at C/2B/3B when called up. Contact oriented approach should allow him to hit for average with double-digit HR. Shows great patience at the plate (43 BB/53 K) and makes hard contact going gap-to-gap. Runs well for a C and swiped a career-best 18 bases. Behind the plate his arm works well with good hands.

Barnes,Barrett — 789 — Pittsburgh
EXP MLB DEBUT: 2017 | H/W: 5-11 209 | FUT: Starting OF | 7C

Bats R Age 25 — 2012 (S-1) Texas Tech
Pwr ++ | BAvg ++ | Spd +++ | Def +++

Year	Lev	Team	AB	R	H	HR	RBI	Avg	OB	Slg	OPS	bb%	ct%	Eye	SB	CS	x/h%	Iso	RC/G
2014	A	West Virginia	13	1	2	0	2	154	267	154	421	13	85	1.00	2	0	0	0	1.17
2014	A+	Bradenton	21	3	5	0	1	238	333	333	667	13	76	0.60	1	0	40	95	4.07
2015	A+	Bradenton	234	45	61	6	24	261	340	423	763	11	82	0.68	13	5	39	162	5.11
2015	AA	Altoona	126	17	31	3	17	246	331	365	696	11	80	0.64	4	4	29	119	4.24
2016	AA	Altoona	405	60	124	9	47	306	370	477	846	9	74	0.39	10	4	35	170	6.25

Had his best season as a pro, slashing .367/.440/.627 after the break at AA. Has good bat speed, solid plate discipline, and fringe-average power. Has above-average speed, covers ground well, and should be able to stick in CF. Loads of potential, but checkered injury history lingers.

Barreto,Franklin — 46 — Oakland
EXP MLB DEBUT: 2017 | H/W: 5-10 190 | FUT: Starting MIF | 8A

Bats R Age 21 — 2012 FA (VZ)
Pwr +++ | BAvg ++++ | Spd +++ | Def ++

Year	Lev	Team	AB	R	H	HR	RBI	Avg	OB	Slg	OPS	bb%	ct%	Eye	SB	CS	x/h%	Iso	RC/G
2013	Rk	Bluefield	54	4	11	0	7	204	232	333	565	4	74	0.14	0	2	55	130	2.39
2014	A-	Vancouver	289	65	90	6	61	311	368	481	849	8	78	0.41	29	5	37	170	6.13
2015	A+	Stockton	338	50	102	13	47	302	331	500	831	4	80	0.22	8	3	37	198	5.51
2016	AA	Midland	462	63	130	10	50	281	333	413	747	7	81	0.40	30	15	29	132	4.68
2016	AAA	Nashville	17	2	6	1	3	353	353	647	1000	0	76	0.00	0	2	33	294	7.45

Athletic INF with solid all-around game and can make impact with bat. Hits for easy BA due to quick hands. Focuses on line drives, though can shorten swing and go opp way. Could exceed average pop projection, but would require change in swing path. Makes easy contact and improved walk rate. Range is solid, though is fringy defender.

Basabe,Luis Alejandro — 46 — Arizona
EXP MLB DEBUT: 2020 | H/W: 5-10 160 | FUT: Starting 2B | 7D

Bats B Age 20 — 2012 FA (VZ)
Pwr ++ | BAvg ++ | Spd ++++ | Def +++

Year	Lev	Team	AB	R	H	HR	RBI	Avg	OB	Slg	OPS	bb%	ct%	Eye	SB	CS	x/h%	Iso	RC/G
2015	Rk	GCL Red Sox	100	22	26	0	6	260	388	310	698	17	67	0.64	8	4	19	50	4.70
2016	A	Greenville	229	39	71	4	25	310	406	467	873	14	75	0.64	14	6	34	157	6.87
2016	A	Kane County	161	16	35	3	13	217	337	323	660	15	63	0.48	3	6	26	106	4.00

Switch-hitting, speedy INF who struggled upon trade from BOS. Has offensive potential with bat speed and level swing path. Provides sneaky pop from lean, athletic frame and projects to average at best. Owns above average speed and average defense could get better with improved footwork.

Basabe,Luis Alex — 8 — Chicago (A)
EXP MLB DEBUT: 2019 | H/W: 6-0 160 | FUT: Starting OF | 8D

Bats B Age 20 — 2012 FA (VZ)
Pwr +++ | BAvg ++ | Spd +++ | Def ++++

Year	Lev	Team	AB	R	H	HR	RBI	Avg	OB	Slg	OPS	bb%	ct%	Eye	SB	CS	x/h%	Iso	RC/G
2014	Rk	DSL Red Sox	148	38	42	0	26	284	404	480	884	17	76	0.83	13	2	43	196	7.38
2014	Rk	GCL Red Sox	105	15	26	1	13	248	331	324	654	11	78	0.57	2	4	23	76	3.73
2015	A-	Lowell	222	36	54	7	23	243	339	401	739	13	70	0.48	15	4	33	158	4.91
2016	A	Greenville	403	61	104	12	52	258	325	447	772	9	71	0.34	25	5	42	189	5.27
2016	A+	Salem	22	5	8	0	1	364	391	545	937	4	86	0.33	0	0	38	182	6.96

Plus athlete who enjoyed breakout season and can impact game with bat and glove. Ranges well in CF and has arm and instincts to win awards. Cleaner swing from right side and has power potential. Fast bat gives him BA potential, though can expand strike zone and struggle with spin. Ingredients are here for 20 HR/20 SB.

Bauers,Jake — 39 — Tampa Bay
EXP MLB DEBUT: 2017 | H/W: 6-1 195 | FUT: Starting OF | 8B

Bats L Age 21 — 2013 (7) HS (CA)
Pwr +++ | BAvg +++ | Spd ++ | Def ++

Year	Lev	Team	AB	R	H	HR	RBI	Avg	OB	Slg	OPS	bb%	ct%	Eye	SB	CS	x/h%	Iso	RC/G
2013	Rk	Azl Padres	163	22	46	1	25	282	339	374	713	8	81	0.45	2	0	24	92	4.39
2014	A	Fort Wayne	406	59	120	8	64	296	374	414	788	11	80	0.64	5	6	24	118	5.42
2015	A+	Charlotte	217	33	58	6	38	267	354	433	787	12	85	0.88	2	3	38	166	5.47
2015	AA	Montgomery	257	36	71	5	36	276	331	405	736	8	84	0.51	6	3	32	128	4.61
2016	AA	Montgomery	493	79	135	14	78	274	367	420	787	13	82	0.82	10	6	32	146	5.49

Patient hitter who has been young for level throughout career. Possesses plus pitch recognition and hand-eye coordination to hit for BA while adding more loft and leverage to line drive stroke. Set career-high in HR and makes easy contact. May not have ideal power for 1B, but moves well around bag with quick hands. Can also play RF.

Bautista,Rafael — 789 — Washington
EXP MLB DEBUT: 2017 | H/W: 6-2 165 | FUT: Starting CF | 7B

Bats R Age 24 — 2012 FA (DR)
Pwr + | BAvg +++ | 4.04 Spd +++++ | Def +++

Year	Lev	Team	AB	R	H	HR	RBI	Avg	OB	Slg	OPS	bb%	ct%	Eye	SB	CS	x/h%	Iso	RC/G
2014	A	Hagerstown	487	97	141	5	54	290	335	382	717	6	85	0.46	69	15	21	92	4.34
2015	Rk	GCL Nationals	16	3	5	1	2	313	313	500	813	0	94	0.00	0	0	20	188	4.79
2015	A-	Auburn	33	6	9	0	4	273	294	364	658	3	79	0.14	3	0	33	91	3.46
2015	A+	Potomac	206	23	56	0	8	272	309	325	634	5	89	0.50	23	4	16	53	3.44
2016	AA	Harrisburg	543	77	153	4	39	282	337	341	677	8	83	0.48	56	10	13	59	3.89

Uses hands and bat speed to pepper all fields with line drives, but doesn't use lower half well and swing often gets out sync. The result is lots of singles and almost no power. More patience means more times on base, where he uses his top-shelf speed effectively. Has glove and range to stick in CF, and is an above-average defender.

Becerra,Wuilmer — 79 — New York (N)
EXP MLB DEBUT: 2018 | H/W: 6-3 225 | FUT: Starting OF | 7C

Bats R Age 22 — 2011 FA (VZ)
Pwr +++ | BAvg +++ | Spd +++ | Def +++

Year	Lev	Team	AB	R	H	HR	RBI	Avg	OB	Slg	OPS	bb%	ct%	Eye	SB	CS	x/h%	Iso	RC/G
2012	Rk	GCL Blue Jays	32	5	8	0	4	250	333	375	708	11	78	0.57	0	1	50	125	4.61
2013	Rk	GCL Mets	173	21	42	1	25	243	321	295	616	10	65	0.33	5	6	17	52	3.17
2014	Rk	Kingsport	207	37	62	7	29	300	344	469	812	6	73	0.25	5	3	31	169	5.53
2015	A	Savannah	449	67	130	9	63	290	338	423	761	7	79	0.34	16	8	30	134	4.87
2016	A+	St. Lucie	247	27	77	1	34	312	336	393	729	4	79	0.17	7	1	23	81	4.30

Gutty OF battled shoulder soreness most of '16, resulting in low power output and shoulder surgery. Hit tool has continually improved since selling out to FB early in career. Quick wrists, strong hands and a better understanding of hitting led to hit tool emergence. Has always had loud BP power until injury.

Bell,Josh — 39 — Pittsburgh
EXP MLB DEBUT: 2016 | H/W: 6-2 240 | FUT: Starting 1B | 9D

Bats B Age 24 — 2011 (2) HS (TX)
Pwr ++++ | BAvg ++++ | Spd ++ | Def +++

Year	Lev	Team	AB	R	H	HR	RBI	Avg	OB	Slg	OPS	bb%	ct%	Eye	SB	CS	x/h%	Iso	RC/G
2014	AA	Altoona	94	13	27	0	7	287	343	309	652	8	87	0.67	4	1	7	21	3.70
2015	AA	Altoona	368	47	113	5	60	307	381	427	808	11	86	0.88	7	4	25	120	5.71
2015	AAA	Indianapolis	121	20	42	2	18	347	444	504	948	15	88	1.40	2	0	29	157	7.66
2016	AAA	Indianapolis	421	57	124	14	60	295	379	468	847	12	82	0.77	3	7	33	173	6.15
2016	MLB	Pittsburgh	128	18	35	3	19	273	376	406	782	14	85	1.11	0	1	31	133	5.55

Strong-bodied 1B impressed in his big-league debut. Has plus bat speed and raw power that should result in 20+ HR down the road. Advanced understanding of strike zone and bat control allow him to shoot lines drives to all fields and his minor league career slash line is .303/.373/.454.

Bellinger,Cody — 3 — Los Angeles (N)
EXP MLB DEBUT: 2018 | H/W: 6-4 210 | FUT: Starting 1B | 9D

Bats L Age 21 — 2013 (4) HS (AZ)
Pwr ++++ | BAvg +++ | Spd ++ | Def ++++

Year	Lev	Team	AB	R	H	HR	RBI	Avg	OB	Slg	OPS	bb%	ct%	Eye	SB	CS	x/h%	Iso	RC/G
2014	Rk	Azl Dodgers	20	2	3	0	0	150	190	200	390	5	75	0.20	0	0	33	50	0.01
2014	Rk	Ogden	195	49	64	3	34	328	373	503	876	7	82	0.40	8	0	34	174	6.34
2015	A+	Rancho Cuca	478	97	126	30	103	264	336	538	874	10	69	0.35	10	2	53	274	6.68
2016	AA	Tulsa	399	61	105	23	65	263	358	484	842	13	76	0.63	8	2	39	221	6.05
2016	AAA	Oklahoma City	11	5	6	3	6	545	583	1364	1947	8	100		0	0	50	818	16.17

Missed the first month of the season with a hip injury, but finished strong and proved his 2015 breakout was no fluke. Quick LH stroke allows him to tap into plus power. Swing can get big as he hunts for balls he can drive, but his BB rate was a career best 12%. Plus defender who moves well with Gold Glove potential. Slashed .314/.424/.557 in the AFL.

Benintendi,Andrew

78 | Boston | EXP MLB DEBUT: 2016 | H/W: 5-10 170 | FUT: Starting CF | 9C

Bats L Age 22
2015 (1) Arkansas
Pwr +++
BAvg ++++
Spd +++
Def +++

Year	Lev	Team	AB	R	H	HR	RBI	Avg	OB	Slg	OPS	bb%	ct%	Eye	SB	CS	x/h%	Iso	RC/G
2015	A-	Lowell	124	19	36	7	15	290	409	540	950	17	88	1.67	7	1	36	250	7.59
2015	A	Greenville	74	17	26	4	16	351	429	581	1010	12	88	1.11	3	2	35	230	7.94
2016	A+	Salem	135	30	46	1	32	341	407	563	970	10	93	1.67	8	2	46	222	7.71
2016	AA	Portland	237	40	70	8	44	295	360	515	875	9	87	0.80	8	7	44	219	6.37
2016	MLB	Boston	105	16	31	2	14	295	357	476	833	9	76	0.40	1	0	45	181	6.03

Consistent producer who was on playoff roster after exceptional season. Doubles machine who can hit RHP and LHP equally well and makes excellent contact in very disciplined approach. Covers plate well and owns textbook stroke. Power could grow to above average in time. Runs well and can patrol CF or LF with average arm.

Benson,Will

89 | Cleveland | EXP MLB DEBUT: 2020 | H/W: 6-5 225 | FUT: Starting OF | 8E

Bats L Age 18
2016 (1) HS (GA)
Pwr ++++
BAvg ++
Spd ++++
Def +++

Year	Lev	Team	AB	R	H	HR	RBI	Avg	OB	Slg	OPS	bb%	ct%	Eye	SB	CS	x/h%	Iso	RC/G
2016	Rk	AZL Indians	158	31	33	6	27	209	306	424	730	12	62	0.37	10	2	58	215	5.09

Tall, physically mature prep OF with toolsy makeup. Strength in forearms/legs generate plus bat speed and raw power, but employs deep load, leading to contact issues. Great athlete with good burst out of box; likes to run; ability to steal bases. Power profiles well in RF with strong arm and enough range to stick there at maturity.

Beras,Jairo

9 | Texas | EXP MLB DEBUT: 2018 | H/W: 6-6 195 | FUT: Starting OF | 8D

Bats R Age 22
2012 FA (DR)
Pwr ++++
BAvg ++
Spd ++
Def ++

Year	Lev	Team	AB	R	H	HR	RBI	Avg	OB	Slg	OPS	bb%	ct%	Eye	SB	CS	x/h%	Iso	RC/G
2013	Rk	Azl Rangers	64	11	16	2	15	250	304	438	742	7	70	0.26	1	0	38	188	4.78
2014	A	Hickory	389	38	94	7	33	242	301	342	643	8	66	0.25	5	4	27	100	3.45
2015	A	Hickory	327	45	95	9	43	291	329	440	770	5	73	0.22	9	4	31	150	4.95
2016	A+	High Desert	409	71	107	22	78	262	303	511	814	6	70	0.20	5	5	50	249	5.59

Lean OF who set easy high in HR after two years in Low-A. Was outstanding late as he used better approach and started to read spin. Still strikes out a lot with holes in swing. Projects to well above average pop and has shown ability to use entire field despite uppercut stroke. Not a pretty defender with crude routes, but has very strong arm.

Betts,Chris

2 | Tampa Bay | EXP MLB DEBUT: 2020 | H/W: 6-2 215 | FUT: Starting C | 8E

Bats L Age 20
2015 (2) HS (CA)
Pwr ++
BAvg ++
Spd +
Def ++

Year	Lev	Team	AB	R	H	HR	RBI	Avg	OB	Slg	OPS	bb%	ct%	Eye	SB	CS	x/h%	Iso	RC/G
2016	Rk	GCL Devil Rays	42	5	9	0	6	214	365	310	675	19	69	0.77	2	0	33	95	4.44
2016	A-	Hudson Valley	70	2	11	0	7	157	322	214	536	20	67	0.74	0	0	36	57	2.23

Strong, sturdy C who may have to move to 1B despite arm strength. Has very mature approach and sees lots of pitches, but lacks ability to make contact. Owns plus power potential, but swing path more conducive to doubles at present. Strikes out a lot as swing mechanics can be funky. Had Tommy John surgery in July '15.

Bichette,Bo

46 | Toronto | EXP MLB DEBUT: 2020 | H/W: 6-0 200 | FUT: Starting SS | 8C

Bats R Age 19
2016 (2) HS (FL)
Pwr +++
BAvg +++
Spd +++
Def ++

Year	Lev	Team	AB	R	H	HR	RBI	Avg	OB	Slg	OPS	bb%	ct%	Eye	SB	CS	x/h%	Iso	RC/G
2016	Rk	GCL Blue Jays	82	21	35	4	36	427	466	732	1198	7	79	0.35	3	0	43	305	10.33

Athletic, steady INF who found pro pitching much to his liking in debut. Bat speed ideal to make hard contact, but inconsistent mechanics may be exploited. Offers power potential with leverage and can go to opposite field. Defense is only ordinary and could very well move off SS. Makes routine plays with strong arm.

Bishop,Braden

8 | Seattle | EXP MLB DEBUT: 2018 | H/W: 6-1 190 | FUT: Starting OF | 8D

Bats R Age 23
2015 (3) Washington
Pwr ++
BAvg ++
Spd +++
Def ++++

Year	Lev	Team	AB	R	H	HR	RBI	Avg	OB	Slg	OPS	bb%	ct%	Eye	SB	CS	x/h%	Iso	RC/G
2015	NCAA	Washington	193	38	57	4	25	295	370	440	811	11	81	0.64	15	5	33	145	5.71
2015	A-	Everett	219	34	70	2	22	320	335	393	728	2	85	0.15	13	3	16	73	4.15
2016	A	Clinton	248	38	72	1	21	290	355	331	686	9	81	0.52	6	1	10	40	4.05
2016	A+	Bakersfield	166	19	41	2	22	247	294	319	613	6	77	0.28	2	0	20	72	2.91

Lean, athletic OF who is standout defender in CF and could move to corner due to strong arm and range. Takes good routes to balls and gets quality jumps. Has inconsistent swing and often chops at balls early in count. Generally makes acceptable contact due to bat speed and focuses on gap power. Exhibits average speed on base.

Blandino,Alex

456 | Cincinnati | EXP MLB DEBUT: 2018 | H/W: 6-0 190 | FUT: Reserve IF | 6C

Bats R Age 24
2014 (1) Stanford
Pwr ++
BAvg ++
Spd ++
Def +++

Year	Lev	Team	AB	R	H	HR	RBI	Avg	OB	Slg	OPS	bb%	ct%	Eye	SB	CS	x/h%	Iso	RC/G
2014	Rk	Billings	110	20	34	4	16	309	397	527	924	13	84	0.89	6	3	44	218	7.18
2014	A	Dayton	134	20	35	4	16	261	327	440	767	9	69	0.31	1	2	43	179	5.26
2015	A+	Daytona	299	46	88	7	35	294	361	438	799	9	81	0.55	7	10	31	144	5.46
2015	AA	Pensacola	115	15	27	3	18	235	338	374	712	14	82	0.86	2	2	37	139	4.60
2016	AA	Pensacola	401	52	93	8	37	232	325	337	661	12	72	0.48	14	5	28	105	3.78

Utility infielder profile took step back in '16. Swing length became issue against Double-A pitching. Lots of swing-and-miss; struggles connecting with ball in hitter's zone. Solid-average power potential, plays down due to hit tool concerns. Solid defender at 3 positions. Role versatility means likely role on MLB bench if hits enough.

Blankenhorn,Travis

45 | Minnesota | EXP MLB DEBUT: 2019 | H/W: 6-2 208 | FUT: Starting 3B | 8C

Bats L Age 20
2015 (3) HS (PA)
Pwr +++
BAvg +++
Spd ++
Def ++

Year	Lev	Team	AB	R	H	HR	RBI	Avg	OB	Slg	OPS	bb%	ct%	Eye	SB	CS	x/h%	Iso	RC/G
2015	Rk	Elizabethton	144	14	35	3	20	243	297	326	623	7	78	0.34	1	0	17	83	3.03
2015	Rk	GCL Twins	49	6	12	0	3	245	339	408	747	13	78	0.64	2	0	50	163	5.25
2016	Rk	Elizabethton	138	30	41	9	29	297	336	558	894	5	76	0.24	3	0	41	261	6.33
2016	A	Cedar Rapids	91	11	26	1	12	286	343	418	761	8	69	0.29	2	1	31	132	5.22

Tall, athletic INF who mostly played 2B in '16, but projects well at 3B. Frame has room for more strength and offers admirable power potential. Can be all-around hitter with smooth swing mechanics. Will need to make more contact and be more selective to flourish. Runs well underway and quickness sufficient for any spot.

Boldt,Ryan

789 | Tampa Bay | EXP MLB DEBUT: 2019 | H/W: 6-2 210 | FUT: Starting OF | 7C

Bats L Age 22
2016 (2) Nebraska
Pwr ++
BAvg +++
Spd +++
Def +++

Year	Lev	Team	AB	R	H	HR	RBI	Avg	OB	Slg	OPS	bb%	ct%	Eye	SB	CS	x/h%	Iso	RC/G
2016	NCAA	Nebraska	257	48	74	5	30	288	339	416	756	7	86	0.56	20	9	28	128	4.84
2016	A-	Hudson Valley	170	17	37	1	15	218	261	276	538	6	86	0.42	8	9	19	59	2.24

Well-rounded OF who can be solid hitter, but hasn't tapped into raw power yet. Excellent OF who gets good jumps and takes efficient routes. Can play all OF spots and may stick in CF due to speed. Offers size and strength and uses entire field in approach. Possesses average raw power, but more content with contact with level stroke.

Bolt,Skye

8 | Oakland | EXP MLB DEBUT: 2018 | H/W: 6-3 190 | FUT: Starting OF | 8E

Bats B Age 23
2015 (4) North Carolina
Pwr ++
BAvg ++
Spd +++
Def +++

Year	Lev	Team	AB	R	H	HR	RBI	Avg	OB	Slg	OPS	bb%	ct%	Eye	SB	CS	x/h%	Iso	RC/G
2015	NCAA	North Carolina	205	44	53	10	45	259	380	449	828	16	80	1.00	7	3	36	190	6.06
2015	A-	Vermont	181	26	43	4	19	238	327	381	708	12	76	0.55	2	1	37	144	4.45
2016	A	Beloit	342	34	79	5	37	231	315	345	660	11	74	0.48	10	5	34	114	3.79

Toolsy, athletic OF who has high ceiling, but lacks polish with bat and glove. Is sound CF with above average speed, though can take inefficient routes. Doesn't recognize pitches well and can be free swinger early in count. Has pull side power and sufficient bat speed from both sides of plate to hit for BA.

Bonifacio,Jorge

79 | Kansas City | EXP MLB DEBUT: 2017 | H/W: 6-1 195 | FUT: Starting OF | 8D

Bats R Age 23
2009 FA (DR)
Pwr ++++
BAvg ++
Spd ++
Def ++

Year	Lev	Team	AB	R	H	HR	RBI	Avg	OB	Slg	OPS	bb%	ct%	Eye	SB	CS	x/h%	Iso	RC/G
2013	A+	Wilmington	206	32	61	2	29	296	367	408	775	10	81	0.58	0	2	26	112	5.27
2013	AA	NW Arkansas	93	15	28	2	19	301	375	441	816	11	75	0.48	2	1	32	140	5.83
2014	AA	NW Arkansas	505	49	116	4	51	230	299	309	608	9	75	0.39	8	3	24	79	3.01
2015	AA	NW Arkansas	483	60	116	17	64	240	301	416	717	8	74	0.33	3	2	42	176	4.33
2016	AAA	Omaha	495	82	137	19	86	277	344	461	805	9	74	0.39	6	2	34	184	5.57

Improving OF who had power breakout after two years in AA. Hitting for consistent pop to all fields and started to show keener eye at plate. Swing and miss will always be part of equation and he will be pull-conscious. Secondary skills are sub-par, particularly speed and defense. Gotten slower and range may relegate to LF.

Bradley,Bobby | 3 | Cleveland | EXP MLB DEBUT: 2018 | H/W: 6-1 225 | FUT: Starting 1B | 8C

Bats L Age 20	Year	Lev	Team	AB	R	H	HR	RBI	Avg	OB	Slg	OPS	bb%	ct%	Eye	SB	CS	x/h%	Iso	RC/G
2014 (3) HS (MS)																				
Pwr ++++	2014	Rk	AZL Indians	155	39	56	8	50	361	421	652	1073	9	77	0.44	3	0	45	290	9.04
BAvg ++	2015	A	Lake County	401	62	108	27	92	269	359	529	888	12	63	0.38	3	0	43	259	7.30
Spd ++	2015	A+	Lynchburg	8	0	0	0	0	0	111	0	111	11	75	0.50	0	0		0	-3.61
Def ++	2016	A+	Lynchburg	485	82	114	29	102	235	338	466	803	13	65	0.44	3	0	46	231	5.90

Big, thick 1B led High-A hitters in HR with elite ISO against older arms. Plus-plus raw power plays to all fields. Some swing-and-miss, but short, simple load and plate coverage allow for decent barrel control. Works counts and willing to walk. Poor runner who won't steal bases. Fringe-average glove/arm; profiles best as 1B long-term.

Brett,Ryan | 4 | Tampa Bay | EXP MLB DEBUT: 2015 | H/W: 5-9 180 | FUT: Starting 2B | 7C

Bats R Age 25	Year	Lev	Team	AB	R	H	HR	RBI	Avg	OB	Slg	OPS	bb%	ct%	Eye	SB	CS	x/h%	Iso	RC/G
2010 (3) HS (WA)	2014	AA	Montgomery	422	64	128	8	38	303	341	448	789	5	82	0.32	27	7	30	145	5.12
Pwr ++	2015	A+	Charlotte	3	2	2	0	0	667	667	1000	1667	0	100		0	1	50	333	13.79
BAvg +++	2015	AAA	Durham	328	48	81	5	30	247	280	354	634	4	80	0.23	4	3	30	107	3.15
Spd +++	2015	MLB	Tampa Bay	3	0	2	0	0	667	750	1000	1750	25	100		0	0	50	333	17.49
Def +++	2016		Did not play (injury)																	

Short, instinctual INF who missed '16 after Tommy John surgery in May. Has feel for bat with plate coverage and bat control. Swings hard when he sees his pitch and can hit hard line drives to gaps. Has enough pop to keep defense honest. Quick feet is highlight of defense and runs very well for SB. Ranges to both sides and has decent arm for 2B.

Brigman,Bryson | 46 | Seattle | EXP MLB DEBUT: 2019 | H/W: 5-11 180 | FUT: Starting 2B | 7C

Bats R Age 21	Year	Lev	Team	AB	R	H	HR	RBI	Avg	OB	Slg	OPS	bb%	ct%	Eye	SB	CS	x/h%	Iso	RC/G
2016 (3) San Diego																				
Pwr +																				
BAvg +++																				
Spd +++	2016	NCAA	San Diego	191	31	71	0	22	372	420	424	844	8	90	0.84	17	7	13	52	5.95
Def +++	2016	A-	Everett	265	51	69	0	19	260	359	291	650	13	84	0.95	17	12	10	30	3.95

Well-rounded INF with plus plate discipline and pitch recognition. Makes easy contact from compact stroke and uses above average speed well. Runs aggressively, but needs better jumps. Offers little power and doesn't have much projection. Needs to add strength to drive ball more. Will likely end up at 2B due to fringy arm.

Brinson,Lewis | 8 | Milwaukee | EXP MLB DEBUT: 2017 | H/W: 6-3 195 | FUT: Starting CF | 9C

Bats R Age 22	Year	Lev	Team	AB	R	H	HR	RBI	Avg	OB	Slg	OPS	bb%	ct%	Eye	SB	CS	x/h%	Iso	RC/G
2012 (1) HS (FL)	2015	AA	Frisco	110	14	32	6	23	291	328	545	873	5	75	0.21	2	1	47	255	6.20
Pwr ++++	2015	AAA	Round Rock	30	9	13	1	4	433	541	567	1107	19	80	1.17	3	0	15	133	9.93
BAvg +++	2016	Rk	Azl Rangers	13	3	3	0	1	231	333	308	641	13	85	1.00	2	0	33	77	3.93
Spd ++++	2016	AA	Frisco	304	46	72	11	40	237	277	431	708	5	79	0.27	11	4	43	194	4.08
Def ++++	2016	AAA	Colorado Springs	89	14	34	4	20	382	396	618	1014	2	76	0.10	4	2	38	236	7.78

Dynamic, quick-twitch athlete with above-average-to-plus tools across the board. Aggressive with fringy ct% in upper minors, but pitch recognition and barrel control have improved. Quick wrists, good bat speed with plus raw power to pull-side; 30-HR upside at peak. Quick first step, good underway speed for solid SB impact and plus range for CF.

Brito,Daniel | 4 | Philadelphia | EXP MLB DEBUT: 2021 | H/W: 6-1 155 | FUT: Starting 2B | 8E

Bats L Age 19	Year	Lev	Team	AB	R	H	HR	RBI	Avg	OB	Slg	OPS	bb%	ct%	Eye	SB	CS	x/h%	Iso	RC/G
2014 FA (VZ)																				
Pwr ++																				
BAvg ++++																				
Spd +++																				
Def +++	2016	Rk	GCL Phillies	190	35	54	2	25	284	355	421	777	10	86	0.78	7	2	31	137	5.35

High-ticket teenager had a great first exposure to pro ball, hitting line drives from gap to gap and showing an advanced plate approach. He has quick hands and good barrel control, along with a projectable body. A solid defender, he'll likely stick at 2B.

Brito,Ronny | 6 | Los Angeles (N) | EXP MLB DEBUT: 2021 | H/W: 6-0 165 | FUT: Starting SS | 8E

Bats B Age 18	Year	Lev	Team	AB	R	H	HR	RBI	Avg	OB	Slg	OPS	bb%	ct%	Eye	SB	CS	x/h%	Iso	RC/G
2015 FA (DR)																				
Pwr ++																				
BAvg ++																				
Spd ++++																				
Def ++++	2016		Did not play in the US																	

Signed out of the DR for $2 million, Brito has the tools to be a plus defender. Has good range, soft hands, and a plus arm. At the plate, needs to prove he can hit. Has good pitch recognition and is patient with good bat speed, but he lacks the strength needed to hit as a pro. Lots of projection left, but lots of work to do.

Brito,Socrates | 789 | Arizona | EXP MLB DEBUT: 2015 | H/W: 6-2 205 | FUT: Starting CF | 7C

Bats L Age 24	Year	Lev	Team	AB	R	H	HR	RBI	Avg	OB	Slg	OPS	bb%	ct%	Eye	SB	CS	x/h%	Iso	RC/G
2010 FA (DR)	2015	MLB	Arizona	33	5	10	0	1	303	324	455	778	3	79	0.14	1	0	40	152	5.06
Pwr +++	2016	Rk	Azl Diamondbacks	7	0	1	0	2	143	143	143	286	0	57	0.00	0	0	0	0	-2.36
BAvg +++	2016	A+	Visalia	9	1	1	1	2	111	111	444	556	0	78	0.00	0	0	100	333	1.54
Spd ++	2016	AAA	Reno	303	46	89	6	39	294	323	439	762	4	80	0.22	7	6	27	145	4.72
Def ++++	2016	MLB	Arizona	95	10	17	4	12	179	196	358	554	2	76	0.09	2	0	47	179	1.88

Late blooming athletic OF. Struggled in a few '16 MLB stints. Continues to refine approach as he adds strength to game. Has cut down swing and smoothed out hands path to ball. Has 15-20 HR potential. Run tool hasn't translated to high SB totals. Can play all OF positions. Arm is best suited for RF. Bat best suited for CF.

Brown,Aaron | 9 | Philadelphia | EXP MLB DEBUT: 2018 | H/W: 6-2 220 | FUT: Reserve OF | 6C

Bats L Age 24	Year	Lev	Team	AB	R	H	HR	RBI	Avg	OB	Slg	OPS	bb%	ct%	Eye	SB	CS	x/h%	Iso	RC/G
2014 (3) Pepperdine	2014	A	Lakewood	55	3	17	1	5	309	321	473	794	2	65	0.05	0	1	41	164	5.62
Pwr ++	2015	A+	Clearwater	389	52	100	11	47	257	305	406	711	6	77	0.31	10	8	32	149	4.18
BAvg ++	2016	Rk	GCL Phillies	11	0	3	0	1	273	273	273	545	0	82	0.00	0	0	0	0	1.78
4.20 Spd ++	2016	A+	Clearwater	69	9	21	2	12	304	400	391	791	14	72	0.58	3	0	10	87	5.55
Def +++	2016	AA	Reading	228	39	51	3	27	224	292	360	652	9	72	0.35	2	4	41	136	3.64

Has grown more patient at the plate as a pro, but contact is still a problem. Though the swing can be balanced, it's also pull-heavy without the power that his frame might suggest. Some speed to his game, but has not been put to use on the basepaths. Arm is the star on defense, but might not hit enough to hold down an outfield corner.

Brugman,Jaycob | 89 | Oakland | EXP MLB DEBUT: 2017 | H/W: 6-0 195 | FUT: Starting OF | 7D

Bats L Age 25	Year	Lev	Team	AB	R	H	HR	RBI	Avg	OB	Slg	OPS	bb%	ct%	Eye	SB	CS	x/h%	Iso	RC/G
2013 (17) Brigham Young	2014	A	Beloit	248	33	69	8	37	278	367	484	851	12	74	0.54	5	2	45	206	6.45
Pwr ++	2014	A+	Stockton	195	34	55	13	35	282	336	533	870	8	74	0.32	3	3	38	251	6.17
BAvg +++	2015	AA	Midland	500	61	130	6	63	260	342	382	724	11	82	0.70	11	7	32	122	4.71
Spd +++	2016	AA	Midland	157	27	41	5	20	261	329	439	769	9	79	0.48	2	3	37	178	5.07
Def +++	2016	AAA	Nashville	386	50	114	7	67	295	355	438	793	9	77	0.41	5	3	32	142	5.42

Emerging prospect who is on verge of majors due to versatility and solid offensive production. Swings hard, though erratic approach conducive to strikeouts and weak contact at times. Can be too selective and needs to turn on pitches to realize average power potential. Can play all OF spots and owns strong arm with average speed and range.

Brusa,Gio | 7 | San Francisco | EXP MLB DEBUT: 2018 | H/W: 6-3 220 | FUT: Starting OF | 8E

Bats B Age 23	Year	Lev	Team	AB	R	H	HR	RBI	Avg	OB	Slg	OPS	bb%	ct%	Eye	SB	CS	x/h%	Iso	RC/G
2016 (6) Pacific																				
Pwr +++																				
BAvg ++																				
Spd ++	2016	NCAA	Pacific	202	38	68	14	46	337	412	614	1026	11	80	0.63	1	2	41	277	8.24
Def ++	2016	A-	Salem-Keizer	220	36	58	10	42	264	299	495	794	5	69	0.16	1	1	48	232	5.42

Free-swinging OF who exhibits above average power when contact is made. Has trouble with selectivity and pull-conscious approach will mute BA potential. Can drive ball a long way from both sides and natural loft could lead to more pop. Secondary skills lag far behind. Not very fast and could move to 1B if range doesn't improve.

Burns,Andy | 456 | Toronto | EXP MLB DEBUT: 2016 | H/W: 6-2 205 | FUT: Utility player | 7D

Bats R Age 26	Year	Lev	Team	AB	R	H	HR	RBI	Avg	OB	Slg	OPS	bb%	ct%	Eye	SB	CS	x/h%	Iso	RC/G
2011 (11) Arizona	2014	AA	New Hampshire	495	71	126	15	63	255	312	430	742	8	80	0.41	18	8	41	176	4.65
Pwr ++	2015	AA	New Hampshire	21	5	5	1	1	238	333	381	714	13	86	1.00	0	0	20	143	4.46
BAvg +++	2015	AAA	Buffalo	478	60	140	4	45	293	345	372	717	7	86	0.55	6	9	21	79	4.41
Spd +++	2016	AAA	Buffalo	418	42	96	8	38	230	286	352	638	7	80	0.40	13	5	35	122	3.36
Def ++	2016	MLB	Toronto	6	2	0	0	0	0	0	0	0	0	67	0.00	0	0		0	-6.12

Versatile INF with athleticism and decent hitting skills. Regressed with bat in '16, but has strong swing that results in hard contact to gaps. HR declined, but power not part of equation. Quick feet give him chance for SB and range. Possesses strong arm, but not proficient with glove at any spot.

Cabbage,Trey — 5 — Minnesota
EXP MLB DEBUT: 2020 | H/W: 6-3 204 | FUT: Starting 3B | 7D

Bats L Age 19 — 2015 (4) HS (TN) — Pwr ++ | BAvg +++ | Spd ++ | Def ++

Year	Lev	Team	AB	R	H	HR	RBI	Avg	OB	Slg	OPS	bb%	ct%	Eye	SB	CS	x/h%	Iso	RC/G
2015	Rk	GCL Twins	119	8	30	0	13	252	294	269	563	6	69	0.19	1	5	7	17	2.16
2016	Rk	Elizabethton	98	16	20	2	8	204	284	337	621	10	61	0.29	2	1	40	133	3.35

Tall INF with limited action due to injuries. Sleeper prospect as he owns nice tools and athleticism to stick at 3B. Very quick bat with natural strength lead to power profile. Not fleet afoot, but has keen instincts on base. Very raw defender, but could grow to average thanks to strong arm, quick hands, and agility. Will take time to develop.

Calhoun,Willie — 4 — Los Angeles (N)
EXP MLB DEBUT: 2017 | H/W: 5-8 187 | FUT: Starting 2B | 8C

Bats L Age 22 — 2015 (4) Yavapai JC — Pwr ++++ | BAvg +++ | Spd + | Def +

Year	Lev	Team	AB	R	H	HR	RBI	Avg	OB	Slg	OPS	bb%	ct%	Eye	SB	CS	x/h%	Iso	RC/G
2015	Rk	Ogden	151	28	42	7	26	278	374	517	890	13	88	1.28	2	1	50	238	6.74
2015	A	Great Lakes	61	9	24	1	8	393	439	492	931	8	89	0.71	0	0	17	98	6.83
2015	A+	Rancho Cuca	73	11	24	3	14	329	388	548	935	9	82	0.54	0	0	42	219	7.04
2016	AA	Tulsa	503	75	128	27	88	254	316	469	785	8	87	0.69	0	0	41	215	5.10

Short 2B hit for power, though contact and walk rates held steady though BA dipped in the 2nd half. Played 3B in college, but has below-average range and will need to work hard to stick at 2B. Speed is not part of his game, but thumps the ball consistently with a good understanding of the strike zone.

Call,Alex — 78 — Chicago (A)
EXP MLB DEBUT: 2019 | H/W: 6-0 185 | FUT: Starting OF | 7C

Bats R Age 22 — 2016 (3) Ball State — Pwr +++ | BAvg +++ | Spd +++ | Def ++

Year	Lev	Team	AB	R	H	HR	RBI	Avg	OB	Slg	OPS	bb%	ct%	Eye	SB	CS	x/h%	Iso	RC/G
2016	NCAA	Ball State	243	67	87	13	44	358	426	667	1093	11	88	1.00	17	4	49	309	8.93
2016	Rk	Great Falls	107	19	33	3	17	308	413	439	852	15	83	1.06	4	4	21	131	6.40
2016	A	Kannapolis	185	23	57	3	18	308	360	449	809	8	78	0.38	10	2	35	141	5.55

Fundamentally sound OF who stands out for grinding and intangibles. Maximizes skills by working counts and playing all-out. Showed improved and surprising pop while maintaining line drive stroke. Can overswing at times and bury ball into ground. Runs fairly well, though isn't a burner. Strong arm headlines fringy CF defense.

Camargo,Johan — 456 — Atlanta
EXP MLB DEBUT: 2017 | H/W: 6-0 160 | FUT: Utility player | 6B

Bats B Age 23 — 2010 FA (PN) — Pwr ++ | BAvg ++ | Spd +++ | Def +++

Year	Lev	Team	AB	R	H	HR	RBI	Avg	OB	Slg	OPS	bb%	ct%	Eye	SB	CS	x/h%	Iso	RC/G
2013	Rk	Danville	228	28	67	0	14	294	346	360	705	7	86	0.58	3	3	16	66	4.33
2014	A	Rome	420	53	112	0	40	267	322	324	645	7	88	0.68	7	6	18	57	3.70
2014	A+	Lynchburg	58	7	15	1	6	259	271	345	616	2	78	0.08	0	0	20	86	2.69
2015	A+	Carolina	391	50	101	1	32	258	311	335	646	7	86	0.56	4	2	22	77	3.64
2016	AA	Mississippi	446	46	119	4	43	267	304	379	683	5	82	0.29	1	2	30	112	3.87

Switch-hitting SS stock climbed after adding strength and defensive versatility to package. Reworked swing, using body more to generate loud contact, losing a little bat-to-ball skills in the process. Added leverage means additional power. Posted career highs in 2B and HR. Doesn't carry offensive struggle with him to field anymore.

Cameron,Daz — 78 — Houston
EXP MLB DEBUT: 2019 | H/W: 6-2 185 | FUT: Starting OF | 8D

Bats R Age 20 — 2015 (S-1) HS (GA) — Pwr ++ | BAvg ++ | Spd +++ | Def ++++

Year	Lev	Team	AB	R	H	HR	RBI	Avg	OB	Slg	OPS	bb%	ct%	Eye	SB	CS	x/h%	Iso	RC/G
2015	Rk	Greeneville	103	20	28	0	11	272	370	350	719	13	70	0.52	11	6	18	78	4.85
2015	Rk	GCL Astros	70	13	15	0	6	214	304	243	547	11	76	0.53	12	4	13	29	2.31
2016	A-	Tri City	79	13	22	2	14	278	329	418	747	7	67	0.23	8	2	27	139	4.92
2016	A	Quad Cities	77	5	11	0	6	143	224	221	444	9	57	0.24	4	3	36	78	0.58

Athletic OF who got off to poor start and was demoted to extended ST. Ended season in July due to broken finger. Has vast amount of talent, mostly instincts and speed. Patrols CF with polished routes. Too much swing and miss and may never hit for BA. Swing mechanics need work, though has plus bat speed. Could grow into average pop.

Candelario,Jeimer — 5 — Chicago (N)
EXP MLB DEBUT: 2016 | H/W: 6-1 210 | FUT: Starting 3B | 8C

Bats B Age 23 — 2010 FA (DR) — Pwr +++ | BAvg +++ | Spd ++ | Def +++

Year	Lev	Team	AB	R	H	HR	RBI	Avg	OB	Slg	OPS	bb%	ct%	Eye	SB	CS	x/h%	Iso	RC/G
2015	A+	Myrtle Beach	318	42	86	5	39	270	314	415	729	6	81	0.32	0	1	38	145	4.47
2015	AA	Tennessee	158	21	46	5	25	291	378	462	840	12	87	1.05	0	0	35	171	6.11
2016	AA	Tennessee	210	30	46	4	23	219	322	367	689	13	78	0.70	0	0	48	148	4.32
2016	AAA	Iowa	264	44	88	9	54	333	417	542	959	13	80	0.72	0	2	39	208	7.68
2016	MLB	Chi Cubs	11	0	1	0	0	91	231	91	322	15	55	0.40	0	0	0	0	-1.94

Strong 3B had mixed results. Struggled at AA, but exploded when moved up to AAA. High energy player has good power, a sweet swing, and a good plate discipline (70 BB/99 K). Above-average defender w/ good hands and a strong arm, but limited range. Smart player with solid skills and stock is on the rise.

Canelo,Malquin — 6 — Philadelphia
EXP MLB DEBUT: 2019 | H/W: 5-10 156 | FUT: Starting SS | 7D

Bats R Age 22 — 2012 FA (DR) — Pwr ++ | BAvg ++ | Spd +++ | Def ++++

Year	Lev	Team	AB	R	H	HR	RBI	Avg	OB	Slg	OPS	bb%	ct%	Eye	SB	CS	x/h%	Iso	RC/G
2014	A	Lakewood	152	19	41	1	18	270	319	355	674	7	80	0.35	4	1	24	86	3.81
2014	A+	Clearwater	48	2	10	0	3	208	255	271	526	6	75	0.25	1	1	30	63	1.84
2015	A	Lakewood	264	48	82	5	23	311	361	466	827	7	85	0.54	10	2	35	155	5.72
2015	A+	Clearwater	248	24	62	3	24	250	295	323	618	6	79	0.30	7	6	18	73	2.99
2016	A+	Clearwater	451	53	111	4	49	246	293	330	624	6	79	0.32	13	8	23	84	3.13

Defensive whiz who has stalled at High-A. Small frame does not allow for much projection, so his ceiling is a BA-and-SB guy that you hide at the bottom of a lineup. Except that his ct% has gotten worse, and though he has a handful of steals, it's more quickness that he uses in the field rather than straightline speed. Has to hit more.

Cantu,Ulysses — 35 — Cleveland
EXP MLB DEBUT: 2021 | H/W: 5-11 220 | FUT: Starting 1B | 7D

Bats R Age 18 — 2016 (6) HS (TX) — Pwr +++ | BAvg +++ | Spd + | Def ++

Year	Lev	Team	AB	R	H	HR	RBI	Avg	OB	Slg	OPS	bb%	ct%	Eye	SB	CS	x/h%	Iso	RC/G
2016	Rk	AZL Indians	109	11	22	1	9	202	281	248	529	10	61	0.29	0	0	14	46	1.78

Stocky, thick with good present strength but will need to firm up as he matures. Short load, good bat speed, strong forearms to get the barrel out front for gap pop; projected 12-15 HR impact. Base-clogger potential with no SB upside. Has arm for 3B, but poor athleticism, footwork could relegate him to 1B, which pressures bat to produce.

Capel,Conner — 89 — Cleveland
EXP MLB DEBUT: 2021 | H/W: 6-1 185 | FUT: Starting OF | 8E

Bats L Age 19 — 2016 (5) HS (TX) — Pwr ++ | BAvg +++ | Spd ++++ | Def +++

Year	Lev	Team	AB	R	H	HR	RBI	Avg	OB	Slg	OPS	bb%	ct%	Eye	SB	CS	x/h%	Iso	RC/G
2016	Rk	AZL Indians	138	22	29	0	13	210	268	290	558	7	86	0.55	10	3	28	80	2.66

Raw, athletic prep OF with chance for four average-or-better tools. Short to ball with compact, level stroke for high BA/ct% floor; gap power now and likely not a HR threat. Quick to full speed out of box with long, fluid strides; will score from 1B on double; future SB source. Enough range for CF; strong arm for RF. Great makeup; wants to succeed.

Caratini,Victor — 23 — Chicago (N)
EXP MLB DEBUT: 2018 | H/W: 6-1 215 | FUT: Starting C | 7C

Bats B Age 23 — 2013 (2) Miami-Dade — Pwr ++ | BAvg +++ | Spd + | Def +++

Year	Lev	Team	AB	R	H	HR	RBI	Avg	OB	Slg	OPS	bb%	ct%	Eye	SB	CS	x/h%	Iso	RC/G
2013	Rk	Danville	200	29	58	1	25	290	406	430	836	16	76	0.80	0	2	43	140	6.57
2014	A	Kane County	53	7	14	0	13	264	316	377	693	7	81	0.40	0	0	36	113	4.19
2014	A	Rome	323	42	90	5	42	279	347	406	753	10	82	0.58	1	1	30	127	4.95
2015	A+	Myrtle Beach	393	39	101	4	53	257	339	372	711	11	81	0.65	0	0	36	115	4.55
2016	AA	Tennessee	412	57	120	6	47	291	373	405	779	12	81	0.68	2	1	28	114	5.38

Switch-hitting C put up solid numbers at AA. Uses line-drive swing to shoot balls into gaps with good plate discipline, but limited future power. Compensates with plus bat speed and ability to make contact. Converted to catching in '14 and continues to improve with a strong arm and should be able to stick at the position.

Carlson,Dylan — 789 — St. Louis
EXP MLB DEBUT: 2021 | H/W: 6-3 195 | FUT: Starting OF | 7C

Bats B Age 18 — 2016 (1) HS (CA) — Pwr +++ | BAvg ++ | Spd ++ | Def ++

Year	Lev	Team	AB	R	H	HR	RBI	Avg	OB	Slg	OPS	bb%	ct%	Eye	SB	CS	x/h%	Iso	RC/G
2016	Rk	GCL Cardinals	183	30	46	3	22	251	312	404	716	8	72	0.31	4	2	41	153	4.51

One of three 1st round picks in '16. Tall, strong switch-hitting corner OF has good across-the-board tools. Projects to have plus power from both sides, though he makes better contact from the right. Fringe runner with an average arm takes solid routes, but could be moved to 1B down the road.

Carpio, Luis — 6 — New York (N)

EXP MLB DEBUT: 2021 | H/W: 6-0 165 | FUT: Starting SS | 8E

Bats R Age 19
2013 FA (VZ)

		Pwr	++
BAvg	+++
Spd	++++
Def	+++

Year	Lev	Team	AB	R	H	HR	RBI	Avg	OB	Slg	OPS	bb%	ct%	Eye	SB	CS	x/h%	Iso	RC/G
2015	Rk	Kingsport	181	31	55	0	22	304	364	359	723	9	81	0.50	9	7	18	55	4.54
2016	Rk	GCL Mets	31	3	9	0	2	290	313	387	700	3	65	0.09	0	0	22	97	4.37
2016	A-	Brooklyn	43	4	6	0	1	140	275	186	461	16	77	0.80	0	0	33	47	1.39

Athletic SS missed most of potential breakout campaign after shoulder surgery to repair labrum. Returned as a DH late in season. Explosiveness was missing from game, as expected. Flashes of extensive tool shed did make sporadic appearances.

Castillo, Diego — 6 — New York (A)

EXP MLB DEBUT: 2021 | H/W: 6-0 170 | FUT: Starting SS | 7E

Bats R Age 19
2014 FA (VZ)

		Pwr	+
BAvg	++
Spd	++
Def	++++

Year	Lev	Team	AB	R	H	HR	RBI	Avg	OB	Slg	OPS	bb%	ct%	Eye	SB	CS	x/h%	Iso	RC/G
2016	Rk	GCL Yankees	165	14	44	1	7	267	324	327	651	8	87	0.67	5	3	18	61	3.71

Fundamentally-solid SS who spent 1st year in US. Has contact approach and advanced feel for hitting. Doesn't make loud contact and uses speed for infield hits. Can be a tough out due to contact and will need to add strength to drive ball. Can be plus defender with quick, clean hands and nimble footwork. Arm strength enough for any infield spot.

Castillo, Henry — 45 — Arizona

EXP MLB DEBUT: 2018 | H/W: 5-11 189 | FUT: Utility player | 6C

Bats B Age 22
2013 FA (DR)

		Pwr	++
BAvg	++
Spd	+++
Def	++

Year	Lev	Team	AB	R	H	HR	RBI	Avg	OB	Slg	OPS	bb%	ct%	Eye	SB	CS	x/h%	Iso	RC/G
2013	Rk	AZL DBacks	32	3	10	0	3	313	333	375	708	3	78	0.14	0	0	20	63	4.02
2014	Rk	AZL DBacks	124	22	41	1	22	331	336	548	884	1	77	0.03	1	2	39	218	6.38
2015	Rk	Missoula	85	7	23	1	4	271	311	341	652	6	81	0.31	1	1	17	71	3.42
2015	A	Kane County	289	36	91	3	32	315	331	429	760	2	81	0.13	5	2	25	114	4.60
2016	A+	Visalia	492	71	127	12	63	258	311	417	728	7	73	0.29	6	9	41	159	4.52

Versatile INF/OF switch hitter sold out to the long ball in '16. Hit 12 HRs after previously high mark was 2. New approach and added leverage in swing path led to uptake in strikeout rate. Bat slowed tremendously. Can play 5 or 6 positions.

Castro, Willi — 6 — Cleveland

EXP MLB DEBUT: 2019 | H/W: 6-1 165 | FUT: Starting SS | 7D

Bats B Age 19
2013 FA (PR)

		Pwr	++
BAvg	++
Spd	+++
Def	+++

Year	Lev	Team	AB	R	H	HR	RBI	Avg	OB	Slg	OPS	bb%	ct%	Eye	SB	CS	x/h%	Iso	RC/G
2014	Rk	AZL Indians	155	31	37	2	11	239	267	348	615	4	79	0.18	9	4	27	110	2.90
2015	A-	Mahoning Valley	273	34	72	1	25	264	290	330	619	4	89	0.32	20	7	18	66	3.15
2016	A	Lake County	518	68	134	7	49	259	285	371	656	4	81	0.20	16	11	27	112	3.41
2016	A+	Lynchburg	9	0	2	0	0	222	222	222	444	0	78	0.00	0	1	0	0	0.46

Young, lean SS showed moderate power and speed in first full pro season. Slap approach and solid contact from both sides, but is aggressive and willing to chase. Flashes modest gap power with potential for fringe HR output at maturity. Above-avg range at SS with good instincts and strong arm to stick there long-term.

Cave, Jake — 789 — New York (A)

EXP MLB DEBUT: 2017 | H/W: 6-0 200 | FUT: Reserve OF | 6B

Bats L Age 24
2011 (6) HS (VA)

		Pwr	++
BAvg	+++
Spd	+++
Def	+++

Year	Lev	Team	AB	R	H	HR	RBI	Avg	OB	Slg	OPS	bb%	ct%	Eye	SB	CS	x/h%	Iso	RC/G
2014	AA	Trenton	176	24	48	4	18	273	340	455	795	9	75	0.41	2	3	40	182	5.55
2015	AA	Trenton	505	68	136	2	37	269	327	345	671	8	81	0.44	17	3	21	75	3.86
2015	AAA	Scranton/WB	24	4	11	0	4	458	519	667	1185	11	67	0.38	0	0	36	208	12.13
2016	AA	Trenton	104	12	30	3	17	288	351	510	860	9	73	0.36	3	4	47	221	6.48
2016	AAA	Scranton/WB	322	47	84	5	38	261	316	401	717	7	76	0.33	3	3	35	140	4.41

High-energy OF who has limited tools. Set high in HR, though has yet to hit 10 HR in season. Plus athlete with decent speed and ranges well in OF. Tends to lengthen swing and can be pull happy when selling out for power. Has chance to hit for BA due to bat speed. Development of power is key as he doesn't hit LHP and has too many Ks.

Cecchini, Gavin — 46 — New York (N)

EXP MLB DEBUT: 2016 | H/W: 6-2 200 | FUT: Starting SS | 7B

Bats R Age 23
2012 (1) HS (LA)

		Pwr	++
BAvg	+++
Spd	+++
Def	+++

Year	Lev	Team	AB	R	H	HR	RBI	Avg	OB	Slg	OPS	bb%	ct%	Eye	SB	CS	x/h%	Iso	RC/G
2014	A+	St. Lucie	233	36	55	5	31	236	328	352	680	12	83	0.80	3	3	29	116	4.15
2014	AA	Binghamton	4	1	1	0	0	250	250	250	500	0	75	0.00	0	0	0	0	1.07
2015	AA	Binghamton	439	64	139	7	51	317	376	442	818	9	87	0.76	3	4	27	125	5.70
2016	AAA	Las Vegas	446	71	145	8	55	325	391	448	839	10	88	0.87	4	1	26	123	5.98
2016	MLB	NY Mets	6	2	2	0	2	333	333	667	1000	0	67	0.00	0	0	100	333	9.06

Tall, slight SS made MLB debut after sparkling Triple-A season. Added additional bat speed, making him a better bet becoming an everyday SS. Lacks raw power but has power apt at turning on inside FB. Also a solid base runner and defender. High baseball IQ plays up overall game.

Cedrola, Lorenzo — 8 — Boston

EXP MLB DEBUT: 2021 | H/W: 5-11 170 | FUT: Starting OF | 8E

Bats R Age 19
2015 FA (VZ)

		Pwr	++
BAvg	++
Spd	++++
Def	+++

Year	Lev	Team	AB	R	H	HR	RBI	Avg	OB	Slg	OPS	bb%	ct%	Eye	SB	CS	x/h%	Iso	RC/G
2016	Rk	GCL Red Sox	214	33	62	2	21	290	324	393	717	5	87	0.39	9	4	27	103	4.30

Speedy OF who spent 1st year in US and showcased plus wheels in CF. Gets great jumps on balls and takes efficient routes. Strong arm enhances defense. Has some upside as hitter. Makes easy contact and hits hard line drives to gaps. Not much power in game, though should produce doubles in time. Plays game aggressively.

Celestino, Gilberto — 8 — Houston

EXP MLB DEBUT: 2021 | H/W: 6-0 170 | FUT: Starting CF | 8E

Bats R Age 18
2015 FA (DR)

		Pwr	++
BAvg	+++
Spd	+++
Def	+++

Year	Lev	Team	AB	R	H	HR	RBI	Avg	OB	Slg	OPS	bb%	ct%	Eye	SB	CS	x/h%	Iso	RC/G
2016	Rk	GCL Astros	55	7	11	0	2	200	302	291	592	13	71	0.50	6	1	36	91	3.01

Lean, fast OF who has potential to be dynamite CF. Swings fast bat and could grow to average power as he adds muscle to frame. Has feel for contact and can differentiate between balls and strikes. Needs to shorten swing when behind in count. Draws walks and uses speed well. True CF who takes efficient routes.

Cespedes, Ricardo — 789 — New York (N)

EXP MLB DEBUT: 2021 | H/W: 6-1 200 | FUT: Starting OF | 8E

Bats L Age 19
2013 FA (DR)

		Pwr	++
BAvg	++
Spd	+++
Def	+++

Year	Lev	Team	AB	R	H	HR	RBI	Avg	OB	Slg	OPS	bb%	ct%	Eye	SB	CS	x/h%	Iso	RC/G
2015	Rk	GCL Mets	165	17	37	0	15	224	281	267	548	7	82	0.45	7	3	14	42	2.35
2016	Rk	Kingsport	227	30	73	1	16	322	347	374	722	4	84	0.25	7	7	11	53	4.19

Quick twitch swing. Uses hands and wrist strength to generate bat speed. Maturing into frame. Hasn't learned importance of balance in base for power yet. An average athlete, relies on good instincts in center and on basepaths to enhance average foot speed.

Chang, Yu-Cheng — 6 — Cleveland

EXP MLB DEBUT: 2018 | H/W: 6-1 175 | FUT: Starting 3B | 7C

Bats R Age 21
2013 FA (TW)

		Pwr	++
BAvg	++
4.50	Spd	+++
Def	+++

Year	Lev	Team	AB	R	H	HR	RBI	Avg	OB	Slg	OPS	bb%	ct%	Eye	SB	CS	x/h%	Iso	RC/G
2014	Rk	AZL Indians	159	39	55	6	25	346	412	566	978	10	82	0.64	6	1	35	220	7.68
2015	A	Lake County	393	52	91	9	52	232	281	361	642	6	74	0.26	5	6	32	130	3.29
2016	A+	Lynchburg	417	78	108	13	70	259	331	463	794	10	74	0.41	11	3	47	204	5.55

Lean INF showed moderate power/speed output in High-A. Flashes good backspin carry to the gaps via short, level stroke; high-volume doubles pop with avg HR potential. Feel for barrel, but will expand zone. Fringy speed; better underway. Has range/hands to stay at SS for now, but move to 3B likely as he adds mass to his frame.

Chapman, Matt — 5 — Oakland

EXP MLB DEBUT: 2017 | H/W: 6-0 210 | FUT: Starting 3B | 8B

Bats R Age 23
2014 (1) Cal State Fullerton

		Pwr	+++++
BAvg	++
Spd	++
Def	++++

Year	Lev	Team	AB	R	H	HR	RBI	Avg	OB	Slg	OPS	bb%	ct%	Eye	SB	CS	x/h%	Iso	RC/G
2014	A	Beloit	190	22	45	5	20	237	264	389	653	4	76	0.15	2	1	36	153	3.31
2014	AA	Midland	3	0	0	0	0	0	0	0	0	0	100		0	0	0	0	-2.66
2015	A+	Stockton	304	60	76	23	57	250	335	566	901	11	74	0.49	4	1	62	316	6.82
2016	AA	Midland	438	78	107	29	83	244	334	521	855	12	66	0.40	7	4	55	276	6.57
2016	AAA	Nashville	76	14	15	7	13	197	282	513	796	11	66	0.35	0	0	60	316	5.45

Strong 3B who led TL in HR and K while finishing 3rd in minors in HR. All or nothing hitter as swing mechanics geared toward hard contact. Has trouble with breaking balls and long swing can be exploited. Natural power as good as any and will draw a ton of walks with keen eye. Very good defender with nice range and incredible arm strength.

Chatham,C.J.

6 | **Boston** | EXP MLB DEBUT: 2019 | H/W: 6-4 185 | FUT: Starting MIF | **8D**

Bats R Age 22 — 2016 (2) Florida Atlantic

Pwr +++ / BAvg ++ / Spd +++ / Def +++

Year	Lev	Team	AB	R	H	HR	RBI	Avg	OB	Slg	OPS	bb%	ct%	Eye	SB	CS	x/h%	Iso	RC/G
2016	NCAA	Florida Atlantic	249	48	89	8	50	357	412	554	966	8	86	0.64	2	1	33	197	7.36
2016	Rk	GCL Red Sox	24	2	4	1	2	167	167	375	542	0	71	0.00	0	0	75	208	1.68
2016	A-	Lowell	108	19	28	4	19	259	310	426	736	7	81	0.40	0	1	32	167	4.46

Tall, athletic INF who sets tone with nifty all-around tools. May move off SS due to size, but has present skills. Has quick first step and smooth actions. Possesses good pop, but tends to swing aggressively early in count. Pitch recognition needs work, but has shown aptitude to make adjustments.

Chavis,Michael

5 | **Boston** | EXP MLB DEBUT: 2019 | H/W: 5-10 190 | FUT: Starting 3B | **7C**

Bats R Age 21 — 2014 (1) HS (GA)

Pwr +++ / BAvg ++ / Spd ++ / Def ++

Year	Lev	Team	AB	R	H	HR	RBI	Avg	OB	Slg	OPS	bb%	ct%	Eye	SB	CS	x/h%	Iso	RC/G
2014	Rk	GCL Red Sox	134	21	36	1	16	269	342	425	768	10	72	0.39	5	3	44	157	5.42
2015	A	Greenville	435	56	97	16	58	223	272	405	676	6	67	0.20	8	5	47	182	3.83
2016	A	Greenville	279	30	68	8	35	244	299	391	690	7	73	0.30	3	1	32	147	3.95
2016	A+	Salem	25	5	4	0	1	160	222	160	382	7	72	0.29	1	0	0	0	-0.25

Short, stout INF who struggled late due to thumb injury. Made better contact with shorter stroke, but power suffered. Hit far less doubles and HR, but plus pop potential remains. Bat speed is impressive, but can be jammed inside and breaking balls give him fits. Has arm for 3B, but lacks quickness and range. May move to 2B.

Chisholm,Jasrado

6 | **Arizona** | EXP MLB DEBUT: 2020 | H/W: 5-11 165 | FUT: Starting SS | **8D**

Bats L Age 19 — 2015 FA (BM)

Pwr ++ / BAvg ++ / Spd ++++ / Def ++++

Year	Lev	Team	AB	R	H	HR	RBI	Avg	OB	Slg	OPS	bb%	ct%	Eye	SB	CS	x/h%	Iso	RC/G
2016	Rk	Missoula	249	42	70	9	37	281	332	446	778	7	71	0.26	13	4	31	165	5.16

Free-swinging, athletic SS with more glove than bat. Quick-twitch swinger w/ good leverage for power despite slight frame. No concept of plate discipline. Will swing at anything close. Average runner developing into a plus-defender. Bat may hold back from future everyday role.

Ciuffo,Nick

2 | **Tampa Bay** | EXP MLB DEBUT: 2019 | H/W: 6-1 205 | FUT: Starting C | **7D**

Bats L Age 22 — 2013 (1) HS (SC)

Pwr ++ / BAvg ++ / Spd ++ / Def +++

Year	Lev	Team	AB	R	H	HR	RBI	Avg	OB	Slg	OPS	bb%	ct%	Eye	SB	CS	x/h%	Iso	RC/G
2013	Rk	GCL Devil Rays	159	11	41	0	25	258	298	308	606	5	75	0.23	0	0	17	50	2.83
2014	Rk	Princeton	192	25	43	4	20	224	287	333	620	8	77	0.38	2	1	28	109	3.08
2015	A	Bowling Green	356	30	92	1	32	258	273	326	599	2	85	0.13	2	3	24	67	2.71
2016	Rk	GCL Devil Rays	15	1	1	0	0	67	176	67	243	12	87	1.00	0	0	0	0	-0.84
2016	A+	Charlotte	229	16	60	0	15	262	290	297	587	4	80	0.20	2	3	13	35	2.54

Toolsy backstop who missed most of June and July with injury. Has promise as hitter with raw power and impressive bat speed. Inability to recognize pitches and too little contact hinders value. Has yet to hit for any power despite strength and leverage. Has tools to be sound receiver with strong arm and blocking ability. Needs to stay on field.

Clark,LeDarious

789 | **Texas** | EXP MLB DEBUT: 2019 | H/W: 5-10 185 | FUT: Starting OF | **7D**

Bats R Age 23 — 2015 (12) West Florida

Pwr +++ / BAvg ++ / Spd ++++ / Def ++

Year	Lev	Team	AB	R	H	HR	RBI	Avg	OB	Slg	OPS	bb%	ct%	Eye	SB	CS	x/h%	Iso	RC/G
2015	A-	Spokane	257	46	71	8	24	276	343	471	814	9	72	0.36	29	9	38	195	5.84
2016	Rk	Azl Rangers	14	4	3	1	1	214	214	500	714	0	71	0.00	1	0	67	286	3.86
2016	A	Hickory	314	43	76	12	34	242	274	439	714	4	68	0.14	25	10	46	197	4.27

Athletic, quick OF with plus speed, but doesn't get on base enough to use it. Pitch selectivity is poor and is free-swinger early in count. Has short, compact stroke and sneaky power for size. Likes to go to opp field in approach and will hit lots of doubles. Plays all OF spots, though still raw. Likely LF due to fringy arm.

Clark,Trent

78 | **Milwaukee** | EXP MLB DEBUT: 2019 | H/W: 6-0 205 | FUT: Starting OF | **8C**

Bats L Age 20 — 2015 (1) HS (TX)

Pwr +++ / BAvg ++++ / Spd +++ / Def +++

Year	Lev	Team	AB	R	H	HR	RBI	Avg	OB	Slg	OPS	bb%	ct%	Eye	SB	CS	x/h%	Iso	RC/G
2015	Rk	Azl Brewers	165	34	51	1	16	309	415	442	858	15	78	0.83	20	5	27	133	6.74
2015	Rk	Helena	42	5	13	1	5	310	431	381	812	18	81	1.13	5	3	8	71	6.01
2016	A	Wisconsin	221	27	51	2	24	231	341	344	685	14	69	0.54	5	10	37	113	4.36

Athletic OF spent extended time on DL in full-season debut. Compact, explosive swing through zone yields high contact for future BA impact; advanced approach. Gap power for now but chance for average HR once matured. SB% declined but shows good first step and underway speed for solid SB ability. Glove profiles best in CF/LF long-term.

Cole,Hunter

49 | **San Francisco** | EXP MLB DEBUT: 2017 | H/W: 6-1 190 | FUT: Starting OF | **7C**

Bats R Age 24 — 2014 (26) Georgia

Pwr +++ / BAvg +++ / Spd +++ / Def ++

Year	Lev	Team	AB	R	H	HR	RBI	Avg	OB	Slg	OPS	bb%	ct%	Eye	SB	CS	x/h%	Iso	RC/G
2014	A-	Salem-Kaizer	92	17	22	4	10	239	300	424	724	8	78	0.40	1	0	41	185	4.33
2015	A	Augusta	40	4	11	0	5	275	356	425	781	11	70	0.42	2	1	55	150	5.77
2015	A+	San Jose	217	28	68	6	37	313	369	493	862	8	81	0.45	4	3	32	180	6.18
2015	AA	Richmond	192	23	56	3	21	292	340	464	803	7	76	0.30	1	1	41	172	5.56
2016	AA	Richmond	469	57	127	13	62	271	316	420	736	6	75	0.27	2	4	32	149	4.50

Aggressive hitter who played OF all season after 2B in '15. Set career-high in HR, though is more of a BA hitter with solid bat speed and strength. Takes vicious hacks at ball and can be fooled by breaking balls. Solid athlete who can take extra base with good speed. Lacks quickness for 2B and will likely stick in RF.

Collins,Zack

2 | **Chicago (A)** | EXP MLB DEBUT: 2018 | H/W: 6-3 220 | FUT: Starting C | **8B**

Bats L Age 22 — 2016 (1) Miami

Pwr +++ / BAvg ++++ / Spd ++ / Def ++

Year	Lev	Team	AB	R	H	HR	RBI	Avg	OB	Slg	OPS	bb%	ct%	Eye	SB	CS	x/h%	Iso	RC/G
2016	NCAA	Miami	190	54	69	16	59	363	549	668	1217	29	72	1.47	1	3	38	305	12.25
2016	Rk	Azl White Sox	11	1	1	0	0	91	91	91	182	0	36	0.00	0	0	0	0	-4.52
2016	A+	Winston-Salem	120	24	31	6	18	258	418	467	885	22	68	0.85	0	0	42	208	7.38

Natural-hitting C who could advance quickly thanks to pro approach and intellect. Not a standout defender; bat trumps glove. Offers plus power to pull side and has short stroke and hand-eye coordination to make contact and hit for high BA. More power should be forthcoming. Very crude defender, but can improve receiving and blocking in time.

Cordell,Ryan

789 | **Milwaukee** | EXP MLB DEBUT: 2017 | H/W: 6-4 195 | FUT: Starting OF | **7B**

Bats R Age 25 — 2013 (11) Liberty

Pwr +++ / BAvg +++ / Spd +++ / Def +++

Year	Lev	Team	AB	R	H	HR	RBI	Avg	OB	Slg	OPS	bb%	ct%	Eye	SB	CS	x/h%	Iso	RC/G
2014	A	Hickory	274	53	88	8	40	321	382	504	886	9	81	0.51	18	3	34	182	6.52
2014	A+	Myrtle Beach	62	12	19	5	19	306	377	645	1022	10	79	0.54	3	1	47	339	8.13
2015	A+	High Desert	286	58	89	13	57	311	373	528	901	9	81	0.53	10	5	35	217	6.59
2015	AA	Frisco	221	26	48	5	18	217	258	335	592	5	67	0.16	10	1	27	118	2.57
2016	AA	Frisco	405	69	107	19	70	264	318	484	802	7	76	0.33	12	4	43	220	5.35

Tall, versatile glove who could contribute in near future. Shows solid-average HR potential with pull-oriented approach. Swing can get long and will chase, but cut back on Ks in '16. Plus runner with quick first step and fluid strides for some SB impact; low OBP history could limit his upside. Defensive acumen will increase opportunity for PT.

Cordero,Franchy

78 | **San Diego** | EXP MLB DEBUT: 2017 | H/W: 6-3 175 | FUT: Reserve OF | **6B**

Bats L Age 22 — 2011 FA (DR)

Pwr ++ / BAvg + / Spd ++++ / Def +++

Year	Lev	Team	AB	R	H	HR	RBI	Avg	OB	Slg	OPS	bb%	ct%	Eye	SB	CS	x/h%	Iso	RC/G
2014	A	Fort Wayne	85	5	16	0	9	188	225	235	460	4	58	0.11	3	3	19	47	0.74
2015	A	Fort Wayne	481	59	117	5	34	243	289	306	595	6	75	0.26	22	11	16	62	2.64
2016	A+	Lake Elsinore	297	47	85	5	35	286	329	444	774	6	72	0.23	11	8	34	158	5.19
2016	AA	San Antonio	245	31	75	6	19	306	351	478	829	6	73	0.25	12	6	29	171	5.89
2016	AAA	El Paso	13	1	1	0	0	77	250	77	327	19	69	0.75	0	0	0	0	-0.97

Speedy former shortstop transitioned to OF full-time. Long-swing, little bat control. Struggles getting bat started against MLB velocity. Makes lots of soft contact. Strikes out a bunch. Sneaky pull power. Plus speed tool only goes so far.

Cordoba,Allen

6 | **San Diego** | EXP MLB DEBUT: 2017 | H/W: 6-1 175 | FUT: Starting SS | **8D**

Bats R Age 21 — 2013 FA (PN)

Pwr ++ / BAvg ++++ / Spd +++ / Def +++

Year	Lev	Team	AB	R	H	HR	RBI	Avg	OB	Slg	OPS	bb%	ct%	Eye	SB	CS	x/h%	Iso	RC/G
2015	Rk	GCL Cardinals	202	40	69	2	20	342	387	421	808	7	90	0.75	11	3	14	79	5.45
2016	Rk	Johnson City	196	49	71	0	18	362	424	495	919	10	90	1.11	22	4	30	133	7.05

Slender, athletic Panamanian SS has been a revelation. Unorthodox approach at the plate, but relies on a quick bat and plus pitch recognition to make consistent, hard contact and has won two consecutive batting titles. Above average runner with good range and enough arm to stick at short. Rule 5 pick from STL. Sleeper alert.

Cozens,Dylan — 9 — Philadelphia — EXP MLB DEBUT: 2017 — H/W: 6-6 235 — FUT: Starting OF — 9D

Bats L Age 22
2012 (2) HS (AZ)
Pwr + + + + +
BAvg + +
4.69 Spd + + +
Def + +

Year	Lev	Team	AB	R	H	HR	RBI	Avg	OB	Slg	OPS	bb%	ct%	Eye	SB	CS	x/h%	Iso	RC/G
2014	A	Lakewood	509	69	126	16	62	248	302	415	717	7	71	0.27	23	7	37	167	4.37
2015	Rk	GCL Phillies	15	1	3	0	4	200	200	267	467	0	73	0.00	0	0	33	67	0.78
2015	A+	Clearwater	365	52	103	5	46	282	330	411	741	7	78	0.33	18	5	31	129	4.65
2015	AA	Reading	40	6	14	3	9	350	395	625	1020	7	83	0.43	2	1	36	275	7.71
2016	AA	Reading	521	106	144	40	125	276	352	591	943	10	64	0.33	21	1	56	315	8.01

The power clicked, as he let it fly and led the minors in HR. But important caveats exist: his home park is a bandbox (on the road: just 11 HR, .766 OPS); and he struck out 186 times. The ball jumps off his bat to all fields, his swing has improved, but is there enough contact? It's a classic RF profile, and he has chipped in a bunch of SB, too.

Craig,Will — 5 — Pittsburgh — EXP MLB DEBUT: 2018 — H/W: 6-3 212 — FUT: Starting 3B — 8C

Bats R Age 22
2016 (1) Wake Forest
Pwr + + +
BAvg + + + +
Spd +
Def + +

Year	Lev	Team	AB	R	H	HR	RBI	Avg	OB	Slg	OPS	bb%	ct%	Eye	SB	CS	x/h%	Iso	RC/G
2016	NCAA	Wake Forest	182	53	69	16	66	379	507	731	1237	21	81	1.34	0	1	46	352	11.42
2016	A-	West Virginia	218	28	61	2	23	280	394	362	756	16	83	1.11	2	0	23	83	5.37

1st round pick has a solid offensive skill set. RH stroke with good bat speed and raw power results in hard contact and over-the-fence power. Advanced understanding of strike zone and contact ability give him tools to hit for power and BA. Lack of quickness and athleticism make him a below-average defender at 3B.

Crawford,J.P. — 6 — Philadelphia — EXP MLB DEBUT: 2017 — H/W: 6-2 180 — FUT: Starting SS — 8A

Bats L Age 22
2013 (1) HS (CA)
Pwr + + +
BAvg + + + +
4.19 Spd + + +
Def + + + +

Year	Lev	Team	AB	R	H	HR	RBI	Avg	OB	Slg	OPS	bb%	ct%	Eye	SB	CS	x/h%	Iso	RC/G
2014	A+	Clearwater	236	32	65	8	29	275	352	407	759	11	84	0.76	10	7	23	131	4.95
2015	A+	Clearwater	79	15	31	1	8	392	484	443	927	15	89	1.56	5	2	6	51	7.33
2015	AA	Reading	351	53	93	5	34	265	355	407	762	12	87	1.09	7	2	35	142	5.33
2016	AA	Reading	136	23	36	3	13	265	398	390	787	18	85	1.43	5	3	31	125	5.84
2016	AAA	Lehigh Valley	336	40	82	4	30	244	328	318	646	11	82	0.71	7	4	20	74	3.70

Hit a speedbump at Triple-A, though maintained solid plate control. At times struggled to stay back on pitches and drive them. Overall, excellent athleticism results in smooth swing that should result in moderate power. Average runner with a plus arm and instincts. With a bit more polish at the plate, he'll soon be a lineup staple.

Cronenworth,Jake — 6 — Tampa Bay — EXP MLB DEBUT: 2018 — H/W: 6-1 185 — FUT: Starting 2B — 7C

Bats L Age 23
2015 (7) Michigan
Pwr + +
BAvg + + +
Spd + + +
Def + + +

Year	Lev	Team	AB	R	H	HR	RBI	Avg	OB	Slg	OPS	bb%	ct%	Eye	SB	CS	x/h%	Iso	RC/G
2015	NCAA	Michigan	269	62	91	6	48	338	413	494	907	11	90	1.21	11	9	30	156	6.88
2015	A-	Hudson Valley	196	31	57	1	16	291	388	398	786	14	70	0.53	12	7	28	107	5.82
2016	A	Bowling Green	314	66	101	3	48	322	421	436	858	15	82	0.95	12	7	24	115	6.59
2016	A+	Charlotte	111	15	19	1	9	171	258	243	501	10	77	0.50	2	1	26	72	1.69

Instinctual INF who is tough out due to willingness to work counts and get on base. Bat speed is average and won't lead to much power, but recognizes pitches and can go to opposite field. Knows strike zone and should have high OBP. Not the most gifted athlete, but ranges well and owns average arm. Led MWL in OBP.

Cruz,Johan — 6 — Chicago (A) — EXP MLB DEBUT: 2019 — H/W: 6-2 190 — FUT: Starting SS — 7D

Bats R Age 21
2012 FA (DR)
Pwr + +
BAvg + + +
Spd + + +
Def + + +

Year	Lev	Team	AB	R	H	HR	RBI	Avg	OB	Slg	OPS	bb%	ct%	Eye	SB	CS	x/h%	Iso	RC/G
2013	Rk	DSL White Sox	244	29	30	0	7	123	204	160	364	9	77	0.44	18	7	27	37	-0.12
2014	Rk	Azl White Sox	78	12	14	1	7	179	264	256	521	10	77	0.50	0	1	29	77	1.92
2014	Rk	DSL White Sox	85	10	28	1	7	329	412	471	883	12	79	0.67	5	4	32	141	6.83
2015	Rk	Great Falls	269	40	84	6	38	312	342	442	784	4	77	0.20	0	0	27	130	4.98
2016	A	Kannapolis	251	31	64	5	26	255	315	371	686	8	76	0.36	2	2	28	116	3.94

Tall INF who is adding strength and more offensive punch to profile. Focuses on hitting hard line drives, though can turn on pitch and pull out of park. Hits LHP well and should add more pop as he ages. Owns double-plus arm that could slide him over to 3B, but has hands/feet to stick at SS.

Curbelo,Luis — 46 — Chicago (A) — EXP MLB DEBUT: 2021 — H/W: 6-3 185 — FUT: Starting MIF — 8E

Bats R Age 19
2016 (6) HS (FL)
Pwr + + +
BAvg + +
Spd + +
Def + +

Year	Lev	Team	AB	R	H	HR	RBI	Avg	OB	Slg	OPS	bb%	ct%	Eye	SB	CS	x/h%	Iso	RC/G
2016	Rk	Azl White Sox	164	20	37	2	14	226	291	323	614	8	74	0.36	4	0	27	98	3.05

Tall, lean INF who split season between 2B and SS. Has good defensive instincts, but lacks ideal range to stick at SS. Arm and hands will work anywhere on diamond. Offers power potential, but needs to add strength to realize. Swings balanced stick with decent approach and has shown ability to go to opposite field.

Daal,Carlton — 6 — Cincinnati — EXP MLB DEBUT: 2018 — H/W: 6-1 180 — FUT: Utility player — 7E

Bats R Age 23
2012 FA (CC)
Pwr +
BAvg + +
Spd + + +
Def + + +

Year	Lev	Team	AB	R	H	HR	RBI	Avg	OB	Slg	OPS	bb%	ct%	Eye	SB	CS	x/h%	Iso	RC/G
2013	Rk	AZL Reds	21	3	3	0	3	143	182	143	325	5	71	0.17	0	0	0	0	-1.16
2013	Rk	Billings	51	5	13	0	4	255	296	275	571	6	75	0.23	2	0	8	20	2.31
2014	A	Dayton	345	46	102	1	29	296	332	351	683	5	83	0.32	13	3	14	55	3.83
2015	A+	Daytona	381	38	103	0	30	270	308	286	595	5	84	0.34	21	5	6	16	2.77
2016	AA	Pensacola	116	15	36	1	6	310	360	379	739	7	78	0.35	5	1	14	69	4.60

Solid defensive SS may not have the strength to endure MLB season. Quick, flat swing produces solid bat-to-ball skills. Tends to loft balls into the OF too much for frame/skill set. Above average defensive SS and runner. Will be asset on bench at very least.

Dalbec,Bobby — 5 — Boston — EXP MLB DEBUT: 2018 — H/W: 6-4 225 — FUT: Starting 3B — 8D

Bats R Age 21
2016 (4) Arizona
Pwr + + + +
BAvg + +
Spd +
Def + +

Year	Lev	Team	AB	R	H	HR	RBI	Avg	OB	Slg	OPS	bb%	ct%	Eye	SB	CS	x/h%	Iso	RC/G
2016	NCAA	Arizona	231	42	60	7	40	260	360	429	788	13	63	0.42	7	3	38	169	6.00
2016	A-	Lowell	132	25	51	7	33	386	426	674	1100	6	75	0.27	2	2	43	288	9.30

Tall, strong 3B who destroyed NYPL in pro debut. Exhibits incredible raw power, especially to pull side, and has swing and bat speed to hit to all fields. Can sell out for power and struggle with breaking balls. Secondary skills are lacking, but has improved with glove and lateral quickness.

Davidson,Braxton — 9 — Atlanta — EXP MLB DEBUT: 2019 — H/W: 6-2 230 — FUT: Starting OF — 7D

Bats L Age 20
2014 (1) HS (NC)
Pwr + + + +
BAvg + +
Spd + +
Def + +

Year	Lev	Team	AB	R	H	HR	RBI	Avg	OB	Slg	OPS	bb%	ct%	Eye	SB	CS	x/h%	Iso	RC/G
2014	Rk	Danville	36	1	6	0	3	167	333	222	556	20	72	0.90	0	0	33	56	2.67
2014	Rk	GCL Braves	111	23	27	0	8	243	368	324	693	17	71	0.69	0	0	30	81	4.58
2015	A	Rome	401	51	97	10	45	242	373	374	747	17	66	0.62	1	6	34	132	5.32
2016	A+	Carolina	428	53	96	10	63	224	335	360	694	14	57	0.39	4	4	38	136	4.85

Swing-and-miss issues became more pronounced in Single-A. Long, looping swing susceptible to hard stuff in and off-speed pitches down. Raw plus power shows brief glimpses in game. Improved as a defender. Might not have arm for right field; may need to move back to first base.

Davidson,Matt — 5 — Chicago (A) — EXP MLB DEBUT: 2013 — H/W: 6-3 230 — FUT: Starting 3B — 7E

Bats R Age 26
2009 (S-1) HS (CA)
Pwr + + + +
BAvg + +
Spd +
Def + + +

Year	Lev	Team	AB	R	H	HR	RBI	Avg	OB	Slg	OPS	bb%	ct%	Eye	SB	CS	x/h%	Iso	RC/G
2013	MLB	Arizona	76	8	18	3	12	237	326	434	760	12	68	0.42	0	1	50	197	5.20
2014	AAA	Charlotte	478	59	95	20	55	199	273	362	635	9	66	0.30	0	0	40	163	3.24
2015	AAA	Charlotte	528	63	107	23	74	203	286	375	661	11	64	0.32	1	0	42	172	3.72
2016	AAA	Charlotte	284	35	76	10	46	268	342	444	785	10	70	0.37	0	0	39	176	5.47
2016	MLB	Chi White Sox	2	1	1	0	1	500	500	500	1000	0	50	0.00	0	0	0	0	11.13

Big, strong 3B who has spent 4 years in AAA. Ended season in June after broken foot. Consistent 20+ HR producer, but too much swing and miss in game. Regressing bat and BA troublesome as he has to hit to have value. OK defender with strong arm and average agility. Rarely runs, but game revolves around power.

Davis,Brendon — 56 — Los Angeles (N) — EXP MLB DEBUT: 2019 — H/W: 6-4 165 — FUT: Starting 3B — 7D

Bats R Age 19
2015 (5) HS (CA)
Pwr + + +
BAvg + +
Spd + +
Def + +

Year	Lev	Team	AB	R	H	HR	RBI	Avg	OB	Slg	OPS	bb%	ct%	Eye	SB	CS	x/h%	Iso	RC/G
2015	Rk	Azl Dodgers	90	14	25	0	14	278	309	322	631	4	71	0.15	2	0	12	44	3.10
2015	Rk	Ogden	24	5	4	1	3	167	231	333	564	8	67	0.25	0	0	50	167	2.14
2016	A	Great Lakes	398	51	96	5	49	241	293	334	627	7	70	0.25	8	3	26	93	3.15

Tall, lanky SS struggled in his full-season debut, hitting just .241 with 27% K rate. Still has plus raw tools and projects to have at least average power once he matures. Moves well with average speed and a strong arm, but isn't likely to stick at SS due to his size. Swing mechanics need refinement, but has good athleticism.

Davis,D.J. — 78 — Toronto

EXP MLB DEBUT: 2018 | H/W: 6-1 180 | FUT: Starting OF | 8E

Bats L Age 22 — 2012 (1) HS (MS)
Pwr ++ | BAvg ++ | Spd ++ | Def ++++

Year	Lev	Team	AB	R	H	HR	RBI	Avg	OB	Slg	OPS	bb%	ct%	Eye	SB	CS	x/h%	Iso	RC/G
2012	A-	Vancouver	18	3	3	0	0	167	348	167	514	22	67	0.83	1	1	0	0	1.84
2013	Rk	Bluefield	225	35	54	6	25	240	319	418	737	10	66	0.34	13	8	39	178	5.00
2014	A	Lansing	494	56	105	8	52	213	266	316	582	7	66	0.22	19	20	27	103	2.52
2015	A	Lansing	496	77	140	7	59	282	335	391	726	7	76	0.33	21	10	24	109	4.47
2016	A+	Dunedin	274	35	54	1	15	197	290	263	553	12	64	0.36	22	6	24	66	2.29

Regressing OF who struggled in High-A after two years in Low-A. Still exhibits offensive potential with exciting bat speed, raw power, and plus wheels. Has major contact issues with free-swinging ways and can't hit LHP. Approach and pitch recognition need work. Split between LF and CF and may not have enough arm strength despite plus range.

Davis,Dylan — 79 — San Francisco

EXP MLB DEBUT: 2018 | H/W: 6-0 205 | FUT: Starting OF | 7C

Bats R Age 23 — 2014 (3) Oregon State
Pwr +++ | BAvg ++ | Spd ++ | Def +++

Year	Lev	Team	AB	R	H	HR	RBI	Avg	OB	Slg	OPS	bb%	ct%	Eye	SB	CS	x/h%	Iso	RC/G
2014	A-	Salem-Kaizer	85	11	17	4	7	200	261	341	602	8	73	0.30	1	0	24	141	2.58
2015	A	Augusta	256	37	64	9	30	250	324	406	730	10	70	0.37	2	1	34	156	4.62
2015	A+	San Jose	107	18	22	3	11	206	298	318	615	12	74	0.50	0	1	27	112	3.06
2016	A	Augusta	236	38	68	8	43	288	368	496	864	11	75	0.52	3	1	43	208	6.50
2016	A+	San Jose	248	36	69	18	49	278	337	544	881	8	75	0.36	1	0	42	266	6.29

Intriguing OF who set high in HR. Owns plus raw power with natural bat speed and strength. Can hit ball over fence to all fields. Can get pull-happy when selling out for power and needs to improve pitch recognition. Will always have K in profile. Sound defender in corner with strong arm. Won't steal many bases.

Davis,J.D. — 5 — Houston

EXP MLB DEBUT: 2017 | H/W: 6-3 225 | FUT: Starting 3B | 8D

Bats R Age 23 — 2014 (3) Cal State Fullerton
Pwr ++++ | BAvg ++ | Spd + | Def ++

Year	Lev	Team	AB	R	H	HR	RBI	Avg	OB	Slg	OPS	bb%	ct%	Eye	SB	CS	x/h%	Iso	RC/G
2014	NCAA	Cal State Fullerton	237	34	80	6	43	338	416	523	940	12	78	0.60	7	0	34	186	7.51
2014	A-	Tri City	111	18	31	5	20	279	365	495	861	12	77	0.60	1	0	42	216	6.34
2014	A	Quad Cities	155	20	47	8	32	303	357	516	873	8	74	0.32	4	0	36	213	6.33
2015	A+	Lancaster	485	93	140	26	101	289	360	520	880	10	68	0.34	5	2	41	231	6.85
2016	AA	Corpus Christi	485	61	130	23	81	268	330	485	815	8	71	0.31	1	3	45	216	5.74

Slugger with well above average raw power and solid eye at plate. Has advanced a level per year and is on verge of majors. Makes loud contact from strong stroke and possesses all fields pop. Power based more on strength than bat speed. Lot of Ks, but OK trade off for HR. Limited mobility and range and is only fringe defender.

Davis,Jaylin — 79 — Minnesota

EXP MLB DEBUT: 2019 | H/W: 6-1 190 | FUT: Starting OF | 7D

Bats R Age 22 — 2015 (24) Appalachian State
Pwr +++ | BAvg ++ | Spd ++ | Def ++

Year	Lev	Team	AB	R	H	HR	RBI	Avg	OB	Slg	OPS	bb%	ct%	Eye	SB	CS	x/h%	Iso	RC/G
2015	NCAA	Appalachian State	65	10	17	2	9	262	368	400	768	14	68	0.52	5	0	29	138	5.45
2016	Rk	Elizabethton	47	12	13	7	12	277	333	745	1078	8	51	0.17	2	0	62	468	11.93
2016	A	Cedar Rapids	192	32	48	9	29	250	324	469	793	10	67	0.33	3	0	48	219	5.66

Strong OF who impresses with natural pop and bat speed. Features above average power potential and could grow into more as he cleans up approach and swing mechanics. BA in doubt as he can lunge at balls and doesn't cover plate. Not a speed merchant, but not a slouch and will steal occasional bag. Average arm in corner OF.

Davis,Jonathan — 79 — Toronto

EXP MLB DEBUT: 2018 | H/W: 5-8 190 | FUT: Reserve OF | 6B

Bats R Age 24 — 2013 (15) Central Arkansas
Pwr ++ | BAvg ++ | Spd ++++ | Def ++

Year	Lev	Team	AB	R	H	HR	RBI	Avg	OB	Slg	OPS	bb%	ct%	Eye	SB	CS	x/h%	Iso	RC/G
2014	Rk	GCL Blue Jays	3	0	0	0	0	0	0	0	0	0	100		0	0		0	-2.66
2014	A-	Vancouver	88	14	19	1	10	216	266	386	652	6	70	0.23	7	1	47	170	3.67
2015	A	Lansing	49	13	20	2	8	408	482	612	1094	13	86	1.00	6	1	25	204	9.10
2015	A+	Dunedin	161	22	37	1	14	230	275	342	616	6	79	0.29	5	6	43	112	3.10
2016	A+	Dunedin	417	74	105	14	54	252	359	441	801	14	73	0.63	33	6	41	189	5.81

Breakout prospect who was 2nd in FSL in SB. Sets career highs in AB, 2B, HR, BB, and SB. Best attribute is plus speed and has honed instincts with reading pitchers. Was healthy for first time and showcased short stroke. Not much natural power, but can turn on FB and pull out of park. Too many Ks, but will see pitches. Passable in OF corner.

Dawson,Ronnie — 79 — Houston

EXP MLB DEBUT: 2019 | H/W: 6-2 225 | FUT: Starting OF | 7C

Bats L Age 21 — 2016 (2) Ohio State
Pwr +++ | BAvg ++ | Spd +++ | Def ++

Year	Lev	Team	AB	R	H	HR	RBI	Avg	OB	Slg	OPS	bb%	ct%	Eye	SB	CS	x/h%	Iso	RC/G
2016	NCAA	Ohio State	257	55	85	13	51	331	415	611	1026	13	83	0.86	21	4	49	280	8.38
2016	A-	Tri City	244	41	55	7	36	225	337	373	710	14	73	0.62	12	6	38	148	4.53

Big, strong OF with ideal power/speed package to provide value. Brings disciplined eye to plate and knows value of working counts. Has average power to all fields, though can be jammed inside. Has struggled with LHP and breaking balls. Fits LF profile despite good speed. Inefficient routes and poor jumps hinder glovework.

De Leon,Michael — 46 — Texas

EXP MLB DEBUT: 2019 | H/W: 6-1 160 | FUT: Starting SS | 7B

Bats B Age 20 — 2013 FA (DR)
Pwr ++ | BAvg +++ | Spd ++ | Def +++

Year	Lev	Team	AB	R	H	HR	RBI	Avg	OB	Slg	OPS	bb%	ct%	Eye	SB	CS	x/h%	Iso	RC/G
2014	A	Hickory	336	42	82	1	26	244	302	295	597	8	88	0.70	3	3	16	51	3.13
2014	A+	Myrtle Beach	24	5	7	1	6	292	370	542	912	11	83	0.75	0	0	57	250	6.94
2014	AA	Frisco	3	1	1	0	0	333	333	667	1000	0	67	0.00	0	0	100	333	9.06
2015	A	Hickory	306	29	68	1	29	222	277	281	558	7	85	0.49	1	1	21	59	2.53
2016	A+	High Desert	454	54	121	9	54	267	303	385	689	5	87	0.42	7	5	29	119	3.94

Young INF who held his own as one of younger players in A+. Set easy high in HR and combines bat control with extreme contact ability to hit for BA. Has sweet swing from both sides and profiles to average power. Quick hands are highlight on defense and possesses solid arm. Can play 2B, but has range and more impact at SS.

Dean,Austin — 7 — Miami

EXP MLB DEBUT: 2017 | H/W: 6-1 190 | FUT: Starting OF | 7C

Bats R Age 23 — 2012 (4) HS (TX)
Pwr +++ | BAvg ++ | Spd ++ | Def +++

Year	Lev	Team	AB	R	H	HR	RBI	Avg	OB	Slg	OPS	bb%	ct%	Eye	SB	CS	x/h%	Iso	RC/G
2013	A-	Batavia	213	28	57	2	19	268	322	418	740	7	78	0.36	0	2	37	150	4.77
2013	A	Greensboro	20	4	4	1	3	200	333	400	733	17	75	0.80	0	0	50	200	4.81
2014	A	Greensboro	403	67	124	9	58	308	367	444	812	9	82	0.53	4	4	27	136	5.56
2015	A+	Jupiter	519	67	139	5	52	268	319	366	685	7	85	0.51	18	10	28	98	4.04
2016	AA	Jacksonville	480	60	114	11	67	238	307	375	682	9	77	0.44	1	2	34	138	3.96

Thick, strong-bodied OF took a step back. Was more aggressive at the plate and doubled his HR output but at the price of low contact. Good bat speed and average to above raw power. Sets up tall with hands low and drives the ball. Has average speed but that isn't going to be part of his game. Covers ground in the OF with average arm.

DeJong,Paul — 56 — St. Louis

EXP MLB DEBUT: 2017 | H/W: 6-1 195 | FUT: Starting 3B | 7C

Bats R Age 23 — 2015 (4) Illinois State
Pwr +++ | BAvg ++ | Spd ++ | Def ++

Year	Lev	Team	AB	R	H	HR	RBI	Avg	OB	Slg	OPS	bb%	ct%	Eye	SB	CS	x/h%	Iso	RC/G
2015	NCAA	Illinois State	210	47	70	14	48	333	412	605	1017	12	76	0.56	2	1	41	271	8.31
2015	Rk	Johnson City	37	10	18	4	15	486	558	973	1531	14	76	0.67	0	0	56	486	15.32
2015	A	Peoria	219	32	63	5	26	288	355	438	794	10	80	0.53	13	4	32	151	5.42
2016	AA	Springfield	496	62	129	22	73	260	315	460	775	7	71	0.28	3	2	41	200	5.12

Has a quick stroke that generates good lift to go along with plus raw power. Can be overly aggressive as he hunts for pitches he can drive, but has good bat speed and did set career high in HR. Below average runner with just enough range, glove work, and arm strength to stick at 3B. Doesn't have huge upside, but fits into the system well.

Delmonico,Nicky — 359 — Chicago (A)

EXP MLB DEBUT: 2017 | H/W: 6-2 230 | FUT: Starting 1B | 7C

Bats L Age 24 — 2011 (6) HS (TN)
Pwr +++ | BAvg ++ | Spd ++ | Def ++

Year	Lev	Team	AB	R	H	HR	RBI	Avg	OB	Slg	OPS	bb%	ct%	Eye	SB	CS	x/h%	Iso	RC/G
2014	A+	Brevard County	141	11	37	4	15	262	297	404	702	5	76	0.21	2	2	32	142	3.95
2015	A	Kannapolis	20	4	8	1	8	400	429	700	1129	5	80	0.25	0	0	38	300	9.26
2015	AA	Birmingham	223	26	53	3	26	238	315	386	700	10	77	0.48	2	1	51	148	4.36
2016	AA	Birmingham	142	25	48	10	31	338	394	676	1070	8	77	0.39	1	0	54	338	8.85
2016	AAA	Charlotte	260	32	64	7	30	246	322	388	710	10	72	0.39	2	0	36	142	4.38

Strong INF who set high in HR and 2B while spending time at multiple positions. Now in 3rd org, but bat leading him to majors. Has vicious stroke, though can be pull happy and sell out for power. Hit for high BA in AA by working counts and allowing bat speed to make contact. Does not run well and lacks quickness to be average with glove.

Demeritte,Travis — 45 — Atlanta

EXP MLB DEBUT: 2018 | H/W: 6-0 180 | FUT: Starting 2B | 8D

Bats R Age 22 — 2013 (1) HS (GA)
Pwr ++++ | BAvg ++ | Spd +++ | Def ++++

Year	Lev	Team	AB	R	H	HR	RBI	Avg	OB	Slg	OPS	bb%	ct%	Eye	SB	CS	x/h%	Iso	RC/G
2014	A	Hickory	398	77	84	25	66	211	299	450	749	11	57	0.29	6	2	51	239	5.49
2015	A-	Spokane	20	0	3	0	0	150	227	150	377	9	45	0.18	0	2	0	0	-0.70
2015	A	Hickory	170	27	41	5	19	241	338	412	750	13	59	0.36	10	1	44	171	5.62
2016	A+	Carolina	124	21	31	3	11	250	380	476	856	17	60	0.52	4	1	55	226	7.67
2016	A+	High Desert	331	73	90	25	59	272	352	583	935	11	62	0.33	13	3	54	311	8.12

Athletic 2B with loud power, patience and lots of swing-and-miss, still looking for consistency. Cannot read the spin of the breaking ball, striking out 175 times in 455 ABs. Has 30 HR potential despite hit tool deficiency. Can run a little and has increased profile due to Gold-Glove caliber defense at 2B.

Denton,Bryce — 5 — St. Louis
EXP MLB DEBUT: 2020 | H/W: 6-0 191 | FUT: Starting 3B | 7D

Bats R | Age 19 | 2015 (2) HS (TN)
Pwr + + | BAvg + + + | Spd + + | Def + +

Year	Lev	Team	AB	R	H	HR	RBI	Avg	OB	Slg	OPS	bb%	ct%	Eye	SB	CS	x/h%	Iso	RC/G
2015	Rk	GCL Cardinals	155	21	30	1	14	194	247	245	492	7	79	0.34	3	0	13	52	1.49
2016	Rk	Johnson City	202	34	57	4	26	282	347	376	723	9	82	0.54	2	1	19	94	4.46

Rebounded from a rough pro debut. Has good bat speed and raw power, and worked hard to shorten swing and make more consistent contact. Swing can still get long.. Below average speed and defense limit him to 3B where he will need to show power to have value.

Devers,Rafael — 5 — Boston
EXP MLB DEBUT: 2018 | H/W: 6-0 195 | FUT: Starting 3B | 9C

Bats L | Age 20 | 2013 FA (DR)
Pwr + + + | BAvg + + + | Spd + + + | Def + + +

Year	Lev	Team	AB	R	H	HR	RBI	Avg	OB	Slg	OPS	bb%	ct%	Eye	SB	CS	x/h%	Iso	RC/G
2014	Rk	GCL Red Sox	157	21	49	4	36	312	368	484	852	8	81	0.47	1	0	35	172	6.07
2014	Rk	DSL Red Sox	104	26	35	3	21	337	448	538	986	17	81	1.05	4	1	34	202	8.32
2015	A	Greenville	469	71	135	11	70	288	323	443	766	5	82	0.29	3	2	37	156	4.80
2016	A+	Salem	503	64	142	11	71	282	335	443	779	7	81	0.43	18	6	36	161	5.13

Powerful 3B with high ceiling who started slow, but ended on fire. Used better plate approach to draw walks and makes good contact for slugger. Hits ton of doubles and will eventually turn on pitches to realize plus power potential. Set high in SB, though will slow down as he ages. Owns tools for 3B, but could slide over to 1B if needed.

Dewees,Donnie — 78 — Chicago (N)
EXP MLB DEBUT: 2019 | H/W: 5-11 180 | FUT: Starting CF | 8D

Bats L | Age 23 | 2015 (2) North Florida
Pwr + + | BAvg + + + + | Spd + + + + | Def + +

Year	Lev	Team	AB	R	H	HR	RBI	Avg	OB	Slg	OPS	bb%	ct%	Eye	SB	CS	x/h%	Iso	RC/G
2015	NCAA	North Florida	251	88	106	18	68	422	484	749	1233	11	94	1.88	23	3	36	327	10.21
2015	A-	Eugene	282	42	75	5	30	266	301	376	677	5	81	0.26	19	7	27	110	3.68
2016	A	South Bend	365	65	103	3	54	282	335	414	749	7	86	0.57	17	5	29	132	4.87
2016	A+	Myrtle Beach	149	25	43	2	19	289	333	423	756	6	76	0.28	14	0	33	134	4.87

Advanced feel for hitting with a good understanding of the strike zone and the ability to make contact. Size and line-drive approach limit long-term power upside, but has strength to hit 10-15 HR. Plus speed is best tool and hit 14 3B with 31 SB. Barrels the ball well, but needs to be more selective (6% BB rate). Should be able to stick in CF.

Diaz,Elias — 2 — Pittsburgh
EXP MLB DEBUT: 2015 | H/W: 6-0 210 | FUT: Starting C | 7B

Bats R | Age 26 | 2008 FA (VZ)
Pwr + + | BAvg + + + | Spd + + | Def + + + +

Year	Lev	Team	AB	R	H	HR	RBI	Avg	OB	Slg	OPS	bb%	ct%	Eye	SB	CS	x/h%	Iso	RC/G
2016	A+	Bradenton	23	6	9	1	5	391	481	522	1003	15	91	2.00	0	1	11	130	8.03
2016	AA	Altoona	7	0	2	0	1	286	375	286	661	13	86	1.00	0	0	0	0	4.04
2016	AAA	Indianapolis	94	4	25	0	10	266	289	298	587	3	82	0.18	1	0	12	32	2.53
2016	MLB	Pittsburgh	4	0	0	0	1	0	0	0	0	0	75	0.00	0	0		0	-5.26

Strong, defensive backstop missed all but 34 games due to elbow surgery. Diaz blocks and receives well and had a plus arm prior to the injury. Frames pitches well and calls a good game. Widely considered one of the best defenders in the minors. Hit well when he returned to action and has a good understanding of the strike zone.

Diaz,Isan — 46 — Milwaukee
EXP MLB DEBUT: 2018 | H/W: 5-10 185 | FUT: Starting 2B | 8C

Bats L | Age 20 | 2014 (S-2) HS (MA)
Pwr + + + + | BAvg + + + | 4.40 Spd + + | Def + + +

Year	Lev	Team	AB	R	H	HR	RBI	Avg	OB	Slg	OPS	bb%	ct%	Eye	SB	CS	x/h%	Iso	RC/G
2014	Rk	Azl Diamondbacks	182	22	34	3	21	187	285	330	615	12	69	0.45	6	5	44	143	3.23
2015	Rk	Missoula	272	58	98	13	51	360	431	640	1071	11	76	0.52	12	7	45	279	9.20
2016	A	Wisconsin	507	71	134	20	75	264	356	469	825	12	71	0.49	11	8	44	205	6.11

Young, emerging INF who led MWL in HR and ISO. Plus bat speed and can turn on a MLB fastball; shows good pop the opposite way. Unrefined approach and will chase, but draws walks. Fringe runner; likely not SB source. Solid-average range and defensive actions. Intriguing HR/RBI potential as middle-of-order bat and above-average 2B.

Diaz,Lewin — 3 — Minnesota
EXP MLB DEBUT: 2020 | H/W: 6-3 180 | FUT: Starting 1B | 8D

Bats L | Age 20 | 2013 FA (DR)
Pwr + + + | BAvg + + + | Spd + | Def + +

Year	Lev	Team	AB	R	H	HR	RBI	Avg	OB	Slg	OPS	bb%	ct%	Eye	SB	CS	x/h%	Iso	RC/G
2015	Rk	GCL Twins	111	12	29	1	15	261	344	369	713	11	78	0.58	2	0	31	108	4.56
2015	Rk	Elizabethton	48	7	8	3	5	167	216	375	591	6	65	0.18	0	0	50	208	2.37
2016	Rk	Elizabethton	174	26	54	9	37	310	355	575	930	6	80	0.34	0	0	48	264	6.86

Offense-first 1B who continues to succeed due to instincts and clean swing. Swings hard with above average bat speed and has power to all fields. Adding strength as he matures and also greater feel for contact. Can hit LHP, though pitch recognition needs work. Limited mobility, though strong arm and soft hands are assets.

Diaz,Yandy — 579 — Cleveland
EXP MLB DEBUT: 2017 | H/W: 6-2 185 | FUT: Utility player | 7B

Bats R | Age 25 | 2013 FA (CU)
Pwr + + | BAvg + + + + | Spd + + + | Def + + +

Year	Lev	Team	AB	R	H	HR	RBI	Avg	OB	Slg	OPS	bb%	ct%	Eye	SB	CS	x/h%	Iso	RC/G
2014	A+	Carolina	283	42	81	2	37	286	392	367	759	15	88	1.40	3	3	17	81	5.44
2015	AA	Akron	476	61	150	7	55	315	412	408	819	14	86	1.20	8	7	17	92	6.02
2015	AAA	Columbus	19	1	3	0	1	158	158	263	421	0	74	0.00	0	0	67	105	0.30
2016	AA	Akron	84	13	24	2	14	286	444	381	825	22	81	1.50	6	2	13	95	6.47
2016	AAA	Columbus	360	53	117	7	44	325	403	461	864	12	81	0.67	5	1	27	136	6.43

Tall INF posted top-10 marks in BA, OBP, Eye among IL bats. Employs short load, quick hands, line-drive plane for plus ct% and BA skills. Low HR ceiling, but pounds gaps and works whole field. Rarely expands zone. Average runner but picks his spots; moderate SB upside. Above-average defender with versatility.

Diaz,Yusniel — 789 — Los Angeles (N)
EXP MLB DEBUT: 2019 | H/W: 6-1 195 | FUT: Starting OF | 8D

Bats R | Age 20 | 2015 FA (CU)
Pwr + + + | BAvg + + + | Spd + + + | Def + + +

Year	Lev	Team	AB	R	H	HR	RBI	Avg	OB	Slg	OPS	bb%	ct%	Eye	SB	CS	x/h%	Iso	RC/G
2016	Rk	Azl Dodgers	14	2	2	1	3	143	143	357	500	0	79	0.00	0	0	50	214	0.98
2016	A+	Rancho Cuca	316	47	86	8	54	272	333	418	751	8	78	0.41	7	8	27	146	4.81

Strong Cuban OF was signed for $15.5 million, but was limited in debut by shoulder injury. Showed solid skills. Can be overly aggressive at the plate leading to a 20% K rate, but does have good pitch recognition and bat speed that should allow him to hit for BA. Has the size and bat speed for power.

Didder,Ray-Patrick — 89 — Atlanta
EXP MLB DEBUT: 2020 | H/W: 6-0 170 | FUT: Reserve OF | 6B

Bats R | Age 22 | 2013 FA (AA)
Pwr + + | BAvg + + | Spd + + + + | Def + + +

Year	Lev	Team	AB	R	H	HR	RBI	Avg	OB	Slg	OPS	bb%	ct%	Eye	SB	CS	x/h%	Iso	RC/G
2013	Rk	DSL Braves	135	34	35	0	12	259	398	289	686	19	75	0.91	8	3	9	30	4.52
2014	Rk	GCL Braves	157	22	43	0	16	274	337	376	713	9	79	0.45	4	4	26	102	4.50
2015	Rk	Danville	223	31	55	0	16	247	309	332	640	8	77	0.39	10	7	22	85	3.51
2016	A	Rome	478	95	131	6	35	274	343	381	724	9	79	0.50	37	12	23	107	4.56

Late developing OF from Aruba enjoyed success after reworking approach and swing. Works counts, lots of hard groundball and lined contact. Will turn around an inside FB but relies on hitting ball in holes and using speed to get on base. Run tool finally showed up on base paths. Athletic defender with a plus arm.

Difo,Wilmer — 46 — Washington
EXP MLB DEBUT: 2015 | H/W: 5-11 200 | FUT: Reserve SS | 7C

Bats B | Age 25 | 2010 FA (DR)
Pwr + + | BAvg + + + | 4.19 Spd + + + + | Def + + + +

Year	Lev	Team	AB	R	H	HR	RBI	Avg	OB	Slg	OPS	bb%	ct%	Eye	SB	CS	x/h%	Iso	RC/G
2015	AA	Harrisburg	359	48	100	2	39	279	302	387	689	3	78	0.15	26	1	29	109	3.85
2015	MLB	Washington	11	1	2	0	0	182	182	182	364	0	82	0.00	0	0	0	0	-0.33
2016	AA	Harrisburg	410	59	106	6	41	259	315	354	669	8	86	0.58	28	11	23	95	3.85
2016	AAA	Syracuse	5	0	1	0	0	200	200	200	400	0	60	0.00	0	0	0	0	-0.49
2016	MLB	Washington	58	14	16	1	7	276	364	379	743	12	79	0.67	3	0	25	103	4.91

Though passed on the org chart by the Trea Turner Express, he made some important gains in plate approach in second tour of AA. Handles both sides of the plate well, and more patient approach will pay SB dividends. Plus defensive instincts and strong arm give him ability to play either MIF slot. Will need to continue to hit to nail down an everyday job.

Dozier,Hunter — 59 — Kansas City
EXP MLB DEBUT: 2016 | H/W: 6-4 220 | FUT: Starting 3B | 8C

Bats R | Age 25 | 2013 (1) SF Austin
Pwr + + + | BAvg + + + | Spd + + | Def + + +

Year	Lev	Team	AB	R	H	HR	RBI	Avg	OB	Slg	OPS	bb%	ct%	Eye	SB	CS	x/h%	Iso	RC/G
2014	AA	NW Arkansas	234	33	49	4	21	209	302	312	614	12	70	0.44	3	2	33	103	3.12
2015	AA	NW Arkansas	475	65	101	12	53	213	281	349	630	9	68	0.30	6	2	40	137	3.24
2016	AA	NW Arkansas	95	14	29	8	21	305	394	642	1037	13	76	0.61	4	0	55	337	8.59
2016	AAA	Omaha	391	65	115	15	54	294	360	506	866	9	74	0.40	3	1	45	212	6.42
2016	MLB	KC Royals	19	4	4	0	1	211	286	263	549	10	58	0.25	0	0	25	53	2.32

Re-vaulted up prospect chart after return of his plus bat. Set highs in 2B and HR by simplifying approach and making better contact. Natural power evolving, and he shortens swing when appropriate. Bat speed still fringy, but swing is cleaner. Errors an issue at 3B and could move to RF with average arm.

Dubon,Mauricio

6 | **Milwaukee** | EXP MLB DEBUT: 2018 | H/W: 6-0 160 | FUT: Starting MIF | **7B**

Bats R Age 22 — 2013 (26) HS (CA)

Pwr ++ · BAvg ++++ · Spd ++++ · Def +++

Year	Lev	Team	AB	R	H	HR	RBI	Avg	OB	Slg	OPS	bb%	ct%	Eye	SB	CS	x/h%	Iso	RC/G
2014	A-	Lowell	256	40	82	3	34	320	343	395	738	3	90	0.35	7	8	15	74	4.40
2015	A	Greenville	236	43	71	4	29	301	350	428	778	7	86	0.53	18	4	27	127	5.11
2015	A+	Salem	237	27	65	1	18	274	338	325	663	9	84	0.61	12	3	15	51	3.83
2016	A+	Salem	235	53	72	0	29	306	392	379	771	12	89	1.32	24	4	19	72	5.49
2016	AA	Portland	251	48	85	6	40	339	366	538	904	4	86	0.31	6	3	38	199	6.41

Advanced INF who hit at least .295 every month. Set highs in HR and SB while exhibiting more advanced approach at plate. Puts bat to ball easily due to hand-eye coordination and should hit for high BA. Limited strength mutes power production, but turns on pitches. Has plus speed and should stick at SS with quick hands and feet.

Duggar,Steven

8 | **San Francisco** | EXP MLB DEBUT: 2017 | H/W: 6-2 195 | FUT: Starting OF | **7B**

Bats L Age 23 — 2015 (6) Clemson

Pwr ++ · BAvg +++ · Spd ++++ · Def +++

Year	Lev	Team	AB	R	H	HR	RBI	Avg	OB	Slg	OPS	bb%	ct%	Eye	SB	CS	x/h%	Iso	RC/G
2015	NCAA	Clemson	227	56	69	5	43	304	438	432	869	19	78	1.10	10	5	26	128	6.94
2015	A-	Salem-Kaizer	229	40	67	1	27	293	386	367	753	13	77	0.67	6	3	21	74	5.18
2016	A+	San Jose	264	43	75	9	30	284	386	462	848	14	75	0.67	6	7	33	178	6.41
2016	AA	Richmond	243	35	78	1	24	321	391	432	823	10	79	0.55	9	7	27	111	5.96

Plus athlete with well above average speed and fundamental hitting techniques. Can hit with two strikes and learning to drive ball more consistently. Could be doubles machine with level stroke and innate ability to take extra base. Can lengthen swing at times and may not develop much pop. Can be very good CF defender with plus arm.

Dykstra,Luke

4 | **St. Louis** | EXP MLB DEBUT: 2020 | H/W: 6-1 195 | FUT: Reserve IF | **6C**

Bats R Age 21 — 2014 (7) HS (CA)

Pwr + · BAvg +++ · Spd +++ · Def +++

Year	Lev	Team	AB	R	H	HR	RBI	Avg	OB	Slg	OPS	bb%	ct%	Eye	SB	CS	x/h%	Iso	RC/G
2014	Rk	GCL Braves	149	16	39	2	28	262	304	376	680	6	92	0.75	7	2	33	114	4.05
2015	Rk	Danville	131	18	39	0	12	298	324	382	705	4	92	0.45	2	1	26	84	4.23
2015	A	Rome	92	9	32	0	10	348	368	478	847	3	95	0.60	1	0	34	130	5.80
2016	A	Rome	322	32	98	0	41	304	317	363	680	2	90	0.19	7	3	18	59	3.75

Hard working 2B with MLB pedigree. Has grit and bat-to-ball skills of father Lenny, lacks athleticism. Approach at plate works to all fields. Lots of contact, zero power in swing or frame. Plays adequately throughout infield. Maximizes opportunity through pure grit.

Engel,Adam

78 | **Chicago (A)** | EXP MLB DEBUT: 2017 | H/W: 6-2 210 | FUT: Starting CF | **7B**

Bats R Age 25 — 2013 (19) Louisville

Pwr ++ · BAvg ++ · Spd ++++ · Def ++++

Year	Lev	Team	AB	R	H	HR	RBI	Avg	OB	Slg	OPS	bb%	ct%	Eye	SB	CS	x/h%	Iso	RC/G
2014	A+	Winston-Salem	88	11	21	0	5	239	287	239	526	6	76	0.29	9	1	0	0	1.76
2015	A+	Winston-Salem	529	90	133	7	43	251	330	369	699	10	75	0.47	65	11	29	117	4.31
2016	A+	Winston-Salem	55	15	18	0	5	327	403	473	876	11	80	0.64	6	0	39	145	6.77
2016	AA	Birmingham	306	56	78	4	25	255	339	412	751	11	77	0.56	31	9	40	157	5.10
2016	AAA	Charlotte	149	19	36	3	16	242	289	369	658	6	66	0.20	8	5	31	128	3.65

Athletic, speedy OF who gets on base and wreaks havoc. Has hit 7 HR in each of last 3 seasons and power isn't game. Can leg out doubles and triples with sound gap power. OBP should be high, though will flail at breaking balls when behind in count. Excellent CF who has plus range and sufficient arm strength to be factor.

Enright,Kole

5 | **Texas** | EXP MLB DEBUT: 2020 | H/W: 6-1 175 | FUT: Starting 3B | **8D**

Bats B Age 19 — 2016 (3) HS (FL)

Pwr +++ · BAvg +++ · Spd ++ · Def ++

Year	Lev	Team	AB	R	H	HR	RBI	Avg	OB	Slg	OPS	bb%	ct%	Eye	SB	CS	x/h%	Iso	RC/G
2016	Rk	Azl Rangers	150	22	47	1	17	313	372	420	792	9	78	0.42	3	1	30	107	5.44

Quick-swinging INF who was surprise producer in debut. Plays multiple positions and exhibits plus arm. Will need to settle into spot and likely to be 3B. Destroys LHP and offers average power potential. Makes good contact for age and hits hard gappers with level stroke. Is adept at hitting from both sides and could use a bit more strength.

Erceg,Lucas

5 | **Milwaukee** | EXP MLB DEBUT: 2018 | H/W: 6-3 200 | FUT: Starting 3B | **8D**

Bats L Age 21 — 2016 (2) Menlo

Pwr ++++ · BAvg +++ · Spd ++ · Def +++

Year	Lev	Team	AB	R	H	HR	RBI	Avg	OB	Slg	OPS	bb%	ct%	Eye	SB	CS	x/h%	Iso	RC/G
2016	Rk	Helena	105	17	42	2	22	400	442	552	995	7	85	0.50	8	1	26	152	7.64
2016	A	Wisconsin	167	17	47	7	29	281	330	497	827	7	77	0.32	1	3	40	216	5.65

Pure hitter who turned in exceptional debut. Tall, lean frame generates good bat speed for plus raw pop; chance for good HR impact with added muscle. Average BA/ct% skills at present; will need to shorten up to handle quality off-speed. Former college closer with plus-plus arm and range for 3B. Under-the-radar name to watch for.

Ervin,Phil

789 | **Cincinnati** | EXP MLB DEBUT: 2018 | H/W: 5-10 205 | FUT: Reserve OF | **7E**

Bats R Age 24 — 2013 (1) Samford

Pwr +++ · BAvg ++ · Spd ++++ · Def +++

Year	Lev	Team	AB	R	H	HR	RBI	Avg	OB	Slg	OPS	bb%	ct%	Eye	SB	CS	x/h%	Iso	RC/G
2013	A	Dayton	43	7	15	1	6	349	451	465	916	16	77	0.80	2	1	20	116	7.37
2014	A	Dayton	498	68	118	7	68	237	301	376	677	8	78	0.42	30	5	41	139	3.96
2015	A+	Daytona	405	68	98	12	63	242	330	375	705	12	80	0.64	30	7	31	133	4.33
2015	AA	Pensacola	51	7	12	2	8	235	391	412	802	20	71	0.87	4	3	42	176	6.05
2016	AA	Pensacola	419	71	100	13	45	239	341	399	739	13	79	0.74	36	10	38	160	4.89

Streaky, stocky RHH with solid approach at plate. Struggles getting his swing moving. Too much soft contact in swing despite strength in frame and bat. Struggling to escape tweener profile. Plus-runner, tries to outrun catcher. Better corner OF than CF, further complicating profile.

Escalera,Alfredo

789 | **Kansas City** | EXP MLB DEBUT: 2018 | H/W: 6-1 185 | FUT: Starting OF | **7D**

Bats R Age 22 — 2012 (8) HS (FL)

Pwr ++ · BAvg +++ · Spd +++ · Def ++

Year	Lev	Team	AB	R	H	HR	RBI	Avg	OB	Slg	OPS	bb%	ct%	Eye	SB	CS	x/h%	Iso	RC/G
2014	A	Lexington	438	62	97	9	38	221	252	340	592	4	75	0.16	11	3	31	119	2.53
2015	A	Lexington	262	40	82	8	33	313	338	477	815	4	78	0.17	12	2	29	164	5.32
2015	A+	Wilmington	199	18	41	2	14	206	269	291	560	8	69	0.28	7	3	27	85	2.26
2016	A+	Wilmington	283	37	76	3	30	269	319	343	662	7	73	0.28	5	3	18	74	3.59
2016	AA	NW Arkansas	202	25	56	2	23	277	298	376	674	3	75	0.12	5	1	29	99	3.59

Fundamentally-sound OF who can impact game in variety of ways and is advancing quickly. Crushes LHP with quick stroke and gap power. Tends to be free swinger and approach could use discipline. Power only projects to gap, though has strength and bat speed to produce more with different approach. Plays all OF spots.

Estevez,Omar

46 | **Los Angeles (N)** | EXP MLB DEBUT: 2020 | H/W: 5-10 168 | FUT: Starting 2B | **8D**

Bats R Age 19 — 2015 FA (CU)

Pwr ++ · BAvg +++ · Spd +++ · Def ++

Year	Lev	Team	AB	R	H	HR	RBI	Avg	OB	Slg	OPS	bb%	ct%	Eye	SB	CS	x/h%	Iso	RC/G
2016	A	Great Lakes	471	46	120	9	61	255	294	389	682	5	74	0.21	3	6	36	134	3.81

Signed for $6 million and has across the board tools. Held his own in the MWL as one of the younger players. At times was over-matched, but has a good all-fields approach and should be able to hit for BA with avg power. Good range with soft hands and an avg arm. Might be pressed at SS, but profiles well at 2B.

Evans,Phillip

456 | **New York (N)** | EXP MLB DEBUT: 2017 | H/W: 5-9 220 | FUT: Utility player | **6C**

Bats R Age 24 — 2011 (15) HS (CA)

Pwr ++ · BAvg ++ · Spd ++ · Def ++

Year	Lev	Team	AB	R	H	HR	RBI	Avg	OB	Slg	OPS	bb%	ct%	Eye	SB	CS	x/h%	Iso	RC/G
2014	Rk	GCL Mets	3	0	2	0	0	667	667	667	1333	0	67	0.00	0	0	0	0	12.86
2014	A+	St. Lucie	389	34	96	4	39	247	315	319	634	9	85	0.66	0	1	21	72	3.51
2015	A+	St. Lucie	252	19	59	0	32	234	301	313	614	9	83	0.55	2	2	29	79	3.29
2016	A+	St. Lucie	28	3	4	0	2	143	273	143	416	15	89	1.67	0	0	0	0	1.51
2016	AA	Binghamton	361	50	121	8	39	335	368	485	853	5	83	0.32	1	1	31	150	5.83

Short, stocky INF had breakout '16 campaign in Double-A and won Eastern League batting title. Employed more patient approach overall, primarily attacking FB in hit zone. Real doubt approach will work in MLB, with below average tools across the board. Biggest attribute is versatility.

Fabian,Sandro

9 | **San Francisco** | EXP MLB DEBUT: 2021 | H/W: 6-1 180 | FUT: Starting OF | **8E**

Bats R Age 19 — 2014 FA (DR)

Pwr ++ · BAvg +++ · Spd ++ · Def +++

Year	Lev	Team	AB	R	H	HR	RBI	Avg	OB	Slg	OPS	bb%	ct%	Eye	SB	CS	x/h%	Iso	RC/G
2016	Rk	Azl Giants	159	30	54	2	35	340	367	522	889	4	82	0.25	3	1	37	182	6.37

Aggressive hitter who shows admirable tools for age. Likes to swing early in count and destroy ball. Needs to become more disciplined. Hit for BA despite being swing-happy, but poor pitch recognition won't work at higher levels. Projects to above average power when body develops, but lacks speed. True RF with plus arm strength.

Farmer,Kyle — 25 — Los Angeles (N)

EXP MLB DEBUT: 2017 | H/W: 6-0 205 | FUT: Reserve C | 6C

Bats R Age 26
2013 (8) Georgia
Pwr +
BAvg + +
Spd +
Def + + +

Year	Lev	Team	AB	R	H	HR	RBI	Avg	OB	Slg	OPS	bb%	ct%	Eye	SB	CS	x/h%	Iso	RC/G
2014	A+	Rancho Cuca	130	8	31	0	15	238	293	292	585	7	78	0.36	2	0	19	54	2.71
2015	A+	Rancho Cuca	163	33	55	1	27	337	383	515	898	7	85	0.48	5	2	38	178	6.67
2015	AA	Tulsa	283	25	77	2	39	272	306	392	699	5	81	0.25	0	1	38	120	4.06
2016	Rk	Azl Dodgers	17	4	5	2	4	294	333	647	980	6	94	1.00	0	0	40	353	6.80
2016	AA	Tulsa	266	31	68	5	31	256	320	395	714	9	83	0.57	2	0	37	139	4.44

Converted backstop continues to progress behind the plate with good hands and a strong arm, but release and blocking skills need work. Broken hand limited him to 74 games at AA and muted his production at the plate. Barrels the ball well and makes consistent contact. A work in progress, but upside is likely as a backup C/3B.

Feliciano,Mario — 2 — Milwaukee

EXP MLB DEBUT: 2021 | H/W: 6-1 195 | FUT: Starting C | 7D

Bats R Age 18
2016 (S-2) HS (PR)
Pwr + +
BAvg + + +
Spd + +
Def + + +

Year	Lev	Team	AB	R	H	HR	RBI	Avg	OB	Slg	OPS	bb%	ct%	Eye	SB	CS	x/h%	Iso	RC/G
2016	Rk	Azl Brewers	117	16	31	0	16	265	306	359	665	6	84	0.37	2	2	26	94	3.77

Raw prep C with moderate offensive upside. Best chance for impact is BA, employing a level stroke conducive to solid-average contact and an ability to spray the ball. Power works gap-to-gap; likely not much HR impact. Defensive actions are raw, but flashes above-average arm strength to remain at position long-term.

Fields,Roemon — 8 — Toronto

EXP MLB DEBUT: 2017 | H/W: 5-11 180 | FUT: Reserve OF | 6B

Bats L Age 26
2013 Bethany College
Pwr +
BAvg + +
Spd + + + +
Def + + + +

Year	Lev	Team	AB	R	H	HR	RBI	Avg	OB	Slg	OPS	bb%	ct%	Eye	SB	CS	x/h%	Iso	RC/G
2014	A-	Vancouver	294	64	79	1	26	269	330	350	681	8	79	0.44	48	9	23	82	4.01
2015	A+	Dunedin	264	34	71	1	21	269	311	348	659	6	80	0.31	21	9	21	80	3.59
2015	AA	New Hampshire	202	28	52	1	11	257	318	292	610	8	83	0.53	23	5	8	35	3.11
2015	AAA	Buffalo	23	1	5	0	1	217	308	261	569	12	83	0.75	2	0	20	43	2.84
2016	AA	New Hampshire	497	65	113	4	32	227	292	296	587	8	80	0.46	44	16	19	68	2.79

Incredibly fast OF who finished 2nd in EL in SB. Possesses slap-hitting approach and rarely drives ball. Set high in HR, but has limited power production or potential. Keeps ball on ground to use wheels. Stolen at least 44 bases each season as pro. Patrols CF with plus range and can track down any ball. Fits reserve profile with good OBP.

Fisher,Derek — 78 — Houston

EXP MLB DEBUT: 2017 | H/W: 6-3 205 | FUT: Starting OF | 8B

Bats L Age 23
2014 (S-1) Virginia
Pwr + + + +
BAvg + + +
Spd + + + +
Def + +

Year	Lev	Team	AB	R	H	HR	RBI	Avg	OB	Slg	OPS	bb%	ct%	Eye	SB	CS	x/h%	Iso	RC/G
2014	A-	Tri City	152	31	46	2	18	303	369	408	777	10	77	0.46	17	4	20	105	5.25
2015	A	Quad Cities	151	32	46	6	24	305	382	510	892	11	75	0.51	8	2	39	205	6.81
2015	A+	Lancaster	344	74	90	16	63	262	350	471	821	12	72	0.49	23	5	37	209	5.92
2016	AA	Corpus Christi	371	54	91	16	59	245	371	431	802	17	65	0.58	23	7	36	186	6.06
2016	AAA	Fresno	107	17	31	5	17	290	345	505	850	8	76	0.35	5	0	42	215	6.00

Tall, fluid OF who was better in AAA and has put together back-to-back 20 HR/20 SB seasons. Uses clean swing with plus bat speed to hit for power and has quality selectivity. Will swing and miss a lot due to long stroke. Has played CF, but not a fit there due to poor reads and fringy arm. Exhibits plus speed on base.

Fisher,Jameson — 7 — Chicago (A)

EXP MLB DEBUT: 2019 | H/W: 6-2 200 | FUT: Starting OF | 7C

Bats L Age 23
2016 (4) SE Louisiana
Pwr + + +
BAvg + + +
Spd + + +
Def + +

Year	Lev	Team	AB	R	H	HR	RBI	Avg	OB	Slg	OPS	bb%	ct%	Eye	SB	CS	x/h%	Iso	RC/G
2016	NCAA	SE Louisiana	198	49	84	11	66	424	548	692	1240	21	84	1.74	15	0	35	268	11.55
2016	Rk	Great Falls	187	39	64	4	25	342	425	487	912	13	77	0.63	13	7	28	144	7.18

Smooth-swinging OF who impressed with high BA. Works counts and knows when/how to use entire field. Should grow into at least average power and has enough speed to leg out doubles and SB on occasion. No plus tool in arsenal and may be liability in field. Bat will have to carry him.

Fletcher,David — 46 — Los Angeles (A)

EXP MLB DEBUT: 2018 | H/W: 5-10 175 | FUT: Starting SS | 7C

Bats R Age 22
2015 (6) Loyola Marymount
Pwr +
BAvg + + +
Spd + +
Def + + + +

Year	Lev	Team	AB	R	H	HR	RBI	Avg	OB	Slg	OPS	bb%	ct%	Eye	SB	CS	x/h%	Iso	RC/G
2015	NCAA	Loyola Marymount	221	32	68	2	27	308	373	416	789	9	92	1.28	14	3	26	109	5.52
2015	Rk	Orem	160	28	53	0	30	331	392	456	848	9	94	1.78	11	4	30	125	6.27
2015	A	Burlington	120	18	34	1	10	283	348	358	707	9	89	0.92	6	1	18	75	4.48
2016	A+	Inland Empire	324	42	89	3	31	275	321	346	666	6	87	0.51	15	3	18	71	3.77
2016	AA	Arkansas	80	10	24	0	6	300	325	375	700	4	84	0.23	1	0	25	75	4.01

Savvy INF who is advancing quickly with improved bat and continued steady defense. Can play both middle INF spots and possesses body control and average arm. Can hit for BA due to hand-eye coordination and level swing. Not much power in profile and needs to draw more walks in order to steal bases. Makes very easy contact.

Florial,Estevan — 8 — New York (A)

EXP MLB DEBUT: 2020 | H/W: 6-1 185 | FUT: Starting OF | 9E

Bats L Age 19
2015 FA (HT)
Pwr + + +
BAvg + +
Spd + + +
Def + + +

Year	Lev	Team	AB	R	H	HR	RBI	Avg	OB	Slg	OPS	bb%	ct%	Eye	SB	CS	x/h%	Iso	RC/G
2016	Rk	Pulaski	236	36	53	7	25	225	307	364	671	11	67	0.36	10	2	34	140	3.89
2016	A	Charleston (Sc)	20	4	6	1	5	300	364	550	914	9	75	0.40	0	0	33	250	6.97
2016	A+	Tampa	8	0	1	0	0	125	125	125	250	0	75	0.00	0	0	0	0	-2.09

Toolsy prospect with immense ceiling, but is far away from reaching it. Few can match raw power and speed and could develop into middle-of-the- order guy. Poor pitch recognition and hitting instincts need to improve. Drives ball a long way when he makes contact. Can be plus runner at times and should steal bases. Plus arm is highlight of OF.

Forbes,Ti'quan — 5 — Texas

EXP MLB DEBUT: 2019 | H/W: 6-3 180 | FUT: Starting 3B | 8E

Bats R Age 20
2014 (2) HS (MS)
Pwr + +
BAvg + +
Spd + + + +
Def + +

Year	Lev	Team	AB	R	H	HR	RBI	Avg	OB	Slg	OPS	bb%	ct%	Eye	SB	CS	x/h%	Iso	RC/G
2014	Rk	Azl Rangers	174	27	42	0	16	241	330	282	612	12	73	0.49	10	1	12	40	3.17
2015	A-	Spokane	217	25	57	0	19	263	307	323	630	6	75	0.26	2	2	21	60	3.20
2016	A	Hickory	427	50	107	4	44	251	292	335	627	6	75	0.24	6	5	22	84	3.09

Long, lean INF who did not fare well in 1st full season, but exhibits all 5 tools. Plus athlete who runs well and shows pull-side power. Has room to add strength and could evolve to average power. Approach needs overhaul, but is still raw batter with sub-par eye. Has chance to be standout 3B with plus arm, but needs work on footwork.

Foster,Jared — 789 — Los Angeles (A)

EXP MLB DEBUT: 2019 | H/W: 6-1 200 | FUT: Starting OF | 8E

Bats R Age 24
2015 (5) LSU
Pwr + +
BAvg + + +
Spd + + +
Def + +

Year	Lev	Team	AB	R	H	HR	RBI	Avg	OB	Slg	OPS	bb%	ct%	Eye	SB	CS	x/h%	Iso	RC/G
2015	NCAA	LSU	212	37	59	10	35	278	323	495	818	6	83	0.38	10	0	41	217	5.40
2015	Rk	Orem	232	36	60	6	38	259	306	392	699	6	82	0.38	13	5	30	134	4.03
2016	A	Burlington	267	26	71	5	33	266	317	412	729	7	82	0.42	3	8	38	146	4.51
2016	A+	Inland Empire	160	23	47	4	23	294	311	438	748	2	79	0.12	6	2	28	144	4.41

Ultra athletic OF with exemplary raw tools. Has nice upside and will need time to add polish. Makes loud contact with balanced approach and has success against LHP. Exhibits average raw power and hits lots of doubles. Held back by aggressive, long stroke. Runs well underway and patrols CF with nifty range.

Fowler,Dustin — 8 — New York (A)

EXP MLB DEBUT: 2018 | H/W: 6-0 195 | FUT: Starting OF | 7B

Bats L Age 22
2013 (18) HS (GA)
Pwr + +
BAvg + + +
Spd + + + +
Def + + + +

Year	Lev	Team	AB	R	H	HR	RBI	Avg	OB	Slg	OPS	bb%	ct%	Eye	SB	CS	x/h%	Iso	RC/G
2013	Rk	GCL Yankees	112	8	27	0	9	241	267	384	651	3	79	0.17	3	1	44	143	3.52
2014	A	Charleston (Sc)	257	33	66	9	41	257	293	459	752	5	79	0.25	3	2	42	202	4.62
2015	A	Charleston (Sc)	241	35	74	4	31	307	337	419	756	4	80	0.23	18	7	22	112	4.63
2015	A+	Tampa	246	29	71	1	39	289	330	370	699	6	83	0.35	12	6	21	81	4.10
2016	AA	Trenton	541	67	152	12	88	281	309	458	767	4	84	0.26	25	11	38	177	4.81

Speedy, athletic OF who finished 2nd in minors in triples. Starting to show natural pop with high in HR and using speed to leg out xbh. Has stolen 25+ bases last two seasons and has 20/20 potential. Can hit LHP with clean swing, though needs to be more selective and up OBP. Solid defender with heady jumps, routes, and range.

Fox,Lucius — 6 — Tampa Bay

EXP MLB DEBUT: 2020 | H/W: 6-1 175 | FUT: Starting MIF | 8D

Bats B Age 19
2015 FA (BA)
Pwr +
BAvg + + +
Spd + + + +
Def + +

Year	Lev	Team	AB	R	H	HR	RBI	Avg	OB	Slg	OPS	bb%	ct%	Eye	SB	CS	x/h%	Iso	RC/G
2016	A	Augusta	285	46	59	2	16	207	298	277	575	11	73	0.49	25	7	20	70	2.65

High-upside INF who ended season in July due to bone bruise in foot. Uses advanced approach at plate and focuses on line drives to gaps. Swing path and lack of strength mute power production, though can turn on pitches with plus bat speed. Tremendous quickness aids range and has average arm to stick at SS. Could move to 2B if necessary.

Fraley,Jake | 78 | Tampa Bay | EXP MLB DEBUT: 2019 | H/W: 6-0 195 | FUT: Starting CF | 7B

Bats L Age 21
2016 (S-2) LSU
Pwr ++
BAvg +++
Spd ++++
Def +++

Year	Lev	Team	AB	R	H	HR	RBI	Avg	OB	Slg	OPS	bb%	ct%	Eye	SB	CS	x/h%	Iso	RC/G
2016	NCAA	LSU	267	61	87	5	36	326	408	464	872	12	88	1.12	28	10	24	139	6.55
2016	A-	Hudson Valley	206	34	49	1	18	238	323	364	687	11	83	0.76	33	9	35	126	4.37

Leadoff-hitting prospect who maximizes skill set with instincts and grinding mentality. Should be able to stick in CF where he ranges well and takes efficient routes. Works counts to advantage to find pitches he can drive or draw walks. Has BA potential thanks to all-fields approach. Only has gap power at most, but can leg out xbh with plus speed.

Franco,Anderson | 5 | Washington | EXP MLB DEBUT: 2021 | H/W: 6-3 190 | FUT: Starting 3B | 8E

Bats R Age 19
2013 FA (DR)
Pwr +++
BAvg +++
Spd ++
Def +++

Year	Lev	Team	AB	R	H	HR	RBI	Avg	OB	Slg	OPS	bb%	ct%	Eye	SB	CS	x/h%	Iso	RC/G
2015	Rk	GCL Nationals	153	19	43	4	19	281	341	412	753	8	83	0.54	2	3	26	131	4.80
2015	A-	Auburn	40	0	9	0	4	225	340	300	640	15	95	3.50	0	0	22	75	4.42
2016	Rk	GCL Nationals	83	9	23	1	9	277	310	349	660	5	87	0.36	1	0	17	72	3.55

Back injury siphoned crucial development time in 2016 for the former high-profile international signee. Owns the physicality, bat speed and raw power to dream on an MLB-caliber third baseman on both sides of the ball. Potential seen in small short-season glimpses in rookie ball so far. But health is now added to the risk factors.

Frazier,Clint | 89 | New York (A) | EXP MLB DEBUT: 2017 | H/W: 6-1 190 | FUT: Starting OF | 9C

Bats R Age 22
2013 (1) HS (GA)
Pwr ++++
BAvg +++
Spd +++
Def +++

Year	Lev	Team	AB	R	H	HR	RBI	Avg	OB	Slg	OPS	bb%	ct%	Eye	SB	CS	x/h%	Iso	RC/G
2014	A	Lake County	474	70	126	13	50	266	343	411	755	11	66	0.35	12	6	29	146	5.21
2015	A+	Lynchburg	501	88	143	16	72	285	371	465	836	12	75	0.54	15	7	38	180	6.14
2016	AA	Akron	341	56	94	13	48	276	353	469	823	11	75	0.48	13	4	41	194	5.87
2016	AAA	Columbus	21	2	5	0	0	238	238	333	571	0	71	0.00	0	0	20	95	2.22
2016	AAA	Scranton/WB	101	17	23	3	7	228	278	396	674	6	70	0.23	0	0	35	168	3.77

High-upside hitter who matched career-high in HR and continues to show positive tools. Has incredible bat speed and makes acceptable contact despite high K totals. Leveraged stroke and natural strength lead to plus pop and is willing to draw walks. Can play CF, though may end up in RF with strong arm and solid-average range.

Friedl,TJ | 78 | Cincinnati | EXP MLB DEBUT: 2019 | H/W: 5-10 170 | FUT: Starting OF | 7C

Bats L Age 21
2016 (NDFA) Nevada
Pwr ++
BAvg +++
Spd ++++
Def ++++

Year	Lev	Team	AB	R	H	HR	RBI	Avg	OB	Slg	OPS	bb%	ct%	Eye	SB	CS	x/h%	Iso	RC/G
2016	NCAA	Nevada	222	68	89	3	35	401	476	563	1039	13	88	1.23	13	5	24	162	8.58
2016	Rk	Billings	121	24	42	3	17	347	410	545	956	10	79	0.52	7	2	38	198	7.55

Speedy LHH CF prospect fell through the cracks during draft process and signed by CIN. Not much of a ceiling left. Good approach at plate, line drive hitter. Swing-and-miss issues exist in swing. Speedy runner. Should contribute in run game. Good defender in CF; should stick there.

Fukofuka,Amalani | 89 | Kansas City | EXP MLB DEBUT: 2019 | H/W: 6-1 180 | FUT: Starting OF | 7E

Bats R Age 21
2013 (5) HS (CA)
Pwr ++
BAvg ++
Spd +++
Def ++

Year	Lev	Team	AB	R	H	HR	RBI	Avg	OB	Slg	OPS	bb%	ct%	Eye	SB	CS	x/h%	Iso	RC/G
2013	Rk	Azl Royals	156	28	38	1	12	244	355	346	701	15	70	0.57	10	2	32	103	4.62
2014	Rk	Burlington	180	19	33	1	12	183	261	289	550	10	63	0.29	7	7	30	106	2.27
2015	Rk	Idaho Falls	280	53	95	3	38	339	395	500	895	8	75	0.37	10	3	32	161	6.92
2016	A	Lexington	404	45	81	5	34	200	254	272	526	7	66	0.21	27	6	23	72	1.66

Tall, lean OF who spent 1st year in full season and never got on track. Adding needed strength to frame and could evolve into average pop. Swings a clean bat, but expands strike zone and struggles to read pitches. Has ability to leg out doubles and steal bases with good speed. Probable LF as fringy arm and range aren't up to snuff.

Galindo,Wladimir | 5 | Chicago (N) | EXP MLB DEBUT: 2021 | H/W: 6-3 210 | FUT: Starting 3B | 8D

Bats R Age 20
2013 FA (VZ)
Pwr +++
BAvg ++
Spd ++
Def +++

Year	Lev	Team	AB	R	H	HR	RBI	Avg	OB	Slg	OPS	bb%	ct%	Eye	SB	CS	x/h%	Iso	RC/G
2016	A-	Eugene	247	46	60	9	40	243	332	462	794	12	67	0.41	3	0	53	219	5.83

Thick, strong bodied, he's been slow to develop and has yet to make his full-season debut, though he did play a full schedule at short-season Eugene. Has above-average raw power, but needs to make more consistent contact and be more selective. Moves well at 3B with a plus arm, but needs better footwork.

Gamel,Ben | 789 | Seattle | EXP MLB DEBUT: 2016 | H/W: 5-11 185 | FUT: Starting OF | 7C

Bats L Age 24
2010 (10) HS (FL)
Pwr ++
BAvg +++
Spd +++
Def +++

Year	Lev	Team	AB	R	H	HR	RBI	Avg	OB	Slg	OPS	bb%	ct%	Eye	SB	CS	x/h%	Iso	RC/G
2014	AA	Trenton	544	58	142	2	51	261	307	340	647	6	84	0.41	13	5	25	79	3.53
2015	AAA	Scranton/WB	500	77	150	10	64	300	359	472	831	8	78	0.43	13	5	35	172	5.91
2016	AAA	Scranton/WB	483	80	149	6	51	308	365	420	785	8	81	0.46	19	8	25	112	5.26
2016	MLB	NY Yankees	8	1	1	0	0	125	222	125	347	11	88	1.00	0	0	0	0	0.40
2016	MLB	Seattle	40	8	8	1	5	200	289	325	614	11	63	0.33	0	0	38	125	3.14

Short OF who spent 2nd year in AAA and won IL MVP. Has shown ability to hit leadoff and works counts to get on base. Runs fairly well underway and is aggressive basestealer. Not much over-the-wall power, but hits loads of doubles. Has shown ability to hit LHP and can shorten swing. Plays all OF spots and is average defender with fringy arm strength.

Garcia,Aramis | 2 | San Francisco | EXP MLB DEBUT: 2018 | H/W: 6-2 220 | FUT: Starting C | 8D

Bats R Age 24
2014 (2) Florida Intl
Pwr +++
BAvg ++
Spd ++
Def ++

Year	Lev	Team	AB	R	H	HR	RBI	Avg	OB	Slg	OPS	bb%	ct%	Eye	SB	CS	x/h%	Iso	RC/G
2014	A-	Salem-Kaizer	70	5	16	2	12	229	280	357	637	7	73	0.26	0	0	31	129	3.18
2015	A	Augusta	319	42	87	15	61	273	345	467	812	10	76	0.45	0	1	36	194	5.57
2015	A+	San Jose	75	10	17	0	5	227	310	280	590	11	71	0.41	1	0	24	53	2.83
2016	Rk	Azl Giants	22	1	5	0	4	227	227	273	500	0	95	0.00	0	0	20	45	1.93
2016	A+	San Jose	144	20	37	2	20	257	323	340	663	9	71	0.33	1	0	22	83	3.70

Strong, compact C who missed time due to facial fracture. Improving defender with quick, strong arm, though receiving and blocking still need attention. Could be bat-first backstop due to short stroke and average power. Has chance to hit for BA, but needs to be more patient and read pitches better.

Garcia,Julio | 456 | Los Angeles (A) | EXP MLB DEBUT: 2020 | H/W: 6-0 175 | FUT: Starting SS | 7D

Bats R Age 19
2014 FA (DR)
Pwr +
BAvg ++
Spd ++
Def +++

Year	Lev	Team	AB	R	H	HR	RBI	Avg	OB	Slg	OPS	bb%	ct%	Eye	SB	CS	x/h%	Iso	RC/G
2015	Rk	Azl Angels	58	5	13	0	6	224	250	259	509	3	72	0.13	4	0	15	34	1.39
2016	Rk	Azl Angels	47	2	7	0	7	149	216	213	428	8	72	0.31	1	0	43	64	0.54

Lean, wiry INF who has struggled to hit in rookie ball. Moved to 3B, though can play 2B and SS. Needs to add more strength to realize bat potential. Swings quick bat, but has little pitch recognition or feel for contact. Could develop power, but lacks loft and leverage. Solid defender with smooth actions, ideal range, and plus arm.

Garcia,Wilkerman | 6 | New York (A) | EXP MLB DEBUT: 2020 | H/W: 6-0 180 | FUT: Starting SS | 8D

Bats B Age 19
2014 FA (VZ)
Pwr ++
BAvg ++
Spd +++
Def +++

Year	Lev	Team	AB	R	H	HR	RBI	Avg	OB	Slg	OPS	bb%	ct%	Eye	SB	CS	x/h%	Iso	RC/G
2016	Rk	Pulaski	222	21	44	1	13	198	249	284	533	6	80	0.34	4	6	32	86	2.08

Fluid athlete who oozes tools and should stick at SS. Clean, quick hands highlight defensive attributes and has plus arm strength. Still makes fair share of errors, but should get better in time. Power potential is only average, though shows bat control and ability to put ball in play. Bat speed and knowledge of K zone should lead to nice BA.

Garcia,Willy | 789 | Pittsburgh | EXP MLB DEBUT: 2017 | H/W: 6-2 215 | FUT: Starting OF | 7D

Bats R Age 24
2010 FA (DR)
Pwr ++
BAvg ++
Spd ++
Def +++

Year	Lev	Team	AB	R	H	HR	RBI	Avg	OB	Slg	OPS	bb%	ct%	Eye	SB	CS	x/h%	Iso	RC/G
2013	A+	Bradenton	449	51	115	16	60	256	292	437	729	5	66	0.15	13	6	37	180	4.62
2014	AA	Altoona	439	59	119	18	63	271	309	478	787	5	67	0.17	8	4	42	207	5.42
2015	AA	Altoona	204	26	64	5	29	314	349	441	790	5	77	0.23	3	2	22	127	5.09
2015	AAA	Indianapolis	276	36	68	10	38	246	278	424	702	4	72	0.16	1	4	37	178	3.96
2016	AAA	Indianapolis	462	53	113	6	43	245	292	366	658	6	72	0.24	5	9	35	121	3.60

Athletic OF took a step back after a breakout in 2015. Has good bat speed and raw power, but can be overly aggressive at the plate, raising concerns about his ability to hit for average (31 BB/131 K). Solid defender with good range and a plus arm. The power is legit, but will need to refine his approach at some point.

Garrett,Stone — 789 — Miami
EXP MLB DEBUT: 2020 | H/W: 6-2 195 | FUT: Starting OF | 8D

Bats R Age 21
2014 (8) HS (TX)

- Pwr ++++
- BAvg ++
- Spd +++
- Def ++

Year	Lev	Team	AB	R	H	HR	RBI	Avg	OB	Slg	OPS	bb%	ct%	Eye	SB	CS	x/h%	Iso	RC/G
2014	Rk	GCL Marlins	148	17	35	0	11	236	271	270	541	5	79	0.23	4	1	11	34	2.00
2015	A-	Batavia	222	36	66	11	46	297	353	581	934	8	73	0.32	8	5	53	284	7.35
2016	Rk	GCL Marlins	7	1	1	0	0	143	333	143	476	22	57	0.67	1	0	0	0	0.93
2016	A	Greensboro	197	21	42	6	16	213	255	371	625	5	64	0.15	1	2	40	157	3.15

Lean, projectable OF struggled at plate and missed extended action due to ill-advised teammate prank. Tends to hit off front foot, but has plus bat speed and raw power if he can fix lower half. MIA worked on it, and he does have 17 HR in 153 career games. Needs to make more consistent contact to fully tap into his raw talent.

Garver,Mitch — 2 — Minnesota
EXP MLB DEBUT: 2017 | H/W: 6-1 220 | FUT: Starting C | 7C

Bats R Age 26
2013 (9) New Mexico

- Pwr +++
- BAvg ++
- Spd +
- Def ++

Year	Lev	Team	AB	R	H	HR	RBI	Avg	OB	Slg	OPS	bb%	ct%	Eye	SB	CS	x/h%	Iso	RC/G
2013	Rk	Elizabethton	202	16	49	2	30	243	308	366	674	9	85	0.61	0	0	39	124	4.04
2014	A	Cedar Rapids	430	65	128	16	79	298	385	481	866	12	85	0.94	7	5	36	184	6.40
2015	A+	Fort Myers	433	46	106	4	58	245	349	333	681	14	81	0.84	5	3	27	88	4.29
2016	AA	Chattanooga	358	44	92	11	66	257	337	419	756	11	76	0.50	1	3	39	162	4.98
2016	AAA	Rochester	76	6	25	1	8	329	386	434	820	8	72	0.33	0	0	24	105	5.87

Strong backstop with decent tools, though has work to do to become average C. Owns strong arm with quick release, but limited agility and sub-par footwork limit upside. Swings a strong bat and combines with patient approach to give him power potential. Puts bat to ball easily and smashes a lot of doubles, especially to pull side.

Gasparini,Marten — 6 — Kansas City
EXP MLB DEBUT: 2020 | H/W: 6-0 195 | FUT: Starting SS | 8E

Bats B Age 19
2013 FA (IT)

- Pwr ++
- BAvg ++
- Spd ++++
- Def ++++

Year	Lev	Team	AB	R	H	HR	RBI	Avg	OB	Slg	OPS	bb%	ct%	Eye	SB	CS	x/h%	Iso	RC/G
2014	Rk	Idaho Falls	11	4	5	1	3	455	500	727	1227	8	82	0.50	2	0	20	273	10.18
2014	Rk	Burlington	68	11	13	0	1	191	225	250	475	4	53	0.09	4	1	23	59	1.20
2015	Rk	Idaho Falls	197	36	51	2	25	259	342	411	754	11	59	0.31	26	9	31	152	5.86
2016	A	Lexington	382	35	75	7	42	196	257	293	550	8	65	0.23	14	10	28	97	2.04

Nimble, quick SS who struggled in 1st full season as pro. Has potential to develop offense, but poor selectivity and pitch recognition not up to snuff. Has double-digit HR potential due to bat speed and improved strength. Owns strong arm and runs well. BA will ultimately decide future.

Gatewood,Jake — 35 — Milwaukee
EXP MLB DEBUT: 2019 | H/W: 6-5 190 | FUT: Starting 3B | 7C

Bats R Age 21
2014 (S-1) HS (CA)

- Pwr ++++
- BAvg ++
- Spd ++
- Def +++

Year	Lev	Team	AB	R	H	HR	RBI	Avg	OB	Slg	OPS	bb%	ct%	Eye	SB	CS	x/h%	Iso	RC/G
2014	Rk	Azl Brewers	204	19	42	3	32	206	253	279	533	6	65	0.18	7	8	21	74	1.72
2015	Rk	Helena	212	38	58	6	41	274	330	476	807	8	68	0.26	3	5	52	203	5.90
2015	A	Wisconsin	177	16	37	4	16	209	267	316	583	7	63	0.22	5	0	27	107	2.54
2016	A	Wisconsin	496	70	119	14	64	240	267	391	658	4	72	0.13	3	2	39	151	3.38

Tall 3B showed more consistency in second A-campaign. Owns plus bat speed and leverage in swing for potential HR impact. Elongated swing and head movement impede his ability to make consistent enough contact; very aggressive approach still an issue. Saw time at 1B, but plus arm and average range profile well for 3B.

Gerber,Michael — 89 — Detroit
EXP MLB DEBUT: 2017 | H/W: 6-0 190 | FUT: Starting OF | 7B

Bats L Age 24
2014 (15) Creighton

- Pwr +++
- BAvg +++
- Spd ++
- Def +++

Year	Lev	Team	AB	R	H	HR	RBI	Avg	OB	Slg	OPS	bb%	ct%	Eye	SB	CS	x/h%	Iso	RC/G
2014	A-	Connecticut	217	40	62	7	37	286	338	493	831	7	78	0.35	8	4	44	207	5.80
2014	A	West Michigan	31	4	12	0	5	387	457	484	941	11	90	1.33	1	0	25	97	7.38
2015	A	West Michigan	513	74	150	13	76	292	354	468	822	9	81	0.51	16	4	36	175	5.74
2016	A+	Lakeland	351	52	99	14	60	282	342	481	824	8	68	0.29	2	3	39	199	6.00
2016	AA	Erie	153	17	40	4	20	261	347	431	778	12	73	0.49	6	0	38	170	5.42

Well-rounded OF who got off to slow start, but heated up in June. Set high in HR and shows keen eye at plate. Balanced swing produces more doubles than HR, but can turn on pitches and make loud contact. Can sell out for power at times. Has fringy speed and can steal bases with instincts and savvy. Solid OF who could play CF in pinch.

Gettys,Michael — 8 — San Diego
EXP MLB DEBUT: 2018 | H/W: 6-1 203 | FUT: Starting OF | 8D

Bats R Age 21
2014 (2) HS (GA)

- Pwr +++
- BAvg ++
- Spd ++++
- Def ++++

Year	Lev	Team	AB	R	H	HR	RBI	Avg	OB	Slg	OPS	bb%	ct%	Eye	SB	CS	x/h%	Iso	RC/G
2014	Rk	Azl Padres	213	29	66	3	38	310	355	437	792	7	69	0.23	14	2	24	127	5.56
2015	A	Fort Wayne	494	62	114	6	44	231	272	346	618	5	67	0.17	20	10	34	115	3.07
2016	A	Fort Wayne	257	37	78	3	27	304	349	416	765	7	73	0.26	24	10	23	113	5.03
2016	A+	Lake Elsinore	248	40	76	9	33	306	351	468	819	6	69	0.22	9	6	29	161	5.77

Athletic OF with lots of swing-and-miss in game. Struggles identifying pitches out of the zone. Expands zone w/ two strikes. Lacks patience. Wastes quick-twitch swing. Solid power in bat. Could hit 18-21 HR at projection. Plus-plus runner and defender. Good route runner in CF.

Gillaspie,Casey — 3 — Tampa Bay
EXP MLB DEBUT: 2017 | H/W: 6-4 240 | FUT: Starting 1B | 8C

Bats B Age 24
2014 (1) Wichita State

- Pwr ++++
- BAvg +++
- Spd +
- Def ++

Year	Lev	Team	AB	R	H	HR	RBI	Avg	OB	Slg	OPS	bb%	ct%	Eye	SB	CS	x/h%	Iso	RC/G
2015	Rk	GCL Devil Rays	6	0	0	0	0	0	0	0	0	0	67	0.00	0	0		0	-6.12
2015	A	Bowling Green	234	37	65	16	44	278	355	530	885	11	82	0.65	4	0	42	252	6.36
2015	A+	Charlotte	41	3	6	1	4	146	222	268	491	9	78	0.44	0	0	33	122	1.48
2016	AA	Montgomery	293	51	79	11	41	270	390	454	844	17	73	0.73	5	1	41	184	6.48
2016	AAA	Durham	179	27	55	7	23	307	383	520	903	11	79	0.58	0	1	40	212	6.85

Offensive 1B who can be a middle-of-the-order run producer with above average power and keen hitting instincts. Knows strike zone and recognizes spin. Will draw walks and all fields pop continues to evolve. Got in better shape in '16, but still relegated to 1B with below average speed and hands.

Gimenez,Andres — 6 — New York (N)
EXP MLB DEBUT: 2021 | H/W: 6-0 165 | FUT: Starting SS | 8E

Bats L Age 18
2015 FA (VZ)

- Pwr ++
- BAvg +++
- Spd ++++
- Def ++

Year	Lev	Team	AB	R	H	HR	RBI	Avg	OB	Slg	OPS	bb%	ct%	Eye	SB	CS	x/h%	Iso	RC/G
2016		Did not play in the US																	

Tall, lanky LHH SS was NYM prize international signing in '15. Dominated the Dominican League with a .350/.469/.523 line. Scouts rave at ability to barrel line drives to all fields. Power lags behind hit tool. Slight frame and foot speed lends itself to becoming lead-off hitter. Defensively, he's rangy but raw.

Giron,Ruddy — 6 — San Diego
EXP MLB DEBUT: 2019 | H/W: 5-11 175 | FUT: Starting 2B | 7D

Bats R Age 20
2013 FA (DR)

- Pwr ++
- BAvg ++
- Spd +++
- Def ++

Year	Lev	Team	AB	R	H	HR	RBI	Avg	OB	Slg	OPS	bb%	ct%	Eye	SB	CS	x/h%	Iso	RC/G
2014	Rk	Azl Padres	185	23	31	0	13	168	202	222	424	4	77	0.19	1	2	32	54	0.51
2015	A	Fort Wayne	386	58	110	9	49	285	335	407	742	7	82	0.43	15	14	23	122	4.58
2016	A	Fort Wayne	401	49	89	2	20	222	283	304	587	8	82	0.46	8	7	30	82	2.85
2016	A+	Lake Elsinore	47	7	20	1	5	426	460	681	1141	6	72	0.23	1	0	45	255	10.32

Young, talented SS came down to earth after successful pro-debut. Quick, compact swing was overpowered by Single-A pitching. Will need to add strength throughout frame. There is room to grow. Average runner. Very mechanical defensively. Likely will move off position long term.

Gomez,Jose — 46 — Colorado
EXP MLB DEBUT: 2021 | H/W: 5-11 175 | FUT: Starting 2B | 7C

Bats R Age 20
2013 FA (VZ)

- Pwr ++
- BAvg ++++
- Spd ++
- Def ++

Year	Lev	Team	AB	R	H	HR	RBI	Avg	OB	Slg	OPS	bb%	ct%	Eye	SB	CS	x/h%	Iso	RC/G
2016	Rk	Grand Junction	267	54	98	3	51	367	417	468	885	8	91	0.96	23	13	19	101	6.41

Contact-oriented Dominican SS had an impressive debut in the Pioneer League. Uses a short, compact stroke to shoot line drives to all fields. Below average defender with stiff hands and limited range, so a move to 2B seems likely. Good understanding of the strike zone should allow him to continue to hit as he moves up.

Gonzalez,Erik — 456 — Cleveland
EXP MLB DEBUT: 2016 | H/W: 6-3 195 | FUT: Utility player | 7D

Bats R Age 25
2008 FA (DR)

- Pwr ++
- BAvg +++
- Spd +++
- Def ++++

Year	Lev	Team	AB	R	H	HR	RBI	Avg	OB	Slg	OPS	bb%	ct%	Eye	SB	CS	x/h%	Iso	RC/G
2014	AA	Akron	129	21	46	1	16	357	390	473	863	5	82	0.30	6	1	22	116	6.03
2015	AA	Akron	311	38	87	6	46	280	304	421	726	3	82	0.20	10	5	32	141	4.24
2015	AAA	Columbus	238	32	53	3	23	223	269	311	580	6	80	0.32	8	2	23	88	2.57
2016	AAA	Columbus	429	62	127	11	53	296	326	450	776	4	79	0.22	12	10	34	154	4.87
2016	MLB	Cleveland	16	2	5	0	0	313	353	313	665	6	50	0.13	0	1	0	0	4.88

Tall, lean, glove-first INF posted first 10 HR/10 SB season and nearly hit .300 in IL. Fringy contact skills, aggressive at plate and prone to lunging at off-speed. Gap power with line-drive stroke. Some speed for moderate SB totals, but not a burner. Great range, instincts, arm to man either 2B or SS long-term.

Gonzalez,Pedro

8 | Colorado | EXP MLB DEBUT: 2021 | H/W: 6-5 190 | FUT: Starting OF | 8E

Bats R Age 19
2014 FA (DR)

- Pwr ++++
- BAvg ++
- Spd +++
- Def ++

Year	Lev	Team	AB	R	H	HR	RBI	Avg	OB	Slg	OPS	bb%	ct%	Eye	SB	CS	x/h%	Iso	RC/G
2016	Rk	Grand Junction	226	32	52	2	19	230	275	394	669	6	66	0.18	6	7	48	164	4.02

Tall, projectable OF was moved from SS and struggled, hitting just .230 in 226 AB. Has plus raw power and bat speed, but needs to make more consistent contact before it becomes game usable. Above-average speed for size and can play any OF position though RF seems most likely. Tons of potential, but very much a work in progress.

Goodwin,Brian

789 | Washington | EXP MLB DEBUT: 2016 | H/W: 6-0 205 | FUT: Reserve OF | 6A

Bats L Age 26
2011 (S-1) Miami-Dade JC

- Pwr +++
- BAvg ++
- Spd +++
- Def ++++

Year	Lev	Team	AB	R	H	HR	RBI	Avg	OB	Slg	OPS	bb%	ct%	Eye	SB	CS	x/h%	Iso	RC/G
2013	AA	Harrisburg	457	82	115	10	40	252	346	407	753	13	74	0.55	19	11	35	155	5.14
2014	AAA	Syracuse	274	31	60	4	32	219	340	328	668	15	65	0.53	6	4	30	109	4.13
2015	AA	Harrisburg	429	58	97	8	46	226	289	340	629	8	78	0.41	15	7	30	114	3.25
2016	AAA	Syracuse	436	51	122	14	68	280	349	438	787	10	76	0.43	15	3	33	158	5.31
2016	MLB	Washington	42	1	12	0	5	286	318	429	747	5	67	0.14	0	0	42	143	5.13

Teetered to the edge of the prospect cliff, only to learn how to make adjustments with a tighter swing that resulted in a very good return to Triple-A. Athleticism allows him to play all three outfield positions, moderate power, some patience and a bit of speed still hold his value. Could be a 10 HR/10 SB guy off the bench.

Gordon,Miles

8 | Cincinnati | EXP MLB DEBUT: 2021 | H/W: 6-1 185 | FUT: Starting OF | 7E

Bats L Age 19
2015 (4) HS (ON)

- Pwr ++
- BAvg ++
- Spd ++++
- Def +++

Year	Lev	Team	AB	R	H	HR	RBI	Avg	OB	Slg	OPS	bb%	ct%	Eye	SB	CS	x/h%	Iso	RC/G
2015	Rk	AZL Reds	118	15	26	0	12	220	264	305	569	6	78	0.27	5	3	27	85	2.48
2016	Rk	Billings	65	11	17	0	11	262	368	369	738	14	78	0.79	3	2	29	108	5.14

Extremely raw, Canadian OF held his own in pro debut. Quick wrists and hands produce plus bat speed. Struggles maintaining plane through swing. Has power projection in frame. Could hit for power at maturity. Still learning how to incorporate speed on both sides of the ball.

Gordon,Nick

6 | Minnesota | EXP MLB DEBUT: 2018 | H/W: 6-0 160 | FUT: Starting SS | 8B

Bats L Age 21
2014 (1) HS (FL)

- Pwr ++
- BAvg ++++
- Spd +++
- Def +++

Year	Lev	Team	AB	R	H	HR	RBI	Avg	OB	Slg	OPS	bb%	ct%	Eye	SB	CS	x/h%	Iso	RC/G
2014	Rk	Elizabethton	235	46	69	1	28	294	325	366	691	4	81	0.24	11	7	16	72	3.89
2015	A	Cedar Rapids	481	79	133	1	58	277	331	360	690	8	82	0.44	25	8	23	83	4.11
2016	A+	Fort Myers	461	56	134	3	52	291	324	386	710	5	81	0.26	19	13	24	95	4.16

Exciting SS with consistent approach. Owns all-around tools that show incremental improvement. Runs well and has quickness and hands to stick at SS. Focuses on line drives with simple swing and should hit for high BA due to bat control. Offers power potential, but will need to improve against LHP. Can impact game on both sides.

Granite,Zack

8 | Minnesota | EXP MLB DEBUT: 2017 | H/W: 6-1 175 | FUT: Starting OF | 7C

Bats L Age 24
2013 (14) Seton Hall

- Pwr ++
- BAvg +++
- Spd ++++
- Def ++

Year	Lev	Team	AB	R	H	HR	RBI	Avg	OB	Slg	OPS	bb%	ct%	Eye	SB	CS	x/h%	Iso	RC/G
2014	Rk	GCL Twins	14	4	3	0	0	214	313	214	527	13	71	0.50	3	0	0	0	1.92
2014	A	Cedar Rapids	79	9	23	0	2	291	325	367	692	5	90	0.50	1	4	17	76	4.11
2015	A	Cedar Rapids	67	17	24	0	5	358	456	463	918	15	91	2.00	7	1	25	104	7.43
2015	A+	Fort Myers	381	59	95	1	26	249	322	304	627	10	83	0.65	21	12	16	55	3.46
2016	AA	Chattanooga	526	86	155	4	52	295	347	382	729	7	92	0.98	56	14	19	87	4.70

Extreme contact hitter with breakout season and led SL in SB. Set highs in doubles, HR, and SB while exhibiting plus K zone knowledge. Fringy power and isn't much of threat, but is leadoff hitter with plus speed. Sound defender who can stick in CF, though arm strength may move to LF eventually. Can hang in against LHP.

Greiner,Grayson

2 | Detroit | EXP MLB DEBUT: 2018 | H/W: 6-6 220 | FUT: Starting C | 8E

Bats R Age 24
2014 (3) South Carolina

- Pwr +++
- BAvg ++
- Spd +
- Def +++

Year	Lev	Team	AB	R	H	HR	RBI	Avg	OB	Slg	OPS	bb%	ct%	Eye	SB	CS	x/h%	Iso	RC/G
2014	A	West Michigan	90	11	29	2	16	322	396	444	840	11	80	0.61	0	0	24	122	6.05
2015	A+	Lakeland	312	24	57	3	21	183	248	250	498	8	71	0.30	0	0	26	67	1.37
2016	A+	Lakeland	109	14	34	0	12	312	380	367	747	10	76	0.46	0	0	18	55	4.93
2016	AA	Erie	208	20	60	7	30	288	321	462	783	5	74	0.18	1	0	32	173	5.05
2016	AAA	Toledo	4	0	0	0	0	0	0	0	0	0	50	0.00	0	0		0	-7.85

Large-framed C who ended season on fire and rebounded from poor '15. Set high in HR and plenty more pop in tank. Swing can be exploited, but willing to work counts and find pitches to drive. Power improving as he learns to read spin, but can get aggressive at times. Provides big frame behind plate and owns strong arm with solid release.

Grier,Anfernee

8 | Arizona | EXP MLB DEBUT: 2020 | H/W: 6-1 180 | FUT: Starting OF | 8E

Bats R Age 21
2016 (S-1) Auburn

- Pwr ++
- BAvg ++
- Spd ++++
- Def ++++

Year	Lev	Team	AB	R	H	HR	RBI	Avg	OB	Slg	OPS	bb%	ct%	Eye	SB	CS	x/h%	Iso	RC/G
2016	NCAA	Auburn	238	56	87	12	41	366	441	576	1016	12	77	0.58	19	5	26	210	8.33
2016	Rk	Missoula	14	2	3	1	2	214	214	500	714	0	64	0.00	0	0	67	286	4.18
2016	A-	Hillsboro	75	8	18	1	6	240	269	307	576	4	72	0.14	9	2	17	67	2.24

Speedy OF who saw stock explode during junior year at Auburn. Hit tool is work in progress despite plus bat speed. Struggles to square up ball due to elongated swing path; compounded when worked inside with fastballs. Did develop power this season; now a 10-15 HR bat at maturity. Best tool is speed. Uses it in the field and on the base paths.

Guerra,Javier

6 | San Diego | EXP MLB DEBUT: 2018 | H/W: 5-11 155 | FUT: Starting SS | 8D

Bats L Age 21
2012 FA (PN)

- Pwr +++
- BAvg ++
- Spd +++
- Def ++++

Year	Lev	Team	AB	R	H	HR	RBI	Avg	OB	Slg	OPS	bb%	ct%	Eye	SB	CS	x/h%	Iso	RC/G
2013	Rk	DSL Red Sox	210	27	52	0	23	248	350	290	640	14	81	0.83	7	4	17	43	3.78
2014	Rk	GCL Red Sox	201	21	54	2	26	269	286	408	694	2	79	0.12	1	5	37	139	3.89
2015	A	Greenville	434	64	121	15	68	279	325	449	775	6	74	0.27	7	9	34	171	5.01
2016	A+	Lake Elsinore	391	49	79	9	41	202	266	325	591	8	64	0.24	4	4	37	123	2.69

Smooth, potentially plus-plus defender plagued by swing-and-miss issues. Long, lumbering swing victimized by High-A pitching. Swings at everything; lacks 2-strike approach. Plus raw power in BP; could hit 20-25 HRs at maturity if hit tool allows it. Heady defender. Great footwork and reactions. Strong arm.

Guerrero,Gabby

79 | Cincinnati | EXP MLB DEBUT: 2017 | H/W: 6-3 215 | FUT: Starting OF | 7E

Bats R Age 23
2011 FA (DR)

- Pwr +++
- BAvg +
- Spd +++
- Def +++

Year	Lev	Team	AB	R	H	HR	RBI	Avg	OB	Slg	OPS	bb%	ct%	Eye	SB	CS	x/h%	Iso	RC/G
2014	A+	High Desert	538	97	165	18	96	307	348	467	814	6	76	0.26	18	6	29	160	5.46
2015	AA	Jackson	177	22	38	2	15	215	265	305	570	6	73	0.25	3	0	32	90	2.35
2015	AA	Mobile	283	29	64	5	32	226	255	367	623	4	79	0.18	8	2	39	141	3.01
2016	AA	Mobile	319	39	77	8	45	241	286	404	691	6	76	0.26	6	3	40	163	3.94
2016	AAA	Reno	99	10	21	1	9	212	278	313	591	8	75	0.36	0	0	33	101	2.78

Toolsy OF with good bat-to-ball skills. Lacks plate discipline. Lots of soft contact. Does not recognize spin out of pitcher's hand. Has raw plus power, though doesn't make enough barreled contact to take advantage of power. Solid defender in RF; and is an average runner.

Guerrero,Vladimir

5 | Toronto | EXP MLB DEBUT: 2020 | H/W: 6-1 200 | FUT: Starting OF | 9D

Bats R Age 18
2015 FA (DR)

- Pwr ++++
- BAvg +++
- Spd ++
- Def +

Year	Lev	Team	AB	R	H	HR	RBI	Avg	OB	Slg	OPS	bb%	ct%	Eye	SB	CS	x/h%	Iso	RC/G
2016	Rk	Bluefield	236	32	64	8	46	271	361	449	810	12	85	0.94	15	5	36	178	5.74

Strong prospect who takes after father and can hit anything in zone. Owns plus hand-eye coordination and bat control to make easy contact. Projects to double-plus power with lightning stroke and reads pitches well. Defensive home in question. Seems likely to move off 3B as arm and range are less than stellar. Steals bases, but more on instincts.

Guillorme,Luis

46 | New York (N) | EXP MLB DEBUT: 2018 | H/W: 5-9 190 | FUT: Reserve IF | 6C

Bats L Age 22
2013 (10) HS (FL)

- Pwr +
- BAvg +++
- Spd +++
- Def ++++

Year	Lev	Team	AB	R	H	HR	RBI	Avg	OB	Slg	OPS	bb%	ct%	Eye	SB	CS	x/h%	Iso	RC/G
2013	Rk	GCL Mets	159	22	41	0	11	258	330	283	613	10	89	1.00	6	4	10	25	3.46
2014	Rk	Kingsport	238	38	67	0	17	282	329	324	653	7	88	0.61	6	4	15	42	3.70
2014	A	Savannah	9	2	3	0	0	333	400	333	733	10	100		0	0	0	0	5.15
2015	A	Savannah	446	67	142	0	55	318	392	354	746	11	84	0.77	18	8	11	36	4.96
2016	A+	St. Lucie	441	47	116	1	46	263	329	315	644	9	86	0.68	4	2	16	52	3.67

Glove-first SS struggled to build on '15 campaign. Gets most out of skill set; average bat speed plays up due to headiness. Power is non-existent. Relies on reactions and exceptional footwork to make difficult plays routine at short. A 50-runner, doesn't get out of the box well.

Gurriel,Yulieski

357 | **Houston** | EXP MLB DEBUT: 2016 | H/W: 6-0 190 | FUT: Starting 3B | **8B**

Bats R Age 32 | 2016 FA (CU)

Pwr +++ | BAvg +++ | Spd +++ | Def ++

Year	Lev	Team	AB	R	H	HR	RBI	Avg	OB	Slg	OPS	bb%	ct%	Eye	SB	CS	x/h%	Iso	RC/G
2016	Rk	GCL Astros	7	0	2	0	0	286	286	429	714	0	71	0.00	0	0	50	143	4.24
2016	A+	Lancaster	14	2	6	1	9	429	429	786	1214	0	79	0.00	0	0	50	357	9.95
2016	AA	Corpus Christi	17	0	2	0	3	118	167	118	284	6	65	0.17	0	0	0	0	-2.05
2016	AAA	Fresno	18	3	4	1	2	222	263	444	708	5	78	0.25	0	0	50	222	3.95
2016	MLB	Houston	130	13	34	3	15	262	289	385	674	4	91	0.42	1	1	29	123	3.75

Natural-hitting prospect who can impact game with bat. Could be middle-of-the-order run producer with hand-eye coordination, pitch recognition, and plenty of pop in bat. Owns bat speed and strength, but level swing path more conducive to doubles. Runs fairly well, though not likely to steal many bases. Could play variety of positions, but best at 3B.

Guzman,Jeison

6 | **Kansas City** | EXP MLB DEBUT: 2021 | H/W: 6-2 180 | FUT: Starting SS | **8E**

Bats B Age 18 | 2015 FA (DR)

Pwr ++ | BAvg +++ | Spd ++ | Def +++

Year	Lev	Team	AB	R	H	HR	RBI	Avg	OB	Slg	OPS	bb%	ct%	Eye	SB	CS	x/h%	Iso	RC/G
2016	Rk	Azl Royals	188	35	49	1	19	261	325	378	703	9	77	0.41	5	3	31	117	4.35

Quick, tall SS with impressive tools, but needs significant polish. Added strength could lead to average power down road. Brings patient approach to plate and sees lots of pitches. Hits hard line drives to both gaps, but offers little in way of speed. Has ideal actions to stick at SS with clean hands, average arm, and quick feet.

Guzman,Ronald

3 | **Texas** | EXP MLB DEBUT: 2017 | H/W: 6-5 205 | FUT: Starting 1B | **7B**

Bats L Age 22 | 2011 FA (DR)

Pwr +++ | BAvg +++ | Spd + | Def ++

Year	Lev	Team	AB	R	H	HR	RBI	Avg	OB	Slg	OPS	bb%	ct%	Eye	SB	CS	x/h%	Iso	RC/G
2014	A	Hickory	445	46	97	6	63	218	278	330	608	8	76	0.35	6	3	39	112	2.98
2015	A	Hickory	97	10	30	3	14	309	350	433	783	6	85	0.40	2	0	20	124	4.93
2015	A+	High Desert	422	54	117	9	73	277	321	434	754	6	76	0.27	3	0	35	156	4.79
2016	AA	Frisco	375	51	108	15	56	288	346	477	823	8	78	0.40	2	1	33	189	5.64
2016	AAA	Round Rock	88	9	19	1	11	216	266	330	596	6	74	0.26	0	1	37	114	2.76

Natural-hitting 1B who finished 2nd in TL in BA while posting career high in HR. Has large frame, but more focused on contact than power. Got off to hot start, but faded late. Long arms lead to holes in swing, but hits hard line drives when contact made. Lacks foot speed and owns below average range. Question is whether he will have enough pop for 1B.

Hampson,Garrett

6 | **Colorado** | EXP MLB DEBUT: 2020 | H/W: 5-11 185 | FUT: Starting SS | **7D**

Bats R Age 22 | 2016 (3) Long Beach State

Pwr ++ | BAvg +++ | Spd ++++ | Def +++

Year	Lev	Team	AB	R	H	HR	RBI	Avg	OB	Slg	OPS	bb%	ct%	Eye	SB	CS	x/h%	Iso	RC/G
2016	NCAA	Long Beach State	245	55	75	2	26	306	380	400	780	11	84	0.74	23	8	23	94	5.36
2016	A-	Boise	256	43	77	2	44	301	411	441	853	16	78	0.86	36	4	31	141	6.69

3rd round pick has a reputation as a hard worker who gets the most from his limited skills. Excellent approach at the plate with an ability to make contact and get on base. Has plus speed and stole 36 in 40 attempts. Moves well on defense with a strong arm, but some see his future at 2B.

Haniger,Mitch

789 | **Seattle** | EXP MLB DEBUT: 2016 | H/W: 6-2 215 | FUT: Starting OF | **7B**

Bats R Age 26 | 2012 (S-1) Cal Poly

Pwr +++ | BAvg +++ | Spd +++ | Def +++

Year	Lev	Team	AB	R	H	HR	RBI	Avg	OB	Slg	OPS	bb%	ct%	Eye	SB	CS	x/h%	Iso	RC/G
2015	A+	Visalia	202	40	67	12	36	332	384	619	1002	8	81	0.44	8	2	46	287	7.78
2015	AA	Mobile	153	23	43	1	19	281	349	379	728	9	79	0.50	4	4	28	98	4.67
2016	AA	Mobile	197	21	58	5	30	294	388	462	850	13	81	0.81	4	3	36	168	6.34
2016	AAA	Reno	261	58	89	20	64	341	427	670	1097	13	76	0.63	8	1	48	330	9.45
2016	MLB	Arizona	109	9	25	5	17	229	306	404	709	10	75	0.44	0	0	32	174	4.20

Acquired by SEA via trade, reestablished self in big way in '16. Reworked swing and removed pronounced hitch, which resulted in uptake in average and power. Hit 30 HR between 3 levels of minors, but still dealing with considerable length in swing. Will be exploited by average or better velocity. Plays all three OF positions well and arm suited for RF.

Hanneman,Jacob

8 | **Chicago (N)** | EXP MLB DEBUT: 2018 | H/W: 6-1 200 | FUT: Starting CF | **7D**

Bats L Age 25 | 2013 (3) Brigham Young

Pwr ++ | BAvg ++ | Spd ++++ | Def ++++

Year	Lev	Team	AB	R	H	HR	RBI	Avg	OB	Slg	OPS	bb%	ct%	Eye	SB	CS	x/h%	Iso	RC/G
2014	A	Kane County	342	57	87	6	39	254	316	377	694	8	77	0.40	32	4	29	123	4.10
2014	A+	Daytona	145	17	35	2	12	241	295	345	640	7	77	0.32	5	3	31	103	3.34
2015	A+	Myrtle Beach	61	12	20	0	4	328	388	393	782	9	75	0.40	7	1	20	66	5.36
2015	AA	Tennessee	434	60	101	6	41	233	285	362	647	7	74	0.28	17	1	35	129	3.47
2016	AA	Tennessee	291	37	72	10	30	247	307	426	733	8	81	0.45	26	8	39	179	4.53

Injuries limited him to 74 games and he struggled at the plate. Plus athlete has a smooth LH stroke and good bat speed, but can be overly aggressive with poor pitch recognition which has prevented him from reaching full potential. Runs well and had a career high in HR.

Hansen,Mitch

789 | **Los Angeles (N)** | EXP MLB DEBUT: 2020 | H/W: 6-4 210 | FUT: Starting OF | **8C**

Bats L Age 20 | 2015 (2) HS (TX)

Pwr +++ | BAvg +++ | Spd +++ | Def ++

Year	Lev	Team	AB	R	H	HR	RBI	Avg	OB	Slg	OPS	bb%	ct%	Eye	SB	CS	x/h%	Iso	RC/G
2015	Rk	Azl Dodgers	149	23	30	0	17	201	274	282	556	9	66	0.29	6	1	30	81	2.35
2016	Rk	Ogden	293	55	91	11	50	311	359	491	850	7	76	0.31	11	4	27	181	5.97

2nd round pick in '15 had a breakout season in the Pioneer League. Has solid across the board tools with good size and above-average raw power, but his swing can get long and he will need to adjust as he progresses and cut down on strikeouts. Runs well but profiles as a corner OF and played all three spots in '16.

Hanson,Alen

457 | **Pittsburgh** | EXP MLB DEBUT: 2016 | H/W: 5-11 175 | FUT: Utility player | **7B**

Bats B Age 24 | 2009 FA (DR)

Pwr ++ | BAvg ++ | Spd ++++ | Def ++

Year	Lev	Team	AB	R	H	HR	RBI	Avg	OB	Slg	OPS	bb%	ct%	Eye	SB	CS	x/h%	Iso	RC/G
2013	AA	Altoona	137	13	35	1	10	255	297	380	676	6	81	0.31	6	2	29	124	3.85
2014	AA	Altoona	482	64	135	11	58	280	324	442	765	6	82	0.35	25	11	33	162	4.89
2015	AAA	Indianapolis	475	66	125	6	43	263	316	387	704	7	81	0.41	35	12	28	124	4.23
2016	AAA	Indianapolis	432	58	115	8	32	266	317	389	706	7	82	0.41	36	15	26	123	4.19
2016	MLB	Pittsburgh	31	5	7	0	1	226	273	258	531	6	84	0.40	2	1	14	32	2.11

Speedy, athletic player has been slow to develop since breakout in 2012. Has plus speed and strokes the ball with surprising pop for his size, but line-drive approach limits HR potential. Makes consistent contact, but needs to be more selective. Below-average defender and played 2B/LF/3B in '16. Has speed, instincts for SB.

Happ,Ian

47 | **Chicago (N)** | EXP MLB DEBUT: 2018 | H/W: 6-0 205 | FUT: Starting 2B | **8B**

Bats B Age 22 | 2015 (1) Cincinnati

Pwr +++ | BAvg ++++ | Spd ++ | Def ++

Year	Lev	Team	AB	R	H	HR	RBI	Avg	OB	Slg	OPS	bb%	ct%	Eye	SB	CS	x/h%	Iso	RC/G
2015	NCAA	Cincinnati	198	47	73	14	44	369	494	672	1166	20	75	1.00	12	8	44	303	10.88
2015	A-	Eugene	106	26	30	4	11	283	411	491	901	18	74	0.82	9	0	43	208	7.36
2015	A	South Bend	145	24	35	5	22	241	321	448	769	10	73	0.44	1	1	49	207	5.23
2016	A+	Myrtle Beach	240	37	71	7	42	296	413	475	888	17	71	0.70	10	3	37	179	7.26
2016	AA	Tennessee	248	35	65	8	31	262	317	415	732	7	76	0.33	6	2	34	153	4.47

Breakout season established him as top 50 prospect. Owns balanced, up-the-middle approach that results in consistent contact. Good plate discipline and bat speed led to career best 15 HR and power should continue to develop. Below average defense at 2B, but has an MLB ready bat so could develop into a super UT type.

Harrison,Monte

789 | **Milwaukee** | EXP MLB DEBUT: 2019 | H/W: 6-3 220 | FUT: Starting OF | **7C**

Bats R Age 21 | 2014 (2) HS (MO)

Pwr +++ | BAvg ++ | Spd ++++ | Def ++++

Year	Lev	Team	AB	R	H	HR	RBI	Avg	OB	Slg	OPS	bb%	ct%	Eye	SB	CS	x/h%	Iso	RC/G
2015	Rk	Helena	97	20	29	3	13	299	387	474	862	13	76	0.61	14	2	31	175	6.49
2015	A	Wisconsin	162	18	24	2	11	148	216	247	463	8	52	0.18	6	4	42	99	0.91
2016	Rk	Azl Brewers	19	4	4	0	1	211	348	368	716	17	79	1.00	0	0	50	158	5.07
2016	A	Wisconsin	267	34	59	6	37	221	275	337	612	7	64	0.21	8	3	31	116	3.00

Muscular, quick-twitch athlete with tools but lacking consistency. Tapped into power and cut back on Ks in second Class-A year, but lengthy swing and aggressive approach yield fringy contact skills. Plus bat speed with chance for average HR pop with time. Premium speed for SB upside and range; strong arm plays well at all OF positions.

Hawkins,Courtney

7 | **Chicago (A)** | EXP MLB DEBUT: 2018 | H/W: 6-3 245 | FUT: Starting OF | **7C**

Bats R Age 23 | 2012 (1) HS (TX)

Pwr ++++ | BAvg + | Spd ++ | Def ++

Year	Lev	Team	AB	R	H	HR	RBI	Avg	OB	Slg	OPS	bb%	ct%	Eye	SB	CS	x/h%	Iso	RC/G
2012	A+	Winston-Salem	17	3	5	1	2	294	294	588	882	0	88	0.00	0	1	60	294	5.74
2013	A+	Winston-Salem	383	48	68	19	62	178	235	384	619	7	58	0.18	10	5	56	206	3.22
2014	A+	Winston-Salem	449	65	112	19	84	249	329	450	779	11	68	0.37	11	3	43	200	5.42
2015	AA	Birmingham	300	39	73	9	41	243	291	410	701	6	67	0.20	1	4	41	167	4.24
2016	AA	Birmingham	418	35	85	12	60	203	253	349	603	6	67	0.20	0	3	44	146	2.76

Regressing prospect who spent repeat year in AA. Still young for level and offers promising tools. Expands strike zone with poor approach and struggles to read spin. Getting slower as body grows, though power emerging to all fields. Bat speed remains well above average and has strong arm. Still has tools to dream on.

Hayes,Ke'Bryan | 5 | Pittsburgh | EXP MLB DEBUT: 2020 | H/W: 6-1 210 | FUT: Starting 3B | 8D

Bats R Age 20
2015 (1) HS (TX)

Skill	Rating
Pwr	+ + +
BAvg	+ + +
Spd	+ +
Def	+ + +

Year	Lev	Team	AB	R	H	HR	RBI	Avg	OB	Slg	OPS	bb%	ct%	Eye	SB	CS	x/h%	Iso	RC/G
2015	Rk	GCL Pirates	144	24	48	0	13	333	422	375	797	13	83	0.92	7	1	10	42	5.73
2015	A-	West Virginia	41	8	9	0	7	220	319	244	563	13	83	0.86	1	1	11	24	2.82
2016	Rk	GCL Pirates	5	0	2	0	0	400	500	600	1100	17	80	1.00	0	0	50	200	10.07
2016	A	West Virginia	247	27	65	6	37	263	308	393	701	6	79	0.31	6	5	29	130	4.02

Strong frame, good bat speed, and plus raw power. Back injury limited him to 247 AB in '16. Patient approach at the plate and ability to barrel the ball give him a chance to hit for power and average down the road. Shows good agility and range at 3B with a plus arm and now profiles as an above-average defender.

Hays,Austin | 79 | Baltimore | EXP MLB DEBUT: 2019 | H/W: 6-1 195 | FUT: Starting OF | 8D

Bats R Age 21
2016 (3) Jacksonville

Skill	Rating
Pwr	+ + +
BAvg	+ + +
Spd	+ +
Def	+ +

Year	Lev	Team	AB	R	H	HR	RBI	Avg	OB	Slg	OPS	bb%	ct%	Eye	SB	CS	x/h%	Iso	RC/G
2016	A-	Aberdeen	140	14	47	4	21	336	384	514	898	7	77	0.34	4	3	32	179	6.66

Sweet-swinging OF who profiles as RF with above average power and strong arm. Makes easy contact with clean swing mechanics and offers leverage for pop. Can be aggressive early in count and can end up in pitcher's counts. Doesn't run particularly well, but not a baseclogger. Handles RF and needs to improve reads and routes.

Herbert,Lucas | 2 | Atlanta | EXP MLB DEBUT: 2021 | H/W: 6-0 200 | FUT: Starting C | 8E

Bats R Age 20
2015 (2) HS (CA)

Skill	Rating
Pwr	+ + +
BAvg	+ +
Spd	+
Def	+ + + +

Year	Lev	Team	AB	R	H	HR	RBI	Avg	OB	Slg	OPS	bb%	ct%	Eye	SB	CS	x/h%	Iso	RC/G
2015	Rk	GCL Braves	4	1	2	1	1	500	500	1250	1750	0	75	0.00	0	0	50	750	16.26
2016	A	Rome	335	29	62	6	30	185	227	278	504	5	71	0.19	2	4	29	93	1.33

Solid catch-and-throw catcher who was overmatched at plate during full season debut. Strong kid with raw power, but struggled against advanced pitching. Length in swing exploited early. Tightened up swing mechanics late in season. Advanced catching skills for Single-A.

Heredia,Starling | 7 | Los Angeles (N) | EXP MLB DEBUT: 2021 | H/W: 6-2 200 | FUT: Starting OF | 8D

Bats R Age 18
2015 FA (DR)

Skill	Rating
Pwr	+ + + +
BAvg	+ +
Spd	+ + +
Def	+ + +

Year	Lev	Team	AB	R	H	HR	RBI	Avg	OB	Slg	OPS	bb%	ct%	Eye	SB	CS	x/h%	Iso	RC/G
2016		Did not play in the US																	

Strong, physically mature OF signed for $2.6 million. Plus athlete with good raw power and impressive bat speed. Crushes quality FB, but as with most players this young, struggles with off-speed offerings. Above-average speed and a strong arm. Has yet to make his state-side debut, but is a player to keep an eye on.

Hernandez,Brayan | 89 | Seattle | EXP MLB DEBUT: 2020 | H/W: 6-2 175 | FUT: Starting OF | 9E

Bats B Age 19
2014 FA (VZ)

Skill	Rating
Pwr	+ +
BAvg	+ + +
Spd	+ + +
Def	+ + +

Year	Lev	Team	AB	R	H	HR	RBI	Avg	OB	Slg	OPS	bb%	ct%	Eye	SB	CS	x/h%	Iso	RC/G
2016	Rk	Azl Mariners	130	13	37	1	19	285	321	400	721	5	72	0.19	9	3	30	115	4.43

Projectable OF with high upside based upon above average tools. Shows advanced instincts with bat and glove. Ranges well in CF and takes efficient routes. Arm may lead him to LF. Has plus power potential and will need to add loft to simple swing. Exceptional bat speed and has chance to hit for BA, but needs better approach.

Hernandez,Marco | 456 | Boston | EXP MLB DEBUT: 2016 | H/W: 6-0 200 | FUT: Utility player | 6A

Bats L Age 24
2009 FA (DR)

Skill	Rating
Pwr	+ +
BAvg	+ + +
Spd	+ +
Def	+ + +

Year	Lev	Team	AB	R	H	HR	RBI	Avg	OB	Slg	OPS	bb%	ct%	Eye	SB	CS	x/h%	Iso	RC/G
2014	A+	Daytona	441	61	119	3	55	270	316	351	668	6	80	0.33	22	8	19	82	3.70
2015	AA	Portland	282	30	92	5	31	326	347	482	829	3	83	0.18	4	2	33	156	5.48
2015	AAA	Pawtucket	181	27	49	4	22	271	302	409	710	4	78	0.21	1	0	31	138	4.07
2016	AAA	Pawtucket	223	26	69	5	29	309	345	444	789	5	77	0.24	4	2	23	135	5.10
2016	MLB	Boston	51	11	15	1	5	294	357	373	730	9	80	0.50	1	0	13	78	4.50

Utility player who was up and down between BOS and AAA. Plays all INF spots with plus quickness and range. Arm strength is OK and likely better at 2B. Swings aggressively early in count, though makes clean contact. Adept at bunting and has hand-eye coordination. Doesn't have power profile and needs to get on base. Below average speed.

Hernandez,Teoscar | 789 | Houston | EXP MLB DEBUT: 2016 | H/W: 6-2 180 | FUT: Starting OF | 8C

Bats R Age 24
2011 FA (DR)

Skill	Rating
Pwr	+ + +
BAvg	+ + +
Spd	+ + + +
Def	+ + +

Year	Lev	Team	AB	R	H	HR	RBI	Avg	OB	Slg	OPS	bb%	ct%	Eye	SB	CS	x/h%	Iso	RC/G
2014	AA	Corpus Christi	95	12	27	4	10	284	299	474	773	2	62	0.06	2	3	33	189	5.36
2015	AA	Corpus Christi	470	92	103	17	48	219	270	362	632	7	73	0.26	33	7	30	143	3.05
2016	AA	Corpus Christi	279	53	85	6	30	305	376	437	813	10	80	0.58	29	11	29	133	5.70
2016	AAA	Fresno	144	20	45	4	23	313	369	500	869	8	83	0.52	5	4	36	188	6.27
2016	MLB	Houston	100	15	23	4	11	230	306	420	726	10	72	0.39	0	2	48	190	4.55

Athletic OF who rebounded from poor '15 and reached majors. Improved contact rate while honing pitch recognition. Has plus speed and will steal bases. Speed enhanced by higher OBP and shows average power potential. Chases balls when behind in count. Ranges well in OF and could play any spot with strong arm.

Herrera,Carlos | 46 | Colorado | EXP MLB DEBUT: 2019 | H/W: 6-0 145 | FUT: Starting SS | 7D

Bats L Age 20
2013 FA (VZ)

Skill	Rating
Pwr	+ +
BAvg	+ +
Spd	+ + +
Def	+ + +

Year	Lev	Team	AB	R	H	HR	RBI	Avg	OB	Slg	OPS	bb%	ct%	Eye	SB	CS	x/h%	Iso	RC/G
2014	Rk	DSL Rockies	139	18	32	0	11	230	287	281	567	7	82	0.44	6	4	22	50	2.59
2015	Rk	DSL Rockies	53	12	18	0	5	340	364	377	741	4	79	0.18	10	2	11	38	4.40
2015	A-	Boise	221	35	59	2	21	267	311	339	650	6	79	0.30	28	5	19	72	3.41
2016	A	Asheville	548	70	120	7	41	219	248	328	576	4	79	0.18	10	11	33	109	2.42

Skinny SS has plus speed and good raw athleticism. Struggled against older competition in the MWL, hitting .238. Should develop at least average power once he matures and has the range and arm to stick at short, but needs to work on his mechanics and footwork. Plus speed and ability to stick at SS give decent fantasy potential.

Herrera,Rosell | 79 | Colorado | EXP MLB DEBUT: 2018 | H/W: 6-3 195 | FUT: Reserve OF | 7D

Bats B Age 24
2009 FA (DR)

Skill	Rating
Pwr	+ + +
BAvg	+ +
Spd	+ +
Def	+ +

Year	Lev	Team	AB	R	H	HR	RBI	Avg	OB	Slg	OPS	bb%	ct%	Eye	SB	CS	x/h%	Iso	RC/G
2012	A	Asheville	213	22	43	1	26	202	274	272	546	9	77	0.43	6	3	26	70	2.25
2013	A	Asheville	472	83	162	16	76	343	418	515	933	11	80	0.64	21	8	30	172	7.23
2014	A+	Modesto	275	31	67	4	23	244	304	335	639	8	81	0.46	9	7	24	91	3.41
2015	A+	Modesto	466	55	121	4	36	260	314	354	668	7	79	0.38	9	8	25	94	3.77
2016	AA	Hartford	425	61	124	5	66	292	374	379	753	12	81	0.71	36	8	19	87	5.04

Switch-hitting OF has stagnated since being moved from SS to OF. Has good size with average power, but can be overly aggressive with below-average ct% and struggles with breaking balls, limiting his long-term upside. Speed is not a big part of his game, but does have good instincts on the bases. Stock is down, but skills remain.

Higgins,P.J. | 23 | Chicago (N) | EXP MLB DEBUT: 2019 | H/W: 5-10 185 | FUT: Starting C | 7C

Bats R Age 23
2015 (12) Old Dominion

Skill	Rating
Pwr	+ +
BAvg	+ + + +
Spd	+ +
Def	+ +

Year	Lev	Team	AB	R	H	HR	RBI	Avg	OB	Slg	OPS	bb%	ct%	Eye	SB	CS	x/h%	Iso	RC/G
2015	NCAA	Old Dominion	239	40	80	3	32	335	398	452	850	9	93	1.56	3	2	28	117	6.18
2015	Rk	Azl Cubs	80	17	23	2	10	288	345	488	832	8	81	0.47	3	0	39	200	5.87
2015	A-	Eugene	57	8	18	0	5	316	350	386	736	5	81	0.27	1	0	22	70	4.49
2016	A	South Bend	445	57	126	0	40	283	383	355	738	14	83	0.96	3	1	25	72	5.10

12th rounder had a solid full-season debut. Played 2B/3B/1B/C in college and C/1B at Low-A. Moves well behind the plate with a quick, accurate arm. Patient approach at the plate with plus plate discipline (72 BB/75 K). Balanced, line-drive approach resulted in 30 2B but 0 HR. If he can stick behind the plate, his bat and OB ability give him value.

Hill,Derek | 89 | Detroit | EXP MLB DEBUT: 2019 | H/W: 6-2 195 | FUT: Starting CF | 8D

Bats R Age 21
2014 (1) HS (IA)

Skill	Rating
Pwr	+ +
BAvg	+ +
Spd	+ + + +
Def	+ + + +

Year	Lev	Team	AB	R	H	HR	RBI	Avg	OB	Slg	OPS	bb%	ct%	Eye	SB	CS	x/h%	Iso	RC/G
2014	Rk	GCL Tigers	99	12	21	2	11	212	322	333	655	14	81	0.84	9	1	29	121	3.91
2014	A-	Connecticut	74	8	15	0	3	203	224	243	467	3	65	0.08	2	1	13	41	0.73
2015	A	West Michigan	210	33	50	0	16	238	304	314	619	9	79	0.45	25	7	22	76	3.27
2016	A	West Michigan	384	66	102	1	31	266	309	349	658	6	73	0.23	35	6	24	83	3.59

Plus athlete who ended season early due to elbow surgery. Finished 2nd in MWL in SB, his 2nd yr at level. Making progress, but still needs significant work. Swings and misses often and seems content with going to opp field. Has strength and bat speed for power, but not realizing it. Plus-plus speed gives him value and is outstanding defender.

Hill,Tyler | 7 | Boston | EXP MLB DEBUT: 2020 | H/W: 6-0 195 | FUT: Starting OF | 7D

Bats R Age 21	Year	Lev	Team	AB	R	H	HR	RBI	Avg	OB	Slg	OPS	bb%	ct%	Eye	SB	CS	x/h%	Iso	RC/G
2014 (19) HS (DE)																				
Pwr ++	2014	Rk	GCL Red Sox	7	1	0	0	0	0	125	0	125	13	71	0.50	0	1		0	-3.77
BAvg +++	2015	Rk	GCL Red Sox	132	16	33	0	16	250	331	280	611	11	83	0.73	11	2	12	30	3.32
Spd ++	2015	A-	Lowell	15	4	6	0	0	400	400	467	867	0	87	0.00	2	0	17	67	5.59
Def ++	2016	A-	Lowell	232	43	77	4	38	332	395	487	882	9	82	0.59	11	11	30	155	6.53

Intriguing OF who led NYP in BA. Being brought along slowly as he owns nice tools, but raw ability. Has LF profile as speed and arm aren't up to snuff and he lacks instincts for routes and jumps. Loose swing and bat speed provide BA and shows ability to turn on good FB for pull power. Swing mechanics are very clean.

Hilliard,Sam | 79 | Colorado | EXP MLB DEBUT: 2019 | H/W: 6-5 225 | FUT: Starting OF | 8E

Bats L Age 23	Year	Lev	Team	AB	R	H	HR	RBI	Avg	OB	Slg	OPS	bb%	ct%	Eye	SB	CS	x/h%	Iso	RC/G
2015 (15) Wichita State																				
Pwr ++++																				
BAvg ++																				
Spd ++++	2015	Rk	Grand Junction	222	45	68	7	42	306	403	532	935	14	75	0.65	12	4	41	225	7.65
Def +++	2016	A	Asheville	461	71	123	17	83	267	346	449	795	11	67	0.37	30	12	37	182	5.73

15th round pick has a nice mix of power and speed, hitting 17 HR w/30 SB in '16. Has good bat speed, but is overly aggressive in search of power (71% CT) and a high BABIP inflated BA. Plus runner despite his 6'5" frame and plus raw power is starting to show in game action. Potential to be a 20/20 guy if he can hit.

Hinojosa,C.J. | 6 | San Francisco | EXP MLB DEBUT: 2018 | H/W: 5-10 175 | FUT: Starting MIF | 7D

Bats R Age 22	Year	Lev	Team	AB	R	H	HR	RBI	Avg	OB	Slg	OPS	bb%	ct%	Eye	SB	CS	x/h%	Iso	RC/G
2015 (11) Texas																				
Pwr ++	2015	NCAA	Texas	211	26	51	7	30	242	316	403	719	10	88	0.92	4	0	35	161	4.57
BAvg +++	2015	A-	Salem-Kaizer	189	24	56	5	19	296	325	481	806	4	92	0.53	2	3	43	185	5.30
Spd ++	2016	A+	San Jose	260	45	77	6	34	296	382	442	824	12	82	0.78	1	4	30	146	5.94
Def ++	2016	AA	Richmond	226	27	56	3	19	248	309	336	645	8	81	0.47	1	0	21	88	3.50

Fundamentally-sound INF who swings a quick bat and brings mature approach to plate. Draws walks and ability to read spin allows him to use all field and hit for BA. Can hit HR on occasion, but more of doubles hitter. Not much speed for MIF and lacks ideal quickness. Could play 2B if needed, but makes routine plays.

Hinshaw,Chad | 78 | Los Angeles (A) | EXP MLB DEBUT: 2018 | H/W: 6-1 205 | FUT: Starting OF | 7D

Bats R Age 26	Year	Lev	Team	AB	R	H	HR	RBI	Avg	OB	Slg	OPS	bb%	ct%	Eye	SB	CS	x/h%	Iso	RC/G
2013 (15) Illinois State	2015	Rk	Azl Angels	26	7	8	0	4	308	438	462	899	19	77	1.00	3	0	38	154	7.59
Pwr ++	2015	AA	Arkansas	263	48	76	1	26	289	377	365	742	12	71	0.49	27	5	24	76	5.05
BAvg ++	2016	Rk	Azl Angels	3	2	3	1	2	1000	1000	2333	3333	25	100		1	0	67	1333	32.68
Spd +++	2016	Rk	Orem	12	0	2	0	0	167	167	417	583	0	50	0.00	0	1	100	250	4.17
Def +++	2016	AA	Arkansas	205	26	39	5	23	190	262	302	565	9	66	0.29	14	6	31	112	2.25

Athletic, savvy OF who repeated AA, though was limited after May due to injuries. Speed is best tool and is instinctual baserunner. Not much pop in level swing path and can be inconsistent with plate discipline. Long swing can be jammed inside and doesn't reach seats enough. Very solid defender with range and quality jumps.

Holder,Kyle | 46 | New York (A) | EXP MLB DEBUT: 2019 | H/W: 6-1 185 | FUT: Starting SS | 7D

Bats L Age 22	Year	Lev	Team	AB	R	H	HR	RBI	Avg	OB	Slg	OPS	bb%	ct%	Eye	SB	CS	x/h%	Iso	RC/G
2015 (1) San Diego																				
Pwr +																				
BAvg ++	2015	NCAA	San Diego	224	45	78	4	31	348	399	482	881	8	92	1.00	5	6	26	134	6.36
Spd +++	2015	A-	Staten Island	225	23	48	0	12	213	269	253	522	7	85	0.50	6	2	17	40	2.12
Def +++++	2016	A	Charleston (Sc)	352	40	102	1	18	290	319	347	665	4	85	0.28	8	6	16	57	3.59

Standout defender who exhibits athleticism and body control. Makes plays with quick, easy actions. Split time between 2B and SS and glove should get him to big leagues. May not hit enough. Makes easy contact, but is aggressive early in count and has poor OBP. Bat speed and power well below average. Needs to get on base.

Hood,Destin | 789 | Miami | EXP MLB DEBUT: 2016 | H/W: 6-2 205 | FUT: Reserve OF | 6B

Bats R Age 27	Year	Lev	Team	AB	R	H	HR	RBI	Avg	OB	Slg	OPS	bb%	ct%	Eye	SB	CS	x/h%	Iso	RC/G
2008 (2) HS (AL)	2015	AA	Akron	140	20	41	3	19	293	340	479	819	7	74	0.28	4	1	41	186	5.77
Pwr +++	2015	AA	Reading	167	19	48	7	37	287	316	503	819	4	75	0.17	1	1	44	216	5.47
BAvg ++	2015	AAA	Columbus	59	3	10	0	2	169	222	271	493	6	64	0.19	1	0	40	102	1.38
Spd +++	2016	AAA	New Orleans	476	61	127	15	80	267	320	435	755	7	76	0.33	11	6	37	168	4.78
Def +++	2016	MLB	Miami	25	3	6	1	2	240	240	400	640	0	56	0.00	0	1	33	160	3.62

Late developing player has a nice mix of power and speed and made his MLB debut at 26. Plus athlete remains raw at the plate and has struggled to stay healthy. Has above-average power and stroked 29 2B and 15 HR. Torches LHP and could earn a platoon role. Average runner on the bases and in the field where he can play all three OF slots.

Hoskins,Rhys | 3 | Philadelphia | EXP MLB DEBUT: 2018 | H/W: 6-4 225 | FUT: Starting 1B | 7C

Bats R Age 24	Year	Lev	Team	AB	R	H	HR	RBI	Avg	OB	Slg	OPS	bb%	ct%	Eye	SB	CS	x/h%	Iso	RC/G
2014 (5) Sacramento State	2014	NCAA	Sacramento State	213	45	68	12	53	319	425	573	997	15	85	1.26	6	0	44	254	8.09
Pwr ++++	2014	A-	Williamsport	245	30	58	9	40	237	297	408	705	8	78	0.39	3	3	41	171	4.13
BAvg +++	2015	A	Lakewood	255	39	82	9	51	322	384	525	910	9	80	0.52	2	4	37	204	6.82
4.70 Spd +	2015	A+	Clearwater	243	47	77	8	39	317	390	510	900	11	80	0.59	2	0	38	193	6.81
Def ++	2016	AA	Reading	498	95	140	38	116	281	371	566	937	12	75	0.57	8	3	46	285	7.27

Has continued to hit and with power at each step. Some stiffness to his swing, is pull-happy, and has trouble tracking quality breaking stuff. But is patient enough to get into FB counts, will take a walk, and has light-tower strength. Lack of speed and only average defense limits his overall projection, so he'll need to keep producing in the box.

Huff,Sam | 2 | Texas | EXP MLB DEBUT: 2020 | H/W: 6-4 215 | FUT: Starting C | 8E

Bats R Age 19	Year	Lev	Team	AB	R	H	HR	RBI	Avg	OB	Slg	OPS	bb%	ct%	Eye	SB	CS	x/h%	Iso	RC/G
2016 (7) HS (AZ)																				
Pwr ++																				
BAvg +++																				
Spd +																				
Def +++	2016	Rk	Azl Rangers	97	19	32	1	17	330	425	485	909	14	70	0.55	0	0	38	155	7.67

Big, sturdy backstop who had standout pro debut. Exhibits average, raw power and feel for contact in smooth stroke. Power development will determine prospect status as he could be more gap guy. More strength than bat speed, but can hit for BA. Is fundamentally-sound behind plate, though footwork and release need attention.

Hughston,Casey | 78 | Pittsburgh | EXP MLB DEBUT: 2020 | H/W: 6-2 200 | FUT: Starting CF | 7E

Bats L Age 22	Year	Lev	Team	AB	R	H	HR	RBI	Avg	OB	Slg	OPS	bb%	ct%	Eye	SB	CS	x/h%	Iso	RC/G
2015 (3) Alabama																				
Pwr +++																				
BAvg +	2015	NCAA	Alabama	235	39	78	6	44	332	389	502	891	9	77	0.40	12	2	31	170	6.68
Spd +++	2015	A-	West Virginia	219	23	49	2	28	224	267	311	578	6	68	0.18	4	1	27	87	2.45
Def +++	2016	A	West Virginia	400	49	76	11	35	190	247	335	582	7	62	0.19	16	8	38	145	2.59

3rd round pick has been a bust so far, hitting .202/.256/.326 over two seasons. Speed and raw power give him interesting potential, but extreme contact issues have plagued him (65% CT). Pirates sent him back to instructs for a month, but the timeout didn't work. Has the range and arm-strength to stick in CF for now.

Ibanez,Andy | 4 | Texas | EXP MLB DEBUT: 2017 | H/W: 5-10 170 | FUT: Starting 2B | 7A

Bats R Age 24	Year	Lev	Team	AB	R	H	HR	RBI	Avg	OB	Slg	OPS	bb%	ct%	Eye	SB	CS	x/h%	Iso	RC/G
2015 FA (CU)																				
Pwr +++																				
BAvg +++																				
Spd ++	2016	A	Hickory	185	28	60	7	35	324	416	546	962	14	85	1.04	10	8	43	222	7.66
Def +++	2016	AA	Frisco	307	39	80	6	31	261	316	391	707	8	85	0.53	5	2	33	130	4.28

Instinctual, advanced 2B who bypassed A+ and could be offensive-minded INF. Works counts and uses controlled, compact stroke for plus contact and average pop. Power mostly to pull side, though uses whole field. Thick frame limits quickness, but is solid defender with arm strength. Exhibits fringy speed, but can leg out doubles.

Ice,Logan | 2 | Cleveland | EXP MLB DEBUT: 2019 | H/W: 5-10 195 | FUT: Starting C | 7E

Bats B Age 21	Year	Lev	Team	AB	R	H	HR	RBI	Avg	OB	Slg	OPS	bb%	ct%	Eye	SB	CS	x/h%	Iso	RC/G
2016 (S-2) Oregon State																				
Pwr ++																				
BAvg +++																				
Spd ++	2016	NCAA	Oregon State	174	42	54	7	39	310	431	563	994	18	86	1.48	2	0	46	253	8.33
Def +++	2016	A-	Mahoning Valley	126	13	25	2	8	198	322	302	624	15	70	0.61	0	0	36	103	3.40

Short, stocky C with playable arm and solid defensive actions. Fluid, level stroke as switch hitter with more polish from left side; can get pull-happy. Power works to gaps; projected low HR impact. Selective, works counts and knows how to get on base. Non-threat for SB. Limited overall upside but chance to be an average everyday C.

Jackson,Alex — 79 — Atlanta

EXP MLB DEBUT: 2019 | H/W: 6-2 215 | FUT: Starting OF | 8C

Bats R Age 21
2014 (1) HS (CA)

Pwr ++++
BAvg ++
Spd ++
Def ++

Year	Lev	Team	AB	R	H	HR	RBI	Avg	OB	Slg	OPS	bb%	ct%	Eye	SB	CS	x/h%	Iso	RC/G
2014	Rk	Azl Mariners	82	11	23	2	16	280	352	476	827	10	71	0.38	0	1	43	195	6.17
2015	A-	Everett	163	31	39	8	25	239	326	466	792	11	63	0.34	2	4	51	227	5.94
2015	A	Clinton	108	10	17	0	13	157	202	213	415	5	68	0.17	1	1	35	56	0.11
2016	A	Clinton	333	43	81	11	55	243	313	408	722	9	69	0.33	2	1	40	165	4.55

Strong, athletic hitter who was better in return trip to Low-A. Still has impressive talent and upside with natural hitting skills. Inconsistent contact a result of selling out for power and aggressive approach, but has feel for bat. Can use all fields and electric bat speed should lead to power. Becoming better defender with plus arm.

Jackson,Drew — 6 — Seattle

EXP MLB DEBUT: 2018 | H/W: 6-2 200 | FUT: Starting SS | 7B

Bats R Age 23
2015 (5) Stanford

Pwr ++
BAvg +++
Spd ++++
Def +++

Year	Lev	Team	AB	R	H	HR	RBI	Avg	OB	Slg	OPS	bb%	ct%	Eye	SB	CS	x/h%	Iso	RC/G
2015	NCAA	Stanford	147	27	47	0	9	320	383	388	770	9	85	0.68	6	2	17	68	5.21
2015	A-	Everett	226	64	81	2	26	358	434	447	880	12	85	0.86	47	4	19	88	6.63
2016	A+	Bakersfield	524	87	135	6	47	258	322	345	668	9	80	0.48	16	8	24	88	3.81

Speedy INF who skipped Low-A and was solid. Has well above average speed and quickness and is steady defender with cannon for arm. Mostly focuses on gap power and has short stroke to make contact and use entire field. Will be selective with keen eye, but doesn't project to much power. Glove and speed good enough.

Jackson,Jhalan — 9 — New York (A)

EXP MLB DEBUT: 2019 | H/W: 6-3 220 | FUT: Starting OF | 7D

Bats R Age 24
2015 (7) Florida Southern

Pwr +++
BAvg ++
Spd +++
Def +++

Year	Lev	Team	AB	R	H	HR	RBI	Avg	OB	Slg	OPS	bb%	ct%	Eye	SB	CS	x/h%	Iso	RC/G
2015	A-	Staten Island	177	35	47	5	34	266	326	452	778	8	67	0.27	4	0	45	186	5.53
2016	A	Charleston (Sc)	386	48	91	11	50	236	304	415	719	9	70	0.33	6	8	47	179	4.53

Tall, strong OF who has tools that could be cultivated, but is raw with bat. Exhibits plus power potential, though lack of contact mutes it. Hits lots of doubles and uses average speed. Struggles to read spin and swing tends to get long. Hitting for BA is out of question, but power-speed combo gives him value. Features plus arm strength.

Jagielo,Eric — 35 — Cincinnati

EXP MLB DEBUT: 2017 | H/W: 6-3 210 | FUT: Starting 3B | 7D

Bats L Age 24
2013 (1) Notre Dame

Pwr +++
BAvg ++
Spd +
Def ++

Year	Lev	Team	AB	R	H	HR	RBI	Avg	OB	Slg	OPS	bb%	ct%	Eye	SB	CS	x/h%	Iso	RC/G
2013	A-	Staten Island	184	19	49	6	27	266	357	451	808	12	71	0.48	0	0	43	185	5.91
2014	Rk	GCL Yankees	23	3	5	2	4	217	308	478	786	12	96	3.00	0	0	40	261	5.33
2014	A+	Tampa	309	43	80	16	54	259	340	460	800	11	70	0.41	0	0	38	201	5.57
2015	AA	Trenton	222	36	63	9	35	284	338	495	833	8	74	0.31	0	0	43	212	5.88
2016	AA	Pensacola	365	26	75	7	26	205	291	310	601	11	65	0.34	0	0	31	104	2.90

Acquired in Aroldis Chapman deal, LHH 3B struggled in CIN debut. Stiff and mechanical at plate. A lot of swing and miss in bat as he struggles with average velocity. Power production dipped. Hasn't been the same since '15 knee injury. Below average defensive 3B and slow runner.

January,Ryan — 2 — Arizona

EXP MLB DEBUT: 2020 | H/W: 6-2 198 | FUT: Starting C | 7D

Bats L Age 19
2016 (8) San Jacinto JC

Pwr ++++
BAvg ++
Spd +
Def ++

Year	Lev	Team	AB	R	H	HR	RBI	Avg	OB	Slg	OPS	bb%	ct%	Eye	SB	CS	x/h%	Iso	RC/G
2016	Rk	Missoula	183	34	50	10	26	273	364	470	834	12	66	0.41	0	1	32	197	6.30

Powerful LHH catcher, making strides behind the plate. A long, looping swing contributed to high strikeout numbers; will need to shorten to be successful. Patient approach, and raw power potential in bat. Made strides in pro ball to become better defender.

Javier,Wander — 6 — Minnesota

EXP MLB DEBUT: 2021 | H/W: 6-1 165 | FUT: Starting SS | 9E

Bats R Age 18
2015 FA (DR)

Pwr +++
BAvg +++
Spd +++
Def +++

Year	Lev	Team	AB	R	H	HR	RBI	Avg	OB	Slg	OPS	bb%	ct%	Eye	SB	CS	x/h%	Iso	RC/G
2017		Did not play in the US																	

Athletic, quick INF who suffered thru hamstring injury. When healthy, features all five tools. Ceiling as high as any in org and could grow into middle-of-the-order producer. Exhibits plus raw power to all fields and makes easy contact. Crude pitch recognition needs work. Strong arm and lateral quickness allow him to stick at SS.

Jebavy,Ronnie — 8 — San Francisco

EXP MLB DEBUT: 2019 | H/W: 6-2 205 | FUT: Reserve OF | 6B

Bats R Age 22
2015 (5) Middle Tenn State

Pwr ++
BAvg ++
Spd ++++
Def ++++

Year	Lev	Team	AB	R	H	HR	RBI	Avg	OB	Slg	OPS	bb%	ct%	Eye	SB	CS	x/h%	Iso	RC/G
2015	NCAA	Middle Tenn State	245	38	88	7	36	359	405	531	936	7	86	0.56	24	4	28	171	6.90
2015	A-	Salem-Kaizer	270	44	71	8	30	263	287	419	705	3	80	0.16	23	4	31	156	3.91
2016	A+	San Jose	535	76	132	12	47	247	292	385	677	6	71	0.22	24	14	34	138	3.78

Speedy, athletic OF who provides value with excellent defense and above average speed. Not much strength in frame and long swing can be exploited. Strikes out far too often and doesn't read pitches well. Can turn on pitch to pull ball out of park, but best when going to opposite field. Exhibits plus range and arm in CF and gets good reads.

Jenkins,Eric — 8 — Texas

EXP MLB DEBUT: 2019 | H/W: 6-1 170 | FUT: Starting OF | 8D

Bats L Age 20
2015 (2) HS (NC)

Pwr ++
BAvg ++
Spd +++++
Def +++

Year	Lev	Team	AB	R	H	HR	RBI	Avg	OB	Slg	OPS	bb%	ct%	Eye	SB	CS	x/h%	Iso	RC/G
2015	Rk	Azl Rangers	177	35	44	0	13	249	335	339	674	12	68	0.40	27	3	23	90	4.18
2015	A	Hickory	18	3	7	0	1	389	421	444	865	5	78	0.25	1	0	14	56	6.12
2016	A	Hickory	506	72	112	8	40	221	278	330	608	7	70	0.26	51	15	27	109	2.91
2016	A+	High Desert	4	0	0	0	0	0	0	0	0	0	25	0.00	0	0		0	-10.45

Ultra-fast OF who was 3rd in minors in SB. One of top athletes in org and has chance to be impact player. Swing mechanics are funky and struggles to put bat to ball. Recognizes pitches and will draw walks, but power isn't part of game. Needs to hit ball on ground in order to use double-plus speed. Solid CF with ample range and average arm.

Jhang,Jin-De — 2 — Pittsburgh

EXP MLB DEBUT: 2017 | H/W: 5-11 220 | FUT: Starting C | 7D

Bats L Age 23
2011 FA (TW)

Pwr ++
BAvg +++
Spd ++
Def +++

Year	Lev	Team	AB	R	H	HR	RBI	Avg	OB	Slg	OPS	bb%	ct%	Eye	SB	CS	x/h%	Iso	RC/G
2013	A-	Jamestown	184	22	51	5	34	277	338	413	751	8	87	0.71	0	1	27	136	4.83
2014	A+	Bradenton	269	29	59	2	35	219	261	301	562	5	87	0.42	3	0	27	82	2.55
2015	A+	Bradenton	370	45	108	5	41	292	332	381	713	6	88	0.51	2	4	20	89	4.27
2016	AA	Altoona	188	20	56	1	21	298	337	383	720	6	94	0.92	1	0	25	85	4.53
2016	AAA	Indianapolis	20	2	4	0	2	200	238	250	488	5	90	0.50	0	0	25	50	1.86

Short, stocky Taiwanese backstop has a nice line-drive approach and double-digit HR potential. Moves well behind the plate and the trade of Reese McGuire created a clearer path to the majors. Has a strong arm and a quick release, but needs more reps to refine his receiving skills. The bat will be his ticket to the show.

Jimenez,Eloy — 79 — Chicago (N)

EXP MLB DEBUT: 2019 | H/W: 6-4 205 | FUT: Starting OF | 9C

Bats R Age 20
2013 FA (DR)

Pwr ++++
BAvg ++++
Spd +++
Def +++

Year	Lev	Team	AB	R	H	HR	RBI	Avg	OB	Slg	OPS	bb%	ct%	Eye	SB	CS	x/h%	Iso	RC/G
2014	Rk	Azl Cubs	150	13	34	3	27	227	275	367	642	6	79	0.31	3	1	38	140	3.35
2015	A-	Eugene	232	36	66	7	33	284	328	418	746	6	81	0.35	3	2	26	134	4.53
2016	A	South Bend	432	65	142	14	81	329	365	532	898	5	78	0.27	8	3	40	204	6.52

Career-best line earned him MWL MVP. Starting to tap into raw tools and projects to have plus power. Uses bat speed and hand-eye coordination to make consistent contact and stroked a career-best 14 HR. Needs to be more selective and hunt for pitches he can drive, but that should come. Solid defender w/strong arm.

Jimenez,Emerson — 6 — Colorado

EXP MLB DEBUT: 2019 | H/W: 6-1 160 | FUT: Starting SS | 7E

Bats L Age 22
2011 FA (DR)

Pwr +
BAvg +++
Spd ++++
Def ++++

Year	Lev	Team	AB	R	H	HR	RBI	Avg	OB	Slg	OPS	bb%	ct%	Eye	SB	CS	x/h%	Iso	RC/G
2013	Rk	DSL Rockies	36	3	8	0	4	222	243	250	493	3	89	0.25	1	2	13	28	1.69
2014	A	Asheville	266	36	69	1	28	259	273	342	615	2	78	0.09	16	7	23	83	2.81
2015	A	Asheville	232	33	43	1	17	185	203	254	457	2	78	0.10	16	5	30	69	0.83
2015	A+	Modesto	153	18	33	1	12	216	231	307	538	2	67	0.06	1	3	30	92	1.79
2016	A+	Modesto	319	40	74	1	21	232	262	279	541	4	76	0.17	28	5	16	47	1.89

Athletic defender has yet to hit as a pro and now has a career slash line of just .242/.269/.279. Continues to have an advanced glove with plus speed, a strong arm, and good range. Has good bat speed and the potential to develop average power, but needs a better understanding of the strike zone. Plus speed and glove are his primary tools.

Joe, Connor — 5 — Pittsburgh

EXP MLB DEBUT: 2019 | H/W: 6-0 205 | FUT: Starting 3B | 7D

Bats R | Age 24 | 2014 (S-1) San Diego

Pwr ++ | BAvg +++ | Spd ++ | Def ++

Year	Lev	Team	AB	R	H	HR	RBI	Avg	OB	Slg	OPS	bb%	ct%	Eye	SB	CS	x/h%	Iso	RC/G
2015	A	West Virginia	290	38	71	1	20	245	356	303	659	15	88	1.47	0	4	20	59	4.29
2016	A+	Bradenton	390	49	108	5	52	277	352	392	744	10	78	0.54	2	4	31	115	4.89

Played catcher in college but has settled in at 3B as a pro. Has been slow to develop though he has a good approach at the plate, making consistent contact and shooting line drives from gap to gap. Hit .316/.398/.433 in 2nd half at A+, but has below-average power for 3B. Has decent speed, good glove and a strong arm, but 3B is a work in progress.

Jones, JaCoby — 58 — Detroit

EXP MLB DEBUT: 2016 | H/W: 6-2 205 | FUT: Starting OF | 7C

Bats R | Age 24 | 2013 (3) LSU

Pwr +++ | BAvg +++ | Spd ++++ | Def +++

Year	Lev	Team	AB	R	H	HR	RBI	Avg	OB	Slg	OPS	bb%	ct%	Eye	SB	CS	x/h%	Iso	RC/G
2015	AA	Altoona	10	2	5	0	2	500	545	500	1045	9	100		1	0	0	0	8.18
2015	AA	Erie	136	26	34	6	20	250	333	463	797	11	62	0.33	10	3	44	213	6.09
2016	AA	Erie	77	11	24	4	20	312	391	597	988	11	70	0.43	2	1	50	286	8.45
2016	AAA	Toledo	292	33	71	3	23	243	310	356	659	8	67	0.26	11	4	31	113	3.78
2016	MLB	Detroit	28	3	6	0	2	214	214	321	536	0	57	0.00	0	0	50	107	2.14

Ahtletic prospect who began year late due to drug suspension, but hit upon returning and found way to DET. Very versatile player who can play variety of positions, but may have found home in CF. Offers plus raw power, though HR output dropped and owns plus speed. Long swing hinders contact and expands zone by chasing breaking balls.

Jones, Jahmai — 8 — Los Angeles (A)

EXP MLB DEBUT: 2019 | H/W: 6-0 215 | FUT: Starting OF | 8C

Bats R | Age 19 | 2015 (2) HS (GA)

Pwr +++ | BAvg +++ | Spd ++++ | Def +++

Year	Lev	Team	AB	R	H	HR	RBI	Avg	OB	Slg	OPS	bb%	ct%	Eye	SB	CS	x/h%	Iso	RC/G
2015	Rk	Azl Angels	160	28	39	2	20	244	316	344	660	10	79	0.52	16	7	26	100	3.77
2016	Rk	Orem	196	49	63	3	20	321	387	459	846	10	85	0.72	19	6	29	138	6.10
2016	A	Burlington	62	8	15	1	10	242	299	306	605	7	79	0.38	1	0	13	65	2.85

Toolsy, improving OF who has impressive, emerging arsenal. Swings fast bat and owns natural strength to hit for power and BA. Needs to add more loft for HR and should come. Plus runner now and aids in true CF range. Could become better defender with more polish. Makes loud, hard contact and makes easy contact due to short swing.

Jones, Nolan — 56 — Cleveland

EXP MLB DEBUT: 2020 | H/W: 6-4 185 | FUT: Starting 3B | 8E

Bats L | Age 18 | 2016 (2) HS (PA)

Pwr ++ | BAvg +++ | Spd ++ | Def +++

Year	Lev	Team	AB	R	H	HR	RBI	Avg	OB	Slg	OPS	bb%	ct%	Eye	SB	CS	x/h%	Iso	RC/G
2016	Rk	AZL Indians	109	10	28	0	9	257	386	339	726	17	55	0.47	3	1	25	83	5.82

Tall, lean 3B with well-rounded game and high floor. Whippy, plus bat speed through zone conducive to solid contact and BA; gap power at present with average HR output projected. Advanced approach and willing to walk; fringy speed projects to decline as he matures. Solid defensive chops with arm to profile at 3B, with 2B as fallback option.

Jones, Thomas — 8 — Miami

EXP MLB DEBUT: 2021 | H/W: 6-4 195 | FUT: Starting CF | 8D

Bats R | Age 19 | 2016 (3) HS (SC)

Pwr ++ | BAvg ++ | Spd ++++ | Def +++

Year	Lev	Team	AB	R	H	HR	RBI	Avg	OB	Slg	OPS	bb%	ct%	Eye	SB	CS	x/h%	Iso	RC/G
2016	Rk	GCL Marlins	64	11	15	0	6	234	347	313	659	15	69	0.55	2	6	27	78	4.03

Two-sport star in high school was lured away from Vanderbilt by a $1 million signing bonus. Was limited to just 19 games due to a hamstring injury. Profiles as a 70-grade runner, but remains raw in his approach at the plate. Does have a quick RH bat, but swing can get long. Has a strong arm and can play all three OF slots.

Judge, Aaron — 9 — New York (A)

EXP MLB DEBUT: 2016 | H/W: 6-7 275 | FUT: Starting OF | 8B

Bats R | Age 24 | 2013 (1) Fresno State

Pwr +++++ | BAvg +++ | Spd ++ | Def +++

Year	Lev	Team	AB	R	H	HR	RBI	Avg	OB	Slg	OPS	bb%	ct%	Eye	SB	CS	x/h%	Iso	RC/G
2014	A+	Tampa	233	44	66	8	33	283	410	442	852	18	69	0.69	0	0	29	159	6.77
2015	AA	Trenton	250	36	71	12	44	284	347	516	863	9	72	0.34	1	0	44	232	6.38
2015	AAA	Scranton/WB	228	27	51	8	28	224	311	373	684	11	68	0.39	6	2	35	149	4.05
2016	AAA	Scranton/WB	352	62	95	19	65	270	356	489	845	12	72	0.48	5	0	40	219	6.18
2016	MLB	NY Yankees	84	10	15	4	10	179	258	345	603	10	50	0.21	0	1	40	167	3.43

Large, athletic OF who earned trip to majors based on consistent plus power and sound RF defense. Long arms lead to exploitable holes in swing, but can reach balls on outer half. Will K, but makes acceptable contact given power profile. Runs well, though isn't much of a SB threat. Ranges well in OF and has incredible arm strength to be factor.

Justus, Connor — 6 — Los Angeles (A)

EXP MLB DEBUT: 2019 | H/W: 6-0 190 | FUT: Utility player | 6B

Bats R | Age 22 | 2016 (5) Georgia Tech

Pwr ++ | BAvg ++ | Spd ++ | Def +++

Year	Lev	Team	AB	R	H	HR	RBI	Avg	OB	Slg	OPS	bb%	ct%	Eye	SB	CS	x/h%	Iso	RC/G
2016	NCAA	Georgia Tech	247	62	80	6	37	324	420	486	906	14	85	1.08	9	3	31	162	7.08
2016	Rk	Orem	93	19	32	0	23	344	450	430	881	16	80	0.95	0	2	22	86	7.06
2016	A	Burlington	139	19	32	2	9	230	301	309	610	9	76	0.41	1	2	19	79	2.99

Fundamental INF who struggled in A-, but has potential as utility player. Has very selective eye at plate and draws walks. Likes to go to opp field and leg out doubles with average wheels. Can swing and miss often when selling out for pop and may not have double-digit HR in profile. Should stick at SS with average range and solid arm strength.

Kelly, Carson — 2 — St. Louis

EXP MLB DEBUT: 2016 | H/W: 6-2 220 | FUT: Starting C | 7C

Bats R | Age 22 | 2012 (2) HS (OR)

Pwr +++ | BAvg +++ | Spd ++ | Def ++

Year	Lev	Team	AB	R	H	HR	RBI	Avg	OB	Slg	OPS	bb%	ct%	Eye	SB	CS	x/h%	Iso	RC/G
2014	A	Peoria	363	41	90	6	49	248	318	366	684	9	85	0.69	1	0	30	118	4.13
2015	A+	Palm Beach	389	30	85	8	51	219	260	332	592	5	84	0.34	0	0	32	113	2.74
2016	AA	Springfield	216	29	62	6	18	287	330	403	733	6	79	0.30	1	1	21	116	4.36
2016	AAA	Memphis	113	14	33	0	9	292	355	381	735	8	85	0.65	0	0	30	88	4.80
2016	MLB	St. Louis	13	1	2	0	1	154	154	231	385	0	85	0.00	0	0	50	77	0.23

Defensive minded C continues to improve at the plate and made his MLB debut. Moves well, blocks balls in the dirt, has a strong arm, and calls a good game. Has good raw power, but it hasn't shown up in game action and hit just 6 HR in '16. Makes consistent contact, but lacks an advanced feel for hitting and can be stiff at the plate.

Kemmer, Jon — 79 — Houston

EXP MLB DEBUT: 2017 | H/W: 6-2 230 | FUT: Reserve OF | 6B

Bats L | Age 26 | 2013 (21) Brewton-Parker

Pwr +++ | BAvg ++ | Spd ++ | Def ++

Year	Lev	Team	AB	R	H	HR	RBI	Avg	OB	Slg	OPS	bb%	ct%	Eye	SB	CS	x/h%	Iso	RC/G
2013	A-	Tri City	199	29	44	4	16	221	282	327	609	8	79	0.41	1	2	27	106	2.97
2014	A	Quad Cities	180	29	52	4	17	289	360	450	810	10	78	0.51	3	1	38	161	5.70
2014	A+	Lancaster	153	32	45	12	33	294	312	608	920	3	78	0.12	0	1	51	314	6.39
2015	AA	Corpus Christi	364	67	119	18	65	327	401	574	975	11	76	0.51	9	1	42	247	7.87
2016	AAA	Fresno	407	53	108	18	69	265	328	477	805	9	69	0.30	8	10	43	211	5.71

Strong OF who continues to exhibit power with at least 16 HR each of last 3 years. Can hit LHP, but has poor approach with inability to make consistent contact. Swings hard early in count and subject to high strikeout totals. Average arm works in OF corner, though doesn't run well and owns limited range. Not much upside, but has value in pop.

Kieboom, Carter — 6 — Washington

EXP MLB DEBUT: 2020 | H/W: 6-2 190 | FUT: Starting SS | 8C

Bats R | Age 19 | 2016 (1) HS (GA)

Pwr ++ | BAvg +++ | Spd ++ | Def +++

Year	Lev	Team	AB	R	H	HR	RBI	Avg	OB	Slg	OPS	bb%	ct%	Eye	SB	CS	x/h%	Iso	RC/G
2016	Rk	GCL Nationals	135	29	33	4	25	244	306	452	758	8	68	0.28	1	2	48	207	5.19

Lean and athletic, features a clean right-handed swing with good bat speed. More selective than he showed in his pro debut, though his power was more than expected. Observers split on future defensive role, specifically if any added bulk will push him to 3B. Currently has adequate SS range, and a strong arm.

Kingery, Scott — 4 — Philadelphia

EXP MLB DEBUT: 2018 | H/W: 5-10 180 | FUT: Starting 2B | 7C

Bats R | Age 22 | 2015 (2) Arizona

Pwr ++ | BAvg +++ | Spd ++++ (4.14) | Def +++

Year	Lev	Team	AB	R	H	HR	RBI	Avg	OB	Slg	OPS	bb%	ct%	Eye	SB	CS	x/h%	Iso	RC/G
2015	NCAA	Arizona	237	53	93	5	36	392	415	561	976	4	92	0.50	11	6	27	169	7.06
2015	A	Lakewood	252	43	63	3	21	250	300	337	637	7	83	0.42	11	1	22	87	3.37
2016	A+	Clearwater	375	60	110	3	28	293	350	411	761	8	86	0.61	26	5	32	117	5.04
2016	AA	Reading	156	16	39	2	18	250	273	333	607	3	77	0.14	4	2	23	83	2.68

Small frame, but has shown doubles power out of a clean, short RH stroke. Has excellent bat control, which has led to very good contact rates, but won't flash much over-the-fence power. Excellent range at second base with average arm, and can turn DP. Puts speed to good use on the basepaths.

Kirilloff, Alex — 9 — Minnesota
EXP MLB DEBUT: 2020 **H/W:** 6-2 195 **FUT:** Starting OF **8C**

Bats L Age 19 2016 (1) HS (PA)

	Pwr	+++
BAvg	++++
Spd	+++
Def	++

Year	Lev	Team	AB	R	H	HR	RBI	Avg	OB	Slg	OPS	bb%	ct%	Eye	SB	CS	x/h%	Iso	RC/G
2016	Rk	Elizabethton	216	33	66	7	33	306	339	454	793	5	85	0.34	0	1	26	148	5.02

Natural-hitting OF with impressive pro debut. Covers plate with textbook stroke and shows ability to hang in against LHP. Started hot with power to all fields, but began to chase late and expand zone. Very athletic in RF with solid average speed and plus arm strength. Still room to develop, but ceiling is high.

Knapp, Andrew — 2 — Philadelphia
EXP MLB DEBUT: 2017 **H/W:** 6-1 195 **FUT:** Starting C **7B**

Bats B Age 25 2013 (2) California

Pwr	++
BAvg	+++
Spd	+
Def	++

Year	Lev	Team	AB	R	H	HR	RBI	Avg	OB	Slg	OPS	bb%	ct%	Eye	SB	CS	x/h%	Iso	RC/G
2014	A	Lakewood	283	39	82	5	25	290	352	438	790	9	75	0.38	3	3	34	148	5.44
2014	A+	Clearwater	83	7	13	1	7	157	205	205	409	6	69	0.19	1	0	15	48	-0.08
2015	A+	Clearwater	244	38	64	2	28	262	341	369	710	11	74	0.46	0	1	30	107	4.50
2015	AA	Reading	214	39	77	11	56	360	419	631	1050	9	80	0.51	1	0	44	271	8.56
2016	AAA	Lehigh Valley	403	55	107	8	46	266	327	390	717	8	73	0.35	2	2	31	124	4.41

Made enough small steps defensively to prove he should at least get a shot at an MLB catching job, and is on the cusp of one. While not an impact player with the bat, is a hit-before-power guy with gap pop and a decent eye. More swing-and-miss than one might expect, but L/R splits have evened out. Will probably take time to settle at MLB level.

Kramer, Kevin — 4 — Pittsburgh
EXP MLB DEBUT: 2019 **H/W:** 6-1 190 **FUT:** Starting 2B **7D**

Bats L Age 23 2015 (2) UCLA

Pwr	++
BAvg	+++
Spd	++
Def	+++

Year	Lev	Team	AB	R	H	HR	RBI	Avg	OB	Slg	OPS	bb%	ct%	Eye	SB	CS	x/h%	Iso	RC/G
2015	NCAA	UCLA	254	55	82	7	34	323	407	476	883	12	85	0.95	7	8	28	154	6.64
2015	A-	West Virginia	177	34	54	0	17	305	391	379	770	12	84	0.89	9	4	19	73	5.40
2015	A-	West Virginia	50	9	12	0	3	240	309	320	629	9	84	0.63	3	0	25	80	3.53
2016	A+	Bradenton	444	56	123	4	57	277	348	378	726	10	86	0.76	3	9	28	101	4.70

Polished hitter with a line-drive, gap-to-gap approach. Good strike zone judgement and contact ability. Played SS in college, but has settled in at 2B in the pros with good hands and an average arm.

Krause, Kevin — 29 — Pittsburgh
EXP MLB DEBUT: 2019 **H/W:** 6-2 200 **FUT:** Reserve OF **6C**

Bats R Age 24 2014 (9) Stony Brook

Pwr	+++
BAvg	+++
Spd	+++
Def	++

Year	Lev	Team	AB	R	H	HR	RBI	Avg	OB	Slg	OPS	bb%	ct%	Eye	SB	CS	x/h%	Iso	RC/G
2013	NCAA	Stony Brook	71	4	15	0	6	211	317	268	585	13	75	0.61	0	0	27	56	2.93
2014	NCAA	Stony Brook	198	46	70	8	51	354	429	551	979	12	86	0.93	8	3	33	197	7.66
2014	A-	Jamestown	134	22	37	7	32	276	353	560	913	11	79	0.57	6	2	54	284	6.96
2015		did not play (injury)																	
2016	A-	West Virginia	176	34	48	3	20	273	393	369	763	17	85	1.35	10	4	21	97	5.48

Missed all of 2015 with TJS, but was back in action in 2016. Mature approach at the plate with average power, good plate discipline, and the ability to make contact. Saw limited action behind the dish, splitting time at DH and RF. Not likely to stick behind at catcher as he moves up.

Krieger, Tyler — 6 — Cleveland
EXP MLB DEBUT: 2018 **H/W:** 6-2 170 **FUT:** Starting 2B **7C**

Bats B Age 23 2015 (4) Clemson

Pwr	+
BAvg	+++
Spd	+++
Def	+++

Year	Lev	Team	AB	R	H	HR	RBI	Avg	OB	Slg	OPS	bb%	ct%	Eye	SB	CS	x/h%	Iso	RC/G
2016	A	Lake County	262	51	82	3	35	313	381	427	809	10	75	0.44	15	8	24	115	5.77
2016	A+	Lynchburg	220	33	62	2	23	282	363	405	767	11	76	0.54	6	7	31	123	5.30

Athletic middle INF who excelled at two levels in pro debut. Quick, fluid stroke from both sides produces gap-to-gap doubles power and solid contact; perhaps more to come as he fills out. Selective approach and willing to walk. Average runner, though likely not a real SB threat down the road. Solid arm and defensive actions profile him best at 2B.

Lara, Garvis — 56 — Miami
EXP MLB DEBUT: 2021 **H/W:** 6-1 170 **FUT:** Starting SS **7D**

Bats B Age 20 2013 FA (DR)

Pwr	++
BAvg	++
Spd	++++
Def	+++

Year	Lev	Team	AB	R	H	HR	RBI	Avg	OB	Slg	OPS	bb%	ct%	Eye	SB	CS	x/h%	Iso	RC/G
2015	Rk	GCL Marlins	192	27	54	0	16	281	340	349	689	8	79	0.41	13	2	15	68	4.10
2016	A-	Batavia	31	2	2	0	1	65	147	65	212	9	65	0.27	0	0	0	0	-3.14

Fast-twitch athlete from the D.R. looked overmatched. Remains raw, but shows plus tools. Has good bat speed and makes consistent contact, especially from the LH side. Has the size and bat speed to develop average power. Moves well on defense with good range, soft hands, and a strong arm.

Lara, Gilbert — 56 — Milwaukee
EXP MLB DEBUT: 2020 **H/W:** 6-2 190 **FUT:** Starting 3B **8E**

Bats R Age 19 2014 FA (DR)

Pwr	+++
BAvg	++
Spd	+++
Def	+++

Year	Lev	Team	AB	R	H	HR	RBI	Avg	OB	Slg	OPS	bb%	ct%	Eye	SB	CS	x/h%	Iso	RC/G
2015	Rk	Azl Brewers	202	29	50	1	25	248	280	332	611	4	80	0.22	3	3	20	84	2.91
2015	Rk	Helena	44	2	9	0	5	205	286	273	558	10	73	0.42	0	0	33	68	2.43
2016	Rk	Helena	228	30	57	2	28	250	288	320	608	5	74	0.20	1	1	21	70	2.78

Tall, lean Dominican INF has yet to convert tools into production as pro. Pairs plus bat speed with leverage for intriguing HR potential, but swing can elongate and his approach remains very unrefined. Average runner with limited SB ability. Signed as SS, but strong arm and projectable build profile best at 3B as he adds bulk to his wiry frame.

Laureano, Ramon — 789 — Houston
EXP MLB DEBUT: 2017 **H/W:** 5-11 185 **FUT:** Starting OF **7C**

Bats R Age 22 2014 (16) NE Oklahoma A&M

Pwr	+++
BAvg	+++
Spd	+++
Def	+++

Year	Lev	Team	AB	R	H	HR	RBI	Avg	OB	Slg	OPS	bb%	ct%	Eye	SB	CS	x/h%	Iso	RC/G
2014	Rk	Greeneville	53	8	10	1	2	189	283	245	529	12	70	0.44	4	0	10	57	1.78
2015	A	Quad Cities	287	43	76	4	34	265	315	415	730	7	71	0.25	18	3	36	150	4.67
2016	A+	Lancaster	293	69	93	10	60	317	417	519	936	15	71	0.58	33	11	37	201	7.86
2016	AA	Corpus Christi	124	20	40	5	13	323	417	548	965	14	73	0.61	10	3	40	226	8.06

Consistent OF who had breakout year by using simple approach and pure hitting ways. Understands balls and strikes and has level swing path for contact. Hit for average power, though more content with line drives to gaps. Can play all OF spots and owns speed to track down balls. Solid all-around player.

LaValley, Gavin — 35 — Cincinnati
EXP MLB DEBUT: 2018 **H/W:** 6-3 235 **FUT:** Reserve 1B **6C**

Bats R Age 22 2014 (4) HS (OK)

Pwr	++++
BAvg	++
Spd	+
Def	++

Year	Lev	Team	AB	R	H	HR	RBI	Avg	OB	Slg	OPS	bb%	ct%	Eye	SB	CS	x/h%	Iso	RC/G
2014	Rk	AZL Reds	189	29	54	5	30	286	372	439	811	12	77	0.59	3	0	31	153	5.80
2014	Rk	Billings	21	2	4	1	2	190	190	333	524	0	52	0.00	0	0	25	143	1.71
2015	A	Dayton	469	52	125	4	53	267	337	358	695	10	76	0.44	4	1	27	92	4.22
2016	A	Dayton	19	2	4	0	0	211	318	263	581	14	63	0.43	0	0	25	53	2.81
2016	A+	Daytona	338	50	93	11	61	275	332	470	803	8	79	0.40	0	0	45	195	5.45

Big-bodied, slow footed 1B cut down swing and added power for a nice '16 campaign. Still, swing is long and will struggle catching up to MLB velocity. Potential of 15-20 HR in swing, even if contact deficiencies regulate to platoon role. Not much of a fielder. Foot speed and defensive instincts relegates to 1B only.

LeBlanc, Charles — 56 — Texas
EXP MLB DEBUT: 2019 **H/W:** 6-3 195 **FUT:** Starting 3B **7C**

Bats R Age 20 2016 (4) Pittsburgh

Pwr	++
BAvg	+++
Spd	++
Def	+++

Year	Lev	Team	AB	R	H	HR	RBI	Avg	OB	Slg	OPS	bb%	ct%	Eye	SB	CS	x/h%	Iso	RC/G
2016	NCAA	Pittsburgh	195	45	79	2	46	405	484	513	997	13	85	1.03	7	1	18	108	8.15
2016	A-	Spokane	228	36	65	1	15	285	371	386	757	12	76	0.57	1	3	26	101	5.21

Tall, rangy INF with stellar pro debut and has chance to be solid hitter. Has very disciplined eye at plate and looks for pitches to drive. Can cover plate, though swing can get long and exploited. Power potential only average. Mostly saw time at SS and can play 3B with strong arm. Likely fits best at 3B long-term.

Lee, Khalil — 89 — Kansas City
EXP MLB DEBUT: 2021 **H/W:** 5-10 170 **FUT:** Starting OF **8D**

Bats L Age 18 2016 (3) HS (VA)

Pwr	+++
BAvg	+++
Spd	++++
Def	++

Year	Lev	Team	AB	R	H	HR	RBI	Avg	OB	Slg	OPS	bb%	ct%	Eye	SB	CS	x/h%	Iso	RC/G
2016	Rk	Azl Royals	182	43	49	6	29	269	381	484	865	15	69	0.58	8	4	43	214	6.99

Plus athlete who surpassed expectations upon signing. Has strength and speed to profile to all-around performer. Impressive bat speed and surprising pop for short stature. Hits hard line drives to gaps and has plus speed for SB and range in OF. Needs work with routes and reads, but owns strong arm for RF.

Leon,Julian

2 | **Los Angeles (N)** | EXP MLB DEBUT: 2018 | H/W: 5-11 200 | FUT: Reserve C | **6C**

Bats R Age 21	Year	Lev	Team	AB	R	H	HR	RBI	Avg	OB	Slg	OPS	bb%	ct%	Eye	SB	CS	x/h%	Iso	RC/G
2012 FA (MX)																				
Pwr +++	2013	Rk	Azl Dodgers	81	12	20	3	19	247	307	420	727	8	74	0.33	0	1	35	173	4.43
BAvg ++	2014	Rk	Ogden	223	39	74	12	57	332	413	565	978	12	76	0.58	1	1	36	233	7.89
Spd +	2015	A	Great Lakes	309	30	62	5	26	201	254	298	552	7	65	0.21	0	1	32	97	2.06
Def ++	2016	A+	Rancho Cuca	220	28	49	8	27	223	266	386	652	6	60	0.15	0	1	41	164	3.68

Stocky backstop continued to struggle at the plate, hitting just .223 with little power in the CAL. Has plus raw power, but swing is long with average bat speed and an overly aggressive approach. Solid behind the dish with a strong arm, but needs to improve his footwork and blocking skills. Heading in the wrong direction.

Lewis,Kyle

8 | **Seattle** | EXP MLB DEBUT: 2018 | H/W: 6-4 210 | FUT: Starting OF | **9D**

Bats R Age 21	Year	Lev	Team	AB	R	H	HR	RBI	Avg	OB	Slg	OPS	bb%	ct%	Eye	SB	CS	x/h%	Iso	RC/G
2016 (1) Mercer																				
Pwr ++++																				
BAvg ++++																				
Spd +++	2016	NCAA	Mercer	223	70	88	20	72	395	533	731	1264	23	78	1.38	6	5	38	336	12.05
Def +++	2016	A-	Everett	117	26	35	3	26	299	383	530	913	12	81	0.73	3	0	46	231	7.16

Talented OF who will start season late after knee surgery in July. Has multitude of tools, led by plus power and arm. Has chance to hit for double-plus pop and could realize sooner than expected. Brings very patient approach to plate and has plus bat speed to hit for BA. Runs fairly well and may eventually move to RF. Owns very strong arm.

Leyba,Domingo

46 | **Arizona** | EXP MLB DEBUT: 2018 | H/W: 5-11 160 | FUT: Starting 2B | **8D**

Bats B Age 21	Year	Lev	Team	AB	R	H	HR	RBI	Avg	OB	Slg	OPS	bb%	ct%	Eye	SB	CS	x/h%	Iso	RC/G
2012 FA (DR)	2014	A-	Connecticut	144	20	38	1	17	264	303	375	678	5	88	0.47	1	2	34	111	3.95
Pwr ++	2014	A	West Michigan	116	20	46	1	7	397	426	483	909	5	89	0.46	1	2	17	86	6.41
BAvg +++	2015	A+	Visalia	514	60	122	2	43	237	274	309	583	5	82	0.29	10	6	23	72	2.65
Spd +++	2016	A+	Visalia	340	48	100	6	40	294	350	426	776	8	82	0.47	5	1	32	132	5.12
Def +++	2016	AA	Mobile	156	21	47	4	20	301	370	436	806	10	86	0.77	4	2	26	135	5.55

Aggressive SS who made it to Double-A as 20-year-old. Tremendous hand/eye coordination allows for lots of contact. Made strides barreling pitches and taking breaking pitches out of zone. Has gap power and can turn on FB inside, especially as LHH, but 10 HR season largely fluke. Gets by at SS with above average range, arm suited for 2B.

Liberato,Luis

789 | **Seattle** | EXP MLB DEBUT: 2019 | H/W: 6-1 175 | FUT: Starting OF | **8E**

Bats L Age 21	Year	Lev	Team	AB	R	H	HR	RBI	Avg	OB	Slg	OPS	bb%	ct%	Eye	SB	CS	x/h%	Iso	RC/G
2012 FA (DR)	2014	Rk	Azl Mariners	175	28	37	2	14	211	324	314	638	14	73	0.62	14	2	30	103	3.63
Pwr ++	2015	A-	Everett	181	34	47	5	31	260	346	453	799	12	74	0.51	10	3	43	193	5.73
BAvg ++	2015	A	Clinton	30	3	4	0	0	133	188	233	421	6	67	0.20	1	0	50	100	0.31
Spd +++	2015	AA	Jackson	10	0	0	0	0	0	0	0	0	0	80	0.00	0	0		0	-4.74
Def +++	2016	A	Clinton	372	65	96	2	29	258	341	368	710	11	73	0.47	4	2	30	110	4.57

Toolsy, fast OF who showed positive talent in first full season. With a pure stroke and ideal bat speed, he should grow into more power with added strength and loft. Works counts and has more speed than SB output indicates. Had inconsistent season and needs time to iron out wrinkles. Plays each OF spot with strong arm.

Lien,Connor

89 | **Atlanta** | EXP MLB DEBUT: 2018 | H/W: 6-3 225 | FUT: Starting CF | **7D**

Bats R Age 23	Year	Lev	Team	AB	R	H	HR	RBI	Avg	OB	Slg	OPS	bb%	ct%	Eye	SB	CS	x/h%	Iso	RC/G
2012 (12) HS (FL)	2012	Rk	GCL Braves	149	30	34	0	11	228	315	282	597	11	67	0.39	15	3	18	54	2.97
Pwr +++	2013	Rk	Danville	212	32	48	6	27	226	274	401	675	6	67	0.20	10	3	44	175	3.89
BAvg ++	2014	A	Rome	309	41	85	5	36	275	321	398	719	6	73	0.25	16	4	29	123	4.39
Spd ++++	2015	A+	Carolina	453	72	129	9	47	285	333	415	748	7	72	0.26	34	12	28	130	4.81
Def ++++	2016	AA	Mississippi	223	29	52	6	17	233	305	408	713	9	62	0.27	12	6	38	175	4.81

Athletic CF battled injuries and poor bat-to-ball skills. Developed more pronounced hitch in load, elongating swing as the season wore on. Can't handle average or better velocity without cheating, though tapped into more power, possible 13-20 HR potential at projection. Plays a plus CF due to instincts and run tool. Steals bases despite poor technique.

Lindsay,Desmond

8 | **New York (N)** | EXP MLB DEBUT: 2020 | H/W: 6-0 200 | FUT: Starting OF | **9D**

Bats R Age 20	Year	Lev	Team	AB	R	H	HR	RBI	Avg	OB	Slg	OPS	bb%	ct%	Eye	SB	CS	x/h%	Iso	RC/G
2015 (2) HS (FL)																				
Pwr +++	2015	Rk	GCL Mets	69	10	21	1	6	304	400	464	864	14	70	0.52	3	2	33	159	6.97
BAvg ++++	2015	A-	Brooklyn	45	3	9	0	7	200	308	267	574	13	58	0.37	0	1	33	67	2.83
Spd ++++	2016	Rk	GCL Mets	10	3	4	0	0	400	600	500	1100	33	50	1.00	0	0	25	100	14.55
Def +++	2016	A-	Brooklyn	111	18	33	4	17	297	405	450	855	15	77	0.77	3	1	27	153	6.46

Stocky OF with good athleticism and advanced approach. Quick wrists and strong hands lend itself to plus bat speed. His line drive approach is a bit detrimental to power output, as he gets lots of topspin off bat. But a plus runner on base paths, and covers ground in CF.

Long,Shedric

45 | **Cincinnati** | EXP MLB DEBUT: 2018 | H/W: 5-8 180 | FUT: Starting 2B | **7C**

Bats L Age 21	Year	Lev	Team	AB	R	H	HR	RBI	Avg	OB	Slg	OPS	bb%	ct%	Eye	SB	CS	x/h%	Iso	RC/G
2013 (12) HS (AL)	2013	Rk	AZL Reds	78	9	20	1	8	256	326	321	646	9	78	0.47	1	1	15	64	3.49
Pwr +++	2014	Rk	Billings	87	6	15	0	6	172	217	207	424	5	79	0.28	2	1	20	34	0.62
BAvg ++	2015	A	Dayton	152	22	43	6	16	283	359	474	833	11	80	0.58	2	3	35	191	5.89
Spd ++++	2016	A	Dayton	335	47	94	11	45	281	364	457	821	12	75	0.52	16	3	38	176	5.92
Def ++	2016	A+	Daytona	143	22	46	4	30	322	366	503	870	7	76	0.29	5	1	30	182	6.31

A short, stocky converted catcher, plus bat speed contributed to his breakout. Lots of swing-and-miss due to lack of balance in swing, but he makes loud contact when he connects with ball. Uses leverage in swing to drive ball out of park despite small stature. Best attribute is run tool. Still learning to use plus-plus speed on base paths.

Longhi,Nick

39 | **Boston** | EXP MLB DEBUT: 2018 | H/W: 6-2 205 | FUT: Starting OF | **8E**

Bats R Age 21	Year	Lev	Team	AB	R	H	HR	RBI	Avg	OB	Slg	OPS	bb%	ct%	Eye	SB	CS	x/h%	Iso	RC/G
2013 (30) HS (FL)																				
Pwr ++	2013	Rk	GCL Red Sox	45	4	8	1	4	178	229	356	585	6	73	0.25	1	0	75	178	2.63
BAvg ++++	2014	A-	Lowell	109	19	36	0	10	330	392	440	832	9	80	0.50	0	3	31	110	6.03
Spd ++	2015	A	Greenville	442	52	124	7	62	281	332	403	735	7	80	0.39	2	0	30	122	4.57
Def +	2016	A+	Salem	471	56	133	2	77	282	351	393	744	10	77	0.47	2	3	34	110	4.92

Natural-hitting prospect who finished 2nd in SAL in doubles. Makes loud contact with level swing path, but won't hit many HR without change in approach. Bat speed and strength suitable for pop, but lacks loft and leverage. Walk rate increased and makes good contact. Secondary skills below average—speed and defense need work. Arm is very strong.

Lopez,Nicky

6 | **Kansas City** | EXP MLB DEBUT: 2019 | H/W: 5-11 175 | FUT: Starting SS | **7D**

Bats L Age 22	Year	Lev	Team	AB	R	H	HR	RBI	Avg	OB	Slg	OPS	bb%	ct%	Eye	SB	CS	x/h%	Iso	RC/G
2016 (5) Creighton																				
Pwr +																				
BAvg +++																				
Spd +++	2016	NCAA	Creighton	196	35	60	2	22	306	387	444	831	12	93	2.00	11	2	30	138	6.21
Def +++	2016	Rk	Burlington	231	54	65	6	29	281	376	429	805	13	87	1.17	24	4	26	147	5.78

Athletic INF who may not have standout tool, but has value in variety of areas. Plays solid defense at SS with ample range and first step quickness. Should stick at position as hands and feet work well. Brings patient approach to plate. Knows strike zone and has above average speed for SB. Not much power nor projection.

Lora,Edwin

6 | **Washington** | EXP MLB DEBUT: 2020 | H/W: 6-1 150 | FUT: Reserve SS | **6C**

Bats R Age 21	Year	Lev	Team	AB	R	H	HR	RBI	Avg	OB	Slg	OPS	bb%	ct%	Eye	SB	CS	x/h%	Iso	RC/G
2012 FA (DR)																				
Pwr +	2013	Rk	DSL Nationals	185	29	38	2	13	205	276	281	557	9	76	0.41	6	4	26	76	2.32
BAvg ++	2014	Rk	GCL Nationals	181	27	53	0	15	293	333	337	670	6	80	0.30	13	6	15	44	3.68
Spd +++	2015	A-	Auburn	116	19	30	2	17	259	295	414	709	5	72	0.18	7	0	40	155	4.26
Def ++++	2016	A	Hagerstown	386	56	89	4	42	231	286	370	657	7	71	0.27	23	4	46	140	3.70

A plus defender at SS with speed, quickness and hands to stay at the position. Unfortunately, the hit tool lags far behind; lot of swing and miss and he doesn't engage his lower half of his skinny frame. Does have some SB potential, but lack of contact and OBP at the lower levels doesn't bode well for actualization at higher levels.

Lowe,Brandon

4 | **Tampa Bay** | EXP MLB DEBUT: 2019 | H/W: 6-0 185 | FUT: Starting 2B | **7D**

Bats L Age 22	Year	Lev	Team	AB	R	H	HR	RBI	Avg	OB	Slg	OPS	bb%	ct%	Eye	SB	CS	x/h%	Iso	RC/G
2015 (3) Maryland																				
Pwr ++																				
BAvg +++																				
Spd +++																				
Def ++	2016	A	Bowling Green	379	67	94	5	42	248	351	343	694	14	80	0.78	6	3	24	95	4.39

Fundamentally-sound INF who doesn't stand out with any tool, but gets job done. Swings quick bat and recognizes pitches well to profile to BA. Needs to stand in better against LHP, but knows limitations and swing path conducive to line drives. Draws walks with solid patience. Not above average with glove, but makes plays with instincts.

Lowe,Joshua

5 | Tampa Bay | EXP MLB DEBUT: 2021 | H/W: 6-4 190 | FUT: Starting 3B | 9D

Bats L Age 19
2016 (1) HS (GA)
Pwr ++++
BAvg +++
Spd +++
Def ++

Year	Lev	Team	AB	R	H	HR	RBI	Avg	OB	Slg	OPS	bb%	ct%	Eye	SB	CS	x/h%	Iso	RC/G
2016	Rk	Princeton	80	11	19	3	11	238	371	400	771	18	60	0.53	1	1	26	163	5.91
2016	Rk	GCL Devil Rays	93	14	24	2	15	258	389	409	798	18	71	0.74	1	1	38	151	6.04

Lean, strong INF with as much raw power as any 2016 draftee. Struggles to put bat to ball at times, but has swing path and bat speed to improve. Shows nimble feet and athleticism at 3B and owns plus arm strength. Needs to shorten swing against LHP and keep consistent stroke to hit for BA. Runs well for size.

Lugo,Dawel

56 | Arizona | EXP MLB DEBUT: 2018 | H/W: 6-0 190 | FUT: Starting 3B | 7D

Bats R Age 22
2011 FA (DR)
Pwr +++
BAvg ++
Spd ++
Def +++

Year	Lev	Team	AB	R	H	HR	RBI	Avg	OB	Slg	OPS	bb%	ct%	Eye	SB	CS	x/h%	Iso	RC/G
2015	A	Kane County	81	12	27	0	3	333	365	370	735	5	84	0.31	2	2	7	37	4.41
2015	A	Lansing	122	15	41	2	23	336	362	451	813	4	80	0.21	3	1	22	115	5.29
2015	A+	Dunedin	260	16	57	2	21	219	245	292	538	3	81	0.18	1	3	23	73	1.96
2016	A+	Visalia	315	61	99	13	42	314	345	514	860	5	87	0.37	2	1	32	200	5.78
2016	AA	Mobile	173	24	53	4	20	306	322	451	773	2	91	0.27	1	1	28	145	4.75

Stocky RHH tapped into raw BP power to slug 17 HR in '16. Power surge did not hurt bat-to-ball skill, but plate approach is raw for age/level. Will put swing on anything close to zone. A below-average defender at SS, a move to 3B has helped highlight plus arm. Below average runner with base clogging potential at maturity.

Luplow,Jordan

7 | Pittsburgh | EXP MLB DEBUT: 2018 | H/W: 6-1 195 | FUT: Starting OF | 7D

Bats R Age 23
2014 (3) Fresno State
Pwr +++
BAvg ++
Spd ++
Def ++

Year	Lev	Team	AB	R	H	HR	RBI	Avg	OB	Slg	OPS	bb%	ct%	Eye	SB	CS	x/h%	Iso	RC/G
2013	NCAA	Fresno State	151	23	42	3	21	278	335	437	772	8	79	0.42	6	1	36	159	5.11
2014	NCAA	Fresno State	215	40	81	9	48	377	466	609	1075	14	90	1.64	10	4	38	233	8.96
2014	A-	Jamestown	220	31	61	6	30	277	356	423	779	11	80	0.61	10	6	31	145	5.27
2015	A	West Virginia	390	74	103	12	67	264	361	464	825	13	83	0.88	11	2	50	200	6.02
2016	A+	Bradenton	354	63	90	10	54	254	362	421	783	14	78	0.77	6	2	40	167	5.55

Moved from 3B to LF in 2016. Patient approach at the plate with a good understanding of the strike zone. Swing is geared towards hard line-drives with good bat speed and did stroke 23 2B and 10 HR, but needs to be more selective when ahead in counts. Below average speed and shoulder injuries result in average arm in LF.

Lux,Gavin

6 | Los Angeles (N) | EXP MLB DEBUT: 2021 | H/W: 6-2 190 | FUT: Starting SS | 8C

Bats L Age 19
2016 (1) HS (WI)
Pwr ++
BAvg +++
Spd +++
Def ++++

Year	Lev	Team	AB	R	H	HR	RBI	Avg	OB	Slg	OPS	bb%	ct%	Eye	SB	CS	x/h%	Iso	RC/G
2016	Rk	Azl Dodgers	192	34	53	0	18	276	359	380	740	12	78	0.58	1	0	28	104	5.00
2016	Rk	Ogden	31	7	12	0	3	387	441	484	925	9	74	0.38	1	0	25	97	7.36

Has plus raw tools. Lux has good bat speed and should add muscle to his large frame and projects to have average to above power. Had some swing-and-miss issues against better competition, but has smooth LH stroke. Moves well at SS with good hands and a plus arm and should be able to stick at the position.

Machado,Dixon

6 | Detroit | EXP MLB DEBUT: 2015 | H/W: 6-1 170 | FUT: Utility player | 6A

Bats R Age 25
2008 FA (VZ)
Pwr ++
BAvg ++
Spd +++
Def ++++

Year	Lev	Team	AB	R	H	HR	RBI	Avg	OB	Slg	OPS	bb%	ct%	Eye	SB	CS	x/h%	Iso	RC/G
2014	AA	Erie	292	45	89	5	32	305	389	442	830	12	88	1.11	8	5	33	137	6.07
2015	AAA	Toledo	509	61	133	4	48	261	310	332	642	7	83	0.42	15	3	20	71	3.43
2015	MLB	Detroit	68	6	16	0	5	235	307	279	586	9	79	0.50	1	0	19	44	2.84
2016	AAA	Toledo	492	59	131	4	48	266	344	356	699	11	85	0.77	17	5	26	89	4.41
2016	MLB	Detroit	10	1	1	0	0	100	308	100	408	23	60	0.75	0	0	0	0	-0.23

Quick, rangy INF who continues to improve with bat. Makes good contact with level stroke and enhanced selectivity for OBP. Owns below average pop, but enough strength to line to gaps. Recognizes pitches and controls bat. Ranges very well to both sides and has terrific arm. Hands and feet work well in tandem and knows positioning.

Machado,Jonathan

8 | St. Louis | EXP MLB DEBUT: 2022 | H/W: 5-9 155 | FUT: Starting CF | 7D

Bats L Age 18
2016 FA (CU)
Pwr +
BAvg ++
Spd ++++
Def +++

Year	Lev	Team	AB	R	H	HR	RBI	Avg	OB	Slg	OPS	bb%	ct%	Eye	SB	CS	x/h%	Iso	RC/G
2017		Did not play in the US																	

Short, slender Cuban OF was signed for $2.35 million. LHH has an aggressive approach at the plate, which raises concerns about his ability to hit for BA. Small frame results in below-average power, but is a plus runner who should be able to stick in CF. Very much a work in progress and has yet to make his U.S. debut.

Maitan,Kevin

56 | Atlanta | EXP MLB DEBUT: 2021 | H/W: 6-2 190 | FUT: Starting 3B | 9D

Bats B Age 17
2016 FA (VZ)
Pwr ++++
BAvg ++++
Spd ++
Def ++++

Year	Lev	Team	AB	R	H	HR	RBI	Avg	OB	Slg	OPS	bb%	ct%	Eye	SB	CS	x/h%	Iso	RC/G
2016		Did not play in the US																	

Switch hitter was top international signing in '16 and has yet to make pro debut. Scouts drop Chipper Jones comps talking about young hitter. Has plus hit and power tool from both sides of the plate. Currently a SS, profiles best at 3B long term.

Mancini,Trey

3 | Baltimore | EXP MLB DEBUT: 2016 | H/W: 6-4 215 | FUT: Starting 1B | 8C

Bats R Age 25
2013 (8) Notre Dame
Pwr +++
BAvg ++++
Spd +
Def ++

Year	Lev	Team	AB	R	H	HR	RBI	Avg	OB	Slg	OPS	bb%	ct%	Eye	SB	CS	x/h%	Iso	RC/G
2015	A+	Frederick	207	28	65	8	32	314	343	527	869	4	83	0.26	4	2	38	213	5.93
2015	AA	Bowie	326	60	117	13	57	359	399	586	985	6	82	0.38	2	1	38	227	7.49
2016	AA	Bowie	63	18	19	7	14	302	397	698	1096	14	73	0.59	0	0	58	397	9.44
2016	AAA	Norfolk	483	60	135	13	54	280	345	427	771	9	75	0.39	2	2	30	147	5.12
2016	MLB	Baltimore	14	3	5	3	5	357	357	1071	1429	0	71	0.00	0	0	80	714	12.97

Tall, strong 1B who reached majors with continued offensive onslaught. Has hit 20+ HR last two seasons and now profiles as starter. Walk rate increased and started to use entire field. Will swing and miss when selling out for power, but controls bat. Limited athleticism hinders defense, but makes routine plays with good hands.

Margot,Manuel

8 | San Diego | EXP MLB DEBUT: 2016 | H/W: 5-11 180 | FUT: Starting CF | 9C

Bats R Age 22
2011 FA (DR)
Pwr +++
BAvg ++++
Spd ++++
Def ++++

Year	Lev	Team	AB	R	H	HR	RBI	Avg	OB	Slg	OPS	bb%	ct%	Eye	SB	CS	x/h%	Iso	RC/G
2014	A+	Salem	50	4	17	2	14	340	365	560	925	4	90	0.40	3	2	41	220	6.49
2015	A+	Salem	181	35	51	3	17	282	323	420	743	6	92	0.73	20	5	27	138	4.74
2015	AA	Portland	258	38	70	3	33	271	326	419	745	8	86	0.58	19	8	40	147	4.84
2016	AAA	El Paso	517	98	157	6	55	304	349	426	775	7	88	0.56	30	11	25	122	5.08
2016	MLB	San Diego	37	4	9	0	3	243	243	405	649	0	81	0.00	2	0	56	162	3.35

Quick OF with tremendous hit tool. Doesn't strike out much despite aggressive approach. Tends to chase pitches out of the zone and may struggle with walk rates. Formerly wiry, has put on lean muscle without compromising run tool. Plus defender.

Marlette,Tyler

2 | Seattle | EXP MLB DEBUT: 2018 | H/W: 5-11 195 | FUT: Starting C | 7D

Bats R Age 24
2011 (5) HS (FL)
Pwr +++
BAvg +++
Spd ++
Def +

Year	Lev	Team	AB	R	H	HR	RBI	Avg	OB	Slg	OPS	bb%	ct%	Eye	SB	CS	x/h%	Iso	RC/G
2014	AA	Jackson	32	3	8	2	2	250	333	500	833	11	69	0.40	0	1	50	250	6.09
2015	A+	Bakersfield	148	17	32	5	20	216	275	365	640	8	76	0.34	2	1	34	149	3.25
2015	AA	Jackson	178	15	46	3	12	258	298	393	691	5	83	0.32	0	0	37	135	3.96
2016	A+	Bakersfield	326	42	89	14	53	273	334	472	807	8	75	0.37	5	3	40	199	5.50
2016	AA	Jackson	50	4	15	1	6	300	340	400	740	6	78	0.27	1	0	20	100	4.46

Short, efficient backstop who spent 3rd year shuffling between A+ and AA. Got off to slow start, but finished hot. Offers good pop from simple stroke and is best against LHP. Can hit for BA thanks to quick bat. Doesn't draw many walks, though. Defense needs lots of work. May have to move off C, which limits value.

Marmolejos,Jose

3 | Washington | EXP MLB DEBUT: 2018 | H/W: 6-1 185 | FUT: Reserve 1B | 6B

Bats L Age 24
2011 FA (DR)
Pwr +++
BAvg +++
Spd ++
Def ++

Year	Lev	Team	AB	R	H	HR	RBI	Avg	OB	Slg	OPS	bb%	ct%	Eye	SB	CS	x/h%	Iso	RC/G
2013	Rk	GCL Nationals	141	27	44	2	21	312	374	433	807	9	81	0.52	1	1	30	121	5.58
2014	A-	Auburn	234	30	62	1	31	265	344	385	728	11	79	0.56	0	1	37	120	4.79
2015	A	Hagerstown	468	63	145	11	87	310	358	485	843	7	81	0.39	3	1	38	175	5.90
2016	A+	Potomac	378	72	108	11	59	286	382	495	877	14	78	0.70	2	3	48	209	6.78
2016	AA	Harrisburg	127	15	38	2	15	299	326	417	743	4	77	0.17	0	0	29	118	4.48

Unheralded prospect has just kept hitting; two-time Nats Minor League Player of the Year. A doubles machine the past two seasons, his lack of over-the-fence pop likely limits his chances of starting at the MLB level. But with a decent batting eye and good approach, could find value as a platoon/bench bat. Limited defensively to 1B.

Marrero,Deven — 456 — Boston
EXP MLB DEBUT: 2015 | H/W: 6-1 195 | FUT: Utility player | 6B

Bats R Age 26 | 2012 (1) Arizona State | Pwr ++ | BAvg ++ | Spd +++ | Def ++++

Year	Lev	Team	AB	R	H	HR	RBI	Avg	OB	Slg	OPS	bb%	ct%	Eye	SB	CS	x/h%	Iso	RC/G
2014	AAA	Pawtucket	186	23	39	1	20	210	258	285	543	6	80	0.32	4	1	31	75	2.16
2015	AAA	Pawtucket	375	49	96	6	29	256	316	344	660	8	77	0.38	12	5	21	88	3.60
2015	MLB	Boston	53	8	12	1	3	226	268	283	551	5	64	0.16	2	1	8	57	1.89
2016	AAA	Pawtucket	363	30	72	1	27	198	244	242	487	6	75	0.24	10	3	18	44	1.26
2016	MLB	Boston	12	0	1	0	0	83	214	83	298	14	58	0.40	0	0	0	0	-2.16

Versatile, instinctual INF who is exceptional defender with quickness, positioning, and smooth actions. Saw time at 2B, 3B, and SS and is above average at all spots. Simply hasn't been consistent with bat. Has pop in stroke, but doesn't get to it as he struggles to make contact. Doesn't hit for BA and rarely walks. Needs to hit to play.

Marsh,Brandon — 789 — Los Angeles (A)
EXP MLB DEBUT: 2021 | H/W: 6-2 190 | FUT: Starting OF | 8E

Bats L Age 19 | 2016 (2) HS (GA) | Pwr ++ | BAvg +++ | Spd ++++ | Def +++

Year	Lev	Team	AB	R	H	HR	RBI	Avg	OB	Slg	OPS	bb%	ct%	Eye	SB	CS	x/h%	Iso	RC/G
2016		Did not play (injury)																	

Very athletic OF who didn't play upon signing due to back injury. Exhibits talent in many areas with both bat and glove. Should grow into average power as he grows into frame. Has bat speed and leveraged stroke. Owns plus speed and should be asset on base and in OF. May need to shorten swing and be more selective.

Martin,Jason — 78 — Houston
EXP MLB DEBUT: 2018 | H/W: 5-11 190 | FUT: Starting OF | 7D

Bats L Age 21 | 2013 (8) HS (CA) | Pwr +++ | BAvg ++ | Spd +++ | Def ++

Year	Lev	Team	AB	R	H	HR	RBI	Avg	OB	Slg	OPS	bb%	ct%	Eye	SB	CS	x/h%	Iso	RC/G
2013	Rk	GCL Astros	179	35	45	0	17	251	356	341	697	14	83	0.94	11	7	27	89	4.61
2014	Rk	Greeneville	164	32	45	0	21	274	367	415	782	13	82	0.80	8	6	38	140	5.66
2014	A-	Tri City	81	7	18	1	2	222	284	321	605	8	84	0.54	5	3	28	99	3.10
2015	A	Quad Cities	396	65	107	8	57	270	348	396	744	11	81	0.64	14	15	25	126	4.86
2016	A+	Lancaster	400	74	108	23	75	270	358	533	891	12	73	0.51	20	12	48	263	6.84

Sleeper prospect who produces despite limited tools. Very selective eye at plate and knows which pitches he can drive. Exhibits pure hitting technique with short, quick stroke, but subject to Ks as he struggles with breaking balls and LHP. Runs fairly well and can steal bases. Not adept with glove and needs polish.

Martin,Richie — 6 — Oakland
EXP MLB DEBUT: 2018 | H/W: 5-11 190 | FUT: Starting SS | 8C

Bats R Age 22 | 2015 (1) Florida | Pwr ++ | BAvg ++ | Spd ++++ | Def ++++

Year	Lev	Team	AB	R	H	HR	RBI	Avg	OB	Slg	OPS	bb%	ct%	Eye	SB	CS	x/h%	Iso	RC/G
2015	NCAA	Florida	265	63	77	6	36	291	373	430	804	12	87	1.00	20	8	27	140	5.68
2015	A-	Vermont	190	31	45	2	16	237	326	342	668	12	75	0.53	7	7	27	105	3.95
2016	A+	Stockton	330	46	76	3	31	230	306	312	618	10	78	0.49	12	8	25	82	3.22
2016	AA	Midland	15	1	5	0	7	333	444	533	978	17	87	1.50	2	1	40	200	8.35

Smooth, athletic SS who started late after knee surgery. Possesses quick hands and nimble footwork to be plus defender. Has strong, accurate arm. Focuses on line drives and has understanding of strike zone. Has fringy power, though could develop to average with different approach. Swing mechanics a bit choppy, but not a liability with bat in hands.

Martinez,Eddy — 9 — Chicago (N)
EXP MLB DEBUT: 2019 | H/W: 6-1 195 | FUT: Starting OF | 8D

Bats R Age 22 | 2015 FA (CU) | Pwr +++ | BAvg ++ | Spd ++++ | Def ++++

Year	Lev	Team	AB	R	H	HR	RBI	Avg	OB	Slg	OPS	bb%	ct%	Eye	SB	CS	x/h%	Iso	RC/G
2016	A	South Bend	460	72	117	10	67	254	327	380	708	10	75	0.44	8	5	31	126	4.33

Has raw power, and is a plus runner who covers ground well with a plus arm. Can be overly aggressive at the plate, resulting in plenty of swing and miss, but did draw 50 BB in 460 AB. Very much a work in progress, but is a plus athlete who could make an impact if he can make adjustments.

Martinez,Jeremy — 2 — St. Louis
EXP MLB DEBUT: 2019 | H/W: 5-11 195 | FUT: Starting C | 7C

Bats R Age 22 | 2016 (4) USC | Pwr ++ | BAvg ++++ | Spd ++ | Def ++

Year	Lev	Team	AB	R	H	HR	RBI	Avg	OB	Slg	OPS	bb%	ct%	Eye	SB	CS	x/h%	Iso	RC/G
2016	NCAA	USC	213	35	80	6	42	376	427	563	990	8	94	1.58	1	2	33	188	7.56
2016	A-	State College	194	28	63	1	32	325	420	433	853	14	92	2.00	1	1	27	108	6.60

4th round pick had a solid pro debut; hard-working grinder in college. Average tools behind the plate, but showed enough to stick for now. Good approach at the plate with an advanced understanding of the strike zone (32 BB/16 K). Should develop at least average power and the bat is his ticket to the majors.

Mateo,Jorge — 46 — New York (A)
EXP MLB DEBUT: 2018 | H/W: 6-0 190 | FUT: Starting SS | 8B

Bats R Age 21 | 2012 FA (DR) | Pwr ++ | BAvg +++ | Spd +++++ | Def ++

Year	Lev	Team	AB	R	H	HR	RBI	Avg	OB	Slg	OPS	bb%	ct%	Eye	SB	CS	x/h%	Iso	RC/G
2013	Rk	DSL Yankees	258	50	74	7	26	287	370	450	819	12	80	0.65	49	10	30	163	5.85
2014	Rk	GCL Yankees	58	14	16	0	1	276	354	397	750	11	71	0.41	11	1	38	121	5.24
2015	A	Charleston (Sc)	365	51	98	2	33	268	334	378	712	9	78	0.45	71	15	29	110	4.47
2015	A+	Tampa	84	15	27	0	7	321	374	452	826	8	79	0.39	11	2	30	131	5.92
2016	A+	Tampa	464	65	119	8	48	256	306	381	687	7	77	0.31	36	15	28	125	3.94

Athletic INF who led FSL in SB. Owns tools galore, highlighted by double-plus speed. Has nimble actions with quick hands, but needs polish. Hit career-high in HR and should evolve into average pop. Makes loud contact to all fields, but chases pitches on outer half. Split between 2B and SS and has strong arm for either spot.

Mathias,Mark — 45 — Cleveland
EXP MLB DEBUT: 2018 | H/W: 6-0 200 | FUT: Starting 2B | 7C

Bats R Age 22 | 2015 (3) Cal Poly | Pwr ++ | BAvg ++++ | Spd ++ | Def ++

Year	Lev	Team	AB	R	H	HR	RBI	Avg	OB	Slg	OPS	bb%	ct%	Eye	SB	CS	x/h%	Iso	RC/G
2015	NCAA	Cal Poly	202	42	72	1	28	356	422	436	858	10	91	1.21	9	4	15	79	6.30
2015	A-	Mahoning Valley	245	38	69	2	32	282	371	408	780	13	85	0.97	5	4	35	127	5.55
2016	A+	Lynchburg	427	70	117	5	60	274	347	405	753	10	80	0.55	9	1	38	131	5.02
2016	AA	Akron	15	1	1	0	1	67	125	133	258	6	60	0.17	0	0	100	67	-2.51

Contact-oriented 2B with plus feel for barrel and ability to get on base. Peppers gaps with high-volume doubles pop, A level bat plane through zone projects a limited HR upside. Average runner and likely not an SB source. Fringe range and hands defensively with passable arm strength to make flatfooted throws as everyday 2B regular.

Mathisen,Wyatt — 5 — Pittsburgh
EXP MLB DEBUT: 2018 | H/W: 6-0 227 | FUT: Reserve 3B | 6C

Bats R Age 23 | 2012 (2) HS (TX) | Pwr ++ | BAvg ++ | Spd ++ | Def ++

Year	Lev	Team	AB	R	H	HR	RBI	Avg	OB	Slg	OPS	bb%	ct%	Eye	SB	CS	x/h%	Iso	RC/G
2013	A-	Jamestown	26	4	7	0	3	269	387	269	656	16	73	0.71	1	0	0	0	3.93
2013	A	West Virginia	119	13	22	0	9	185	242	210	452	7	82	0.41	1	0	14	25	1.12
2014	A	West Virginia	375	48	105	3	42	280	338	360	698	8	86	0.61	6	2	21	80	4.24
2015	A+	Bradenton	403	46	106	4	34	263	334	342	677	10	82	0.60	0	1	20	79	4.00
2016	A+	Bradenton	115	13	34	1	18	296	357	409	766	9	82	0.52	0	1	32	113	5.10

Former 2nd round pick has been plagued by injuries. Was moved from behind the plate to 3B, but a sore shoulder limited him to 115 AB. Good approach when healthy and makes consistent contact. Has a good understanding of the strike zone, but power has yet to develop. Needs to show more and prove he can stay healthy.

Matias,Seuly — 89 — Kansas City
EXP MLB DEBUT: 2021 | H/W: 6-3 200 | FUT: Starting OF | 9E

Bats R Age 18 | 2015 FA (DR) | Pwr ++++ | BAvg ++ | Spd +++ | Def ++

Year	Lev	Team	AB	R	H	HR	RBI	Avg	OB	Slg	OPS	bb%	ct%	Eye	SB	CS	x/h%	Iso	RC/G
2016	Rk	Azl Royals	172	32	43	8	29	250	335	477	812	11	58	0.30	2	4	49	227	6.73

Tall, physical OF with exceptional bat speed and offensive profile. Very swing-happy approach mutes OBP, and can be guilty of pulling everything. Expands zone, but owns high ceiling with tools aplenty. Projects to plus power, though hits HR now, even as a teenager. Can play CF, but will likely move to RF as he ages.

Maxwell,Bruce — 2 — Oakland
EXP MLB DEBUT: 2016 | H/W: 6-1 235 | FUT: Starting C | 7D

Bats L Age 26 | 2012 (2) Birmingham So | Pwr +++ | BAvg ++ | Spd + | Def +++

Year	Lev	Team	AB	R	H	HR	RBI	Avg	OB	Slg	OPS	bb%	ct%	Eye	SB	CS	x/h%	Iso	RC/G
2014	A+	Stockton	289	33	79	6	35	273	364	381	744	12	80	0.71	0	1	23	107	4.92
2014	AA	Midland	85	8	12	0	2	141	223	176	400	10	62	0.28	0	1	25	35	-0.21
2015	AA	Midland	338	32	82	2	48	243	321	308	629	10	84	0.72	0	1	22	65	3.52
2016	AAA	Nashville	193	27	62	10	41	321	396	539	935	11	80	0.63	1	0	35	218	7.12
2016	MLB	Oakland	92	8	26	1	14	283	340	402	742	8	74	0.33	0	0	31	120	4.80

Stocky, sturdy backstop who set high in HR in 1st year above AA. Lacks agility and speed, but gives big target and is improving receiver. Hits RHP well and could operate in platoon if necessary. Natural power predicated on quick bat, though lacks hitting instincts for BA. Intriguing prospect who works hard and maximizes limited tools.

May,Jacob | 8 | Chicago (A)

EXP MLB DEBUT: 2017 | H/W: 5-10 180 | FUT: Starting OF | 7C

Bats B Age 25
2013 (3) Coastal Carolina
Pwr +
BAvg + + +
Spd + + + +
Def + + +

Year	Lev	Team	AB	R	H	HR	RBI	Avg	OB	Slg	OPS	bb%	ct%	Eye	SB	CS	x/h%	Iso	RC/G
2013	A	Kannapolis	206	36	59	8	28	286	338	461	799	7	79	0.37	19	5	29	175	5.25
2014	A+	Winston-Salem	415	66	107	2	27	258	326	395	721	9	83	0.59	37	8	40	137	4.67
2015	Rk	Azl White Sox	16	4	4	0	3	250	294	313	607	6	81	0.33	1	0	25	63	2.98
2015	AA	Birmingham	389	47	107	2	32	275	325	334	660	7	81	0.40	37	17	17	59	3.63
2016	AAA	Charlotte	301	38	80	1	24	266	301	352	653	5	76	0.21	19	8	28	86	3.45

Extremely fast OF who missed time with oblique injury, but advancing as solid speed/defense prospect. Mans CF with exceptional range, though very poor arm holds him back. Runs bases very well and could become decent hitter with cleaner swing. Not much power, and needs to get on base more consistently with better approach.

Mazeika,Patrick | 2 | New York (N)

EXP MLB DEBUT: 2020 | H/W: 6-3 210 | FUT: Starting C | 7E

Bats L Age 23
2015 (8) Stetson
Pwr + +
BAvg + + +
Spd +
Def + +

Year	Lev	Team	AB	R	H	HR	RBI	Avg	OB	Slg	OPS	bb%	ct%	Eye	SB	CS	x/h%	Iso	RC/G
2015	NCAA	Stetson	202	43	62	7	53	307	404	485	889	14	92	2.06	1	0	34	178	6.84
2015	Rk	Kingsport	226	44	80	5	48	354	416	540	956	10	88	0.92	1	0	40	186	7.36
2016	A	Columbia	239	34	73	3	35	305	401	402	802	14	84	0.97	2	0	23	96	5.80

LHH continued strong '15 short-season performance during exceptional Single-A debut. Patient hitter with significant barrel potential. Short, flat compact swing aides in overall approach. Swing plane not conducive to big power numbers despite size. Defense behind the dish a work in progress, though scouts impressed with inroads made in 2016.

McBroom,Ryan | 3 | Toronto

EXP MLB DEBUT: 2018 | H/W: 6-3 230 | FUT: Starting 1B | 7D

Bats R Age 24
2014 (15) West Virginia
Pwr + + +
BAvg + + +
Spd +
Def +

Year	Lev	Team	AB	R	H	HR	RBI	Avg	OB	Slg	OPS	bb%	ct%	Eye	SB	CS	x/h%	Iso	RC/G
2014	NCAA	West Virginia	211	32	72	8	49	341	403	512	915	9	83	0.63	1	1	28	171	6.77
2014	A-	Vancouver	273	37	81	11	59	297	329	502	831	5	81	0.25	1	0	42	205	5.50
2015	A	Lansing	461	72	145	12	90	315	380	482	862	10	79	0.51	5	4	36	167	6.29
2016	A+	Dunedin	468	58	128	21	83	274	323	468	791	7	76	0.30	10	4	38	194	5.15
2016	AA	New Hampshire	29	3	4	1	2	138	219	241	460	9	79	0.50	0	0	25	103	1.04

Powerful 1B who finished 3rd in FSL in HR. Continues to showcase power with plenty of loft in leveraged stroke. Ball comes off bat loudly, but is aggressive early in count. Doesn't recognize pitches and can be jammed inside from long swing. Set high in SB, though has well below average speed. Bat-only prospect as he is limited with glove.

McCarthy,Joe | 379 | Tampa Bay

EXP MLB DEBUT: 2018 | H/W: 6-3 225 | FUT: Starting OF | 8D

Bats L Age 23
2015 (5) Virginia
Pwr + +
BAvg + + +
Spd + + +
Def + + +

Year	Lev	Team	AB	R	H	HR	RBI	Avg	OB	Slg	OPS	bb%	ct%	Eye	SB	CS	x/h%	Iso	RC/G
2015	NCAA	Virginia	112	19	22	2	11	196	338	277	615	18	82	1.20	3	0	23	80	3.59
2015	A-	Hudson Valley	184	24	51	0	21	277	342	337	679	9	88	0.78	18	3	18	60	4.15
2016	A	Bowling Green	153	31	44	3	29	288	414	425	839	18	80	1.10	11	2	34	137	6.48
2016	A+	Charlotte	198	20	56	5	31	283	372	434	806	12	81	0.74	8	3	30	152	5.72

All-around player who played mostly 1B in Low-A before promotion to High-A where he also played OF. Has solid power-speed combo, though focuses more on working counts and making loud contact to gaps. Struggles with LHP and can lengthen swing. Gets by defensively with instincts, though arm and range best at 1B.

McClanahan,Chad | 5 | Milwaukee

EXP MLB DEBUT: 2021 | H/W: 6-5 200 | FUT: Starting 3B | 7D

Bats L Age 19
2016 (11) HS (AZ)
Pwr + + +
BAvg + + +
Spd + +
Def + +

Year	Lev	Team	AB	R	H	HR	RBI	Avg	OB	Slg	OPS	bb%	ct%	Eye	SB	CS	x/h%	Iso	RC/G
2016	Rk	Azl Brewers	144	22	30	3	14	208	265	333	598	7	69	0.24	1	2	37	125	2.74

Tall, lean 3B who has far to go, but has tools for solid impact. Flashes above-average raw power via smooth, leveraged stroke; barrel can get long and will need to refine his approach. Good athlete, though not a base stealer. Raw defensive actions at 3B with strong arm for hot corner; could end up at 1B as he fills out.

McGuire,Reese | 2 | Toronto

EXP MLB DEBUT: 2017 | H/W: 5-11 215 | FUT: Starting C | 7B

Bats L Age 22
2013 (1) HS (WA)
Pwr + +
BAvg + + +
Spd + +
Def + + + +

Year	Lev	Team	AB	R	H	HR	RBI	Avg	OB	Slg	OPS	bb%	ct%	Eye	SB	CS	x/h%	Iso	RC/G
2013	A-	Jamestown	16	3	4	0	0	250	294	250	544	6	94	1.00	1	0	0	0	2.62
2014	A	West Virginia	389	46	102	3	45	262	305	334	639	6	89	0.55	7	2	18	72	3.50
2015	A+	Bradenton	374	32	95	0	34	254	303	294	597	7	90	0.67	14	7	16	40	3.11
2016	AA	Altoona	266	29	69	1	37	259	332	346	678	10	90	1.12	4	4	28	86	4.30
2016	AA	New Hampshire	53	5	12	0	5	226	317	264	581	12	85	0.88	2	2	17	38	3.07

Mobile, agile C who makes consistent contact with picturesque swing. Approach and lack of leverage in swing hinder power development, and has struggled with LHP. Defense ahead of offense at present. Calls good games and is plus receiver. Hands and feet work well with strong arm that neutralizes running game. Just needs to hit.

McKinney,Billy | 79 | New York (A)

EXP MLB DEBUT: 2017 | H/W: 6-1 205 | FUT: Starting OF | 7C

Bats L Age 22
2013 (1) HS (TX)
Pwr + +
BAvg + + +
Spd + +
Def + + +

Year	Lev	Team	AB	R	H	HR	RBI	Avg	OB	Slg	OPS	bb%	ct%	Eye	SB	CS	x/h%	Iso	RC/G
2014	A+	Daytona	176	30	53	1	36	301	388	432	820	12	76	0.60	1	0	32	131	6.11
2015	A+	Myrtle Beach	103	19	35	4	25	340	433	544	977	14	87	1.31	0	2	31	204	7.83
2015	AA	Tennessee	274	29	78	3	39	285	349	420	769	9	83	0.57	0	0	38	135	5.17
2016	AA	Tennessee	298	37	75	1	31	252	354	322	676	14	77	0.69	2	4	21	70	4.18
2016	AA	Trenton	128	15	30	3	13	234	300	375	675	9	77	0.41	2	2	37	141	3.85

Natural-hitting OF who is now in third org and brings plus BA potential to table. Has hand-eye coordination and knowledge of strike zone to get on base. Swings quick bat, but level path hinders power production. Inconsistent approach results in vulnerability to breaking balls, and he lacks power and speed. Can play all OF spots with fringy arm.

McMahon,Ryan | 35 | Colorado

EXP MLB DEBUT: 2017 | H/W: 6-2 185 | FUT: Starting 1B | 9D

Bats L Age 22
2013 (2) HS (CA)
Pwr + + + +
BAvg + +
Spd + +
Def + +

Year	Lev	Team	AB	R	H	HR	RBI	Avg	OB	Slg	OPS	bb%	ct%	Eye	SB	CS	x/h%	Iso	RC/G
2013	Rk	Grand Junction	218	42	70	11	52	321	398	583	981	11	73	0.47	4	6	46	261	8.13
2014	A	Asheville	482	93	136	18	102	282	354	502	857	10	70	0.38	8	5	49	220	6.52
2015	A+	Modesto	496	85	149	18	75	300	363	520	883	9	69	0.32	6	13	45	220	6.94
2016	AA	Hartford	466	49	113	12	75	242	322	399	722	11	65	0.34	11	6	39	157	4.78

Strong, athletic 3B took a step back. McMahon has good bat speed and plus raw power with a good understanding of the strike zone, but has significant contact issues. Split time between 3B and 1B where he has soft hands, good range, and a strong arm. Still has impressive tools, but future is less clear.

Meadows,Austin | 8 | Pittsburgh

EXP MLB DEBUT: 2017 | H/W: 6-3 200 | FUT: Starting OF | 9C

Bats L Age 21
2013 (1) HS (GA)
Pwr + + + +
BAvg + + + +
Spd + + +
Def + +

Year	Lev	Team	AB	R	H	HR	RBI	Avg	OB	Slg	OPS	bb%	ct%	Eye	SB	CS	x/h%	Iso	RC/G
2015	A+	Bradenton	508	72	156	7	54	307	359	407	766	7	84	0.52	20	7	21	100	4.96
2015	AA	Altoona	25	5	9	0	1	360	407	680	1087	7	80	0.40	1	0	56	320	9.46
2016	A-	West Virginia	15	0	3	0	0	200	294	333	627	12	93	2.00	0	0	67	133	4.08
2016	AA	Altoona	167	33	52	6	23	311	372	611	982	9	81	0.50	9	3	58	299	7.84
2016	AAA	Indianapolis	126	16	27	6	24	214	298	460	758	11	73	0.44	8	2	59	246	5.03

Athletic OF has compact stroke and ball jumps off bat. Was limited by a hamstring injury and then missed the AFL with a strained oblique. Plus runner who covers ground well in CF, but a below-average arm could result in a shift to LF. Shows good patience at plate and makes consistent contact. Has tools to be impact player.

Mejia,Francisco | 2 | Cleveland

EXP MLB DEBUT: 2018 | H/W: 5-10 175 | FUT: Starting C | 8B

Bats B Age 21
2012 FA (DR)
Pwr + +
BAvg + + + +
4.30 Spd + + +
Def + + +

Year	Lev	Team	AB	R	H	HR	RBI	Avg	OB	Slg	OPS	bb%	ct%	Eye	SB	CS	x/h%	Iso	RC/G
2013	Rk	AZL Indians	105	16	32	4	24	305	336	524	860	5	83	0.28	3	1	44	219	5.88
2014	A-	Mahoning Valley	248	32	70	2	36	282	331	407	738	7	81	0.38	2	4	33	125	4.67
2015	A	Lake County	391	45	95	9	53	243	310	345	655	9	80	0.49	4	1	23	102	3.58
2016	A	Lake County	239	41	83	7	51	347	386	531	917	6	84	0.38	1	0	33	184	6.64
2016	A+	Lynchburg	168	22	56	4	29	333	381	488	869	7	86	0.54	1	2	30	155	6.15

Young catcher had first breakout, posting 50-game hit streak with elite OPS in Low/High-A. Plus contact/BA via short load and level plane through zone, though can get aggressive. Not a big HR/SB threat, but shoots the gaps often for doubles and has good underway speed. Plus arm behind dish, though blocking/framing remain raw.

Mejia,Gabriel | 8 | Cleveland

EXP MLB DEBUT: 2019 | H/W: 5-11 160 | FUT: Starting CF | 8E

Bats B Age 21
2013 FA (DR)
Pwr +
BAvg + + + +
3.88 Spd + + + + +
Def + + +

Year	Lev	Team	AB	R	H	HR	RBI	Avg	OB	Slg	OPS	bb%	ct%	Eye	SB	CS	x/h%	Iso	RC/G
2015	Rk	AZL Indians	168	41	60	0	18	357	429	417	845	11	88	1.05	34	10	15	60	6.21
2015	A-	Mahoning Valley	56	9	17	0	4	304	316	321	637	2	86	0.13	6	1	6	18	3.08
2016	A-	Mahoning Valley	264	55	85	0	16	322	378	375	753	8	81	0.47	28	9	13	53	4.89

Lean, premium athlete with chance for impact BA/SB. High-contact spray hitter who puts ball in play from both sides; works counts. Quick to full speed and elite underway running ability; profiles atop MLB order. HR pop not a factor to his game, but should leg out a high volume of doubles. Has range and closing speed to stick in CF.

Mercado,Oscar | 468 | St. Louis | EXP MLB DEBUT: 2019 | H/W: 6-2 175 | FUT: Utility player | 6C

Bats R Age 22		Year	Lev	Team	AB	R	H	HR	RBI	Avg	OB	Slg	OPS	bb%	ct%	Eye	SB	CS	x/h%	Iso	RC/G
2013 (2) HS (FL)																					
Pwr	+	2013	Rk	GCL Cardinals	163	18	34	1	14	209	283	307	590	9	76	0.44	12	4	29	98	2.87
BAvg	++	2014	Rk	Johnson City	245	41	55	3	25	224	283	306	589	8	85	0.54	26	7	24	82	2.89
Spd	++++	2015	A	Peoria	472	70	120	4	44	254	289	341	630	5	87	0.38	50	19	25	87	3.29
Def	++++	2016	A+	Palm Beach	442	50	95	0	27	215	286	271	558	9	84	0.62	33	20	25	57	2.64

Slick-fielding SS with plus speed looks like a bust. Has a good line-drive approach and makes decent contact, but has failed to hit as a pro and now owns a career slash line of .230/.297/.307. Solid defender with good instincts and good range, but struggles with accuracy on his throws. UT player at best.

Mercedes,Miguel | 3 | Oakland | EXP MLB DEBUT: 2019 | H/W: 6-4 255 | FUT: Starting 1B | 8E

Bats R Age 21		Year	Lev	Team	AB	R	H	HR	RBI	Avg	OB	Slg	OPS	bb%	ct%	Eye	SB	CS	x/h%	Iso	RC/G
2013 FA (DR)																					
Pwr	+++	2013	Rk	DSL Athletics	213	29	36	0	10	169	269	230	499	12	66	0.40	5	5	31	61	1.50
BAvg	++	2014	Rk	Azl Athletics	113	9	25	1	12	221	290	283	574	9	62	0.26	0	0	20	62	2.51
Spd	++	2015	Rk	Azl Athletics	167	15	36	2	28	216	288	347	635	9	58	0.24	1	2	44	132	3.83
Def	++	2016	A-	Vermont	248	32	64	12	43	258	321	448	769	8	70	0.31	0	0	34	190	5.03

Strong-framed prospect who has yet to play above short-season ball, but carries plus power potential. May struggle to hit for BA due to inability to make contact and fringy plate coverage. Doesn't run well and was moved to 1B due to lack of agility at 3B. Future relies on bat and he has the power and bat speed to realize potential.

Mercedes,Yermin | 2 | Baltimore | EXP MLB DEBUT: 2018 | H/W: 5-11 175 | FUT: Starting C | 7E

Bats R Age 24		Year	Lev	Team	AB	R	H	HR	RBI	Avg	OB	Slg	OPS	bb%	ct%	Eye	SB	CS	x/h%	Iso	RC/G
2011 FA (DR)																					
Pwr	+++																				
BAvg	+++	2015	A	Delmarva	239	33	65	8	42	272	304	456	760	4	83	0.27	1	0	40	184	4.67
Spd	+	2016	A	Delmarva	340	58	120	14	60	353	412	579	991	9	81	0.54	1	1	37	226	7.77
Def	+	2016	A+	Frederick	107	20	34	6	17	318	376	542	918	9	82	0.53	0	0	35	224	6.68

Offense-first backstop who led SAL in BA and OBP. Hit all year long and showed surprising pop for limited strength and size. Pure hitting technique allows all-field usage and destroys LHP. Struggles with glove, particularly with throwing. Not much agility or quickness behind plate. Good story as he was found in indy ball in 2014.

Michalczewski,Trey | 5 | Chicago (A) | EXP MLB DEBUT: 2018 | H/W: 6-3 210 | FUT: Starting 3B | 8D

Bats B Age 22		Year	Lev	Team	AB	R	H	HR	RBI	Avg	OB	Slg	OPS	bb%	ct%	Eye	SB	CS	x/h%	Iso	RC/G
2013 (7) HS (OK)		2013	Rk	Bristol	195	25	46	3	21	236	317	328	645	11	71	0.41	2	0	22	92	3.51
Pwr	+++	2014	A	Kannapolis	432	57	118	10	70	273	342	433	775	9	68	0.32	6	3	36	160	5.47
BAvg	+++	2014	A+	Winston-Salem	72	5	14	0	5	194	284	222	506	11	71	0.43	1	0	14	28	1.61
Spd	++	2015	A+	Winston-Salem	474	59	123	7	75	259	330	395	725	10	76	0.44	4	3	37	135	4.62
Def	+++	2016	AA	Birmingham	487	62	110	11	59	226	306	363	669	10	69	0.37	4	0	36	138	3.89

Projectable INF who set high in HR, though finished 2nd in SL in K. Still young for level and has room to grow. Leaps in pitch recognition should lead to better contact and has above average pull pop. Swings with more authority from left and uses hands well. Despite athleticism, lacks foot speed.

Mieses,Johan | 789 | Los Angeles (N) | EXP MLB DEBUT: 2020 | H/W: 6-2 185 | FUT: Starting OF | 8E

Bats R Age 21		Year	Lev	Team	AB	R	H	HR	RBI	Avg	OB	Slg	OPS	bb%	ct%	Eye	SB	CS	x/h%	Iso	RC/G
2013 FA (DR)																					
Pwr	++++																				
BAvg	+	2015	A	Great Lakes	166	16	46	5	20	277	322	440	762	6	81	0.35	7	4	35	163	4.79
Spd	+++	2015	A+	Rancho Cuca	196	35	48	6	19	245	292	439	731	6	71	0.23	3	1	52	194	4.58
Def	+++	2016	A+	Rancho Cuca	461	72	114	28	78	247	302	510	812	7	68	0.24	3	7	54	262	5.71

Tall, athletic OF showed impressive pop, leadling the CAL in HR. Athletic, instinctual player with plus raw power and good bat speed, but can be overly aggressive and poor pitch recognition results in poor contact (147 K). Good speed for his size with a plus arm that profiles best in RF.

Miller,Anderson | 789 | Kansas City | EXP MLB DEBUT: 2019 | H/W: 6-3 205 | FUT: Starting OF | 7D

Bats L Age 22		Year	Lev	Team	AB	R	H	HR	RBI	Avg	OB	Slg	OPS	bb%	ct%	Eye	SB	CS	x/h%	Iso	RC/G
2015 (3) Western Kentucky		2015	NCAA	Western Kentucky	193	47	57	12	35	295	419	560	978	18	77	0.93	5	4	42	264	8.12
Pwr	+++	2015	Rk	Burlington	38	6	13	2	7	342	342	579	921	0	82	0.00	3	0	38	237	6.20
BAvg	++	2015	A	Lexington	169	15	44	2	21	260	317	355	672	8	83	0.50	0	1	25	95	3.86
Spd	+++	2016	A	Lexington	155	24	44	3	18	284	373	432	805	12	67	0.43	3	1	36	148	6.09
Def	+++	2016	A+	Wilmington	144	18	29	3	16	201	263	361	624	8	65	0.24	5	0	48	160	3.27

Athletic, strong OF who was good in A-, but slumped upon promotion to A+. Gets on base and showcases raw power. Doesn't get to power, though, as his long swing can be exploited by good pitching. Lot of swing and miss; needs to shorten stroke at times. Runs well underway and is a sound defender with range and plus arm.

Miller,Jalen | 4 | San Francisco | EXP MLB DEBUT: 2019 | H/W: 5-11 175 | FUT: Starting 2B | 7D

Bats R Age 20		Year	Lev	Team	AB	R	H	HR	RBI	Avg	OB	Slg	OPS	bb%	ct%	Eye	SB	CS	x/h%	Iso	RC/G
2015 (3) HS (GA)																					
Pwr	++																				
BAvg	++																				
Spd	+++	2015	Rk	Azl Giants	174	28	38	0	13	218	288	259	547	9	76	0.40	11	2	16	40	2.22
Def	+++	2016	A	Augusta	457	65	102	5	44	223	265	322	587	5	77	0.24	11	5	29	98	2.59

Nimble, athletic INF with positive tools and plenty of projection. Pitch selection needs work and can struggle with breaking balls. Uses simple swing to make contact and can use speed to beat out grounders. Can overswing at times in attempt for power and needs to understand limitations. Sound 2B with quick hands and sufficient range.

Minier,Amaurys | 3 | Minnesota | EXP MLB DEBUT: 2020 | H/W: 6-2 190 | FUT: Starting 1B | 8E

Bats B Age 21		Year	Lev	Team	AB	R	H	HR	RBI	Avg	OB	Slg	OPS	bb%	ct%	Eye	SB	CS	x/h%	Iso	RC/G
2012 FA (DR)		2013	Rk	GCL Twins	112	10	24	6	17	214	254	455	710	5	74	0.21	1	1	54	241	4.05
Pwr	++++	2014	Rk	GCL Twins	171	25	50	8	33	292	395	520	915	15	70	0.56	2	2	42	228	7.53
BAvg	++	2015	Rk	Elizabethton	175	19	34	2	21	194	269	280	549	9	62	0.27	0	1	32	86	2.15
Spd	+	2015	Rk	GCL Twins	6	1	2	0	0	333	333	333	667	0	67	0.00	0	0	0	0	3.37
Def	+	2016	Rk	Elizabethton	167	20	37	10	32	222	319	449	768	13	63	0.39	0	0	49	228	5.43

Tall, powerful hitter with plus raw power from both sides of plate. Doesn't make enough contact for power to play up, though can drive ball a long way when makes contact. Not much talent other than power. Spent 4 years in rookie/short-season ball and only .233 career hitter. Poor foot speed, hands, and footwork limit him to 1B long-term.

Miranda,Jose | 56 | Minnesota | EXP MLB DEBUT: 2021 | H/W: 6-2 180 | FUT: Starting 3B | 7C

Bats R Age 18		Year	Lev	Team	AB	R	H	HR	RBI	Avg	OB	Slg	OPS	bb%	ct%	Eye	SB	CS	x/h%	Iso	RC/G
2016 (S-2) HS (PR)																					
Pwr	++																				
BAvg	++																				
Spd	+++																				
Def	+++	2016	Rk	GCL Twins	185	14	42	1	20	227	299	292	591	9	81	0.53	4	5	21	65	2.92

Lean, quick INF who split time between SS and 3B. More of speed/defense prospect at present, but offense upside is solid. Makes easy contact with balanced approach and projects to at least average pop when fully grown. Flashes excellent glove with fast, soft hands and arm strength. Footwork still a bit crude, but has chance to be above average.

Molina,Leonardo | 789 | New York (A) | EXP MLB DEBUT: 2020 | H/W: 6-2 180 | FUT: Starting OF | 8E

Bats R Age 19		Year	Lev	Team	AB	R	H	HR	RBI	Avg	OB	Slg	OPS	bb%	ct%	Eye	SB	CS	x/h%	Iso	RC/G
2013 FA (DR)																					
Pwr	+++																				
BAvg	++	2015	Rk	GCL Yankees	162	15	40	2	17	247	291	364	655	6	77	0.27	6	5	33	117	3.51
Spd	+++	2016	Rk	Pulaski	175	23	43	7	23	246	320	440	760	10	74	0.42	4	3	42	194	4.97
Def	++	2016	A	Charleston (Sc)	126	12	25	2	13	198	246	302	548	6	73	0.24	0	2	32	103	2.02

Young, projectable OF with high upside. Started in Low-A, but demoted in June. Ended year on fire and could develop into 20 HR/20 SB producer. Has loads of power potential due to natural strength and has speed to be factor. Very raw approach and expands strike zone. Has tools to be standout defender, but instincts are raw.

Moncada,Yoan | 45 | Chicago (A) | EXP MLB DEBUT: 2016 | H/W: 6-2 205 | FUT: Starting 3B | 9A

Bats B Age 21		Year	Lev	Team	AB	R	H	HR	RBI	Avg	OB	Slg	OPS	bb%	ct%	Eye	SB	CS	x/h%	Iso	RC/G
2015 FA (CU)																					
Pwr	+++	2015	A	Greenville	306	61	85	8	38	278	365	438	803	12	73	0.51	49	3	35	160	5.78
BAvg	++++	2016	A+	Salem	228	57	70	4	34	307	421	496	917	16	74	0.75	36	8	46	189	7.69
Spd	+++++	2016	AA	Portland	177	37	49	11	28	277	373	531	904	13	64	0.42	9	4	41	254	7.57
Def	++	2016	MLB	Boston	19	3	4	0	1	211	250	263	513	5	37	0.08	0	0	25	53	4.00

Explosive athlete who reached BOS after dynamic production. Moved to 3B in August and may profile better there. Owns plus-plus speed and plus power potential. Swings aggressively, but willing to draw walks. Exceptional bat speed and makes hard contact to all fields. Needs polish with pitch recognition and defense.

Moniak,Mickey — 789 — Philadelphia
EXP MLB DEBUT: 2020 | H/W: 6-2 185 | FUT: Starting CF | 8C

Bats L Age 18 — 2016 (1) HS (CA)
Pwr ++ | BAvg ++++ | Spd ++++ | Def ++++

Year	Lev	Team	AB	R	H	HR	RBI	Avg	OB	Slg	OPS	bb%	ct%	Eye	SB	CS	x/h%	Iso	RC/G
2016	Rk	GCL Phillies	176	27	50	1	28	284	326	409	735	6	80	0.31	10	4	32	125	4.60

Sweet-swinging lefty was drafted #1 overall and is touted as the Phillies' CF of the future. Exceptional bat-to-ball ability, with a plus run tool and outstanding defender. Lean frame at present, but hopes are that with added strength/growth, additional power would emerge. Potential top-of-the-order hitter.

Montgomery,Troy — 789 — Los Angeles (A)
EXP MLB DEBUT: 2019 | H/W: 5-10 185 | FUT: Starting OF | 7C

Bats L Age 22 — 2016 (8) Ohio State
Pwr +++ | BAvg ++ | Spd ++++ | Def +++

Year	Lev	Team	AB	R	H	HR	RBI	Avg	OB	Slg	OPS	bb%	ct%	Eye	SB	CS	x/h%	Iso	RC/G
2016	NCAA	Ohio State	236	51	70	8	34	297	420	466	886	17	83	1.22	21	7	33	169	6.96
2016	Rk	Orem	88	16	30	4	17	341	437	557	994	15	77	0.75	10	4	30	216	8.25
2016	A	Burlington	142	15	37	3	13	261	335	401	737	10	79	0.53	3	2	32	141	4.75

Short, speedy OF with impressive tools across board. Plays solid defense in CF and owns strong arm suitable for corner spot. Plus speed accentuates quick jumps and reads. Takes vicious cuts at ball and long swing will result in Ks. Approach needs to be cleaned up. Possesses average power, though doesn't hit to opposite field often.

Morales,Jonathan — 2 — Atlanta
EXP MLB DEBUT: 2019 | H/W: 5-11 180 | FUT: Starting C | 6C

Bats R Age 22 — 2015 (25) Miami-Dade JC
Pwr ++ | BAvg +++ | Spd ++ | Def +++

Year	Lev	Team	AB	R	H	HR	RBI	Avg	OB	Slg	OPS	bb%	ct%	Eye	SB	CS	x/h%	Iso	RC/G
2015	Rk	GCL Braves	135	24	41	7	22	304	369	511	880	9	90	1.00	2	2	34	207	6.28
2016	A	Rome	424	49	114	4	55	269	310	356	666	6	87	0.45	3	4	25	87	3.74

Old-for-level C (though new to the position) with solid bat-to-ball skills. Approach improved as the season wore on. Stocky frame has power in it—though when he sold out for power in May and June, struggled as result. Solid defender, with above-average pop times.

Moran,Colin — 5 — Houston
EXP MLB DEBUT: 2016 | H/W: 6-4 205 | FUT: Starting 3B | 7B

Bats L Age 24 — 2013 (1) North Carolina
Pwr ++ | BAvg ++++ | Spd + | Def ++

Year	Lev	Team	AB	R	H	HR	RBI	Avg	OB	Slg	OPS	bb%	ct%	Eye	SB	CS	x/h%	Iso	RC/G
2014	A+	Jupiter	361	34	106	5	33	294	344	393	738	7	85	0.53	1	2	25	100	4.62
2014	AA	Corpus Christi	112	12	34	2	22	304	355	411	766	7	79	0.39	0	1	24	107	4.93
2015	AA	Corpus Christi	366	47	112	9	67	306	379	459	838	11	78	0.54	1	0	32	153	6.05
2016	AAA	Fresno	459	50	119	10	69	259	328	368	696	9	73	0.38	3	2	24	109	4.13
2016	MLB	Houston	23	1	3	0	2	130	167	174	341	4	65	0.13	0	0	33	43	-1.10

Tall, natural-hitting 3B who set high in HR, though doesn't have much sock in balanced swing and approach. Should hit for a high BA as he uses whole field and can hang in against LHP. Has keen understanding of strike zone and owns ideal plate coverage. Very slow foot speed and lacks quickness with hands/feet. Strong arm is asset at 3B.

Morgan,Gareth — 789 — Seattle
EXP MLB DEBUT: 2020 | H/W: 6-4 220 | FUT: Starting OF | 8E

Bats R Age 20 — 2014 (S-2) HS (ON)
Pwr +++ | BAvg + | Spd ++ | Def ++

Year	Lev	Team	AB	R	H	HR	RBI	Avg	OB	Slg	OPS	bb%	ct%	Eye	SB	CS	x/h%	Iso	RC/G
2014	Rk	Azl Mariners	155	15	23	2	12	148	228	252	480	9	53	0.22	4	1	48	103	1.20
2015	Rk	Azl Mariners	222	31	50	5	30	225	265	383	648	5	60	0.13	5	1	42	158	3.78
2016	Rk	Azl Mariners	125	17	27	1	11	216	263	344	607	6	54	0.14	5	1	37	128	3.67
2016	A+	Bakersfield	13	3	5	0	4	385	385	615	1000	0	46	0.00	0	0	60	231	13.26

Huge-framed OF who spent 2nd year in rookie ball and continues to rack up Ks due to lack of feel for bat. Can overswing and lunge at breaking balls, but hits ball a long way when contact made. Bat speed among the best in org, but useless without better approach. Doesn't run well and will likely end up in RF as arm is strong.

Morgan,Josh — 456 — Texas
EXP MLB DEBUT: 2018 | H/W: 5-11 185 | FUT: Starting 2B | 8D

Bats R Age 21 — 2014 (3) HS (CA)
Pwr ++ | BAvg ++++ | Spd +++ | Def +++

Year	Lev	Team	AB	R	H	HR	RBI	Avg	OB	Slg	OPS	bb%	ct%	Eye	SB	CS	x/h%	Iso	RC/G
2014	Rk	Azl Rangers	113	26	38	0	10	336	432	372	803	14	88	1.46	2	2	8	35	5.95
2014	A-	Spokane	89	11	27	0	9	303	374	315	688	10	89	1.00	1	1	4	11	4.30
2015	A	Hickory	351	59	101	3	36	288	369	362	731	11	85	0.85	9	4	19	74	4.81
2016	A+	High Desert	470	74	141	7	64	300	360	394	754	9	87	0.72	4	2	20	94	4.90

Smart INF with keen plate discipline and advanced bat for age. Makes easy, plus contact with balanced swing. Power starting to emerge, but focuses more on bat control and putting ball in play. More of average runner, but can pick his spots to steal. Shrewd, steady defender with good hands, though range may lead him to 2B full-time.

Moroff,Max — 456 — Pittsburgh
EXP MLB DEBUT: 2016 | H/W: 5-10 185 | FUT: Utility player | 6B

Bats B Age 23 — 2012 (16) HS (FL)
Pwr ++ | BAvg ++ | Spd ++ | Def +++

Year	Lev	Team	AB	R	H	HR	RBI	Avg	OB	Slg	OPS	bb%	ct%	Eye	SB	CS	x/h%	Iso	RC/G
2013	A	West Virginia	429	75	100	8	48	233	334	345	679	13	76	0.64	8	8	29	112	4.11
2014	A+	Bradenton	467	57	114	1	50	244	322	340	663	10	72	0.42	21	15	32	96	3.90
2015	AA	Altoona	523	79	153	7	51	293	376	409	785	12	79	0.63	17	13	27	117	5.49
2016	AAA	Indianapolis	421	61	97	8	45	230	366	349	715	18	69	0.70	9	7	31	119	4.81
2016	MLB	Pittsburgh	2	0	0	0	0	0	0	0	0	0	0	0.00	0	0		0	

Athletic 2B failed to duplicate his breakout of '15. Good understanding of the strike zone results in plus walk rate, but can be too selective and contact skills are problematic. Needs to put more balls in play. Has moderate power, but can get in trouble when he searches for more. Is at his best when he hits the ball in the gaps.

Mountcastle,Ryan — 6 — Baltimore
EXP MLB DEBUT: 2019 | H/W: 6-3 195 | FUT: Starting 3B | 8D

Bats R Age 20 — 2015 (1) HS (FL)
Pwr +++ | BAvg +++ | Spd ++ | Def ++

Year	Lev	Team	AB	R	H	HR	RBI	Avg	OB	Slg	OPS	bb%	ct%	Eye	SB	CS	x/h%	Iso	RC/G
2015	Rk	GCL Orioles	163	21	51	3	14	313	349	411	760	5	78	0.25	10	4	20	98	4.70
2015	A-	Aberdeen	33	2	7	1	5	212	212	303	515	0	70	0.00	0	1	14	91	1.13
2016	A	Delmarva	455	53	128	10	51	281	319	426	745	5	79	0.26	5	4	33	145	4.57

Tall, athletic INF who was consistent producer in first full season as pro. Exhibits nice bat speed and shortens swing to make good contact. Aggressive, free-swinging ways could be issue at higher levels, but smashes LHP and has power profile. May not stick at SS due to size and arm, but hands and range good for 2B or 3B.

Moyer,Hutton — 456 — Los Angeles (A)
EXP MLB DEBUT: 2018 | H/W: 6-1 185 | FUT: Utility player | 7E

Bats B Age 23 — 2015 (7) Pepperdine
Pwr +++ | BAvg ++ | Spd ++ | Def ++

Year	Lev	Team	AB	R	H	HR	RBI	Avg	OB	Slg	OPS	bb%	ct%	Eye	SB	CS	x/h%	Iso	RC/G
2015	NCAA	Pepperdine	220	52	65	14	45	295	382	564	946	12	74	0.53	15	8	42	268	7.54
2015	Rk	Orem	137	27	33	4	29	241	288	438	726	6	76	0.27	4	2	45	197	4.44
2016	A	Burlington	96	15	30	3	13	313	353	510	863	6	79	0.30	2	1	40	198	6.09
2016	A+	Inland Empire	389	60	104	14	59	267	318	455	773	7	68	0.24	11	3	40	188	5.23

Promising INF who reached A+ in May and ended year strong. Showed surprising pop and hit loads of doubles. Uses both gaps effectively and can turn on pitches for pop. Swings aggressively and rarely draws walks. Long swing can be exploited. Steals bases more on savvy than speed. Plays all over infield, though not a standout at any spot.

Mundell,Brian — 3 — Colorado
EXP MLB DEBUT: 2019 | H/W: 6-3 230 | FUT: Starting 1B | 7C

Bats R Age 23 — 2015 (7) Cal Poly
Pwr ++++ | BAvg +++ | Spd + | Def +

Year	Lev	Team	AB	R	H	HR	RBI	Avg	OB	Slg	OPS	bb%	ct%	Eye	SB	CS	x/h%	Iso	RC/G
2015	NCAA	Cal Poly	170	24	48	5	34	282	378	447	825	13	84	0.96	0	2	35	165	5.99
2015	A-	Boise	244	35	67	4	36	275	359	410	769	12	82	0.71	7	1	36	135	5.27
2016	A	Asheville	537	94	168	14	83	313	378	503	881	9	85	0.67	7	8	43	190	6.48

Tall, strong-bodied 1B has plus raw power and stroked a minor league record 59 doubles in his full-season debut. Makes consistent contact with good bat speed and strike zone awareness so should be able to hit for average and power. Below-average runner and defender limits him to 1B, but his bat gives him a chance.

Munoz,Yairo — 456 — Oakland
EXP MLB DEBUT: 2018 | H/W: 6-1 165 | FUT: Starting SS | 7B

Bats R Age 22 — 2012 FA (DR)
Pwr +++ | BAvg ++ | Spd +++ | Def ++

Year	Lev	Team	AB	R	H	HR	RBI	Avg	OB	Slg	OPS	bb%	ct%	Eye	SB	CS	x/h%	Iso	RC/G
2014	A-	Vermont	252	29	75	5	20	298	317	448	765	3	83	0.17	14	6	33	151	4.67
2015	A	Beloit	369	48	87	9	48	236	279	363	642	6	83	0.35	10	2	30	127	3.33
2015	A+	Stockton	150	21	48	4	26	320	366	480	846	7	87	0.55	1	1	33	160	5.84
2016	AA	Midland	387	44	93	9	39	240	283	367	650	6	80	0.30	6	7	30	127	3.38

Versatile INF who began year late due to heel/foot issues. Can play variety of INF positions with soft hands and very strong arm. Has tendency to be careless with glove. Hits for power to all fields and smashes LHP. Swings hard at everything and can get himself out with poor plate coverage. Runs well and could be power/speed guy.

Murphy,Alex | 23 | Baltimore | EXP MLB DEBUT: 2019 | H/W: 5-11 210 | FUT: Starting C | 7C

Bats R Age 22
2013 (6) HS (MD)
Pwr + + +
BAvg + +
Spd +
Def + +

Year	Lev	Team	AB	R	H	HR	RBI	Avg	OB	Slg	OPS	bb%	ct%	Eye	SB	CS	x/h%	Iso	RC/G
2014	A	Delmarva	15	0	3	0	1	200	200	267	467	0	60	0.00	0	0	33	67	0.78
2015	Rk	GCL Orioles	8	0	0	0	0	0	111	0	111	11	88	1.00	0	0		0	-2.31
2015	A-	Aberdeen	55	8	16	2	8	291	371	527	898	11	82	0.70	0	0	56	236	6.83
2015	A	Delmarva	120	17	31	2	28	258	321	408	729	8	74	0.35	0	0	39	150	4.65
2016	A	Delmarva	456	54	115	16	63	252	325	423	748	10	70	0.36	0	0	39	171	4.91

Short, strong hitter who had career year while staying healthy. Split time between 1B and C and showed surprising pop. Owns bat speed and all-fields ability, but lacks swing mechanics to hit for BA. Power faded after June, though should add durability as he ages. Receiving and blocking are average, but throwing mechanics a bit suspect.

Murphy,Sean | 2 | Oakland | EXP MLB DEBUT: 2019 | H/W: 6-3 215 | FUT: Starting C | 7C

Bats R Age 22
2016 (3) Wright State
Pwr + + +
BAvg +
Spd + +
Def + + +

Year	Lev	Team	AB	R	H	HR	RBI	Avg	OB	Slg	OPS	bb%	ct%	Eye	SB	CS	x/h%	Iso	RC/G
2016	NCAA	Wright State	136	38	39	6	34	287	398	507	905	16	87	1.39	6	0	36	221	7.05
2016	Rk	Azl Athletics	3	1	0	0	0	0	0	0	0	0	100		0	0		0	-2.66
2016	A-	Vermont	76	10	18	2	7	237	318	329	647	11	84	0.75	1	0	17	92	3.62

Tall, agile backstop with large frame and ideal strength for blocking and receiving. Has above average athleticism for catcher and already adequate with glove. Poor hitter at present as he has fringy bat speed and limited pitch recognition. Because of strength, he owns decent power potential. Could revamp swing mechanics.

Murphy,Tom | 2 | Colorado | EXP MLB DEBUT: 2015 | H/W: 6-1 220 | FUT: Starting C | 7B

Bats R Age 26
2012 (3) Buffalo
Pwr + + +
BAvg + +
Spd + +
Def + + +

Year	Lev	Team	AB	R	H	HR	RBI	Avg	OB	Slg	OPS	bb%	ct%	Eye	SB	CS	x/h%	Iso	RC/G
2015	AA	New Britain	265	36	66	13	44	249	309	468	777	8	70	0.29	5	2	47	219	5.20
2015	AAA	Albuquerque	129	19	35	7	19	271	299	535	833	4	67	0.12	0	1	51	264	6.04
2015	MLB	Colorado	35	5	9	3	9	257	333	543	876	10	71	0.40	0	0	44	286	6.37
2016	AAA	Albuquerque	303	53	99	19	59	327	361	647	1007	5	74	0.21	1	1	53	320	8.03
2016	MLB	Colorado	44	8	12	5	13	273	333	659	992	8	57	0.21	1	0	58	386	9.43

Strong backstop has developed into one of the better offensive catchers in the minors. Has a good approach at the plate that generates above average power to all fields. Good bat speed, but struggles to make consistent contact. Moves well behind the plate with a strong throwing arm.

Naylor,Josh | 3 | San Diego | EXP MLB DEBUT: 2019 | H/W: 6-0 225 | FUT: Starting 1B | 8D

Bats L Age 19
2015 (1) HS (ON)
Pwr + + +
BAvg + + + +
Spd +
Def + +

Year	Lev	Team	AB	R	H	HR	RBI	Avg	OB	Slg	OPS	bb%	ct%	Eye	SB	CS	x/h%	Iso	RC/G
2015	Rk	GCL Marlins	98	8	32	1	16	327	353	418	771	4	89	0.36	1	0	19	92	4.83
2016	A	Greensboro	342	42	92	9	54	269	313	430	743	6	82	0.35	10	3	38	161	4.58
2016	A+	Lake Elsinore	139	17	35	3	21	252	268	353	620	2	84	0.14	1	1	23	101	2.86

Slow-footed, big-bodied 1B with natural hit tool. Advanced to High-A as 19-year-old. Excellent bat-to-ball control results in lots of hard contact. Raw plus-plus power present in BP. Body will need attention as he ages. Questions about effort have plagued some of the hype.

Neuse,Sheldon | 5 | Washington | EXP MLB DEBUT: 2019 | H/W: 6-0 195 | FUT: Starting 3B | 7C

Bats R Age 22
2016 (2) Oklahoma
Pwr + + +
BAvg + +
Spd + +
Def + + +

Year	Lev	Team	AB	R	H	HR	RBI	Avg	OB	Slg	OPS	bb%	ct%	Eye	SB	CS	x/h%	Iso	RC/G
2016	NCAA	Oklahoma	198	42	73	10	48	369	473	646	1119	16	78	0.91	12	2	41	278	10.01
2016	A-	Auburn	126	16	29	1	11	230	302	341	643	9	79	0.50	2	2	31	111	3.61

Two-way player at Oklahoma with a big junior season. Plus approach in first crack at pro ball; good contact ability and willingness to take a walk. Used opposite field, but will likely need to pull the ball more to realize average power potential. Below-average speed and plus arm, defensively best suited to 3B, rather than the SS he played in college.

Nevin,Tyler | 5 | Colorado | EXP MLB DEBUT: 2020 | H/W: 6-4 200 | FUT: Starting 3B | 9D

Bats R Age 19
2015 (S-1) HS (CA)
Pwr + + +
BAvg + + + +
Spd + + +
Def + +

Year	Lev	Team	AB	R	H	HR	RBI	Avg	OB	Slg	OPS	bb%	ct%	Eye	SB	CS	x/h%	Iso	RC/G
2015	Rk	Grand Junction	189	29	50	2	18	265	362	386	749	13	78	0.69	3	7	36	122	5.14
2016	A-	Boise	1	1	1	0	0	1000	1000	2000	3000	0	100		0	0	100	1000	27.71

Hamstring injury sidelined him all season and cost a year of development. Prior to the injury, he showed good bat speed, plus raw power, and a willingness to work the count and get on base. An average runner, he will have to work hard to stick at 3B, but should be able to hit for average with moderate power.

Newman,Kevin | 6 | Pittsburgh | EXP MLB DEBUT: 2019 | H/W: 6-1 180 | FUT: Starting SS | 8C

Bats R Age 23
2015 (1) Arizona
Pwr +
BAvg + + + +
Spd + + +
Def + + +

Year	Lev	Team	AB	R	H	HR	RBI	Avg	OB	Slg	OPS	bb%	ct%	Eye	SB	CS	x/h%	Iso	RC/G
2015	NCAA	Arizona	227	53	84	2	36	370	421	489	910	8	93	1.33	22	3	26	119	6.75
2015	A	West Virginia	98	14	30	0	8	306	364	367	732	8	92	1.13	6	1	17	61	4.82
2016	A+	Bradenton	164	24	60	3	24	366	425	494	919	9	93	1.42	4	1	23	128	6.89
2016	AA	Altoona	233	41	67	2	28	288	359	378	737	10	90	1.08	6	3	22	90	4.91

Had a breakout season, hitting .320/.389/.426 between A+/AA. Plus hand-eye coordination and strike zone judgment allow him to make consistent contact. Should be able to hit for average as he moves up, but it also results in below-average power. Runs well with good range and arm and looks to be able to stick at SS.

Ngoepe,Gift | 46 | Pittsburgh | EXP MLB DEBUT: 2017 | H/W: 5-8 200 | FUT: Utility player | 6C

Bats B Age 27
2008 FA (SA)
Pwr +
BAvg + +
Spd + + +
Def + + + + +

Year	Lev	Team	AB	R	H	HR	RBI	Avg	OB	Slg	OPS	bb%	ct%	Eye	SB	CS	x/h%	Iso	RC/G
2013	AA	Altoona	220	29	39	3	16	177	270	282	552	11	63	0.34	10	3	38	105	2.24
2014	AA	Altoona	437	58	104	9	52	238	318	380	697	10	69	0.38	13	8	34	142	4.33
2015	AA	Altoona	246	31	64	3	25	260	326	362	688	9	73	0.36	3	6	27	102	4.08
2015	AAA	Indianapolis	61	5	15	0	1	246	313	311	625	9	75	0.40	1	2	27	66	3.29
2016	AAA	Indianapolis	332	40	72	8	27	217	284	355	639	9	61	0.24	5	2	40	139	3.60

Athletic infielder is one of the better defenders in the minors and his defense is major league ready. Unfortunately, he has yet to prove that he can hit and faltered again in 2016, hitting .217/.289/.355 at AAA. Struggles to make consistent contact and breaking balls give him fits. Runs well but is not a base-stealing threat.

Nicholas,Brett | 23 | Texas | EXP MLB DEBUT: 2016 | H/W: 6-2 220 | FUT: Reserve C | 6B

Bats L Age 28
2010 (6) Missouri
Pwr + + +
BAvg + +
Spd +
Def + +

Year	Lev	Team	AB	R	H	HR	RBI	Avg	OB	Slg	OPS	bb%	ct%	Eye	SB	CS	x/h%	Iso	RC/G
2013	AA	Frisco	506	71	146	21	91	289	348	474	822	8	76	0.37	2	1	34	186	5.66
2014	AAA	Round Rock	452	40	124	10	58	274	315	389	705	6	75	0.24	4	1	25	115	4.04
2015	AAA	Round Rock	403	49	108	12	63	268	314	412	726	6	80	0.34	2	2	31	144	4.32
2016	AAA	Round Rock	400	57	115	13	58	288	349	458	807	9	78	0.43	2	2	36	170	5.50
2016	MLB	Texas	40	5	11	2	4	275	341	550	891	9	78	0.44	0	0	64	275	6.64

Offensive-minded backstop who has hit double-digit HR each of last four years. Makes acceptable contact with average power. Can hit for passable BA as he recognizes pitches and knows strike zone. Spent 3rd year in AAA and is an unpolished C. Has seen action at 1B and has utility upside. Arm may not be strong enough to stick at catcher.

Nido,Tomas | 2 | New York (N) | EXP MLB DEBUT: 2018 | H/W: 6-0 205 | FUT: Starting C | 8E

Bats R Age 22
2012 (8) HS (FL)
Pwr + + +
BAvg + +
Spd +
Def + + +

Year	Lev	Team	AB	R	H	HR	RBI	Avg	OB	Slg	OPS	bb%	ct%	Eye	SB	CS	x/h%	Iso	RC/G
2012	Rk	Kingsport	124	15	30	2	15	242	309	339	648	9	81	0.52	1	0	27	97	3.56
2013	A-	Brooklyn	119	3	22	1	11	185	211	261	472	3	82	0.19	0	1	32	76	1.22
2014	A-	Brooklyn	188	20	52	1	21	277	327	335	662	7	78	0.34	2	2	15	59	3.62
2015	A	Savannah	317	39	82	6	40	259	286	372	658	4	73	0.14	1	1	27	114	3.38
2016	A+	St. Lucie	344	38	110	7	46	320	355	459	815	5	88	0.45	0	1	29	140	5.40

RHH catcher showed vast improvements on both sides of the ball. Hit tool shaky despite leading Florida State League in hitting, as he has a significant hitch in his load. Will struggle getting around higher velocity. Hangs tough against breaking pitches, reads spins well, but very impatient at the plate. Has made himself into catcher after struggling previously.

Nimmo,Brandon | 78 | New York (N) | EXP MLB DEBUT: 2016 | H/W: 6-3 205 | FUT: Starting OF | 7B

Bats L Age 24
2011 (1) HS (WY)
Pwr + + +
BAvg + + +
Spd + + +
Def + + +

Year	Lev	Team	AB	R	H	HR	RBI	Avg	OB	Slg	OPS	bb%	ct%	Eye	SB	CS	x/h%	Iso	RC/G
2015	A+	St. Lucie	16	3	2	0	2	125	300	188	488	20	81	1.33	0	0	50	63	2.15
2015	AA	Binghamton	269	26	75	2	16	279	342	368	710	9	80	0.47	0	2	23	89	4.38
2015	AAA	Las Vegas	91	19	24	3	8	264	385	418	803	17	78	0.90	5	4	29	154	5.84
2016	AAA	Las Vegas	392	72	138	11	61	352	420	541	961	11	81	0.63	7	8	32	189	7.55
2016	MLB	NY Mets	73	12	20	1	6	274	329	329	658	8	73	0.30	0	0	10	55	3.50

Inconsistent performer enjoyed '16 breakout, finishing 2nd in batting in PCL. Showed a tendency to barrel balls to all fields against RHP. Struggles picking up spin against LHP. Showed more power than expected in limited big league duty. Could hit 15-20 HRs w/ regular at-bats. Solid in the field. Likely a below-average CF.

Nottingham,Jacob
2 | **Milwaukee** | EXP MLB DEBUT: 2018 | H/W: 6-2 230 | FUT: Starting C | **7C**

Bats R Age 22
2013 (6) HS (CA)
Pwr +++
BAvg +++
4.40 Spd +
Def +

Year	Lev	Team	AB	R	H	HR	RBI	Avg	OB	Slg	OPS	bb%	ct%	Eye	SB	CS	x/h%	Iso	RC/G
2014	Rk	Greeneville	174	25	40	5	28	230	302	385	687	9	69	0.33	3	2	40	155	4.08
2015	A	Quad Cities	230	34	75	10	46	326	375	543	918	7	78	0.35	1	2	39	217	6.82
2015	A+	Lancaster	71	14	23	4	14	324	351	606	957	4	86	0.30	0	0	48	282	6.87
2015	A+	Stockton	164	25	49	3	22	299	347	409	755	7	77	0.32	1	0	24	110	4.77
2016	AA	Biloxi	415	46	97	11	37	234	284	347	631	7	67	0.21	9	2	26	113	3.13

Big, hulking C whose bat struggled in first tour of upper minors and AFL. Chance for solid-average HR production, but lack of contact and free-swinging mentality could be roadblocks. Flashes of plus arm, but inaccurate throws and raw blocking and receiving skills may necessitate a move to 1B. Still fairly young with time to learn.

Nunez,Amado
6 | **Chicago (A)** | EXP MLB DEBUT: 2021 | H/W: 6-2 178 | FUT: Starting 3B | **8D**

Bats R Age 19
2014 FA (DR)
Pwr ++
BAvg +++
Spd +++
Def +++

Year	Lev	Team	AB	R	H	HR	RBI	Avg	OB	Slg	OPS	bb%	ct%	Eye	SB	CS	x/h%	Iso	RC/G
2016	Rk	Azl White Sox	216	19	62	1	26	287	319	370	689	4	76	0.19	9	2	23	83	3.88

Lean, spry INF who showcases fluid actions and quickness at SS. Spent 2 years in rookie ball and ready for next step. Offers no plus skills, though has quick bat and power potential. Swing mechanics suitable to hit for BA and will need better two-strike approach. Has strong arm with quick release and could move to 3B if he continues to grow.

Nunez,Dom
2 | **Colorado** | EXP MLB DEBUT: 2018 | H/W: 6-0 175 | FUT: Starting C | **7C**

Bats L Age 22
2013 (6) HS, CA
Pwr +++
BAvg +++
Spd ++
Def +++

Year	Lev	Team	AB	R	H	HR	RBI	Avg	OB	Slg	OPS	bb%	ct%	Eye	SB	CS	x/h%	Iso	RC/G
2013	Rk	Grand Junction	195	24	39	3	23	200	268	323	591	8	83	0.53	11	8	44	123	2.94
2014	Rk	Grand Junction	176	30	55	8	40	313	386	517	903	11	84	0.75	5	7	36	205	6.68
2015	A	Asheville	373	61	105	13	53	282	371	448	819	12	85	0.96	7	7	34	166	5.83
2016	A+	Modesto	390	44	94	10	51	241	326	362	687	11	77	0.54	8	1	27	121	4.07

Defensive-minded C took a step back. Has a strong, accurate arm with quick release and good game calling instincts. Good approach at plate with compact stroke that is geared towards making contact and putting ball into play. Swing does generate some loft so expect moderate power with the potential for more as he matures.

Nunez,Renato
5 | **Oakland** | EXP MLB DEBUT: 2016 | H/W: 6-1 220 | FUT: Starting 3B | **8B**

Bats R Age 23
2010 FA (VZ)
Pwr ++++
BAvg +++
Spd ++
Def ++

Year	Lev	Team	AB	R	H	HR	RBI	Avg	OB	Slg	OPS	bb%	ct%	Eye	SB	CS	x/h%	Iso	RC/G
2013	A	Beloit	508	69	131	19	85	258	297	423	720	5	73	0.21	2	2	35	165	4.20
2014	A+	Stockton	509	75	142	29	96	279	324	517	841	6	78	0.30	2	0	42	238	5.69
2015	AA	Midland	381	62	106	18	61	278	328	480	808	7	83	0.42	1	0	39	202	5.29
2016	AAA	Nashville	505	61	115	23	75	228	272	412	684	6	76	0.26	2	0	39	184	3.70
2016	MLB	Oakland	15	0	2	0	1	133	133	133	267	0	80	0.00	0	0	0	0	-1.57

Power-hitting INF who has improved across the board and reached OAK in '16. Features potential double-plus power to all fields and can hit ball a long way. Will expand strike zone and not draw many walks, but is better BA hitter than stats suggest. Has clean, direct path to ball and ideal strength. Improved footwork at 3B, but has also seen action in LF.

O'Brien,Peter
37 | **Kansas City** | EXP MLB DEBUT: 2015 | H/W: 6-4 235 | FUT: Reserve OF | **6C**

Bats R Age 26
2012 (2) Miami
Pwr ++++
BAvg ++
Spd +
Def ++

Year	Lev	Team	AB	R	H	HR	RBI	Avg	OB	Slg	OPS	bb%	ct%	Eye	SB	CS	x/h%	Iso	RC/G
2014	AA	Mobile	13	1	5	1	4	385	429	615	1044	7	62	0.20	0	0	20	231	9.59
2015	AAA	Reno	490	77	139	26	107	284	326	551	877	6	75	0.25	1	3	50	267	6.34
2015	MLB	Arizona	10	1	4	1	3	400	500	800	1300	17	50	0.40	0	0	50	400	17.39
2016	AAA	Reno	406	64	103	24	75	254	294	505	799	5	64	0.16	2	0	48	251	5.71
2016	MLB	Arizona	64	6	9	5	9	141	179	391	570	4	58	0.11	0	0	67	250	2.14

Power-hitting former catcher continues to struggle with quality breaking pitches. Had a rough 28-game stint in majors; struck out in 40% of plate appearances. Power is real; could hit 20 HR even in platoon role. But as a poor runner and defender, he's relegated to 1B or LF long term.

Ockimey,Josh
3 | **Boston** | EXP MLB DEBUT: 2019 | H/W: 6-1 215 | FUT: Starting 1B | **7C**

Bats L Age 21
2014 (5) HS (PA)
Pwr ++++
BAvg ++
Spd +
Def ++

Year	Lev	Team	AB	R	H	HR	RBI	Avg	OB	Slg	OPS	bb%	ct%	Eye	SB	CS	x/h%	Iso	RC/G
2014	Rk	GCL Red Sox	112	17	21	0	10	188	278	232	510	11	67	0.38	1	0	19	45	1.63
2015	A-	Lowell	199	30	53	4	38	266	348	422	770	11	61	0.32	2	2	38	156	5.90
2016	A	Greenville	407	60	92	18	62	226	364	425	789	18	68	0.68	3	1	48	199	5.79

Big, strong 1B who got off to hot start in first full year, but struggled mightily last two months. Works counts and gets on base, but long swing and pull-happy approach hinder BA potential. Hits with plus power due to leveraged, uppercut stroke, but will strike out in bunches. Defense and foot speed are both well below average. Bat only prospect.

O'Conner,Justin
2 | **Tampa Bay** | EXP MLB DEBUT: 2017 | H/W: 6-0 190 | FUT: Starting C | **7D**

Bats R Age 25
2010 (1) HS (IN)
Pwr +++
BAvg +
Spd ++
Def ++++

Year	Lev	Team	AB	R	H	HR	RBI	Avg	OB	Slg	OPS	bb%	ct%	Eye	SB	CS	x/h%	Iso	RC/G
2014	A+	Charlotte	319	40	90	10	44	282	314	486	800	4	76	0.19	0	0	48	204	5.31
2014	AA	Montgomery	80	9	21	2	3	263	272	388	659	1	75	0.05	0	0	29	125	3.22
2015	AA	Montgomery	429	50	99	9	53	231	253	371	624	3	70	0.10	10	2	39	140	2.97
2016	Rk	GCL Devil Rays	40	8	13	2	5	325	400	525	925	11	83	0.71	0	0	31	200	6.95
2016	AA	Montgomery	25	2	4	1	3	160	160	280	440	0	64	0.00	0	0	25	120	0.01

Athletic catcher who was beset by back strain and saw limited action. Plus defender who could be asset in majors now. Has exceptional arm strength with accuracy and is solid leader of pitching staff. Problem has been offensive production. Hits for average power to all fields, but struggles to make contact and flails at pitches outside of zone.

O'Hearn,Ryan
37 | **Kansas City** | EXP MLB DEBUT: 2017 | H/W: 6-3 200 | FUT: Starting 1B | **7B**

Bats L Age 23
2014 (8) Sam Houston St
Pwr ++++
BAvg +++
Spd +
Def ++

Year	Lev	Team	AB	R	H	HR	RBI	Avg	OB	Slg	OPS	bb%	ct%	Eye	SB	CS	x/h%	Iso	RC/G
2014	Rk	Idaho Falls	249	61	90	13	54	361	448	590	1038	14	76	0.66	3	2	33	229	8.77
2015	A	Lexington	314	44	87	19	56	277	351	494	845	10	72	0.41	7	2	34	217	6.04
2015	A+	Wilmington	161	14	38	8	21	236	317	447	764	11	66	0.35	0	0	47	211	5.21
2016	A+	Wilmington	88	13	31	7	18	352	406	670	1077	8	69	0.30	0	0	45	318	9.39
2016	AA	NW Arkansas	414	49	107	15	60	258	335	437	773	10	68	0.37	3	5	39	179	5.35

Strong INF prospect who continues to hit for consistent pop and improved his ability to hit LHP. Has significant raw power and uses hands well in swing. Can be too aggressive with stick and swing tends to lengthen, which leads to strikeouts. Offers very little speed, but has gotten better with glove at 1B and LF.

Ohlman,Mike
23 | **Toronto** | EXP MLB DEBUT: 2018 | H/W: 6-5 240 | FUT: Reserve C | **6C**

Bats R Age 26
2009 (11) HS (FL)
Pwr ++
BAvg ++
Spd ++
Def +

Year	Lev	Team	AB	R	H	HR	RBI	Avg	OB	Slg	OPS	bb%	ct%	Eye	SB	CS	x/h%	Iso	RC/G
2013	A+	Frederick	361	61	113	13	53	313	405	524	929	13	74	0.60	5	0	41	211	7.52
2014	AA	Bowie	403	40	95	2	33	236	309	318	627	10	79	0.50	0	0	29	82	3.38
2015	AA	Springfield	366	53	100	12	69	273	354	418	772	11	79	0.60	0	1	29	145	5.15
2016	AA	Springfield	83	9	25	1	16	301	376	373	750	11	77	0.53	0	2	16	72	4.92
2016	AAA	Memphis	168	34	47	6	28	280	339	464	803	8	68	0.28	1	0	36	185	5.71

Huge, powerful backstop has a decent bat with moderate raw power and a good understanding of the strike zone. Will have to work hard to stick behind the plate. He has a strong arm, but struggles blocking the ball and is slow in his actions—not surprising given his size. Profiles as a backup catcher.

Okey,Chris
2 | **Cincinnati** | EXP MLB DEBUT: 2019 | H/W: 5-11 195 | FUT: Starting C | **7C**

Bats R Age 22
2016 (2) Clemson
Pwr +++
BAvg ++
Spd ++
Def +++

Year	Lev	Team	AB	R	H	HR	RBI	Avg	OB	Slg	OPS	bb%	ct%	Eye	SB	CS	x/h%	Iso	RC/G
2016	NCAA	Clemson	239	61	81	15	74	339	455	611	1066	18	77	0.94	4	3	41	272	9.30
2016	Rk	Billings	37	5	6	0	1	162	184	189	373	3	78	0.13	0	0	17	27	-0.20
2016	A	Dayton	148	21	36	6	21	243	309	432	741	9	67	0.29	5	0	42	189	4.85

Quality athlete for a catcher, but slow, lumbering swing makes it unlikely for him to succeed against plus velocity. Lots of strength in swing; 15 to 20 HR power potential. A solid receiver, gets high marks for how he handles a pitching staff.

Olson,Matt
39 | **Oakland** | EXP MLB DEBUT: 2016 | H/W: 6-5 230 | FUT: Starting 1B | **8C**

Bats L Age 23
2012 (S-1) HS (GA)
Pwr ++++
BAvg ++
Spd +
Def ++

Year	Lev	Team	AB	R	H	HR	RBI	Avg	OB	Slg	OPS	bb%	ct%	Eye	SB	CS	x/h%	Iso	RC/G
2013	A	Beloit	481	69	108	23	93	225	325	435	760	13	69	0.49	4	3	51	210	5.16
2014	A+	Stockton	512	111	134	37	97	262	399	543	942	19	73	0.85	2	0	51	281	7.72
2015	AA	Midland	466	82	116	17	75	249	387	438	825	18	70	0.76	5	1	47	189	6.37
2016	AAA	Nashville	464	69	109	17	60	235	336	422	759	13	72	0.54	1	0	48	188	5.18
2016	MLB	Oakland	21	3	2	0	0	95	321	143	464	25	81	1.75	0	0	50	48	1.97

Big, strong prospect who combines power and patience to provide value. Saw action at both 1B and RF to add versatility. Has hit at least 31 doubles each of last 4 years and has 25+ HR pop. Has very patient approach, though holes in swing lead to K and low BA. Has leverage and loft in strong stroke. Very poor foot speed.

Ona,Jorge
789 | San Diego | EXP MLB DEBUT: 2021 | H/W: 6-0 220 | FUT: Starting OF | 8E

Bats R Age 20
2016 FA (CU)
Pwr ++++
BAvg +++
Spd ++
Def +++

Year	Lev	Team	AB	R	H	HR	RBI	Avg	OB	Slg	OPS	bb%	ct%	Eye	SB	CS	x/h%	Iso	RC/G
2016		Did not play in U.S.																	

Cuban teenager on verge of making US debut. Impressed during SD instructional game at PETCO. Raw all-around, but showed significant raw power. Uses the entire field with approach. Below-average speed, likely a corner outfielder long-term.

O'Neill,Tyler
9 | Seattle | EXP MLB DEBUT: 2017 | H/W: 5-11 210 | FUT: Starting OF | 8B

Bats R Age 21
2013 (3) HS (BC)
Pwr ++++
BAvg +++
Spd +++
Def ++

Year	Lev	Team	AB	R	H	HR	RBI	Avg	OB	Slg	OPS	bb%	ct%	Eye	SB	CS	x/h%	Iso	RC/G
2014	Rk	Azl Mariners	2	0	0	0	0	0	0	0	0	0	50	0.00	0	0		0	-7.85
2014	A-	Everett	10	2	4	0	2	400	455	600	1055	9	50	0.20	0	0	50	200	13.24
2014	A	Clinton	219	31	54	13	38	247	310	466	775	8	64	0.25	5	0	41	219	5.36
2015	A+	Bakersfield	407	68	106	32	87	260	310	558	867	7	66	0.21	16	5	52	297	6.49
2016	AA	Jackson	492	68	144	24	102	293	372	508	880	11	70	0.41	12	2	38	215	6.82

Compact OF who led SL in SLG, 2nd in HR en route to MVP honors. Can impact game with bat as he gets on base, has electric bat speed, and hits for power to all fields. Balls flies off bat, though will overswing and have fair share of strikeouts. Strong arm in OF, but not a standout defender. Raw routes and reads, but speed makes up for mistakes.

Orimoloye,Demi
79 | Milwaukee | EXP MLB DEBUT: 2020 | H/W: 6-4 225 | FUT: Starting OF | 8E

Bats R Age 20
2015 (4) HS (ON)
Pwr ++++
BAvg ++
Spd ++++
Def +++

Year	Lev	Team	AB	R	H	HR	RBI	Avg	OB	Slg	OPS	bb%	ct%	Eye	SB	CS	x/h%	Iso	RC/G
2015	Rk	Azl Brewers	137	23	40	6	26	292	307	518	825	2	72	0.08	19	6	43	226	5.59
2016	Rk	Helena	219	26	45	5	17	205	281	324	605	10	74	0.40	18	5	29	119	2.91

Freak athlete who remains undeveloped, but has power-speed potential. Lacks ideal contact skills, though ball travels when he connects. Learning to use entire field and selectivity improved in second year. Plus runner with legit SB upside. Crude defensive reads now, but cannon arm profiles well as RF. Very high upside OF worth following.

Ortiz,Jhailyn
9 | Philadelphia | EXP MLB DEBUT: 2021 | H/W: 6-3 215 | FUT: Starting 1B | 9D

Bats R Age 18
2015 FA (DR)
Pwr ++++
BAvg ++
Spd +
Def ++

Year	Lev	Team	AB	R	H	HR	RBI	Avg	OB	Slg	OPS	bb%	ct%	Eye	SB	CS	x/h%	Iso	RC/G
2016	Rk	GCL Phillies	173	29	40	8	27	231	300	434	734	9	69	0.32	8	2	45	202	4.63

Huge physical kid with broad shoulders and developed lower half. Plus-plus raw power that showed up in first pro exposure. Has bat speed, but swing can get long and like many teenagers, will need to work on recognizing spin. High upside. Adequate in RF now, but more likely to end up at 1B as body matures.

Osuna,Jose
37 | Pittsburgh | EXP MLB DEBUT: 2017 | H/W: 6-2 213 | FUT: Reserve 1B | 6C

Bats R Age 24
2009 FA (VZ)
Pwr +++
BAvg +++
Spd ++
Def ++

Year	Lev	Team	AB	R	H	HR	RBI	Avg	OB	Slg	OPS	bb%	ct%	Eye	SB	CS	x/h%	Iso	RC/G
2014	A+	Bradenton	365	47	108	10	57	296	346	458	804	7	80	0.39	4	2	33	162	5.38
2015	A+	Bradenton	174	23	49	4	29	282	335	431	766	7	81	0.42	1	1	35	149	4.95
2015	AA	Altoona	323	46	93	8	52	288	324	437	760	5	81	0.28	6	3	32	149	4.71
2016	AA	Altoona	253	34	68	6	38	269	330	435	764	8	83	0.52	1	1	40	166	5.01
2016	AAA	Indianapolis	220	27	64	7	31	291	330	482	812	6	84	0.36	2	3	42	191	5.38

Strong bodied player put up solid offensive numbers hitting .279/.331/.457. Uses a quick bat to make consistent, hard contact. Line-drive approach results in gap power and hit 37 doubles and 13 HR. Runs well, but speed isn't a big part of game. Good arm and good hands allowed him to split time between 1B/OF.

Padlo,Kevin
5 | Tampa Bay | EXP MLB DEBUT: 2019 | H/W: 6-2 205 | FUT: Starting 3B | 7C

Bats R Age 20
2014 (5) HS (CA)
Pwr +++
BAvg ++
Spd +++
Def +++

Year	Lev	Team	AB	R	H	HR	RBI	Avg	OB	Slg	OPS	bb%	ct%	Eye	SB	CS	x/h%	Iso	RC/G
2014	Rk	Grand Junction	160	32	48	8	44	300	414	594	1007	16	76	0.82	6	1	56	294	8.64
2015	A-	Boise	255	44	75	9	46	294	400	502	902	15	76	0.73	33	5	44	208	7.19
2015	A	Asheville	83	11	12	2	7	145	268	277	545	14	69	0.54	2	1	58	133	2.15
2016	A	Bowling Green	414	71	95	16	66	229	353	413	766	16	68	0.59	14	9	43	184	5.45

Strong INF who can hit for power with advanced approach, but troubles loom due to being pull-conscious and FB-only hitter. Making contact is often difficult, and unlikely to hit for BA. Draws walks, and set high in HR. Speed and quickness suitable for 3B and makes all routine plays. Production may trail off without better contact.

Palacios,Jermaine
6 | Minnesota | EXP MLB DEBUT: 2019 | H/W: 6-0 155 | FUT: Starting MIF | 7D

Bats R Age 20
2013 FA (VZ)
Pwr ++
BAvg +++
Spd +++
Def ++

Year	Lev	Team	AB	R	H	HR	RBI	Avg	OB	Slg	OPS	bb%	ct%	Eye	SB	CS	x/h%	Iso	RC/G
2015	Rk	Elizabethton	140	23	47	2	23	336	350	507	857	2	86	0.15	5	2	38	171	5.75
2015	Rk	GCL Twins	95	13	40	1	14	421	471	589	1061	9	88	0.82	4	2	30	168	8.54
2016	A	Cedar Rapids	261	34	58	1	28	222	272	287	560	6	85	0.46	3	4	21	65	2.54

Athletic, lithe INF who is advanced hitter despite limited strength. Controls strike zone like veteran and uses bat control for easy contact. Uses entire field and can shoot gaps. Not much power in profile and only has average speed. Makes careless errors and needs to clean up footwork to stick at SS.

Palacios,Joshua
89 | Toronto | EXP MLB DEBUT: 2019 | H/W: 6-1 193 | FUT: Starting OF | 7C

Bats B Age 21
2016 (4) Auburn
Pwr ++
BAvg +++
Spd +++
Def +++

Year	Lev	Team	AB	R	H	HR	RBI	Avg	OB	Slg	OPS	bb%	ct%	Eye	SB	CS	x/h%	Iso	RC/G
2016	NCAA	Auburn	143	34	55	5	23	385	457	608	1065	12	81	0.70	12	5	33	224	8.93
2016	Rk	GCL Blue Jays	49	10	13	0	4	265	308	327	634	6	88	0.50	4	1	23	61	3.46
2016	A-	Vancouver	110	15	39	0	13	355	427	473	900	11	85	0.82	4	2	26	118	6.96
2016	A	Lansing	38	2	13	0	1	342	359	421	780	3	92	0.33	0	2	23	79	4.93

Fundamentally-sound hitter who returned from broken wrist and showed natural bat work. Differentiates between balls and strikes. Exhibits occasional pull power, though drives ball to all fields. Benefits by hitting LHP well. Speed and defense are admirable, though neither are above average. Can play CF and has decent range.

Palka,Daniel
9 | Minnesota | EXP MLB DEBUT: 2017 | H/W: 6-2 220 | FUT: Starting OF | 7C

Bats L Age 25
2013 (3) Georgia Tech
Pwr ++++
BAvg ++
Spd ++
Def ++

Year	Lev	Team	AB	R	H	HR	RBI	Avg	OB	Slg	OPS	bb%	ct%	Eye	SB	CS	x/h%	Iso	RC/G
2013	A-	Hillsboro	47	10	16	2	10	340	426	574	1000	13	66	0.44	1	0	31	234	9.07
2014	A	South Bend	455	63	113	22	82	248	331	466	797	11	72	0.43	9	3	44	218	5.55
2015	A+	Visalia	511	95	143	29	90	280	351	532	883	10	68	0.34	24	7	48	252	6.89
2016	AA	Chattanooga	300	42	81	21	65	270	352	547	899	11	67	0.38	7	4	46	277	7.16
2016	AAA	Rochester	203	31	47	13	25	232	294	483	777	8	58	0.21	2	1	53	251	5.89

Ultra-strong prospect with plus power to all fields. Finished 4th in minors in HR, though also 2nd in K. Lot of swing and miss in game and BA is in doubt. Draws walks, but cheats on FB as bat speed a tad short. Runs fairly well for size, though secondary skills behind true pop. Has improved in RF with better routes and can play 1B.

Palmeiro,Preston
3 | Baltimore | EXP MLB DEBUT: 2019 | H/W: 5-11 180 | FUT: Starting 1B | 7D

Bats L Age 22
2016 (7) NC State
Pwr ++
BAvg +++
Spd ++
Def ++

Year	Lev	Team	AB	R	H	HR	RBI	Avg	OB	Slg	OPS	bb%	ct%	Eye	SB	CS	x/h%	Iso	RC/G
2016	NCAA	NC State	243	53	82	9	55	337	408	539	947	11	83	0.69	1	0	37	202	7.30
2016	A-	Aberdeen	128	13	33	0	18	258	301	320	622	6	72	0.22	2	2	21	63	3.09

Natural-hitting 1B who maximizes talent in batter's box. Has smooth swing and has keen hand-eye coordination. Makes good contact with solid bat speed and can use entire field in line drive approach. May not hit enough HR for 1B, though can exhibit pull power. Lacks speed to be proficient on base and not enough arm for OF. Limited to 1B.

Papi,Mike
379 | Cleveland | EXP MLB DEBUT: 2018 | H/W: 6-2 190 | FUT: Starting OF | 7C

Bats L Age 24
2014 (S-1) Virginia
Pwr +++
BAvg ++
Spd ++
Def +++

Year	Lev	Team	AB	R	H	HR	RBI	Avg	OB	Slg	OPS	bb%	ct%	Eye	SB	CS	x/h%	Iso	RC/G
2014	A-	Mahoning Val	9	2	2	0	3	222	222	222	444	0	100		0	0	0	0	1.56
2014	A	Lake County	135	21	24	3	15	178	311	274	585	16	76	0.81	2	0	29	96	2.91
2015	A+	Lynchburg	416	53	98	4	45	236	360	356	716	16	72	0.69	6	7	41	120	4.86
2016	A+	Lynchburg	140	22	33	7	18	236	371	450	821	18	70	0.71	0	1	48	214	6.17
2016	AA	Akron	259	33	59	8	40	228	333	398	731	14	72	0.57	4	0	44	170	4.82

Virginia product broke through to AA and set career-highs in HR, ISO, x/h%. Walks often with patient, selective demeanor; future OBP league target. Flashes avg HR pop to all fields with good bat speed and slight uphill plane through zone; high-volume doubles at a minimum. Strong arm and enough range to profile at either RF/LF; 1B fallback option.

Paredes, Isaac — 6 — Chicago (N)

EXP MLB DEBUT: 2022 | H/W: 5-11 175 | FUT: Starting SS | 7D

Bats R Age 18
2016 FA (MX)

			Pwr	++
			BAvg	+++
			Spd	+++
			Def	+++

Year	Lev	Team	AB	R	H	HR	RBI	Avg	OB	Slg	OPS	bb%	ct%	Eye	SB	CS	x/h%	Iso	RC/G
2016	Rk	Azl Cubs	167	23	51	1	26	305	356	443	799	7	88	0.65	4	0	35	138	5.48
2016	A	South Bend	12	0	2	0	0	167	167	167	333	0	83	0.00	0	0	0	0	-0.59

SS prospect from Mexico started strong in rookie ball, earning a brief stint in the MWL. Good range with a strong arm, but will need to work hard to stick at short. Some concerns about his conditioning and work ethic, but held his own. Good bat speed with solid contact ability give him offensive upside even if he moves off of SS.

Park, Hoy Jun — 46 — New York (A)

EXP MLB DEBUT: 2019 | H/W: 6-1 175 | FUT: Starting MIF | 8E

Bats L Age 20
2014 FA (KR)

			Pwr	++
			BAvg	++
			Spd	++++
			Def	+++

Year	Lev	Team	AB	R	H	HR	RBI	Avg	OB	Slg	OPS	bb%	ct%	Eye	SB	CS	x/h%	Iso	RC/G
2015	Rk	Pulaski	222	48	53	5	30	239	340	383	723	13	77	0.68	12	7	36	144	4.72
2016	A	Charleston (Sc)	435	60	98	2	34	225	329	329	657	13	72	0.56	32	3	30	103	3.94

Quick INF who is still raw with bat, but is developing nicely with glove. Spent most of year at SS, though has seen action at 2B. Possesses range and arm for either spot and makes difficult plays look routine. Gets on base at high clip and effectively uses plus speed for SB. Strikes out far too much for lack of pop. Weak contact drives down value.

Paroubeck, Jordan — 79 — Los Angeles (N)

EXP MLB DEBUT: 2019 | H/W: 6-2 190 | FUT: Starting OF | 8D

Bats B Age 22
2013 (S-2) HS (CA)

			Pwr	+++
			BAvg	+++
			Spd	+++
			Def	+++

Year	Lev	Team	AB	R	H	HR	RBI	Avg	OB	Slg	OPS	bb%	ct%	Eye	SB	CS	x/h%	Iso	RC/G
2014	Rk	Azl Padres	140	26	40	4	24	286	346	457	804	8	70	0.31	4	2	35	171	5.71
2015	Rk	Azl Dodgers	49	11	12	1	8	245	327	429	756	11	73	0.46	0	0	50	184	5.16
2016	Rk	Ogden	104	13	24	5	15	231	310	413	724	10	52	0.24	4	1	38	183	5.62
2016	A	Great Lakes	60	8	12	1	3	200	262	317	578	8	45	0.15	1	0	33	117	3.88

Tall, lanky switch-hitting OF is with his third org in three years. Has been limited by injuries (shoulder and hamstring), but has plus bat speed and strength to hit for above-average power. Continues to have contact issues due to high leg kick and timing, but has the tools to hit. Average speed and good arm means he could play either corner slot.

Patterson, Jordan — 379 — Colorado

EXP MLB DEBUT: 2016 | H/W: 6-4 215 | FUT: Starting OF | 7C

Bats L Age 25
2013 (4) South Alabama

			Pwr	+++
			BAvg	+++
			Spd	+++
			Def	+++

Year	Lev	Team	AB	R	H	HR	RBI	Avg	OB	Slg	OPS	bb%	ct%	Eye	SB	CS	x/h%	Iso	RC/G
2014	A	Asheville	453	69	126	14	66	278	345	430	775	9	74	0.39	25	8	33	152	5.17
2015	A+	Modesto	303	62	92	10	43	304	345	568	912	6	71	0.22	9	6	52	264	7.21
2015	AA	New Britain	185	26	53	7	32	286	327	503	829	6	77	0.26	9	4	49	216	5.66
2016	AAA	Albuquerque	427	75	125	14	61	293	363	480	843	10	72	0.40	10	0	36	187	6.22
2016	MLB	Colorado	18	1	8	0	2	444	474	500	974	5	94	1.00	0	1	13	56	7.14

OF/1B has a good approach at the plate with a career slash line of .290/.369/.487. Has good raw power but needs to prove that he can make enough contact to hit for average. Moves well on the bases and at 1B. Also saw time at 1B. Has the tools to be a 20/20 player in the majors, but needs to be more selective.

Pentecost, Max — 2 — Toronto

EXP MLB DEBUT: 2018 | H/W: 6-2 195 | FUT: Starting C | 8D

Bats R Age 24
2014 (1) Kennesaw State

			Pwr	+++
			BAvg	+++
			Spd	++
			Def	++

Year	Lev	Team	AB	R	H	HR	RBI	Avg	OB	Slg	OPS	bb%	ct%	Eye	SB	CS	x/h%	Iso	RC/G
2014	Rk	GCL Blue Jays	22	2	8	0	3	364	364	455	818	0	86	0.00	0	1	25	91	5.11
2014	A-	Vancouver	83	15	26	0	9	313	329	410	739	2	78	0.11	2	1	19	96	4.43
2015		Did not play (injury)																	
2016	A	Lansing	239	36	75	7	34	314	369	490	859	8	79	0.41	4	2	33	176	6.15
2016	A+	Dunedin	49	6	12	3	7	245	288	469	758	6	65	0.18	1	1	42	224	4.91

Athletic backstop who did not play in '15 and was DH for all of '16. Has quality hitting ability with quick, short stroke and offers above average raw power. At best when hitting hard line drives to gaps. Runs well for catcher. Rebuilding arm strength and should be fine in '17 and will need to attend to deficient receiving and footwork.

Perez, Arvicent — 2 — Detroit

EXP MLB DEBUT: 2019 | H/W: 5-10 180 | FUT: Starting C | 7D

Bats R Age 23
2011 FA (VZ)

			Pwr	++
			BAvg	+++
			Spd	+
			Def	+++

Year	Lev	Team	AB	R	H	HR	RBI	Avg	OB	Slg	OPS	bb%	ct%	Eye	SB	CS	x/h%	Iso	RC/G
2014	Rk	GCL Tigers	81	14	25	3	20	309	317	519	836	1	91	0.14	3	0	40	210	5.34
2014	A-	West Michigan	46	7	16	0	6	348	362	391	753	2	89	0.20	1	1	13	43	4.49
2015	A-	Connecticut	19	3	5	0	1	263	263	316	579	0	89	0.00	0	1	20	53	2.50
2015	A	West Michigan	118	7	27	0	5	229	248	263	511	2	83	0.15	1	0	15	34	1.64
2016	A	West Michigan	271	28	82	0	30	303	320	391	711	3	87	0.19	1	0	24	89	4.12

Improving prospect who has shown ability to hit for BA while showing advances in receiving and blocking. Controls bat with simple, level swing and makes exemplary contact. Rarely works counts and is free-swinger. Only projects to gap power, but should be acceptable as he is sound backstop. Bat will determine future.

Perez, Delvin — 6 — St. Louis

EXP MLB DEBUT: 2020 | H/W: 6-3 175 | FUT: Starting SS | 8C

Bats R Age 18
2016 (1) HS (PR)

			Pwr	++
			BAvg	+++
			Spd	+++
			Def	++++

Year	Lev	Team	AB	R	H	HR	RBI	Avg	OB	Slg	OPS	bb%	ct%	Eye	SB	CS	x/h%	Iso	RC/G
2016	Rk	GCL Cardinals	163	19	48	0	19	294	343	393	735	7	83	0.43	12	1	25	98	4.67

23rd pick was considered a lock to go in the top 10, but a failed drug test caused him to drop. Plus athlete with true SS actions. 70-grade runner with good first-step quickness, range, and a plus arm. Good approach at the plate with a quick bat, but needs to make more contact and improve pitch recognition. Below-average power is only flaw.

Perez, Yanio — 57 — Texas

EXP MLB DEBUT: 2018 | H/W: 6-2 205 | FUT: Starting 3B | 8D

Bats R Age 21
2016 FA (CU)

			Pwr	+++
			BAvg	+++
			Spd	+++
			Def	++

Year	Lev	Team	AB	R	H	HR	RBI	Avg	OB	Slg	OPS	bb%	ct%	Eye	SB	CS	x/h%	Iso	RC/G
2017		Did not play in the US																	

Pure-hitting INF who DNP in '16 after signing for large bonus out of Cuba. Lacks big tool, but does everything with bat well. Has short stroke for good contact and enough leverage and strength to hit for average pop. Runs well and could be potent basestealer. Not much of a defender and could move to OF in time.

Perkins, Blake — 8 — Washington

EXP MLB DEBUT: 2020 | H/W: 6-1 165 | FUT: Starting CF | 7D

Bats B Age 20
2015 (2) HS (AZ)

			Pwr	+
			BAvg	++
			Spd	++++
			Def	++++

Year	Lev	Team	AB	R	H	HR	RBI	Avg	OB	Slg	OPS	bb%	ct%	Eye	SB	CS	x/h%	Iso	RC/G
2015	Rk	GCL Nationals	166	21	35	1	12	211	268	283	551	7	78	0.36	4	5	23	72	2.27
2016	A-	Auburn	209	31	49	1	16	234	316	282	599	11	81	0.64	10	3	14	48	3.08
2016	A	Hagerstown	25	4	5	0	2	200	333	200	533	17	76	0.83	0	1	0	0	2.31

New to switch-hitting, it didn't go well (.205/.315/.246 as LHH). Still has athletic ability and owns a quick bat from RH side, as he makes good contact. Plus speed shows up on bases and in CF, where has an above-average defender. Young, but slight frame suggests power unlikely to come.

Peter, Jake — 45 — Chicago (A)

EXP MLB DEBUT: 2017 | H/W: 6-1 185 | FUT: Utility player | 6A

Bats R Age 24
2014 (7) Creighton

			Pwr	++
			BAvg	+++
			Spd	++
			Def	+++

Year	Lev	Team	AB	R	H	HR	RBI	Avg	OB	Slg	OPS	bb%	ct%	Eye	SB	CS	x/h%	Iso	RC/G
2014	Rk	Great Falls	152	26	59	2	21	388	436	579	1015	8	91	1.00	1	1	32	191	7.94
2014	A+	Winston-Salem	89	8	21	0	5	236	269	303	572	4	85	0.31	1	0	24	67	2.60
2015	A+	Winston-Salem	497	76	129	3	57	260	331	348	679	10	82	0.60	23	3	26	89	4.08
2016	AA	Birmingham	253	27	77	4	29	304	380	407	787	11	79	0.60	5	1	23	103	5.42
2016	AAA	Charlotte	228	30	59	2	24	259	310	342	652	7	81	0.39	3	1	25	83	3.54

Versatile prospect who played all over diamond in '16. Limited power in profile, but makes good contact and hits line drives to gaps. Can hit LHP with all-fields approach and knows strike zone. Should hit for BA. SB dropped and doesn't have quick legs. Versatility trumps natural defensive skills.

Peters, DJ — 789 — Los Angeles (N)

EXP MLB DEBUT: 2020 | H/W: 6-6 225 | FUT: Starting OF | 8D

Bats R Age 21
2016 (4) Western NV JC

			Pwr	++++
			BAvg	++
			Spd	+++
			Def	++

Year	Lev	Team	AB	R	H	HR	RBI	Avg	OB	Slg	OPS	bb%	ct%	Eye	SB	CS	x/h%	Iso	RC/G
2016	Rk	Ogden	262	63	92	13	48	351	428	615	1042	12	75	0.53	5	3	43	263	8.88

JuCo OF has huge raw power. Torched pitchers in the Pioneer League, with good understanding of strike zone combined with bat speed and raw power. Does have swing-and-miss due to length, but pitch recognition mitigates downside. Plus athlete with good speed and a plus arm. Could become a fourth-round steal.

Peterson,D.J. — 3 — Seattle

EXP MLB DEBUT: 2017 | H/W: 6-1 210 | FUT: Starting 1B | 8D

Bats R Age 25
2013 (1) New Mexico

- Pwr +++
- BAvg +++
- Spd +
- Def ++

Year	Lev	Team	AB	R	H	HR	RBI	Avg	OB	Slg	OPS	bb%	ct%	Eye	SB	CS	x/h%	Iso	RC/G
2014	AA	Jackson	222	32	58	13	38	261	328	473	801	9	77	0.43	1	1	36	212	5.28
2015	AA	Jackson	358	39	80	7	44	223	285	346	632	8	75	0.34	5	0	35	123	3.25
2015	AAA	Tacoma	14	0	3	0	0	214	214	286	500	0	79	0.00	0	1	33	71	1.33
2016	AA	Jackson	277	31	75	11	43	271	336	466	801	9	75	0.40	1	1	43	195	5.46
2016	AAA	Tacoma	178	26	45	8	35	253	296	438	734	6	71	0.22	0	1	36	185	4.43

Powerful slugger who had nice rebound season. Power returned and showcased smoother swing. Will expand strike zone and overswing, but has chance to hit for both BA and power. Uses entire field when on, but can often be pull-conscious. Spent most of season at 1B and seems to be permanent home. Former 3B with strong arm.

Peterson,Dustin — 7 — Atlanta

EXP MLB DEBUT: 2017 | H/W: 6-2 210 | FUT: Starting OF | 7C

Bats R Age 22
2013 (2) HS (AZ)

- Pwr +++
- BAvg ++
- Spd +++
- Def +++

Year	Lev	Team	AB	R	H	HR	RBI	Avg	OB	Slg	OPS	bb%	ct%	Eye	SB	CS	x/h%	Iso	RC/G
2013	Rk	Azl Padres	157	20	46	0	18	293	331	344	675	5	79	0.27	3	0	17	51	3.74
2014	A	Fort Wayne	527	64	123	10	79	233	268	361	629	5	74	0.18	1	3	36	127	3.06
2015	A+	Carolina	446	58	112	8	62	251	318	348	666	9	80	0.48	6	3	22	96	3.75
2016	AA	Mississippi	524	65	148	12	88	282	339	431	770	8	81	0.45	4	1	35	149	5.04

After several lackluster campaigns, frm 3B turned OF had an under-the-radar breakout. Cutting down on his swing had immense impact on increasing contact rate and line drive rate. Working all fields with gap-to-gap power, RH showed makings of high double potential. Still struggles with velocity and MLB caliber secondaries from RHP.

Phillips,Brett — 89 — Milwaukee

EXP MLB DEBUT: 2017 | H/W: 6-0 185 | FUT: Starting OF | 8C

Bats L Age 22
2012 (6) HS (FL)

- Pwr +++
- BAvg +++
- 4.13 Spd ++++
- Def ++++

Year	Lev	Team	AB	R	H	HR	RBI	Avg	OB	Slg	OPS	bb%	ct%	Eye	SB	CS	x/h%	Iso	RC/G
2014	A+	Lancaster	109	19	37	4	10	339	415	560	974	11	82	0.70	5	4	38	220	7.74
2015	A+	Lancaster	291	68	93	15	53	320	367	588	955	7	78	0.34	8	6	44	268	7.29
2015	AA	Biloxi	80	14	20	0	6	250	362	413	774	15	63	0.47	2	1	50	163	6.21
2015	AA	Corpus Christi	134	22	43	1	18	321	359	463	822	6	81	0.31	7	2	30	142	5.65
2016	AA	Biloxi	441	60	101	16	62	229	331	397	728	13	65	0.44	12	7	36	168	4.86

Athletic OF who endured setbacks at AA. Plus defender with rocket arm for RF; hustles and has plus speed for SB ability. Swing is herky-jerky and not conducive to tons of raw power; will lunge at breaking balls and needs to work on pitch recognition. Has quality overall tools, but may need more time in minors than previously thought.

Pieters,Chris — 37 — Chicago (N)

EXP MLB DEBUT: 2020 | H/W: 6-3 185 | FUT: Starting OF | 7D

Bats L Age 22
2011 FA (CC)

- Pwr ++
- BAvg ++
- Spd ++++
- Def +++

Year	Lev	Team	AB	R	H	HR	RBI	Avg	OB	Slg	OPS	bb%	ct%	Eye	SB	CS	x/h%	Iso	RC/G
2015	Rk	DSL Cubs	180	38	56	3	33	311	436	428	864	18	82	1.25	25	4	23	117	6.83
2015	Rk	AZL Cubs	35	6	9	0	6	257	278	400	678	3	71	0.10	0	0	56	143	3.90
2016	A-	Eugene	252	36	62	3	30	246	321	337	659	10	71	0.38	20	3	23	91	3.72

International FA from Curacao was converted from pitching. Late bloomer has a quick bat with the ability to make hard contact. Can be overly aggressive at the plate and managed only 3 HR, but should develop more as he matures. Plus speed plays well on the bases and in LF where he has a good arm. Still raw in many aspects of his game.

Pinder,Chad — 46 — Oakland

EXP MLB DEBUT: 2016 | H/W: 6-2 195 | FUT: Starting MIF | 7B

Bats R Age 25
2013 (S-2) Virginia Tech

- Pwr +++
- BAvg +++
- Spd ++
- Def ++

Year	Lev	Team	AB	R	H	HR	RBI	Avg	OB	Slg	OPS	bb%	ct%	Eye	SB	CS	x/h%	Iso	RC/G
2013	A-	Vermont	140	14	28	3	8	200	263	293	556	8	71	0.29	1	0	25	93	2.10
2014	A+	Stockton	403	61	116	13	55	288	325	489	814	5	75	0.22	12	9	43	201	5.51
2015	AA	Midland	477	71	151	15	86	317	354	486	841	6	78	0.27	7	5	32	170	5.74
2016	AAA	Nashville	426	72	110	14	51	258	299	425	724	6	75	0.23	5	1	36	167	4.30
2016	MLB	Oakland	51	4	12	1	4	235	278	373	650	6	73	0.21	0	0	42	137	3.42

Savvy INF who maximizes talent and has ability to play SS or 2B. Has fluid, level swing path and hand-eye coordination to hit for BA and offers good power to all fields. Can be free swinger at times and could stand to be more patient. Hits LHP very well. Doesn't run well and won't be impact defender despite strong arm. Range best at 2B.

Plummer,Nick — 78 — St. Louis

EXP MLB DEBUT: 2020 | H/W: 5-10 200 | FUT: Starting OF | 8D

Bats L Age 20
2015 (1) HS (MI)

- Pwr +++
- BAvg +++
- Spd +++
- Def +++

Year	Lev	Team	AB	R	H	HR	RBI	Avg	OB	Slg	OPS	bb%	ct%	Eye	SB	CS	x/h%	Iso	RC/G
2015	Rk	GCL Cardinals	180	43	41	1	22	228	365	344	710	18	69	0.70	8	6	34	117	4.89
2016		Did not play (injury)																	

Quick, athletic OF missed all of '16 due to hand/wrist injury that required surgery. Showed an advanced feel for hitting in HS with the potential for above-average power. Quick LH stroke with a gap-to-gap approach. Average runner with good speed when under way. Not likely to stick in CF over the long-term, but has nice offensive upside.

Potts,Hudson — 456 — San Diego

EXP MLB DEBUT: 2021 | H/W: 6-3 205 | FUT: Starting 3B | 7E

Bats R Age 18
2016 (1) HS (TX)

- Pwr ++
- BAvg +++
- Spd ++
- Def ++

Year	Lev	Team	AB	R	H	HR	RBI	Avg	OB	Slg	OPS	bb%	ct%	Eye	SB	CS	x/h%	Iso	RC/G
2016	Rk	Azl Padres	183	35	54	1	21	295	328	399	727	5	81	0.26	8	4	28	104	4.39
2016	A-	Tri-City	60	7	14	0	6	233	333	267	600	13	78	0.69	2	1	7	33	3.16

An intriguing first-round pick, who was a 3B on most boards, but SD drafted as a SS. Likely lacks range and footwork for MIF. Good contact skills, and showed patience and gap-to-gap power in pro debut. Scouts believe average power potential will emerge at maturity.

Powell,Boog — 78 — Seattle

EXP MLB DEBUT: 2017 | H/W: 5-10 185 | FUT: Reserve OF | 6B

Bats L Age 24
2012 (20) Orange Coast CC

- Pwr +
- BAvg +++
- Spd +++
- Def +++

Year	Lev	Team	AB	R	H	HR	RBI	Avg	OB	Slg	OPS	bb%	ct%	Eye	SB	CS	x/h%	Iso	RC/G
2014	A	Beloit	254	43	85	3	17	335	450	429	879	17	81	1.08	16	13	16	94	6.99
2014	A+	Stockton	61	11	23	0	11	377	449	459	908	12	93	2.00	0	2	17	82	7.03
2015	AA	Montgomery	238	44	78	1	22	328	401	416	817	11	84	0.76	11	8	17	88	5.85
2015	AAA	Durham	206	22	53	2	18	257	357	364	721	13	80	0.78	7	6	28	107	4.79
2016	AAA	Tacoma	248	39	67	3	27	270	330	359	689	8	83	0.52	10	6	21	89	4.07

Aggressive OF who ended season in June due to 80-game PED suspension. Lacks standout tools to profile as starter, but can impact game with speed and nose for contact. Will work counts and find pitches to drive, but lacks power (3 HR each of past 3 seasons). Is a career .301 hitter, but has limited bat speed. Solid defender.

Pruitt,Reggie — 8 — Toronto

EXP MLB DEBUT: 2019 | H/W: 6-0 170 | FUT: Starting OF | 7D

Bats R Age 19
2015 (24) HS (GA)

- Pwr +
- BAvg ++
- Spd ++++
- Def +++

Year	Lev	Team	AB	R	H	HR	RBI	Avg	OB	Slg	OPS	bb%	ct%	Eye	SB	CS	x/h%	Iso	RC/G
2015	Rk	GCL Blue Jays	121	23	27	0	12	223	293	289	582	9	69	0.32	15	2	26	66	2.69
2016	Rk	Bluefield	173	36	41	0	10	237	290	266	556	7	75	0.30	16	2	10	29	2.22

Rangy, fast OF who is all about athleticism. Has good instincts for game and optimally utilizes speed on base and in CF. Ranges well and takes efficient routes. Not much power at present and hope is that he adds loft to short stroke. Swing mechanics get out of whack at times, but likely to improve. Should add strength as he matures.

Pujols,Jose — 9 — Philadelphia

EXP MLB DEBUT: 2020 | H/W: 6-3 175 | FUT: Starting OF | 8D

Bats R Age 21
2012 FA (DR)

- Pwr ++++
- BAvg +
- 4.48 Spd ++
- Def +++

Year	Lev	Team	AB	R	H	HR	RBI	Avg	OB	Slg	OPS	bb%	ct%	Eye	SB	CS	x/h%	Iso	RC/G
2013	Rk	GCL Phillies	160	27	30	6	18	188	274	369	642	11	65	0.34	1	3	50	181	3.49
2014	Rk	GCL Phillies	151	21	35	5	28	232	288	411	699	7	64	0.22	1	2	43	179	4.35
2014	A-	Williamsport	61	3	13	0	5	213	213	295	508	0	66	0.00	0	0	38	82	1.36
2015	A-	Williamsport	256	43	61	4	30	238	306	359	665	9	68	0.31	5	4	34	121	3.83
2016	A	Lakewood	498	67	120	24	82	241	303	440	742	8	64	0.25	5	3	40	199	4.91

Showed off his immense power; led the SAL in HRs but also in Ks. Power now ranges from pole to pole, coming from incredible bat speed and a loose, fluid swing. Can too often become unbalanced on soft stuff low/away, and attempts to hit pitches he can't get to. Defense has improved and has a strong RF arm. Exciting, but still very raw.

Quinn,Heath — 9 — San Francisco

EXP MLB DEBUT: 2019 | H/W: 6-2 190 | FUT: Starting OF | 8D

Bats R Age 21
2016 (3) Samford

- Pwr +++
- BAvg +++
- Spd ++
- Def +++

Year	Lev	Team	AB	R	H	HR	RBI	Avg	OB	Slg	OPS	bb%	ct%	Eye	SB	CS	x/h%	Iso	RC/G
2016	NCAA	Samford	242	62	83	21	77	343	444	682	1126	15	77	0.80	4	2	47	339	9.82
2016	Rk	Azl Giants	5	4	3	0	0	600	714	800	1514	29	80	2.00	0	0	33	200	16.58
2016	A-	Salem-Keizer	205	37	69	9	34	337	411	571	982	11	76	0.52	3	0	42	234	8.01
2016	A+	San Jose	17	2	6	0	0	353	421	412	833	11	59	0.29	0	0	17	59	7.15

Tall, natural-hitting OF who impressed in pro debut with admirable offensive traits. Can crush balls to all fields and has potential to hit for plus power. Makes hard contact with balanced approach. Can get aggressive and chase pitches and has holes that need to be closed. Runs OK and is decent defender in RF.

Quinn,Roman — 8 — Philadelphia

EXP MLB DEBUT: 2016 | **H/W:** 5-10 170 | **FUT:** Starting CF | **8C**

Bats B Age 23
2011 (2) HS (FL)

- Pwr + +
- BAvg + + +
- 3.87 Spd + + + + +
- Def + + +

Year	Lev	Team	AB	R	H	HR	RBI	Avg	OB	Slg	OPS	bb%	ct%	Eye	SB	CS	x/h%	Iso	RC/G
2014	A+	Clearwater	327	51	84	7	36	257	331	370	701	10	76	0.45	32	12	24	113	4.21
2015	AA	Reading	232	44	71	4	15	306	356	435	791	7	82	0.43	29	10	23	129	5.26
2016	Rk	GCL Phillies	22	6	11	0	0	500	522	591	1113	4	86	0.33	5	1	18	91	8.76
2016	AA	Reading	286	58	82	6	25	287	354	441	795	9	76	0.44	31	8	32	154	5.51
2016	MLB	Philadelphia	57	10	15	0	6	263	354	333	687	12	67	0.42	5	1	27	70	4.39

Enough patience to get on base; enough bat control and pop to get hits; an embarrassment of speed to cause havoc once on. Not been able to stay healthy during any minor league season. Outfield play improving; held his own during September MLB cameo. Electric player fraught with risk.

Ramirez,Harold — 789 — Toronto

EXP MLB DEBUT: 2017 | **H/W:** 5-10 220 | **FUT:** Starting OF | **7B**

Bats R Age 22
2011 FA (CB)

- Pwr + +
- BAvg + + + +
- Spd + +
- Def + + +

Year	Lev	Team	AB	R	H	HR	RBI	Avg	OB	Slg	OPS	bb%	ct%	Eye	SB	CS	x/h%	Iso	RC/G
2013	A-	Jamestown	274	42	78	5	40	285	340	409	749	8	81	0.44	23	11	26	124	4.76
2014	A	West Virginia	204	30	63	1	24	309	344	402	746	5	83	0.31	12	3	25	93	4.63
2015	A+	Bradenton	306	45	103	4	47	337	387	458	844	8	84	0.52	22	15	22	121	5.92
2016	AA	Altoona	379	58	116	2	49	306	343	401	744	5	83	0.32	7	10	22	95	4.61
2016	AA	New Hampshire	4	2	3	0	1	750	800	1000	1800	20	100		0	0	33	250	17.38

Thick, compact OF who hits for a high BA by smashing hard line drives to entire field. Swings hard, but under control, but doesn't project to much over-the-wall pop. Doesn't walk much as he puts bat to ball easily. Plays mostly CF, but profiles better in LF as arm strength and speed a little short.

Ramirez,Juan — 8 — Detroit

EXP MLB DEBUT: 2021 | **H/W:** 5-9 160 | **FUT:** Starting CF | **8E**

Bats L Age 17
2015 FA (DR)

- Pwr +
- BAvg + + +
- Spd + + +
- Def + + +

Year	Lev	Team	AB	R	H	HR	RBI	Avg	OB	Slg	OPS	bb%	ct%	Eye	SB	CS	x/h%	Iso	RC/G
2017		Did not play in the US																	

Small, quick OF with advanced bat control and pitch recognition for age. Is a very tough out with keen eye and plate discipline. Lacks strength to hit for power and needs to grow into lithe frame. Only exhibits average speed on base, though is solid CF defender. More of a long-term project, but could be high BA guy.

Ramos,Henry — 89 — Los Angeles (N)

EXP MLB DEBUT: 2017 | **H/W:** 6-2 220 | **FUT:** Starting OF | **7D**

Bats B Age 24
2010 (5) HS (PR)

- Pwr + + +
- BAvg + +
- Spd + + +
- Def + + +

Year	Lev	Team	AB	R	H	HR	RBI	Avg	OB	Slg	OPS	bb%	ct%	Eye	SB	CS	x/h%	Iso	RC/G
2015	Rk	GCL Red Sox	24	4	7	0	2	292	414	292	705	17	88	1.67	2	0	0	0	4.92
2015	A-	Lowell	12	1	4	0	1	333	333	333	667	0	67	0.00	0	0	0	0	3.37
2015	AA	Portland	131	8	32	0	8	244	317	359	676	10	80	0.54	0	0	41	115	4.12
2016	AA	Portland	171	20	48	3	11	281	324	404	728	6	85	0.44	3	3	25	123	4.44
2016	AAA	Pawtucket	190	18	47	5	29	247	289	400	689	5	77	0.25	4	2	34	153	3.86

Strong, athletic OF split between AA and AAA and had a productive season. Can play CF with good speed and range and his arm good enough for a corner spot. Injury history has muted potential, but features above average raw power. Has leverage in stroke to realize pop, but strikes out too much and approach is substandard.

Ramos,Milton — 6 — New York (N)

EXP MLB DEBUT: 2020 | **H/W:** 5-11 180 | **FUT:** Starting SS | **7E**

Bats R Age 21
2014 (3) HS (FL)

- Pwr +
- BAvg + +
- Spd + + + +
- Def + + + +

Year	Lev	Team	AB	R	H	HR	RBI	Avg	OB	Slg	OPS	bb%	ct%	Eye	SB	CS	x/h%	Iso	RC/G
2014	Rk	GCL Mets	166	20	40	0	29	241	300	355	655	8	80	0.41	6	6	35	114	3.76
2015	Rk	GCL Mets	36	3	7	0	3	194	216	222	438	3	75	0.11	1	2	14	28	0.49
2015	Rk	Kingsport	164	22	52	1	24	317	345	415	760	4	82	0.23	3	6	25	98	4.72
2016	A	Columbia	363	31	80	0	35	220	284	273	556	8	76	0.36	5	4	21	52	2.33

Light-hitting, glove first SS. Hit tool has been question mark since HS. Worked on driving hands through zone quicker in '16. Was woeful down the stretch. Potential plus-plus defensively with a strong arm. Bat will need to come around significantly to become MLB player.

Ramsey,James — 789 — Seattle

EXP MLB DEBUT: 2017 | **H/W:** 6-0 200 | **FUT:** Starting OF | **7D**

Bats L Age 27
2012 (1) Florida State

- Pwr + + +
- BAvg + + +
- Spd + + +
- Def + + +

Year	Lev	Team	AB	R	H	HR	RBI	Avg	OB	Slg	OPS	bb%	ct%	Eye	SB	CS	x/h%	Iso	RC/G
2014	AA	Springfield	243	47	73	13	36	300	380	527	906	11	73	0.47	4	2	38	226	7.01
2014	AAA	Columbus	109	17	31	3	16	284	361	468	829	11	69	0.38	1	0	42	183	6.26
2015	AAA	Columbus	440	46	107	12	42	243	325	382	706	11	71	0.41	3	4	33	139	4.36
2016	AAA	Oklahoma City	254	33	67	8	38	264	327	433	760	9	69	0.30	5	4	36	169	5.12
2016	AAA	Tacoma	97	12	26	1	6	268	349	371	720	11	66	0.36	0	1	27	103	4.81

Athletic OF who is now in fourth organization and spent last 2 1/2 years in AAA. Started slow, but finished strong and could win spot. Runs well, though not a burner, possible he could steal more bases in time. Lot of strikeouts, and he struggles with LHP. Could be platoon partner as he owns average power and can play all OF spots.

Randolph,Cornelius — 7 — Philadelphia

EXP MLB DEBUT: 2020 | **H/W:** 5-11 205 | **FUT:** Starting OF | **8D**

Bats L Age 19
2015 (1) HS (GA)

- Pwr + + +
- BAvg + + + +
- Spd + +
- Def + +

Year	Lev	Team	AB	R	H	HR	RBI	Avg	OB	Slg	OPS	bb%	ct%	Eye	SB	CS	x/h%	Iso	RC/G
2015	Rk	GCL Phillies	172	35	52	1	24	302	412	442	854	16	81	1.00	7	5	37	140	6.68
2016	Rk	GCL Phillies	12	1	1	0	0	83	214	83	298	14	75	0.67	0	0	0	0	-1.03
2016	A	Lakewood	241	33	66	2	27	274	345	357	701	10	76	0.46	5	4	23	83	4.29

Pure hitter lost two months with a shoulder/back injury. Was swinging much better by the end of season. Lightning hands create great bat speed, and has simple mechanics, along with pitch recognition beyond years. The question is how much power he'll generate. Still learning the OF, and is a good athlete despite thick build.

Ravelo,Rangel — 3 — Oakland

EXP MLB DEBUT: 2017 | **H/W:** 6-1 225 | **FUT:** Starting 1B | **7D**

Bats R Age 24
2010 (6) HS (FL)

- Pwr + +
- BAvg + + +
- Spd +
- Def + + +

Year	Lev	Team	AB	R	H	HR	RBI	Avg	OB	Slg	OPS	bb%	ct%	Eye	SB	CS	x/h%	Iso	RC/G
2014	AA	Birmingham	476	72	147	11	66	309	382	473	854	11	84	0.73	10	6	35	164	6.23
2015	Rk	Azl Athletics	25	7	9	0	7	360	500	560	1060	22	88	2.33	1	0	44	200	9.69
2015	AA	Midland	88	13	28	2	17	318	381	477	859	9	81	0.53	0	1	32	159	6.23
2015	AAA	Nashville	101	10	28	1	18	277	324	376	700	6	78	0.32	0	0	25	99	4.11
2016	AAA	Nashville	367	60	96	8	54	262	324	395	719	8	83	0.54	1	1	33	134	4.44

Pure-hitting 1B who sees a lot of pitches and willing to draw walks in mature approach. Doesn't have ideal power for 1B, but hits lots of doubles with level swing path. Secondary skills are limited as he is well below average runner and is relegated to 1B with immobility. Has strong arm, though.

Ray,Corey — 8 — Milwaukee

EXP MLB DEBUT: 2018 | **H/W:** 5-11 185 | **FUT:** Starting OF | **9D**

Bats L Age 22
2016 (1) Louisville

- Pwr + + +
- BAvg + + + +
- Spd + + + +
- Def + + +

Year	Lev	Team	AB	R	H	HR	RBI	Avg	OB	Slg	OPS	bb%	ct%	Eye	SB	CS	x/h%	Iso	RC/G
2016	NCAA	Louisville	268	55	83	15	60	310	391	545	936	12	85	0.88	44	0	39	235	7.10
2016	A	Wisconsin	12	2	1	0	0	83	267	83	350	20	67	0.75	1	1	0	0	-0.79
2016	A+	Brevard County	231	24	57	5	17	247	307	385	692	8	77	0.37	9	5	35	139	4.05

Collegiate standout underwent knee surgery after pro debut. Stocky, nimble athlete with quick-twitch attributes. Speed is best tool; likes to run and will be SB asset. Short load, sprays ball with smooth stroke for high BA as leadoff type. More pop than build lets on; bat speed could yield above-avg HR. Range for CF, but reads will need to improve.

Read,Raudy — 2 — Washington

EXP MLB DEBUT: 2018 | **H/W:** 6-0 170 | **FUT:** Starting C | **7D**

Bats R Age 23
2011 FA (DR)

- Pwr + + +
- BAvg + + +
- Spd +
- Def + + +

Year	Lev	Team	AB	R	H	HR	RBI	Avg	OB	Slg	OPS	bb%	ct%	Eye	SB	CS	x/h%	Iso	RC/G
2013	Rk	GCL Nationals	147	9	37	2	17	252	281	327	608	4	88	0.35	2	6	19	75	2.97
2014	A-	Auburn	210	27	59	6	35	281	326	462	788	6	82	0.38	0	3	44	181	5.15
2015	A	Hagerstown	295	38	72	5	36	244	303	369	673	8	83	0.50	4	3	36	125	3.88
2015	A+	Potomac	18	1	7	0	5	389	450	500	950	10	83	0.67	0	0	29	111	7.47
2016	A+	Potomac	386	54	101	9	51	262	317	415	731	7	86	0.58	6	3	40	153	4.58

Improved already solid bat-to-ball skills, used entire field, and both doubles and HR power showed up in game action. Still can be impatient at times, but bat will need to carry him. Has a strong arm behind the dish, but rest of defense—receiving/blocking, game calling—still needs work.

Reed,Buddy — 789 — San Diego

EXP MLB DEBUT: 2020 | **H/W:** 6-4 210 | **FUT:** Starting OF | **8D**

Bats B Age 21
2016 (2) Florida

- Pwr + +
- BAvg + + +
- Spd + + + +
- Def + + + +

Year	Lev	Team	AB	R	H	HR	RBI	Avg	OB	Slg	OPS	bb%	ct%	Eye	SB	CS	x/h%	Iso	RC/G
2016	NCAA	Florida	256	57	67	4	32	262	359	395	754	13	76	0.63	24	0	30	133	5.18
2016	A-	Tri-City	205	31	52	0	13	254	326	337	663	10	74	0.42	15	5	25	83	3.86

Speedy, switch hitting OF dropped in draft due to inconsistent performance. Tall athlete with good bat-to-ball skills from both sides of plate. Swing not conducive to high power output despite large frame. Plus-plus speed weapon on basepaths and in field. Needs to tighten up route running to stay in CF.

Reed,Michael

789 | Milwaukee | EXP MLB DEBUT: 2015 | H/W: 6-0 215 | FUT: Reserve OF | 6A

Bats R Age 24
2011 (5) HS (TX)

- Pwr +
- BAvg + + +
- Spd + + +
- Def + + +

Year	Lev	Team	AB	R	H	HR	RBI	Avg	OB	Slg	OPS	bb%	ct%	Eye	SB	CS	x/h%	Iso	RC/G
2015	AA	Biloxi	313	43	87	5	49	278	383	422	804	14	74	0.66	25	7	34	144	5.96
2015	AAA	Colorado Springs	126	19	31	0	21	246	349	381	730	14	75	0.65	1	0	48	135	5.05
2015	MLB	Milwaukee	6	2	2	0	0	333	333	500	833	0	50	0.00	0	0	50	167	8.60
2016	AAA	Colorado Springs	411	68	102	8	45	248	363	365	728	15	70	0.60	20	8	29	117	4.91
2016	MLB	Milwaukee	22	3	4	0	0	182	250	182	432	8	68	0.29	1	0	0	0	0.33

Strong, athletic hitter with look of well-rounded fourth OF. Displays solid-average contact and works counts exceptionally well for OBP value. High-volume doubles power profile sans many HR. Good runner with on-base skills for 25+ SB upside with regular PT. Covers ground well enough for CF; strong arm profiles best as RF long-term.

Reinheimer,Jack

6 | Arizona | EXP MLB DEBUT: 2017 | H/W: 6-1 185 | FUT: Utility player | 6A

Bats R Age 24
2013 (5) East Carolina

- Pwr +
- BAvg + + +
- Spd + + +
- Def + + +

Year	Lev	Team	AB	R	H	HR	RBI	Avg	OB	Slg	OPS	bb%	ct%	Eye	SB	CS	x/h%	Iso	RC/G
2014	A	Clinton	436	69	115	2	46	264	324	335	659	8	83	0.51	34	9	20	71	3.75
2014	A+	High Desert	85	15	29	1	12	341	371	459	830	4	86	0.33	5	2	24	118	5.54
2015	AA	Jackson	202	25	56	1	16	277	324	351	676	6	81	0.36	12	1	21	74	3.82
2015	AA	Mobile	283	39	75	4	26	265	350	371	721	12	81	0.69	9	5	27	106	4.65
2016	AAA	Reno	500	64	144	2	48	288	350	384	734	9	81	0.52	20	11	26	96	4.73

Solid MIF on both sides of ball gets most out of ability due to plus-makeup. Headiness at plate, on the bases and in field plays up average tool set. Contact righthanded hitter, able to pepper liners to all fields. Little power in swing and frame. Plays average defense throughout the middle infield.

Renfroe,Hunter

9 | San Diego | EXP MLB DEBUT: 2016 | H/W: 6-1 220 | FUT: Starting OF | 9C

Bats R Age 25
2013 (1) Mississippi State

- Pwr + + + +
- BAvg + + +
- Spd + + +
- Def + + +

Year	Lev	Team	AB	R	H	HR	RBI	Avg	OB	Slg	OPS	bb%	ct%	Eye	SB	CS	x/h%	Iso	RC/G
2014	AA	San Antonio	224	17	52	5	23	232	309	353	662	10	76	0.47	2	1	33	121	3.72
2015	AA	San Antonio	421	50	109	14	54	259	313	425	738	7	73	0.29	4	1	36	166	4.59
2015	AAA	El Paso	90	15	30	6	24	333	362	633	995	4	78	0.20	1	0	43	300	7.54
2016	AAA	El Paso	533	95	163	30	105	306	333	557	891	4	78	0.19	5	2	42	251	6.19
2016	MLB	San Diego	35	8	13	4	14	371	389	800	1189	3	86	0.20	0	0	54	429	9.17

Cutting down on his swing path in 2016 paid huge dividends, as he corralled his strikeout rate without compromising power potential. Slugged 34 HRs between Triple-A & MLB. Struggles with patience and is prone to extend the zone. When he hits the ball, it barrels off the bat. Bulked up some last off-season but didn't lose athleticism.

Reyes,Franmil

9 | San Diego | EXP MLB DEBUT: 2018 | H/W: 6-5 240 | FUT: Starting OF | 7D

Bats R Age 21
2011 FA (DR)

- Pwr + + +
- BAvg + +
- Spd +
- Def + +

Year	Lev	Team	AB	R	H	HR	RBI	Avg	OB	Slg	OPS	bb%	ct%	Eye	SB	CS	x/h%	Iso	RC/G
2013	Rk	Azl Padres	165	24	52	3	30	315	389	467	856	11	76	0.51	5	5	33	152	6.40
2013	A-	Eugene	44	4	9	1	4	205	222	295	518	2	77	0.10	0	0	22	91	1.45
2014	A	Fort Wayne	508	67	126	11	59	248	300	368	668	7	77	0.32	1	5	29	120	3.66
2015	A	Fort Wayne	455	52	116	8	62	255	323	393	717	9	80	0.51	10	5	34	138	4.48
2016	A+	Lake Elsinore	493	63	137	16	83	278	341	452	793	9	78	0.44	2	3	37	174	5.34

Big-bodied, slugging OF made strides in 2016 with hit tool. Shortened trigger, making swing path more direct to ball, though still some inconsistency in swing balance. Raw-plus power transitioned to CAL well. A 20-grade runner, he's relegated long term to corner OF or 1B.

Reyes,Jomar

5 | Baltimore | EXP MLB DEBUT: 2019 | H/W: 6-3 220 | FUT: Starting 3B | 8C

Bats R Age 20
2014 FA (DR)

- Pwr + + +
- BAvg + +
- Spd +
- Def + +

Year	Lev	Team	AB	R	H	HR	RBI	Avg	OB	Slg	OPS	bb%	ct%	Eye	SB	CS	x/h%	Iso	RC/G
2014	Rk	GCL Orioles	186	23	53	4	29	285	338	425	763	7	80	0.39	1	0	30	140	4.92
2015	Rk	GCL Orioles	16	2	4	0	4	250	333	375	708	11	69	0.40	1	0	50	125	4.71
2015	A	Delmarva	309	36	86	5	44	278	318	440	758	6	76	0.25	1	0	42	162	4.87
2016	A+	Frederick	464	53	106	10	51	228	268	336	604	5	78	0.25	3	0	26	108	2.74

Big, strong 3B with dazzling combination of bat speed and strength. All about power, though aggressive approach negates best tool. Has potential for 30+ HR, but unlikely to hit for BA. Draws few walks and can struggle with spin. Has well below average speed, and poor footwork and range could move him to 1B. Payoff could be huge if patient.

Reyes,Victor

789 | Arizona | EXP MLB DEBUT: 2018 | H/W: 6-3 170 | FUT: Reserve OF | 6B

Bats L Age 22
2011 FA (VZ)

- Pwr + +
- BAvg + + +
- Spd + +
- Def + + +

Year	Lev	Team	AB	R	H	HR	RBI	Avg	OB	Slg	OPS	bb%	ct%	Eye	SB	CS	x/h%	Iso	RC/G
2013	Rk	Danville	81	12	26	0	4	321	345	358	703	4	89	0.33	0	0	12	37	4.04
2013	Rk	GCL Braves	112	22	40	0	21	357	419	446	866	10	82	0.60	5	1	23	89	6.41
2014	A	Rome	332	32	86	0	34	259	309	298	607	7	83	0.41	12	7	15	39	3.02
2015	A	Kane County	424	57	132	2	59	311	345	389	734	5	86	0.38	13	4	18	78	4.48
2016	A+	Visalia	469	62	142	6	54	303	349	416	764	7	83	0.42	20	8	20	113	4.91

Contact-first OF developed some power in CAL, but hit tool pushing plus, with tremendous hand-eye coordination. Swing path conducive to high number of groundballs. Used more leverage this season to drive balls down the line. Fringe-speed despite 20 SB output. Rangy corner defender with poor arm. Best bet as LF.

Reynolds,Bryan

8 | San Francisco | EXP MLB DEBUT: 2018 | H/W: 6-3 200 | FUT: Starting OF | 8C

Bats B Age 22
2016 (2) Vanderbilt

- Pwr + + +
- BAvg + + +
- Spd + + +
- Def + + +

Year	Lev	Team	AB	R	H	HR	RBI	Avg	OB	Slg	OPS	bb%	ct%	Eye	SB	CS	x/h%	Iso	RC/G
2016	NCAA	Vanderbilt	224	59	74	13	57	330	451	603	1053	18	74	0.84	8	5	43	272	9.36
2016	A-	Salem-Keizer	154	28	48	5	30	312	358	500	858	7	73	0.27	2	0	38	188	6.21
2016	A	Augusta	63	11	20	1	8	317	348	444	793	5	68	0.15	1	0	30	127	5.49

Tall, rangy OF who efficiently uses smooth stroke to use all fields and hit for BA. No one tool stands out, but he does multiple things very well. Has decent power from both sides and can drive ball to gaps. Doesn't own great speed, but is good runner and sound defender. May swing and miss as he can overswing. Will likely move to corner OF.

Reynolds,Sean

89 | Miami | EXP MLB DEBUT: 2021 | H/W: 6-7 205 | FUT: Starting OF | 8E

Bats L Age 18
2016 (4) HS (CA)

- Pwr + + + +
- BAvg + +
- Spd + + +
- Def + +

Year	Lev	Team	AB	R	H	HR	RBI	Avg	OB	Slg	OPS	bb%	ct%	Eye	SB	CS	x/h%	Iso	RC/G
2016	Rk	GCL Marlins	148	17	23	0	11	155	265	196	461	13	57	0.34	3	3	17	41	0.78

Huge, muscular OF has the potential to develop plus power, but remains raw at the plate and struggled in his debut. Most teams viewed him as a pitcher, as he showed a good low-90s FB. Moves well in the OF with a plus arm and average speed. Good tools, but lots of work to do.

Riddle,J.T.

456 | Miami | EXP MLB DEBUT: 2017 | H/W: 6-1 180 | FUT: Utility player | 6B

Bats L Age 25
2013 (13) Kentucky

- Pwr +
- BAvg + +
- Spd + + +
- Def + + +

Year	Lev	Team	AB	R	H	HR	RBI	Avg	OB	Slg	OPS	bb%	ct%	Eye	SB	CS	x/h%	Iso	RC/G
2015	A+	Jupiter	185	30	50	0	9	270	311	314	625	6	84	0.38	7	3	14	43	3.21
2015	AA	Jacksonville	173	26	50	5	20	289	320	422	742	4	86	0.33	0	0	24	133	4.43
2015	AAA	New Orleans	3	2	2	0	0	667	800	667	1467	40	100		0	0	0	0	15.92
2016	AA	Jacksonville	389	49	108	3	51	278	334	368	702	8	81	0.46	5	1	23	90	4.23
2016	AAA	New Orleans	56	4	15	1	2	268	281	357	638	2	84	0.11	1	0	20	89	3.04

Gritty, aggressive player has a solid offensive game. Short, compact stroke and a line drive approach allows him to barrel the ball consistently, but without much power. Held his own at AA/AAA, slashing .276/.326/.366. Has seen action at 3B/SS/2B and has a plus arm, good hands, and solid range.

Riley,Austin

5 | Atlanta | EXP MLB DEBUT: 2019 | H/W: 6-3 220 | FUT: Starting 3B | 8D

Bats R Age 20
2015 (S-1) HS (MS)

- Pwr + + + +
- BAvg + +
- Spd + +
- Def + +

Year	Lev	Team	AB	R	H	HR	RBI	Avg	OB	Slg	OPS	bb%	ct%	Eye	SB	CS	x/h%	Iso	RC/G
2015	Rk	Danville	111	18	39	5	19	351	424	586	1010	11	75	0.50	0	1	38	234	8.41
2015	Rk	GCL Braves	106	18	27	7	21	255	331	500	831	10	65	0.32	2	1	44	245	6.17
2016	A	Rome	495	68	134	20	80	271	324	479	803	7	70	0.27	3	3	46	208	5.58

Strong RHH had solid full season debut. Slugged 20 HR in pitcher's league and has more raw power to tap into. Hit tool has question marks, including swing/miss tendency, and hitch in load causes trouble against velocity. Learned to cheat on FB as season wore on. Not the greatest athlete, but will pass at third, especially with plus arm.

Rios,Edwin

35 | Los Angeles (N) | EXP MLB DEBUT: 2018 | H/W: 6-3 220 | FUT: Starting 1B | 7D

Bats L Age 22
2015 (6) Florida Intl

- Pwr + + + +
- BAvg + +
- Spd + +
- Def + +

Year	Lev	Team	AB	R	H	HR	RBI	Avg	OB	Slg	OPS	bb%	ct%	Eye	SB	CS	x/h%	Iso	RC/G
2015	Rk	Azl Dodgers	7	1	3	0	0	429	429	429	857	0	86	0.00	0	1	0	0	5.35
2015	Rk	Ogden	68	8	16	3	13	235	307	471	777	9	57	0.24	0	0	63	235	6.17
2016	A	Great Lakes	119	17	30	6	13	252	299	487	787	6	63	0.18	3	1	50	235	5.67
2016	A+	Rancho Cuca	177	37	65	16	46	367	395	712	1106	4	80	0.23	0	0	43	345	8.65
2016	AA	Tulsa	122	14	31	5	17	254	300	434	734	6	75	0.26	0	0	39	180	4.42

Has good size and plus raw power. Mashed his way through three different levels, hitting .301/.341/.567 with 27 HR. Aggressive approach at the plate with strength results in plus power, but average bat speed and contact issues limit BA potential. Below-avg defender limits him to 1B.

Rivera, TJ — 45 — New York (N)

Bats R **Age** 28
2011 (NDFA) Troy

Pwr	++
BAvg	++++
Spd	++
Def	+++

EXP MLB DEBUT: 2016 **H/W:** 6-1 205 **FUT:** Utility player **6A**

Year	Lev	Team	AB	R	H	HR	RBI	Avg	OB	Slg	OPS	bb%	ct%	Eye	SB	CS	x/h%	Iso	RC/G
2014	AA	Binghamton	201	28	72	1	28	358	392	438	829	5	87	0.41	1	0	19	80	5.57
2015	AA	Binghamton	220	37	75	5	27	341	375	455	830	5	90	0.55	1	1	20	114	5.50
2015	AAA	Las Vegas	183	26	56	2	21	306	332	443	774	4	86	0.28	0	0	36	137	4.90
2016	AAA	Las Vegas	405	67	143	11	85	353	388	516	904	5	87	0.43	3	3	30	163	6.39
2016	MLB	NY Mets	105	10	35	3	16	333	352	476	828	3	84	0.18	0	0	23	143	5.30

Scrappy undrafted FA benefited from several injuries at 2B to break through as a late-season surprise. High baseball IQ has made up for swing speed deficiencies throughout pro career. Led PCL in batting average in '16. Doesn't profile for anything more than a utility player due to power profile and lack of patience.

Rivero, Sebastian — 2 — Kansas City

Bats R **Age** 18
2015 FA (VZ)

Pwr	+
BAvg	+++
Spd	+
Def	++++

EXP MLB DEBUT: 2021 **H/W:** 6-1 180 **FUT:** Starting C **7D**

Year	Lev	Team	AB	R	H	HR	RBI	Avg	OB	Slg	OPS	bb%	ct%	Eye	SB	CS	x/h%	Iso	RC/G
2016	Rk	Azl Royals	134	15	36	0	20	269	300	343	643	4	79	0.21	0	0	28	75	3.33

Defensive-oriented backstop who is very advanced for age with glove. Shows leadership qualities and is adept at both blocking and receiving. Owns solid average arm with quick release. More of a spray hitter at present and lacks strength for current pop. Makes OK contact, but free swinging ways need to be tamed to have BA potential.

Rizzo, Joe — 5 — Seattle

Bats L **Age** 19
2016 (2) HS (VA)

Pwr	++
BAvg	++
Spd	++
Def	+

EXP MLB DEBUT: 2020 **H/W:** 5-9 195 **FUT:** Starting 3B **8E**

Year	Lev	Team	AB	R	H	HR	RBI	Avg	OB	Slg	OPS	bb%	ct%	Eye	SB	CS	x/h%	Iso	RC/G
2016	Rk	Azl Mariners	148	21	43	2	21	291	364	392	756	10	76	0.47	2	1	23	101	5.02

Short, compact 3B with natural-hitting skills and chance to grow into prototypical slugger. Offers above average strength and plus, raw power from left side. Bat speed sufficient and could use better pitch recognition to hit for BA. Very raw defender and needs to improve footwork. Hands and actions can both be too stiff.

Robbins, Walker — 7 — St. Louis

Bats L **Age** 19
2016 (5) HS (MS)

Pwr	++
BAvg	++++
Spd	++
Def	++

EXP MLB DEBUT: 2021 **H/W:** 6-3 215 **FUT:** Starting OF **7D**

Year	Lev	Team	AB	R	H	HR	RBI	Avg	OB	Slg	OPS	bb%	ct%	Eye	SB	CS	x/h%	Iso	RC/G
2016	Rk	GCL Cardinals	108	14	20	0	6	185	221	194	416	4	71	0.16	3	0	5	9	0.09

Tall, strong-bodied prospect was the Cards 5th round pick. LHH is a bat only prospect with average athleticism. Has good bat speed and plus raw power, but will need to work on pitch recognition and making more consistent contact. Does have a good arm and is likely limited to 1B or LF.

Robertson, Daniel — 456 — Tampa Bay

Bats R **Age** 23
2012 (S-1) HS (CA)

Pwr	++
BAvg	+++
Spd	++
Def	+++

EXP MLB DEBUT: 2017 **H/W:** 6-1 205 **FUT:** Starting SS **7B**

Year	Lev	Team	AB	R	H	HR	RBI	Avg	OB	Slg	OPS	bb%	ct%	Eye	SB	CS	x/h%	Iso	RC/G
2013	A	Beloit	401	59	111	9	46	277	344	401	745	9	80	0.52	1	7	28	125	4.77
2014	A+	Stockton	548	110	170	15	60	310	390	471	861	12	83	0.77	4	4	32	161	6.34
2015	Rk	GCL Devil Rays	8	2	1	0	0	125	364	125	489	27	75	1.50	1	0	0	0	1.95
2015	AA	Montgomery	299	49	82	4	41	274	346	415	761	10	81	0.57	2	3	35	140	5.12
2016	AAA	Durham	436	50	113	5	43	259	346	356	702	12	77	0.58	2	1	26	96	4.39

Instinctual, versatile INF who has regressed after a breakout 2014, but still has value. Natural hitter who combines mature eye with bat speed. Power and SB have declined. Ability to play all INF spots enhances his game as he has quick first step and OK range.

Robles, Victor — 8 — Washington

Bats R **Age** 19
2013 FA (DR)

Pwr	++
BAvg	++++
Spd	++++
Def	++++

EXP MLB DEBUT: 2018 **H/W:** 6-0 185 **FUT:** Starting CF **9B**

Year	Lev	Team	AB	R	H	HR	RBI	Avg	OB	Slg	OPS	bb%	ct%	Eye	SB	CS	x/h%	Iso	RC/G
2015	Rk	GCL Nationals	73	19	27	2	11	370	446	562	1007	12	84	0.83	12	1	33	192	8.18
2015	A-	Auburn	140	29	48	3	16	343	378	479	857	5	85	0.38	12	4	23	136	5.93
2016	Rk	GCL Nationals	20	3	3	1	1	150	150	300	450	0	65	0.00	0	1	33	150	0.13
2016	A	Hagerstown	233	48	71	5	30	305	355	459	814	7	84	0.47	19	8	28	155	5.53
2016	A+	Potomac	168	24	44	3	11	262	319	387	706	8	81	0.44	18	5	30	125	4.23

Premium athleticism meets advanced plate approach and keen baseball instincts—all in a teenager's body. Has the total package: fluid, loose swing that drives his exceptional hit tool and growing power, electric speed on bases and in the field and highlight-level defense. An impact player in the making who makes the game look easy.

Rodgers, Brendan — 46 — Colorado

Bats R **Age** 20
2015 (1) HS (FL)

Pwr	++++
BAvg	++++
Spd	+++
Def	+++

EXP MLB DEBUT: 2019 **H/W:** 6-0 180 **FUT:** Starting SS **9C**

Year	Lev	Team	AB	R	H	HR	RBI	Avg	OB	Slg	OPS	bb%	ct%	Eye	SB	CS	x/h%	Iso	RC/G
2015	Rk	Grand Junction	143	22	39	3	20	273	342	420	761	9	74	0.41	4	3	33	147	5.08
2016	A	Asheville	442	73	124	19	73	281	333	480	813	7	78	0.36	6	3	40	199	5.46

3rd pick in 2015 draft has plus raw power, good bat speed, and a solid understanding of the strike zone. Already starting to add bulk and muscle and blasted 31 doubles along with 19 HR at Low-A. Above-average runner with good range, soft hands, and a strong arm. No longer any questions about his ability to stick at short. A star in the making.

Rodriguez, Alfredo — 6 — Cincinnati

Bats R **Age** 22
2016 FA (CU)

Pwr	++
BAvg	++
Spd	++++
Def	++++

EXP MLB DEBUT: 2018 **H/W:** 6-0 190 **FUT:** Starting SS **7D**

Year	Lev	Team	AB	R	H	HR	RBI	Avg	OB	Slg	OPS	bb%	ct%	Eye	SB	CS	x/h%	Iso	RC/G
2016		Did not play in the US																	

Glove-first Cuban SS, compared defensively to former LA prospect Erisbel Arruebarrena without the arm. Swing-and-miss concerns exist in swing. Overall, solid approach at plate. Works counts. Has power potential in build; 10-15 HRs at maturity. A plus runner, utilizes strength on both sides of ball. Extremely heady base runner.

Rodriguez, Carlos — 37 — St. Louis

Bats R **Age** 20
2013 FA (VZ)

Pwr	+++
BAvg	+++
Spd	++
Def	++

EXP MLB DEBUT: 2020 **H/W:** 6-2 215 **FUT:** Starting 1B **7D**

Year	Lev	Team	AB	R	H	HR	RBI	Avg	OB	Slg	OPS	bb%	ct%	Eye	SB	CS	x/h%	Iso	RC/G
2016	Rk	GCL Cardinals	95	12	23	1	7	242	339	358	697	13	68	0.47	0	1	26	116	4.49

Strong, powerful 1B prospect struggled in his U.S. debut. Moves well defensively with soft hands and a good feel for 1B. Has a quick bat and good raw power, but needs to make more consistent contact and failed to make adjustments as the season progressed. A work in progress.

Rodriguez, David — 2 — Tampa Bay

Bats R **Age** 21
2012 FA (VZ)

Pwr	+
BAvg	++
Spd	++
Def	+++

EXP MLB DEBUT: 2019 **H/W:** 6-1 215 **FUT:** Starting C **8E**

Year	Lev	Team	AB	R	H	HR	RBI	Avg	OB	Slg	OPS	bb%	ct%	Eye	SB	CS	x/h%	Iso	RC/G
2014	Rk	GCL Devil Rays	128	15	35	0	23	273	321	383	704	7	76	0.29	3	0	34	109	4.29
2015	Rk	Princeton	178	20	46	4	27	258	316	376	692	8	78	0.38	1	1	26	118	4.00
2016	A	Bowling Green	416	54	100	9	62	240	313	349	662	10	79	0.50	4	3	26	108	3.70

Strong defensive C who is developing quickly and showing vast improvements across board. Has excellent catch-and-throw skills. Footwork getting better as well as receiving. Draws walks in simple approach and offers average power at best. Lacks bat speed and fringy bat control may lead to bottom of order hitter.

Rodriguez, Nellie — 3 — Cleveland

Bats R **Age** 22
2012 (15) HS (NY)

Pwr	++++
BAvg	++
Spd	+
Def	++

EXP MLB DEBUT: 2017 **H/W:** 6-2 225 **FUT:** Starting 1B **7D**

Year	Lev	Team	AB	R	H	HR	RBI	Avg	OB	Slg	OPS	bb%	ct%	Eye	SB	CS	x/h%	Iso	RC/G
2013	A	Lake County	160	18	31	1	13	194	306	256	563	14	67	0.49	0	0	26	63	2.46
2014	A	Lake County	485	67	130	22	88	268	349	482	831	11	71	0.42	0	0	44	214	6.09
2015	A+	Lynchburg	396	65	109	17	84	275	358	495	853	11	69	0.42	1	0	47	220	6.53
2015	AA	Akron	93	7	11	4	14	118	196	269	465	9	60	0.24	0	0	55	151	0.55
2016	AA	Akron	492	66	123	26	85	250	349	474	823	13	62	0.40	1	0	46	224	6.45

Big, thick 1B posted top-five marks in HR, ISO, BB% among EL bats. Creates natural loft in swing for big-time raw power, though poor ct% could cap his HR upside. Draws walks and works counts for OBP value; hits LH/RH well. Below-average athlete with stiff hands and fringy arm. Limited to 1B defensively where his power profiles well.

Rogers, Jake — 2 — Houston

Bats R Age 21
2016 (3) Tulane
EXP MLB DEBUT: 2018 H/W: 6-1 190 FUT: Starting C **7C**

Pwr	++
BAvg	++
Spd	++
Def	++++

Year	Lev	Team	AB	R	H	HR	RBI	Avg	OB	Slg	OPS	bb%	ct%	Eye	SB	CS	x/h%	Iso	RC/G
2016	NCAA	Tulane	211	46	55	7	28	261	366	403	769	14	81	0.85	13	1	29	142	5.27
2016	A-	Tri City	87	11	22	2	12	253	350	425	775	13	79	0.72	0	2	45	172	5.42
2016	A	Quad Cities	72	7	15	1	4	208	288	319	607	10	65	0.32	1	0	33	111	3.05

Defensive-oriented C who receives accolades for glovework. Owns cannon for an arm and can neutralize running game with quick release. Receives with proficiency and calls good game. Offense not nearly as polished. Can chop at ball, though works counts to get on base. Not much power in game and long swing leads to Ks.

Romero, Avery — 45 — Miami

Bats R Age 23
2012 (3) HS (FL)
EXP MLB DEBUT: 2018 H/W: 5-11 195 FUT: Utility player **6C**

Pwr	++
BAvg	++
Spd	++
Def	+++

Year	Lev	Team	AB	R	H	HR	RBI	Avg	OB	Slg	OPS	bb%	ct%	Eye	SB	CS	x/h%	Iso	RC/G
2014	A	Greensboro	366	51	117	5	46	320	363	429	792	6	87	0.53	6	4	25	109	5.22
2014	A+	Jupiter	100	12	32	0	10	320	364	400	764	7	87	0.54	4	1	25	80	4.99
2015	A+	Jupiter	455	47	118	3	42	259	316	314	631	8	84	0.54	3	4	15	55	3.38
2016	A+	Jupiter	269	28	68	3	27	253	304	335	639	7	86	0.51	1	0	24	82	3.46
2016	AA	Jacksonville	100	13	19	1	10	190	296	290	586	13	83	0.88	2	0	32	100	3.13

Struggled against more advanced pitching. Uses a short, compact stroke with good bat speed to barrel the ball, but failed to hit with authority at AA. Tick below average on the bases, but is a good baserunner. Solid defender with good hands and an average arm, but future now looks to be in a utility role.

Rondon, Adrian — 6 — Tampa Bay

Bats R Age 18
2014 FA (DR)
EXP MLB DEBUT: 2020 H/W: 6-1 190 FUT: Starting SS **9E**

Pwr	+++
BAvg	++
Spd	+++
Def	+++

Year	Lev	Team	AB	R	H	HR	RBI	Avg	OB	Slg	OPS	bb%	ct%	Eye	SB	CS	x/h%	Iso	RC/G
2015	Rk	GCL Devil Rays	145	3	24	0	11	166	253	234	488	10	61	0.30	0	2	38	69	1.28
2016	Rk	Princeton	193	29	48	7	36	249	296	430	726	6	70	0.22	1	5	40	181	4.46

Raw, developing INF with high ceiling, but long way to go. Incredible bat speed gives him power projection and makes loud contact when he puts bat to ball. Strikes out far too often when swing lengthens and long arms are exploitable. Exhibits average speed, but doesn't steal. May not have enough range for SS, but has quickness.

Rondon, Jose — 6 — San Diego

Bats R Age 23
2011 FA (VZ)
EXP MLB DEBUT: 2016 H/W: 6-1 195 FUT: Starting SS **7B**

Pwr	++
BAvg	+++
Spd	+++
Def	+++

Year	Lev	Team	AB	R	H	HR	RBI	Avg	OB	Slg	OPS	bb%	ct%	Eye	SB	CS	x/h%	Iso	RC/G
2015	A+	Lake Elsinore	237	50	71	3	22	300	357	414	770	8	84	0.55	17	6	25	114	5.08
2015	AA	San Antonio	100	6	19	0	9	190	221	230	451	4	85	0.27	1	3	16	40	1.13
2016	AA	San Antonio	376	45	105	5	44	279	307	386	693	4	82	0.23	13	4	27	106	3.86
2016	AAA	El Paso	80	8	24	1	9	300	309	388	696	1	85	0.08	0	1	21	88	3.73
2016	MLB	San Diego	25	1	3	0	1	120	154	120	274	4	84	0.25	0	0	0	0	-1.04

Well-rounded SS made MLB debut after splitting most of '16 between AA and AAA. High floor, low ceiling. Ready to contribute with bat and at SS soon. Sprays ball to all fields; good bat-to-ball ability. Aggressive around the strike zone results in soft contact. Average runner, but uses good footwork and instincts defensively and on basepaths.

Rortvedt, Ben — 2 — Minnesota

Bats L Age 19
2016 (2) HS (WI)
EXP MLB DEBUT: 2021 H/W: 5-10 190 FUT: Starting C **8D**

Pwr	+++
BAvg	++
Spd	++
Def	++

Year	Lev	Team	AB	R	H	HR	RBI	Avg	OB	Slg	OPS	bb%	ct%	Eye	SB	CS	x/h%	Iso	RC/G
2016	Rk	GCL Twins	59	3	12	0	3	203	266	254	520	8	86	0.63	0	0	25	51	2.23
2016	Rk	Elizabethton	40	2	10	0	7	250	333	250	583	11	95	2.50	0	0	0	0	3.46

Short, stout backstop who will take time to develop, but upside is high. Lots of power packed in short stroke and has chance to hit for BA and HR. Swings smoothly, though will chase breaking balls out of zone. Receiving needs attention, but tools there to be solid defender. Throws with accuracy and strength and understands game-calling.

Rosario, Amed — 6 — New York (N)

Bats R Age 21
2012 FA (DR)
EXP MLB DEBUT: 2017 H/W: 6-2 190 FUT: Starting SS **9C**

Pwr	+++
BAvg	++++
Spd	++++
Def	+++

Year	Lev	Team	AB	R	H	HR	RBI	Avg	OB	Slg	OPS	bb%	ct%	Eye	SB	CS	x/h%	Iso	RC/G
2014	A	Savannah	30	2	4	1	4	133	161	300	461	3	63	0.09	0	0	50	167	0.60
2015	A+	St. Lucie	385	41	99	0	25	257	299	335	634	6	81	0.32	12	4	25	78	3.32
2015	AA	Binghamton	10	1	1	0	1	100	100	100	200	0	50	0.00	1	0	0	0	-4.05
2016	A+	St. Lucie	265	27	82	3	40	309	360	442	802	7	86	0.58	13	6	26	132	5.45
2016	AA	Binghamton	214	38	73	2	31	341	395	481	876	8	76	0.37	6	2	29	140	6.58

Athletic SS was the talk of the Eastern League in 2016. Owns a dynamic hit tool as he barrels line drives to all fields. Power has begun to develop in BP as frame fills out. A plus runner, still learning how to use speed on basepaths. Improved footwork at SS; potential plus defender.

Ruiz, Esteury — 46 — Kansas City

Bats R Age 18
2015 FA (DR)
EXP MLB DEBUT: 2022 H/W: 6-0 150 FUT: Starting MIF **8E**

Pwr	++
BAvg	+++
Spd	+++
Def	++

Year	Lev	Team	AB	R	H	HR	RBI	Avg	OB	Slg	OPS	bb%	ct%	Eye	SB	CS	x/h%	Iso	RC/G
2016		Did not play in the US																	

High-upside INF with exciting talent and tools. Spent most of season at 2B in DR, though has range and quickness for SS. Has very lean frame that needs strength, though plus bat speed results in gap power at present. Can turn on pitches, yet has bat control and pitch recognition. Can be inefficient runner, but has very good speed.

Ruiz, Keibert — 2 — Los Angeles (N)

Bats B Age 18
2014 FA (VZ)
EXP MLB DEBUT: 2022 H/W: 6-0 165 FUT: Starting C **7C**

Pwr	++
BAvg	+++
Spd	++
Def	+++

Year	Lev	Team	AB	R	H	HR	RBI	Avg	OB	Slg	OPS	bb%	ct%	Eye	SB	CS	x/h%	Iso	RC/G
2016	Rk	Ogden	189	28	67	2	33	354	393	503	896	6	88	0.52	0	0	33	148	6.45
2016	Rk	Azl Dodgers	33	5	16	0	15	485	528	667	1194	8	88	0.75	0	0	31	182	10.14

Had an impressive state-side debut, hitting .374/.412/.527 and was youngest player in Pioneer League. Has good approach from both sides, using quick bat and contact approach to shoot line drives to all fields. Approach results in average power, could add more as he matures. Plus defender with good hands, an average arm, and a quick release.

Ruiz, Rio — 5 — Atlanta

Bats L Age 22
2012 (4) HS (CA)
EXP MLB DEBUT: 2016 H/W: 6-1 230 FUT: Starting 3B **6C**

Pwr	+++
BAvg	+++
Spd	+
Def	++

Year	Lev	Team	AB	R	H	HR	RBI	Avg	OB	Slg	OPS	bb%	ct%	Eye	SB	CS	x/h%	Iso	RC/G
2013	A	Quad Cities	416	46	108	12	63	260	339	430	769	11	78	0.54	12	3	43	171	5.17
2014	A+	Lancaster	516	76	151	11	77	293	390	436	826	14	82	0.90	4	4	33	143	6.07
2015	AA	Mississippi	420	48	98	5	46	233	333	324	657	13	78	0.67	2	4	28	90	3.87
2016	AAA	Gwinnett	465	52	126	10	62	271	356	400	756	12	75	0.53	1	4	29	129	5.06
2016	MLB	Atlanta	7	1	2	0	2	286	286	571	857	0	71	0.00	1	0	50	286	6.52

Sturdy 3B rebounded after woeful '15. Shortened up swing, cut down on swing-and-miss. Plus raw power has yet to work into game. Struggles making consistent hard contact. Extremely slow runner, has little positional flexibility. Likely a second division starter at 1B or 3B.

Rutherford, Blake — 8 — New York (A)

Bats L Age 19
2016 (1) HS (CA)
EXP MLB DEBUT: 2020 H/W: 6-3 195 FUT: Starting OF **9D**

Pwr	+++
BAvg	++++
Spd	++
Def	+++

Year	Lev	Team	AB	R	H	HR	RBI	Avg	OB	Slg	OPS	bb%	ct%	Eye	SB	CS	x/h%	Iso	RC/G
2016	Rk	Pulaski	89	13	34	2	9	382	439	618	1057	9	73	0.38	0	2	38	236	9.27

Powerful OF who could evolve into offensive behemoth. Has existing strength to hit for above average pop, but can be pull happy and free-swinger. Plate coverage and bat control are sufficient and can hit LHP. Focuses more on line drives with level swing path. Will likely move to OF corner due to iffy speed and crude routes.

Sanchez, Ali — 2 — New York (N)

Bats R Age 20
2013 FA (VZ)
EXP MLB DEBUT: 2020 H/W: 6-1 200 FUT: Reserve C **7D**

Pwr	++
BAvg	+++
Spd	++
Def	++++

Year	Lev	Team	AB	R	H	HR	RBI	Avg	OB	Slg	OPS	bb%	ct%	Eye	SB	CS	x/h%	Iso	RC/G
2015	Rk	GCL Mets	162	20	45	0	17	278	328	315	642	7	84	0.46	2	0	13	37	3.48
2015	Rk	Kingsport	11	2	2	0	3	182	182	182	364	0	82	0.00	0	0	0	0	-0.33
2016	A-	Brooklyn	171	15	37	0	11	216	260	275	535	6	85	0.38	2	0	27	58	2.21

A defensive-minded catcher, his offense declined in 2016. Never known as an offensive juggernaut, his contact skills took a step back. No longer barreling pitches with regular consistency, weak contact became hallmark to game. Approach isn't conducive to much power.

Sanchez,Jesus — 8 — Tampa Bay

EXP MLB DEBUT: 2020 | H/W: 6-2 185 | FUT: Starting CF | 9E

Bats L Age 19
2014 FA (DR)
Pwr +++
BAvg +++
Spd +++
Def +++

Year	Lev	Team	AB	R	H	HR	RBI	Avg	OB	Slg	OPS	bb%	ct%	Eye	SB	CS	x/h%	Iso	RC/G
2016	Rk	Princeton	49	8	17	3	8	347	385	612	997	6	76	0.25	1	0	41	265	7.76
2016	Rk	GCL Devil Rays	164	25	53	4	31	323	347	530	878	4	81	0.19	1	5	34	207	6.15

Projectable, athletic OF who stood out in all phases of game. Has added strength to complement sweet lefty stroke. Has shown ability to hit LHP and shorten stroke when necessary for contact. Controls bat and projects to plus power down line. Runs very well and is solid in CF with advanced instincts.

Sands,Donny — 2 — New York (A)

EXP MLB DEBUT: 2020 | H/W: 6-2 190 | FUT: Starting C | 7D

Bats R Age 20
2015 (8) HS (AZ)
Pwr ++
BAvg +++
Spd ++
Def ++

Year	Lev	Team	AB	R	H	HR	RBI	Avg	OB	Slg	OPS	bb%	ct%	Eye	SB	CS	x/h%	Iso	RC/G
2016	Rk	GCL Yankees	52	3	14	0	3	269	283	327	610	2	92	0.25	1	0	21	58	3.07
2016	Rk	Pulaski	60	7	18	2	10	300	364	417	780	9	85	0.67	1	0	17	117	5.09

Tall, athletic prospect who converted to C in '16. Will take years to develop, but natural tools conducive to solid backstop. Owns strong arm with flashes of agility. Makes exceptional contact due to bat speed and short stroke. Balanced approach mutes power, but could grow to average. Long-term project, but payoff could be worth it.

Sanger,Brendon — 4 — Los Angeles (A)

EXP MLB DEBUT: 2019 | H/W: 6-0 195 | FUT: Reserve INF | 6B

Bats L Age 23
2015 (4) Florida Atlantic
Pwr ++
BAvg +++
Spd ++
Def ++

Year	Lev	Team	AB	R	H	HR	RBI	Avg	OB	Slg	OPS	bb%	ct%	Eye	SB	CS	x/h%	Iso	RC/G
2015	NCAA	Florida Atlantic	230	57	85	7	48	370	493	583	1076	20	87	1.87	2	0	36	213	9.48
2015	Rk	Orem	217	45	65	4	29	300	420	456	876	17	82	1.15	13	3	38	157	6.95
2016	A	Burlington	443	47	102	4	39	230	321	325	646	12	80	0.66	4	5	30	95	3.73

Natural-hitting 2B with disciplined approach and strike zone knowledge. Can put bat to ball and use all fields. Lacks power and defense to profile as everyday player, but has talent to warrant a look. Gets on base consistently, but doesn't run often. Range is limited at 2B, though arm is OK.

Santander,Anthony — 379 — Baltimore

EXP MLB DEBUT: 2018 | H/W: 6-2 190 | FUT: Starting OF | 7C

Bats B Age 22
2011 FA (VZ)
Pwr ++++
BAvg ++
Spd ++
Def +++

Year	Lev	Team	AB	R	H	HR	RBI	Avg	OB	Slg	OPS	bb%	ct%	Eye	SB	CS	x/h%	Iso	RC/G
2013	A	Lake County	219	27	53	5	31	242	284	370	654	6	80	0.30	6	3	34	128	3.44
2014	A	Lake County	163	16	30	1	10	184	261	270	531	9	70	0.35	2	0	37	86	1.95
2015	A-	Mahoning Valley	31	6	13	3	9	419	486	903	1389	11	74	0.50	0	0	69	484	13.52
2015	A	Lake County	248	46	68	10	42	274	323	460	783	7	79	0.34	4	2	38	185	5.04
2016	A+	Lynchburg	500	90	145	20	95	290	359	494	853	10	76	0.46	10	5	43	204	6.18

Muscular OF posted top-five marks in HR, ISO, OPS among CAR bats. Above-average power from both sides with big leg kick, though latter can lead to contact issues. Willing to walk; target for OBP owners. Thick build projects minimal SB impact. Fringy range with strong arm to profile as LF/RF; 1B potential fallback. Rule 5 pick from CLE.

Scavuzzo,Jacob — 78 — Los Angeles (N)

EXP MLB DEBUT: 2018 | H/W: 6-4 185 | FUT: Reserve OF | 6C

Bats R Age 23
2012 (21) HS (CA)
Pwr +++
BAvg ++
Spd ++
Def ++

Year	Lev	Team	AB	R	H	HR	RBI	Avg	OB	Slg	OPS	bb%	ct%	Eye	SB	CS	x/h%	Iso	RC/G
2014	Rk	Ogden	45	6	13	1	5	289	333	489	822	6	78	0.30	2	0	54	200	5.72
2014	A	Great Lakes	402	46	84	5	35	209	267	311	578	7	69	0.25	17	4	32	102	2.51
2015	A	Great Lakes	213	30	56	5	20	263	286	427	714	3	79	0.16	4	1	39	164	4.09
2015	A+	Rancho Cuca	227	47	70	13	49	308	367	568	935	8	76	0.39	3	4	46	260	7.12
2016	AA	Tulsa	421	59	112	10	39	266	312	397	708	6	76	0.28	4	2	29	131	4.14

Tall, athletic OF was a 21st round pick and has worked hard to become a legit prospect. Added bulk; has plus bat speed and aggressive swing to gain above-average power, but also lots of swing-and-miss. Average speed and arm strength fit best in LF. Failed to repeat his '15 breakout.

Schrock,Max — 4 — Oakland

EXP MLB DEBUT: 2017 | H/W: 5-8 180 | FUT: Starting 2B | 7C

Bats L Age 22
2015 (13) South Carolina
Pwr ++
BAvg ++++
Spd ++
Def ++

Year	Lev	Team	AB	R	H	HR	RBI	Avg	OB	Slg	OPS	bb%	ct%	Eye	SB	CS	x/h%	Iso	RC/G
2015	A-	Auburn	172	31	53	2	14	308	357	448	804	7	91	0.81	2	1	30	140	5.52
2016	A	Hagerstown	270	46	88	4	39	326	377	459	836	8	93	1.10	15	3	30	133	5.89
2016	A+	Potomac	232	30	79	5	29	341	365	453	818	4	91	0.41	7	2	20	112	5.28
2016	A+	Stockton	9	0	1	0	0	111	111	111	222	0	100		0	0	0	0	-0.55
2016	AA	Midland	23	3	9	0	3	391	391	435	826	0	100		0	1	11	43	5.26

Short, natural hitter who rarely strikes out. Can be tough out and has enough bat speed and strength to hit hard line drives to gaps. Can pull ball out on occasion and reads spin well. Not much speed, but savvy baserunning allows for SB. Not a proficient defender and relegated to 2B with limited range and arm.

Senzel,Nick — 5 — Cincinnati

EXP MLB DEBUT: 2018 | H/W: 6-1 205 | FUT: Starting 3B | 9C

Bats R Age 21
2016 (1) Tennessee
Pwr +++
BAvg ++++
Spd +++
Def ++++

Year	Lev	Team	AB	R	H	HR	RBI	Avg	OB	Slg	OPS	bb%	ct%	Eye	SB	CS	x/h%	Iso	RC/G
2016	NCAA	Tennessee	210	57	74	8	59	352	456	595	1051	16	90	1.90	25	4	46	243	8.85
2016	Rk	Billings	33	3	5	0	4	152	282	182	464	15	85	1.20	3	0	20	30	1.84
2016	A	Dayton	210	38	69	7	36	329	417	567	984	13	77	0.65	15	7	48	238	8.22

The best college hitter in '16 draft. Exhibits an average or better tools across board. A worker. Improved swing path to lift more without compromising line drive approach. Should hit for more power than college numbers indicated. Will stick at 3B long term after tremendous improvements in '16.

Sepulveda,Carlos — 4 — Chicago (N)

EXP MLB DEBUT: 2021 | H/W: 5-10 170 | FUT: Utility player | 7D

Bats L Age 20
2014 FA (MX)
Pwr +
BAvg +++
Spd +++
Def +++

Year	Lev	Team	AB	R	H	HR	RBI	Avg	OB	Slg	OPS	bb%	ct%	Eye	SB	CS	x/h%	Iso	RC/G
2016	A	South Bend	332	55	103	1	24	310	360	373	734	7	88	0.63	4	11	17	63	4.65

Got off to a slow start after missing 6 weeks. When healthy, he tore the cover off the ball, hitting .330 in June and .337 in July. Quick LH stroke results in line drives to all fields. Good approach at the plate leads to consistent contact. Might be shorter than his listed 5-10, but moves well at 2B with a good glove and solid arm.

Seymour,Anfernee — 6 — Atlanta

EXP MLB DEBUT: 2020 | H/W: 5-11 165 | FUT: Starting SS | 8E

Bats B Age 21
2014 (7) HS (FL)
Pwr +
BAvg ++
Spd +++++
Def ++

Year	Lev	Team	AB	R	H	HR	RBI	Avg	OB	Slg	OPS	bb%	ct%	Eye	SB	CS	x/h%	Iso	RC/G
2014	Rk	GCL Marlins	98	24	24	0	3	245	327	265	593	11	72	0.44	11	2	4	20	2.83
2015	A-	Batavia	238	39	65	0	14	273	329	349	678	8	78	0.38	29	6	22	76	3.96
2016	A	Greensboro	409	61	103	1	26	252	290	306	596	5	77	0.23	36	12	17	54	2.68
2016	A	Rome	82	11	23	0	5	280	314	293	607	5	73	0.18	7	1	4	12	2.71

Athletic SS, but considerable rawness throughout game. Quick, compact swing leads to barreled contact, but doesn't read spin well. Lots of swing and miss on breaking balls close to zone. No power in frame, but 80-grade speed with 43 SB in '16. Could be 60-plus SB type at full projection. Rangy but raw at SS, could move to OF.

Shaffer,Richie — 359 — Cincinnati

EXP MLB DEBUT: 2015 | H/W: 6-3 220 | FUT: Starting 3B | 7C

Bats R Age 26
2012 (1) Clemson
Pwr ++++
BAvg ++
Spd ++
Def ++

Year	Lev	Team	AB	R	H	HR	RBI	Avg	OB	Slg	OPS	bb%	ct%	Eye	SB	CS	x/h%	Iso	RC/G
2015	AA	Montgomery	149	22	39	7	27	262	360	470	830	13	67	0.47	3	0	44	208	6.31
2015	AAA	Durham	244	42	66	19	45	270	353	582	935	11	70	0.42	1	1	56	311	7.47
2015	MLB	Tampa Bay	74	11	14	4	6	189	286	392	678	12	57	0.31	0	1	50	203	4.29
2016	AAA	Durham	428	49	97	11	48	227	329	367	695	13	68	0.48	4	1	39	140	4.35
2016	MLB	Tampa Bay	48	5	12	1	4	250	321	438	758	9	63	0.28	0	1	58	188	5.60

Tall, versatile prospect who hits for power and draws walks, but little else. Hasn't found success in limited time in majors, but has found LHP to his liking. Doesn't often tap into natural pop as he can lunge at balls and expand K zone. Plays 1B, 3B, and RF with strong arm, but poor speed.

Shaw,Chris — 3 — San Francisco

EXP MLB DEBUT: 2017 | H/W: 6-4 235 | FUT: Starting 1B | 8B

Bats L Age 23
2015 (1) Boston College
Pwr ++++
BAvg +++
Spd +
Def ++

Year	Lev	Team	AB	R	H	HR	RBI	Avg	OB	Slg	OPS	bb%	ct%	Eye	SB	CS	x/h%	Iso	RC/G
2015	NCAA	Boston College	144	25	46	11	43	319	402	611	1014	12	82	0.77	0	0	43	292	8.02
2015	A-	Salem-Kaizer	178	22	51	12	30	287	355	551	906	10	77	0.46	0	0	45	264	6.68
2016	A+	San Jose	270	47	77	16	55	285	352	544	897	9	74	0.40	0	0	49	259	6.73
2016	AA	Richmond	232	26	57	5	30	246	306	414	719	8	76	0.36	0	0	44	168	4.46

Hulking slugger with feel for bat. Has 30+ HR potential by natural strength and plus bat speed. Very fluid swing from left side and has ability to use all fields. Swing can get long and susceptible to K, but trade off for power is more than OK. Improving defender at 1B, though has very slow foot speed. Can struggle with LHP.

Shepherd,Zac

5 | Detroit | EXP MLB DEBUT: 2019 | H/W: 6-3 185 | FUT: Starting 3B | 8D

Bats R Age 21 — 2012 FA (AU)

Pwr +++ · BAvg ++ · Spd ++ · Def ++

Year	Lev	Team	AB	R	H	HR	RBI	Avg	OB	Slg	OPS	bb%	ct%	Eye	SB	CS	x/h%	Iso	RC/G
2014	Rk	GCL Tigers	173	34	52	4	29	301	376	497	873	11	75	0.48	5	1	40	197	6.72
2015	A	West Michigan	383	48	94	5	51	245	328	339	667	11	69	0.40	4	3	26	94	3.89
2016	A+	Lakeland	409	62	76	15	50	186	296	350	646	14	61	0.40	0	0	47	164	3.68

Lanky 3B who led FSL in Ks in miserable season. Long swing and poor instincts exploited by good pitchers, though showed signs of tapping into natural power. Swings hard and has leverage in stroke to hit for pop to all fields. Swing and miss part of game. Has hands and arm for 3B, but needs help with feet and throwing accuracy.

Sierra,Anibal

6 | Houston | EXP MLB DEBUT: 2018 | H/W: 6-1 190 | FUT: Starting SS | 7C

Bats R Age 23 — 2016 FA (CU)

Pwr ++ · BAvg +++ · Spd +++ · Def +++

Year	Lev	Team	AB	R	H	HR	RBI	Avg	OB	Slg	OPS	bb%	ct%	Eye	SB	CS	x/h%	Iso	RC/G
2016		Did not play in the US																	

Quick, agile INF who could advance quickly on basis of offensive potential and solid defense. Swings a quick bat and exhibits good raw power. May not get to power as he is content with using entire field with simple, balanced stroke. Very quick defender with clean hands and textbook footwork. Can make careless errors, but easily correctable.

Sierra,Magneuris

8 | St. Louis | EXP MLB DEBUT: 2019 | H/W: 5-11 160 | FUT: Starting CF | 8C

Bats L Age 20 — 2012 FA (DR)

Pwr ++ · BAvg +++ · Spd ++++ · Def +++

Year	Lev	Team	AB	R	H	HR	RBI	Avg	OB	Slg	OPS	bb%	ct%	Eye	SB	CS	x/h%	Iso	RC/G
2014	Rk	GCL Cardinals	202	42	78	2	30	386	431	505	936	7	85	0.53	13	3	22	119	6.99
2015	Rk	Johnson City	216	38	68	3	15	315	370	394	764	8	81	0.45	15	2	16	79	4.92
2015	A	Peoria	178	19	34	1	7	191	222	247	469	4	71	0.13	4	5	15	56	0.83
2016	A	Peoria	524	78	161	3	60	307	335	395	730	4	81	0.23	31	17	22	88	4.35

Toolsy, athletic OF continues his rapid development. Has plus eye-hand coordination and barrels the ball well. Strike zone judgment fluctuated and he struggled with breaking balls down in the zone. Above-average speed led to a career high 31 SB. Gap power is only average tool and has the speed and arm to stick in CF.

Sierra,Miguelangel

46 | Houston | EXP MLB DEBUT: 2020 | H/W: 5-11 165 | FUT: Starting SS | 8E

Bats R Age 19 — 2014 FA (VZ)

Pwr +++ · BAvg ++ · Spd +++ · Def +++

Year	Lev	Team	AB	R	H	HR	RBI	Avg	OB	Slg	OPS	bb%	ct%	Eye	SB	CS	x/h%	Iso	RC/G
2016	Rk	Greeneville	121	23	35	11	19	289	353	620	973	9	67	0.30	6	6	46	331	8.04
2016	A-	Tri City	93	6	13	0	5	140	200	183	383	7	63	0.21	0	3	23	43	-0.46

Rangy, instinctual INF with impressive set of skills. Growing into lean frame and showcased surprising pop. Uses all fields in approach, though expands strike zone and can sell out for power. Needs to learn bat control to hit for BA. Has ample range and soft hands along with arm strength suitable for SS, but can make careless errors.

Simcox,A.J.

6 | Detroit | EXP MLB DEBUT: 2018 | H/W: 6-3 185 | FUT: Starting SS | 7C

Bats R Age 22 — 2015 (14) Tennessee

Pwr ++ · BAvg +++ · Spd +++ · Def +++

Year	Lev	Team	AB	R	H	HR	RBI	Avg	OB	Slg	OPS	bb%	ct%	Eye	SB	CS	x/h%	Iso	RC/G
2015	NCAA	Tennessee	188	29	55	1	27	293	357	378	735	9	84	0.63	15	3	20	85	4.76
2015	Rk	GCL Tigers	15	4	5	0	1	333	375	333	708	6	80	0.33	2	0	0	0	4.10
2015	A-	Connecticut	100	14	27	0	12	270	305	340	645	5	86	0.36	5	2	22	70	3.48
2015	A	West Michigan	85	11	34	1	8	400	433	471	904	6	87	0.45	4	2	12	71	6.36
2016	A+	Lakeland	527	76	138	5	51	262	299	345	644	5	80	0.26	7	5	21	83	3.32

Instinctual INF who combines savvy with smooth stroke to be viable prospect. Doesn't stand out, but focuses on contact and use of entire field. All 5 HR hit in July, but power not part of equation. Needs to get on base more to use average speed. Arm is best defensive tool, though uses smooth actions and average range to make plays.

Sisco,Chance

2 | Baltimore | EXP MLB DEBUT: 2017 | H/W: 6-2 195 | FUT: Starting C | 8C

Bats L Age 22 — 2013 (2) HS (CA)

Pwr ++ · BAvg ++++ · Spd ++ · Def ++

Year	Lev	Team	AB	R	H	HR	RBI	Avg	OB	Slg	OPS	bb%	ct%	Eye	SB	CS	x/h%	Iso	RC/G
2014	A	Delmarva	426	56	145	5	63	340	400	448	848	9	81	0.53	1	2	23	108	6.08
2015	A+	Frederick	263	30	81	4	26	308	385	422	807	11	84	0.80	8	1	23	114	5.70
2015	AA	Bowie	74	9	19	2	8	257	337	392	729	11	81	0.64	0	1	32	135	4.64
2016	AA	Bowie	408	52	130	4	44	319	405	422	826	13	80	0.72	2	2	25	103	6.07
2016	AAA	Norfolk	16	4	4	2	7	250	333	625	958	11	69	0.40	0	0	50	375	7.47

Smooth backstop who led EL in OBP and hit HR in Futures Game. Advanced hitter who works counts, makes contact with clean swing path, and hits hard line drives to all fields. Game power hasn't yet developed and has struggled against LHP. Improving defender, especially catch and throw skills, but only average at best. Bat will carry him.

Slater,Austin

78 | San Francisco | EXP MLB DEBUT: 2017 | H/W: 6-2 215 | FUT: Starting OF | 7C

Bats R Age 24 — 2014 (8) Stanford

Pwr +++ · BAvg +++ · Spd ++ · Def ++

Year	Lev	Team	AB	R	H	HR	RBI	Avg	OB	Slg	OPS	bb%	ct%	Eye	SB	CS	x/h%	Iso	RC/G
2014	A-	Salem-Kaizer	118	21	41	2	23	347	398	449	848	8	86	0.59	7	1	20	102	5.91
2015	A+	San Jose	250	25	73	3	34	292	319	396	715	4	82	0.23	4	3	26	104	4.14
2015	AA	Richmond	199	21	59	0	13	296	343	362	705	7	76	0.29	1	1	20	65	4.21
2016	AA	Richmond	145	20	46	5	25	317	414	490	904	14	75	0.67	6	1	30	172	7.14
2016	AAA	Sacramento	245	36	73	13	42	298	381	506	887	12	78	0.62	2	6	34	208	6.58

Improving prospect who set easy high in HR while drastically improving walk rate. Very successful against LHP and has strong feel for contact. Should hit for nice BA with at least average pop. Added loft to stroke to better utilize natural bat speed. Not much of a runner and needs to find defensive home. Played 2B in '15 and OF in '16.

Smith,Dominic

3 | New York (N) | EXP MLB DEBUT: 2017 | H/W: 6-0 250 | FUT: Starting 1B | 8C

Bats L Age 21 — 2013 (1) HS (CA)

Pwr +++ · BAvg ++++ · Spd ++ · Def +++

Year	Lev	Team	AB	R	H	HR	RBI	Avg	OB	Slg	OPS	bb%	ct%	Eye	SB	CS	x/h%	Iso	RC/G
2013	Rk	GCL Mets	167	23	48	3	22	287	377	407	784	13	78	0.65	2	4	27	120	5.49
2013	Rk	Kingsport	6	2	4	0	4	667	750	1333	2083	25	100		0	0	100	667	21.29
2014	A	Savannah	461	52	125	1	44	271	344	338	682	10	83	0.66	5	4	22	67	4.16
2015	A+	St. Lucie	456	58	139	6	79	305	354	417	771	7	84	0.47	2	1	28	112	5.02
2016	AA	Binghamton	484	64	146	14	91	302	367	457	824	9	85	0.68	2	1	31	155	5.72

Polarizing, hefty 1B w ith solid all-around tools. Line-drive hitter has become adept at a gap-to-gap approach. Unafraid to turn on FB and pull it for a HR. Skill set never a question, but effort and desire has held him back. A good athlete, weight gain has robbed him of some flexibility and foot speed.

Smith,Dwight

7 | Toronto | EXP MLB DEBUT: 2017 | H/W: 5-11 195 | FUT: Starting OF | 7C

Bats L Age 24 — 2011 (S-1) HS (GA)

Pwr +++ · BAvg +++ · Spd +++ · Def +++

Year	Lev	Team	AB	R	H	HR	RBI	Avg	OB	Slg	OPS	bb%	ct%	Eye	SB	CS	x/h%	Iso	RC/G
2012	A-	Vancouver	63	5	11	0	8	175	246	254	500	9	83	0.55	0	0	36	79	1.93
2013	A	Lansing	423	57	120	7	46	284	362	388	750	11	81	0.63	25	5	23	104	4.94
2014	A+	Dunedin	472	83	134	12	60	284	362	453	816	11	85	0.84	15	4	36	169	5.79
2015	AA	New Hampshire	460	74	122	7	44	265	333	376	709	9	86	0.73	4	3	29	111	4.45
2016	AA	New Hampshire	471	56	125	15	74	265	329	433	763	9	81	0.49	12	7	35	168	4.94

Natural-hitting OF who repeated AA and set high in HR. Tough out with disciplined eye and ease of putting bat to ball. Hand-eye coordination is above average, though modest power may limit him to reserve role. Strikeout rate increased as he swung for fences frequently. Exhibits average speed, though fringy arm limits him to LF.

Smith,Will

2 | Los Angeles (N) | EXP MLB DEBUT: 2019 | H/W: 6-0 192 | FUT: Starting C | 8C

Bats R Age 22 — 2016 (1) Louisville

Pwr ++ · BAvg +++ · Spd +++ · Def ++++

Year	Lev	Team	AB	R	H	HR	RBI	Avg	OB	Slg	OPS	bb%	ct%	Eye	SB	CS	x/h%	Iso	RC/G
2016	NCAA	Louisville	157	40	60	7	43	382	449	567	1016	11	91	1.36	9	0	25	185	7.91
2016	Rk	Ogden	28	4	9	1	5	321	406	429	835	13	96	4.00	0	0	11	107	6.13
2016	A	Great Lakes	81	12	21	1	7	259	348	309	656	12	78	0.61	2	1	10	49	3.73
2016	A+	Rancho Cuca	97	13	21	2	12	216	315	320	635	13	68	0.45	1	0	29	103	3.43

Was the most athletic backstop in the 2016 draft. Features quickness on the bases and behind the plate. Uses a compact RH stroke to shoot line drives to all fields, but approach results in below-average power. Plus pitch recognition and plate discipline should allow him to hit for BA and get on base. Plus defender with a strong arm.

Solak,Nick

4 | New York (A) | EXP MLB DEBUT: 2019 | H/W: 5-11 175 | FUT: Starting 2B | 7C

Bats R Age 22 — 2016 (2) Louisville

Pwr ++ · BAvg ++++ · Spd +++ · Def ++

Year	Lev	Team	AB	R	H	HR	RBI	Avg	OB	Slg	OPS	bb%	ct%	Eye	SB	CS	x/h%	Iso	RC/G
2016	NCAA	Louisville	165	49	62	5	29	376	466	564	1030	15	87	1.27	9	0	32	188	8.54
2016	A-	Staten Island	240	48	77	3	25	321	396	421	817	11	84	0.77	8	0	22	100	5.82

Fundamentally-sound INF with a line-drive approach and offensive talent. Won't be factor in hitting for pop, but easily puts bat to ball and sprays to all fields. Sees lot of pitches and gets on base via walk or hit. Offers good speed for SB, though is fringy defender. Makes routine plays, but doesn't wow with glove.

Sosa,Edmundo | 6 | St. Louis | EXP MLB DEBUT: 2019 | H/W: 5-11 170 | FUT: Starting SS | 7C

Bats R Age 21	Year	Lev	Team	AB	R	H	HR	RBI	Avg	OB	Slg	OPS	bb%	ct%	Eye	SB	CS	x/h%	Iso	RC/G
2012 FA (PN)	2014	Rk	GCL Cardinals	207	37	57	1	23	275	333	377	710	8	86	0.62	8	5	25	101	4.45
Pwr ++	2014	A-	State College	5	0	1	0	0	200	200	200	400	0	60	0.00	0	0	0	0	-0.49
BAvg +++	2015	Rk	Johnson City	200	30	60	7	16	300	352	485	837	7	81	0.42	6	2	32	185	5.77
Spd +++	2016	A	Peoria	351	42	94	3	30	268	305	336	642	5	80	0.27	5	4	18	68	3.27
Def ++++	2016	A+	Palm Beach	34	3	10	0	4	294	314	412	726	3	76	0.13	0	0	20	118	4.37

Solid season at plate despite low contact and walk rates. Good all-around skills and understands how to play game. Barrels ball consistently but can be overly aggressive. Not likely to hit for power, but has good gap ability and has the swing for more as he matures. Defensively is quick with good hands and range, but a below-average arm.

Soto,Isael | 9 | Miami | EXP MLB DEBUT: 2020 | H/W: 6-0 190 | FUT: Starting OF | 8D

Bats L Age 20	Year	Lev	Team	AB	R	H	HR	RBI	Avg	OB	Slg	OPS	bb%	ct%	Eye	SB	CS	x/h%	Iso	RC/G
2013 FA (DR)	2014	Rk	GCL Marlins	183	26	46	7	23	251	290	426	716	5	74	0.21	1	2	37	175	4.15
Pwr +++	2015	Rk	GCL Marlins	26	3	9	1	5	346	452	615	1067	16	77	0.83	0	1	44	269	9.48
BAvg ++	2015	A-	Batavia	21	1	2	0	0	95	136	95	232	5	52	0.10	0	0	0	0	-3.48
Spd ++	2015	A	Greensboro	64	2	8	0	1	125	164	141	305	4	58	0.11	0	0	13	16	-1.96
Def ++	2016	A	Greensboro	401	51	99	9	38	247	320	399	719	10	71	0.37	3	0	38	152	4.56

Was healthy after missing most of 2015 with a knee injury. Remains raw at the plate, but does have plus bat speed and should develop average to above power. Soto is a free swinger and is overly aggressive, striking out 115 times in 401 AB. An average to below runner, but does have a good arm and should settle in as a corner OF.

Soto,Juan | 9 | Washington | EXP MLB DEBUT: 2020 | H/W: 6-1 185 | FUT: Starting OF | 9D

Bats L Age 18	Year	Lev	Team	AB	R	H	HR	RBI	Avg	OB	Slg	OPS	bb%	ct%	Eye	SB	CS	x/h%	Iso	RC/G
2015 FA (DR)																				
Pwr +++																				
BAvg ++++																				
Spd ++	2016	Rk	GCL Nationals	169	25	61	5	31	361	410	550	960	8	85	0.56	5	2	31	189	7.24
Def +++	2016	A-	Auburn	21	3	9	0	1	429	500	571	1071	13	81	0.75	0	0	33	143	9.27

A top international signee from 2015, Soto raked his way through rookie ball and won the MVP of the GCL. Has strong hands and an impeccable approach for a teenager, using the whole field and barreling up all types of pitches. Power is emerging, but his polished hit tool is the story. Average defense will limit him to an OF corner.

Sparks,Taylor | 5 | Cincinnati | EXP MLB DEBUT: 2018 | H/W: 6-4 200 | FUT: Reserve 3B | 7E

Bats R Age 24	Year	Lev	Team	AB	R	H	HR	RBI	Avg	OB	Slg	OPS	bb%	ct%	Eye	SB	CS	x/h%	Iso	RC/G
2014 (2) UC-Irvine	2014	NCAA	UC Irvine	253	45	78	5	37	308	375	506	881	10	72	0.39	8	8	40	198	6.89
Pwr +++	2014	Rk	Billings	198	41	46	10	30	232	336	490	826	14	58	0.37	14	1	52	258	7.03
BAvg +	2015	A+	Daytona	446	68	110	13	54	247	294	401	695	6	64	0.19	14	4	35	155	4.27
Spd +++	2016	A+	Daytona	245	26	54	6	34	220	254	359	613	4	77	0.19	6	4	39	139	2.83
Def +++	2016	AA	Pensacola	224	23	40	8	28	179	237	313	549	7	63	0.20	2	0	33	134	1.92

Contact issues reared its ugly head between Double-A and High-A in '16, as he features long, looping swings. Takes a while for hands to get started. Can get beaten by below-average velocity and struggles against breaking ball, but has plus power potential. Hit 13 HRs between two levels despite .200 BA. Can stick at 3B and runs well for size.

Starling,Bubba | 8 | Kansas City | EXP MLB DEBUT: 2017 | H/W: 6-4 210 | FUT: Reserve OF | 6B

Bats R Age 24	Year	Lev	Team	AB	R	H	HR	RBI	Avg	OB	Slg	OPS	bb%	ct%	Eye	SB	CS	x/h%	Iso	RC/G
2011 (1) HS (KS)	2014	A+	Wilmington	482	67	105	9	54	218	290	338	628	9	69	0.33	17	2	34	120	3.26
Pwr +++	2015	A+	Wilmington	44	6	17	2	12	386	471	614	1084	14	61	0.41	2	1	35	227	10.97
BAvg +	2015	AA	NW Arkansas	331	51	84	10	32	254	316	426	742	8	73	0.33	4	5	39	172	4.75
Spd +++	2016	AA	NW Arkansas	233	28	43	5	23	185	234	322	556	6	65	0.19	10	1	49	137	2.14
Def ++++	2016	AAA	Omaha	166	14	30	2	17	181	214	265	479	4	61	0.11	1	0	33	84	0.93

Athletic, aggressive OF who is terrific CF and exhibits above average speed, but lacks instincts and feel for bat. Struggles to hit breaking balls and rarely works counts. Raw power hasn't developed, but projects to at least average. Making contact comes difficult. Runs bases well and should stick at CF long-term.

Stassi,Max | 2 | Houston | EXP MLB DEBUT: 2013 | H/W: 5-10 200 | FUT: Starting C | 7D

Bats R Age 26	Year	Lev	Team	AB	R	H	HR	RBI	Avg	OB	Slg	OPS	bb%	ct%	Eye	SB	CS	x/h%	Iso	RC/G
2009 (4) HS (CA)	2014	MLB	Houston	20	2	7	0	4	350	350	450	800	0	70	0.00	0	0	29	100	5.34
Pwr +++	2015	AAA	Fresno	294	37	62	13	43	211	275	384	659	8	68	0.28	1	1	37	173	3.51
BAvg ++	2015	MLB	Houston	15	4	6	1	2	400	438	600	1038	6	67	0.20	0	0	17	200	8.85
Spd ++	2016	AAA	Fresno	243	21	56	7	32	230	289	374	663	8	73	0.31	1	0	36	144	3.60
Def +++	2016	MLB	Houston	13	1	1	0	0	77	77	77	154	0	62	0.00	0	0	0	0	-4.28

Short, powerful C who started year late after wrist surgery. Has spent time in majors over last four years and still decent prospect. Solid-average defender with average arm and keen pitch framing. Doesn't make enough contact and long swing hinders BA. Has good power to pull side, but has to stay healthy to become ensconced in majors.

Staton,Allen | 457 | St. Louis | EXP MLB DEBUT: 2019 | H/W: 5-10 190 | FUT: Utility player | 6C

Bats R Age 24	Year	Lev	Team	AB	R	H	HR	RBI	Avg	OB	Slg	OPS	bb%	ct%	Eye	SB	CS	x/h%	Iso	RC/G
2015 (NDFA) N Greenville																				
Pwr +++																				
BAvg +																				
Spd ++	2016	A+	Palm Beach	192	15	42	3	26	219	261	307	568	5	79	0.27	0	0	26	89	2.34
Def ++	2016	AA	Springfield	180	23	50	3	20	278	337	394	731	8	81	0.46	2	0	26	117	4.57

Hard-nosed player who gets the most of his ability. Shows sure hands on defense with a strong arm and split time between 3B, 2B, RF, and LF, though 3B will be his long-term position due to lack of range. Gets surprising pop from his short RH stroke with above-average raw power.

Stephenson,Tyler | 2 | Cincinnati | EXP MLB DEBUT: 2020 | H/W: 6-4 225 | FUT: Starting C | 7C

Bats R Age 20	Year	Lev	Team	AB	R	H	HR	RBI	Avg	OB	Slg	OPS	bb%	ct%	Eye	SB	CS	x/h%	Iso	RC/G
2015 (1) HS (GA)																				
Pwr +++																				
BAvg ++	2015	Rk	Billings	194	28	52	1	16	268	343	361	703	10	78	0.52	0	2	31	93	4.39
Spd ++	2016	Rk	AZL Reds	20	4	5	1	2	250	318	450	768	9	65	0.29	0	0	40	200	5.27
Def +++	2016	A	Dayton	139	17	30	3	16	216	278	324	602	8	68	0.27	0	0	27	108	2.79

Strong, physical receiver struggled with a wrist injury and concussion in '16. RHH struggled reading spin off breaking ball and lost bat speed due to injury. Plus raw power evident in BP. Made strides with footwork behind the plate, enhancing receiver skills while also aiding plus arm in running game.

Stevenson,Andrew | 78 | Washington | EXP MLB DEBUT: 2017 | H/W: 6-0 185 | FUT: Starting CF | 8C

Bats L Age 22	Year	Lev	Team	AB	R	H	HR	RBI	Avg	OB	Slg	OPS	bb%	ct%	Eye	SB	CS	x/h%	Iso	RC/G
2015 (2) LSU	2015	Rk	GCL Nationals	5	1	1	0	0	200	333	200	533	17	60	0.50	0	0	0	0	1.98
Pwr ++	2015	A-	Auburn	72	11	26	0	9	361	418	431	848	9	83	0.58	7	3	12	69	6.10
BAvg +++	2015	A	Hagerstown	137	28	39	1	16	285	324	358	682	6	88	0.50	16	4	15	73	3.94
4.12 Spd ++++	2016	A+	Potomac	273	37	83	1	18	304	360	418	778	8	84	0.55	27	9	25	114	5.25
Def ++++	2016	AA	Harrisburg	256	38	63	2	16	246	301	328	629	7	80	0.39	12	5	24	82	3.27

Possible future top-of-the-order hitter knows his game: hits hard grounders, uses middle of the field, emphasis on contact over power, and runs like the wind. With some added lower-half strength, could become a doubles gap hitter. Solid eye at the plate, though can still struggle with soft stuff away. Excellent glove in CF, but arm is suspect.

Stewart,Christin | 7 | Detroit | EXP MLB DEBUT: 2017 | H/W: 6-0 205 | FUT: Starting OF | 8C

Bats L Age 23	Year	Lev	Team	AB	R	H	HR	RBI	Avg	OB	Slg	OPS	bb%	ct%	Eye	SB	CS	x/h%	Iso	RC/G
2015 (1) Tennessee	2015	Rk	GCL Tigers	22	5	8	1	2	364	440	682	1122	12	77	0.60	2	1	50	318	9.93
Pwr ++++	2015	A-	Connecticut	49	7	12	2	11	245	315	490	805	9	63	0.28	0	0	50	245	6.16
BAvg +++	2015	A	West Michigan	185	29	53	7	31	286	350	492	842	9	76	0.40	3	2	38	205	6.03
Spd ++	2016	A+	Lakeland	355	59	93	23	67	262	389	524	913	17	70	0.70	3	1	49	262	7.42
Def +	2016	AA	Erie	87	17	19	6	19	218	313	448	761	12	70	0.46	0	0	42	230	4.93

Very strong hitter who led FSL in HR, OBP, and SLG before promotion to AA. Exhibited consistent pop and has bat speed and leveraged stroke to reach seats at any level. Draws walks, but can be too patient. BA in question as he swings for fences with long stroke. Doesn't run and likely to be baseclogger in time. Defense is suspect.

Stewart,D.J. | 7 | Baltimore | EXP MLB DEBUT: 2018 | H/W: 6-0 230 | FUT: Starting OF | 7C

Bats L Age 23	Year	Lev	Team	AB	R	H	HR	RBI	Avg	OB	Slg	OPS	bb%	ct%	Eye	SB	CS	x/h%	Iso	RC/G
2015 (1) Florida State																				
Pwr +++	2015	NCAA	Florida State	214	62	68	15	59	318	484	593	1078	24	78	1.47	12	3	40	276	9.74
BAvg +++	2015	A-	Aberdeen	238	25	52	6	24	218	287	345	632	9	78	0.44	4	1	31	126	3.28
Spd ++	2016	A	Delmarva	213	27	49	4	25	230	357	352	709	16	73	0.72	16	6	35	122	4.67
Def ++	2016	A+	Frederick	201	41	56	6	30	279	388	448	836	15	77	0.78	10	3	36	169	6.28

Big-framed OF who was better in A+ than A-. Swings a vicious stick with plus bat speed. Combines pitch recognition with contact to be formidable, but may not have enough game power. Has potential for 20+ HR, but more comfortable with line drives. Runs well for size and steals bags on instincts. Owns LF profile with sub-par range.

Stobbe,Cole

6 | Philadelphia | EXP MLB DEBUT: 2022 | H/W: 6-1 200 | FUT: Starting 3B | 7C

Bats R Age 19
2016 (3) HS (NE)
Pwr +++
BAvg ++
Spd +++
Def ++

Year	Lev	Team	AB	R	H	HR	RBI	Avg	OB	Slg	OPS	bb%	ct%	Eye	SB	CS	x/h%	Iso	RC/G
2016	Rk	GCL Phillies	148	23	40	4	13	270	333	405	739	9	80	0.47	3	6	30	135	4.62

Solid but unspectacular tools across the board. With above average raw power and current line drive ability, many see him growing into game power once he's acclimated to pro ball. Hit tool and speed should be solid-average also. Most feel he'll need to move off shortstop due to limited range, though he played there in the GCL.

Stuart,Champ

8 | New York (N) | EXP MLB DEBUT: 2018 | H/W: 6-0 185 | FUT: Reserve OF | 6E

Bats R Age 24
2013 (6) Brevard
Pwr ++
BAvg +
Spd ++++
Def +++

Year	Lev	Team	AB	R	H	HR	RBI	Avg	OB	Slg	OPS	bb%	ct%	Eye	SB	CS	x/h%	Iso	RC/G
2013	Rk	Kingsport	150	26	36	1	14	240	380	353	734	18	61	0.59	11	2	33	113	5.51
2014	A	Savannah	285	50	73	3	28	256	340	340	680	11	66	0.37	29	4	18	84	4.17
2015	A+	St. Lucie	330	43	58	4	17	176	265	242	507	11	57	0.28	21	3	22	67	1.50
2016	A+	St. Lucie	275	49	73	6	24	265	340	407	747	10	65	0.33	25	3	29	142	5.17
2016	AA	Binghamton	184	23	37	2	10	201	258	261	518	7	60	0.19	15	3	16	60	1.59

Raw, athletic OF continues to struggle against age appropriate pitching. Swings in parts, long and looping. Struggles with spins of breaking pitches. Top flight athlete; lots of SB potential in legs. Time is running out on bat, though.

Stubbs,Garrett

2 | Houston | EXP MLB DEBUT: 2018 | H/W: 5-10 175 | FUT: Starting C | 7D

Bats L Age 23
2015 (8) USC
Pwr ++
BAvg +++
Spd +++
Def +++

Year	Lev	Team	AB	R	H	HR	RBI	Avg	OB	Slg	OPS	bb%	ct%	Eye	SB	CS	x/h%	Iso	RC/G
2015	NCAA	USC	228	51	79	1	25	346	416	434	850	11	86	0.87	20	7	22	88	6.23
2015	A-	Tri City	34	5	8	0	2	235	366	235	601	17	91	2.33	2	0	0	0	3.85
2015	A	Quad Cities	84	15	23	0	5	274	378	333	711	14	98	7.00	1	0	22	60	5.23
2016	A+	Lancaster	206	35	60	6	38	291	379	442	820	12	82	0.78	10	3	32	150	5.86
2016	AA	Corpus Christi	120	23	39	4	16	325	396	517	912	10	91	1.27	5	0	36	192	6.85

Emerging prospect who makes extreme contact and starting to grow into average power potential. Exhibits more athleticism than most C and is adept at stealing bases. Hits LHP with aplomb and has chance to hit for BA. Lacks ideal size for C, though receives and blocks well with strong arm. Interesting profile.

Sullivan,Brett

2 | Tampa Bay | EXP MLB DEBUT: 2018 | H/W: 6-1 195 | FUT: Starting C | 7D

Bats L Age 23
2015 (17) Pacific
Pwr +++
BAvg +++
Spd +++
Def +

Year	Lev	Team	AB	R	H	HR	RBI	Avg	OB	Slg	OPS	bb%	ct%	Eye	SB	CS	x/h%	Iso	RC/G
2015	NCAA	Pacific	193	28	53	7	28	275	314	492	806	5	89	0.52	6	4	43	218	5.33
2015	Rk	Princeton	265	47	69	11	31	260	287	483	770	4	87	0.29	5	0	49	223	4.76
2016	A	Bowling Green	470	75	133	13	81	283	318	438	756	5	85	0.34	17	4	35	155	4.66

Raw C who moved behind plate in '16. Very athletic and smooth actions give him upside as defender. Strong arm is best attribute, but poor footwork and release hinder it. Makes very easy contact with simple stroke and has fine hand-eye coordination. Covers plate well and can hit for average power. Runs well, though will slow down in time.

Swanson,Dansby

6 | Atlanta | EXP MLB DEBUT: 2016 | H/W: 6-1 190 | FUT: Starting SS | 9B

Bats R Age 23
2015 (1) Vanderbilt
Pwr +++
BAvg ++++
Spd ++++
Def ++++

Year	Lev	Team	AB	R	H	HR	RBI	Avg	OB	Slg	OPS	bb%	ct%	Eye	SB	CS	x/h%	Iso	RC/G
2015	NCAA	Vanderbilt	281	76	94	15	64	335	423	623	1046	13	81	0.80	16	2	48	288	8.73
2015	A-	Hillsboro	83	19	24	1	11	289	392	482	874	14	83	1.00	0	0	46	193	6.86
2016	A+	Carolina	78	14	26	1	10	333	441	526	967	16	83	1.15	7	1	50	192	8.10
2016	AA	Mississippi	333	54	87	8	45	261	332	402	734	10	79	0.49	6	2	30	141	4.65
2016	MLB	Atlanta	129	20	39	3	17	302	366	442	808	9	74	0.38	3	0	28	140	5.67

Former #1 overall pick made MLB debut in August of '16 and was as advertised. Advanced approach at the plate and quick hands, plus uses all fields. Hit 12 HR between the minors and majors; expect 15-20 HR power in prime. Was very good defensively. Very heady player, plays up his SB totals.

Tapia,Raimel

789 | Colorado | EXP MLB DEBUT: 2016 | H/W: 6-2 160 | FUT: Starting CF | 8C

Bats L Age 23
2010 FA (DR)
Pwr +++
BAvg +++
Spd ++++
Def +++

Year	Lev	Team	AB	R	H	HR	RBI	Avg	OB	Slg	OPS	bb%	ct%	Eye	SB	CS	x/h%	Iso	RC/G
2014	A	Asheville	481	93	157	9	72	326	372	453	825	7	81	0.39	33	16	27	127	5.63
2015	A+	Modesto	544	74	166	12	71	305	335	467	801	4	81	0.23	26	10	33	162	5.21
2016	AA	Hartford	424	79	137	8	34	323	361	450	811	6	88	0.51	17	14	24	127	5.38
2016	AAA	Albuquerque	104	14	36	0	14	346	358	490	849	2	88	0.17	6	3	28	144	5.71
2016	MLB	Colorado	38	4	10	0	3	263	300	263	563	5	71	0.18	3	0	0	0	2.11

Forced his way to COL by slashing .328/.361/.458 between AA/AAA. Was more aggressive at plate, but good eye-hand coordination, bat speed, and ability to make hard contact allow him to hit for BA. Power was muted in the upper minors, but speed continues to be an asset and should stick in CF. Top of the order hitter.

Tatis Jr.,Fernando

56 | San Diego | EXP MLB DEBUT: 2020 | H/W: 6-3 185 | FUT: Starting 3B | 8E

Bats R Age 18
2015 FA (DR)
Pwr +++
BAvg +++
Spd ++
Def ++++

Year	Lev	Team	AB	R	H	HR	RBI	Avg	OB	Slg	OPS	bb%	ct%	Eye	SB	CS	x/h%	Iso	RC/G
2016	Rk	Azl Padres	176	35	48	4	20	273	312	426	738	5	75	0.23	14	2	38	153	4.54
2016	A-	Tri-City	44	4	12	0	5	273	319	455	774	6	70	0.23	1	1	50	182	5.50

Acquired in mid-season trade, had solid short-season debut. Raw hit tool. Will need to clean up swing to take advantage of his quick wrists and strong hands. Raw power potential in bat and frame. Hit 24 XBH in 55 games. Plus-defender potential at 3B. Has better natural movements at 3B than his father.

Taveras,Leody

8 | Texas | EXP MLB DEBUT: 2020 | H/W: 6-1 170 | FUT: Starting OF | 9D

Bats B Age 18
2015 FA (DR)
Pwr ++
BAvg +++
Spd ++++
Def ++++

Year	Lev	Team	AB	R	H	HR	RBI	Avg	OB	Slg	OPS	bb%	ct%	Eye	SB	CS	x/h%	Iso	RC/G
2016	Rk	Azl Rangers	144	22	40	1	15	278	329	382	711	7	83	0.46	11	4	25	104	4.35
2016	A-	Spokane	123	14	28	0	9	228	275	293	567	6	79	0.31	3	1	25	65	2.47

Athletic, lean OF with all requisite tools to be impact player. Plus defender with great range and accurate arm. Needs to add strength and polish up approach, but has bat talent. Makes consistent, hard contact from both sides and could hit for above average pop at peak. Instinctual hitter who knows strike zone and can shorten stroke with two strikes.

Taylor,Tyrone

789 | Milwaukee | EXP MLB DEBUT: 2017 | H/W: 6-0 185 | FUT: Starting OF | 7C

Bats R Age 23
2012 (2) HS (CA)
Pwr ++
BAvg +++
Spd +++
Def +++

Year	Lev	Team	AB	R	H	HR	RBI	Avg	OB	Slg	OPS	bb%	ct%	Eye	SB	CS	x/h%	Iso	RC/G
2013	A	Wisconsin	485	69	133	8	57	274	323	400	723	7	87	0.56	19	8	32	126	4.47
2014	A+	Brevard County	507	69	141	6	68	278	330	396	726	7	89	0.67	22	6	32	118	4.59
2014	AA	Huntsville	13	0	1	0	0	77	143	77	220	7	62	0.20	1	0	0	0	-3.22
2015	AA	Biloxi	454	48	118	3	43	260	307	337	644	6	88	0.56	10	6	22	77	3.58
2016	AA	Biloxi	465	51	108	9	34	232	290	327	617	8	84	0.52	9	5	23	95	3.16

Athletic OF whose production and stock has fallen in upper minors. Tapped into more power with swing tweaks, but projects to have minimal HR totals. Quick hands and simple load for high contact for solid BA. Above-average runner with potential for 20+ SB annually as everyday, low-offense CF. More real-life value than fantasy value at this point.

Tejeda,Anderson

6 | Texas | EXP MLB DEBUT: 2020 | H/W: 5-11 160 | FUT: Starting SS | 8D

Bats L Age 18
2014 FA (DR)
Pwr +++
BAvg +++
Spd ++
Def ++

Year	Lev	Team	AB	R	H	HR	RBI	Avg	OB	Slg	OPS	bb%	ct%	Eye	SB	CS	x/h%	Iso	RC/G
2016	Rk	Azl Rangers	133	22	39	1	21	293	333	496	830	6	73	0.22	1	0	49	203	6.09
2016	A-	Spokane	94	15	26	8	19	277	313	553	866	5	65	0.15	1	0	35	277	6.39

Short, lean INF with pure-hitting stroke and surprising pop for size. Plays all over infield and owns soft hands and plus arm. Has decent range, but lacks ideal quickness for SS. Exhibits plus hand-eye coordination to make acceptable contact, but has far too aggressive approach. Can sell out for power and flail at breakers.

Telis,Tomas

23 | Miami | EXP MLB DEBUT: 2014 | H/W: 5-8 175 | FUT: Reserve C | 6B

Bats B Age 25
2007 FA (VZ)
Pwr ++
BAvg +++
Spd +
Def +++

Year	Lev	Team	AB	R	H	HR	RBI	Avg	OB	Slg	OPS	bb%	ct%	Eye	SB	CS	x/h%	Iso	RC/G
2015	AAA	New Orleans	48	3	16	0	4	333	396	333	730	9	88	0.83	2	0	0	0	4.67
2015	MLB	Miami	27	1	4	0	0	148	179	148	327	4	89	0.33	0	0	0	0	-0.12
2015	MLB	Texas	11	1	2	0	2	182	182	182	364	0	91	0.00	0	0	0	0	0.19
2016	AAA	New Orleans	336	46	104	6	45	310	361	429	789	7	88	0.64	4	2	24	119	5.25
2016	MLB	Miami	13	1	4	1	4	308	308	538	846	0	85	0.00	0	0	25	231	5.06

Stocky backstop has a solid approach at the plate and makes consistent contact, shooting line-drives to all fields. That approach gives him value, but limits his power upside. Has an average arm behind the plate, but has worked hard in other areas and is now a solid defender.

Tellez,Rowdy — 3 — Toronto

EXP MLB DEBUT: 2017 | H/W: 6-4 220 | FUT: Starting 1B | 8B

Bats L Age 22
2013 (30) HS (CA)
Pwr ++++
BAvg +++
Spd +
Def ++

Year	Lev	Team	AB	R	H	HR	RBI	Avg	OB	Slg	OPS	bb%	ct%	Eye	SB	CS	x/h%	Iso	RC/G
2014	Rk	Bluefield	191	26	56	4	36	293	357	424	781	9	86	0.70	3	2	29	131	5.24
2014	A	Lansing	42	6	15	2	7	357	449	500	949	14	76	0.70	0	0	13	143	7.54
2015	A	Lansing	270	36	80	7	49	296	354	444	798	8	79	0.43	2	2	33	148	5.37
2015	A+	Dunedin	131	17	36	7	28	275	345	473	818	10	79	0.50	3	0	33	198	5.54
2016	AA	New Hampshire	438	71	130	23	81	297	385	530	915	13	79	0.68	4	3	42	233	7.01

Big-framed 1B with lightning-quick bat who finished 2nd in EL in OBP. Got off to slow start, but picked up pace and had dynamite season. Becoming well-rounded hitter with keen eye and easy contact. Set easy high in HR and projects well. Bat-only prospect, as he is fringy defender with well below average wheels.

Thaiss,Matt — 23 — Los Angeles (A)

EXP MLB DEBUT: 2018 | H/W: 6-0 195 | FUT: Starting 1B | 8C

Bats L Age 21
2016 (1) Virginia
Pwr ++
BAvg ++++
Spd ++
Def ++

Year	Lev	Team	AB	R	H	HR	RBI	Avg	OB	Slg	OPS	bb%	ct%	Eye	SB	CS	x/h%	Iso	RC/G
2016	NCAA	Virginia	232	55	87	10	59	375	465	578	1043	14	93	2.44	0	1	29	203	8.53
2016	Rk	Orem	65	16	22	2	12	338	377	569	946	6	94	1.00	2	4	45	231	6.96
2016	A	Burlington	199	24	55	4	31	276	348	427	776	10	86	0.79	1	0	35	151	5.28

Natural-hitting prospect who moved from C to 1B upon signing. Brings mature approach to plate and works counts to find pitches to drive to all fields. Has raw power, but mostly hits hard line drives to gaps. Increased HR could result in lower BA. Has nice swing and shows aptitude against LHP. Not much speed and still learning nuances of 1B.

Thomas,Cody — 789 — Los Angeles (N)

EXP MLB DEBUT: 2020 | H/W: 6-4 211 | FUT: Starting OF | 7D

Bats L Age 22
2016 (13) Oklahoma
Pwr ++++
BAvg ++
Spd +++
Def ++

Year	Lev	Team	AB	R	H	HR	RBI	Avg	OB	Slg	OPS	bb%	ct%	Eye	SB	CS	x/h%	Iso	RC/G
2016	NCAA	Oklahoma	117	26	35	6	27	299	349	556	905	7	74	0.29	2	0	46	256	6.81
2016	Rk	Ogden	210	41	58	16	44	276	333	576	910	8	60	0.21	9	3	48	300	7.82
2016	Rk	Azl Dodgers	22	10	11	3	6	500	560	1045	1605	12	86	1.00	1	0	45	545	14.68

Backup QB for Oklahoma so had limited baseball reps. Has good size and strength that translated well and finished 2nd in Pioneer League in HR. Aggressive approach results in poor contact and needs to improve pitch recognition. Plus OF arm with average speed and played all three OF positions in debut. LH power bat.

Thompson,David — 5 — New York (N)

EXP MLB DEBUT: 2018 | H/W: 6-0 208 | FUT: Reserve IF | 6C

Bats R Age 23
2015 (4) Miami
Pwr +++
BAvg ++
Spd +
Def ++

Year	Lev	Team	AB	R	H	HR	RBI	Avg	OB	Slg	OPS	bb%	ct%	Eye	SB	CS	x/h%	Iso	RC/G
2015	NCAA	Miami	253	59	83	19	90	328	426	640	1066	15	89	1.48	1	3	47	312	8.71
2015	A-	Brooklyn	206	22	45	3	22	218	258	320	578	5	79	0.25	3	0	31	102	2.48
2016	A	Columbia	228	45	67	5	58	294	335	474	808	6	79	0.29	3	0	43	180	5.47
2016	A+	St. Lucie	204	29	54	6	37	265	315	412	727	7	80	0.37	3	0	33	147	4.37

Stocky corner infielder with raw power potential. Big time slugger in college has struggled catching up to velocity in pro ball. Hit 11 HR between Single-A and High-A, and more power should come. Not a great athlete. Struggles defensively at corner; would likely DH if AL player. Not enough hit tool to satisfy regular MLB time.

Tilson,Charlie — 78 — Chicago (A)

EXP MLB DEBUT: 2016 | H/W: 5-11 195 | FUT: Starting OF | 7B

Bats L Age 24
2011 (2) HS (IL)
Pwr ++
BAvg +++
Spd ++++
Def ++++

Year	Lev	Team	AB	R	H	HR	RBI	Avg	OB	Slg	OPS	bb%	ct%	Eye	SB	CS	x/h%	Iso	RC/G
2014	A+	Palm Beach	370	54	114	5	36	308	350	414	764	6	79	0.32	10	7	18	105	4.85
2014	AA	Springfield	139	19	33	2	17	237	269	324	593	4	80	0.21	2	3	21	86	2.60
2015	AA	Springfield	539	85	159	4	32	295	350	388	738	8	87	0.64	46	19	21	93	4.73
2016	AAA	Memphis	351	53	99	4	34	282	344	407	751	9	85	0.65	15	3	28	125	4.94
2016	MLB	Chi White Sox	2	0	1	0	0	500	500	500	1000	0	100		0	0	0	0	6.83

Improving and consistent OF who was injured in MLB debut. Does everything well on diamond except hit for power. Gets on base with pro approach and has compact stroke to make easy contact. Uses all fields, has plus speed for xbh and SB. Drives ball with authority, but won't reach seats often. True CF, but arm strength a bit short.

Tobias,Josh — 4 — Boston

EXP MLB DEBUT: 2019 | H/W: 5-9 195 | FUT: Starting 2B | 7D

Bats R Age 24
2015 (10) Florida
Pwr +++
BAvg +++
4.17 Spd ++
Def +++

Year	Lev	Team	AB	R	H	HR	RBI	Avg	OB	Slg	OPS	bb%	ct%	Eye	SB	CS	x/h%	Iso	RC/G
2015	NCAA	Florida	231	60	82	5	46	355	413	524	937	9	84	0.62	11	2	29	169	7.13
2015	A-	Williamsport	240	31	77	4	37	321	358	475	833	6	83	0.33	12	10	34	154	5.70
2016	A	Lakewood	365	49	111	7	55	304	359	444	802	8	84	0.53	6	4	31	140	5.43
2016	A+	Clearwater	126	21	32	2	14	254	319	357	676	9	76	0.40	4	1	28	103	3.87

Short, strong infielder with a knack for hitting. Can square up velocity from both sides, shows some power when gets his pitch. A hustling, hard-nosed player on offense. Shows good defensive range, but suffers from sloppy footwork and limited agility and only average arm likely keeps him at 2B. Will need to prove himself at each level.

Tocci,Carlos — 8 — Philadelphia

EXP MLB DEBUT: 2018 | H/W: 6-2 160 | FUT: Starting CF | 7D

Bats R Age 21
2011 FA (VZ)
Pwr ++
BAvg +++
Spd +++
Def ++++

Year	Lev	Team	AB	R	H	HR	RBI	Avg	OB	Slg	OPS	bb%	ct%	Eye	SB	CS	x/h%	Iso	RC/G
2013	A	Lakewood	421	40	88	0	26	209	248	249	498	5	82	0.29	6	7	19	40	1.60
2014	A	Lakewood	487	59	118	2	30	242	279	324	604	5	80	0.26	10	11	24	82	2.87
2015	A	Lakewood	234	35	75	2	25	321	374	423	797	8	87	0.65	14	2	24	103	5.41
2015	A+	Clearwater	275	31	71	2	18	258	289	313	602	4	81	0.23	3	9	15	55	2.74
2016	A+	Clearwater	500	66	142	3	50	284	330	362	692	6	85	0.45	13	6	22	78	4.06

Improved in his second shot at High-A, but hasn't added much bulk or strength to his wiry, athletic frame. The result is mostly singles and an occasional stolen base. Hit tool is passable, and defensive skills in CF, including a strong arm, means an MLB floor. But the likelihood that it's an impact profile is slim, even though he's still young.

Torrens,Luis — 2 — San Diego

EXP MLB DEBUT: 2017 | H/W: 6-0 175 | FUT: Starting C | 8D

Bats R Age 20
2012 FA (VZ)
Pwr ++
BAvg ++
Spd ++
Def +++

Year	Lev	Team	AB	R	H	HR	RBI	Avg	OB	Slg	OPS	bb%	ct%	Eye	SB	CS	x/h%	Iso	RC/G
2014	A-	Staten Island	185	27	50	2	18	270	322	405	727	7	78	0.34	1	2	36	135	4.54
2014	A	Charleston (Sc)	26	4	4	1	3	154	313	269	582	19	73	0.86	0	0	25	115	2.72
2015		Did not play (injury)																	
2016	A-	Staten Island	45	6	14	0	5	311	367	400	767	8	84	0.57	1	1	29	89	5.13
2016	A	Charleston (Sc)	139	9	32	2	10	230	335	317	652	14	81	0.85	1	1	25	86	3.87

Under the radar backstop who returned after missing all of '15 (shoulder). Solid present defender with nimble feet, agility, and receiving. Asset with strong arm and quick release. Has potential with bat, particularly with power. Works counts to get on base and finding pitch to drive. Has chance to be all-around talent. Rule 5 pick from NYY.

Torres,Christopher — 6 — Seattle

EXP MLB DEBUT: 2021 | H/W: 5-11 170 | FUT: Starting SS | 8D

Bats B Age 19
2014 FA (DR)
Pwr ++
BAvg ++
Spd ++++
Def ++++

Year	Lev	Team	AB	R	H	HR	RBI	Avg	OB	Slg	OPS	bb%	ct%	Eye	SB	CS	x/h%	Iso	RC/G
2016	Rk	Azl Mariners	167	31	43	0	17	257	333	359	693	10	74	0.43	12	4	30	102	4.33

Standout SS who enjoyed 1st year in US. Has hands, range, and feet to stick at SS long-term and is consistent defender. Owns plus speed at present and should be more useful as he gets on base consistently. Has work to do with bat as he needs to add muscle to lean frame. His hard line drives, but can be overpowered by quick FB.

Torres,Gleyber — 6 — New York (A)

EXP MLB DEBUT: 2018 | H/W: 6-1 175 | FUT: Starting SS | 9C

Bats R Age 20
2013 FA (VZ)
Pwr ++
BAvg +++
Spd +++
Def +++

Year	Lev	Team	AB	R	H	HR	RBI	Avg	OB	Slg	OPS	bb%	ct%	Eye	SB	CS	x/h%	Iso	RC/G
2014	A-	Boise	28	4	11	1	4	393	469	786	1254	13	75	0.57	2	0	55	393	12.14
2015	A	South Bend	464	53	136	3	62	293	353	386	739	8	77	0.40	22	13	24	93	4.74
2015	A+	Myrtle Beach	23	1	4	0	2	174	208	174	382	4	70	0.14	0	1	0	0	-0.46
2016	A+	Myrtle Beach	356	62	98	9	47	275	352	433	784	11	76	0.48	19	10	36	157	5.40
2016	A+	Tampa	122	19	31	2	19	254	341	385	726	12	81	0.70	2	3	32	131	4.73

Exciting prospect who is evolving into terrific overall player. Starting to hit for power as he set high in HR. Has feel for bat and covers plate. Uses entire field and will hit loads of doubles. Runs bases aggressively with good speed and is average defender with strong arm. Has advanced skills for age and will only get better.

Torres,Nick — 79 — San Diego

EXP MLB DEBUT: 2017 | H/W: 6-1 220 | FUT: Reserve OF | 6B

Bats R Age 23
2014 (4) Cal Poly
Pwr ++
BAvg +++
Spd ++
Def +++

Year	Lev	Team	AB	R	H	HR	RBI	Avg	OB	Slg	OPS	bb%	ct%	Eye	SB	CS	x/h%	Iso	RC/G
2014	A-	Eugene	169	20	43	3	23	254	284	373	657	4	75	0.17	2	2	33	118	3.39
2015	A	Fort Wayne	288	45	94	2	40	326	366	462	828	6	82	0.35	4	1	35	135	5.71
2015	A+	Lake Elsinore	211	21	58	3	30	275	305	408	712	4	79	0.20	5	1	34	133	4.15
2016	AA	San Antonio	373	40	105	6	40	282	311	416	727	4	74	0.17	10	4	34	134	4.36
2016	AAA	El Paso	130	15	40	6	18	308	333	508	841	4	73	0.14	0	2	35	200	5.72

Quick moving OF made it to Triple-A in '16, but is a tweener bat. May struggle to hold starting MLB job due to fringe-average power in maxed-out frame. Solid approach with some swing and miss issues. Can play either corner OF positions.

Toups,Corey

4 | Kansas City | EXP MLB DEBUT: 2017 | H/W: 5-10 170 | FUT: Utility player | 6B

Bats R Age 24	Year	Lev	Team	AB	R	H	HR	RBI	Avg	OB	Slg	OPS	bb%	ct%	Eye	SB	CS	x/h%	Iso	RC/G
2014 (15) Sam Houston St	2014	NCAA	Sam Houston St	187	43	58	7	29	310	392	513	905	12	83	0.78	11	2	41	203	6.86
Pwr ++	2014	Rk	Idaho Falls	203	49	68	3	32	335	451	507	959	17	81	1.13	7	0	38	172	8.09
BAvg ++	2015	A	Lexington	388	75	113	7	44	291	363	441	804	10	79	0.54	31	5	35	149	5.65
Spd ++	2016	A+	Wilmington	155	21	39	2	11	252	345	419	764	12	77	0.63	6	1	44	168	5.35
Def +++	2016	AA	NW Arkansas	338	61	93	10	38	275	345	450	795	10	72	0.38	16	3	40	175	5.57

Short, reliable INF who set highs in doubles and HR in mature approach. Uses all fields and offers OK pop despite size. Produces by understanding limitations, but fails to make contact as much as hoped. Will draw walks to get on base. Speed isn't great, but steals bases with savvy. Makes routine plays at 2B more on feel than quickness.

Trahan,Blake

6 | Cincinnati | EXP MLB DEBUT: 2018 | H/W: 5-9 180 | FUT: Starting SS | 7C

Bats R Age 23	Year	Lev	Team	AB	R	H	HR	RBI	Avg	OB	Slg	OPS	bb%	ct%	Eye	SB	CS	x/h%	Iso	RC/G
2015 (3) LA-Lafayette																				
Pwr ++	2015	NCAA	La-Lafayette	254	51	80	2	29	315	404	406	810	13	87	1.19	17	0	23	91	5.91
BAvg +++	2015	Rk	Billings	186	32	58	1	15	312	393	403	797	12	90	1.32	10	3	21	91	5.74
Spd ++++	2015	A+	Daytona	35	1	4	0	0	114	114	114	229	0	86	0.00	0	0	0	0	-1.61
Def +++	2016	A+	Daytona	521	90	137	4	47	263	326	361	687	9	86	0.67	25	8	25	98	4.19

Solid, collegiate SS established self as best SS in CIN system with good defense and plus-speed. Has solid bat-to-ball skills. Can work counts and take walks. Not much power in stature. Uses leverage in swing in gap-to-gap approach. Not a question he sticks at SS.

Trammell,Taylor

789 | Cincinnati | EXP MLB DEBUT: 2021 | H/W: 6-2 195 | FUT: Starting OF | 9E

Bats L Age 19	Year	Lev	Team	AB	R	H	HR	RBI	Avg	OB	Slg	OPS	bb%	ct%	Eye	SB	CS	x/h%	Iso	RC/G
2016 (S-1) HS (GA)																				
Pwr ++++																				
BAvg +++																				
Spd ++++																				
Def ++++	2016	Rk	Billings	228	39	69	2	34	303	367	421	788	9	75	0.40	24	7	25	118	5.47

Multi-sport athlete chose baseball over football senior year of high school, so very raw on diamond. Abundant tool shed; average or better tools across the board. Best attribute is his legs. Strong, solid base will help on basepaths, in CF and will propel his power potential.

Travis,Sam

3 | Boston | EXP MLB DEBUT: 2017 | H/W: 6-0 205 | FUT: Starting 1B | 7B

Bats R Age 23	Year	Lev	Team	AB	R	H	HR	RBI	Avg	OB	Slg	OPS	bb%	ct%	Eye	SB	CS	x/h%	Iso	RC/G
2014 (2) Indiana	2014	A-	Lowell	165	28	55	4	30	333	349	448	798	2	89	0.22	5	1	18	115	4.92
Pwr +++	2014	A	Greenville	107	12	31	3	14	290	333	495	829	6	87	0.50	0	1	48	206	5.67
BAvg ++++	2015	A+	Salem	246	35	77	5	40	313	379	467	846	10	83	0.60	10	6	31	154	6.09
Spd ++	2015	AA	Portland	243	35	73	4	38	300	384	436	820	12	86	0.97	9	6	32	136	5.94
Def ++	2016	AAA	Pawtucket	173	26	47	6	29	272	330	434	763	8	77	0.38	1	0	34	162	4.88

Strong, advanced hitter whose season ended in May after knee surgery. Swings a level bat and makes easy, hard contact. Uses whole-field approach and can pull balls out on occasion. May lack ideal pop for 1B, but covers plate well and will hit for BA thanks to bat control. Not terribly athletic, but is passable defender with average hands.

Trevino,Jose

2 | Texas | EXP MLB DEBUT: 2018 | H/W: 5-11 195 | FUT: Starting C | 7C

Bats R Age 24	Year	Lev	Team	AB	R	H	HR	RBI	Avg	OB	Slg	OPS	bb%	ct%	Eye	SB	CS	x/h%	Iso	RC/G
2014 (6) Oral Roberts	2013	NCAA	Oral Roberts	195	32	47	8	37	241	321	410	731	11	85	0.79	0	0	36	169	4.63
Pwr +++	2014	NCAA	Oral Roberts	230	37	70	10	43	304	360	491	851	8	89	0.80	4	0	31	187	5.90
BAvg +++	2014	A-	Spokane	288	58	74	9	49	257	312	448	760	7	83	0.46	2	0	46	191	4.88
Spd +	2015	A	Hickory	424	62	111	14	63	262	292	415	707	4	86	0.30	1	4	32	153	4.00
Def ++	2016	A+	High Desert	433	67	131	9	68	303	342	434	776	6	89	0.53	2	1	30	132	4.99

Improving defender who is in 2nd year of catching. Has plus arm and emerging receiving ability, but lacks athleticism and agility. Makes extreme contact with plus bat control and hand-eye coordination. Uses whole field, though can be aggressive swinger and only has fringy power. Had success against LHP.

Tucker,Cole

6 | Pittsburgh | EXP MLB DEBUT: 2020 | H/W: 6-3 185 | FUT: Starting SS | 8D

Bats B Age 20	Year	Lev	Team	AB	R	H	HR	RBI	Avg	OB	Slg	OPS	bb%	ct%	Eye	SB	CS	x/h%	Iso	RC/G
2014 (1) HS (AZ)																				
Pwr ++	2014	Rk	GCL Pirates	180	39	48	2	13	267	359	356	715	13	79	0.68	13	5	21	89	4.61
BAvg +++	2015	A	West Virginia	300	46	88	2	25	293	329	377	706	5	84	0.33	25	6	20	83	4.12
Spd +++	2016	A	West Virginia	61	9	16	1	2	262	308	443	750	6	85	0.44	1	1	44	180	4.82
Def +++	2016	A+	Bradenton	269	36	64	1	25	238	312	301	613	10	77	0.47	5	6	22	63	3.16

Tall 1st rounder had torn labrum in '15 and was limited to 80 games in '16. Has a good approach at the plate and makes consistent contact, but has been slow to develop and has yet to show much power. Moves well on defense with good range, soft hands, and an above-average arm. Still has some projection left, but remains raw.

Tucker,Kyle

789 | Houston | EXP MLB DEBUT: 2019 | H/W: 6-4 190 | FUT: Starting OF | 9C

Bats L Age 20	Year	Lev	Team	AB	R	H	HR	RBI	Avg	OB	Slg	OPS	bb%	ct%	Eye	SB	CS	x/h%	Iso	RC/G
2015 (1) HS (FL)																				
Pwr ++++	2015	Rk	GCL Astros	119	18	25	2	13	210	260	319	579	6	88	0.57	4	2	28	109	2.84
BAvg ++++	2015	Rk	Greeneville	112	11	32	1	20	286	328	393	721	6	87	0.47	14	2	31	107	4.41
Spd +++	2016	A	Quad Cities	373	43	103	6	56	276	346	402	748	10	80	0.53	31	9	29	126	4.89
Def +++	2016	A+	Lancaster	59	13	20	3	13	339	435	661	1096	14	90	1.67	1	3	55	322	9.25

Lean, athletic OF who is advanced for age. Has all requisite tools to be standout. Has plus bat speed and effortless swing to produce both power and BA. Could add more strength and gets pull conscious at times. Very proficient OF with smarts, range, and arm. Makes game look very easy and could hit leadoff or in middle of order.

Twine,Justin

4 | Miami | EXP MLB DEBUT: 2019 | H/W: 5-11 205 | FUT: Utility player | 7E

Bats R Age 21	Year	Lev	Team	AB	R	H	HR	RBI	Avg	OB	Slg	OPS	bb%	ct%	Eye	SB	CS	x/h%	Iso	RC/G
2014 (2) HS (TX)																				
Pwr ++																				
BAvg ++	2014	Rk	GCL Marlins	166	19	38	1	16	229	256	355	611	3	69	0.12	5	1	37	127	2.96
Spd ++++	2015	A	Greensboro	451	44	93	7	39	206	217	310	527	1	76	0.06	8	4	32	104	1.60
Def +++	2016	A	Greensboro	353	42	88	3	33	249	288	334	622	5	67	0.16	8	6	25	85	3.08

2nd round pick has failed to live up to expectations. Has good bat speed and raw strength, but is overly aggressive with a long swing and poor contact. Plus, plus speed with good range and a strong arm, but poor footwork and inconsistent throws resulted in a move to 2B. Needs to be more selective at the plate to remain a viable prospect.

Urena,Jhoan

35 | New York (N) | EXP MLB DEBUT: 2019 | H/W: 6-1 230 | FUT: Starting 3B | 7E

Bats B Age 22	Year	Lev	Team	AB	R	H	HR	RBI	Avg	OB	Slg	OPS	bb%	ct%	Eye	SB	CS	x/h%	Iso	RC/G
2011 FA (DR)	2013	Rk	GCL Mets	157	19	47	0	20	299	353	376	729	8	78	0.38	4	1	19	76	4.59
Pwr +++	2014	A-	Brooklyn	283	30	85	5	47	300	361	431	792	9	80	0.47	7	9	31	131	5.38
BAvg ++	2015	Rk	GCL Mets	15	4	5	2	2	333	474	800	1274	21	100		1	0	60	467	11.09
Spd ++	2015	A+	St. Lucie	210	15	45	0	18	214	253	267	520	5	81	0.28	2	0	18	52	1.86
Def ++	2016	A+	St. Lucie	383	52	86	9	53	225	301	350	651	10	80	0.56	0	1	33	125	3.62

Promsing, switch-hitting 3B has struggled regaining form after fracturing hamate bone in both wrists. Bat speed evaporated in '16, and hit tool downgraded as a result. Maxed-out physically. Has made strides defensively at 3B. Should stick at position long term, but has base-clogging speed.

Urena,Richard

6 | Toronto | EXP MLB DEBUT: 2018 | H/W: 6-0 185 | FUT: Starting SS | 8B

Bats B Age 21	Year	Lev	Team	AB	R	H	HR	RBI	Avg	OB	Slg	OPS	bb%	ct%	Eye	SB	CS	x/h%	Iso	RC/G
2012 FA (DR)	2014	A-	Vancouver	33	3	8	0	5	242	306	364	669	8	85	0.60	1	0	38	121	4.05
Pwr +++	2015	A	Lansing	384	62	102	15	58	266	290	438	727	3	78	0.15	5	5	31	172	4.13
BAvg +++	2015	A+	Dunedin	124	9	31	1	8	250	268	315	582	2	79	0.12	3	1	16	65	2.37
Spd ++	2016	A+	Dunedin	394	52	120	8	41	305	346	447	793	6	84	0.39	9	6	28	142	5.19
Def +++	2016	AA	New Hampshire	124	14	33	0	18	266	289	395	684	3	85	0.21	0	2	33	129	3.91

Projectable INF who finished 2nd in FSL in BA. Better hitter from left, but has enough strength and quick bat from both sides. Power declined, but did better job of closing holes in swing. At his best when using whole field and working counts. Soft hands, strong arm and smooth actions highlight defense, but needs to clean up footwork.

Urias,Luis

456 | San Diego | EXP MLB DEBUT: 2018 | H/W: 5-9 160 | FUT: Starting 2B | 7A

Bats R Age 19	Year	Lev	Team	AB	R	H	HR	RBI	Avg	OB	Slg	OPS	bb%	ct%	Eye	SB	CS	x/h%	Iso	RC/G
2013 FA (MX)	2014	Rk	Azl Padres	155	29	48	0	14	310	382	355	736	10	92	1.38	10	6	13	45	4.99
Pwr ++	2015	A-	Tri-City	31	6	11	0	1	355	444	387	832	14	97	5.00	3	3	9	32	6.40
BAvg ++++	2015	A	Fort Wayne	193	28	56	0	16	290	344	326	671	8	91	0.89	5	10	11	36	4.03
Spd +++	2016	A+	Lake Elsinore	466	71	154	5	52	330	383	440	823	8	92	1.11	7	13	23	109	5.77
Def +++	2016	AAA	El Paso	9	6	4	1	3	444	643	778	1421	36	89	5.00	1	0	25	333	14.29

Incredibly advanced 19-year-old infielder impressed against better competition. Advanced approach at plate; he rarely strikes out. Started lining ball to gaps in '16. Very slight power potential. Doesn't drive the ball regularly. Relies on spraying the field with liners. Likely 2B at maturity.

Valentin,Jesmuel — 4 — Philadelphia

EXP MLB DEBUT: 2017 | H/W: 5-9 180 | FUT: Reserve 2B | 6B

Bats B Age 22 / 2012 (S-1) HS (PR)	Year	Lev	Team	AB	R	H	HR	RBI	Avg	OB	Slg	OPS	bb%	ct%	Eye	SB	CS	x/h%	Iso	RC/G
Pwr ++	2014	A+	Clearwater	44	8	9	0	0	205	255	250	505	6	86	0.50	1	1	22	45	1.96
BAvg ++	2015	A+	Clearwater	99	18	27	1	14	273	351	424	776	11	85	0.80	0	2	44	152	5.41
4.50 Spd ++	2016	AA	Reading	341	59	94	5	38	276	348	399	747	10	84	0.68	4	3	29	123	4.93
Def +++	2016	AAA	Lehigh Valley	105	17	26	4	14	248	325	381	706	10	77	0.50	0	1	23	133	4.17

Small-framed INF with a smattering of tools that add up to MLB-worthy. Has a nice, easy short swing from both sides of the plate. Doesn't have loft or strength for home run power, but stings line drives past infielders and into the gaps. Good pitch recognition; puts together good at bats. Strong defender at 2B, with the arm for SS in a pinch.

Valera,Breyvic — 456 — St. Louis

EXP MLB DEBUT: 2017 | H/W: 5-11 160 | FUT: Utility player | 6B

Bats B Age 24 / 2010 FA (VZ)	Year	Lev	Team	AB	R	H	HR	RBI	Avg	OB	Slg	OPS	bb%	ct%	Eye	SB	CS	x/h%	Iso	RC/G
	2014	AA	Springfield	227	31	65	0	20	286	331	339	670	6	90	0.68	4	5	15	53	3.94
Pwr +	2015	A+	Palm Beach	51	9	18	0	7	353	468	451	919	18	96	5.50	0	3	22	98	7.69
BAvg +++	2015	AA	Springfield	360	37	85	3	31	236	302	297	599	9	93	1.26	2	4	16	61	3.37
Spd +++	2016	AA	Springfield	178	16	46	0	12	258	294	298	592	5	90	0.50	3	1	13	39	2.96
Def +++	2016	AAA	Memphis	217	32	74	0	31	341	423	415	838	13	90	1.41	8	4	20	74	6.28

Switch-hitting INF started the season slowly at AA, but was red-hot when moved up to AAA. Hits well from both sides of the plate and uses the whole field. Doesn't have much power, but has good speed. Solid range and actions and can play multiple positions.

Vallot,Chase — 2 — Kansas City

EXP MLB DEBUT: 2019 | H/W: 6-0 215 | FUT: Starting C | 8D

Bats R Age 20 / 2014 (S-1) HS (LA)	Year	Lev	Team	AB	R	H	HR	RBI	Avg	OB	Slg	OPS	bb%	ct%	Eye	SB	CS	x/h%	Iso	RC/G
Pwr ++++	2014	Rk	Burlington	186	29	40	7	27	215	311	403	715	12	56	0.32	0	1	53	188	5.16
BAvg ++	2015	A	Lexington	279	46	61	13	40	219	319	427	745	13	62	0.39	1	0	48	208	5.21
Spd ++	2016	Rk	Azl Royals	30	5	4	2	2	133	212	367	579	9	53	0.21	0	0	75	233	2.62
Def ++	2016	A	Lexington	272	37	67	13	44	246	341	463	804	13	57	0.33	0	0	49	217	6.67

Power-hitting backstop who got off to great start, but cooled off after return from injury. Uses disciplined approach and leveraged stroke to hit for plus pop, though has crude swing and pitch recognition. Will fan a lot and BA in question. Below average receiver and footwork needs attention. Owns cannon for an arm that is asset against runners.

Van Hoosier,Evan — 45 — Texas

EXP MLB DEBUT: 2018 | H/W: 5-11 185 | FUT: Utility player | 6B

Bats R Age 23 / 2013 (8) JC of Southern NV	Year	Lev	Team	AB	R	H	HR	RBI	Avg	OB	Slg	OPS	bb%	ct%	Eye	SB	CS	x/h%	Iso	RC/G
	2013	A-	Spokane	169	21	42	2	9	249	314	361	674	9	82	0.52	3	1	31	112	3.95
Pwr ++	2014	A	Hickory	437	79	117	11	58	268	335	442	776	9	81	0.52	14	2	39	174	5.21
BAvg ++	2015	Rk	Azl Rangers	28	5	8	0	1	286	333	393	726	7	79	0.33	2	0	38	107	4.56
Spd +++	2015	A+	High Desert	257	40	85	2	33	331	375	494	869	7	78	0.32	5	3	33	163	6.39
Def ++	2016	AA	Frisco	80	8	21	0	4	263	298	325	623	5	83	0.29	1	1	14	63	3.13

Versatile prospect who started late due to PED suspension, then was injured in June. Has quick stroke and feel for contact with line drive approach. Lacks over-the-wall power, but has strength to hit to gaps. Runs well and is efficient basestealer. Mostly plays 2B and 3B and lacks arm strength, but makes routine plays.

Verdugo,Alex — 89 — Los Angeles (N)

EXP MLB DEBUT: 2017 | H/W: 6-0 205 | FUT: Starting OF | 8C

Bats L Age 20 / 2014 (2) HS (AZ)	Year	Lev	Team	AB	R	H	HR	RBI	Avg	OB	Slg	OPS	bb%	ct%	Eye	SB	CS	x/h%	Iso	RC/G
	2014	Rk	Azl Dodgers	170	28	59	3	33	347	416	518	933	11	92	1.43	8	0	34	171	7.19
Pwr +++	2014	Rk	Ogden	20	3	8	0	8	400	400	450	850	0	80	0.00	3	0	13	50	5.47
BAvg +++	2015	A	Great Lakes	421	50	124	5	42	295	322	394	716	4	87	0.32	13	5	24	100	4.20
Spd +++	2015	A+	Rancho Cuca	91	20	35	4	19	385	411	659	1070	4	87	0.33	1	0	43	275	8.22
Def +++	2016	AA	Tulsa	477	58	130	13	63	273	334	407	741	8	86	0.66	2	6	28	134	4.69

Another solid season at Double-A, has a good approach at the plate with solid bat-to-ball skills. Doubled his walk total, but can still be overly aggressive. Just 20 years old, he should develop more power as he matures. Solid defender with a plus arm.

Vielma,Engelb — 456 — Minnesota

EXP MLB DEBUT: 2018 | H/W: 5-11 155 | FUT: Starting SS | 7D

Bats B Age 22 / 2011 FA (VZ)	Year	Lev	Team	AB	R	H	HR	RBI	Avg	OB	Slg	OPS	bb%	ct%	Eye	SB	CS	x/h%	Iso	RC/G
	2013	Rk	Elizabethton	23	7	5	0	1	217	250	217	467	4	70	0.14	1	0	0	0	0.73
Pwr +	2014	A	Cedar Rapids	418	63	111	1	33	266	312	323	635	6	83	0.39	10	6	16	57	3.34
BAvg ++	2015	A+	Fort Myers	441	49	119	1	29	270	324	306	630	7	84	0.49	35	12	10	36	3.33
Spd +++	2016	A+	Fort Myers	25	5	5	0	0	200	333	200	533	17	68	0.63	2	0	0	0	2.07
Def +++++	2016	AA	Chattanooga	314	47	85	0	21	271	342	318	660	10	80	0.55	10	8	13	48	3.82

Defensive-oriented INF who could win Gold Glove, but may not hit enough to become starter. Small, lean with incredible quickness and plus hands/feet. Focuses on contact with simple stroke, but lacks strength for power. Only 2 HR in 1500+ AB and doesn't drive ball enough. Runs OK and can steal bases on shrewd instincts.

Viloria,Meibrys — 2 — Kansas City

EXP MLB DEBUT: 2020 | H/W: 5-11 175 | FUT: Starting C | 7C

Bats L Age 20 / 2013 FA (CB)	Year	Lev	Team	AB	R	H	HR	RBI	Avg	OB	Slg	OPS	bb%	ct%	Eye	SB	CS	x/h%	Iso	RC/G
Pwr ++																				
BAvg +++	2014	Rk	Burlington	40	4	8	1	5	200	360	325	685	20	75	1.00	0	0	38	125	4.41
Spd ++	2015	Rk	Burlington	150	20	39	0	16	260	335	260	595	10	85	0.74	0	0	0	0	3.08
Def +	2016	Rk	Idaho Falls	226	54	85	6	55	376	427	606	1033	8	84	0.56	1	1	44	230	8.26

Short, strong C who was MVP of Pioneer League after leading league in BA. Only offers average bat speed, but makes easy contact and possesses very selective eye. Makes hard contact to gaps and has evolving power. Doesn't run much and is considered poor defender as he lacks instincts for C. Ideal arm strength with OK release.

Vincej,Zach — 46 — Cincinnati

EXP MLB DEBUT: 2017 | H/W: 5-11 177 | FUT: Reserve SS | 6B

Bats R Age 25 / 2012 (37) Pepperdine	Year	Lev	Team	AB	R	H	HR	RBI	Avg	OB	Slg	OPS	bb%	ct%	Eye	SB	CS	x/h%	Iso	RC/G
	2012	Rk	Billings	143	27	48	1	17	336	375	434	809	6	84	0.39	4	4	25	98	5.40
Pwr +	2013	A	Dayton	377	51	99	3	31	263	327	358	685	9	81	0.50	13	7	25	95	4.08
BAvg ++	2014	A+	Bakersfield	428	72	116	1	40	271	339	336	675	9	83	0.60	11	8	22	65	4.03
Spd +++	2015	AA	Pensacola	286	39	69	5	22	241	342	329	671	13	83	0.92	7	7	22	87	4.11
Def ++++	2016	AA	Pensacola	399	45	112	3	47	281	323	378	702	6	79	0.29	7	6	27	98	4.11

Solid, defensive SS impressed with hit tool in Double-A and AFL. A contact hitter, Vincej sprays the ball to all fields. Will turn on an occasional fastball for a HR. Looking to attack the FB, willing to expand. Sound defensively. Good footwork and soft hands.

Vogelbach,Dan — 3 — Seattle

EXP MLB DEBUT: 2016 | H/W: 6-0 250 | FUT: Starting 1B | 7B

Bats L Age 24 / 2011 (2) HS (FL)	Year	Lev	Team	AB	R	H	HR	RBI	Avg	OB	Slg	OPS	bb%	ct%	Eye	SB	CS	x/h%	Iso	RC/G
	2015	Rk	Azl Cubs	11	4	5	0	0	455	647	636	1283	35	91	6.00	0	0	40	182	13.39
Pwr ++++	2015	AA	Tennessee	254	41	69	7	39	272	405	425	830	18	76	0.93	1	1	35	154	6.37
BAvg +++	2016	AAA	Iowa	305	53	97	16	64	318	422	548	970	15	78	0.82	0	0	37	230	7.90
Spd +	2016	AAA	Tacoma	154	26	37	7	32	240	403	422	825	21	78	1.24	0	0	38	182	6.29
Def +	2016	MLB	Seattle	12	0	1	0	0	83	154	83	237	8	50	0.17	0	0	0	0	-3.55

Thick, sturdy 1B with excellent approach and plate discipline along with plus power to all fields. Set career high in HR and makes decent contact for slugger. Draws high number of walks with selectivity, but that's where accolades stop. Has well below average speed and athleticism. Lacks hands and quickness at 1B.

Wade,LaMonte — 78 — Minnesota

EXP MLB DEBUT: 2018 | H/W: 6-1 189 | FUT: Starting OF | 7C

Bats L Age 23 / 2015 (9) Maryland	Year	Lev	Team	AB	R	H	HR	RBI	Avg	OB	Slg	OPS	bb%	ct%	Eye	SB	CS	x/h%	Iso	RC/G
	2015	NCAA	Maryland	158	30	53	4	32	335	441	468	910	16	87	1.50	7	2	23	133	7.19
Pwr ++	2015	Rk	Elizabethton	231	36	72	9	44	312	426	506	932	17	85	1.35	12	1	31	195	7.46
BAvg +++	2015	A	Cedar Rapids	14	1	2	0	1	143	200	143	343	7	86	0.50	0	0	0	0	0.01
Spd +++	2016	A	Cedar Rapids	207	32	58	4	27	280	406	396	803	18	87	1.63	5	3	22	116	6.05
Def +++	2016	A+	Fort Myers	110	17	35	4	24	318	375	518	893	8	85	0.59	1	1	37	200	6.48

Well-rounded OF who exceeds expectations with simple approach. Very disciplined hitter with more BB than K. Makes hard contact to gaps and can pull ball out of park. Would hit for more pop if pulled ball more. Could hit for high BA due to balanced swing. Runs fairly well and is average defender in corner. Not quick enough for CF.

Wade,Tyler — 46 — New York (A)

EXP MLB DEBUT: 2017 | H/W: 6-1 185 | FUT: Starting MIF | 7C

Bats L Age 22 / 2013 (4) HS (CA)	Year	Lev	Team	AB	R	H	HR	RBI	Avg	OB	Slg	OPS	bb%	ct%	Eye	SB	CS	x/h%	Iso	RC/G
	2013	A-	Staten Island	13	0	1	0	1	77	200	77	277	13	69	0.50	0	0	0	0	-1.77
Pwr ++	2014	A	Charleston (Sc)	507	77	138	1	51	272	346	349	695	10	77	0.48	22	13	22	77	4.28
BAvg ++	2015	A+	Tampa	368	51	103	2	28	280	349	353	702	10	82	0.60	31	15	17	73	4.34
Spd ++++	2015	AA	Trenton	113	6	23	1	3	204	217	265	483	2	79	0.08	2	1	22	62	1.11
Def +++	2016	AA	Trenton	505	90	131	5	27	259	345	349	694	12	80	0.64	27	8	21	89	4.30

Versatile prospect who split between 2B and SS during season and played OF in AFL. Set high in HR, though isn't much of power threat. Expands zone at times, but generally uses short stroke and disciplined eye to get on base. Steals lots of bases with above average speed and uses smooth actions to make plays in field despite sub-par arm.

Wakamatsu,Luke — 6 — Cleveland

EXP MLB DEBUT: 2019 | H/W: 6-3 185 | FUT: Starting SS | 8E

Bats B Age 20
2015 (20) HS (TX)
Pwr ++
BAvg ++
Spd +++
Def +++

Year	Lev	Team	AB	R	H	HR	RBI	Avg	OB	Sig	OPS	bb%	ct%	Eye	SB	CS	x/h%	Iso	RC/G
2015	Rk	AZL Indians	105	8	28	1	12	267	336	400	736	9	62	0.28	4	2	32	133	5.30
2016	A-	Mahoning Valley	69	4	16	0	9	232	293	304	598	8	83	0.50	1	1	31	72	3.05

Tall, lean SS missed latter half of '17 with shoulder injury. Fluid stroke from both sides yields average contact with good approach for age. Gap pop for now and will require added muscle to tap into average HR potential. Speed better underway; projects to decline as he fills out. Instinctual, well-rounded glove with enough arm to play 3B if needed.

Walker,Adam Brett — 7 — Baltimore

EXP MLB DEBUT: 2017 | H/W: 6-5 225 | FUT: Starting OF | 8D

Bats R Age 25
2012 (3) Jacksonville
Pwr +++++
BAvg ++
Spd ++
Def ++

Year	Lev	Team	AB	R	H	HR	RBI	Avg	OB	Sig	OPS	bb%	ct%	Eye	SB	CS	x/h%	Iso	RC/G
2012	Rk	Elizabethton	232	44	58	14	45	250	307	496	802	8	67	0.25	4	0	43	246	5.60
2013	A	Cedar Rapids	508	83	141	27	109	278	319	526	845	6	77	0.27	10	0	46	248	5.78
2014	A+	Fort Myers	505	78	124	25	94	246	306	436	742	8	69	0.28	9	5	36	190	4.65
2015	AA	Chattanooga	502	75	120	31	106	239	309	498	807	9	61	0.26	13	4	54	259	6.15
2016	AAA	Rochester	478	61	116	27	75	243	307	479	786	8	58	0.22	7	4	47	236	6.10

Power-packed OF who led minors in Ks, but 2nd in IL in HR. Has smashed at least 25 HR each of past 4 years and offers as much pop as any prospect. Has long swing path that can be exploited, but drives ball when contact made. Fails to recognize spin and holds little BA potential. Regressing defense, but shows range and arm.

Walker,Christian — 37 — Baltimore

EXP MLB DEBUT: 2014 | H/W: 6-0 220 | FUT: Starting OF | 7C

Bats R Age 26
2012 (4) South Carolina
Pwr +++
BAvg ++
Spd +
Def ++

Year	Lev	Team	AB	R	H	HR	RBI	Avg	OB	Sig	OPS	bb%	ct%	Eye	SB	CS	x/h%	Iso	RC/G
2014	AAA	Norfolk	166	15	43	6	19	259	332	428	759	10	70	0.37	0	0	37	169	5.04
2014	MLB	Baltimore	18	1	3	1	1	167	211	389	599	5	50	0.11	0	0	67	222	3.47
2015	AAA	Norfolk	534	68	137	18	74	257	319	423	742	8	75	0.36	1	3	38	167	4.68
2015	MLB	Baltimore	9	0	1	0	0	111	333	111	444	25	56	0.75	0	0	0	0	0.23
2016	AAA	Norfolk	504	64	133	18	64	264	318	437	755	7	73	0.29	1	3	37	173	4.82

Strong hitter who has spent 2 1/2 yrs in AAA and has changed game to power approach. Recognizes pitches he can drive and uses bat speed and strength to reach seats. Strikeout rate has increased as his swing lengthens, but can go to opp field. Mostly LF in '16 and lack of athleticism and speed mute value. Needs to hit to play.

Wall,Forrest — 4 — Colorado

EXP MLB DEBUT: 2018 | H/W: 6-0 176 | FUT: Starting 2B | 8C

Bats L Age 21
2014 (S-1) HS (FL)
Pwr ++
BAvg ++++
Spd ++++
Def +++

Year	Lev	Team	AB	R	H	HR	RBI	Avg	OB	Sig	OPS	bb%	ct%	Eye	SB	CS	x/h%	Iso	RC/G
2014	Rk	Grand Junction	157	48	50	3	24	318	418	490	909	15	80	0.84	18	5	30	172	7.27
2015	A-	Boise	10	4	5	0	1	500	688	500	1188	38	80	3.00	2	2	0	0	12.68
2015	A	Asheville	361	57	101	7	46	280	353	438	791	10	80	0.57	23	9	33	158	5.48
2016	A+	Modesto	459	57	121	6	56	264	324	355	679	8	79	0.42	22	11	21	92	3.90

1st rounder had a sub-par season in the hitter-friendly CAL, but was young for the level. Quick stroke along with plus bat speed should lead to average gap power, but approach is geared towards line drives. Makes solid contact with a good understanding of the strike zone. Solid defender and should stick at 2B.

Wallach,Chad — 2 — Cincinnati

EXP MLB DEBUT: 2018 | H/W: 6-3 230 | FUT: Reserve C | 6B

Bats R Age 25
2013 (5) Cal State Fullerton
Pwr ++
BAvg ++
Spd ++
Def +++

Year	Lev	Team	AB	R	H	HR	RBI	Avg	OB	Sig	OPS	bb%	ct%	Eye	SB	CS	x/h%	Iso	RC/G
2013	A-	Batavia	146	19	33	0	13	226	280	267	547	7	82	0.41	0	0	18	41	2.30
2014	A	Greensboro	271	50	87	7	49	321	427	476	903	16	86	1.28	3	0	31	155	7.10
2014	A+	Jupiter	64	4	21	0	8	328	434	375	809	16	89	1.71	0	0	14	47	6.14
2015	A+	Daytona	370	41	91	3	32	246	318	351	669	10	79	0.51	2	3	35	105	3.92
2016	AA	Pensacola	200	27	48	8	30	240	359	410	769	16	77	0.80	0	1	38	170	5.30

Reserve catcher profile with power. Son of former MLB 3B Tim Wallach. Works counts as hitter, looking for pitch to drive. Gets beat by better FB due to length in swing. Has average power potential and improved footwork behind the plate. Easy target to throw to.

Walton,Donnie — 46 — Seattle

EXP MLB DEBUT: 2018 | H/W: 5-10 184 | FUT: Starting MIF | 7C

Bats B Age 22
2016 (5) Oklahoma State
Pwr ++
BAvg ++
Spd +++
Def +++

Year	Lev	Team	AB	R	H	HR	RBI	Avg	OB	Sig	OPS	bb%	ct%	Eye	SB	CS	x/h%	Iso	RC/G
2016	NCAA	Oklahoma State	246	45	83	3	44	337	414	447	861	12	85	0.89	14	0	24	110	6.38
2016	A-	Everett	178	43	50	5	23	281	360	421	781	11	87	0.92	6	0	28	140	5.33

Short, nimble INF who could advance quickly due to advanced instincts and defense. Plays both 2B and SS and is very reliable. Not flashy, but gets job done. Better hitter from left side and makes simple contact with short stroke. Punches ball to all fields and can pull ball out of park on occasion. Has average speed, though not a burner.

Ward,Drew — 5 — Washington

EXP MLB DEBUT: 2018 | H/W: 6-3 215 | FUT: Starting 3B | 7C

Bats L Age 22
2013 (3) HS (OK)
Pwr +++
BAvg ++
4.52 Spd ++
Def ++

Year	Lev	Team	AB	R	H	HR	RBI	Avg	OB	Sig	OPS	bb%	ct%	Eye	SB	CS	x/h%	Iso	RC/G
2014	A	Hagerstown	431	45	116	10	73	269	334	413	747	9	72	0.35	2	2	34	144	4.88
2015	Rk	GCL Nationals	13	2	2	1	2	154	313	385	697	19	38	0.38	0	0	50	231	6.64
2015	A+	Potomac	377	47	94	6	47	249	320	358	678	9	71	0.35	2	1	29	109	3.96
2016	A+	Potomac	230	36	64	11	32	278	371	491	863	13	70	0.49	0	1	42	213	6.65
2016	AA	Harrisburg	178	19	39	3	24	219	305	309	614	11	71	0.43	0	1	26	90	3.08

Gameday power finally manifested in 2016, as he earned a promotion to AA after a hot start. Has some bat speed, but straddles the line between patience and passivity, and his tendency to lengthen his swing results in contact problems. Has worked to improve defense, but will need to maintain it to stay at hot corner.

Ward,Taylor — 2 — Los Angeles (A)

EXP MLB DEBUT: 2018 | H/W: 6-1 185 | FUT: Starting C | 7B

Bats R Age 23
2015 (1) Fresno State
Pwr +++
BAvg +++
Spd ++
Def +++

Year	Lev	Team	AB	R	H	HR	RBI	Avg	OB	Sig	OPS	bb%	ct%	Eye	SB	CS	x/h%	Iso	RC/G
2015	NCAA	Fresno State	214	39	65	7	42	304	402	486	888	14	84	1.03	7	0	35	182	6.80
2015	Rk	Orem	109	20	38	2	19	349	486	459	944	21	93	3.63	5	2	18	110	8.03
2015	A	Burlington	92	10	32	1	12	348	412	413	825	10	84	0.67	1	1	13	65	5.78
2016	A+	Inland Empire	466	61	116	10	56	249	319	337	656	9	83	0.59	0	0	18	88	3.65

Strong defender who hit for power at end of season. Uses simple swing and keen eye to make contact and get on base consistently. More gap power at present, but could evolve into more HR pop. Can be too passive at plate and pull happy. Quick feet accentuates agility behind plate. Receives well and shows strong arm with textbook release.

Washington,Kyri — 7 — Boston

EXP MLB DEBUT: 2020 | H/W: 5-11 220 | FUT: Starting OF | 7E

Bats R Age 22
2015 (23) Longwood
Pwr ++++
BAvg ++
Spd +++
Def ++

Year	Lev	Team	AB	R	H	HR	RBI	Avg	OB	Sig	OPS	bb%	ct%	Eye	SB	CS	x/h%	Iso	RC/G
2015	NCAA	Longwood	208	40	58	15	52	279	356	548	904	11	68	0.37	10	3	43	269	7.11
2015	Rk	GCL Red Sox	38	6	10	1	7	263	364	368	732	14	71	0.55	0	1	20	105	4.79
2015	A-	Lowell	80	13	21	0	15	263	330	388	717	9	64	0.28	4	1	43	125	4.97
2016	A	Greenville	382	51	100	16	73	262	320	487	807	8	68	0.27	16	7	45	225	5.79

Short, strong athlete who broke out in power department in first full season. Exhibits plus pop, especially to pull side, and could develop other tools. Runs well, though likely to slow down as he ages. Doesn't bring much discipline to plate and is free swinger early in count. Needs to read spin to hit for BA. LF profile with average arm.

Welker,Colton — 5 — Colorado

EXP MLB DEBUT: 2021 | H/W: 6-2 195 | FUT: Starting 3B | 8D

Bats R Age 19
2016 (4) HS (FL)
Pwr +++
BAvg +++
Spd ++
Def +++

Year	Lev	Team	AB	R	H	HR	RBI	Avg	OB	Sig	OPS	bb%	ct%	Eye	SB	CS	x/h%	Iso	RC/G
2016	Rk	Grand Junction	210	38	69	5	36	329	368	490	858	6	87	0.46	6	4	32	162	5.93

Had an impressive pro debut in the Pioneer League. Has good bat speed and makes consistent, hard contact with average to above power. Swing is a bit funky and can get long, but has good hand-eye coordination. Average runner and with good hands and a strong arm. Profiles as plus 3B if power develops.

Wendle,Joey — 4 — Oakland

EXP MLB DEBUT: 2016 | H/W: 6-1 190 | FUT: Starting 2B | 7C

Bats L Age 26
2012 (6) West Chester
Pwr ++
BAvg +++
Spd ++
Def +++

Year	Lev	Team	AB	R	H	HR	RBI	Avg	OB	Sig	OPS	bb%	ct%	Eye	SB	CS	x/h%	Iso	RC/G
2014	Rk	AZL Indians	22	8	10	0	4	455	538	591	1129	15	82	1.00	1	1	20	136	10.17
2014	AA	Akron	336	46	85	8	50	253	307	414	720	7	83	0.46	4	2	39	161	4.41
2015	AAA	Nashville	577	80	167	10	57	289	316	442	757	4	80	0.19	12	2	36	153	4.68
2016	AAA	Nashville	491	81	137	12	61	279	315	452	767	5	77	0.23	14	4	38	173	4.89
2016	MLB	Oakland	96	11	25	1	11	260	304	302	606	6	83	0.38	2	0	8	42	2.89

Steady INF who reached majors with consistent performance. Covers plate to make good contact. Uses whole field and can hit LHP. Not much over wall pop, but can reach seats on occasion while smashing doubles to gaps. Has become aggressive hitter early in count. Plays mostly 2B and is consistent defender with fringy arm.

Westbrook,Jamie

4 | Arizona | EXP MLB DEBUT: 2017 | H/W: 5-9 170 | FUT: Reserve IF | **6C**

Bats R Age 21 — 2013 (5) HS (AZ)

Pwr ++ / BAvg ++ / Spd +++ / Def +++

Year	Lev	Team	AB	R	H	HR	RBI	Avg	OB	Slg	OPS	bb%	ct%	Eye	SB	CS	x/h%	Iso	RC/G
2013	Rk	Azl Diamondbacks	154	31	45	1	20	292	363	468	830	10	86	0.81	3	3	38	175	6.07
2013	Rk	Missoula	67	12	17	1	13	254	315	343	658	8	70	0.30	1	0	24	90	3.62
2014	A	South Bend	509	69	132	8	49	259	311	375	686	7	81	0.39	6	3	30	116	3.95
2015	A+	Visalia	480	75	153	17	72	319	351	510	862	5	86	0.35	14	4	35	192	5.85
2016	AA	Mobile	435	50	114	5	36	262	304	349	653	6	86	0.43	10	5	24	87	3.57

Smallish MIF came down to earth with bat in '16. Average and power both slumped from '15 career highs. A free-swinging RHH, pitchers exploited his willingness to swing at anything close. Lots of soft contact in bat. Cannot differentiate between good and bad pitches to swing at around zone. Average defender and runner.

White,Isaiah

78 | Miami | EXP MLB DEBUT: 2020 | H/W: 6-0 170 | FUT: Starting CF | **7C**

Bats R Age 20 — 2015 (3) HS (NC)

Pwr ++ / BAvg + / Spd +++++ / Def ++++

Year	Lev	Team	AB	R	H	HR	RBI	Avg	OB	Slg	OPS	bb%	ct%	Eye	SB	CS	x/h%	Iso	RC/G
2015	Rk	GCL Marlins	126	19	37	0	8	294	310	381	691	2	65	0.07	13	0	24	87	4.15
2016	A-	Batavia	173	23	37	1	17	214	303	301	603	11	65	0.37	5	4	27	87	3.07

Looked over-matched in short-season ball, as he can be overly aggressive at the plate. He does have impressive raw tools and some of the best speed in the system, but needs to prove he can make enough contact to hit. Plus-plus runner who covers ground well and is a true CF. Speed is his best asset.

White,Mikey

46 | Oakland | EXP MLB DEBUT: 2018 | H/W: 6-1 200 | FUT: Starting SS | **7E**

Bats R Age 23 — 2015 (2) Alabama

Pwr ++ / BAvg ++ / Spd ++ / Def +++

Year	Lev	Team	AB	R	H	HR	RBI	Avg	OB	Slg	OPS	bb%	ct%	Eye	SB	CS	x/h%	Iso	RC/G
2015	NCAA	Alabama	218	48	74	4	35	339	422	537	958	12	78	0.66	8	1	39	197	7.85
2015	A-	Vermont	111	18	35	2	16	315	392	459	851	11	74	0.48	0	2	34	144	6.42
2015	A	Beloit	130	16	26	1	12	200	257	262	519	7	77	0.33	0	1	23	62	1.77
2016	A+	Stockton	469	65	116	6	50	247	306	352	658	8	72	0.31	4	2	29	104	3.63

Savvy INF who suffered thru poor first half, but was better at end of year. Strikes out too often and gives away at bats with limited contact. Mostly doubles power and should grow into more as he learns to read pitches better. Relies on instincts in field and can play all INF spots with quickness and average arm.

Whitley,Garrett

8 | Tampa Bay | EXP MLB DEBUT: 2020 | H/W: 6-1 205 | FUT: Starting OF | **9D**

Bats R Age 20 — 2015 (1) HS (NY)

Pwr +++ / BAvg +++ / Spd ++++ / Def +++

Year	Lev	Team	AB	R	H	HR	RBI	Avg	OB	Slg	OPS	bb%	ct%	Eye	SB	CS	x/h%	Iso	RC/G
2015	Rk	GCL Devil Rays	96	12	18	3	13	188	304	365	668	14	74	0.64	5	4	50	177	3.97
2015	A-	Hudson Valley	42	3	6	0	4	143	234	190	425	11	71	0.42	3	1	17	48	0.51
2016	A-	Hudson Valley	256	38	68	1	31	266	343	379	722	10	71	0.40	21	5	29	113	4.77

Explosive athlete who started slow, but ended strong. Has well above average bat speed and exhibits plus power potential. Working on putting ball in play now, but pop will determine ceiling. Runs very well on base and in CF, where he owns plus range. Struggles to recognize spin and swing can get long. Very high upside.

Williams,Justin

9 | Tampa Bay | EXP MLB DEBUT: 2018 | H/W: 6-2 215 | FUT: Starting OF | **8C**

Bats L Age 21 — 2013 (2) HS (LA)

Pwr +++ / BAvg +++ / Spd ++ / Def +++

Year	Lev	Team	AB	R	H	HR	RBI	Avg	OB	Slg	OPS	bb%	ct%	Eye	SB	CS	x/h%	Iso	RC/G
2014	A	South Bend	102	16	29	2	23	284	330	461	791	6	77	0.30	0	1	38	176	5.32
2015	A	Bowling Green	387	43	110	7	42	284	308	413	721	3	80	0.17	3	1	31	129	4.16
2015	A+	Charlotte	83	8	20	0	6	241	250	301	551	1	83	0.07	3	1	25	60	2.09
2016	A+	Charlotte	194	23	64	4	31	330	350	448	798	3	87	0.23	0	1	23	119	5.00
2016	AA	Montgomery	148	20	37	6	28	250	275	446	720	3	80	0.17	0	1	41	196	4.08

Projectable OF who was great in A+ before promotion to AA. Set career-high in HR and has sound feel for bat despite all-or-nothing approach. Possesses clean swing from left side and has average raw power. Rarely steals bases, but has good enough speed for ideal range. Waiting for breakout.

Williams,Mason

789 | New York (A) | EXP MLB DEBUT: 2015 | H/W: 6-1 185 | FUT: Starting OF | **7D**

Bats L Age 25 — 2010 (4) HS (FL)

Pwr ++ / BAvg +++ / Spd +++ / Def ++++

Year	Lev	Team	AB	R	H	HR	RBI	Avg	OB	Slg	OPS	bb%	ct%	Eye	SB	CS	x/h%	Iso	RC/G
2015	MLB	NY Yankees	21	3	6	1	3	286	318	571	890	5	86	0.33	0	0	67	286	6.23
2016	Rk	GCL Yankees	4	0	0	0	0	0	0	0	0	0	75	0.00	0	0		0	-5.26
2016	A+	Tampa	42	2	14	0	1	333	349	429	777	2	90	0.25	0	0	21	95	4.89
2016	AAA	Scranton/WB	125	19	37	0	23	296	323	376	699	4	83	0.24	1	1	24	80	4.01
2016	MLB	NY Yankees	27	4	8	0	2	296	321	333	655	4	56	0.08	0	0	13	37	4.14

Athletic OF who missed most of season after shoulder surgery. Drop in prospect status, but has good wheels and is above average defender. Has plus range in OF and has polished routes. Gets on base and can use speed, but is more of a slap hitter with limited power. Rarely hits HR, though has natural bat speed and wiry strength.

Williams,Nick

789 | Philadelphia | EXP MLB DEBUT: 2017 | H/W: 6-3 195 | FUT: Starting OF | **8C**

Bats L Age 23 — 2012 (2) HS (TX)

Pwr +++ / BAvg ++ / 4.26 Spd +++ / Def +++

Year	Lev	Team	AB	R	H	HR	RBI	Avg	OB	Slg	OPS	bb%	ct%	Eye	SB	CS	x/h%	Iso	RC/G
2014	A+	Myrtle Beach	377	61	110	13	68	292	326	491	816	5	69	0.16	5	7	41	199	5.76
2014	AA	Frisco	62	4	14	0	4	226	250	290	540	3	66	0.10	1	1	21	65	1.88
2015	AA	Frisco	378	56	113	13	45	299	354	479	832	8	80	0.42	10	8	34	180	5.75
2015	AA	Reading	97	21	31	4	10	320	340	536	876	3	79	0.15	3	0	35	216	6.00
2016	AAA	Lehigh Valley	497	78	128	13	64	258	285	427	711	4	73	0.14	6	4	41	169	4.15

Gifted with elite physical tools (fast hands, bat speed, footspeed), his shoddy plate approach returned in 2016 and put his once-lofty projection at risk. Still has considerable BA and HR potential due to his fluid swing, but pitch recognition has been a challenge. Has shown solid defensive skills as an OF corner.

Williams,Nonie

6 | Los Angeles (A) | EXP MLB DEBUT: 2021 | H/W: 6-2 200 | FUT: Starting SS | **9E**

Bats B Age 18 — 2016 (3) HS (KS)

Pwr ++ / BAvg ++ / Spd ++++ / Def ++

Year	Lev	Team	AB	R	H	HR	RBI	Avg	OB	Slg	OPS	bb%	ct%	Eye	SB	CS	x/h%	Iso	RC/G
2016	Rk	Azl Angels	156	23	38	0	11	244	280	282	563	5	74	0.20	8	3	13	38	2.21

Big, athletic INF with immense upside. Explosive bat speed is highlight and could evolve into double-plus power at peak. Has excellent speed now, though may slow down as he matures. Swing mechanics aren't pretty and struggles to read spin. Raw defender with limited range and may outgrow SS. Will take time to develop.

Wilson,D.J.

8 | Chicago (N) | EXP MLB DEBUT: 2020 | H/W: 5-8 177 | FUT: Starting CF | **7C**

Bats R Age 20 — 2015 (4) HS (OH)

Pwr ++ / BAvg +++ / Spd ++++ / Def ++++

Year	Lev	Team	AB	R	H	HR	RBI	Avg	OB	Slg	OPS	bb%	ct%	Eye	SB	CS	x/h%	Iso	RC/G
2015	Rk	Azl Cubs	79	12	21	0	6	266	318	354	672	7	81	0.40	5	1	24	89	3.89
2016	A-	Eugene	245	37	63	3	29	257	313	371	685	8	77	0.36	21	8	32	114	3.98

Speedy, but undersized OF has a short, compact stroke and a good understanding of strike zone should allow him to hit for average though he drew just 20 BB. Scouts are mixed on his power upside, but he has just 3 HR in 324 pro AB. Covers ground well in CF with an average arm and is plus defender.

Wilson,Marcus

8 | Arizona | EXP MLB DEBUT: 2020 | H/W: 6-3 175 | FUT: Starting CF | **7D**

Bats R Age 20 — 2014 (S-2) HS (CA)

Pwr ++ / BAvg ++ / Spd ++++ / Def ++++

Year	Lev	Team	AB	R	H	HR	RBI	Avg	OB	Slg	OPS	bb%	ct%	Eye	SB	CS	x/h%	Iso	RC/G
2014	Rk	Azl Diamondbacks	131	15	27	1	22	206	293	275	567	11	69	0.40	4	2	19	69	2.46
2015	Rk	Missoula	213	42	55	1	22	258	358	338	696	13	71	0.54	7	4	25	80	4.45
2016	A-	Hillsboro	136	24	34	0	15	250	414	316	730	22	71	0.95	18	3	21	66	5.31
2016	A	Kane County	99	11	25	1	5	253	339	384	723	12	68	0.41	7	2	40	131	4.88

Super-athletic OF made significant strides with bat in '16. Cleaned up load issues, quicker bat-to-ball skills. Cut down on strikeouts adjusting game plan and swing. Power will come as he fills out his body. Speed is greatest asset. Showed advanced skill on the bases and in the field.

Winker,Jesse

7 | Cincinnati | EXP MLB DEBUT: 2017 | H/W: 6-3 215 | FUT: Starting OF | **8C**

Bats L Age 23 — 2012 (S-1) HS (FL)

Pwr +++ / BAvg ++++ / Spd ++ / Def ++

Year	Lev	Team	AB	R	H	HR	RBI	Avg	OB	Slg	OPS	bb%	ct%	Eye	SB	CS	x/h%	Iso	RC/G
2014	A+	Bakersfield	205	42	65	13	49	317	429	580	1009	16	78	0.87	5	1	43	263	8.43
2014	AA	Pensacola	77	15	16	2	8	208	330	351	680	15	71	0.64	0	0	44	143	4.18
2015	AA	Pensacola	443	69	125	13	55	282	385	433	818	14	81	0.89	8	4	31	151	5.95
2016	Rk	AZL Reds	13	6	6	2	6	462	533	923	1456	13	69	0.50	0	0	33	462	14.68
2016	AAA	Louisville	380	39	115	3	45	303	396	384	781	13	84	1.00	0	0	22	82	5.55

Production has been up and down past three seasons. An advanced hitter, went back to basics concentrating on hit tool, cutting down strikeouts at the expense of his power. Wrist and hand strength hasn't been the same since suffering tendon injury in right wrist in '14. A below average defender, his flexiblity is limited.

Wiseman,Rhett | 9 | Washington | EXP MLB DEBUT: 2019 | H/W: 6-0 200 | FUT: Starting OF | 7C

Bats L Age 22	Year	Lev	Team	AB	R	H	HR	RBI	Avg	OB	Slg	OPS	bb%	ct%	Eye	SB	CS	x/h%	Iso	RC/G
2015 (3) Vanderbilt																				
Pwr +++																				
BAvg ++	2015	NCAA	Vanderbilt	290	70	92	15	49	317	400	566	966	12	75	0.55	12	2	41	248	7.82
4.26 Spd +++	2015	A-	Auburn	210	25	52	5	35	248	307	376	683	8	75	0.35	6	2	33	129	3.89
Def ++	2016	A	Hagerstown	478	71	122	13	75	255	315	410	725	8	78	0.40	19	10	35	155	4.46

Solid first full season. Has some raw power, but swing can get "sweepy," and doesn't yet use opposite field very much. Adequate contact, good patience, and more footspeed than one might expect, though limited to OF corner. Heady player who takes good ABs. Will need to continue to hit.

Woodman,J.B. | 89 | Toronto | EXP MLB DEBUT: 2019 | H/W: 6-2 195 | FUT: Starting OF | 8D

Bats L Age 22	Year	Lev	Team	AB	R	H	HR	RBI	Avg	OB	Slg	OPS	bb%	ct%	Eye	SB	CS	x/h%	Iso	RC/G
2016 (2) Mississippi																				
Pwr +++																				
BAvg +++	2016	NCAA	Mississippi	232	53	75	14	55	323	408	578	985	12	79	0.69	12	7	40	254	7.85
Spd +++	2016	A-	Vancouver	195	28	53	3	24	272	369	421	789	13	63	0.42	10	2	42	149	6.16
Def +++	2016	A	Lansing	34	5	15	1	5	441	500	588	1088	11	62	0.31	0	1	20	147	10.84

Instinctual, athletic OF with impressive power/speed combo. Lacks a prominent tool, though does everything well. Likes to see pitches and focus on line drives to gaps. Hits breaking balls, but has tendency to be too patient at plate and expand zone. Will steal bases aggressively and has speed to play CF. Good arm would work well in RF.

Wrenn,Stephen | 8 | Houston | EXP MLB DEBUT: 2019 | H/W: 6-2 185 | FUT: Starting OF | 7D

Bats R Age 22	Year	Lev	Team	AB	R	H	HR	RBI	Avg	OB	Slg	OPS	bb%	ct%	Eye	SB	CS	x/h%	Iso	RC/G
2016 (6) Georgia																				
Pwr ++																				
BAvg ++	2016	NCAA	Georgia	209	34	62	5	26	297	355	435	791	8	78	0.40	12	4	24	139	5.31
Spd ++++	2016	A-	Tri City	149	30	42	9	27	282	359	544	903	11	73	0.45	8	1	45	262	6.91
Def +++	2016	A	Quad Cities	140	16	33	3	12	236	272	393	665	5	73	0.18	7	2	39	157	3.60

Speedy OF who is adding polish to his offensive repertoire. Surprised with power output in pro debut and could grow to average power down line. Pop mostly to pull side and may struggle to hit for BA as he doesn't put bat to ball consistently. Exhibits plus speed and is strong defender in CF with above average arm.

Yastrzemski,Mike | 789 | Baltimore | EXP MLB DEBUT: 2017 | H/W: 5-11 180 | FUT: Reserve OF | 6B

Bats L Age 26	Year	Lev	Team	AB	R	H	HR	RBI	Avg	OB	Slg	OPS	bb%	ct%	Eye	SB	CS	x/h%	Iso	RC/G
2013 (14) Vanderbilt	2014	A+	Frederick	93	21	29	1	19	312	366	462	829	8	83	0.50	5	0	34	151	5.85
Pwr ++	2014	AA	Bowie	184	23	46	3	12	250	303	413	716	7	82	0.41	1	2	43	163	4.42
BAvg ++	2015	AA	Bowie	476	63	117	6	59	246	308	372	680	8	79	0.43	8	7	36	126	3.99
Spd +++	2016	AA	Bowie	127	27	34	6	27	268	363	449	812	13	84	0.95	4	0	32	181	5.69
Def +++	2016	AAA	Norfolk	339	41	75	7	32	221	307	369	676	11	71	0.43	10	3	43	147	4.02

Well-rounded OF who struggled in AAA, but brings enough talent and tools to warrant reserve spot. Set high in HR, but focuses more on hitting line drives to gaps. Uses all fields and recognizes pitches. Average bat speed leads to limited pop and bails out against LHP. Strikes out too often for his limited power. Can play all OF spots with average arm.

Yerzy,Andy | 2 | Arizona | EXP MLB DEBUT: 2021 | H/W: 6-3 215 | FUT: Starting C | 7E

Bats L Age 18	Year	Lev	Team	AB	R	H	HR	RBI	Avg	OB	Slg	OPS	bb%	ct%	Eye	SB	CS	x/h%	Iso	RC/G
2016 (2) HS (ON)																				
Pwr ++																				
BAvg ++																				
Spd ++	2016	Rk	Azl Diamondbacks	102	5	20	1	15	196	226	255	481	4	78	0.18	0	0	20	59	1.16
Def +	2016	Rk	Missoula	60	2	15	0	1	250	250	283	533	0	73	0.00	0	1	13	33	1.56

Canadian LHH catcher with loud raw power tool. Swing was complete mess in pro debut, with lack of hitting approach. Power is calling card; uses solid balance and swing leverage to drive ball out of park. 20 HR-plus potential if bat can come around. Defense is a work-in-progress. Not good enough an athlete for OF. C/1B or bust type.

Ynfante,Wadye | 78 | St. Louis | EXP MLB DEBUT: 2020 | H/W: 6-0 160 | FUT: Starting CF | 8D

Bats R Age 19	Year	Lev	Team	AB	R	H	HR	RBI	Avg	OB	Slg	OPS	bb%	ct%	Eye	SB	CS	x/h%	Iso	RC/G
2014 FA (DR)																				
Pwr +++																				
BAvg +++																				
Spd +++																				
Def +++	2016	Rk	GCL Cardinals	17	1	1	0	0	59	111	59	170	6	76	0.25	0	1	0	0	-2.82

Wiry, athletic OF from the D.R. finally made his state-side debut. Moves well defensively with good range and a decent arm. Has a good approach at the plate with plus bat speed and impressive raw power. Still raw in some aspects of his game, but worth watching.

Young,Chesny | 457 | Chicago (N) | EXP MLB DEBUT: 2018 | H/W: 6-0 170 | FUT: Utility player | 6A

Bats R Age 24	Year	Lev	Team	AB	R	H	HR	RBI	Avg	OB	Slg	OPS	bb%	ct%	Eye	SB	CS	x/h%	Iso	RC/G
2014 (14) Mercer	2014	A-	Boise	48	13	17	0	9	354	446	417	863	14	83	1.00	1	0	18	63	6.65
Pwr +	2014	A	Kane County	105	14	34	0	9	324	355	419	774	5	79	0.23	2	1	24	95	4.99
BAvg ++++	2015	A	South Bend	108	23	34	0	14	315	383	380	763	10	94	1.71	9	3	18	65	5.33
Spd ++	2015	A+	Myrtle Beach	402	65	129	1	30	321	389	388	777	10	89	1.02	12	5	17	67	5.37
Def +++	2016	AA	Tennessee	491	60	149	4	37	303	376	387	763	10	87	0.89	16	14	21	84	5.17

14th round pick has done nothing but hit as a pro. Uses a compact stroke to shoot line drives to all fields and has some of the best bat control in the minors. Won the Southern League batting title and has a career slash line of .314/.384/.390. Is a jack-of-all-trades and played 2B, SS, 3B, LF, 1B and DH in '16.

Yrizarri,Yeyson | 6 | Texas | EXP MLB DEBUT: 2019 | H/W: 6-0 175 | FUT: Starting SS | 8E

Bats R Age 20	Year	Lev	Team	AB	R	H	HR	RBI	Avg	OB	Slg	OPS	bb%	ct%	Eye	SB	CS	x/h%	Iso	RC/G
2013 FA (VZ)	2014	Rk	Azl Rangers	190	23	45	1	19	237	271	332	603	5	81	0.25	5	3	33	95	2.87
Pwr ++	2014	Rk	DSL Rangers	43	7	13	0	6	302	348	419	766	7	91	0.75	1	1	31	116	5.13
BAvg ++	2015	A-	Spokane	245	27	65	2	29	265	283	339	622	2	81	0.13	8	6	20	73	2.90
Spd +++	2015	AAA	Round Rock	33	2	9	0	4	273	294	364	658	3	85	0.20	0	1	22	91	3.52
Def +++	2016	A	Hickory	450	53	121	7	53	269	283	389	672	2	80	0.10	20	15	31	120	3.49

Intriguing INF who has upside with bat. Free-swinging and all-or-nothing approach needs to be tamed, though he's been successful with it. Could steal many more bases if OBP higher. Tends to be pull-conscious, but has surprising pop in frame. Swings very fast bat and should hit lots of doubles with 15+ HR at peak. Should stick at SS with ample range.

Zagunis,Mark | 79 | Chicago (N) | EXP MLB DEBUT: 2017 | H/W: 6-0 205 | FUT: Starting OF | 8D

Bats R Age 24	Year	Lev	Team	AB	R	H	HR	RBI	Avg	OB	Slg	OPS	bb%	ct%	Eye	SB	CS	x/h%	Iso	RC/G
2014 (3) Virginia Tech	2014	A-	Boise	154	32	46	2	27	299	416	422	838	17	80	1.00	11	2	28	123	6.47
Pwr ++	2014	A	Kane County	50	11	14	0	4	280	400	440	840	17	82	1.11	5	0	50	160	6.64
BAvg +++	2015	A+	Myrtle Beach	413	78	112	8	54	271	389	412	801	16	79	0.93	12	10	33	140	5.92
Spd +++	2016	AA	Tennessee	179	30	54	4	24	302	402	453	854	14	80	0.83	1	2	33	151	6.48
Def +++	2016	AAA	Iowa	179	31	49	6	25	274	353	486	839	11	77	0.52	4	0	45	212	6.14

Converted backstop was in the midst of a breakout season when he broke his foot. Mature approach at the plate. Compact, line-drive stroke and good plate discipline give him the tools to hit for average. Should develop average power, but not a real masher. Has the arm-strength and speed to be an asset on defense. Career .401 OBP.

Zangari,Corey | 3 | Chicago (A) | EXP MLB DEBUT: 2020 | H/W: 6-4 240 | FUT: Starting 1B | 8E

Bats R Age 19	Year	Lev	Team	AB	R	H	HR	RBI	Avg	OB	Slg	OPS	bb%	ct%	Eye	SB	CS	x/h%	Iso	RC/G
2015 (6) HS (OK)																				
Pwr ++++	2015	Rk	Azl White Sox	195	29	63	6	40	323	359	492	852	5	75	0.22	1	0	32	169	5.97
BAvg ++	2015	Rk	Great Falls	17	0	4	0	1	235	350	353	703	15	82	1.00	0	0	50	118	4.78
Spd +	2016	Rk	Great Falls	202	31	52	7	27	257	327	426	753	9	65	0.30	2	2	37	168	5.15
Def +	2016	A	Kannapolis	223	22	37	8	24	166	235	314	548	8	52	0.19	0	2	46	148	2.32

Behemoth slugger who was demoted to short-season in June after disastrous Low-A performance. Fails to recognize pitches and consistently expands strike zone. When contact made, can drive ball to any part of park and beyond. Needs to shorten stroke with two strikes. Poor defender with sub-par speed and range. Stuck at 1B or DH.

Zimmer,Bradley | 89 | Cleveland | EXP MLB DEBUT: 2017 | H/W: 6-4 185 | FUT: Starting OF | 9C

Bats L Age 24	Year	Lev	Team	AB	R	H	HR	RBI	Avg	OB	Slg	OPS	bb%	ct%	Eye	SB	CS	x/h%	Iso	RC/G
2014 (1) San Francisco	2014	A	Lake County	11	4	3	2	2	273	385	909	1294	15	73	0.67	1	0	100	636	11.97
Pwr +++	2015	A+	Lynchburg	285	59	87	10	38	305	385	488	873	11	73	0.48	32	5	33	182	6.66
BAvg +++	2015	AA	Akron	187	24	41	6	24	219	288	374	662	9	71	0.33	12	2	39	155	3.63
4.06 Spd ++++	2016	AA	Akron	340	58	86	14	53	253	359	471	829	14	66	0.49	33	13	47	218	6.45
Def ++++	2016	AAA	Columbus	128	18	31	1	9	242	349	305	654	14	56	0.38	5	1	19	63	4.22

Tall, lean OF with potential for five above-average tools. Selective, works counts and can get on base. Works middle of field well, peppers gaps and will flash power to all fences. Swing can get long, as evidenced by unspectacular ct%. Quick first step and good range for CF; arm can play in RF. Smart baserunner with speed for SB impact.

Pitchers are classified as Starters (SP) or Relievers (RP).

THROWS: Handedness — right (RH) or left (LH).

AGE: Pitcher's age, as of April 1, 2017.

DRAFTED: The year, round, and school that the pitcher performed at as an amateur if drafted, or the year and country where the player was signed from, if a free agent.

EXP MLB DEBUT: The year a player is expected to debut in the major leagues.

H/W: The player's height and weight.

FUT: The role that the pitcher is expected to have for the majority of his major league career, not necessarily his greatest upside.

PITCHES: Each pitch that a pitcher throws is graded and designated with a "+", indicating the quality of the pitch, taking into context the pitcher's age and level pitched. Pitches are graded for their velocity, movement, and command. An average pitch will receive three "+" marks. If known, a pitcher's velocity for each pitch is indicated.

FB	fastball
CB	curveball
SP	split-fingered fastball
SL	slider
CU	change-up
CT	cut-fastball
KC	knuckle-curve
KB	knuckle-ball
SC	screwball
SU	slurve

PLAYER STAT LINES: Pitchers receive statistics for the last five teams that they played for (if applicable), including college and the major leagues.

TEAM DESIGNATIONS: Each team that the pitcher performed for during a given year is included.

LEVEL DESIGNATIONS: The level for each team a player performed is included. "AAA" means Triple-A, "AA" means Double-A, "A+" means high Class-A, "A-" means low Class-A and "Rk" means rookie level.

SABERMETRIC CATEGORIES: Descriptions of all the sabermetric categories appear in the glossary.

CAPSULE COMMENTARIES: For each pitcher, a brief analysis of their skills/statistics, and their future potential is provided.

ELIGIBILITY: Eligibility for inclusion is the standard for which Major League Baseball adheres to; 50 innings pitched or 45 days on the 25-man roster, not including the month of September.

POTENTIAL RATINGS: The Potential Ratings are a two-part system in which a player is assigned a number rating based on his upside potential (1-10) and a letter rating based on the probability of reaching that potential (A-E).

Potential

10:	Hall of Famer	5:	MLB reserve
9:	Elite player	4:	Top minor leaguer
8:	Solid regular	3:	Average minor leaguer
7:	Average regular	2:	Minor league reserve
6:	Platoon player	1:	Minor league roster filler

Probability Rating

- A: 90% probability of reaching potential
- B: 70% probability of reaching potential
- C: 50% probability of reaching potential
- D: 30% probability of reaching potential
- E: 10% probability of reaching potential

FASTBALL: Scouts grade a fastball in terms of both velocity and movement. Movement of a pitch is purely subjective, but one can always watch the hitter to see how he reacts to a pitch or if he swings and misses. Pitchers throw four types of fastballs with varying movement. A two-seam fastball is often referred to as a sinker. A four-seam fastball appears to maintain its plane at high velocities. A cutter can move in different directions and is caused by the pitcher both cutting-off his extension out front and by varying the grip. A split-fingered fastball (forkball) is thrown with the fingers spread apart against the seams and demonstrates violent downward movement. Velocity is often graded on the 20-80 scale and is indicated by the chart below.

Scout Grade	Velocity (mph)
80	96+
70	94-95
60	92-93
50 (avg)	89-91
40	87-88
30	85-86
20	82-84

PITCHER RELEASE TIMES: The speed (in seconds) that a pitcher releases a pitch from the stretch is extremely important in terms of halting the running game and establishing good pitching mechanics. Pitchers are timed from the movement of the front leg until the baseball reaches the catcher's mitt. The phrases "slow to the plate" or "quick to the plate" may appear in the capsule commentary box.

1.0-1.2	+
1.3-1.4	MLB average
1.5+	−

Abreu,Albert — SP — New York (A)

EXP MLB DEBUT: 2019 | H/W: 6-2 175 | FUT: #3 starter | 8C

Thrws R Age 21 — 2013 FA (DR)

Velo	Pitch	Grade
92-96	FB	+ + + +
79-81	CB	+ + +
82-85	SL	+ + +
84-88	CU	+ + +

Year	Lev	Team	W	L	Sv	IP	K	ERA	WHIP	BF/G	OBA	H%	S%	xERA	Ctl	Dom	Cmd	hr/9	BPV
2015	Rk	Greeneville	2	3	1	46	51	2.53	1.21	14.3	212	29	80	2.56	4.1	9.9	2.4	0.4	86
2016	A	Quad Cities	2	8	4	90	104	3.50	1.23	17.4	196	28	72	2.53	4.9	10.4	2.1	0.5	73
2016	A+	Lancaster	1	0	0	11	11	5.63	1.88	17.5	275	33	74	6.22	7.2	8.8	1.2	1.6	-18

Athletic, quick-armed SP who dominated in first full season. Power arsenal highlighted by plus FB and above average SL. Poor control is significant problem, but can improve as he gets mechanics down. Sequencing getting better and hard CU evolving into dependable pitch. Long way from ceiling, but could pay dividends.

Acevedo,Domingo — SP — New York (A)

EXP MLB DEBUT: 2017 | H/W: 6-7 242 | FUT: #2 starter | 9D

Thrws R Age 22 — 2012 FA (DR)

Velo	Pitch	Grade
93-99	FB	+ + + + +
80-84	SL	+ +
85-87	CU	+ + +

Year	Lev	Team	W	L	Sv	IP	K	ERA	WHIP	BF/G	OBA	H%	S%	xERA	Ctl	Dom	Cmd	hr/9	BPV
2014	Rk	GCL Yankees 2	0	1	0	15	21	4.17	1.46	12.9	273	43	68	3.59	3.6	12.5	3.5	0.0	147
2015	A-	Staten Island	3	0	0	48	53	1.69	1.08	17.0	215	30	86	2.26	2.8	9.9	3.5	0.4	121
2015	A	Charleston (Sc)	0	0	0	1	1	7.50	2.50	6.4	371	46	67	7.88	7.5	7.5	1.0	0.0	-50
2016	A	Charleston (Sc)	3	1	0	42	48	1.92	0.97	20.0	222	32	80	1.92	1.5	10.2	6.9	0.2	162
2016	A+	Tampa	2	3	0	50	54	3.23	1.28	20.5	258	35	75	3.46	2.7	9.7	3.6	0.5	120

Big, strong SP who has advanced feel and mechanics for size. Moving quickly through org based upon plus-plus FB that exhibits vicious late life. Above average CU gives him chance against LHH, but needs to add consistency and polish to fringy SL. Can overthrow at times and delivery may be best served in pen. Huge upside if all comes together.

Adames,Jose — RP — Cincinnati

EXP MLB DEBUT: 2018 | H/W: 6-2 165 | FUT: Setup reliever | 7E

Thrws R Age 24 — 2010 FA (DR)

Velo	Pitch	Grade
94-98	FB	+ + +
	CB	+ +
	CU	+

Year	Lev	Team	W	L	Sv	IP	K	ERA	WHIP	BF/G	OBA	H%	S%	xERA	Ctl	Dom	Cmd	hr/9	BPV
2014	A	Greensboro	2	2	0	44	38	3.07	1.45	18.8	270	33	82	4.36	3.7	7.8	2.1	0.8	59
2015	A	Greensboro	1	3	0	38	26	2.36	1.34	19.8	240	28	85	3.58	4.0	6.1	1.5	0.7	20
2015	A+	Jupiter	5	6	0	78	64	4.72	1.57	19.1	278	35	67	4.01	4.4	7.4	1.7	0.0	33
2016	A	Greensboro	0	0	0	0	0			2.0	1000	100	0				0.0		
2016	A+	Jupiter	1	5	7	48	43	6.00	1.63	5.9	274	35	61	4.42	5.1	8.1	1.6	0.4	26

Dominican hurler has been slow to develop. He signed in 2010 but has yet to pitch above A+ ball. Was moved to relief with disappointing results. He does have a plus mid-to-upper 90s FB and a sharp-breaking CB, but below-average command has stalled his development.

Adams,Austin — RP — Washington

EXP MLB DEBUT: 2017 | H/W: 6-2 225 | FUT: Setup reliever | 6B

Thrws R Age 25 — 2012 (8) South Florida

Velo	Pitch	Grade
91-97	FB	+ + +
84-87	SL	+ + +
	CU	+

Year	Lev	Team	W	L	Sv	IP	K	ERA	WHIP	BF/G	OBA	H%	S%	xERA	Ctl	Dom	Cmd	hr/9	BPV
2015	A+	Inland Empire	2	1	0	14	21	2.54	1.20	6.3	200	34	76	1.98	4.4	13.3	3.0	0.0	138
2015	AA	Arkansas	1	1	1	36	49	2.98	1.46	5.7	177	29	77	2.41	7.7	12.2	1.6	0.0	29
2015	AAA	Salt Lake	0	0	0	3	1	11.25	3.13	9.5	100	11	60	5.91	25.3	2.8	0.1	0.0	-615
2016	Rk	Azl Angels	0	0	0	3	2	3.00	0.33	4.7	106	13	0		0.0	6.0		0.0	126
2016	AA	Arkansas	0	1	4	41	61	3.07	1.29	5.3	200	33	76	2.63	5.3	13.4	2.5	0.4	117

Hard-throwing RP who saw limited action in 2nd half of year. Tough to hit and pitches aggressively to all quadrants of zone. Poor control limits quality of pitches. Moving FB tough to command, though can blow ball by hitters up in zone. Throws with lots of effort and SL features incredible break when on. Spent entire career in pen.

Adams,Chance — SP — New York (A)

EXP MLB DEBUT: 2017 | H/W: 6-0 215 | FUT: #3 starter | 8C

Thrws R Age 22 — 2015 (5) Dallas Baptist

Velo	Pitch	Grade
92-96	FB	+ + + +
81-83	SL	+ + +
	CU	+ +

Year	Lev	Team	W	L	Sv	IP	K	ERA	WHIP	BF/G	OBA	H%	S%	xERA	Ctl	Dom	Cmd	hr/9	BPV
2015	A-	Staten Island	1	0	0	9	13	0.98	0.87	8.5	162	28	88	0.74	2.9	12.7	4.3	0.0	168
2015	A	Charleston (Sc)	1	1	0	11	16	3.21	0.98	8.5	181	31	64	1.24	3.2	12.9	4.0	0.0	163
2015	A+	Tampa	1	0	0	14	16	1.29	1.00	10.7	233	34	86	1.92	1.3	10.3	8.0	0.0	168
2016	A+	Tampa	5	0	0	57	73	2.67	0.98	18.1	203	30	75	2.08	2.4	11.5	4.9	0.6	161
2016	AA	Trenton	8	1	0	69	71	2.08	0.85	19.5	152	19	80	1.24	3.1	9.2	3.0	0.7	100

Compact SP who moved to rotation in '16 and found success in AA. Pitches aggressively with pure arm speed and can retire hitters with FB/SL combo. Lacks height, so plane to plate is flat and he allows high amount of flyballs. Velocity keeps him afloat and could return to pen without better CU. K rate and low oppBA are highlights.

Adams,Spencer — SP — Chicago (A)

EXP MLB DEBUT: 2018 | H/W: 6-3 171 | FUT: #3 starter | 8D

Thrws R Age 20 — 2014 (2) HS (GA)

Velo	Pitch	Grade
89-93	FB	+ + +
80-83	SL	+ + +
82-84	CU	+ +

Year	Lev	Team	W	L	Sv	IP	K	ERA	WHIP	BF/G	OBA	H%	S%	xERA	Ctl	Dom	Cmd	hr/9	BPV
2014	Rk	Azl White Sox	3	3	0	41	59	3.71	1.29	16.9	297	44	73	4.32	0.9	12.9	14.8	0.9	226
2015	A	Kannapolis	9	5	0	100	73	3.24	1.22	21.3	282	33	75	3.78	1.0	6.6	6.6	0.6	110
2015	A+	Winston-Salem	3	0	0	29	23	2.16	1.31	24.0	274	34	84	3.57	2.2	7.1	3.3	0.3	88
2016	A+	Winston-Salem	8	7	0	107	74	4.03	1.32	24.6	284	33	69	4.01	1.8	6.2	3.5	0.6	82
2016	AA	Birmingham	2	5	0	55	26	3.92	1.25	24.9	275	31	67	3.49	1.6	4.2	2.6	0.3	50

Projectable SP who continues to post low K rate, but has effortless delivery and impeccable feel for pitching. Repeats delivery and uses downhill plane to get groundball outs. Has potential to throw harder, but relies on FB location and control. Doesn't use CU enough, though shows glimpses of becoming average pitch. Needs CU to combat LHH.

Adcock,Brett — SP — Houston

EXP MLB DEBUT: 2019 | H/W: 6-1 225 | FUT: #4 starter | 7D

Thrws L Age 21 — 2016 (4) Michigan

Velo	Pitch	Grade
90-95	FB	+ + +
78-82	CB	+ + +
84-86	CU	+ +

Year	Lev	Team	W	L	Sv	IP	K	ERA	WHIP	BF/G	OBA	H%	S%	xERA	Ctl	Dom	Cmd	hr/9	BPV
2016	NCAA	Michigan	7	5	0	78	100	3.23	1.46	22.3	191	29	77	2.89	7.1	11.5	1.6	0.3	33
2016	A-	Tri City	0	0	0	4	6	6.59	1.22	5.5	206	35	40	2.11	4.4	13.2	3.0	0.0	137

Durable, stocky SP who has chance as either SP or RP. Some see move to pen due to lots of effort in delivery and inability to command plate. Has sneaky quick FB, but tends to be flat, and CB that is tough to make hard contact against. Can retire via K or groundballs. Lacks feel for CU and tends to telegraph.

Adon,Melvin — SP — San Francisco

EXP MLB DEBUT: 2019 | H/W: 6-3 195 | FUT: #3 starter | 8E

Thrws R Age 22 — 2015 FA (DR)

Velo	Pitch	Grade
92-99	FB	+ + + +
84-86	SL	+ +
85-88	CU	+

Year	Lev	Team	W	L	Sv	IP	K	ERA	WHIP	BF/G	OBA	H%	S%	xERA	Ctl	Dom	Cmd	hr/9	BPV
2016	A-	Salem-Keizer	5	5	0	67	55	5.50	1.77	22.0	310	38	67	5.37	4.6	7.4	1.6	0.4	28

Strong-armed SP with excellent natural stuff, but hasn't been tested in full season yet. Holds velocity deep into games with plus FB. Can reach high 90s with minimal effort, though better at lower velocities due to movement. Surprisingly hittable given his arsenal, but telegraphs CU by slowing arm speed. Inconsistent release point on SL.

Aiken,Brady — SP — Cleveland

EXP MLB DEBUT: 2019 | H/W: 6-4 205 | FUT: #2 starter | 9E

Thrws L Age 20 — 2015 (1) HS (FL)

Velo	Pitch	Grade
88-92	FB	+ + +
71-75	CB	+ + + +
81-83	CU	+ + + +

Year	Lev	Team	W	L	Sv	IP	K	ERA	WHIP	BF/G	OBA	H%	S%	xERA	Ctl	Dom	Cmd	hr/9	BPV
2015	na	Did not play in minors																	
2016	Rk	AZL Indians	0	4	0	24	35	7.13	1.88	12.5	321	49	59	5.72	4.9	13.1	2.7	0.4	123
2016	A-	Mahoning Vall	2	1	0	22	22	4.48	1.27	18.1	243	30	68	3.88	3.3	9.0	2.8	1.2	91

Two-time first round draftee's debut yielded mixed bag. Stockpiled strikeouts with late-fading CU and CB that flashes plus 12/6 shape, but struggled to spot FB, which now tops out at 92. Low-effort delivery, clean/fast arm action, athleticism should allow command to improve. If velo bounces back, potential for three plus pitches as front-line type.

Akin,Keegan — SP — Baltimore

EXP MLB DEBUT: 2019 | H/W: 6-0 225 | FUT: #3 starter | 8D

Thrws L Age 22 — 2016 (2) W Michigan

Velo	Pitch	Grade
91-95	FB	+ + +
81-84	SL	+ + +
	CU	+ + +

Year	Lev	Team	W	L	Sv	IP	K	ERA	WHIP	BF/G	OBA	H%	S%	xERA	Ctl	Dom	Cmd	hr/9	BPV
2016	NCAA	West Michigan	7	4	0	109	133	1.82	0.94	24.1	190	29	79	1.31	2.5	11.0	4.4	0.1	149
2016	A-	Aberdeen	0	1	0	26	29	1.04	0.85	10.6	170	25	86	0.79	2.4	10.0	4.1	0.0	133

Fast-armed lefty who was potent upon signing after draft. Tough to hit when three pitches working in tandem. None of pitches grade as plus, but none are sub-par either. Lacks ideal size and projection, but has good velocity and moves ball around quadrants of zone. Could use better breaking ball, but doesn't miss up despite plane to plate.

Albertos,Jose — SP — Chicago (N)

EXP MLB DEBUT: 2020 | H/W: 6-1 185 | FUT: #3 starter | 8D

Thrws R Age 18 — 2015 FA (MX)

Velo	Pitch	Grade
93-95	FB	+ + + +
	SL	+ + +
	CU	+ + +

Year	Lev	Team	W	L	Sv	IP	K	ERA	WHIP	BF/G	OBA	H%	S%	xERA	Ctl	Dom	Cmd	hr/9	BPV
2016	Rk	Azl Cubs	0	0	0	4	7	0.00	0.50	13.3	81	19	100		2.3	15.8	7.0	0.0	241

Small, athletic righty was signed out of Mexico for $1.5 million. Comes after hitters with a plus 93-95 mph FB that hits 97. Locates the FB well and backs it up with a SL that flashes plus and a CU with good fade. Off-speed offerings need refinement, but show potential. Shoulder soreness limited him, but should be ready to return in the spring.

Alcantara,Raul — SP — Oakland

EXP MLB DEBUT: 2016 | H/W: 6-4 220 | FUT: #4 starter | 7C

Thrws R Age 24 — 2009 FA (DR)

Velo	Pitch	Grade
90-95	FB	+++
80-84	SL	++
77-80	CB	++
80-83	CU	+++

Year	Lev	Team	W	L	Sv	IP	K	ERA	WHIP	BF/G	OBA	H%	S%	xERA	Ctl	Dom	Cmd	hr/9	BPV
2014	AA	Midland	2	0	0	19	10	2.34	1.15	25.4	239	28	77	2.42	2.3	4.7	2.0	0.0	39
2015	A+	Stockton	0	2	0	48	29	3.92	1.29	13.2	284	32	69	3.92	1.5	5.4	3.6	0.6	75
2016	AA	Midland	5	6	0	90	73	4.80	1.41	22.4	283	33	68	4.70	2.7	7.3	2.7	1.1	77
2016	AAA	Nashville	4	0	0	45	32	1.19	0.91	21.1	230	28	88	1.87	0.6	6.4	10.7	0.2	117
2016	MLB	Oakland	1	3	0	22	14	7.33	1.58	19.5	332	31	65	8.33	1.6	5.7	3.5	3.7	77

Tall, control-oriented SP who reached majors for first time. Can be too hittable as he lives in fat part of plate. Has good natural stuff, but prefers to pitch to contact. CU can be out pitch, but needs better CB or SL to keep hitters honest. Works down in zone when on and sequences pitches like veteran.

Alcantara,Sandy — SP — St. Louis

EXP MLB DEBUT: 2020 | H/W: 6-4 170 | FUT: #2 SP/closer | 9D

Thrws R Age 21 — 2013 FA (DR)

Velo	Pitch	Grade
94-98	FB	+++++
80-82	SL	+
	CB	++
88-90	CU	++

Year	Lev	Team	W	L	Sv	IP	K	ERA	WHIP	BF/G	OBA	H%	S%	xERA	Ctl	Dom	Cmd	hr/9	BPV
2015	Rk	GCL Cardinals	4	4	0	64	51	3.23	1.23	21.6	246	30	74	3.10	2.8	7.2	2.6	0.4	71
2016	A	Peoria	5	7	0	90	119	4.10	1.37	22.2	235	35	69	3.23	4.5	11.9	2.6	0.4	111
2016	A+	Palm Beach	0	4	0	32	34	3.64	1.21	21.6	216	31	67	2.26	3.9	9.5	2.4	0.0	84

Long, lean 21-year-old from the Dominican Republic has a lightning quick arm. Added size and strength and now owns a plus 94-98 mph FB that has been clocked as high as 102 mph. Mixes in a CU that is raw but shows potential and has some feel for a CB. Lots of projection left.

Alcantara,Victor — RP — Detroit

EXP MLB DEBUT: 2017 | H/W: 6-2 190 | FUT: Setup reliever | 8E

Thrws R Age 24 — 2011 FA (DR)

Velo	Pitch	Grade
92-96	FB	+++
84-88	SL	++
84-87	CU	++

Year	Lev	Team	W	L	Sv	IP	K	ERA	WHIP	BF/G	OBA	H%	S%	xERA	Ctl	Dom	Cmd	hr/9	BPV
2013	Rk	Orem	2	5	0	59	48	7.47	1.83	16.1	305	35	60	6.49	5.3	7.3	1.4	1.5	6
2014	A	Burlington	7	6	1	125	117	3.81	1.26	18.9	217	28	69	2.81	4.3	8.4	2.0	0.4	53
2015	A+	Inland Empire	7	12	0	136	125	5.63	1.54	22.0	284	35	63	4.63	3.8	8.3	2.2	0.7	63
2016	AA	Arkansas	3	7	0	111	79	4.30	1.47	16.4	253	29	71	4.09	4.6	6.4	1.4	0.7	9

Big, strong pitcher who led TL in walks. Moved to pen at mid-season and likely to stay there. Could develop into power RP, but is more thrower than pitcher. Doesn't throw strikes, has no pitch for LHH, and K rate has dropped. Has potential for electric FB, but has a lot of effort in delivery that is difficult to repeat.

Alexander,Tyler — SP — Detroit

EXP MLB DEBUT: 2017 | H/W: 6-2 200 | FUT: #4 starter | 7C

Thrws L Age 22 — 2015 (2) Texas Christian

Velo	Pitch	Grade
87-92	FB	+++
74-78	CB	+++
77-80	SL	++
81-83	CU	++

Year	Lev	Team	W	L	Sv	IP	K	ERA	WHIP	BF/G	OBA	H%	S%	xERA	Ctl	Dom	Cmd	hr/9	BPV
2015	NCAA	Texas Christian	6	3	0	93	72	3.09	1.09	21.5	259	31	74	3.17	1.0	7.0	7.2	0.7	117
2015	A-	Connecticut	0	2	0	37	33	0.97	0.59	10.5	140	16	95	0.55	1.2	8.0	6.6	0.7	130
2016	A+	Lakeland	6	7	0	101	82	2.14	1.00	21.5	232	28	81	2.44	1.3	7.3	5.5	0.5	113
2016	AA	Erie	2	1	0	34	23	3.17	1.17	22.7	272	30	78	3.92	1.1	6.1	5.8	1.1	99

Command/control SP who thrives with location and deception. Not much velocity in tank, but regularly hits spots and keeps ball on ground. Uses two breaking balls and sequences well. Has fringy stuff at best, though ability to keep hitters off-guard is paramount. Rarely allows walks as he repeats delivery, slot, and arm speed consistently.

Allard,Kolby — SP — Atlanta

EXP MLB DEBUT: 2020 | H/W: 6-1 180 | FUT: #1 starter | 9D

Thrws L Age 19 — 2015 (1) HS (CA)

Velo	Pitch	Grade
90-94	FB	++++
74-77	CB	++++
82-84	CU	++

Year	Lev	Team	W	L	Sv	IP	K	ERA	WHIP	BF/G	OBA	H%	S%	xERA	Ctl	Dom	Cmd	hr/9	BPV
2015	Rk	GCL Braves	0	0	0	6	12	0.00	0.17	6.0	56	17	100		0.0	18.0		0.0	342
2016	Rk	Danville	3	0	0	27	33	1.33	0.85	19.9	191	29	83	1.02	1.7	11.0	6.6	0.0	170
2016	A	Rome	5	3	0	60	62	3.74	1.23	22.1	242	31	71	3.33	3.0	9.3	3.1	0.7	104

Back surgery caused delay in his '16 debut. Struggled out of gate, regained form after July demotion to Rookie ball. Struggles repeating delivery. Throws across his body, causing FB to bleed over plate. 12/6 CB has plus-plus potential and is deadly when changing eye levels with FB. CU is work-in-progress; needs to gain separation from FB.

Allen,Logan — SP — San Diego

EXP MLB DEBUT: 2019 | H/W: 6-3 200 | FUT: #4 starter | 7C

Thrws L Age 19 — 2015 (8) HS (FL)

Velo	Pitch	Grade
89-92	FB	+++
81-83	SL	+++
76-79	CB	++
	CU	+++

Year	Lev	Team	W	L	Sv	IP	K	ERA	WHIP	BF/G	OBA	H%	S%	xERA	Ctl	Dom	Cmd	hr/9	BPV
2015	Rk	GCL Red Sox	0	0	0	20	24	0.90	0.65	9.9	175	27	85	0.35	0.5	10.8	24.0	0.0	200
2015	A-	Lowell	0	0	0	4	2	2.20	1.46	17.6	342	39	83	4.76	0.0	4.4		0.0	97
2016	Rk	Azl Padres	0	0	0	6	8	3.00	1.00	7.6	228	36	67	1.84	1.5	12.0	8.0	0.0	194
2016	A-	Tri-City	0	1	0	2	4	8.57	2.38	10.9	403	68	60	8.12	4.3	17.1	4.0	0.0	211
2016	A	Fort Wayne	3	4	0	54	47	3.33	1.30	14.8	240	30	74	3.09	3.7	7.8	2.1	0.3	60

Tall, durable LHP can attack hitters with an assortment of options. 2-seam FB has good life but lost some velocity as starts wore on. SL has two-plane break, could develop into plus pitch. CB tended to loop more than it broke. Has average feel for CU. Advanced pitchability marks, especially setting up hitters for SL & CU.

Almonte,Miguel — SP — Kansas City

EXP MLB DEBUT: 2015 | H/W: 6-2 210 | FUT: #3 starter | 8D

Thrws R Age 24 — 2010 FA (DR)

Velo	Pitch	Grade
92-96	FB	++++
76-79	CB	++
83-87	CU	++++

Year	Lev	Team	W	L	Sv	IP	K	ERA	WHIP	BF/G	OBA	H%	S%	xERA	Ctl	Dom	Cmd	hr/9	BPV
2015	AA	NW Arkansas	4	4	0	67	55	4.03	1.37	16.5	256	31	70	3.70	3.6	7.4	2.0	0.5	53
2015	AAA	Omaha	2	2	0	36	41	5.47	1.33	13.6	244	33	58	3.59	3.7	10.2	2.7	0.7	101
2015	MLB	KC Royals	0	2	0	8	10	6.59	1.71	4.1	232	19	80	7.82	7.7	11.0	1.4	4.4	8
2016	AA	NW Arkansas	2	1	0	16	15	7.31	1.75	6.6	347	40	63	7.65	2.3	8.4	3.8	2.3	109
2016	AAA	Omaha	3	7	0	60	57	5.55	1.75	13.1	271	34	68	5.05	6.3	8.6	1.4	0.8	2

Strong pitcher who has electric stuff, but has trouble finding plate. Demoted to AA late in season and has to clean up control. Lively FB has been difficult to locate and has tendency to overthrow. CU flashes double-plus and throws with plus arm speed. CB hasn't improved and may scrap in favor of SL. Needs to determine role as he is regressing.

Almonte,Yency — SP — Colorado

EXP MLB DEBUT: 2019 | H/W: 6-3 205 | FUT: #4 starter | 7C

Thrws R Age 22 — 2012 (17) HS (FL)

Velo	Pitch	Grade
93-96	FB	++++
83-85	SL	+++
	CU	++

Year	Lev	Team	W	L	Sv	IP	K	ERA	WHIP	BF/G	OBA	H%	S%	xERA	Ctl	Dom	Cmd	hr/9	BPV
2014	A	Burlington	2	5	0	42	32	4.93	1.29	19.2	252	29	63	3.94	3.0	6.9	2.3	1.1	60
2015	A	Kannapolis	8	4	0	92	71	3.90	1.28	22.2	261	31	71	3.77	2.5	6.9	2.7	0.8	74
2015	A+	Winston-Salem	3	3	0	44	39	2.44	0.90	23.5	183	24	72	1.30	2.4	7.9	3.3	0.2	95
2016	A+	Modesto	8	9	0	138	134	3.71	1.18	25.1	242	30	71	3.36	2.5	8.7	3.4	0.9	107
2016	AA	Hartford	3	1	0	30	22	3.00	1.27	24.5	206	22	82	3.43	4.8	6.6	1.4	1.2	7

Breakout season, going 11-10 w/ 3.58 ERA. Plus 93-96 mph FB that tops at 98 mph is backed up by a good hard SL and fringe CU. Dom jumped from 6.9 to 8.7 w/ improved Cmd and gives him a chance to make an impact in the majors. CU needs to improve to remain a starter, but plus velocity makes him a power reliever at worst.

Altavilla,Dan — RP — Seattle

EXP MLB DEBUT: 2016 | H/W: 5-11 200 | FUT: Setup reliever | 7C

Thrws R Age 24 — 2014 (5) Mercyhurst Coll

Velo	Pitch	Grade
91-96	FB	+++
84-86	SL	+++
81-82	CU	+

Year	Lev	Team	W	L	Sv	IP	K	ERA	WHIP	BF/G	OBA	H%	S%	xERA	Ctl	Dom	Cmd	hr/9	BPV
2014	A-	Everett	5	3	0	66	66	4.36	1.61	20.9	284	36	75	5.06	4.4	9.0	2.1	1.0	62
2015	A+	Bakersfield	6	12	0	148	134	4.07	1.29	21.7	248	31	69	3.50	3.2	8.1	2.5	0.7	78
2016	AA	Jackson	7	3	16	56	65	1.92	1.10	5.1	202	28	85	2.25	3.5	10.4	3.0	0.5	110
2016	MLB	Seattle	0	0	0	12	10	0.74	0.99	3.1	244	31	92	2.07	0.7	7.4	10.0	0.0	132

Short, powerful RP who was moved to pen for '16 and was dominant. Reached SEA and showcased quality hard stuff. Increased velocity in pen and also kept electric, late life to FB. SL showed more consistency with power break and consistently misses bats. Key is to get ahead in count. Lot of effort in delivery and lacks feel for changing speeds.

Alvarez,Yadier — SP — Los Angeles (N)

EXP MLB DEBUT: 2018 | H/W: 6-3 175 | FUT: #2 SP/closer | 9D

Thrws R Age 21 — 2015 FA (CU)

Velo	Pitch	Grade
92-97	FB	+++++
83-86	SL	+++
	CU	++

Year	Lev	Team	W	L	Sv	IP	K	ERA	WHIP	BF/G	OBA	H%	S%	xERA	Ctl	Dom	Cmd	hr/9	BPV
2016	Rk	Azl Dodgers	1	1	0	20	26	1.80	0.95	15.1	138	23	79	0.70	4.5	11.7	2.6	0.0	107
2016	A	Great Lakes	3	2	0	39	55	2.30	1.07	16.9	219	35	78	2.13	2.5	12.7	5.0	0.2	178

Cuban flamethrower was signed for $16 million. Has a plus-plus fastball that sits at 92-97 mph, topping out at 100. Backs up the heater with a good hard SL that flashes as plus and a below-average CU. Showed improved Cmd when moved to the MWL, but has below-average control of all three offerings. Mechanics and release point can be inconsistent.

Anderson,Chris — RP — Los Angeles (N)

EXP MLB DEBUT: 2017 | H/W: 6-3 245 | FUT: Setup reliever | 7D

Thrws R Age 24 — 2013 (1) Jacksonville

Velo	Pitch	Grade
92-94	FB	+++
78-81	CB	++
80-83	CU	+++

Year	Lev	Team	W	L	Sv	IP	K	ERA	WHIP	BF/G	OBA	H%	S%	xERA	Ctl	Dom	Cmd	hr/9	BPV
2014	A+	Rancho Cuca	7	7	0	134	146	4.63	1.57	21.8	280	37	71	4.68	4.2	9.8	2.3	0.7	80
2015	AA	Tulsa	9	7	0	126	98	4.06	1.44	23.4	257	30	74	4.19	4.2	7.0	1.7	0.9	30
2015	AAA	Oklahoma City	0	3	0	6	2	19.18	3.77	13.4	449	44	48	15.57	13.3	3.0	0.2	3.0	-287
2016	A+	Rancho Cuca	1	2	0	27	26	3.31	1.14	6.0	207	25	75	2.90	3.6	8.6	2.4	1.0	75
2016	AA	Tulsa	3	6	0	39	25	5.97	1.84	10.1	251	28	67	4.95	8.0	5.7	0.7	0.7	-96

Former 1st rounder has been slow to develop and was moved to relief in '16. Pounds the strike zone with a solid three-pitch mix. Best offering is a 92-94 mph FB that tops out at 97 mph. Mixes in a quality SL with an avg CU. Control continues to be a huge issue and walked 46 in 67.1 IP. Hard to see any success unless his command improves.

Anderson,Ian
SP | **Atlanta** | EXP MLB DEBUT: 2020 | H/W: 6-3 170 | FUT: #2 starter | **8C**

Thrws R Age 18
2016 (1) HS (NY)

Velo	Pitch	Grade
91-95	FB	++++
83-85	SL	+++
83-84	CU	+++

Year	Lev	Team	W	L	Sv	IP	K	ERA	WHIP	BF/G	OBA	H%	S%	xERA	Ctl	Dom	Cmd	hr/9	BPV
2016	Rk	Danville	0	2	0	21	18	3.82	1.27	17.4	241	30	69	3.14	3.4	7.6	2.3	0.4	64
2016	Rk	GCL Braves	1	0	0	18	18	0.00	1.00	13.8	216	30	100	1.73	2.0	9.0	4.5	0.0	126

#3 pick in '16 draft, shot up draft boards due to signability and advanced pitchability skills. FB 91-95 in pro debut, around the plate. Complements with a potentially plus SL and average CU. SL is true swing-and-miss offering, helping overall projection as #2 starter. Can add muscle to slight frame to help add velocity to FB.

Anderson,Shaun
SP | **Boston** | EXP MLB DEBUT: 2019 | H/W: 6-4 225 | FUT: #3 starter | **8E**

Thrws R Age 22
2016 (3) Florida

Velo	Pitch	Grade
90-95	FB	++++
84-88	SL	+++
77-79	CB	++
	CU	++

Year	Lev	Team	W	L	Sv	IP	K	ERA	WHIP	BF/G	OBA	H%	S%	xERA	Ctl	Dom	Cmd	hr/9	BPV
2016	NCAA	Florida	3	0	13	46	60	0.98	0.82	4.7	193	30	89	1.16	1.4	11.7	8.6	0.2	192
2016	A-	Lowell	0	0	0	2	4	36.82	5.45	9.1	659	83	27	29.14	0.0	16.4		4.1	313

Tall, strong pitcher who served as RP in college, but appears to be in line to start as pro. Uses four pitches to advantage and works from high 3/4 slot to provide tough downhill plane. Lacks true out pitch and needs to find consistent 2nd offering to complement plus FB. SL features drastic cutting action, but doesn't throw for strikes.

Appel,Mark
SP | **Philadelphia** | EXP MLB DEBUT: 2017 | H/W: 6-5 220 | FUT: #3 starter | **8C**

Thrws R Age 25
2013 (1) Stanford

Velo	Pitch	Grade
91-94	FB	+++
83-86	SL	+++
81-85	CU	+++

Year	Lev	Team	W	L	Sv	IP	K	ERA	WHIP	BF/G	OBA	H%	S%	xERA	Ctl	Dom	Cmd	hr/9	BPV
2014	A+	Lancaster	2	5	0	44		9.80	1.93	17.4	373	44	49	8.19	2.2	8.2	3.6	1.8	104
2014	AA	Corpus Christi	1	2	0	39	38	3.69	1.23	22.6	241	31	70	3.06	3.0	8.8	2.9	0.5	95
2015	AA	Corpus Christi	5	1	0	63	49	4.28	1.44	20.7	276	32	73	4.59	3.3	7.0	2.1	1.0	55
2015	AAA	Fresno	5	2	0	68	61	4.49	1.40	23.9	259	32	69	4.02	3.7	8.1	2.2	0.8	63
2016	AAA	Lehigh Valley	3	3	0	38	34	4.49	1.57	20.9	271	34	72	4.57	4.7	8.0	1.7	0.7	35

Season cut short by shoulder injury and then elbow surgery (bone spurs). In eight starts, control problems worsened, starting with sloppy FB command. What once was a promising three-pitch (SL and CU) arsenal looked only average. Good size, and still has velocity, but needs better results with runners on base which could quell the bullpen talk.

Arano,Victor
RP | **Philadelphia** | EXP MLB DEBUT: 2017 | H/W: 6-2 200 | FUT: Setup reliever | **8D**

Thrws R Age 22
2013 FA (MX)

Velo	Pitch	Grade
94-96	FB	++++
85-87	SL	+++
85-86	CU	++

Year	Lev	Team	W	L	Sv	IP	K	ERA	WHIP	BF/G	OBA	H%	S%	xERA	Ctl	Dom	Cmd	hr/9	BPV
2013	Rk	Azl Dodgers	3	2	0	49	49	4.22	1.32	15.7	273	35	69	3.98	2.4	9.0	3.8	0.7	115
2014	A	Great Lakes	4	7	3	86	83	4.08	1.26	15.9	266	33	71	4.11	2.1	8.7	4.2	1.2	118
2015	A+	Clearwater	4	12	0	124	69	4.72	1.27	21.1	273	31	61	3.65	1.9	5.0	2.7	0.5	57
2016	A+	Clearwater	4	1	4	63	71	2.29	1.06	7.0	226	31	81	2.54	2.1	10.1	4.7	0.6	143
2016	AA	Reading	1	1	1	16	24	2.22	0.93	5.5	194	29	85	2.28	2.2	13.3	6.0	1.1	198

Shortened up for bullpen work, he added several mph on his FB that now works in the mid-90s with ease. Moves it in/out and commands it well. SL also got harder, and batters have a tough time squaring him up. Delivery is compact and repeatable, and could move quickly through the system as bullpen piece.

Araujo,Pedro
RP | **Chicago (N)** | EXP MLB DEBUT: 2019 | H/W: 6-3 214 | FUT: Setup reliever | **7C**

Thrws R Age 23
2011 FA (DR)

Velo	Pitch	Grade
90-94	FB	++++
	CB	++
	CU	++

Year	Lev	Team	W	L	Sv	IP	K	ERA	WHIP	BF/G	OBA	H%	S%	xERA	Ctl	Dom	Cmd	hr/9	BPV
2014	Rk	Azl Cubs	0	0	1	16	27	2.80	1.24	6.5	209	37	79	2.71	4.5	15.1	3.4	0.6	169
2014	Rk	DSL Cubs	2	1	0	20	14	1.35	1.15	19.9	232	29	87	2.32	2.7	6.3	2.3	0.0	59
2015	A-	Eugene	0	2	1	50	70	2.69	1.04	9.2	233	37	73	2.17	1.6	12.6	7.8	0.2	201
2016	A	South Bend	3	0	3	34	45	1.59	0.88	7.9	165	26	83	1.07	2.9	11.9	4.1	0.3	154
2016	A+	Myrtle Beach	0	2	1	19	22	5.21	1.63	6.5	251	34	69	4.64	6.2	10.4	1.7	0.9	39

Tall, strong reliever signed out of the D.R. started well in the MWL, but faltered when moved up to High-A. Inconsistent mechanics and release point have resulted in below-average control, but also has a good 90-94 mph FB that gets on hitters quickly. Has been slow to develop, but has the power arm needed to make an impact.

Armenteros,Rogelio
SP | **Houston** | EXP MLB DEBUT: 2018 | H/W: 6-1 215 | FUT: #4 starter | **7D**

Thrws R Age 22
2014 FA (CU)

Velo	Pitch	Grade
88-94	FB	+++
73-77	CB	+++
80-83	CU	+++

Year	Lev	Team	W	L	Sv	IP	K	ERA	WHIP	BF/G	OBA	H%	S%	xERA	Ctl	Dom	Cmd	hr/9	BPV
2016	A	Quad Cities	0	2	0	18	20	1.98	0.82	16.6	190	28	73	0.96	1.5	9.9	6.7	0.0	156
2016	A+	Lancaster	6	4	1	90	107	4.20	1.38	19.9	255	33	74	4.38	3.7	10.7	2.9	1.3	111
2016	AA	Corpus Christi	2	0	0	18	13	1.99	1.16	24.0	250	30	85	3.05	2.0	6.5	3.3	0.5	81

Big-framed SP who showcased value in first full season. Repeats delivery well despite size and effort. FB tends to flatten, but has solid pitch mix. Keeps ball low in zone and hitters bury into ground. Has ability to retire hitters with all pitches and can use any in any count. Could make for ideal setup guy.

Armstrong,Shawn
RP | **Cleveland** | EXP MLB DEBUT: 2015 | H/W: 6-2 225 | FUT: Setup reliever | **7B**

Thrws R Age 26
2011 (18) East Carolina

Velo	Pitch	Grade
92-95	FB	++++
88-91	CT	+++
82-85	SL	++

Year	Lev	Team	W	L	Sv	IP	K	ERA	WHIP	BF/G	OBA	H%	S%	xERA	Ctl	Dom	Cmd	hr/9	BPV
2014	AAA	Columbus	0	0	0	5	4	5.40	1.40	4.2	221	23	67	4.50	5.4	7.2	1.3	1.8	2
2015	AAA	Columbus	1	2	16	49	80	2.38	1.28	4.4	211	39	79	2.31	4.8	14.6	3.1	0.0	153
2015	MLB	Cleveland	0	0	0	8	11	2.25	0.88	3.7	181	26	83	2.03	2.3	12.4	5.5	1.1	180
2016	AAA	Columbus	3	1	9	49	72	1.84	1.14	4.1	163	29	82	1.44	5.3	13.2	2.5	0.0	112
2016	MLB	Cleveland	0	0	0	10	7	2.65	1.37	4.3	238	27	85	3.80	4.4	6.2	1.4	0.9	10

Strong, matured RP led IL in Dom/OBA (min. 40 IP) and didn't allow a HR as closer. High SwK floor via plus, sinking FB and tight CT combination. Will need to work ahead in the count and throw more strikes to be trusted in high-leverage situations. If that happens, a late-inning arm with Dom upside worth keeping an eye on.

Aro,Jonathan
RP | **Seattle** | EXP MLB DEBUT: 2015 | H/W: 6-0 235 | FUT: Middle reliever | **6B**

Thrws R Age 26
2011 FA (DR)

Velo	Pitch	Grade
90-94	FB	+++
81-84	SL	+++
81-83	CU	+

Year	Lev	Team	W	L	Sv	IP	K	ERA	WHIP	BF/G	OBA	H%	S%	xERA	Ctl	Dom	Cmd	hr/9	BPV
2015	AA	Portland	3	2	0	22	19	2.85	1.04	10.7	194	26	70	1.58	3.3	7.7	2.4	0.0	69
2015	AAA	Pawtucket	0	1	2	51	53	3.16	1.04	7.6	229	31	69	2.31	1.8	9.3	5.3	0.4	138
2015	MLB	Boston	0	1	0	10	8	7.13	1.88	7.9	345	39	65	7.52	3.6	7.1	2.0	1.8	50
2016	AAA	Tacoma	3	2	1	36	25	2.49	1.08	5.9	222	26	78	2.49	2.5	6.2	2.5	0.5	63
2016	MLB	Seattle	0	0	0	0	0	0.00	10.00	2.6	639	64	100	35.71	45.0	0.0	0.0	0.0	

Sturdy-framed RP who ended season in June due to injury. Uses three pitches, though none grade as plus. Finds success with deception in arm speed and slot. Can be flyball pitcher and attributed to height. Can spot FB low in zone, but tends to live up with SL and CU. Strong body allows him to pitch in back-to-back games and for multiple innings.

Avila,Pedro
SP | **San Diego** | EXP MLB DEBUT: 2020 | H/W: 5-11 170 | FUT: #4 starter | **8E**

Thrws R Age 20
2014 FA (VZ)

Velo	Pitch	Grade
91-94	FB	++++
	CB	+++
	CU	++

Year	Lev	Team	W	L	Sv	IP	K	ERA	WHIP	BF/G	OBA	H%	S%	xERA	Ctl	Dom	Cmd	hr/9	BPV
2016	A	Hagerstown	7	7	0	93	92	3.48	1.33	19.3	247	31	77	3.87	3.7	8.9	2.4	1.0	79

Big fastball heads his arsenal, even though it lacks plane coming from his small stature. Strikeouts came easy in first full-season exposure, but there is work to do. CB is a potential second weapon, but overall command has been a sore spot so far. Will also need to improve his CU to stick in the rotation. Still raw.

Baez,Joan
SP | **Washington** | EXP MLB DEBUT: 2020 | H/W: 6-3 190 | FUT: #3 starter | **8D**

Thrws R Age 22
2014 FA (DR)

Velo	Pitch	Grade
92-95	FB	++++
77-79	CB	+++
84-87	CU	++

Year	Lev	Team	W	L	Sv	IP	K	ERA	WHIP	BF/G	OBA	H%	S%	xERA	Ctl	Dom	Cmd	hr/9	BPV
2014	Rk	DSL Nationals	4	1	0	54	49	1.16	0.92	18.4	178	24	88	1.25	2.8	8.1	2.9	0.2	88
2015	Rk	GCL Nationals	1	3	0	42	42	2.14	1.19	18.7	207	29	80	2.09	4.1	9.0	2.2	0.0	70
2015	A-	Auburn	2	2	0	17	17	7.33	2.03	16.7	302	40	60	5.51	7.3	8.9	1.2	0.0	-20
2015	A	Hagerstown	0	1	0	10	6	11.58	1.88	15.8	313	35	33	6.17	5.3	5.3	1.0	0.9	-30
2016	A	Hagerstown	9	7	0	125	119	3.95	1.47	19.9	254	33	72	3.73	4.6	8.6	1.9	0.4	48

Hard thrower who reaches high-90s and registers strikeouts with FB. CB shows some depth and drop with plus potential, though CU lags behind. Overall command profile is below-average due to inconsistent mechanics, which affect release point and efficiency. Stuff is accounted for, but unable to repeat delivery. Young enough to improve.

Baez,Sandy
SP | **Detroit** | EXP MLB DEBUT: 2018 | H/W: 6-2 180 | FUT: #4 starter | **7C**

Thrws R Age 23
2011 FA (DR)

Velo	Pitch	Grade
91-96	FB	++++
79-83	CB	+++
	CU	++

Year	Lev	Team	W	L	Sv	IP	K	ERA	WHIP	BF/G	OBA	H%	S%	xERA	Ctl	Dom	Cmd	hr/9	BPV
2013	Rk	DSL Tigers	8	1	1	61	50	2.06	0.93	16.4	192	25	75	1.29	2.4	7.4	3.1	0.0	87
2014	Rk	GCL Tigers	1	2	0	61	48	3.09	1.27	20.9	264	32	76	3.48	2.4	7.1	3.0	0.4	82
2015	A-	Connecticut	3	4	0	65	52	4.15	1.46	19.9	285	34	71	4.33	3.0	7.2	2.4	0.6	65
2016	A	West Michigan	7	9	0	113	88	3.82	1.35	22.5	282	34	72	4.03	2.2	7.0	3.1	0.6	84

Durable SP who thrived in 1st full season as pro. Added strength to frame and throws pinpoint strikes with impressive arsenal. FB exhibits plus movement and spots in zone despite erratic mechanics. Power CB shows flashes of becoming plus and he has nice arm speed on sub-par CU. Too inconsistent, but has athleticism to get better.

Ball,Trey — SP — Boston

EXP MLB DEBUT: 2018 | H/W: 6-6 185 | FUT: #3 starter | 7C

Thrws L Age 22
2013 (1) HS (IN)

89-94	FB	+++
74-78	CB	++
80-84	SL	++
78-82	CU	+++

Year	Lev	Team	W	L	Sv	IP	K	ERA	WHIP	BF/G	OBA	H%	S%	xERA	Ctl	Dom	Cmd	hr/9	BPV
2013	Rk	GCL Red Sox	0	1	0	7	5	6.43	2.29	7.1	336	38	73	7.93	7.7	6.4	0.8	1.3	-75
2014	A	Greenville	5	10	0	100	68	4.68	1.50	19.6	282	32	70	4.66	3.5	6.1	1.7	0.8	33
2015	A+	Salem	9	13	0	129	77	4.74	1.46	22.1	262	28	70	4.57	4.2	5.4	1.3	1.1	2
2016	A+	Salem	8	6	0	117	86	3.84	1.61	22.6	268	32	77	4.55	5.2	6.6	1.3	0.6	-4

Tall, projectable SP who repeated High-A and showed better results. Still hasn't dominated, though increased his velocity slightly. Keeps ball on ground as he lives in lower half of zone. Uses height and consistent mechanics to provide hint of deception. CU is best pitch, but can't find effective breaking ball. Finished 2nd in CAR in walks.

Banda,Anthony — SP — Arizona

EXP MLB DEBUT: 2017 | H/W: 6-2 190 | FUT: #4 starter | 7A

Thrws L Age 23
2012 (10) San Jacinto JC

90-93	FB	+++
77-80	CB	+++
82-84	CU	++

Year	Lev	Team	W	L	Sv	IP	K	ERA	WHIP	BF/G	OBA	H%	S%	xERA	Ctl	Dom	Cmd	hr/9	BPV
2014	A	South Bend	3	0	0	35	34	1.54	1.11	23.0	245	32	89	2.86	1.8	8.7	4.9	0.5	127
2014	A	Wisconsin	6	6	2	83	83	3.68	1.47	17.8	264	35	75	3.92	4.1	9.0	2.2	0.4	69
2015	A+	Visalia	8	8	0	151	152	3.33	1.25	22.0	260	34	73	3.37	2.3	9.0	3.9	0.5	118
2016	AA	Mobile	6	2	0	76	84	2.13	1.29	24.0	246	34	85	3.26	3.3	9.9	3.0	0.5	107
2016	AAA	Reno	4	4	0	73	68	3.69	1.37	23.6	261	33	74	3.93	3.3	8.4	2.5	0.7	79

Took giant leap forward in '16. Picked up 2 to 3 mph on 2-seam FB without losing arm side fade. Spike CB showing signs of becoming out pitch. CU started showing signs of becoming workable MLB option. Still inconsistent, features solid fade and good speed differential.

Banuelos,Manny — SP — Los Angeles (A)

EXP MLB DEBUT: 2015 | H/W: 5-10 215 | FUT: #4 starter | 7C

Thrws L Age 26
2008 FA (MX)

89-92	FB	+++
87-89	CT	++
75-78	CB	+++
	CU	+++

Year	Lev	Team	W	L	Sv	IP	K	ERA	WHIP	BF/G	OBA	H%	S%	xERA	Ctl	Dom	Cmd	hr/9	BPV
2015	AAA	Gwinnett	6	2	0	84	69	2.24	1.24	21.3	212	27	81	2.49	4.3	7.4	1.7	0.2	35
2015	MLB	Atlanta	1	4	0	26		5.17	1.61	16.5	290	32	71	5.57	4.1	6.6	1.6	1.4	24
2016	A	Rome	0	1	0	2	4	13.50	3.50	12.6	470	75	57	12.51	9.0	18.0	2.0	0.0	99
2016	AA	Mississippi	0	2	0	18	19	5.47	1.71	20.5	311	37	74	6.69	4.0	9.4	2.4	2.0	81
2016	AAA	Gwinnett	0	2	0	30	21	4.78	1.76	15.3	268	31	73	4.90	6.6	6.3	1.0	0.6	-47

Short, savvy SP who started in May due to elbow soreness. Very tough on LHH with solid CB and CU, though velocity hasn't returned after elbow injury in past. Used to hit mid-90s, but sits lower now and needs pinpoint command to succeed. Cuts and sinks FB well and has solid arm speed on CU. Needs control to return to realize potential.

Barlow,Scott — SP — Los Angeles (N)

EXP MLB DEBUT: 2018 | H/W: 6-3 170 | FUT: #5 SP/swingman | 7D

Thrws R Age 24
2011 (6) HS (CA)

89-93	FB	+++
80-83	SL	++
75-78	CB	++
83-85	CU	++

Year	Lev	Team	W	L	Sv	IP	K	ERA	WHIP	BF/G	OBA	H%	S%	xERA	Ctl	Dom	Cmd	hr/9	BPV
2015	Rk	Azl Dodgers	0	1	0	9	11	4.00	1.33	12.5	240	33	73	3.78	4.0	11.0	2.8	1.0	108
2015	A	Great Lakes	0	1	0	4	1	6.43	2.14	20.8	403	36	86	11.69	2.1	2.1	1.0	4.3	-1
2015	A+	Rancho Cuca	8	3	0	71	64	2.53	1.31	21.0	233	29	82	3.20	4.1	8.1	2.0	0.5	54
2015	AAA	Oklahoma City	0	1	0	3	3	16.88	3.13	19.0	437	54	40	10.83	8.4	8.4	1.0	0.0	-58
2016	AA	Tulsa	4	7	0	124	102	3.99	1.43	22.0	263	32	73	4.04	3.8	7.4	2.0	0.7	49

Tall, lanky RHP had his best season as a pro at AA. Comes after hitters from a high 3/4 arm slot and has a decent low-90s FB with some arm-side run. Mixes in a quality SL that is swing-and-miss. CB and CU have chance to play average. Struggles with control continue and now has a career 3.7 Ctl rate. Back-end starter.

Barnes,Danny — RP — Toronto

EXP MLB DEBUT: 2016 | H/W: 6-1 195 | FUT: Setup reliever | 6A

Thrws R Age 27
2010 (35) Princeton

89-94	FB	+++
74-77	CB	+++
82-85	SL	++
	CU	++

Year	Lev	Team	W	L	Sv	IP	K	ERA	WHIP	BF/G	OBA	H%	S%	xERA	Ctl	Dom	Cmd	hr/9	BPV
2014	A+	Dunedin	0	5	7	38	49	4.24	1.26	4.3	250	35	68	3.67	2.8	11.5	4.1	0.9	149
2015	AA	New Hampshire	3	2	4	60	74	2.99	1.38	6.3	274	38	81	4.12	2.8	11.1	3.9	0.7	140
2016	AA	New Hampshire	2	1	1	35	40	1.02	0.60	5.0	146	19	94	0.63	1.0	10.2	10.0	0.8	174
2016	AAA	Buffalo	1	0	5	25	37	0.36	0.32	4.7	78	15	88		0.7	13.2	18.5	0.0	237
2016	MLB	Toronto	0	0	0	13	14	4.09	1.44	4.7	273	38	68	3.58	3.4	9.5	2.8	0.0	98

Breakout RP prospect who reached TOR after stellar campaign. Posts high K rate thanks to sneaky, lively FB action. Uses simple, clean delivery to generate arm speed and pitch movement. Very tough to hit with low oppBA. Has some deception, though tends to be flyball pitcher. Lacks consistency in secondary offerings, though slow CB shows flashes.

Barria,Jaime — SP — Los Angeles (A)

EXP MLB DEBUT: 2019 | H/W: 6-1 210 | FUT: #4 starter | 7C

Thrws R Age 20
2013 FA (PN)

88-93	FB	+++
79-82	CB	+++
	CU	++

Year	Lev	Team	W	L	Sv	IP	K	ERA	WHIP	BF/G	OBA	H%	S%	xERA	Ctl	Dom	Cmd	hr/9	BPV
2015	Rk	Orem	2	4	0	33	30	6.25	1.57	18.2	325	39	60	5.74	1.9	8.2	4.3	1.1	113
2015	Rk	Azl Angels	3	0	0	36	31	2.00	1.19	20.6	283	36	81	3.11	0.8	7.8	10.3	0.0	137
2016	A	Burlington	8	6	0	117	78	3.85	1.32	19.4	287	34	70	3.94	1.6	6.0	3.7	0.5	82

Strong, durable SP with clean arm action and pinpoint control. Can be hittable as he pitches to contact, but keeps live and heavy FB ball low in zone. Has fast arm on all offerings and can miss some bats with hard CB. CU has glimpses of excellence, but ability to hit spots is best present attribute. Would be standout if he threw harder.

Beck,Chris — RP — Chicago (A)

EXP MLB DEBUT: 2015 | H/W: 6-3 225 | FUT: #4 starter | 7D

Thrws R Age 26
2012 (2) Georgia Southern

90-94	FB	+++
84-87	SL	+++
81-85	CU	+++

Year	Lev	Team	W	L	Sv	IP	K	ERA	WHIP	BF/G	OBA	H%	S%	xERA	Ctl	Dom	Cmd	hr/9	BPV
2014	AAA	Charlotte	1	3	0	33	28	4.08	1.48	20.3	278	35	71	4.03	3.5	7.6	2.2	0.3	60
2015	AAA	Charlotte	3	2	0	54	40	3.16	1.18	21.7	247	29	74	3.07	2.3	6.7	2.9	0.5	75
2015	MLB	Chi White Sox	0	1	0	6	3	6.00	2.33	30.9	371	42	71	7.49	6.0	4.5	0.8	0.0	-63
2016	AAA	Charlotte	5	4	0	66	50	4.22	1.54	13.1	292	35	73	4.78	3.4	6.8	2.0	0.7	49
2016	MLB	Chi White Sox	2	2	0	25	20	6.45	1.91	4.8	305	36	67	6.27	6.1	7.2	1.2	1.1	-17

Durable arm who was moved to pen and struggled with pitch-to-contact ways. All pitches are at least average and poor K rate is rather surprising. Throws with plus arm speed and sinker very tough to elevate. Hard SL returning to above average status, though CU can be too firm. Missed more bats in pen, but still not good enough given natural stuff.

Beede,Tyler — SP — San Francisco

EXP MLB DEBUT: 2017 | H/W: 6-3 210 | FUT: #3 starter | 8B

Thrws R Age 23
2014 (1) Vanderbilt

92-97	FB	++++
77-78	CB	+++
83-86	CU	+++

Year	Lev	Team	W	L	Sv	IP	K	ERA	WHIP	BF/G	OBA	H%	S%	xERA	Ctl	Dom	Cmd	hr/9	BPV
2014	Rk	Azl Giants	0	1	0	8	11	3.29	1.46	8.8	257	40	75	3.39	4.4	12.1	2.8	0.0	117
2014	A-	Salem-Kaizer	0	0	0	6	7	2.90	1.77	14.2	314	43	82	5.03	4.4	10.2	2.3	0.0	83
2015	A+	San Jose	2	2	0	52	37	2.25	1.15	23.0	258	31	81	2.99	1.6	6.4	4.1	0.3	91
2015	AA	Richmond	3	8	0	72	49	5.24	1.35	23.1	234	27	59	3.31	4.4	6.1	1.4	0.5	10
2016	AA	Richmond	8	7	0	147	135	2.81	1.28	25.2	247	31	79	3.36	3.2	8.3	2.5	0.6	79

Athletic, tall SP who led EL in ERA and 2nd in K. Attacks hitters with splendid trio of pitches. Cuts and sinks FB and can rear back and fire by hitters up in zone. K rate has increased while he's learned to mix, though could improve control. CU can be plus at times with heavy life and CB is becoming top offering. Was outstanding late in season.

Bickford,Phil — SP — Milwaukee

EXP MLB DEBUT: 2018 | H/W: 6-4 200 | FUT: #3 starter | 8C

Thrws R Age 21
2015 (1) JC of So Nevada

90-93	FB	+++
80-83	SL	+++
82-83	CU	++

Year	Lev	Team	W	L	Sv	IP	K	ERA	WHIP	BF/G	OBA	H%	S%	xERA	Ctl	Dom	Cmd	hr/9	BPV
2015	Rk	Azl Giants	0	1	0	22	32	2.04	0.86	8.1	173	30	74	0.83	2.4	13.0	5.3	0.0	187
2016	A	Augusta	3	4	0	60	69	2.70	1.07	21.2	225	32	74	2.26	2.3	10.4	4.6	0.3	144
2016	A+	Brevard County	2	1	0	27	30	3.67	1.52	19.5	255	35	75	3.83	5.0	10.0	2.0	0.3	63
2016	A+	San Jose	2	2	0	33	36	2.73	1.00	21.0	184	24	77	2.11	3.3	9.8	3.0	0.8	106

Athletic, wiry RH with explosive arm speed and Dom history. Touched 98 mph as a prep but now sits 90-93 with lively FB; chance to regain a tick with added mass. Tight SL flashes plus and will blend in CU as fringe third pitch. Effortful delivery that often finishes offline; command still a ways off. Closer profile if rotation project fizzles out.

Bieber,Shane — SP — Cleveland

EXP MLB DEBUT: 2019 | H/W: 6-3 195 | FUT: #5 SP/swingman | 7C

Thrws R Age 21
2016 (4) UC-Santa Barbara

90-92	FB	+++
	SL	+++
	CU	+++

Year	Lev	Team	W	L	Sv	IP	K	ERA	WHIP	BF/G	OBA	H%	S%	xERA	Ctl	Dom	Cmd	hr/9	BPV
2016	NCAA	UC SantaBarbara	12	4	0	134	109	2.75	1.06	28.9	250	31	74	2.63	1.1	7.3	6.8	0.3	121
2016	A-	Mahoning Vall	0	0	0	24	21	0.38	0.50	8.9	129	18	92		0.8	7.9	10.5	0.0	140

Tall, athletic, strike-throwing RH who displays feel for and advanced command of three solid-average offerings. Works ahead with low-90s FB and will throw average SL/CU to both RH and LH. Smooth, online, repeatable delivery and arm action. Creates good extension off rubber and keeps ball down in zone for lots of ground balls. Limited Dom ceiling.

Bird,Zachary — RP — Texas

EXP MLB DEBUT: 2018 | H/W: 6-4 205 | FUT: Setup reliever | 7E

Thrws R Age 22
2012 (9) HS (MS)

93-95	FB	++++
85-87	SL	+++
83-84	CU	+

Year	Lev	Team	W	L	Sv	IP	K	ERA	WHIP	BF/G	OBA	H%	S%	xERA	Ctl	Dom	Cmd	hr/9	BPV
2013	A	Great Lakes	2	5	0	60	50	5.10	1.68	14.2	249	30	70	4.58	6.8	7.5	1.1	0.8	-29
2014	A	Great Lakes	6	17	0	118	110	4.26	1.46	19.5	261	33	71	4.13	4.2	8.4	2.0	0.7	56
2015	A+	Rancho Cuca	5	7	0	89	95	4.75	1.37	19.6	228	30	65	3.37	4.9	9.6	2.0	0.6	60
2015	AA	Mississippi	1	1	0	12	8	4.43	1.64	18.1	189	23	70	3.04	8.9	5.9	0.7	0.0	-115
2016	A+	Carolina	3	3	0	47	34	8.96	2.14	8.4	318	37	56	6.76	7.4	6.5	0.9	0.8	-66

Inconsistently wild, hard-throwing RHP had dreadful '16 season in pen. Struggled mightily with control and FB command. FB 93-95 with late arm-side movement. Depth of SL disappeared. CU is not a factor. Did not appear in any games after August 9 for undisclosed reasons.

Blach,Ty — SP — San Francisco

EXP MLB DEBUT: 2016 | H/W: 6-2 200 | FUT: #4 starter | 7B

Thrws L Age 26
2012 (5) Creighton

Pitches	Year	Lev	Team	W	L	Sv	IP	K	ERA	WHIP	BF/G	OBA	H%	S%	xERA	Ctl	Dom	Cmd	hr/9	BPV
88-92 FB +++	2013	A+	San Jose	12	4	0	130	117	2.91	1.09	23.1	253	32	75	2.95	1.2	8.1	6.5	0.6	130
81-83 SL ++	2014	AA	Richmond	8	8	0	141	91	3.13	1.28	23.1	263	30	76	3.56	2.5	5.8	2.3	0.5	55
75-78 CB ++	2015	AAA	Sacramento	11	12	0	165	93	4.47	1.33	25.4	289	32	68	4.40	1.7	5.1	3.0	0.9	64
80-82 CU +++	2016	AAA	Sacramento	14	7	0	162	113	3.44	1.14	24.7	243	29	70	2.92	2.1	6.3	3.0	0.5	74
	2016	MLB	SF Giants	1	0	0	17	10	1.06	0.76	15.2	143	16	92	0.85	2.6	5.3	2.0	0.5	42

Durable SP with back-end profile, but saw K rate increase in repeat year in AAA. Has pitched at least 130 IP in each season as pro and limits LHH with variety of offerings. Keeps ball down in zone and throws any pitch in any count. Mostly fringy stuff and can be guilty of too many strikes. CU is best pitch with nice arm action.

Black,Corey — RP — Chicago (N)

EXP MLB DEBUT: 2017 | H/W: 5-11 175 | FUT: Setup reliever | 7C

Thrws R Age 25
2012 (4) Faulkner

Pitches	Year	Lev	Team	W	L	Sv	IP	K	ERA	WHIP	BF/G	OBA	H%	S%	xERA	Ctl	Dom	Cmd	hr/9	BPV
94-96 FB ++++	2013	A+	Daytona	4	0	0	25	28	2.88	1.28	20.5	238	31	83	3.71	3.6	10.1	2.8	1.1	102
85-88 SL +++	2014	AA	Tennessee	6	7	0	124	119	3.48	1.38	20.0	222	27	78	3.64	5.1	8.6	1.7	0.9	34
76-78 CB ++	2015	AA	Tennessee	3	5	0	86	101	4.92	1.41	9.8	234	32	65	3.64	4.9	10.6	2.1	0.7	75
80-83 CU ++	2016	AA	Tennessee	0	3	8	22	25	3.24	1.49	4.8	223	32	76	3.03	6.1	10.1	1.7	0.0	36
	2016	AAA	Iowa	0	3	6	30	37	5.08	1.69	4.9	261	38	68	4.32	6.3	11.1	1.8	0.3	48

Short, hard-throwing righty continues to blow hitters away with a high-octane FB. Heater sits at 94-96, topping out at 100 mph and is backed up by a quality SL. As a starter also had an average CB and CU. Command and control continue to be an issue and he walked 36 in 53 innings of work. Has the velocity and breaking ball to be an impact reliever.

Black,Ray — RP — San Francisco

EXP MLB DEBUT: 2017 | H/W: 6-5 225 | FUT: Closer | 8E

Thrws R Age 26
2011 (7) Pittsburgh

Pitches	Year	Lev	Team	W	L	Sv	IP	K	ERA	WHIP	BF/G	OBA	H%	S%	xERA	Ctl	Dom	Cmd	hr/9	BPV
94-99 FB ++++	2014	A	Augusta	1	3	1	31		3.76	0.96	3.6	154	39	59	1.11	4.1	18.5	4.6	0.3	242
85-88 SL ++++	2014	A+	San Jose	1	0	0	4	7	2.25	0.75	3.6	81	19	67		4.5	15.8	3.5	0.0	180
CU ++	2015	A+	San Jose	2	1	0	25	51	2.88	1.52	5.4	156	36	83	2.93	9.0	18.4	2.0	0.7	105
	2016	AA	Richmond	1	4	6	31	53	4.92	1.58	3.9	162	32	67	2.77	9.3	15.3	1.7	0.3	44

Strong-armed RP who can't stay on mound. Limited after June due to undisclosed injury and has been beset by number of ailments in past, including TJS. When healthy, can dominate hitters from both sides. Posts low oppBA and incredibly high K rate due to plus FB and plus hard SL. Everything comes out of hand hard, though struggles to throw strikes.

Blackburn,Clayton — SP — San Francisco

EXP MLB DEBUT: 2017 | H/W: 6-3 230 | FUT: #5 SP/swingman | 6B

Thrws R Age 24
2011 (16) HS (OK)

Pitches	Year	Lev	Team	W	L	Sv	IP	K	ERA	WHIP	BF/G	OBA	H%	S%	xERA	Ctl	Dom	Cmd	hr/9	BPV
	2013	A+	San Jose	7	5	0	133	138	3.65	1.10	22.7	228	29	69	2.88	2.4	9.3	3.9	0.8	122
89-93 FB +++	2014	Rk	Azl Giants	0	1	0	5	9	3.60	0.80	9.1	221	44	50	1.21	0.0	16.2		0.0	310
82-84 SL +++	2014	AA	Richmond	5	6	0	93	85	3.29	1.23	20.9	264	34	71	3.01	1.9	8.2	4.3	0.1	114
77-78 CB ++	2015	AAA	Sacramento	10	4	0	123	99	2.85	1.29	22.0	268	33	78	3.57	2.3	7.2	3.1	0.4	85
CU +++	2016	AAA	Sacramento	7	10	0	136	101	4.36	1.30	22.4	270	30	70	4.33	2.3	6.7	2.9	1.2	76

Durable SP who repeated AAA and continued to exhibit plus control. Keeps ball down in zone with sinker and induces high amount of groundballs. Repeats simple delivery and works efficiently. Can be hittable with pitch to contact ways and lacks frontline pitch. Mixes four pitches well with tight SL being best offering.

Blackburn,Paul — SP — Oakland

EXP MLB DEBUT: 2017 | H/W: 6-1 195 | FUT: #4 starter | 7C

Thrws R Age 23
2012 (S-1) HS (CA)

Pitches	Year	Lev	Team	W	L	Sv	IP	K	ERA	WHIP	BF/G	OBA	H%	S%	xERA	Ctl	Dom	Cmd	hr/9	BPV
	2013	A-	Boise	2	3	0	46	38	3.33	1.52	15.4	240	29	79	3.91	5.7	7.4	1.3	0.6	-1
91-94 FB +++	2014	A	Kane County	9	4	0	117	75	3.23	1.19	19.5	247	29	73	3.05	2.4	5.8	2.4	0.5	57
75-79 CB +++	2015	A+	Myrtle Beach	7	5	0	89	63	3.13	1.24	20.1	261	31	74	3.24	2.2	6.4	2.9	0.3	72
CU +++	2016	AA	Jackson	3	1	0	40	27	3.58	1.27	20.5	270	32	71	3.56	2.0	6.0	3.0	0.4	72
	2016	AA	Tennessee	6	4	0	102	72	3.17	1.19	22.8	250	29	74	3.17	2.3	6.3	2.8	0.5	70

Command/control SP who is now in third org upon trade from SEA. Works down in zone with three average offerings. Has limited durability, but can be effective early in game. Works off quality FB while above average CB can get Ks. Shows feel for CU and has been OK against LHH.

Blewett,Scott — SP — Kansas City

EXP MLB DEBUT: 2018 | H/W: 6-6 210 | FUT: #3 starter | 8D

Thrws R Age 20
2014 (2) HS (NY)

Pitches	Year	Lev	Team	W	L	Sv	IP	K	ERA	WHIP	BF/G	OBA	H%	S%	xERA	Ctl	Dom	Cmd	hr/9	BPV
90-94 FB +++																				
77-80 CB +++	2014	Rk	Burlington	1	2	0	28	29	4.82	1.50	15.1	255	32	69	4.38	4.8	9.3	1.9	1.0	56
83-85 CU ++	2015	A	Lexington	3	5	0	81	60	5.22	1.38	18.9	278	33	61	4.15	2.7	6.7	2.5	0.7	66
	2016	A	Lexington	8	11	0	129	121	4.32	1.46	22.1	275	34	71	4.33	3.6	8.4	2.4	0.7	74

Tall, promising SP who repeated Low-A and was solid late in year. Posted higher K rate and showed more consistency in downhill delivery. Still offers projection and could throw harder as he grows into frame. FB exhibits sink, though has been hit hard by LHH. Needs to upgrade fringy CU and has athleticism to repeat slot and arm speed.

Borucki,Ryan — SP — Toronto

EXP MLB DEBUT: 2018 | H/W: 6-4 175 | FUT: #3 starter | 8E

Thrws L Age 23
2012 (15) HS (IL)

Pitches	Year	Lev	Team	W	L	Sv	IP	K	ERA	WHIP	BF/G	OBA	H%	S%	xERA	Ctl	Dom	Cmd	hr/9	BPV
	2014	A-	Vancouver	1	1	1	23	22	1.94	0.69	16.3	166	22	73	0.73	1.2	8.5	7.3	0.4	140
88-94 FB +++	2015	Rk	GCL Blue Jays	0	0	0	1	1	0.00	1.00	3.8	262	35	100	2.32	0.0	9.0		0.0	180
79-82 SL ++	2015	A-	Vancouver	0	1	0	4	6	4.29	2.14	10.4	336	51	78	6.29	6.4	12.9	2.0	0.0	76
80-83 CU ++++	2016	A	Lansing	10	4	0	115	107	2.42	1.14	22.8	244	32	77	2.51	2.0	8.4	4.1	0.1	114
	2016	A+	Dunedin	1	4	0	20	10	14.40	2.60	18.1	415	39	48	13.28	5.4	4.5	0.8	4.5	-47

Tall SP who finished 2nd in MWL in ERA. Blew up in A+, but has average pitch mix that could get better. Throws strikes with deceptive FB and has plus CU in arsenal. Uses excellent arm speed on CU that features late, tumbling action. Has injury history, though was healthy all year. Needs to upgrade SL to give him true swing-and-miss offering.

Bowden,Ben — RP — Colorado

EXP MLB DEBUT: 2018 | H/W: 6-4 235 | FUT: Setup reliever | 7C

Thrws L Age 22
2016 (2) Vanderbilt

Pitches	Year	Lev	Team	W	L	Sv	IP	K	ERA	WHIP	BF/G	OBA	H%	S%	xERA	Ctl	Dom	Cmd	hr/9	BPV
90-95 FB +++																				
83-85 SL ++																				
CU ++	2016	NCAA	Vanderbilt	2	1	10	48	65	3.55	1.29	8.2	261	39	73	3.52	2.6	12.1	4.6	0.6	166
	2016	A	Asheville	0	1	0	23	29	3.10	1.64	4.0	260	38	81	4.24	5.8	11.3	1.9	0.4	63

Lefty reliever from Vanderbilt was Rockies 2nd round pick in 2016. Comes after hitters with a 90-95 mph heater, CU, and SL—all of which could become above-average. Strong frame and collegiate experience should allow him to move up quickly.

Brakeman,Marc — RP — Boston

EXP MLB DEBUT: 2018 | H/W: 6-2 185 | FUT: Setup reliever | 7C

Thrws R Age 22
2015 (16) Stanford

Pitches	Year	Lev	Team	W	L	Sv	IP	K	ERA	WHIP	BF/G	OBA	H%	S%	xERA	Ctl	Dom	Cmd	hr/9	BPV
90-94 FB +++																				
83-85 SL ++	2015	NCAA	Stanford	2	4	0	52	35	2.93	1.19	23.2	257	30	75	3.08	1.9	6.0	3.2	0.3	75
CU +++	2015	Rk	GCL Red Sox	0	0	0	1	0	0.00	2.00	4.8	415	41	100	7.58	0.0	0.0		0.0	18
	2016	A	Greenville	5	5	1	72	76	4.36	1.29	12.4	267	35	67	3.81	2.4	9.5	4.0	0.7	125

Quick-armed RP who was moved to pen in June and will likely stay there. Lacks strength and durability to maintain velocity. Arm action produces movement to FB that was quicker in short stints. Best pitch is sinking CU that hitters rarely square up. Not much break in middling SL. Performed poorly against LHH (.330 BA).

Brault,Steven — SP — Pittsburgh

EXP MLB DEBUT: 2016 | H/W: 6-0 200 | FUT: #4 starter | 7C

Thrws L Age 24
2013 (11) Regis

Pitches	Year	Lev	Team	W	L	Sv	IP	K	ERA	WHIP	BF/G	OBA	H%	S%	xERA	Ctl	Dom	Cmd	hr/9	BPV
	2015	A+	Bradenton	4	1	0	65	45	3.04	1.27	20.5	252	30	76	3.29	2.9	6.2	2.1	0.4	52
89-93 FB +++	2015	AA	Altoona	9	3	0	90	80	2.00	1.01	23.0	221	29	79	1.92	1.9	8.0	4.2	0.1	111
80-83 SL ++	2016	A-	West Virginia	0	0	0	4	5	0.00	0.25	12.3	81	14	100		0.0	11.3		0.0	221
84-87 CU ++	2016	AAA	Indianapolis	2	7	0	71	81	3.92	1.42	18.8	248	33	74	3.89	4.4	10.3	2.3	0.8	83
	2016	MLB	Pittsburgh	0	3	0	33	29	4.89	1.87	19.4	325	38	77	6.76	4.6	7.9	1.7	1.4	35

Short strike-throwing lefty held his own in 7 big league starts. Comes after hitters from a low 3/4 slot with a low-90 FB that has good late sink. Mixes in an improved SL and a decent CU. Succeeds by keeping hitters off balance and when able to work the edges with above-average control. Simple, repeatable mechanics could allow him to thrive.

Brice,Austin — RP — Miami

EXP MLB DEBUT: 2016 | H/W: 6-4 235 | FUT: #5 SP/swingman | 7C

Thrws R Age 24
2010 (9) HS (NC)

Pitches	Year	Lev	Team	W	L	Sv	IP	K	ERA	WHIP	BF/G	OBA	H%	S%	xERA	Ctl	Dom	Cmd	hr/9	BPV
	2014	A+	Jupiter	8	9	0	127	109	3.61	1.33	21.1	241	30	72	3.22	3.9	7.7	2.0	0.4	52
90-94 FB +++	2015	AA	Jacksonville	6	9	0	125	127	4.68	1.46	21.4	244	31	69	3.99	5.0	9.1	1.8	0.8	48
83-85 SL ++	2016	AA	Jacksonville	4	7	2	93	79	2.90	1.16	13.7	231	29	76	2.78	2.8	7.6	2.7	0.5	80
80-82 CB +++	2016	AAA	New Orleans	0	0	2	8	10	1.10	0.49	5.4	115	13	100	0.35	1.1	11.0	10.0	1.1	186
80-83 CU ++	2016	MLB	Miami	0	1	0	14	14	7.07	1.00	3.6	186	22	25	2.58	3.2	9.0	2.8	1.3	93

Strong-bodied hurler had a breakout season. Works off a low-90s FB that tops out at 94 mph. Throws both a CB and a SL and a mixes in a show-me CU that projects as average. Raw stuff is good and mechanics were more consistent in '16 leading to improved FB command. Worked in relief once he reached the majors.

Bridwell,Parker

RP | Baltimore | EXP MLB DEBUT: 2016 | H/W: 6-4 185 | FUT: #5 SP/swingman | 7D

Thrws R Age 25
2010 (9) HS (TX)

Velo	Pitch	Grade
90-95	FB	+++
80-83	SL	++
81-84	CU	+++

Year	Lev	Team	W	L	Sv	IP	K	ERA	WHIP	BF/G	OBA	H%	S%	xERA	Ctl	Dom	Cmd	hr/9	BPV
2016	Rk	GCL Orioles	2	0	0	6	7	0.00	1.00	7.6	151	23	100	0.97	4.5	10.5	2.3	0.0	86
2016	A-	Aberdeen	1	1	0	5	4	5.40	0.40	8.1	124	9		0.92	0.0	7.2		1.8	148
2016	AA	Bowie	1	1	1	55	38	4.57	1.52	13.3	265	29	73	4.77	4.6	6.2	1.4	1.1	6
2016	AAA	Norfolk	1	0	0	10	14	1.80	0.50	8.3	124	17	75	0.27	0.9	12.6	14.0	0.9	221
2016	MLB	Baltimore	0	0	0	3	3	14.52	1.94	7.4	364	34	25	11.76	2.9	8.7	3.0	5.8	96

Tall, athletic pitcher who moved to pen at midseason and reached majors. Has always shown positive pitch mix, but failed to find consistency with command or control. Has improved ability to hit spots and CU remains top offering. Uses height to throw downhill and may stay in bullpen due to effort in delivery and uptick in velocity.

Brigham,Jeff

SP | Miami | EXP MLB DEBUT: 2018 | H/W: 6-0 200 | FUT: #5 SP/swingman | 7C

Thrws R Age 25
2014 (4) Washington

Velo	Pitch	Grade
93-96	FB	++++
80-83	SL	++
	CU	+

Year	Lev	Team	W	L	Sv	IP	K	ERA	WHIP	BF/G	OBA	H%	S%	xERA	Ctl	Dom	Cmd	hr/9	BPV
2014	Rk	Ogden	0	3	0	32	33	3.63	1.49	12.6	261	34	76	4.06	4.5	9.2	2.1	0.6	63
2015	A	Great Lakes	2	0	0	7	11	1.29	0.71	12.4	132	26	80	0.03	2.6	14.1	5.5	0.0	203
2015	A+	Jupiter	2	2	0	33	22	1.90	1.30	22.8	266	32	84	3.15	2.4	6.0	2.4	0.0	59
2015	A+	Rancho Cuca	4	5	0	68	64	5.96	1.68	18.0	289	35	65	5.41	4.8	8.5	1.8	1.1	42
2016	A+	Jupiter	7	8	1	122	112	4.05	1.33	18.8	250	32	69	3.40	3.5	8.2	2.4	0.4	73

Stocky, strong-bodied righty has a good 93-96 mph FB that tops out at 98 mph. Throws with effort and can rush his delivery, resulting in below-average control, though he showed some improvement in 2016. Flashes a decent SL with good late break and a below-average CU. Profiles as a back-end guy or a middle reliever. At 24, he was old for High-A in 2016.

Buehler,Walker

SP | Los Angeles (N) | EXP MLB DEBUT: 2019 | H/W: 6-2 175 | FUT: #2 starter | 9D

Thrws R Age 22
2015 (1) Vanderbilt

Velo	Pitch	Grade
93-96	FB	++++
80-85	SL	+++
76-80	CB	+++
	CU	++

Year	Lev	Team	W	L	Sv	IP	K	ERA	WHIP	BF/G	OBA	H%	S%	xERA	Ctl	Dom	Cmd	hr/9	BPV
2015	NCAA	Vanderbilt	5	2	0	88	92	2.96	1.31	22.7	255	34	79	3.56	3.1	9.4	3.1	0.6	104
2016	Rk	Azl Dodgers	1	0	0	2	3	0.00	0.00	5.6	0	0			0.0	13.5		0.0	261
2016	A	Great Lakes	0	0	0	3	3	0.00	1.00	5.7	0	0	100		9.0	9.0	1.0	0.0	-63

Athletic RHP was 24th overall pick in '15. Had Tommy John surgery and was limited to just 5 IP. FB velocity was in mid-to-upper 90s when he returned and he was in better shape. Has a four-pitch mix that includes a plus 93-96 mph FB. CB and SL can be good and he shows an ability to spin the ball. Max effort delivery remains a red-flag going forward.

Burdi,Nick

RP | Minnesota | EXP MLB DEBUT: 2017 | H/W: 6-5 220 | FUT: Closer | 8D

Thrws R Age 24
2014 (2) Louisville

Velo	Pitch	Grade
93-98	FB	++++
85-88	SL	+++
84-87	CU	+

Year	Lev	Team	W	L	Sv	IP	K	ERA	WHIP	BF/G	OBA	H%	S%	xERA	Ctl	Dom	Cmd	hr/9	BPV
2014	A	Cedar Rapids	0	0	4	13	26	4.15	1.23	4.1	179	43	63	1.79	5.5	18.0	3.3	0.0	192
2014	A+	Fort Myers	2	0	1	7	12	0.00	0.99	3.9	200	38	100	1.43	2.5	15.2	6.0	0.0	223
2015	A+	Fort Myers	2	2	2	20	29	2.25	0.75	5.5	175	29	71	1.01	1.4	13.1	9.7	0.5	216
2015	AA	Chattanooga	3	4	2	43	54	4.58	1.67	6.5	247	35	72	4.36	6.7	11.3	1.7	0.6	41
2016	AA	Chattanooga	1	0	0	3	1	9.00	1.67	4.5	321	35	40	4.94	3.0	3.0	1.0	0.0	-9

Hard-throwing RP who ended season in April due to bruised elbow. Has prized arm and potential to serve as closer. Spent entire career in pen and has power arsenal; likes to challenge hitters. Uses max effort delivery, but gives him sneaky stuff. Plus FB sets up effective SL and either registers Ks or gets groundballs. Should be healthy for 2017.

Burdi,Zack

RP | Chicago (A) | EXP MLB DEBUT: 2017 | H/W: 6-3 205 | FUT: Closer | 8C

Thrws R Age 22
2016 (1) Louisville

Velo	Pitch	Grade
93-98	FB	++++
85-88	SL	++++
	CU	+++

Year	Lev	Team	W	L	Sv	IP	K	ERA	WHIP	BF/G	OBA	H%	S%	xERA	Ctl	Dom	Cmd	hr/9	BPV
2016	NCAA	Louisville	1	3	11	30	47	3.30	0.87	4.1	167	27	65	1.62	2.7	14.1	5.2	0.9	199
2016	Rk	Azl White Sox	0	0	0	1	1	0.00	1.00	3.8	262	35	100	2.32	0.0	9.0		0.0	180
2016	A+	Winston-Salem	0	0	0	5	4	5.40	1.20	5.0	299	33	60	5.06	0.0	7.2		1.8	148
2016	AA	Birmingham	0	0	0	16	24	3.94	1.00	5.1	134	19	64	1.83	5.1	13.5	2.7	1.1	124
2016	AAA	Charlotte	1	0	1	16	22	2.25	1.25	7.2	166	28	80	1.75	6.2	12.4	2.0	0.0	74

Hard-throwing RP who could be first player from draft class to reach majors. Hits triple digits with plus FB, and incredible SL shows ideal break. Both pitches miss bats and can even throw occasional CU to keep hitters off balance. Lot of effort in delivery and FB can be flat at times. Control and command need work, but can be effectively wild.

Burnes,Corbin

SP | Milwaukee | EXP MLB DEBUT: 2019 | H/W: 6-2 205 | FUT: #3 starter | 8E

Thrws R Age 22
2016 (4) St. Mary's (CA)

Velo	Pitch	Grade
92-94	FB	++++
80-82	SL	+++
75-77	CB	++
86-87	CU	+++

Year	Lev	Team	W	L	Sv	IP	K	ERA	WHIP	BF/G	OBA	H%	S%	xERA	Ctl	Dom	Cmd	hr/9	BPV
2016	NCAA	St. Mary's (CA)	9	2	0	101	120	2.49	1.08	24.6	210	29	80	2.50	2.9	10.7	3.6	0.7	131
2016	Rk	Azl Brewers	0	0	0	7	10	1.29	0.71	8.2	132	24	80	0.04	2.6	12.9	5.0	0.0	180
2016	A	Wisconsin	3	0	0	28	31	2.23	1.28	12.8	201	28	83	2.53	5.1	9.9	1.9	0.3	58

Quick-armed RH whose Dom ability translated seamlessly to pro ball. Creates sinking action to 92-94 mph FB for tons of ground balls. Mixes SL with late-fading CU for two solid-average potential pitches; uses CB as good pace-changer. Split time as SP/RP in debut; effortful delivery could place him in a late-inning bullpen role long term.

Burrows,Beau

SP | Detroit | EXP MLB DEBUT: 2019 | H/W: 6-2 200 | FUT: #3 starter | 8C

Thrws R Age 20
2015 (1) HS (TX)

Velo	Pitch	Grade
92-96	FB	++++
76-79	CB	++
84-86	CU	++

Year	Lev	Team	W	L	Sv	IP	K	ERA	WHIP	BF/G	OBA	H%	S%	xERA	Ctl	Dom	Cmd	hr/9	BPV
2015	Rk	GCL Tigers	1	0	0	28	33	1.61	1.04	10.8	186	28	83	1.44	3.5	10.6	3.0	0.0	113
2016	A	West Michigan	6	4	0	97	67	3.15	1.21	18.6	241	29	72	2.76	2.8	6.2	2.2	0.2	55

Compact, athletic SP with electric stuff and ability to repeat delivery. Pitch counts were strictly monitored and showed flashes of having three solid offerings. Hits spots with plus FB and power CB could miss more bats in future. Pitches to contact now, though working on consistent release and offspeed stuff. Can leave ball up in zone.

Burrows,Thomas

RP | Seattle | EXP MLB DEBUT: 2018 | H/W: 6-1 205 | FUT: Setup reliever | 6B

Thrws L Age 22
2016 (4) Alabama

Velo	Pitch	Grade
90-95	FB	++++
80-83	SL	+++
	CU	+

Year	Lev	Team	W	L	Sv	IP	K	ERA	WHIP	BF/G	OBA	H%	S%	xERA	Ctl	Dom	Cmd	hr/9	BPV
2016	NCAA	Alabama	2	1	12	28	41	0.96	1.00	5.1	193	32	93	1.71	2.9	13.1	4.6	0.3	177
2016	A-	Everett	0	1	6	24	37	2.60	1.40	5.1	252	41	82	3.51	4.1	13.8	3.4	0.4	155

Physical RP who could advance quickly due to live arm and advanced pitchability. Lacks ideal CU and will stay in pen. College closer who works off plus FB and complements with sharp SL. Very tough on LHH, particularly with low 3/4 slot. FB exhibits great movement, though can be tough to command. Good prospect with high floor.

Campos,Vicente

SP | Los Angeles (A) | EXP MLB DEBUT: 2016 | H/W: 6-3 230 | FUT: #3 starter | 8E

Thrws R Age 24
2009 FA (VZ)

Velo	Pitch	Grade
90-95	FB	++++
79-83	CB	+++
81-85	CU	++

Year	Lev	Team	W	L	Sv	IP	K	ERA	WHIP	BF/G	OBA	H%	S%	xERA	Ctl	Dom	Cmd	hr/9	BPV
2016	AA	Mobile	1	2	0	20	15	3.60	1.35	20.9	281	35	70	3.49	2.3	6.8	3.0	0.0	79
2016	AA	Trenton	5	1	0	56	48	3.04	1.05	24.2	221	28	69	2.08	2.2	7.7	3.4	0.2	96
2016	AAA	Reno	0	0	0	1	0	0.00	0.00	3.4	0	0			0.0	0.0		0.0	18
2016	AAA	Scranton/WB	0	0	0	5	1	1.80	1.80	23.1	362	38	89	6.00	1.8	1.8	1.0	0.0	2
2016	MLB	Arizona	0	0	0	5	4	3.46	1.15	20.7	214	16	100	5.36	3.5	6.9	2.0	3.5	49

Tall, strong SP who was claimed off waivers, but will miss half of '17 after Tommy John surgery. Injury prone throughout career, but has exciting arm and ability to pump electric FB into zone. Owns solid arsenal and improving command. Made MLB debut in '16 and has talent to stick over long term. Hard CB is K pitch while CU has improved.

Casadilla,Franyel

SP | St. Louis | EXP MLB DEBUT: 2021 | H/W: 6-3 175 | FUT: #3 starter | 7D

Thrws R Age 20
2013 FA (VZ)

Velo	Pitch	Grade
90-94	FB	++++
	CB	++
	CU	+

Year	Lev	Team	W	L	Sv	IP	K	ERA	WHIP	BF/G	OBA	H%	S%	xERA	Ctl	Dom	Cmd	hr/9	BPV
2016	Rk	GCL Cardinals	5	2	0	50	35	2.34	1.32	18.8	261	32	82	3.31	2.9	6.3	2.2	0.2	54

Lean, projectable hurler was signed out of Venezuela in '13. FB velocity was up a tick from when signed and now sits at 90-94 mph. Mixes in a CB and CU that show potential, but need refinement. Saw limited action in his U.S. debut; showed good command for a young player. Pounds the strike zone.

Cash,Ralston

RP | Los Angeles (N) | EXP MLB DEBUT: 2017 | H/W: 6-3 215 | FUT: Setup reliever | 7C

Thrws R Age 25
2010 (2) HS (GA)

Velo	Pitch	Grade
92-95	FB	+++
75-77	CB	++
83-85	CU	++

Year	Lev	Team	W	L	Sv	IP	K	ERA	WHIP	BF/G	OBA	H%	S%	xERA	Ctl	Dom	Cmd	hr/9	BPV
2014	AA	Chattanooga	0	0	0	8	10	3.33	1.36	5.6	180	28	73	2.18	6.7	11.1	1.7	0.0	38
2015	AA	Tulsa	2	6	3	57	56	3.47	1.21	4.7	207	25	76	3.19	4.3	8.8	2.1	1.1	62
2015	AAA	Oklahoma City	0	0	0	1	2	0.00	3.00	5.8	415	71	100	9.92	9.0	18.0	2.0	0.0	99
2016	AA	Tulsa	5	3	1	45	56	3.00	1.29	6.4	221	33	75	2.68	4.4	11.2	2.5	0.2	101
2016	AAA	Oklahoma City	4	0	1	24	28	2.63	1.08	5.5	181	26	76	1.87	4.1	10.5	2.5	0.4	96

Reliever had best season yet, going 9-3 with a 2.87 ERA between AA/AAA. FB control remains an issue but is balanced by a high Dom; struck out 84 in 69 IP. Arm action is clean, but needs more consistent mechanics. FB velocity sits in the mid-90s with good sink. 12/6 CB has good depth, but is inconsistent; CU is a usable third pitch.

Castellani,Ryan

SP | Colorado | EXP MLB DEBUT: 2018 | H/W: 6-3 193 | FUT: #2 starter | 8C

Thrws R Age 21 — 2014 (2) HS (AZ)

Velo	Pitch	Grade
91-95	FB	++++
73-75	CB	+++
79-83	CU	++
77-80	SL	++

Year	Lev	Team	W	L	Sv	IP	K	ERA	WHIP	BF/G	OBA	H%	S%	xERA	Ctl	Dom	Cmd	hr/9	BPV
2014	A-	Tri-City	1	2	0	37	25	3.65	1.19	14.8	251	29	69	3.13	2.2	6.1	2.8	0.5	68
2015	A	Asheville	2	7	0	113	94	4.46	1.44	17.8	296	36	68	4.31	2.3	7.5	3.2	0.4	90
2016	A+	Modesto	7	8	0	167	142	3.82	1.23	26.1	249	31	68	3.14	2.7	7.6	2.8	0.4	83

2nd round pick saw his velocity jump from 88-91 to 92-95 mph, topping at 96 with good, late sink. Was the top pitching prospect in the CAL. SL and CU improved as well, as he does a good job of throwing downhill. Pounds the strike zone and now profiles as a possible #2 starter if his CU continues to improve.

Castillo,Diego

RP | Tampa Bay | EXP MLB DEBUT: 2018 | H/W: 6-3 240 | FUT: Setup reliever | 7E

Thrws R Age 23 — 2014 FA (DR)

Velo	Pitch	Grade
93-99	FB	++++
82-84	SL	++

Year	Lev	Team	W	L	Sv	IP	K	ERA	WHIP	BF/G	OBA	H%	S%	xERA	Ctl	Dom	Cmd	hr/9	BPV
2015	A-	Hudson Valley	1	2	4	23	24	2.34	1.13	7.0	226	30	80	2.52	2.7	9.4	3.4	0.4	113
2015	A	Bowling Green	0	0	1	9	4	4.95	1.32	7.5	238	27	58	2.85	4.0	4.0	1.0	0.0	-18
2016	A	Bowling Green	1	3	7	40	50	2.03	1.13	6.6	232	34	82	2.42	2.5	11.3	4.5	0.2	154
2016	A+	Charlotte	2	3	3	20	17	4.93	1.69	6.5	331	39	74	6.38	2.7	7.6	2.8	1.3	82

Big-framed RP who has been unheralded despite ability to dominate. Has exceptional arm speed and velocity. Could solely become FB pitcher, but also has potentially-solid SL in arsenal. Everything comes out of hand quickly and has tenacity. Can pitch multiple innings or on back-to-back games. Rarely changes speeds and needs to polish command.

Castillo,Jesus

SP | Los Angeles (A) | EXP MLB DEBUT: 2019 | H/W: 6-2 165 | FUT: #4 starter | 7D

Thrws R Age 21 — 2011 FA (VZ)

Velo	Pitch	Grade
88-92	FB	+++
75-78	CB	+++
81-82	CU	++

Year	Lev	Team	W	L	Sv	IP	K	ERA	WHIP	BF/G	OBA	H%	S%	xERA	Ctl	Dom	Cmd	hr/9	BPV
2014	Rk	Azl Cubs	1	0	0	30	23	2.69	1.46	11.7	248	31	80	3.31	4.8	6.9	1.4	0.0	13
2015	Rk	Azl Cubs	1	2	0	19	17	4.69	1.82	8.1	324	40	74	5.78	4.2	8.0	1.9	0.5	48
2016	A-	Eugene	2	3	0	33	38	3.27	1.18	18.9	231	31	75	3.13	3.0	10.4	3.5	0.8	124
2016	A	Burlington	3	2	0	29	23	2.47	1.37	20.4	286	35	82	3.90	2.2	7.1	3.3	0.3	87

Long, lean SP who is in third org and it appears LAA will use as starter. Lot of projection in frame and smooth arm action. Lacks plus pitch now, though FB should add velocity and CB could become more consistent with added usage. Telegraphs CU by slowing arm and can be too firm. Struggles with LHH at present. Ability to sequence already apparent.

Castillo,Luis

SP | Miami | EXP MLB DEBUT: 2018 | H/W: 6-2 170 | FUT: #2 SP/closer | 9D

Thrws R Age 24 — 2011 FA (DR)

Velo	Pitch	Grade
96-99	FB	++++
82-84	SL	+++
87-89	CU	++

Year	Lev	Team	W	L	Sv	IP	K	ERA	WHIP	BF/G	OBA	H%	S%	xERA	Ctl	Dom	Cmd	hr/9	BPV
2014	A	Augusta	2	2	10	58	66	3.09	1.39	5.1	254	34	81	4.06	3.9	10.2	2.6	0.9	97
2015	A	Greensboro	4	3	4	63	63	3.00	1.24	10.2	249	34	74	2.87	2.7	9.0	3.3	0.1	107
2015	A+	Jupiter	2	3	0	43	31	3.54	1.34	18.0	265	31	75	3.84	2.9	6.5	2.2	0.6	56
2016	A+	Jupiter	8	4	0	117	91	2.07	0.96	19.3	223	28	77	1.89	1.4	7.0	5.1	0.2	106
2016	AA	Jacksonville	0	2	0	14	12	3.86	1.36	19.5	233	29	72	3.45	4.5	7.7	1.7	0.6	35

Dominican hurler was to be included in the Colin Rea deal, but ended up back with the Marlins. Has a plus FB that sits at 96-99, topping out 101 mph. Mixes in a power SL and an improved CU. The Marlins moved him back into a starting role with good results (8-6 w/ 2.26 ERA in 24 starts), but his future is likely as a power RP or closer.

Cease,Dylan

SP | Chicago (N) | EXP MLB DEBUT: 2019 | H/W: 6-2 190 | FUT: #2 starter | 9D

Thrws R Age 21 — 2014 (6) HS (GA)

Velo	Pitch	Grade
94-96	FB	+++++
80-83	CB	+++
80-83	CU	++

Year	Lev	Team	W	L	Sv	IP	K	ERA	WHIP	BF/G	OBA	H%	S%	xERA	Ctl	Dom	Cmd	hr/9	BPV
2015	Rk	Azl Cubs	1	2	0	24	25	2.63	1.17	8.7	151	22	75	1.40	6.0	9.4	1.6	0.0	25
2016	A-	Eugene	2	0	0	44	66	2.24	1.18	14.7	178	31	80	1.87	5.1	13.4	2.6	0.2	122

Elbow injury that led to Tommy John surgery caused him to drop in '14 draft. Plus FB sits at 94-96, hitting 100 mph with good late life. Power CB gives him a second plus pitch along with an average CU. Blew hitters away in the NWL, but also struggled with control. Leaves pitches up in the zone and control was not all the way back. Upside play.

Chacin,Alejandro

RP | Cincinnati | EXP MLB DEBUT: 2017 | H/W: 6-0 204 | FUT: Middle reliever | 7C

Thrws R Age 23 — 2010 FA (VZ)

Velo	Pitch	Grade
93-96	FB	++++
81-84	SL	++
83-85	CU	+++

Year	Lev	Team	W	L	Sv	IP	K	ERA	WHIP	BF/G	OBA	H%	S%	xERA	Ctl	Dom	Cmd	hr/9	BPV
2013	A	Dayton	4	3	9	65	72	2.91	1.15	5.9	186	25	76	2.27	4.6	10.0	2.2	0.6	74
2014	A	Dayton	4	4	20	65	84	2.35	1.23	5.5	221	33	81	2.59	3.9	11.6	3.0	0.3	123
2015	A	Dayton	1	0	1	14	16	5.70	1.41	6.0	285	40	55	3.67	2.5	10.1	4.0	0.0	132
2015	A+	Daytona	2	0	10	36	56	2.49	0.94	4.7	184	30	77	1.85	2.7	13.9	5.1	0.7	195
2016	AA	Pensacola	5	2	30	60	75	1.79	1.28	4.7	231	34	87	2.87	3.9	11.2	2.9	0.3	115

Small-statured RH with funky side-armed delivery. 2-seam fastball has incredible late sink. Slurvy breaking ball continues to improve. CU is best secondary offering. May be a reverse-split guy in MLB. CIN staff made adjustment in mechanics mid-season to corral command issues.

Chalmers,Dakota

SP | Oakland | EXP MLB DEBUT: 2020 | H/W: 6-3 175 | FUT: #2 starter | 8D

Thrws R Age 20 — 2015 (3) HS (GA)

Velo	Pitch	Grade
91-95	FB	+++
75-78	CB	++
82-86	SL	++
	CU	++

Year	Lev	Team	W	L	Sv	IP	K	ERA	WHIP	BF/G	OBA	H%	S%	xERA	Ctl	Dom	Cmd	hr/9	BPV
2015	Rk	Azl Athletics	0	1	0	20	18	2.69	1.59	8.1	209	28	81	3.14	7.6	8.1	1.1	0.0	-42
2016	A-	Vermont	5	4	0	67	62	4.70	1.37	18.7	225	27	68	3.80	5.0	8.3	1.7	1.1	34

Lean, projectable SP who has yet to play in full season ball, but showed improved FB command and exciting arm speed. Still will take time to develop, but has standout ingredients. Throws hard now and could add more down line. Uses two breaking balls and CU could grow into plus pitch. Needs to learn nuances of pitch mixing.

Chargois,J.T.

RP | Minnesota | EXP MLB DEBUT: 2016 | H/W: 6-3 200 | FUT: Closer | 7B

Thrws R Age 26 — 2012 (2) Rice

Velo	Pitch	Grade
94-99	FB	++++
81-84	SL	+++
84-86	CU	+

Year	Lev	Team	W	L	Sv	IP	K	ERA	WHIP	BF/G	OBA	H%	S%	xERA	Ctl	Dom	Cmd	hr/9	BPV
2015	A+	Fort Myers	1	0	4	15	19	2.40	1.13	3.7	221	34	76	2.10	3.0	11.4	3.8	0.0	142
2015	AA	Chattanooga	1	1	11	33	34	2.73	1.39	4.3	218	30	80	3.00	5.5	9.3	1.7	0.3	38
2016	AA	Chattanooga	0	0	7	11	14	1.61	1.16	4.1	202	28	92	2.69	4.0	11.3	2.8	0.8	112
2016	AAA	Rochester	2	1	9	35	41	1.29	1.00	4.8	215	31	88	1.93	2.1	10.5	5.1	0.3	152
2016	MLB	Minnesota	1	1	0	23	17	4.70	1.61	4.1	278	34	68	4.10	4.7	6.7	1.4	0.0	11

Max-effort RP who showed glimpses of becoming reliable, late-innings arm. Stayed healthy after years of injuries. Short arm action keeps him in pen, but provides deception which allows plus FB to play up. Violent arm speed adds to SL and CU. Generally keeps ball in zone and induces weak contact, especially when FB shows heavy, late sink.

Chavez,Lupe

SP | Houston | EXP MLB DEBUT: 2020 | H/W: 6-2 170 | FUT: #4 starter | 7C

Thrws R Age 19 — 2014 FA (MX)

Velo	Pitch	Grade
88-93	FB	+++
77-80	CB	++
	CU	+++

Year	Lev	Team	W	L	Sv	IP	K	ERA	WHIP	BF/G	OBA	H%	S%	xERA	Ctl	Dom	Cmd	hr/9	BPV
2016	Rk	GCL Blue Jays	4	1	0	32	26	1.69	1.03	20.5	243	30	84	2.43	1.1	7.3	6.5	0.3	119
2016	Rk	GCL Astros	0	0	0	6	5	0.00	0.67	7.0	151	20	100	0.16	1.5	7.5	5.0	0.0	113
2016	Rk	Greeneville	0	0	0	7	10	1.25	1.25	14.7	165	28	89	1.73	6.3	12.5	2.0	0.0	74

Lean SP who was acquired at deadline. Shows advanced skills despite being converted OF. Has exemplary arm strength, but most effective at lower velocity where he gets lots of sinking action. Could throw harder due to loose arm action. Has vintage control and rarely walks hitters. Keeps ball low in zone. Next step is to upgrade CB that is too loopy.

Church,Andrew

SP | New York (N) | EXP MLB DEBUT: 2018 | H/W: 6-2 200 | FUT: Middle reliever | 7C

Thrws R Age 22 — 2013 (2) HS (NV)

Velo	Pitch	Grade
89-94	FB	+++
83-85	SL	+++
	CU	++

Year	Lev	Team	W	L	Sv	IP	K	ERA	WHIP	BF/G	OBA	H%	S%	xERA	Ctl	Dom	Cmd	hr/9	BPV
2015	Rk	GCL Mets	1	0	0	3	3	3.00	1.67	6.7	321	35	100	7.70	3.0	9.0	3.0	3.0	99
2015	A-	Brooklyn	2	3	0	41	22	5.24	1.46	19.6	297	33	63	4.63	2.4	4.8	2.0	0.7	40
2016	A	Columbia	5	2	0	56	52	2.24	0.85	22.9	193	24	77	1.70	1.6	8.3	5.2	0.6	125
2016	A+	St. Lucie	2	1	0	35	22	3.60	1.29	24.0	239	28	70	3.01	3.6	5.7	1.6	0.3	23
2016	AAA	Las Vegas	0	1	0	4	4	6.75	2.00	19.3	383	49	63	6.83	2.3	9.0	4.0	0.0	119

Former 2nd rd pick surprised with solid full-season debut. Of his three pitches, best is 2-seam FB with good late bore. Struggles maintaining velocity from start to start. Can touch 95. SL is solid but unspectacular. Still tinkering with feel for CU. At physical projection.

Civale,Aaron

SP | Cleveland | EXP MLB DEBUT: 2019 | H/W: 6-2 215 | FUT: #5 SP/swingman | 7C

Thrws R Age 21 — 2016 (3) Northeastern

Velo	Pitch	Grade
90-93	FB	+++
86-88	CT	++++
	CB	++
	CU	++

Year	Lev	Team	W	L	Sv	IP	K	ERA	WHIP	BF/G	OBA	H%	S%	xERA	Ctl	Dom	Cmd	hr/9	BPV
2016	NCAA	Northeastern	9	3	0	114	121	1.74	0.93	28.5	220	29	85	2.11	1.2	9.5	8.1	0.6	158
2016	A-	Mahoning Vall	0	2	0	37	28	1.69	0.83	10.5	180	23	77	0.90	1.9	6.8	3.5	0.0	88

Mature RH lacks big-time velo, but thrives on plus command and weak contact. FB will touch 94 mph with arm-side bore for ground balls; CT is out pitch with good length and late 3/4 bite for whiffs. Will need to pitch deeper into starts and mix in CB/CH more to remain SP. FB/CT combo could play well in long relief with chance to add tick of velo.

Clark,Bailey

SP | **Chicago (N)** | EXP MLB DEBUT: 2019 | H/W: 6-4 185 | FUT: #3 starter | **7D**

Thrws R Age 22
2016 (5) Duke

92-95	FB	+++
83-95	SL	+++
87-90	SP	+

Year	Lev	Team	W	L	Sv	IP	K	ERA	WHIP	BF/G	OBA	H%	S%	xERA	Ctl	Dom	Cmd	hr/9	BPV
2016	NCAA	Duke	4	4	0	59	64	5.63	1.59	17.4	290	38	64	4.91	4.0	9.7	2.5	0.8	87
2016	Rk	Azl Cubs	0	0	0	5	4	0.00	0.60	8.6	175	23	100	0.26	0.0	7.2		0.0	148
2016	A-	Eugene	0	0	0	6	9	2.90	1.29	12.7	314	45	86	5.14	0.0	13.1		1.5	253

5th round pick has a plus mid-90s sinking FB that hit 98 mph in college. Second best offering is a quality cut SL that can be swing-and-miss. Hard split CU is a work in progress and will need to improve for him to remain a starter. Some scouts see him as an impact reliever, but he showed enough in his limited debut to remain a starter for now.

Clark,Brian

RP | **Chicago (A)** | EXP MLB DEBUT: 2017 | H/W: 6-3 225 | FUT: Setup reliever | **7D**

Thrws L Age 23
2014 (9) Kent State

90-94	FB	+++
83-84	SL	+++
	CU	++

Year	Lev	Team	W	L	Sv	IP	K	ERA	WHIP	BF/G	OBA	H%	S%	xERA	Ctl	Dom	Cmd	hr/9	BPV
2014	NCAA	Kent State	6	7	0	88	70	3.78	1.25	22.4	232	29	67	2.66	3.6	7.2	2.0	0.1	50
2014	Rk	Great Falls	3	4	0	48	52	3.37	1.27	13.1	257	35	72	3.10	2.6	9.7	3.7	0.2	122
2015	A+	Winston-Salem	10	4	0	89	85	2.33	1.30	12.7	237	32	80	2.76	3.8	8.6	2.2	0.0	69
2016	AA	Birmingham	0	4	4	47	42	2.29	1.29	6.3	281	36	82	3.51	1.7	8.0	4.7	0.2	116
2016	AAA	Charlotte	0	1	0	9	6	5.00	1.33	6.2	262	32	58	3.19	3.0	6.0	2.0	0.0	45

Big, physical RP who was on shuttle between AA and AAA. Establishes control with solid-average sinker, thrown from clean, repeatable delivery. Hits spots with FB and rarely allows HR. SL shows plus potential with late break and depth. Fringy CU gives him third pitch, may can be too firm.

Clarke,Taylor

SP | **Arizona** | EXP MLB DEBUT: 2018 | H/W: 6-4 200 | FUT: #4 starter | **7C**

Thrws R Age 23
2015 (3) Charleston

91-94	FB	+++
78-80	SL	+++
82-85	CU	+++

Year	Lev	Team	W	L	Sv	IP	K	ERA	WHIP	BF/G	OBA	H%	S%	xERA	Ctl	Dom	Cmd	hr/9	BPV
2015	A-	Hillsboro	0	0	3	21	27	0.00	0.57	5.5	119	20	100		1.7	11.6	6.8	0.0	180
2016	A	Kane County	3	2	0	28	24	2.87	1.03	18.1	232	29	71	2.30	1.6	7.7	4.8	0.3	113
2016	A+	Visalia	1	1	0	23	22	2.74	1.13	22.7	227	27	83	3.29	2.7	8.6	3.1	1.2	99
2016	AA	Mobile	8	6	0	97	72	3.61	1.23	23.2	265	31	73	3.76	1.9	6.7	3.4	0.8	86

Over-the-top, high pitchability RH cruised through 3 levels in full-season debut. Spots low 90s FB throughout lower part of zone. Will have command issues if pitch misses high due to delivery. SL slurvy; an effective pitch since he commands it well, but not a swing-and-miss offering. CU has become solid 3rd pitch. Borderline starting pitcher.

Clarkin,Ian

SP | **New York (A)** | EXP MLB DEBUT: 2018 | H/W: 6-2 190 | FUT: #3 starter | **8D**

Thrws L Age 22
2013 (1) HS (CA)

88-93	FB	+++
73-76	CB	+++
82-83	SL	++
80-83	CU	+++

Year	Lev	Team	W	L	Sv	IP	K	ERA	WHIP	BF/G	OBA	H%	S%	xERA	Ctl	Dom	Cmd	hr/9	BPV
2013	Rk	GCL Yankees	0	2	0	5	4	10.80	1.80	7.7	262	23	43	7.73	7.2	7.2	1.0	3.6	-47
2014	A	Charleston (Sc)	3	3	0	70	71	3.21	1.23	17.7	245	31	76	3.39	2.8	9.1	3.2	0.8	106
2014	A+	Tampa	1	0	0	5	4	1.80	1.60	22.1	332	41	88	4.91	1.8	7.2	4.0	0.0	99
2016	A+	Tampa	6	9	0	98	72	3.31	1.33	22.6	266	32	75	3.56	2.8	6.6	2.4	0.4	63

Injury-prone SP who needs innings to realize potential. Ended season in July due to knee surgery. Did not pitch in '15 due to elbow. When healthy, uses deep arsenal of potent offerings including big-breaking CB and very good CU. Added hard SL, but varies arm slot. Heavy FB spotted to both sides of plate and used as groundball inducer.

Cleavinger,Garrett

RP | **Baltimore** | EXP MLB DEBUT: 2018 | H/W: 6-1 210 | FUT: Setup reliever | **7C**

Thrws L Age 22
2015 (3) Oregon

90-94	FB	+++
75-79	CB	+++
	CU	+

Year	Lev	Team	W	L	Sv	IP	K	ERA	WHIP	BF/G	OBA	H%	S%	xERA	Ctl	Dom	Cmd	hr/9	BPV
2015	NCAA	Oregon	6	2	9	40	66	1.58	0.93	4.0	151	28	86	1.16	3.8	14.9	3.9	0.5	182
2015	A-	Aberdeen	6	1	1	25	32	2.16	1.28	5.4	166	24	87	2.50	6.5	11.5	1.8	0.7	50
2016	A	Delmarva	5	0	4	39	53	1.38	0.92	8.6	185	28	91	1.79	2.5	12.2	4.8	0.7	170
2016	A+	Frederick	2	3	0	37	49	4.85	1.56	8.1	251	37	68	4.01	5.6	11.9	2.1	0.5	81

Powerful reliever who dominated Low-A en route to A+. Has proven difficult to hit with solid-average FB and CB combo. Deceptive delivery and slot allow pitches to play up. Has ability to retire hitters with weak contact or swings and misses. Command needs to be cleaned up and get in pitcher's counts, but FB location has improved.

Clifton,Trevor

SP | **Chicago (N)** | EXP MLB DEBUT: 2018 | H/W: 6-1 170 | FUT: #3 starter | **7C**

Thrws R Age 21
2013 (12) HS (TN)

92-95	FB	++++
80-83	CB	+++
	CU	++

Year	Lev	Team	W	L	Sv	IP	K	ERA	WHIP	BF/G	OBA	H%	S%	xERA	Ctl	Dom	Cmd	hr/9	BPV
2013	Rk	Azl Cubs	0	0	0	10	15	7.13	2.08	6.2	313	49	62	5.75	7.1	13.4	1.9	0.0	66
2014	A-	Boise	4	2	0	61	54	3.69	1.46	20.1	255	32	74	3.81	4.4	8.0	1.8	0.4	42
2015	A	South Bend	8	10	0	108	103	3.99	1.28	19.3	230	29	69	3.14	3.9	8.6	2.2	0.6	67
2016	A+	Myrtle Beach	7	7	0	119	129	2.72	1.16	20.6	224	31	76	2.50	3.1	9.8	3.1	0.3	110

Short, athletic righty continues to climb the Cubs depth chart after an impressive breakout at High-A. FB sits at 92-95, topping out at 97 mph. Hard, low-80s power CB is now above-average and CU shows some potential, Strong lower half and good mechanics give him the potential to develop into a solid mid-rotation starter.

Cole,A.J.

SP | **Washington** | EXP MLB DEBUT: 2015 | H/W: 6-5 215 | FUT: #4 starter | **7A**

Thrws R Age 25
2010 (4) HS (FL)

91-93	FB	+++
82-84	SL	++
83-86	CU	+++
74-76	CB	++

Year	Lev	Team	W	L	Sv	IP	K	ERA	WHIP	BF/G	OBA	H%	S%	xERA	Ctl	Dom	Cmd	hr/9	BPV
2014	AAA	Syracuse	7	0	0	63	50	3.43	1.37	24.0	280	32	81	4.72	2.4	7.1	2.9	1.3	81
2015	AAA	Syracuse	5	6	0	105	76	3.17	1.19	20.1	235	27	76	3.18	2.9	6.5	2.2	0.8	56
2015	MLB	Washington	0	0	1	9	9	5.93	1.65	13.6	353	44	64	6.31	1.0	8.9	9.0	1.0	152
2016	AAA	Syracuse	8	8	0	124	109	4.28	1.34	23.5	272	32	71	4.41	2.5	7.9	3.1	1.2	92
2016	MLB	Washington	1	2	0	38	39	5.20	1.34	19.8	256	30	66	4.64	3.3	9.2	2.8	1.7	95

Mixes and matches four pitches, but none are exceptional. Good control of low-90s FB, and CU is best secondary, but he has stalled in upper minors and has been hittable in short MLB stints. Athletic and repeatable delivery, but time is running out to develop that knockout pitch.

Cooney,Tim

SP | **Cleveland** | EXP MLB DEBUT: 2015 | H/W: 6-3 195 | FUT: #4 starter | **7B**

Thrws L Age 26
2012 (3) Wake Forest

88-92	FB	+++
80-82	SL	+++
73-75	CB	+++
82-84	CU	+++

Year	Lev	Team	W	L	Sv	IP	K	ERA	WHIP	BF/G	OBA	H%	S%	xERA	Ctl	Dom	Cmd	hr/9	BPV
2013	AA	Springfield	7	10	0	118	125	3.81	1.27	24.2	284	37	70	3.88	1.4	9.5	6.9	0.6	152
2014	AAA	Memphis	14	6	0	158	119	3.47	1.30	25.0	262	30	78	4.21	2.7	6.8	2.5	1.2	68
2015	AAA	Memphis	6	4	0	88	63	2.76	0.87	23.3	197	22	74	2.07	1.6	6.4	3.9	0.9	90
2015	MLB	St. Louis	1	0	0	31	29	3.18	1.22	21.0	242	30	77	3.43	2.9	8.4	2.9	0.9	91
2016		did not pitch (injury)																	

Crafty southpaw missed all of 2016 after undergoing shoulder surgery. Sequences and locates average four-pitch mix well to keep hitters guessing; CU is best bat-misser with good velo separation from FB. SwK/GB production has dwindled in upper minors and should be considered a low-risk, low-reward #4/5 SP type profile long-term.

Coonrod,Sam

SP | **San Francisco** | EXP MLB DEBUT: 2017 | H/W: 6-2 225 | FUT: #3 starter | **8C**

Thrws R Age 24
2014 (5) Southern Illinois

90-95	FB	++++
81-84	SL	+++
	CU	++

Year	Lev	Team	W	L	Sv	IP	K	ERA	WHIP	BF/G	OBA	H%	S%	xERA	Ctl	Dom	Cmd	hr/9	BPV
2014	NCAA	Southern Illinois	2	6	0	84	77	2.89	1.39	23.6	228	29	79	3.16	5.0	8.2	1.6	0.3	31
2014	Rk	Azl Giants	1	0	0	27	25	3.97	1.40	7.6	294	38	68	3.79	2.0	8.3	4.2	0.0	113
2015	A	Augusta	7	5	0	111	114	3.16	1.23	19.6	247	33	73	2.93	2.8	9.2	3.4	0.2	110
2016	A+	San Jose	5	3	0	63	42	1.99	1.08	22.4	205	24	83	2.22	3.1	6.0	1.9	0.4	41
2016	AA	Richmond	4	3	0	77	52	3.04	1.26	24.2	213	24	79	3.14	4.4	6.1	1.4	0.8	7

Under-the-radar SP who may not post high K rate, but he toys with hitters by advanced sequencing and repeatable delivery. Owns plus FB that is tough to elevate and can work up in zone. Mixes in hard SL with good shape and depth. Should see return in K rate once he masters CU that is currently below average. Very tough to hit when on.

Cosart,Jake

RP | **Boston** | EXP MLB DEBUT: 2018 | H/W: 6-2 175 | FUT: Closer | **8D**

Thrws R Age 23
2014 (3) SeminoleSt JC

93-98	FB	++++
85-88	SP	++
74-78	CB	++

Year	Lev	Team	W	L	Sv	IP	K	ERA	WHIP	BF/G	OBA	H%	S%	xERA	Ctl	Dom	Cmd	hr/9	BPV
2014	Rk	GCL Red Sox	0	1	0	16	16	2.25	1.13	9.0	134	19	78	1.14	6.2	9.0	1.5	0.0	13
2015	A-	Lowell	2	2	0	33	27	5.45	1.39	15.5	218	26	60	3.53	5.5	7.4	1.4	0.8	3
2016	A	Greenville	4	1	2	52	76	2.07	1.17	7.2	197	32	83	2.20	4.3	13.1	3.0	0.3	137
2016	A+	Salem	0	0	0	18	28	1.00	1.00	8.6	121	24	89	0.64	5.5	14.0	2.5	0.0	122

Hard-throwing pitcher who was converted to RP in '16 to terrific results. Bumped to High-A in August and continued to post high Dom. Can register Ks with splitter and CB while FB effective in all quadrants. Has max-effort delivery that is tough to repeat and walks many as a result. Has been tough to hit, but must command FB better.

Cotton,Jharel

SP | **Oakland** | EXP MLB DEBUT: 2016 | H/W: 5-11 195 | FUT: #3 starter | **8C**

Thrws R Age 25
2012 (20) East Carolina

90-96	FB	++++
77-79	CB	++
82-85	SL	++
75-79	CU	++++

Year	Lev	Team	W	L	Sv	IP	K	ERA	WHIP	BF/G	OBA	H%	S%	xERA	Ctl	Dom	Cmd	hr/9	BPV
2015	AA	Tulsa	5	2	0	62	71	2.32	1.13	22.3	218	30	82	2.60	3.0	10.3	3.4	0.6	121
2015	AAA	Oklahoma City	0	0	0	7	9	5.07	1.55	6.2	310	45	64	4.39	2.5	11.4	4.5	0.0	155
2016	AAA	Nashville	3	1	0	38	36	2.83	0.92	23.7	207	26	72	2.08	1.7	8.5	5.1	0.7	126
2016	AAA	Oklahoma City	8	5	0	97	119	4.91	1.15	17.5	226	29	62	3.69	3.0	11.0	3.7	1.6	136
2016	MLB	Oakland	2	0	0	29	23	2.16	0.82	21.2	196	21	85	2.22	1.2	7.1	5.8	1.2	113

Short, ultra-athletic SP who led PCL in Ks. Keeps walks to minimum by commanding heavy FB to both sides of plate. Can cut and sink FB at will and has two breaking balls at disposal. Some effort in delivery, but has fast arm that results in plus CU with wacky action. Repeats delivery, but plane to plate could be problematic.

Covey,Dylan — SP — Chicago (A)

EXP MLB DEBUT: 2017 | H/W: 6-2 195 | FUT: #4 starter | 7C

Thrws R Age 25
2013 (4) San Diego

Velo	Pitch	Grade
89-94	FB	+++
79-81	CB	+++
81-83	SL	++
81-83	CU	+++

Year	Lev	Team	W	L	Sv	IP	K	ERA	WHIP	BF/G	OBA	H%	S%	xERA	Ctl	Dom	Cmd	hr/9	BPV
2013	A	Beloit	1	1	0	47	31	4.78	1.72	21.4	325	37	73	5.83	3.2	5.9	1.8	0.8	37
2014	A	Beloit	4	9	0	101	70	4.81	1.24	22.8	258	31	58	3.14	2.3	6.2	2.7	0.3	68
2014	A+	Stockton	3	5	0	39	22	7.15	1.64	21.7	308	35	53	5.08	3.5	5.1	1.5	0.5	16
2015	A+	Stockton	8	9	0	140	100	3.60	1.27	22.0	255	29	74	3.71	2.8	6.4	2.3	0.8	59
2016	AA	Midland	2	1	0	29	26	1.86	1.31	20.0	204	25	89	2.94	5.3	8.0	1.5	0.6	21

Power-armed SP who ended season in early May, but returned with aplomb in AFL. Has long had potential. Hits spots with terrific FB and can keep ball down in zone for groundballs. Likes to use sinker early in count. Has big-breaking CB for Ks, but has trouble controlling it. Good CU gives him third average offering. Rule 5 pick from OAK.

Crawford,Leo — SP — Los Angeles (N)

EXP MLB DEBUT: 2020 | H/W: 6-0 180 | FUT: #3 starter | 8D

Thrws L Age 20
2015 FA (NI)

Velo	Pitch	Grade
90-92	FB	+++
	CB	++
	CU	++

Year	Lev	Team	W	L	Sv	IP	K	ERA	WHIP	BF/G	OBA	H%	S%	xERA	Ctl	Dom	Cmd	hr/9	BPV
2016	Rk	Azl Dodgers	2	1	0	38	39	2.60	1.00	18.2	224	30	73	2.03	1.7	9.2	5.6	0.2	139
2016	A	Great Lakes	4	1	0	28	24	2.23	1.10	18.4	217	25	86	2.89	2.9	7.7	2.7	1.0	78

Short, athletic lefty from Nicaragua had a solid U.S. debut, going 6-2 with a 2.42 ERA. Uses a high leg kick to drive home a good low-90 FB and has the arm strength for more velocity as he matures. Also mixes in a CB and a rudimentary CU, both of which need work but show potential.

Crick,Kyle — SP — San Francisco

EXP MLB DEBUT: 2017 | H/W: 6-4 220 | FUT: #3 starter | 8E

Thrws R Age 24
2011 (S-1) HS (TX)

Velo	Pitch	Grade
90-94	FB	+++
82-85	SL	+++
74-76	CB	++
	CU	+

Year	Lev	Team	W	L	Sv	IP	K	ERA	WHIP	BF/G	OBA	H%	S%	xERA	Ctl	Dom	Cmd	hr/9	BPV
2012	A	Augusta	7	6	0	111		2.51	1.28	19.8	193	29	79	2.22	5.4	10.4	1.9	0.1	58
2013	A+	San Jose	3	1	0	68	95	1.58	1.28	20.0	200	33	87	2.31	5.1	12.5	2.4	0.1	105
2014	AA	Richmond	6	7	0	90	111	3.80	1.54	17.1	235	33	77	3.96	6.1	11.1	1.8	0.7	53
2015	AA	Richmond	3	4	0	63	73	3.29	1.79	8.1	209	30	81	3.90	9.4	10.4	1.1	0.3	-49
2016	AA	Richmond	4	11	0	109	86	5.04	1.62	21.1	264	32	69	4.55	5.5	7.1	1.3	0.7	-4

Regressing SP who spent 3rd year in AA and still can't find plate. Owns impressive, clean arm with ideal FB to be potent. SL can be out pitch at times, but inconsistent mechanics and release point hinder effectiveness. Has well below average CU and has become more hittable. The hope is that stuff will return and he can throw strikes.

Crismatt,Nabil — SP — New York (N)

EXP MLB DEBUT: 2018 | H/W: 6-1 200 | FUT: #4 starter | 7C

Thrws R Age 22
2011 FA (CB)

Velo	Pitch	Grade
90-92	FB	+++
77-78	CB	+++
83-85	CU	+++

Year	Lev	Team	W	L	Sv	IP	K	ERA	WHIP	BF/G	OBA	H%	S%	xERA	Ctl	Dom	Cmd	hr/9	BPV
2014	Rk	GCL Mets	1	1	2	28	33	2.25	0.89	5.5	160	23	75	1.10	3.2	10.6	3.3	0.3	122
2015	Rk	Kingsport	6	1	0	62	63	2.90	1.03	19.9	229	29	76	2.79	1.7	9.1	5.3	0.9	136
2016	A-	Brooklyn	0	1	1	31	35	3.19	0.97	14.7	229	30	73	2.89	1.2	10.2	8.8	1.2	170
2016	A	Columbia	1	2	0	28	32	1.91	0.78	25.4	201	29	76	1.28	0.6	10.2	16.0	0.3	185
2016	AA	Binghamton	0	1	0	6	7	1.50	1.00	22.9	228	29	100	3.27	1.5	10.5	7.0	1.5	167

Command/control RH pitched effectively between 3 levels. Throws three average offerings. His best pitch is his FB with classic 2-seam arm-side run. Can hit spots on both sides of the plate. SL and CU round out resume. Pitchability is off the charts.

Danish,Tyler — SP — Chicago (A)

EXP MLB DEBUT: 2016 | H/W: 6-0 200 | FUT: #4 starter | 7C

Thrws R Age 22
2013 (2) HS (FL)

Velo	Pitch	Grade
88-93	FB	+++
77-80	SL	++
79-82	CU	+++

Year	Lev	Team	W	L	Sv	IP	K	ERA	WHIP	BF/G	OBA	H%	S%	xERA	Ctl	Dom	Cmd	hr/9	BPV
2014	A+	Winston-Salem	5	3	0	91	78	2.66	1.21	20.4	253	31	81	3.37	2.3	7.7	3.4	0.7	95
2015	AA	Birmingham	8	12	0	142	90	4.50	1.65	24.4	304	34	74	5.39	3.8	5.7	1.5	0.8	18
2016	AA	Birmingham	3	7	0	75	47	4.43	1.16	24.9	251	29	60	2.94	1.9	5.6	2.9	0.4	68
2016	AAA	Charlotte	1	3	0	29	21	5.88	1.68	18.7	322	39	61	4.97	3.1	6.5	2.1	0.0	51
2016	MLB	Chi White Sox	0	0	0	1	0	15.00	7.50	4.1	639	64	78	29.41	22.5	0.0	0.0	0.0	-590

Short, strong SP who reached CHW though season ended in late August after undisclosed injury. Very hittable stuff, though gets plus movement on pitch mix. Induces high amount of groundballs and CU has nasty late action. Throws from low 3/4 slot for deception, though SL is below average. Doesn't have velocity to be dominant.

Davila,Garrett — SP — Kansas City

EXP MLB DEBUT: 2020 | H/W: 6-2 180 | FUT: #4 starter | 7D

Thrws L Age 20
2015 (4) HS (NC)

Velo	Pitch	Grade
88-92	FB	++
75-77	CB	++
81-84	CU	+++

Year	Lev	Team	W	L	Sv	IP	K	ERA	WHIP	BF/G	OBA	H%	S%	xERA	Ctl	Dom	Cmd	hr/9	BPV
2016	Rk	Burlington	7	0	0	65	55	2.77	1.28	22.2	234	30	78	2.92	3.7	7.6	2.0	0.3	54

Smooth SP who may lack frontline velocity, but he gets outs with advanced sequencing and guile. Tough on LHH and keeps ball low in zone with solid sinker. Commands FB to both sides of plate and counters with slow CB and average CU. Pitches aggressively and likes to work inside. Has tools to be back-end starter.

Davis,Rookie — SP — Cincinnati

EXP MLB DEBUT: 2017 | H/W: 6-5 245 | FUT: #4 starter | 7B

Thrws R Age 23
2011 (14) HS (NC)

Velo	Pitch	Grade
92-95	FB	++++
77-80	CB	+++
81-84	CU	+++

Year	Lev	Team	W	L	Sv	IP	K	ERA	WHIP	BF/G	OBA	H%	S%	xERA	Ctl	Dom	Cmd	hr/9	BPV
2014	A	Charleston (Sc)	7	8	0	126	106	4.93	1.40	19.7	274	34	63	3.97	3.0	7.6	2.5	0.5	73
2015	A+	Tampa	6	6	0	97	105	3.71	1.15	20.3	256	35	67	2.96	1.7	9.7	5.8	0.4	148
2015	AA	Trenton	2	1	0	33	24	4.35	1.39	23.2	289	35	67	3.97	2.2	6.5	3.0	0.3	77
2016	AA	Pensacola	10	3	0	101	62	2.94	1.17	21.2	236	26	79	3.27	2.7	5.5	2.1	0.9	45
2016	AAA	Louisville	0	2	0	24	15	7.50	1.88	22.5	360	40	60	7.16	2.6	5.6	2.1	1.1	48

Strong, tall RH with advanced command of his repertoire. FB sits low-to-mid 90s with solid sink but little arm-side movement. Generates tons of groundballs but few swings and misses. Strikeout rate nosedived. CB/CU both average offerings. Can command each pitch in and out of the strike zone. Innings-eating 4th starter upside. High floor.

De La Cruz,Oscar — SP — Chicago (N)

EXP MLB DEBUT: 2019 | H/W: 6-4 200 | FUT: #3 starter | 8D

Thrws R Age 22
2012 FA (DR)

Velo	Pitch	Grade
92-95	FB	++++
80-82	CB	+++
	CU	++

Year	Lev	Team	W	L	Sv	IP	K	ERA	WHIP	BF/G	OBA	H%	S%	xERA	Ctl	Dom	Cmd	hr/9	BPV
2015	A-	Eugene	6	3	0	73	73	2.84	1.00	21.5	214	28	72	2.16	2.1	9.0	4.3	0.5	123
2016	Rk	Azl Cubs	0	1	0	3	2	6.00	1.33	12.5	262	24	67	6.01	3.0	6.0	2.0	3.0	45
2016	A-	Eugene	0	0	0	8	14	1.11	0.86	14.9	180	31	100	1.94	2.2	15.6	7.0	1.1	238
2016	A	South Bend	1	2	0	27	35	3.31	1.10	17.8	223	35	67	2.04	2.6	11.6	4.4	0.0	155

Tall Dominican was impressive again, but was limited to 39 innings due to a sore elbow. Plus FB sits at 92-95 mph with room for more as he matures. CB and CU show potential, but lack consistency. Keeps the ball down in the zone and showed solid command (2 HR and 11 BB).

De Leon,Jose — SP — Los Angeles (N)

EXP MLB DEBUT: 2016 | H/W: 6-2 190 | FUT: #2 starter | 9D

Thrws R Age 24
2013 (24) Southern

Velo	Pitch	Grade
90-93	FB	++++
80-83	SL	+++
83-85	CU	+++

Year	Lev	Team	W	L	Sv	IP	K	ERA	WHIP	BF/G	OBA	H%	S%	xERA	Ctl	Dom	Cmd	hr/9	BPV
2014	A	Great Lakes	2	0	0	22	42	1.22	0.72	19.7	183	39	87	0.93	0.8	17.0	21.0	0.4	303
2015	A+	Rancho Cuca	4	1	0	37	58	1.69	0.91	19.8	199	35	82	1.48	1.9	14.0	7.3	0.2	218
2015	AA	Tulsa	2	6	0	76	105	3.66	1.18	19.1	221	31	75	3.43	3.4	12.4	3.6	1.3	149
2016	AAA	Oklahoma City	7	1	0	86	111	2.61	0.94	20.2	201	28	78	2.25	2.1	11.6	5.6	0.9	170
2016	MLB	LA Dodgers	2	0	0	17	15	6.35	1.53	18.5	284	30	67	6.46	3.7	7.9	2.1	2.6	61

Pounds the strike zone with a good 90-93 mph FB that hits 96 mph. Also showed an improved low-80s slurve and an average CU. Ability to miss bats while attacking the strike zone is among the best in the minors (20 BB/111 K in 86.1 IP). Tends to pitch up in the zone, but velocity, late life, and a bit of deception allow him to stay out of trouble.

de los Santos,Enyel — SP — San Diego

EXP MLB DEBUT: 2019 | H/W: 6-3 170 | FUT: #4 starter | 8C

Thrws R Age 21
2015 FA (DR)

Velo	Pitch	Grade
92-94	FB	+++
75-78	CB	+++
	CU	+++

Year	Lev	Team	W	L	Sv	IP	K	ERA	WHIP	BF/G	OBA	H%	S%	xERA	Ctl	Dom	Cmd	hr/9	BPV
2015	A-	Everett	3	0	0	37	42	4.11	1.34	19.4	261	36	69	3.61	3.1	10.2	3.2	0.5	116
2015	Rk	AZL Mariners	3	0	0	24	29	2.60	1.20	19.4	260	37	79	3.12	1.9	10.8	5.8	0.4	162
2016	A	Fort Wayne	3	2	0	52	45	2.93	1.00	18.1	205	26	70	1.92	2.4	7.8	3.2	0.3	92
2016	A+	Lake Elsinore	5	3	0	68	52	4.36	1.38	19.1	267	30	73	4.74	3.2	6.9	2.2	1.5	56

Promising, lean RHP flashes 3 average or better pitches. 2-seam FB sits 92-94, touching 96, with late life down in the zone. CB has solid 12/6 action, but not a swing-and-miss pitch. CU has plus potential with terrific fade and good deception. Easy delivery but struggles with repeating release point.

DeJong,Chase — SP — Los Angeles (N)

EXP MLB DEBUT: 2017 | H/W: 6-4 205 | FUT: #4 starter | 7D

Thrws R Age 23
2012 (2) HS (CA)

Velo	Pitch	Grade
90-92	FB	+++
75-78	CB	+++
	CU	++

Year	Lev	Team	W	L	Sv	IP	K	ERA	WHIP	BF/G	OBA	H%	S%	xERA	Ctl	Dom	Cmd	hr/9	BPV
2015	A	Lansing	7	4	0	86	77	3.14	1.08	24.0	236	28	75	3.07	1.9	8.0	4.3	0.9	112
2015	A+	Rancho Cuca	4	3	0	50	52	3.96	1.18	18.2	238	30	70	3.46	2.7	9.4	3.5	1.1	114
2016	AA	Tulsa	14	5	0	141	125	2.87	1.03	21.7	210	25	77	2.63	2.5	8.0	3.2	1.0	94
2016	AAA	Oklahoma City	1	0	0	5	8	1.76	1.37	21.4	294	48	86	3.67	1.8	14.1	8.0	0.0	224

Durable RHP had a breakout season, going 15-5 with a 2.82 ERA. FB velocity was a tick better, sitting at 90-92 and topping out at 94 with location and improved movement. Mixes in an above-average CB and an improved, but fringy CU. Delivery is somewhat stiff and he isn't particularly athletic, but knows how to pitch and looks like a back-end starter.

Diaz,Miguel

SP | **San Diego** | EXP MLB DEBUT: 2017 | H/W: 6-1 175 | FUT: #3 starter | **8D**

Thrws R Age 22
2011 FA (DR)

Velo	Pitch	Grade
94-96	FB	++++
77-79	SL	+++
86-87	CU	++

Year	Lev	Team	W	L	Sv	IP	K	ERA	WHIP	BF/G	OBA	H%	S%	xERA	Ctl	Dom	Cmd	hr/9	BPV
2013	Rk	DSL Brewers	3	2	0	48	34	2.43	1.18	17.5	209	26	77	2.13	3.9	6.3	1.6	0.0	26
2014	Rk	Azl Brewers	4	2	0	47	53	4.21	1.32	15.0	241	33	68	3.37	3.8	10.1	2.7	0.6	97
2015	Rk	Azl Brewers	0	3	0	20	23	2.24	1.24	11.7	261	36	83	3.32	2.2	10.3	4.6	0.4	143
2016	A	Wisconsin	1	8	3	94	91	3.73	1.19	14.5	238	30	70	3.11	2.8	8.7	3.1	0.7	100

Dominican RH posted nearly a K-per-IP average. Short, quick arm action produces tailing mid-90s heat; will touch 98 mph. Feel for SL as best secondary; CU still raw but gets good separation and flashes above-average. More control than command; could stand to get more extension toward home. Late-inning RP as fallback. Rule 5 pick from MIL.

Diaz,Yennsy

SP | **Toronto** | EXP MLB DEBUT: 2019 | H/W: 6-1 160 | FUT: #3 starter | **8D**

Thrws R Age 20
2014 FA (DR)

Velo	Pitch	Grade
91-95	FB	++++
78-80	CB	++
83-86	CU	++

Year	Lev	Team	W	L	Sv	IP	K	ERA	WHIP	BF/G	OBA	H%	S%	xERA	Ctl	Dom	Cmd	hr/9	BPV
2016	Rk	Bluefield	4	6	0	56	48	5.79	1.54	20.3	272	31	65	5.18	4.3	7.7	1.8	1.4	40

Lean, projectable pitcher with exciting, loose arm. Incredible arm speed produces plus velocity and could add more with additional strength. Secondary offerings remain crude, though CU shows promise due to arm action and slot. Can rush delivery which negatively impacts command and control. Long-term project with high upside.

Dietz,Matthias

SP | **Baltimore** | EXP MLB DEBUT: 2020 | H/W: 6-5 220 | FUT: #3 starter | **8D**

Thrws R Age 21
2016 (2) Logan CC

Velo	Pitch	Grade
91-96	FB	+++
82-85	SL	++
	CU	++

Year	Lev	Team	W	L	Sv	IP	K	ERA	WHIP	BF/G	OBA	H%	S%	xERA	Ctl	Dom	Cmd	hr/9	BPV
2016	A-	Aberdeen	0	3	0	18	8	4.95	1.76	11.9	300	34	69	4.83	4.9	4.0	0.8	0.0	-44

Big-framed SP who is far from majors, but has ingredients to be mid-rotation workhorse. Has ideal frame and power repertoire to dominate, but focuses more on pitch movement and efficiency than Ks. Lively FB is best pitch, but hard SL and CU have potential to be average. Needs pitch to battle LHH and cleaner delivery would help.

Diplan,Marcos

SP | **Milwaukee** | EXP MLB DEBUT: 2019 | H/W: 6-0 160 | FUT: #3 starter | **8E**

Thrws R Age 20
2013 FA (DR)

Velo	Pitch	Grade
91-94	FB	++++
77-79	SL	++++
83-86	CU	++

Year	Lev	Team	W	L	Sv	IP	K	ERA	WHIP	BF/G	OBA	H%	S%	xERA	Ctl	Dom	Cmd	hr/9	BPV
2015	Rk	Helena	2	2	2	50	54	3.77	1.36	16.1	250	33	73	3.72	3.8	9.7	2.6	0.7	91
2016	A	Wisconsin	6	2	1	70	89	1.80	1.16	16.4	199	30	86	2.25	4.1	11.4	2.8	0.4	113
2016	A+	Brevard County	1	2	0	43	40	5.01	1.51	18.7	279	35	67	4.63	3.8	8.4	2.2	0.8	67

Young, lean SP with smallish frame but big-time stuff. Will reach back for 97-98 mph with fastball and sit lower-90s, blending in plus SL with late bite for high Dom ability. Split time between rotation and bullpen due to raw CU. Command a ways off, but is athletic and should be able to develop it. Mid-rotation upside; could use FB/SL in late relief.

Dominguez,Seranthony

SP | **Philadelphia** | EXP MLB DEBUT: 2020 | H/W: 6-1 185 | FUT: #3 starter | **8E**

Thrws R Age 22
2011 FA (DR)

Velo	Pitch	Grade
93-95	FB	++++
80-83	CB	+++
85-86	CU	++

Year	Lev	Team	W	L	Sv	IP	K	ERA	WHIP	BF/G	OBA	H%	S%	xERA	Ctl	Dom	Cmd	hr/9	BPV
2014	Rk	GCL Phillies	2	2	0	26	24	3.12	1.54	8.1	262	34	79	4.00	4.8	8.3	1.7	0.3	37
2015	Rk	GCL Phillies	1	1	0	7	9	2.50	1.81	16.7	228	31	92	5.06	8.8	11.3	1.3	1.3	-16
2016	A-	Williamsport	1	1	0	17	15	2.12	0.71	20.0	143	20	67	0.18	2.1	7.9	3.8	0.0	104
2016	A	Lakewood	5	2	0	48	50	2.43	1.12	19.0	200	27	79	2.19	3.7	9.4	2.5	0.4	85

Comes at hitters from a high 3/4s slot, and easy motion and strong lower half results in low-to-mid-90s velocity. FB has some life and will get swings and misses, though he can struggle to command it. CB flashes plus, and CU shows good fade at times. Ingredients are here for a SP package, but still a raw product that needs reps more than anything.

Donatella,Justin

SP | **Arizona** | EXP MLB DEBUT: 2018 | H/W: 6-6 236 | FUT: #5 SP/swingman | **7C**

Thrws R Age 22
2015 (15) UC-San Diego

Velo	Pitch	Grade
90-93	FB	++++
84-86	SL	+++
83-85	CU	++

Year	Lev	Team	W	L	Sv	IP	K	ERA	WHIP	BF/G	OBA	H%	S%	xERA	Ctl	Dom	Cmd	hr/9	BPV
2015	Rk	Azl Dbacks	1	0	0	18	15	0.99	0.61	6.9	150	20	82	0.01	1.0	7.5	7.5	0.0	125
2015	A-	Hillsboro	1	0	0	8	5	3.33	0.86	9.9	208	25	57	1.32	1.1	5.6	5.0	0.0	88
2016	A	Kane County	7	4	0	79	57	3.64	1.15	21.0	259	30	70	3.42	1.5	6.5	4.4	0.8	95
2016	A+	Visalia	6	4	0	65	54	3.04	1.14	21.5	240	28	78	3.29	2.2	7.5	3.4	1.0	93

Tall, command/control RH pitched solidly between Single-A and High-A. Low 90s two-seam FB acts as sinker due to good leverage in delivery. SL consistently got better throughout '16 with average movement. CU is behind other offerings. Won't be a high strikeout type but should provide quality innings in the back end of a rotation.

Drake,Oliver

RP | **Baltimore** | EXP MLB DEBUT: 2015 | H/W: 6-4 215 | FUT: Setup reliever | **6B**

Thrws R Age 30
2008 (43) Navy

Velo	Pitch	Grade
90-94	FB	+++
84-87	SP	+++

Year	Lev	Team	W	L	Sv	IP	K	ERA	WHIP	BF/G	OBA	H%	S%	xERA	Ctl	Dom	Cmd	hr/9	BPV
2014	AA	Bowie	2	4	31	52	71	3.10	1.11	4.1	218	34	71	2.32	2.9	12.2	4.2	0.3	159
2015	AAA	Norfolk	1	2	23	44	66	0.82	0.89	3.9	156	27	92	0.91	3.3	13.5	4.1	0.2	173
2015	MLB	Baltimore	0	0	0	15	17	2.96	1.64	5.2	272	37	83	4.63	5.3	10.1	1.9	0.6	55
2016	AAA	Norfolk	1	4	10	56	79	2.73	1.23	4.8	218	33	81	3.04	4.0	12.7	3.2	0.8	138
2016	MLB	Baltimore	1	0	0	18	21	4.00	1.00	4.9	178	23	63	2.21	3.5	10.5	3.0	1.0	113

Strong RP who reached majors based upon two solid-average offerings. Walk rate rose, but continued to miss bats with FB and SPL. Lacks FB command, though aggressively pitches inside. Both pitches are rarely straight and generally keeps ball low in zone. Upside limited based on age, but has closer experience and could be dependable late-inning arm.

Dunn,Justin

SP | **New York (N)** | EXP MLB DEBUT: 2019 | H/W: 6-2 185 | FUT: #3 starter | **8C**

Thrws R Age 21
2016 (1) Boston College

Velo	Pitch	Grade
91-95	FB	++++
81-84	SL	++++
77-79	CB	+++
83-85	CU	++

Year	Lev	Team	W	L	Sv	IP	K	ERA	WHIP	BF/G	OBA	H%	S%	xERA	Ctl	Dom	Cmd	hr/9	BPV
2016	NCAA	Boston College	4	2	2	65	72	2.07	1.07	14.1	220	30	82	2.34	2.5	9.9	4.0	0.4	130
2016	A-	Brooklyn	1	1	0	30	35	1.50	1.17	10.9	228	33	88	2.56	3.0	10.5	3.5	0.3	126

Former college reliever, converted to starter in '16 and stock skyrocketed. FB is best pitch, flashing 96, with late life through the zone. SL had good two plane break and could develop into plus pitch. CB too slurvy for a pitcher featuring a SL. CU is a work in progress.

Dunning,Dane

SP | **Chicago (A)** | EXP MLB DEBUT: 2019 | H/W: 6-4 200 | FUT: #3 starter | **8C**

Thrws R Age 22
2016 (1) Florida

Velo	Pitch	Grade
92-95	FB	++++
82-84	SL	+++
83-84	CU	++

Year	Lev	Team	W	L	Sv	IP	K	ERA	WHIP	BF/G	OBA	H%	S%	xERA	Ctl	Dom	Cmd	hr/9	BPV
2016	NCAA	Florida	6	3	2	78	88	2.30	1.02	9.1	236	33	78	2.34	1.4	10.1	7.3	0.3	163
2016	Rk	GCL Nationals	0	0	0	2	3	0.00	0.00	5.6	0	0			0.0	13.5		0.0	261
2016	A-	Auburn	3	2	0	33	29	2.17	0.99	18.1	217	28	78	1.99	1.9	7.9	4.1	0.3	108

Polished starter with ability to locate low-90s FB down in the zone resulting in tons of ground balls. SL and CU both have enough potential to dream on a mid-rotation upside. Throws strikes with all three pitches. Though was mostly a reliever in college, he has a starter's body with broad shoulders, long arms and tapered lower half.

Duplantier,Jon

SP | **Arizona** | EXP MLB DEBUT: 2020 | H/W: 6-4 225 | FUT: #3 starter | **8D**

Thrws R Age 22
2016 (3) Rice

Velo	Pitch	Grade
91-94	FB	++++
79-83	CB	++++
	CU	++

Year	Lev	Team	W	L	Sv	IP	K	ERA	WHIP	BF/G	OBA	H%	S%	xERA	Ctl	Dom	Cmd	hr/9	BPV
2016	NCAA	Rice	7	7	0	111	148	3.24	1.12	25.7	197	30	71	2.15	3.8	12.0	3.1	0.4	131
2016	A-	Hillsboro	0	0	0	1	3	0.00	2.00	4.8	0	0	100	2.00	18.0	27.0	1.5	0.0	18

Tall, projectable RH with two plus pitches. Low 90s FB plays up due to extension in delivery and solid arm-side sink. Must tighten up FB command. Power CB is a swing-and-miss pitch. CU flashes average fade and deception. Best bet in AZ draft to be a significant contributor.

Ecker,Mark

RP | **Detroit** | EXP MLB DEBUT: 2018 | H/W: 6-0 180 | FUT: Setup reliever | **6B**

Thrws R Age 21
2016 (5) Texas A&M

Velo	Pitch	Grade
92-97	FB	++++
84-86	SL	++
	CU	+++

Year	Lev	Team	W	L	Sv	IP	K	ERA	WHIP	BF/G	OBA	H%	S%	xERA	Ctl	Dom	Cmd	hr/9	BPV
2016	NCAA	Texas A&M	4	2	8	46	56	0.39	0.67	6.5	156	24	97	0.37	1.4	10.9	8.0	0.2	178
2016	A-	Connecticut	2	0	4	18	21	0.50	0.56	5.5	121	19	90		1.5	10.5	7.0	0.0	167
2016	A	West Michigan	0	0	5	9	10	1.96	1.20	4.1	258	33	90	3.66	2.0	9.8	5.0	1.0	141

Short reliever with plus velocity and pitch movement. FB rarely comes out straight and is tough to elevate due to late, heavy life. Works with ideal arm speed and throws good strikes despite complicated arm action and mechanics. Doesn't show much break in SL, but improving CU is best secondary with tumbling action.

Edwards,Andrew — RP — Kansas City

EXP MLB DEBUT: 2017 | H/W: 6-6 265 | FUT: Setup reliever | 6B

Thrws R Age 25
2013 (19) Westrn Kentucky

Velo	Pitch	Grade
91-96	FB	++++
84-87	SL	+++
82-85	CU	+

Year	Lev	Team	W	L	Sv	IP	K	ERA	WHIP	BF/G	OBA	H%	S%	xERA	Ctl	Dom	Cmd	hr/9	BPV
2014	A	Lexington	3	5	1	68	48	4.76	1.71	14.0	312	37	70	5.11	3.8	6.4	1.7	0.3	29
2014	A+	Wilmington	0	4	1	18	15	5.93	1.59	7.3	300	37	61	4.85	3.5	7.4	2.1	0.5	58
2015	A+	Wilmington	0	2	2	42	30	3.86	1.24	5.9	218	26	68	2.77	4.1	6.4	1.6	0.4	24
2016	AA	NW Arkansas	0	0	2	18	23	0.50	1.00	6.9	216	34	94	1.70	2.0	11.5	5.8	0.0	171
2016	AAA	Omaha	0	1	5	43	51	5.43	1.69	6.1	266	34	71	5.48	6.1	10.6	1.8	1.5	46

Strong, durable RP who operates with plus FB had a vastly improved K rate in 2016. Lot of effort in delivery keeps him in pen and can cut and sink FB at will. Doesn't locate FB yet and control comes and goes. Not much touch for CU, though improving, hard SL can be go to pitch when having trouble commanding FB.

Ellis,Christopher — SP — St. Louis

EXP MLB DEBUT: 2017 | H/W: 6-5 205 | FUT: Middle reliever | 7C

Thrws R Age 24
2014 (3) Mississippi

Velo	Pitch	Grade
90-92	FB	+++
83-85	SL	+++
81-83	CU	+++

Year	Lev	Team	W	L	Sv	IP	K	ERA	WHIP	BF/G	OBA	H%	S%	xERA	Ctl	Dom	Cmd	hr/9	BPV
2014	Rk	Orem	0	1	0	15	16	7.11	1.64	7.5	284	36	57	5.36	4.7	9.5	2.0	1.2	61
2015	A+	Inland Empire	4	5	0	62	70	3.91	1.17	22.6	232	31	69	3.16	2.9	10.1	3.5	0.9	122
2015	AA	Arkansas	7	4	0	78	62	3.92	1.54	22.7	259	30	77	4.63	5.0	7.2	1.4	1.0	13
2016	AA	Mississippi	8	2	0	78	61	2.76	1.14	23.8	197	25	75	2.08	4.0	7.0	1.7	0.2	36
2016	AAA	Gwinnett	4	7	0	67	65	6.56	1.79	20.6	264	34	61	4.83	7.0	8.7	1.3	0.5	-13

RHP pitcher had disastrous Triple-A debut as command and control issues continue to plague him. FB has average velocity but plays up due to late arm-side run and sink. Power slurve has solid 2-plane movement. CU has average upside. Command is better suited for pen.

Enns,Dietrich — SP — New York (A)

EXP MLB DEBUT: 2017 | H/W: 6-1 210 | FUT: #4 starter | 7C

Thrws L Age 25
2012 (19) Central Mich

Velo	Pitch	Grade
87-92	FB	+++
80-83	SL	+++
74-77	CB	++
79-82	CU	+++

Year	Lev	Team	W	L	Sv	IP	K	ERA	WHIP	BF/G	OBA	H%	S%	xERA	Ctl	Dom	Cmd	hr/9	BPV
2015	Rk	GCL Yankees 2	1	0	0	11	15	0.00	1.08	14.4	161	27	100	1.27	4.9	12.2	2.5	0.0	106
2015	A+	Tampa	1	1	0	47	40	0.76	0.87	17.4	169	23	90	0.87	2.7	7.6	2.9	0.0	83
2016	AA	Trenton	7	2	0	70	74	1.93	1.21	23.5	218	30	85	2.64	3.9	9.5	2.5	0.4	85
2016	AAA	Scranton/WB	7	2	1	65	50	1.52	1.12	18.3	204	25	89	2.30	3.6	6.9	1.9	0.4	45

Breakout prospect who didn't allow an ER in April and flourished despite mediocre repertoire. Hides ball well in deceptive delivery and arm speed adds sneaky quick FB and movement to impressive CU. Lacks put away pitch, but can be effectively wild. Could be interesting situational RP as he is terrific against LHH.

Escobar,Luis — SP — Pittsburgh

EXP MLB DEBUT: 2020 | H/W: 6-1 155 | FUT: #3 starter | 7D

Thrws R Age 20
2013 FA (CB)

Velo	Pitch	Grade
90-93	FB	++++
	CB	++
84-84	CU	+++

Year	Lev	Team	W	L	Sv	IP	K	ERA	WHIP	BF/G	OBA	H%	S%	xERA	Ctl	Dom	Cmd	hr/9	BPV
2015	Rk	GCL Pirates	2	1	0	40	37	3.58	1.04	14.1	204	27	63	1.91	2.9	8.3	2.8	0.2	89
2015	A-	West Virginia	0	0	0	6	5	5.90	1.80	14.1	289	36	64	4.75	5.9	7.4	1.3	0.0	-9
2016	A-	West Virginia	6	5	0	67	61	2.95	1.16	17.8	209	26	76	2.55	3.8	8.2	2.2	0.5	64

Short, slender RHP from Columbia has a live arm and attacks hitters with a plus 90-93 mph FB that has good, late life and tops out at 96 mph. Mixes a CB that flashes as plus, but is inconsistent, and an average CU. FB command is fringy, but he's athletic and hitters in the NYPL had difficulty squaring him up.

Eshelman,Thomas — SP — Philadelphia

EXP MLB DEBUT: 2017 | H/W: 6-3 210 | FUT: #4 starter | 7C

Thrws R Age 22
2015 (2) Cal State Fullerton

Velo	Pitch	Grade
89-92	FB	+++
75-77	CB	++
	CU	++

Year	Lev	Team	W	L	Sv	IP	K	ERA	WHIP	BF/G	OBA	H%	S%	xERA	Ctl	Dom	Cmd	hr/9	BPV
2015	NCAA	Cal St Fullerton	8	5	1	137	139	1.58	0.82	26.2	214	29	82	1.54	0.5	9.1	19.9	0.3	170
2015	Rk	GCL Astros	0	1	0	4	3	4.50	1.25	8.1	210	27	60	2.30	4.5	6.8	1.5	0.0	18
2015	A	Quad Cities	0	0	0	6	5	4.43	1.97	14.6	343	42	75	6.03	4.4	7.4	1.7	0.0	31
2016	A+	Clearwater	4	2	0	59	64	3.35	1.17	21.4	258	33	76	3.68	1.7	9.7	5.8	1.1	148
2016	AA	Reading	5	5	0	61	55	5.16	1.57	20.6	314	39	66	5.10	2.5	8.1	3.2	0.6	96

Continued to fill up the strike zone, but was hit hard upon mid-season promotion to Double-A. With FB command as his top skill, keeping hitters off balance will be his ticket to the majors. Strikeout rate held up, so that's a good sign, but the upper minors will be the test of whether his future is a back-end starter or middle reliever.

Espada,Jose — SP — Toronto

EXP MLB DEBUT: 2020 | H/W: 6-0 170 | FUT: #4 starter | 7D

Thrws R Age 20
2015 (5) HS (PR)

Velo	Pitch	Grade
88-92	FB	+++
77-79	CB	+++
	CU	++

Year	Lev	Team	W	L	Sv	IP	K	ERA	WHIP	BF/G	OBA	H%	S%	xERA	Ctl	Dom	Cmd	hr/9	BPV
2015	Rk	GCL Blue Jays	0	2	0	34	31	3.43	0.97	12.9	206	25	67	2.28	2.1	8.2	3.9	0.8	108
2016	Rk	Bluefield	3	4	1	53	32	4.92	1.25	18.0	265	29	62	3.98	2.0	5.4	2.7	1.0	61

Short, polished SP with athletic, clean delivery. Possesses above average command, though low K rate due to lack of out pitch. Likes to sequence and set up hitters with best pitch being CB. Spots FB low in zone and throws CB for strikes. CU in infancy stage and lacks size and projection for frontline guy.

Espinoza,Anderson — SP — San Diego

EXP MLB DEBUT: 2019 | H/W: 6-0 160 | FUT: #1 starter | 9C

Thrws R Age 19
2014 FA (VZ)

Velo	Pitch	Grade
93-97	FB	++++
76-78	CB	++++
83-86	CU	+++

Year	Lev	Team	W	L	Sv	IP	K	ERA	WHIP	BF/G	OBA	H%	S%	xERA	Ctl	Dom	Cmd	hr/9	BPV
2015	Rk	GCL Red Sox	0	1	0	40	40	0.68	0.83	14.6	175	25	91	0.81	2.0	9.0	4.4	0.0	125
2015	A	Greenville	0	1	0	3	4	11.61	1.94	14.7	314	46	33	5.42	5.8	11.6	2.0	0.0	70
2016	A	Fort Wayne	1	3	0	32	28	4.77	1.43	17.1	296	37	64	4.17	2.2	7.9	3.5	0.3	99
2016	A	Greenville	5	8	0	76	72	4.38	1.37	18.7	264	35	66	3.51	3.2	8.5	2.7	0.2	85

Hard-throwing teenage RH acquired in Drew Pomeranz with number 1 starter upside. FB lives in the mid-90s with advanced command to all quadrants of zone. Plus CB and above-average CU more advanced than age/level. Small stature may be lone limitation. Can't rule out near-future growth spurt.

Faria,Jacob — SP — Tampa Bay

EXP MLB DEBUT: 2017 | H/W: 6-4 200 | FUT: #4 starter | 7B

Thrws R Age 23
2011 (10) HS (CA)

Velo	Pitch	Grade
90-95	FB	+++
78-80	CB	+++
82-85	CU	+++

Year	Lev	Team	W	L	Sv	IP	K	ERA	WHIP	BF/G	OBA	H%	S%	xERA	Ctl	Dom	Cmd	hr/9	BPV
2014	A	Bowling Green	7	9	0	119	107	3.47	1.22	20.9	252	31	73	3.37	2.4	8.1	3.3	0.7	98
2015	A+	Charlotte	10	1	0	74	63	1.34	0.99	23.5	196	26	86	1.58	2.7	7.7	2.9	0.1	84
2015	AA	Montgomery	7	3	0	75	96	2.52	1.09	22.6	197	29	79	2.27	3.6	11.5	3.2	0.6	128
2016	AA	Montgomery	1	6	0	83	93	4.22	1.20	23.9	215	29	64	2.72	3.9	10.1	2.6	0.5	94
2016	AAA	Durham	4	4	0	67	64	3.75	1.16	20.6	195	24	70	2.77	4.3	8.6	2.0	0.9	57

Tall, deceptive SP is advancing quickly as stuff has ticked up. Throws sinking FB with conviction and induces fair share of groundballs. Uses high 3/4 slot to pitch downhill and hitters have difficulty elevating FB. Repeats delivery and shows feel for changing speeds. Walk rate needs to be tamed in order to realize potential.

Faulkner,Andrew — RP — Texas

EXP MLB DEBUT: 2015 | H/W: 6-3 205 | FUT: Setup reliever | 6A

Thrws L Age 24
2011 (14) HS (SC)

Velo	Pitch	Grade
91-96	FB	+++
78-82	SL	++
82-85	CU	+++

Year	Lev	Team	W	L	Sv	IP	K	ERA	WHIP	BF/G	OBA	H%	S%	xERA	Ctl	Dom	Cmd	hr/9	BPV
2015	AA	Frisco	7	4	1	92	90	4.20	1.42	14.0	244	31	72	3.97	4.6	8.8	1.9	0.9	52
2015	AAA	Round Rock	0	0	0	8	13	0.00	0.38	4.3	81	17	100		1.1	14.6	13.0	0.0	251
2015	MLB	Texas	0	0	0	9	10	2.93	1.20	3.4	236	27	89	4.29	2.9	9.8	3.3	2.0	115
2016	AAA	Round Rock	5	3	4	45	39	3.99	1.31	4.5	235	29	70	3.31	4.0	7.8	2.0	0.6	50
2016	MLB	Texas	0	0	0	6	1	7.26	1.94	3.3	314	23	78	9.61	5.8	1.5	0.3	4.4	-113

Deceptive, strong pitcher who was converted to RP in '15 and will likely stay there. Made Opening Day roster and has success against LHH. FB features late, heavy life and throws strikes with it. Has short-arm delivery that makes pitches quicker, but lacks breaking ball. CU can be fierce at times with late sinking action.

Fedde,Erick — SP — Washington

EXP MLB DEBUT: 2018 | H/W: 6-4 180 | FUT: #3 starter | 8B

Thrws R Age 24
2014 (1) UNLV

Velo	Pitch	Grade
92-96	FB	++++
81-83	SL	++++
85-87	CU	++

Year	Lev	Team	W	L	Sv	IP	K	ERA	WHIP	BF/G	OBA	H%	S%	xERA	Ctl	Dom	Cmd	hr/9	BPV
2015	A-	Auburn	4	1	0	35	36	2.57	1.31	18.1	278	37	80	3.57	2.1	9.3	4.5	0.3	129
2015	A	Hagerstown	1	2	0	29	23	4.34	1.10	19.0	227	28	58	2.43	2.5	7.1	2.9	0.3	79
2016	A+	Potomac	6	4	0	91	95	2.86	1.14	20.1	248	32	77	3.13	1.9	9.4	5.0	0.7	136
2016	AA	Harrisburg	2	1	0	29	28	4.02	1.48	25.0	287	37	71	4.17	3.1	8.7	2.8	0.3	90

Former first-rounder regained strength and velocity as season went on in first full year since Tommy John surgery. Showcases lively mid-90s FB and hard SL that both get swings and misses. CU still work in progress. Athletic, repeatable delivery, bulldog worker, classic pitcher's frame.

Fenter,Gray — SP — Baltimore

EXP MLB DEBUT: 2020 | H/W: 6-0 200 | FUT: #3 starter | 8E

Thrws R Age 21
2015 (7) HS (AR)

Velo	Pitch	Grade
89-94	FB	+++
75-80	CB	+++
81-84	SL	++
82-84	CU	+

Year	Lev	Team	W	L	Sv	IP	K	ERA	WHIP	BF/G	OBA	H%	S%	xERA	Ctl	Dom	Cmd	hr/9	BPV
2015	Rk	GCL Orioles	0	0	0	21	18	1.70	0.99	9.0	201	26	81	1.53	2.5	7.6	3.0	0.0	87

Short, stout SP who missed entire season after Tommy John surgery in April. When healthy, owns a solid, though inconsistent, four pitch mix. Likes to locate his FB low in zone and mix in CB that exhibits big-bending action. Doesn't have much projection, but can get by with existing FB. May be candidate for bullpen if secondary pitches don't develop as hoped.

Fernandez,Junior

SP | St. Louis | EXP MLB DEBUT: 2019 | H/W: 6-1 180 | FUT: #2 SP/closer | 9D

Thrws R Age 20
2014 FA (DR)

Pitch	Year	Lev	Team	W	L	Sv	IP	K	ERA	WHIP	BF/G	OBA	H%	S%	xERA	Ctl	Dom	Cmd	hr/9	BPV
94-98 FB +++++	2015	Rk	GCL Cardinals	3	2	0	51	58	3.88	1.35	19.3	273	39	68	3.35	2.6	10.2	3.9	0.0	131
85-88 SL ++	2015	A+	Palm Beach	0	0	0	6	5	1.45	1.61	13.7	314	39	90	4.65	2.9	7.3	2.5	0.0	70
78-81 CU +++	2016	A	Peoria	6	5	0	78	63	3.34	1.34	23.2	244	30	75	3.28	3.9	7.3	1.9	0.3	43
	2016	A+	Palm Beach	2	2	0	43	25	5.42	1.57	19.0	283	31	66	4.88	4.2	5.2	1.3	0.8	-1

Lean, athletic hurler comes after hitters with a double plus 94-98 mph FB that tops at 100. Ditched his CB for a potentially plus hard SL and mixes in average CU. Started well in the MWL, but High-A hitters squared him up. Inconsistent mechanics and a tendency to overthrow limit his effectiveness for now, but the upside is huge.

Fernandez,Pedro

SP | Kansas City | EXP MLB DEBUT: 2017 | H/W: 6-0 175 | FUT: #4 starter | 7C

Thrws R Age 22
2011 FA (DR)

Pitch	Year	Lev	Team	W	L	Sv	IP	K	ERA	WHIP	BF/G	OBA	H%	S%	xERA	Ctl	Dom	Cmd	hr/9	BPV
	2014	A	Lexington	1	8	3	61	60	5.01	1.36	16.0	225	28	64	3.57	4.9	8.8	1.8	0.9	46
91-94 FB +++	2015	A	Lexington	6	2	0	78	89	3.12	1.03	16.7	194	28	68	1.73	3.1	10.3	3.3	0.2	119
80-83 SL ++	2015	A+	Wilmington	0	6	0	32	25	8.94	1.99	22.1	381	45	52	7.31	2.2	7.0	3.1	0.6	83
74-76 CB ++	2016	A+	Wilmington	3	1	0	33	31	2.17	1.05	21.4	204	28	77	1.72	3.0	8.4	2.8	0.0	89
81-84 CU +++	2016	AA	NW Arkansas	1	2	0	29	19	4.03	1.34	15.1	262	30	70	3.80	3.1	5.9	1.9	0.6	40

Short, consistent SP who ended season in July. Throws from lower slot and has added polish last few seasons. Cleaned up delivery and arm slot and now has much better command and control. Pitches often lack movement and can be victimized by flyballs. FB is best pitch, though CU can be dynamite weapon against LHH. Added SL to repertoire.

Ferrell,Riley

RP | Houston | EXP MLB DEBUT: 2018 | H/W: 6-2 200 | FUT: Setup reliever | 7C

Thrws R Age 23
2015 (3) Texas Christian

Pitch	Year	Lev	Team	W	L	Sv	IP	K	ERA	WHIP	BF/G	OBA	H%	S%	xERA	Ctl	Dom	Cmd	hr/9	BPV
92-96 FB ++++																				
83-87 SL +++	2015	NCAA	Texas Christian	1	3	14	31	53	2.60	0.96	3.7	102	19	75	0.89	5.8	15.3	2.7	0.6	137
CU ++	2015	A	Quad Cities	0	0	1	16	17	1.11	1.42	5.7	180	26	91	2.35	7.2	9.4	1.3	0.0	-7
	2016	A+	Lancaster	0	1	4	10	14	1.80	1.10	4.9	242	36	90	3.11	1.8	12.6	7.0	0.9	196

Quick-armed SP who underwent shoulder surgery due to aneurysm. Has terrific arm strength and can pump double-plus FB impeccably. Uses overhand delivery and pure strength to throw everything hard. Wipeout SL can be go-to pitch when ahead, though has tendency to overthrow in short stints. Lot of effort in delivery and will stay in pen.

Fillmyer,Heath

SP | Oakland | EXP MLB DEBUT: 2018 | H/W: 6-1 180 | FUT: #4 starter | 7B

Thrws R Age 22
2014 (5) Mercer Co CC

Pitch	Year	Lev	Team	W	L	Sv	IP	K	ERA	WHIP	BF/G	OBA	H%	S%	xERA	Ctl	Dom	Cmd	hr/9	BPV
90-96 FB +++	2014	Rk	Azl Athletics	1	0	0	9	10	2.93	1.09	6.0	162	24	70	1.31	4.9	9.8	2.0	0.0	62
79-80 CB ++	2015	A	Beloit	3	13	0	99	77	4.99	1.70	19.5	286	34	72	5.29	5.1	7.0	1.4	0.9	7
84-88 CU +++	2016	A+	Stockton	5	6	0	95	89	3.60	1.39	22.2	274	35	73	3.83	2.9	8.4	2.9	0.4	90
	2016	AA	Midland	2	0	0	39	29	2.54	1.00	18.6	220	26	78	2.44	1.8	6.7	3.6	0.7	89

Emerging prospect who was elevated to AA and pitched well all year. Has impact arm with FB that can feature devastating, late action. Has athleticism and quick-armed delivery while CU continues to show promise. Has some effort and may move to pen without better CB. No problem throwing strikes.

Finley,Drew

SP | New York (A) | EXP MLB DEBUT: 2019 | H/W: 6-3 200 | FUT: #4 starter | 7D

Thrws R Age 20
2015 (3) HS (CA)

Pitch	Year	Lev	Team	W	L	Sv	IP	K	ERA	WHIP	BF/G	OBA	H%	S%	xERA	Ctl	Dom	Cmd	hr/9	BPV
88-92 FB +++																				
77-79 CB +++																				
82-84 CU ++	2015	Rk	Pulaski	0	1	0	32	41	3.94	1.63	11.9	268	33	88	6.33	5.3	11.5	2.2	2.5	81
	2016	A-	Staten Island	0	3	0	27	20	4.32	1.11	17.7	216	25	61	2.63	3.0	6.6	2.2	0.7	57

Young pitcher who doesn't get much pub, but has makings of solid SP. Learning to polish mechanics and repeat delivery consistently. No pitches are plus at present, though FB gets good movement and hard CB can be effective. Uses height to throw downhill and features average command. Gaining confidence and could be sleeper.

Flaherty,Jack

SP | St. Louis | EXP MLB DEBUT: 2019 | H/W: 6-4 205 | FUT: #3 starter | 8C

Thrws R Age 21
2014 (1) HS (CA)

Pitch	Year	Lev	Team	W	L	Sv	IP	K	ERA	WHIP	BF/G	OBA	H%	S%	xERA	Ctl	Dom	Cmd	hr/9	BPV
88-92 FB +++																				
73-75 CB ++	2014	Rk	GCL Cardinals	1	1	0	22	28	1.62	0.99	10.6	223	33	86	2.15	1.6	11.4	7.0	0.4	179
77-80 SL +++	2015	A	Peoria	9	3	0	95	97	2.84	1.29	21.7	256	34	77	3.15	2.9	9.2	3.1	0.2	104
80-83 CU +++	2016	A+	Palm Beach	5	9	0	134	126	3.56	1.30	23.0	254	32	73	3.48	3.0	8.5	2.8	0.5	89

Former 1st rounder has a good four-pitch mix and was solid in the FSL. FB sits at 88-92 most nights. Also throws a SL, CB, and CU, all of which have the potential to be average or better but none project as plus. Good athlete with repeatable mechanics. Fills up the strike zone and knows how to pitch.

Flexen,Chris

SP | New York (N) | EXP MLB DEBUT: 2018 | H/W: 6-3 235 | FUT: #4 starter | 7D

Thrws R Age 22
2012 (14) HS (CA)

Pitch	Year	Lev	Team	W	L	Sv	IP	K	ERA	WHIP	BF/G	OBA	H%	S%	xERA	Ctl	Dom	Cmd	hr/9	BPV
	2014	A	Savannah	3	5	0	69	46	4.83	1.62	23.6	278	32	70	4.76	4.8	6.0	1.2	0.7	-4
90-92 FB +++	2015	Rk	GCL Mets	0	0	0	6	5	0.00	0.50	6.6	106	14	100		1.5	7.5	5.0	0.0	113
74-77 CB +++	2015	A-	Brooklyn	0	2	0	12	13	5.21	1.90	19.0	305	42	70	5.21	6.0	9.7	1.6	0.0	31
CU ++	2015	A	Savannah	4	0	0	33	33	1.90	1.05	21.4	230	32	80	2.04	1.9	8.9	4.7	0.0	128
	2016	A+	St. Lucie	10	9	0	134	95	3.56	1.31	22.2	249	30	72	3.33	3.4	6.4	1.9	0.4	40

Physically filled out RHP with very average repertoire on mound. Walk rate continues to climb. Control guy prior to '14 TJS. FB sits low 90s. Can reach back for mid-90s heat. Depth on CB has improved and has a feel for a CU. Feel for pitching gives shot at back-end ceiling. Likely middle reliever if swing-and-miss pitch does not develop.

Flores,Bernardo

SP | Chicago (A) | EXP MLB DEBUT: 2019 | H/W: 6-3 170 | FUT: #3 starter | 8E

Thrws L Age 21
2016 (7) USC

Pitch	Year	Lev	Team	W	L	Sv	IP	K	ERA	WHIP	BF/G	OBA	H%	S%	xERA	Ctl	Dom	Cmd	hr/9	BPV
90-94 FB +++																				
81-87 CT +++	2016	NCAA	USC	1	0	0	41	36	6.77	1.60	11.4	301	37	56	5.03	3.5	7.9	2.3	0.7	65
78-82 CB ++	2016	Rk	Great Falls	6	1	0	59	45	3.66	1.27	21.9	275	33	72	3.77	1.8	6.9	3.8	0.6	92
CU +++	2016	Rk	Azl White Sox	0	1	0	6	7	1.50	0.67	7.0	191	29	75	0.58	0.0	10.5		0.0	207

Quick-armed SP who had impressive pro debut with extreme groundball tendencies. Keeps ball down with solid-average FB with heavy, late action. Throws on downhill plane which allows FB to play up. Mixes in nifty CT and average CU. Lacks consistency in fringy CB and fails to repeat arm speed and slot. Very tough on LHH.

Flores,Kendry

SP | St. Louis | EXP MLB DEBUT: 2015 | H/W: 6-2 195 | FUT: #5 SP/swingman | 6B

Thrws R Age 25
2009 FA (DR)

Pitch	Year	Lev	Team	W	L	Sv	IP	K	ERA	WHIP	BF/G	OBA	H%	S%	xERA	Ctl	Dom	Cmd	hr/9	BPV
	2015	MLB	Miami	1	2	0	12	9	5.16	1.64	7.8	317	39	65	4.78	3.0	6.6	2.3	0.0	58
88-93 FB +++	2016	A+	Jupiter	0	0	0	5	2	0.00	0.40	16.1	124	14	100		0.0	3.6		0.0	83
CB +++	2016	AA	Jacksonville	0	0	0	5	4	1.73	1.35	21.7	323	40	86	4.13	0.0	6.9		0.0	143
SL +++	2016	AAA	New Orleans	3	6	0	91	74	4.54	1.56	22.2	286	34	72	4.83	3.9	7.3	1.9	0.8	46
CU +++	2016	MLB	Miami	0	0	0	3	1	0.00	1.33	12.5	106	12	100	1.45	9.0	3.0	0.3	0.0	-171

Athletic RHP comes after hitters with a 89-93 mph FB that he locates well to both sides of the plate. He backs up the FB with an above-avg CU, SL, and CB. He spots the FB well and has good command. Knows how to pitch and keeps hitters off balance by changing speeds. Profiles as a back-end starter with limited fantasy value.

Franklin,Austin

SP | Tampa Bay | EXP MLB DEBUT: 2020 | H/W: 6-3 215 | FUT: #3 starter | 8D

Thrws R Age 19
2016 (3) HS (FL)

Pitch	Year	Lev	Team	W	L	Sv	IP	K	ERA	WHIP	BF/G	OBA	H%	S%	xERA	Ctl	Dom	Cmd	hr/9	BPV
90-95 FB +++																				
77-80 CB ++																				
CU ++																				
	2016	Rk	GCL Devil Rays	1	2	1	43	40	2.71	1.07	15.2	198	27	72	1.68	3.3	8.4	2.5	0.0	78

Young, promising SP who enjoyed pro debut with advanced FB location and solid angle to plate. CB developing into true swing-and-miss pitch while CU needs significant work. Adds sink to FB at lower velocities and can rear back and hit mid-90s at times. Needs time to iron out consistency of arm slot and ability to throw strikes.

Freeland,Kyle

SP | Colorado | EXP MLB DEBUT: 2017 | H/W: 6-3 170 | FUT: #3 starter | 8C

Thrws L Age 23
2014 (1) Evansville

Pitch	Year	Lev	Team	W	L	Sv	IP	K	ERA	WHIP	BF/G	OBA	H%	S%	xERA	Ctl	Dom	Cmd	hr/9	BPV
	2014	A	Asheville	2	0	0	21	18	0.85	0.85	15.6	190	24	94	1.45	1.7	7.6	4.5	0.4	110
91-94 FB ++++	2015	Rk	Grand Junction	0	0	0	7	9	0.00	0.57	11.9	92	16	100		2.6	11.6	4.5	0.0	157
80-83 SL +++	2015	A+	Modesto	3	2	0	39	19	4.82	1.43	23.8	303	32	69	5.12	1.8	4.4	2.4	1.1	47
86-88 CT ++	2016	AA	Hartford	5	7	0	88	51	3.88	1.24	25.5	253	28	71	3.69	2.6	5.2	2.0	0.9	43
86-88 CU ++	2016	AAA	Albuquerque	6	3	0	73	57	3.93	1.37	25.5	282	33	73	4.35	2.3	7.0	3.0	0.9	81

8th overall pick in '14 was finally healthy, but posted pedestrian numbers. FB sits in at 91-94 mph and tops at 96 mph with good late sink. SL can be plus, but remains inconsistent. Mixes in CT and good CU with fade to keep hitters at bay. Spots his FB to all parts of the plate and has a high pitching IQ, but needs to show more.

Fried,Max — SP — Atlanta

EXP MLB DEBUT: 2018 | H/W: 6-4 185 | FUT: #3 starter | 8D

Thrws L Age 23
2012 (1) HS (CA)

Velo	Pitch	Grade
91-93	FB	+++
75-77	CB	++++
81-84	CU	+++

Year	Lev	Team	W	L	Sv	IP	K	ERA	WHIP	BF/G	OBA	H%	S%	xERA	Ctl	Dom	Cmd	hr/9	BPV
2012	Rk	Azl Padres	0	1	0	17	17	3.66	1.16	6.9	224	29	68	2.72	3.1	8.9	2.8	0.5	93
2013	A	Fort Wayne	6	7	0	118	100	3.50	1.38	21.6	243	30	75	3.53	4.3	7.6	1.8	0.5	40
2014	Rk	Azl Padres	0	0	0	5	8	5.40	2.20	8.4	362	57	73	6.88	5.4	14.4	2.7	0.0	131
2014	A	Fort Wayne	0	1	0	5	2	5.19	1.73	11.8	323	32	75	6.76	3.5	3.5	1.0	1.7	-13
2016	A	Rome	8	7	0	103	112	3.93	1.30	20.2	230	30	72	3.47	4.1	9.8	2.4	0.9	83

Missing almost two full seasons after Tommy John surgery, it took half the season to regain past form. FB command is reminiscent of traditional California prep lefties Barry Zito & Tyler Skaggs. Command needs to be good enough to unleash plus CB. CU came along way in short period of time to up profile back to #3 starter.

Fry,Paul — RP — Seattle

EXP MLB DEBUT: 2017 | H/W: 6-0 190 | FUT: Setup reliever | 6B

Thrws L Age 24
2013 (17) St. Clair Co CC

Velo	Pitch	Grade
89-94	FB	++++
83-85	SL	+++
84-85	CU	++

Year	Lev	Team	W	L	Sv	IP	K	ERA	WHIP	BF/G	OBA	H%	S%	xERA	Ctl	Dom	Cmd	hr/9	BPV
2013	Rk	Azl Mariners	2	3	1	34	34	4.50	1.44	10.3	300	38	70	4.72	2.1	9.0	4.3	0.8	123
2014	A	Clinton	4	4	2	66	77	2.72	1.29	7.1	218	32	77	2.58	4.5	10.5	2.3	0.1	85
2015	A+	Bakersfield	4	3	2	55	70	2.13	1.09	7.7	229	35	78	2.09	2.3	11.5	5.0	0.0	162
2015	AA	Jackson	0	2	7	25	43	1.80	1.28	4.7	238	44	84	2.64	3.6	15.5	4.3	0.0	199
2016	AAA	Tacoma	3	1	0	55	65	2.78	1.44	4.9	236	34	79	3.21	5.1	10.6	2.1	0.2	72

Short RP with outstanding sinker and induces high amount of groundballs. Flown under radar, but continues to post high K rates with hard SL and deceptive CU. Rarely allows HR (5 HR in 235 career innings). Hitters have difficulty making hard contact against him. Lacks stamina and durability so pen is only option.

Fulmer,Carson — SP — Chicago (A)

EXP MLB DEBUT: 2016 | H/W: 6-0 195 | FUT: #2 SP/closer | 8B

Thrws R Age 23
2015 (1) Vanderbilt

Velo	Pitch	Grade
92-96	FB	++++
79-81	CB	++++
82-84	CU	++

Year	Lev	Team	W	L	Sv	IP	K	ERA	WHIP	BF/G	OBA	H%	S%	xERA	Ctl	Dom	Cmd	hr/9	BPV
2015	Rk	Azl White Sox	0	0	0	1		0.00	1.00	3.8	262	35	100	2.32	0.0	9.0		0.0	180
2015	A+	Winston-Salem	0	0	0	22	25	2.05	1.14	10.9	205	27	87	2.69	3.7	10.2	2.8	0.8	103
2016	AA	Birmingham	4	9	0	87	90	4.76	1.53	22.3	251	33	69	4.17	5.3	9.3	1.8	0.7	43
2016	AAA	Charlotte	2	1	0	16	14	3.94	1.19	16.0	237	29	67	3.00	2.8	7.9	2.8	0.6	84
2016	MLB	Chi White Sox	0	2	0	11	10	8.84	1.70	6.3	275	32	47	5.78	5.6	8.0	1.4	1.6	11

Short, max-effort pitcher who was SP in minors, but RP upon recall to CHW. Has nifty power arsenal, led by plus FB and CB. Gets terrific break and spin on CB and can blow FB by hitters in short stints. Throws with violent arm action and has shown feel for CU at times. Command will come and go and could lead to pen full time.

Funkhouser,Kyle — SP — Detroit

EXP MLB DEBUT: 2018 | H/W: 6-2 220 | FUT: #3 starter | 8D

Thrws R Age 23
2016 (4) Louisville

Velo	Pitch	Grade
89-95	FB	+++
81-85	SL	+++
77-80	CB	++
81-83	CU	++

Year	Lev	Team	W	L	Sv	IP	K	ERA	WHIP	BF/G	OBA	H%	S%	xERA	Ctl	Dom	Cmd	hr/9	BPV
2016	NCAA	Louisville	9	3	0	93	95	3.87	1.26	23.7	210	27	71	3.03	4.5	9.2	2.0	0.8	61
2016	A-	Connecticut	0	2	0	37	34	2.67	1.13	11.3	245	32	74	2.43	1.9	8.2	4.3	0.0	114

Physical SP who fell in draft, but showed impressive mix in pros. Could eventually end up in pen, but has four pitches and good velocity. Uses two and four-seam FB and gets ample movement with sinker. SL ahead of CB at present and both could be K pitches in time. CU thrown with ideal arm speed, but lacks ideal movement. Needs to address command.

Gallen,Zac — SP — St. Louis

EXP MLB DEBUT: 2019 | H/W: 6-2 191 | FUT: #4 starter | 7C

Thrws R Age 21
2016 (3) North Carolina

Velo	Pitch	Grade
88-92	FB	+++
85-88	CT	+++
74-77	CB	+
80-83	CU	+++

Year	Lev	Team	W	L	Sv	IP	K	ERA	WHIP	BF/G	OBA	H%	S%	xERA	Ctl	Dom	Cmd	hr/9	BPV
2016	NCAA	North Carolina	5	6	0	90	95	2.69	0.99	26.4	211	29	71	1.81	2.1	9.5	4.5	0.2	132
2016	Rk	GCL Cardinals	0	0	1	9	15	1.96	0.76	5.5	212	39	71	1.02	0.0	14.7		0.0	282

Cards 3rd round pick in 2016 features four-pitch mix, three of which are average to above. Works of a low-90s FB that has good late life. Mixes in a CT, CU, and below-average CB. Was solid in limited pro debut and will likely start 2017 in the MWL. Profiles as a solid back-end starter.

Gant,John — RP — St. Louis

EXP MLB DEBUT: 2016 | H/W: 6-3 200 | FUT: Middle reliever | 6A

Thrws R Age 24
2011 (21) HS (FL)

Velo	Pitch	Grade
89-93	FB	+++
73-76	CB	+++
79-81	CU	+++

Year	Lev	Team	W	L	Sv	IP	K	ERA	WHIP	BF/G	OBA	H%	S%	xERA	Ctl	Dom	Cmd	hr/9	BPV
2015	AA	Binghamton	4	5	0	59	43	4.72	1.57	23.6	287	34	68	4.43	4.0	6.5	1.7	0.3	29
2015	AA	Mississippi	4	0	0	40	43	2.01	1.04	22.2	198	28	80	1.83	3.1	9.6	3.1	0.2	107
2016	A	Rome	0	0	0	3	2	0.00	0.67	10.5	106	13	100		3.0	6.0	2.0	0.0	45
2016	AAA	Gwinnett	3	3	0	56	57	4.18	1.43	19.8	269	34	72	4.24	3.5	9.2	2.6	0.8	87
2016	MLB	Atlanta	1	4	0	50	49	4.86	1.50	10.8	277	34	71	4.97	3.8	8.8	2.3	1.3	75

RHP spent most of '16 driving I-85 between ATL & Gwinnett. Funky delivery creates issues with batter readiness. Controls and commands 3 average pitches. Struggles a couple times through the order, lacking swing-and-miss option to continually give hitters fits. Package plays up in pen. Over-the-top FB is groundball machine.

Garcia,Edgar — RP — Philadelphia

EXP MLB DEBUT: 2020 | H/W: 6-1 180 | FUT: Middle reliever | 7D

Thrws R Age 20
2014 FA (DR)

Velo	Pitch	Grade
91-94	FB	++++
80-83	SL	+++
	CU	++

Year	Lev	Team	W	L	Sv	IP	K	ERA	WHIP	BF/G	OBA	H%	S%	xERA	Ctl	Dom	Cmd	hr/9	BPV
2015	Rk	GCL Phillies	1	2	2	32	34	3.35	1.09	10.5	229	31	68	2.36	2.2	9.5	4.3	0.3	129
2016	A	Lakewood	4	1	2	61	59	2.80	1.21	9.1	255	32	81	3.60	2.2	8.7	3.9	0.9	115

Another under-the-radar young PHI hurler. Quick arm yields a low-to-mid 90s fastball and a SL, which both have plus potential. Also throws a work-in-progress change-up. Worked both out of bullpen and as a starter in Low-A, though many feel his eventual role is as a reliever due to his high-effort delivery. Fielded excellent K/BB ratios so far.

Garcia,Elniery — SP — Philadelphia

EXP MLB DEBUT: 2019 | H/W: 6-0 155 | FUT: #4 starter | 7C

Thrws L Age 22
2011 FA (DR)

Velo	Pitch	Grade
91-94	FB	+++
74-77	CB	+++
83-86	CU	+++

Year	Lev	Team	W	L	Sv	IP	K	ERA	WHIP	BF/G	OBA	H%	S%	xERA	Ctl	Dom	Cmd	hr/9	BPV
2013	Rk	GCL Phillies	1	3	0	36	31	5.22	1.57	17.7	296	37	64	4.51	3.5	7.7	2.2	0.2	63
2014	Rk	GCL Phillies	2	2	0	26	23	2.08	1.15	14.8	262	34	80	2.71	1.4	8.0	5.8	0.0	124
2014	A-	Williamsport	0	0	0	4	5	6.43	1.90	5.0	336	42	71	7.73	4.3	10.7	2.5	2.1	95
2015	A	Lakewood	8	9	0	120	66	3.23	1.34	23.8	270	30	77	3.82	2.7	5.0	1.8	0.5	34
2016	A+	Clearwater	12	4	0	117	91	2.69	1.11	23.0	221	26	78	2.66	2.8	7.0	2.5	0.6	69

Small-framed lefty with good control and smooth, easy motion. Bumped up his FB velocity in 2016, which raises his ceiling. Tight-breaking CB is best secondary, which he also controls well. Good deception on his CU, which with some improvement would give him three average or better pitches. Little physical projection left, but ready for high minors.

Garcia,Jarlin — SP — Miami

EXP MLB DEBUT: 2018 | H/W: 6-3 215 | FUT: #4 starter | 7C

Thrws L Age 24
2011 FA (DR)

Velo	Pitch	Grade
90-95	FB	++++
82-85	CU	+++
	SL	++
	CB	+++

Year	Lev	Team	W	L	Sv	IP	K	ERA	WHIP	BF/G	OBA	H%	S%	xERA	Ctl	Dom	Cmd	hr/9	BPV
2015	A+	Jupiter	3	5	0	97	69	3.06	1.23	21.8	260	31	75	3.23	2.1	6.4	3.0	0.4	76
2015	AA	Jacksonville	1	3	0	36	35	4.97	1.52	22.4	271	34	69	4.69	4.2	8.7	2.1	1.0	61
2016	Rk	GCL Marlins	0	0	0	4	6	0.00	0.25	4.1	81	16	100		0.0	13.5		0.0	261
2016	A+	Jupiter	0	0	0	7	5	1.29	0.71	4.9	168	17	100	1.69	1.3	6.4	5.0	1.3	99
2016	AA	Jacksonville	1	3	0	39	27	4.59	1.25	17.7	256	29	64	3.76	2.5	6.2	2.5	0.9	61

Talented Dominican lefty can't stay healthy and was limited to 50.2 IP in 2016 (triceps injury). FB sits at 90-95 mph and backs it up with a decent CU, CB, and a power SL. CB is his 2nd best offering, but needs consistency. Delivery is max-effort and given injury history, a move to relief is likely. Pounds the zone and has the stuff make an impact.

Garcia,Jason — SP — Baltimore

EXP MLB DEBUT: 2015 | H/W: 6-0 185 | FUT: Closer | 7C

Thrws R Age 24
2010 (17) HS (FL)

Velo	Pitch	Grade
91-97	FB	+++
82-87	SL	+++
	CU	+

Year	Lev	Team	W	L	Sv	IP	K	ERA	WHIP	BF/G	OBA	H%	S%	xERA	Ctl	Dom	Cmd	hr/9	BPV
2014	A	Greenville	2	1	3	35	37	3.84	1.36	16.4	238	33	69	2.91	4.3	9.5	2.2	0.0	71
2015	AA	Bowie	1	2	0	15	14	4.20	1.40	7.0	221	26	74	3.93	5.4	8.4	1.6	1.2	23
2015	MLB	Baltimore	1	0	0	29	22	4.32	1.44	5.9	233	27	72	3.93	5.2	6.8	1.3	0.9	-1
2016	AA	Bowie	6	10	0	123	71	4.75	1.55	22.4	283	32	68	4.38	3.9	5.2	1.3	0.4	5

Short, power-armed pitcher who returned to rotation after serving as RP in '15. Low K rate is surprising given power arsenal. Owns both a two seam FB and hard four-seamer and uses hard SL as his go-to pitch when ahead in count. Needs offspeed pitch against LHH as CU is well below average. Has proven healthy after injuries in past.

Garcia,Yeudy — SP — Pittsburgh

EXP MLB DEBUT: 2018 | H/W: 6-2 203 | FUT: #3 starter | 8D

Thrws R Age 24
2013 FA (DR)

Velo	Pitch	Grade
93-96	FB	++++
83-86	SL	++
85-87	CU	++

Year	Lev	Team	W	L	Sv	IP	K	ERA	WHIP	BF/G	OBA	H%	S%	xERA	Ctl	Dom	Cmd	hr/9	BPV
2015	A	West Virginia	12	5	1	124	112	2.10	1.07	16.1	208	27	81	2.09	3.0	8.1	2.7	0.3	84
2016	A+	Bradenton	6	8	1	127	127	2.76	1.38	20.6	254	33	81	3.64	3.8	9.0	2.4	0.5	77

Tall RHP from the D.R. had another solid season in the FSL. Attacks hitters with a plus 93-96 mph FB that tops out at 98 mph. He pitches effectively off the heater and keeps hitters honest with an above-avg hard SL and a show-me CU. Struggled at times with control, but misses plenty of bats.

Gardeck,Ian
RP | **San Francisco** | EXP MLB DEBUT: 2018 | H/W: 6-2 220 | FUT: Setup reliever | **7D**

Thrws R Age 26	
2012 (16) Alabama	
92-97 FB	++++
85-87 SL	++++
CU	+

Year	Lev	Team	W	L	Sv	IP	K	ERA	WHIP	BF/G	OBA	H%	S%	xERA	Ctl	Dom	Cmd	hr/9	BPV
2013	A	Augusta	4	3	1	56	66	3.21	1.52	5.5	222	32	78	3.38	6.4	10.6	1.7	0.3	35
2014	A-	Salem-Kaizer	2	1	1	13	24	2.75	1.37	4.6	159	35	78	1.95	7.6	16.5	2.2	0.0	111
2014	A+	San Jose	1	2	0	24	19	9.38	2.13	7.0	254	30	53	5.76	10.5	7.1	0.7	0.8	-137
2015	A+	San Jose	3	4	3	86	104	3.55	1.16	5.6	238	34	69	2.78	2.5	10.9	4.3	0.4	146
2016		did not pitch (injury)																	

Hard-throwing RP who missed season due to Tommy John surgery; should return in May/June. Throws with live arm and pitches aggressively to intimidate hitters. Has minimal effort in delivery and adds to plus FB. SL can overpower hitters from both sides, though shows little touch for changing speeds. Will have to prove health, but one to keep an eye on.

Garrett,Amir
SP | **Cincinnati** | EXP MLB DEBUT: 2017 | H/W: 6-5 210 | FUT: #3 starter | **8C**

Thrws L Age 24	
2011 (22) HS (NV)	
92-94 FB	++++
77-80 SL	+++
80-83 CU	+++

Year	Lev	Team	W	L	Sv	IP	K	ERA	WHIP	BF/G	OBA	H%	S%	xERA	Ctl	Dom	Cmd	hr/9	BPV
2013	A	Dayton	1	3	0	34	15	6.88	1.65	19.0	294	31	58	5.46	4.2	4.0	0.9	1.1	-25
2014	A	Dayton	7	8	0	133	127	3.65	1.25	20.0	235	30	72	3.28	3.4	8.6	2.5	0.7	79
2015	A+	Daytona	9	7	0	140	133	2.44	1.23	21.8	228	30	80	2.70	3.5	8.5	2.4	0.3	76
2016	AA	Pensacola	5	3	0	77	78	1.75	1.04	22.9	193	27	81	1.55	3.3	9.1	2.8	0.0	94
2016	AAA	Louisville	2	5	0	67	54	3.48	1.18	22.4	202	24	73	2.77	4.2	7.2	1.7	0.8	36

Former college hoopster who continues to make progress in his third year as full time baseball player. Consistency, especially commanding fastball, is lone sticking point of his ascent to CIN. Did a better job in '16 repeating delivery. FB is heavy and works away, and SL is potentially a tremendous weapon. CU has taken step forward.

Garrett,Braxton
SP | **Miami** | EXP MLB DEBUT: 2020 | H/W: 6-3 190 | FUT: #2 starter | **9D**

Thrws L Age 19	
2016 (1) HS (AL)	
91-94 FB	++++
75-78 CB	+++
CU	+++

Year	Lev	Team	W	L	Sv	IP	K	ERA	WHIP	BF/G	OBA	H%	S%	xERA	Ctl	Dom	Cmd	hr/9	BPV
2016		Did not pitch																	

7th pick in draft features a plus 91-94 mph FB with good, late life. Backs up the heater with a good 11/5 CB and a CU that flashes plus. Has good size and a strong, projectable frame. Mechanics and high 3/4 arm slot are consistent; comes after hitters with good fastball command. Has the size and frame to develop into a workhorse.

Gatto,Joe
SP | **Los Angeles (A)** | EXP MLB DEBUT: 2019 | H/W: 6-3 220 | FUT: #4 starter | **7D**

Thrws R Age 21	
2014 (2) HS (NJ)	
90-95 FB	+++
77-80 CB	++
81-85 CU	++

Year	Lev	Team	W	L	Sv	IP	K	ERA	WHIP	BF/G	OBA	H%	S%	xERA	Ctl	Dom	Cmd	hr/9	BPV
2014	Rk	Azl Angels	2	1	0	25	15	5.40	1.68	11.3	319	37	66	5.25	3.2	5.4	1.7	0.4	28
2014	Rk	Orem	0	0	0	2	1	4.50	1.50	8.6	347	30	100	9.18	0.0	4.5		4.5	99
2015	Rk	Orem	2	3	0	54	38	4.33	1.66	20.2	324	38	74	5.57	2.8	6.3	2.2	0.7	55
2016	A	Burlington	3	8	0	64	54	7.03	1.89	20.1	328	40	61	6.23	4.6	7.6	1.6	0.7	29

Athletic SP who struggled in first full year. Ended season in June after injury. Very hittable stuff, but is working to upgrade secondary offerings. Cuts and sinks FB with ease, though fails to command. Telegraphs CU by slowing arm and arm slot not conducive to consistent CB. Has tools to be solid, though could move to pen where FB would play up.

German,Domingo
SP | **New York (A)** | EXP MLB DEBUT: 2018 | H/W: 6-2 175 | FUT: #4 starter | **7C**

Thrws R Age 24	
2009 FA (DR)	
90-96 FB	+++
79-82 CB	++
80-83 CU	+++

Year	Lev	Team	W	L	Sv	IP	K	ERA	WHIP	BF/G	OBA	H%	S%	xERA	Ctl	Dom	Cmd	hr/9	BPV
2014	A	Greensboro	9	3	0	123	113	2.49	1.15	19.5	250	32	79	2.95	1.8	8.3	4.5	0.4	117
2015		did not pitch (injured)																	
2016	A	Charleston (Sc)	1	1	0	26	18	3.12	0.65	18.1	170	19	53	1.00	0.7	6.2	9.0	0.7	111
2016	A+	Tampa	0	2	0	23	20	3.10	1.51	20.1	284	35	79	4.29	3.5	7.8	2.2	0.4	63

Under-the-radar SP who returned in late June after Tommy John surgery in '15. Showed remarkable poise and command despite layoff, and needs to regain lost velocity. Throws with easy arm action to generate sink to pitches, and hard CB continues to miss bats. Could be moved to bullpen where heavy FB could work wonders.

Gibson,Daniel
RP | **Arizona** | EXP MLB DEBUT: 2017 | H/W: 6-3 215 | FUT: Setup reliever | **7D**

Thrws L Age 25	
2013 (7) Florida	
92-95 FB	++++
83-86 SL	+++

Year	Lev	Team	W	L	Sv	IP	K	ERA	WHIP	BF/G	OBA	H%	S%	xERA	Ctl	Dom	Cmd	hr/9	BPV
2014	A+	Visalia	4	3	0	22	22	9.32	1.94	5.0	331	41	50	6.87	4.9	8.9	1.8	1.2	47
2015	A+	Visalia	2	1	1	28	38	1.61	0.82	3.8	168	27	82	1.00	2.3	12.2	5.4	0.3	177
2015	AA	Mobile	1	0	2	24	20	1.50	1.33	3.8	210	27	88	2.51	5.3	7.5	1.4	0.0	11
2016	AA	Mobile	4	1	0	22	17	0.41	1.35	3.9	260	33	97	3.20	3.2	6.9	2.1	0.0	54
2016	AAA	Reno	2	0	0	21	17	6.86	1.86	4.7	297	33	66	6.61	6.0	7.3	1.2	1.7	-13

Lefty reliever had up-and-down season between Triple-A and Double-A. Struggled commanding FB at both spots. Pure stuff overpowered lesser hitters, struggled in Triple-A with bleeding fastballs up. SL has wipeout potential. Struggles combining power and movement. Isn't as far away from full development as it may seem.

Giolito,Lucas
SP | **Chicago (A)** | EXP MLB DEBUT: 2016 | H/W: 6-6 240 | FUT: #1 starter | **10C**

Thrws R Age 22	
2012 (1) HS (CA)	
93-95 FB	+++++
80-82 CB	++++
84-85 CU	+++

Year	Lev	Team	W	L	Sv	IP	K	ERA	WHIP	BF/G	OBA	H%	S%	xERA	Ctl	Dom	Cmd	hr/9	BPV
2015	AA	Harrisburg	4	2	0	47	45	3.82	1.38	24.7	265	34	71	3.69	3.2	8.6	2.6	0.4	85
2016	A	Hagerstown	0	0	0	7	4	5.14	0.86	25.7	233	20	50	4.03	0.0	5.1		2.6	111
2016	AA	Harrisburg	5	3	0	71	72	3.17	1.42	21.5	251	34	77	3.47	4.3	9.1	2.1	0.3	66
2016	AAA	Syracuse	1	2	0	37	40	2.18	1.11	20.8	229	30	84	2.82	2.4	9.7	4.0	0.7	127
2016	MLB	Washington	0	1	0	21	11	6.82	1.80	16.3	304	28	71	7.80	5.1	4.7	0.9	3.0	-36

Experienced some extended in-game troubles early on in AA, but a mechanical tweak got him back on track. Dominated afterwards in minors, but was wild and got hit around in several MLB appearances. Exceptional stuff: plus-plus FB and CB along with useable CU still screams high ceiling. Just has to translate it to MLB level.

Glasnow,Tyler
SP | **Pittsburgh** | EXP MLB DEBUT: 2016 | H/W: 6-8 220 | FUT: #1 starter | **9C**

Thrws R Age 23	
2011 (5) HS (CA)	
93-95 FB	+++++
75-78 CB	+++
85-87 CU	+++

Year	Lev	Team	W	L	Sv	IP	K	ERA	WHIP	BF/G	OBA	H%	S%	xERA	Ctl	Dom	Cmd	hr/9	BPV
2015	AA	Altoona	5	3	0	63	82	2.43	0.95	19.8	188	29	74	1.51	2.7	11.7	4.3	0.3	156
2015	AAA	Indianapolis	2	1	0	41	48	2.20	1.34	21.3	222	32	83	2.85	4.8	10.5	2.2	0.2	77
2016	AA	Altoona	0	0	0	6	11	3.00	1.67	13.5	191	34	89	4.45	9.0	16.5	1.8	1.5	72
2016	AAA	Indianapolis	8	3	0	110	133	1.88	1.15	21.9	173	26	85	1.90	5.1	10.9	2.1	0.3	77
2016	MLB	Pittsburgh	0	2	0	23	24	4.29	1.52	14.3	252	33	73	4.22	5.1	9.4	1.8	0.8	50

Dominated at AAA, but a shoulder injury limited him once in the majors. Has a plus-plus 93-95 mph FB that tops out 98 mph. Gets good downhill tilt from his 6-8 frame and has late life on FB with arm-side run. Upper-70s CB is now above-average and flashes as plus. CU remains a work in progress, but has potential. Control is the only red flag.

Glover,Koda
RP | **Washington** | EXP MLB DEBUT: 2016 | H/W: 6-5 225 | FUT: Setup reliever | **8D**

Thrws R Age 23	
2015 (8) Oklahoma State	
94-98 FB	++++
89-91 SL	++++
80-82 CB	++

Year	Lev	Team	W	L	Sv	IP	K	ERA	WHIP	BF/G	OBA	H%	S%	xERA	Ctl	Dom	Cmd	hr/9	BPV
2015	A	Hagerstown	1	1	4	24	27	2.25	0.92	5.6	237	32	80	2.47	0.4	10.1	27.0	0.8	190
2016	A+	Potomac	0	0	2	9	15	0.00	0.76	4.7	104	22	100		3.9	14.7	3.8	0.0	176
2016	AA	Harrisburg	2	0	4	22	29	3.26	1.22	5.3	243	36	73	2.98	2.9	11.8	4.1	0.4	154
2016	AAA	Syracuse	1	1	2	24	22	2.25	0.79	5.4	191	23	76	1.62	1.1	8.3	7.3	0.8	136
2016	MLB	Washington	2	0	0	19	16	5.16	1.15	4.0	217	24	58	3.44	3.3	7.5	2.3	1.4	64

Blasted through the system in 13 months, surprising many with a lethal fastball/slider combination out of the bullpen. Hitters have a tough time squaring him up, as both pitches exhibit excellent movement. Aggressive demeanor rounds out the potential late-innings package.

Gohara,Luiz
SP | **Seattle** | EXP MLB DEBUT: 2019 | H/W: 6-3 210 | FUT: #3 starter | **8C**

Thrws L Age 20	
2012 FA (BR)	
91-95 FB	++++
81-84 SL	+++
81-85 CU	++

Year	Lev	Team	W	L	Sv	IP	K	ERA	WHIP	BF/G	OBA	H%	S%	xERA	Ctl	Dom	Cmd	hr/9	BPV
2014	A-	Everett	0	6	0	37	37	8.25	1.89	15.9	305	37	56	6.56	5.8	9.0	1.5	1.5	22
2015	A-	Everett	3	7	0	53	62	6.26	1.86	17.8	309	42	65	5.79	5.4	10.5	1.9	0.7	61
2015	A	Clinton	0	1	0	9	5	1.96	1.74	21.0	278	32	88	4.45	5.9	4.9	0.8	0.0	-52
2016	A-	Everett	2	0	0	15	21	1.79	1.06	19.5	234	36	87	2.62	1.8	12.5	7.0	0.6	195
2016	A	Clinton	5	2	0	54	60	1.83	1.18	21.7	224	32	84	2.43	3.3	10.0	3.0	0.2	108

Big-bodied SP who has ingredients to be stud bulldog. Has tweaked delivery to throw with more consistent power and is doing better job of repeating it. Control has improved and keeps ball in lower half of zone. Plus FB is best pitch and can cut and sink it. Likes to use SL as chase pitch and can register Ks. CU still in developmental phase.

Gomber,Austin
SP | **St. Louis** | EXP MLB DEBUT: 2019 | H/W: 6-5 235 | FUT: #4 starter | **7D**

Thrws L Age 23	
2014 (4) Florida Atlantic	
90-92 FB	+++
80-83 CB	+++
CU	+++

Year	Lev	Team	W	L	Sv	IP	K	ERA	WHIP	BF/G	OBA	H%	S%	xERA	Ctl	Dom	Cmd	hr/9	BPV
2014	NCAA	Florida Atlantic	3	6	0	77	72	3.27	1.21	25.9	264	34	73	3.31	1.8	8.4	4.8	0.5	122
2014	A-	State College	2	2	0	47	36	2.30	1.55	18.7	293	35	87	4.72	3.4	6.9	2.0	0.6	49
2015	A	Peoria	15	3	0	135	140	2.67	0.97	23.3	203	27	75	2.12	2.3	9.3	4.1	0.7	125
2016	A+	Palm Beach	6	8	0	107	101	2.94	1.07	24.5	231	30	73	2.50	2.0	8.5	4.2	0.4	116
2016	AA	Springfield	1	0	0	19	15	1.41	1.05	18.5	170	22	85	1.33	4.2	7.1	1.7	0.0	31

Tall lefty has a nice three-pitch mix that includes a 90-92 mph FB, CB, and CU. CB was slow, sweeping variety in college, but was better as a pro and shows above-average potential. CU is average and he commands the strike zone well. Has some deception in his delivery and understands how to pitch and keep hitters off-balance.

Gonsalves,Stephen — SP — Minnesota — EXP MLB DEBUT: 2017 — H/W: 6-5 215 — FUT: #3 starter — 8C

Thrws L Age 22 — 2013 (4) HS (CA)

Velo	Pitch	Grade
89-94	FB	+ + +
77-80	CB	+ + +
81-83	SL	+ +
81-83	CU	+ + + +

Year	Lev	Team	W	L	Sv	IP	K	ERA	WHIP	BF/G	OBA	H%	S%	xERA	Ctl	Dom	Cmd	hr/9	BPV
2014	A	Cedar Rapids	2	3	0	36	44	3.23	1.16	18.0	233	34	71	2.55	2.7	10.9	4.0	0.2	141
2015	A	Cedar Rapids	6	1	0	55	77	1.15	0.80	22.1	158	26	88	0.83	2.5	12.6	5.1	0.3	179
2015	A+	Fort Myers	7	2	0	79	55	2.62	1.31	21.8	228	28	79	2.91	4.3	6.3	1.4	0.2	14
2016	A+	Fort Myers	5	4	0	65	66	2.35	0.97	22.4	190	26	75	1.58	2.8	9.1	3.3	0.3	107
2016	AA	Chattanooga	8	1	0	74	89	1.82	1.08	22.2	171	26	82	1.50	4.5	10.8	2.4	0.1	91

Tall, lanky SP who uses effortless delivery and FB command to retire hitters. Uses 4 pitches effectively, including plus CU that features late, sinking action. FB velo is only average, but mixes in two breaking balls that result in low oppBA. K rate increased, but needs to watch efficiency and control. Rarely allows HR and ended year on fire.

Gonzales,Marco — SP — St. Louis — EXP MLB DEBUT: 2015 — H/W: 6-1 195 — FUT: #4 starter — 7C

Thrws L Age 25 — 2013 (1) Gonzaga

Velo	Pitch	Grade
88-92	FB	+ +
75-77	CB	+ +
83-86	SL	+ +
78-81	CU	+ + + +

Year	Lev	Team	W	L	Sv	IP	K	ERA	WHIP	BF/G	OBA	H%	S%	xERA	Ctl	Dom	Cmd	hr/9	BPV
2015	A+	Palm Beach	0	0	0	4		0.00	1.19	8.4	297	39	100	3.31	0.0	8.6		0.0	172
2015	AA	Springfield	0	0	0	6	6	0.00	0.97	11.7	255	34	100	2.15	0.0	8.7		0.0	175
2015	AAA	Memphis	1	5	0	69	51	5.47	1.66	22.1	318	36	70	6.08	3.1	6.6	2.1	1.3	53
2015	MLB	St. Louis	0	0	0	2	1	16.36	3.64	14.2	530	54	57	18.65	4.1	4.1	1.0	4.1	-19

Short LHP had TJS in April and will be out until mid-2017. Has a fluid delivery that leads to plus command of four-pitch mix. FB lacks premium velo and sits at 88-92 mph, but he locates it well. Best offering is a plus CU that he will throw in any count He also mixes in a good, but inconsistent CB and a seldom-used slider.

Gonzalez,Brian — SP — Baltimore — EXP MLB DEBUT: 2019 — H/W: 6-3 230 — FUT: #4 starter — 7D

Thrws L Age 21 — 2014 (3) HS (FL)

Velo	Pitch	Grade
88-94	FB	+ + +
75-79	CB	+ + +
81-84	CU	+ +

Year	Lev	Team	W	L	Sv	IP	K	ERA	WHIP	BF/G	OBA	H%	S%	xERA	Ctl	Dom	Cmd	hr/9	BPV
2014	Rk	GCL Orioles	0	0	0	24	25	0.00	0.79	10.9	139	20	100	0.32	3.0	9.3	3.1	0.0	105
2014	A-	Aberdeen	0	1	0	9	11	5.00	1.33	18.7	283	41	58	3.43	2.0	11.0	5.5	0.0	162
2015	A	Delmarva	4	9	0	105	81	5.73	1.49	19.7	248	29	60	4.04	5.0	6.9	1.4	0.7	6
2016	A	Delmarva	10	8	0	147	111	2.51	1.31	22.5	245	29	83	3.42	3.5	6.8	1.9	0.6	44

Durable SP who repeated Low-A and was 3rd in league in ERA. Much improved across board and was consistent in delivery, stuff, and results. Held LHH to .197 BA and kept ball on ground. More pitchability than pure stuff with average pitch mix. Lacks true swing-and-miss offering, though saw slight uptick in velo. Pitches with good angle to plate.

Gonzalez,Merandy — SP — New York (N) — EXP MLB DEBUT: 2020 — H/W: 6-1 195 — FUT: #4 starter — 7D

Thrws R Age 21 — 2013 FA (DR)

Velo	Pitch	Grade
91-94	FB	+ + +
78-82	CB	+ + + +
84-87	CU	+

Year	Lev	Team	W	L	Sv	IP	K	ERA	WHIP	BF/G	OBA	H%	S%	xERA	Ctl	Dom	Cmd	hr/9	BPV
2015	Rk	Kingsport	2	2	0	44	39	2.85	1.33	20.4	243	31	78	3.11	3.9	7.9	2.1	0.2	56
2015	Rk	GCL Mets	2	1	0	22	25	2.05	0.55	18.5	127	18	64		1.2	10.2	8.3	0.4	169
2016	A-	Brooklyn	6	3	0	69	71	2.87	1.33	20.5	250	34	78	3.24	3.5	9.3	2.6	0.3	90

Dominican RH with pitchability history struggled with release point and command throughout '16. FB is low-to-mid nineties with little arm-side movement. CB is best secondary pitch but struggles with identity. Sometimes slurve, sometimes curve. CU is in it's infancy in development.

Gossett,Daniel — SP — Oakland — EXP MLB DEBUT: 2017 — H/W: 6-2 185 — FUT: #3 starter — 8D

Thrws R Age 24 — 2014 (2) Clemson

Velo	Pitch	Grade
90-94	FB	+ + +
85-87	SL	+ +
79-82	CB	+ + +
79-82	CU	+ + +

Year	Lev	Team	W	L	Sv	IP	K	ERA	WHIP	BF/G	OBA	H%	S%	xERA	Ctl	Dom	Cmd	hr/9	BPV
2014	A-	Vermont	1	0	0	24	25	2.25	0.71	7.1	191	26	69	1.04	0.4	9.4	25.0	0.4	177
2015	A	Beloit	5	13	0	144	112	4.74	1.41	22.6	271	31	68	4.43	3.2	7.0	2.2	1.0	56
2016	A+	Stockton	4	1	0	46	53	3.33	1.15	20.3	236	32	73	3.07	2.5	10.4	4.1	0.8	136
2016	AA	Midland	5	5	0	94	94	2.49	1.06	22.8	221	29	77	2.30	2.4	9.0	3.8	0.4	115
2016	AAA	Nashville	1	0	0	13	4	2.05	0.98	25.1	212	23	77	1.70	2.0	2.7	1.3	0.0	12

Durable SP who was potent on three levels in breakout campaign. Has deep repertoire and extreme groundball tendencies. Sequences well and throws quality strikes, especially with commandable FB. Clean, smooth delivery provides pitch movement. Added SL/CT to arsenal to give him another weapon.

Gowdy,Kevin — SP — Philadelphia — EXP MLB DEBUT: 2021 — H/W: 6-4 170 — FUT: #3 starter — 8E

Thrws R Age 19 — 2016 (2) HS (CA)

Velo	Pitch	Grade
91-94	FB	+ + +
86-88	SL	+ + +
83-84	CU	+ +

Year	Lev	Team	W	L	Sv	IP	K	ERA	WHIP	BF/G	OBA	H%	S%	xERA	Ctl	Dom	Cmd	hr/9	BPV
2016	Rk	GCL Phillies	0	1	0	9	9	4.00	1.22	9.1	262	35	64	2.88	2.0	9.0	4.5	0.0	126

Three-pitch mix with quite a bit of current polish. Stays tall in delivery and high-3/4s release results in good downhill plane. FB velocity fluctuated in 2016, but commands it well; hard SL is already a chase pitch, and shows a feel for CU and importance of changing speeds. Has a projectable body and clean mechanics.

Green,Chad — SP — New York (A) — EXP MLB DEBUT: 2016 — H/W: 6-3 210 — FUT: #4 starter — 7C

Thrws R Age 25 — 2013 (11) Louisville

Velo	Pitch	Grade
90-95	FB	+ + +
80-82	SL	+ +
81-84	CU	+ +

Year	Lev	Team	W	L	Sv	IP	K	ERA	WHIP	BF/G	OBA	H%	S%	xERA	Ctl	Dom	Cmd	hr/9	BPV
2013	A+	Lakeland	3	0	1	17	10	3.68	1.29	7.0	249	30	68	2.90	3.2	5.3	1.7	0.0	27
2014	A	West Michigan	6	4	0	130	125	3.11	1.15	22.4	248	32	74	3.02	1.9	8.6	4.5	0.6	121
2015	AA	Erie	5	14	0	148	137	3.95	1.44	23.4	289	36	73	4.33	2.6	8.3	3.2	0.5	97
2016	AAA	Scranton/WB	7	6	0	94	100	1.53	0.94	22.2	204	28	85	1.70	2.0	9.6	4.8	0.3	136
2016	MLB	NY Yankees	2	4	1	45	52	4.78	1.42	16.0	278	33	77	5.82	3.0	10.4	3.5	2.4	124

Durable-framed SP who enjoyed incredible season, culminating in action with NYY. Keeps ball down in zone and spots FB impeccably to all quadrants. Counters FB with SL and CU, though both need polish. Commands plate and maintains consistency with downhill plane and clean mechanics. Posted high K rate, but should drop without better SL.

Greene,Conner — SP — Toronto — EXP MLB DEBUT: 2017 — H/W: 6-3 185 — FUT: #3 starter — 8C

Thrws R Age 22 — 2013 (7) HS (CA)

Velo	Pitch	Grade
92-96	FB	+ + + +
74-77	CB	+ +
83-86	SL	+ + +
81-85	CU	+ +

Year	Lev	Team	W	L	Sv	IP	K	ERA	WHIP	BF/G	OBA	H%	S%	xERA	Ctl	Dom	Cmd	hr/9	BPV
2015	A	Lansing	7	3	0	67	65	3.89	1.40	20.2	284	36	72	4.14	2.5	8.7	3.4	0.5	106
2015	A+	Dunedin	2	3	0	40	35	2.25	1.10	22.4	242	31	79	2.52	1.8	7.9	4.4	0.2	111
2015	AA	New Hampshire	3	1	0	25	15	4.68	1.48	21.5	262	30	67	3.90	4.3	5.4	1.3	0.4	-1
2016	A+	Dunedin	4	4	0	77	51	2.91	1.45	22.0	254	29	81	3.92	4.4	5.9	1.3	0.6	5
2016	AA	New Hampshire	6	5	0	68	48	4.22	1.32	23.5	229	26	68	3.33	4.4	6.3	1.5	0.7	14

Tall, loose SP who continues to add weight and durability. Uses four pitches and can vary release point for movement. Electric FB is best pitch and can miss bats. Can be inefficient with mixing and could use better control. SL has chance to be plus pitch while sinking CU has moments. Can be tough to hit, but K rate not reflective of natural stuff.

Gregorio,Joan — SP — San Francisco — EXP MLB DEBUT: 2017 — H/W: 6-7 180 — FUT: #4 starter — 7C

Thrws R Age 25 — 2010 FA (DR)

Velo	Pitch	Grade
91-95	FB	+ + +
82-85	SL	+ + +
84-86	CU	+ +

Year	Lev	Team	W	L	Sv	IP	K	ERA	WHIP	BF/G	OBA	H%	S%	xERA	Ctl	Dom	Cmd	hr/9	BPV
2014	A	Augusta	2	7	1	68	65	3.57	1.13	20.7	207	27	67	2.20	3.6	8.6	2.4	0.3	76
2014	A+	San Jose	2	2	0	22	27	6.89	1.80	17.1	301	41	61	5.65	5.3	10.9	2.1	0.8	73
2015	AA	Richmond	3	2	1	78	72	3.11	1.23	8.6	225	28	77	3.06	3.7	8.3	2.3	0.7	68
2016	AA	Richmond	0	2	0	27	30	2.33	0.78	19.4	165	23	70	0.88	2.0	10.0	5.0	0.3	144
2016	AAA	Sacramento	6	8	0	107	122	5.29	1.45	21.8	271	35	65	4.58	3.6	10.3	2.8	1.1	105

Very tall, large-framed SP who was hit hard in AAA, but has chance to be high K guy. May eventually move to pen where he can blow ball by hitters with max effort delivery. Has worked to improve control, especially with FB and has amped up SL to near-plus status. Fringy CU could use upgrade, but repeats arm speed.

Griffin,Foster — SP — Kansas City — EXP MLB DEBUT: 2018 — H/W: 6-3 200 — FUT: #3 starter — 8E

Thrws L Age 21 — 2014 (1) HS (FL)

Velo	Pitch	Grade
89-94	FB	+ + +
75-79	CB	+ +
79-82	CU	+ + +

Year	Lev	Team	W	L	Sv	IP	K	ERA	WHIP	BF/G	OBA	H%	S%	xERA	Ctl	Dom	Cmd	hr/9	BPV
2014	Rk	Burlington	0	2	0	28	19	3.21	1.11	10.0	194	22	72	2.36	3.9	6.1	1.6	0.6	24
2015	A	Lexington	4	6	0	102	71	5.46	1.55	20.3	299	35	64	4.92	3.1	6.3	2.0	0.7	47
2016	A	Lexington	1	4	0	37	29	3.40	1.19	21.2	251	30	73	3.34	2.2	7.0	3.2	0.7	86
2016	A+	Wilmington	5	10	0	95	76	6.25	1.82	22.1	326	39	65	6.17	4.1	7.2	1.8	0.9	38

Tall, durable SP who was hit hard in A+ upon promotion, but has pitch mix and delivery to be productive. Works down in zone with high arm slot and locates FB well. Best pitch is deceptive CU with ideal arm speed and late movement. Can be around plate too much and get hit hard, particularly loose CB. Breaking ball needs to improve.

Grimes,Matthew — SP — Baltimore — EXP MLB DEBUT: 2017 — H/W: 6-5 185 — FUT: #4 starter — 7D

Thrws R Age 25 — 2014 (18) Georgia Tech

Velo	Pitch	Grade
90-94	FB	+ + +
81-84	SL	+ +
77-79	CB	+ +
82-84	CU	+ + +

Year	Lev	Team	W	L	Sv	IP	K	ERA	WHIP	BF/G	OBA	H%	S%	xERA	Ctl	Dom	Cmd	hr/9	BPV
2016	A+	Frederick	8	4	0	80	54	1.46	1.06	22.2	234	28	88	2.44	1.8	6.1	3.4	0.3	79
2016	AA	Bowie	3	5	0	57	37	4.72	1.45	22.2	271	31	68	4.35	3.6	5.8	1.6	0.8	25

Tall, angular SP who has flown under radar despite results. Found A+ to be easy and finished in AA. Added velocity to average FB and has polished CU to give him weapon against LHH. Throws with little effort in smooth delivery and live in bottom half of zone. Owns two breaking balls, but neither are up to snuff as swing-and-miss offerings.

Groome,Jason — SP — Boston

EXP MLB DEBUT: 2020 | H/W: 6-6 220 | FUT: #1 starter | 9D

Thrws L Age 18 — 2016 (1) HS (NJ)

- 90-97 FB +++
- 77-79 CB ++++
- 82-85 CU +

Year	Lev	Team	W	L	Sv	IP	K	ERA	WHIP	BF/G	OBA	H%	S%	xERA	Ctl	Dom	Cmd	hr/9	BPV
2016	Rk	GCL Red Sox	0	0	0	4	8	2.25	0.75	7.1	210	48	67	0.93	0.0	18.0		0.0	342
2016	A-	Lowell	0	0	0	2	2	4.09	1.82	10.2	0	0	75	1.73	16.4	8.2	0.5	0.0	-277

Big, physical SP with extreme upside based upon arm strength and advanced pitches for age. Locates potential plus FB to both sides of plate and terrific CB misses bats. Throws three pitches for strikes and could have more velocity in tank. Throws with clean arm action and shows feel for changing speeds. Needs consistency, but could move quickly.

Gsellman,Robert — SP — New York (N)

EXP MLB DEBUT: 2016 | H/W: 6-4 205 | FUT: #3 starter | 7B

Thrws R Age 23 — 2011 (13) HS (CA)

- 91-94 FB +++
- 86-88 SL ++++
- 79-82 CB +++
- 85-87 CU ++

Year	Lev	Team	W	L	Sv	IP	K	ERA	WHIP	BF/G	OBA	H%	S%	xERA	Ctl	Dom	Cmd	hr/9	BPV
2015	A+	St. Lucie	6	0	0	51	37	1.76	0.94	24.0	205	25	81	1.63	1.9	6.5	3.4	0.2	83
2015	AA	Binghamton	7	7	0	92	49	3.52	1.25	23.4	255	29	71	3.26	2.5	4.8	1.9	0.4	36
2016	AA	Binghamton	3	4	0	66	48	2.72	1.09	23.5	234	28	74	2.46	2.0	6.5	3.2	0.3	80
2016	AAA	Las Vegas	1	5	0	48	40	5.79	1.49	23.1	292	33	64	5.41	3.0	7.5	2.5	1.5	72
2016	MLB	NY Mets	4	2	0	44	42	2.44	1.29	22.7	252	33	80	3.11	3.1	8.6	2.8	0.2	89

Came out of nowhere to be team's 3rd best starter in '16 playoff race. 91-94 FB plays up due to explosive late movement. Command was still an issue despite MLB success. SL was a real revelation, flashing two-plane plus movement; this is his swing-and-miss offering. CB is workable but unspectacular. CU is still a work in progress.

Guduan,Reymin — RP — Houston

EXP MLB DEBUT: 2017 | H/W: 6-4 205 | FUT: Closer | 8E

Thrws L Age 25 — 2009 FA (DR)

- 93-96 FB ++++
- 82-86 SL ++
- CU +

Year	Lev	Team	W	L	Sv	IP	K	ERA	WHIP	BF/G	OBA	H%	S%	xERA	Ctl	Dom	Cmd	hr/9	BPV
2015	A	Quad Cities	3	0	0	12		0.75	0.75	7.1	151	24	89	0.34	2.3	11.3	5.0	0.0	160
2015	A+	Lancaster	0	3	4	17	25	3.16	1.35	5.5	199	34	74	2.35	5.8	13.2	2.3	0.0	99
2015	AA	Corpus Christi	1	3	0	16	19	11.74	2.42	5.3	306	39	50	8.10	10.6	10.6	1.0	1.7	-78
2016	AA	Corpus Christi	1	0	2	13	19	0.69	0.77	5.2	160	25	100	1.12	2.1	13.2	6.3	0.7	199
2016	AAA	Fresno	2	3	0	43	44	5.23	1.79	5.8	262	35	69	4.70	7.1	9.2	1.3	0.4	-8

High-risk/high-reward arm who has spent most of career in pen. Has big frame and is stingy against LHH. Can rear back and hit triple-digits and counters with hard SL that flashes average. Cannot throw consistent strikes and walks too many batters. FB can be too straight and shows very little feel for changing speeds. Can dominate in short stints.

Guerrero,Jordan — SP — Chicago (A)

EXP MLB DEBUT: 2017 | H/W: 6-3 195 | FUT: #4 starter | 7C

Thrws L Age 22 — 2012 (15) HS (CA)

- 89-93 FB +++
- 80-82 SL ++
- 78-82 CU +++

Year	Lev	Team	W	L	Sv	IP	K	ERA	WHIP	BF/G	OBA	H%	S%	xERA	Ctl	Dom	Cmd	hr/9	BPV
2013	Rk	Bristol	0	3	0	25	15	4.30	1.43	21.4	305	33	75	5.42	1.8	5.4	3.0	1.4	66
2014	A	Kannapolis	6	2	0	78	80	3.46	1.38	12.1	269	35	76	3.93	3.1	9.2	3.0	0.6	100
2015	A	Kannapolis	6	1	0	55	60	2.29	0.94	23.0	213	30	75	1.69	1.6	9.8	6.0	0.2	150
2015	A+	Winston-Salem	7	3	0	93	88	3.57	1.11	22.9	238	30	68	2.81	2.0	8.5	4.2	0.6	116
2016	AA	Birmingham	7	8	0	136	108	4.83	1.51	23.6	257	30	69	4.38	4.8	7.1	1.5	0.9	16

Lean, deceptive SP who led SL in walks. Had trouble controlling heavy FB that features devastating late life. Can cut and sink FB for weak contact. CU may be best pitch and throws with deceptive arm speed. Dom dropped and will need to enhance breaking ball to miss bats in the future.

Guerrero,Tayron — RP — Miami

EXP MLB DEBUT: 2016 | H/W: 6-8 210 | FUT: Setup reliever | 7C

Thrws R Age 26 — 2009 FA (CL)

- 95-98 FB ++++
- 80-83 SL ++

Year	Lev	Team	W	L	Sv	IP	K	ERA	WHIP	BF/G	OBA	H%	S%	xERA	Ctl	Dom	Cmd	hr/9	BPV
2015	AAA	El Paso	0	0	1	13	15	4.09	1.44	5.1	177	26	68	2.36	7.5	10.2	1.4	0.0	0
2016	AA	Jacksonville	1	1	4	14	15	1.93	1.00	4.5	218	31	79	1.74	1.9	9.6	5.0	0.0	140
2016	AA	San Antonio	0	3	0	23	25	5.04	1.29	5.0	234	31	61	3.41	3.9	9.7	2.5	0.8	88
2016	AAA	El Paso	0	0	0	12	11	6.00	1.75	4.2	262	30	68	5.62	6.8	8.3	1.2	1.5	-16
2016	MLB	San Diego	0	0	0	2	0	4.50	2.00	9.6	347	35	75	6.25	4.5	0.0	0.0	0.0	-104

Long, lanky RP came over to the Marlins in the Andrew Cashner deal. Plus FB that sits at 95-98 and hits 100 mph at the top end, but with little movement and below-average command. Mixes in a low-80 swing-and-miss SL to give him a nice 1-2 punch. FB gets on batters quick with some deception, making him tough to square up.

Guerrieri,Taylor — SP — Tampa Bay

EXP MLB DEBUT: 2017 | H/W: 6-3 195 | FUT: #3 starter | 8C

Thrws R Age 24 — 2011 (1) HS (SC)

- 90-94 FB +++
- 77-81 CB +++
- 80-83 SL +++
- 80-83 CB +++

Year	Lev	Team	W	L	Sv	IP	K	ERA	WHIP	BF/G	OBA	H%	S%	xERA	Ctl	Dom	Cmd	hr/9	BPV
2013	A	Bowling Green	6	2	0	67	51	2.01	0.99	18.2	222	26	84	2.42	1.6	6.9	4.3	0.7	98
2014	Rk	GCL Devil Rays	0	0	0	9	10	0.00	0.99	6.9	214	31	100	1.67	2.0	9.9	5.0	0.0	143
2015	A+	Charlotte	2	2	0	42	44	2.14	1.14	13.9	238	33	79	2.35	2.4	9.4	4.0	0.0	124
2015	AA	Montgomery	3	1	0	36	28	1.50	1.00	17.2	216	26	88	2.22	2.0	7.0	3.5	0.5	90
2016	AA	Montgomery	12	6	1	146	89	3.76	1.21	21.0	240	27	70	3.21	2.8	5.5	1.9	0.7	40

Tall, lean SP who got better as season progressed, but has seen Dom fall while Ctl has risen. Set career high in IP and succeeds with spotting sinker low in zone. FB exhibits late movement while he owns two quality breaking balls. Neither SL or CB miss many bats, but he pitches well to contact. Seems to be past injuries and sketchy makeup.

Gustave,Jandel — RP — Houston

EXP MLB DEBUT: 2016 | H/W: 6-2 210 | FUT: Closer | 8D

Thrws R Age 24 — 2010 FA (DR)

- 94-98 FB +++++
- 84-88 SL ++++
- CU ++

Year	Lev	Team	W	L	Sv	IP	K	ERA	WHIP	BF/G	OBA	H%	S%	xERA	Ctl	Dom	Cmd	hr/9	BPV
2013	Rk	Greeneville	2	3	0	43	49	2.71	1.41	18.3	238	33	81	3.41	4.8	10.2	2.1	0.4	72
2014	A	Quad Cities	5	5	2	79	82	5.01	1.56	15.0	297	39	66	4.54	3.3	9.3	2.8	0.3	97
2015	AA	Corpus Christi	5	2	20	58	49	2.16	1.31	5.2	237	30	84	3.06	3.9	7.6	2.0	0.3	50
2016	AAA	Fresno	3	3	3	57	55	3.79	1.21	4.9	223	30	66	2.48	3.6	8.7	2.4	0.2	76
2016	MLB	Houston	1	0	0	15	16	3.58	1.13	4.3	234	29	73	3.38	2.4	9.5	4.0	1.2	125

Fast-armed RP who earned way to majors with vastly improved control and ability to keep ball on ground. FB flashes double-plus and lives in lower half of zone. Tough to elevate when on and arm speed adds effectiveness and break to hard SL. Has little need for CU, though has struggled with LHH at times. Could be high K, groundball pitcher.

Gutierrez,Vladimir — SP — Cincinnati

EXP MLB DEBUT: 2018 | H/W: 6-5 205 | FUT: #3 starter | 8D

Thrws R Age 21 — 2016 FA (CU)

- 90-93 FB ++++
- 76-78 CB ++++
- CU ++

Year	Lev	Team	W	L	Sv	IP	K	ERA	WHIP	BF/G	OBA	H%	S%	xERA	Ctl	Dom	Cmd	hr/9	BPV
2016		did not pitch																	

Cuban RH has yet to make US pro debut. Worked as reliever in Cuba. CIN has history of converting relievers with solid secondary pitches into starters. 2-seam FB has solid drop and induces plenty of grounders. Scouts differ on CU effectiveness. Wiry physique with room to grow between the shoulders.

Hader,Josh — SP — Milwaukee

EXP MLB DEBUT: 2017 | H/W: 6-3 185 | FUT: #2 SP/closer | 9E

Thrws L Age 23 — 2012 (19) HS (MD)

- 91-95 FB ++++
- 77-81 SL +++
- 81-83 CU ++

Year	Lev	Team	W	L	Sv	IP	K	ERA	WHIP	BF/G	OBA	H%	S%	xERA	Ctl	Dom	Cmd	hr/9	BPV
2014	AA	Corpus Christi	1	1	0	20	24	6.30	1.60	17.7	221	30	60	4.12	7.2	10.8	1.5	0.9	18
2015	AA	Biloxi	1	4	0	38	50	2.83	0.99	20.8	200	29	74	2.16	2.6	11.8	4.5	0.7	160
2015	AA	Corpus Christi	3	3	1	65	69	3.18	1.29	15.7	246	32	77	3.48	3.3	9.5	2.9	0.7	100
2016	AA	Biloxi	2	1	0	57	73	0.95	1.00	19.8	191	30	91	1.55	3.0	11.5	3.8	0.2	144
2016	AAA	Colorado Springs	1	7	0	69	88	5.22	1.43	21.0	245	35	63	3.77	4.7	11.5	2.4	0.7	98

Tall, lean southpaw recorded 11.5 Dom as PCL's second-youngest starter. Elite K track record supported by lively FB thrown from low slot and flashes of plus SL. CU still used sparingly and command of inner-third remains in question. Easy, cross-fire motion; full arm circle in back. Needs to pitch deeper into starts, but FB/SL could work from 'pen.

Hall,Matt — SP — Detroit

EXP MLB DEBUT: 2018 | H/W: 6-0 200 | FUT: #4 starter | 7C

Thrws L Age 23 — 2015 (6) Missouri State

- 85-90 FB ++
- 76-79 CB ++++
- 82-83 SL ++
- 81-84 CU +++

Year	Lev	Team	W	L	Sv	IP	K	ERA	WHIP	BF/G	OBA	H%	S%	xERA	Ctl	Dom	Cmd	hr/9	BPV
2015	NCAA	Missouri State	12	2	1	125	171	2.02	1.06	25.5	198	32	81	1.82	3.2	12.3	3.8	0.2	152
2015	Rk	GCL Tigers	0	0	0	3	4	3.00	1.67	13.5	321	47	80	4.85	3.0	12.0	4.0	0.0	153
2015	A-	Connecticut	0	1	0	31	30	2.90	1.16	12.3	249	31	79	3.37	2.0	8.7	4.3	0.9	120
2016	A	West Michigan	8	0	0	66	72	1.09	1.06	21.4	208	30	89	1.77	2.9	9.8	3.4	0.0	117
2016	A+	Lakeland	3	2	0	60	54	4.19	1.48	21.6	264	32	73	4.41	4.2	8.1	1.9	0.9	50

Short, durable SP who opened eyes despite fringy stuff. Very tough on LHH by changing speeds and eye levels. Below average FB with fringy velocity, but spots to all quadrants of zone. CB is dynamite offering with big breaking action. Gets swings and misses with CB. Mixes in occasional SL and decent CU. Not much upside.

Hanifee,Brenan — SP — Baltimore

EXP MLB DEBUT: 2021 | H/W: 6-5 180 | FUT: #3 starter | 8E

Thrws R Age 18 — 2016 (4) HS (VA)

- 87-93 FB +++
- 81-83 SL +++
- CU +

Year	Lev	Team	W	L	Sv	IP	K	ERA	WHIP	BF/G	OBA	H%	S%	xERA	Ctl	Dom	Cmd	hr/9	BPV
2016		did not pitch																	

Lean, athletic SP who did not pitch upon signing, but has high ceiling based upon projection and solid-average FB at present. Should add velo to FB as he gains strength and repeats delivery. Needs mechanical adjustments to improve SL and well below average CU. Rarely threw CU in HS, but will need for LHH as pro.

Hansen,Alec — SP — Chicago (A)

EXP MLB DEBUT: 2018 | H/W: 6-7 235 | FUT: #2 starter | 9D

Thrws R Age 22
2016 (2) Oklahoma

Velo	Pitch	Grade
93-97	FB	++++
83-87	SL	++++
76-78	CB	++
83-86	CU	++

Year	Lev	Team	W	L	Sv	IP	K	ERA	WHIP	BF/G	OBA	H%	S%	xERA	Ctl	Dom	Cmd	hr/9	BPV
2016	NCAA	Oklahoma	3	5	0	51	75	5.45	1.62	16.2	234	38	64	3.80	6.9	13.2	1.9	0.4	70
2016	Rk	Azl White Sox	0	0	0	7	11	0.00	0.71	8.2	48	10	100		5.1	14.1	2.8	0.0	134
2016	Rk	Great Falls	2	0	0	36	59	1.24	0.66	18.0	105	17	90	0.34	3.0	14.7	4.9	0.7	201
2016	A	Kannapolis	0	1	0	11	11	2.45	1.36	23.0	262	35	80	3.23	3.3	9.0	2.8	0.0	92

Long, powerful SP who dominated minors upon signing. Has plus stuff and can be impossible to hit when sequencing effectively. Threw with better command as pro, though still needs work to iron out mechanics. Can bring serious heat on downward angle to plate and wipe out hitters with plus SL. Delivery could lead to injury issues.

Hanson,Nick — SP — Cincinnati

EXP MLB DEBUT: 2021 | H/W: 6-6 205 | FUT: #4 starter | 7E

Thrws R Age 18
2016 (3) HS (MN)

Velo	Pitch	Grade
91-95	FB	++++
	CB	+++
	CU	++

Year	Lev	Team	W	L	Sv	IP	K	ERA	WHIP	BF/G	OBA	H%	S%	xERA	Ctl	Dom	Cmd	hr/9	BPV
2016	Rk	AZL Reds	0	2	0	16	15	9.44	2.47	10.7	354	44	59	7.99	8.3	8.3	1.0	0.6	-57

Tall, projectable RH struggled in pro debut. FB sits low 90s with solid sink. CB flashes plus with tremendous break. Still developing feel for CU. Struggles mightily repeating delivery. Induced lots of hard contact in debut.

Harris,Greg — SP — Tampa Bay

EXP MLB DEBUT: 2018 | H/W: 6-2 170 | FUT: #4 starter | 7D

Thrws R Age 22
2013 (17) HS (CA)

Velo	Pitch	Grade
89-94	FB	+++
77-79	CB	+++
	CU	++

Year	Lev	Team	W	L	Sv	IP	K	ERA	WHIP	BF/G	OBA	H%	S%	xERA	Ctl	Dom	Cmd	hr/9	BPV
2014	A	Great Lakes	7	6	0	87		4.45	1.33	16.4	264	35	67	3.86	2.9	9.5	3.3	0.7	111
2015	A	Bowling Green	7	5	0	83	84	2.17	1.23	21.0	240	33	81	2.70	3.0	9.1	3.0	0.1	100
2015	A+	Charlotte	1	4	0	39	24	3.44	1.38	18.3	266	31	74	3.57	3.2	5.5	1.7	0.2	30
2016	A+	Charlotte	10	6	0	147	134	3.12	1.20	22.8	223	28	75	2.91	3.6	8.2	2.3	0.6	70
2016	AAA	Durham	0	0	0	3	6	9.00	2.67	16.5	371	67	63	8.20	9.0	18.0	2.0	0.0	99

Emerging SP who led FSL in Ks. Lacks true put-away pitch, but lively, heavy FB plays up. Cuts FB to give different look and is extreme groundball guy. Velocity has inched up with cleaner mechanics, but CU needs to improve to last as SP. Mixes pitches well and CB flashes above average with outstanding shape.

Harris,Jon — SP — Toronto

EXP MLB DEBUT: 2018 | H/W: 6-4 175 | FUT: #3 starter | 8C

Thrws R Age 23
2015 (1) Missouri State

Velo	Pitch	Grade
90-95	FB	+++
83-85	SL	+++
77-79	CB	+++
82-87	CU	+++

Year	Lev	Team	W	L	Sv	IP	K	ERA	WHIP	BF/G	OBA	H%	S%	xERA	Ctl	Dom	Cmd	hr/9	BPV
2015	NCAA	Missouri State	8	2	0	103	116	2.45	1.08	26.8	205	29	76	1.94	3.1	10.1	3.2	0.2	116
2015	A-	Vancouver	0	5	0	36	32	6.75	1.92	14.2	321	40	62	5.76	5.3	8.0	1.5	0.3	20
2016	A	Lansing	8	2	0	84	73	2.24	1.16	21.0	238	31	79	2.52	2.6	7.8	3.0	0.1	89
2016	A+	Dunedin	3	2	0	45	26	3.60	1.13	22.2	226	26	67	2.59	2.8	5.2	1.9	0.4	36

Athletic SP who improved mechanics in solid season and throws four pitches for strikes. Establishes plate with lively FB and can miss bats with SL that features cutting action. Throws heavy ball and rarely allows HR. Struggles to maintain velocity deep into games and may not have true out pitch. CB and CU could turn into strikeout offerings.

Harvey,Hunter — SP — Baltimore

EXP MLB DEBUT: 2019 | H/W: 6-3 175 | FUT: #2 starter | 9D

Thrws R Age 22
2013 (1) HS (NC)

Velo	Pitch	Grade
91-95	FB	++++
72-78	CB	++++
81-84	CU	++

Year	Lev	Team	W	L	Sv	IP	K	ERA	WHIP	BF/G	OBA	H%	S%	xERA	Ctl	Dom	Cmd	hr/9	BPV
2013	Rk	GCL Orioles	0	0	0	13	18	1.37	0.92	9.8	213	35	83	1.44	1.4	12.4	9.0	0.0	203
2013	A-	Aberdeen	0	1	0	12	15	2.25	1.25	16.3	245	37	80	2.70	3.0	11.3	3.8	0.0	140
2014	A	Delmarva	7	5	0	87	106	3.20	1.14	20.3	212	30	72	2.48	3.4	10.9	3.2	0.5	123
2016	Rk	GCL Orioles	0	0	0	5	11	0.00	0.60	8.6	175	49	100	0.14	0.0	19.8		0.0	374
2016	A-	Aberdeen	0	1	0	7	7	3.75	2.08	11.8	307	40	80	5.71	7.5	8.8	1.2	0.0	-27

Injury-prone SP who briefly pitched after missing 2015 and succumbed to TJS in July. Will likely miss most of '17, but has frontline stuff when healthy. Misses bats with two plus pitches in FB and big-breaking CB while CU is advanced for age. Clean, fluid arm action adds movement to all offerings and has ability to sequence like a veteran.

Hatch,Thomas — SP — Chicago (N)

EXP MLB DEBUT: 2020 | H/W: 6-1 190 | FUT: #3 starter | 8D

Thrws R Age 22
2016 (3) Oklahoma State

Velo	Pitch	Grade
89-94	FB	++++
84-87	CT	+++
78-83	SL	++
78-82	CU	++

Year	Lev	Team	W	L	Sv	IP	K	ERA	WHIP	BF/G	OBA	H%	S%	xERA	Ctl	Dom	Cmd	hr/9	BPV
2016		Did not pitch																	

Strong-armed collegiate hurler was the Cubs 1st pick in '16 draft. Featured four average to above offerings including a 90-94 mph sinking FB, a low-80s SL that shows some swing-and-miss potential, a CT, and an usable circle CU. Keeps the ball down in the zone. Concerns about his elbow caused him to slide to round 3 and he has yet to make pro debut.

Hearn,Taylor — RP — Pittsburgh

EXP MLB DEBUT: 2018 | H/W: 6-5 210 | FUT: Setup reliever | 7D

Thrws L Age 22
2015 (5) OK Baptist

Velo	Pitch	Grade
94-97	FB	++++
84-87	SL	+++
	CU	+

Year	Lev	Team	W	L	Sv	IP	K	ERA	WHIP	BF/G	OBA	H%	S%	xERA	Ctl	Dom	Cmd	hr/9	BPV
2015	Rk	GCL Nationals	0	0	0	5	7	0.00	1.20	10.1	221	36	100	2.25	3.6	12.6	3.5	0.0	148
2015	A-	Auburn	1	5	0	43	38	3.98	1.44	18.3	288	36	72	4.20	2.7	8.0	2.9	0.4	88
2016	Rk	GCL Nationals	0	0	0	6	8	1.48	1.31	12.6	104	10	100	2.67	8.9	11.8	1.3	1.5	-9
2016	A	Hagerstown	1	0	0	22	31	3.24	1.44	11.8	285	41	83	4.87	2.8	12.6	4.4	1.2	168
2016	A	West Virginia	1	1	0	22	36	2.03	1.13	11.0	193	33	87	2.48	4.1	14.6	3.6	0.8	171

Big, physical lefty came over from the Nationals in the Melancon deal and worked in relief and as a starter. Blows hitters away with a plus 94-97 mph FB that bumps 99. Above-average SL gives him a second solid offering, but CU is below-average. Whiffed 75 in 57.1 IP.

Heller,Ben — RP — New York (A)

EXP MLB DEBUT: 2016 | H/W: 6-3 205 | FUT: Setup reliever | 6B

Thrws R Age 25
2013 (22) Olivet Nazarene

Velo	Pitch	Grade
93-98	FB	++++
81-85	SL	+++

Year	Lev	Team	W	L	Sv	IP	K	ERA	WHIP	BF/G	OBA	H%	S%	xERA	Ctl	Dom	Cmd	hr/9	BPV
2015	AA	Akron	0	0	0	6	15	1.50	1.00	4.6	228	72	83	1.74	1.5	22.5	15.0	0.0	383
2016	AA	Akron	1	0	7	16	23	0.56	0.50	3.6	62	8	100		2.8	12.9	4.6	0.6	174
2016	AAA	Columbus	2	2	5	25	25	2.51	1.08	3.5	220	29	77	2.30	2.5	9.0	3.6	0.4	112
2016	AAA	Scranton/WB	0	1	1	6	7	1.48	0.82	3.7	149	23	80	0.50	3.0	10.3	3.5	0.0	124
2016	MLB	NY Yankees	1	0	0	7	6	6.43	2.14	3.5	358	37	83	10.35	5.1	7.7	1.5	3.9	18

Hard-throwing RP was acquired at deadline and could be dependable, late-innings arm. Can blow FB by hitters up in zone while missing bats with SL. Two K pitches in arsenal, but value increased as walk rate declined. Has tendency to overthrow which flattens FB and has zero feel for changing speeds. Everything comes out hard, but has valued arm.

Helsley,Ryan — SP — St. Louis

EXP MLB DEBUT: 2019 | H/W: 6-1 195 | FUT: #3 starter | 7C

Thrws R Age 22
2015 (5) Northeastern St

Velo	Pitch	Grade
93-96	FB	++++
75-78	CB	++
83-86	CU	++

Year	Lev	Team	W	L	Sv	IP	K	ERA	WHIP	BF/G	OBA	H%	S%	xERA	Ctl	Dom	Cmd	hr/9	BPV
2015	Rk	Johnson City	1	1	0	40	35	2.02	1.30	15.0	226	29	84	2.82	4.3	7.9	1.8	0.2	44
2016	A	Peoria	10	2	0	95	109	1.61	1.01	21.4	223	32	85	2.09	1.8	10.3	5.7	0.3	155

Short, hard-throwing righty has plus arm speed and comes after hitters with a good 92-95 mph FB that hits 97 mph from a high 3/4 arm slot. Mixes in a fringe CB and and improved CU. Improved control fueled the breakout and raises his profile.

Heredia,Luis — RP — Pittsburgh

EXP MLB DEBUT: 2018 | H/W: 6-5 250 | FUT: Setup reliever | 7D

Thrws R Age 22
2010 FA (MX)

Velo	Pitch	Grade
90-93	FB	++++
	CB	++
84-86	CU	++
	SL	++

Year	Lev	Team	W	L	Sv	IP	K	ERA	WHIP	BF/G	OBA	H%	S%	xERA	Ctl	Dom	Cmd	hr/9	BPV
2012	A-	State College	4	2	0	66	40	2.72	1.10	18.5	221	26	75	2.34	2.7	5.4	2.0	0.3	43
2013	A	West Virginia	7	3	0	65	55	3.05	1.37	19.5	221	27	80	3.38	5.1	7.6	1.5	0.7	17
2014	A	West Virginia	2	4	0	89	43	4.15	1.35	20.6	257	27	71	4.04	3.3	4.3	1.3	0.9	6
2015	A+	Bradenton	5	6	0	86	54	5.44	1.73	18.6	302	35	66	5.08	4.6	5.7	1.2	0.3	-5
2016	A+	Bradenton	4	6	12	54	42	3.66	1.59	5.3	265	33	75	4.02	5.2	7.0	1.4	0.2	5

Tall, strong-armed hurler was moved to relief in 2016. Started well, posting a 0.67 ERA through July, but fell apart in the 2nd half posting a 6.59 ERA. Control continues to be the main issue, walking 23 in 27.1 2nd half IP. Still has a good 90-93 mph FB, but it lacks the zip it once had. His CB, SL, and CU are average to below-average offerings.

Hildenberger,Trevor — RP — Minnesota

EXP MLB DEBUT: 2017 | H/W: 6-2 211 | FUT: Setup reliever | 6A

Thrws R Age 26
2014 (22) California

Velo	Pitch	Grade
89-93	FB	+++
77-81	SL	++
81-84	CU	+++

Year	Lev	Team	W	L	Sv	IP	K	ERA	WHIP	BF/G	OBA	H%	S%	xERA	Ctl	Dom	Cmd	hr/9	BPV
2014	Rk	Elizabethton	0	0	0	1	2	0.00	0.00	2.8	0	0			0.0	18.0		0.0	342
2015	A	Cedar Rapids	2	1	14	45	59	0.80	0.64	5.6	159	26	86	0.15	1.0	11.8	11.8	0.0	203
2015	A+	Fort Myers	1	1	3	19	21	3.32	0.89	5.4	219	32	59	1.48	0.9	9.9	10.5	0.0	171
2016	A+	Fort Myers	1	1	3	9	8	0.99	1.21	6.1	300	38	91	3.41	0.0	7.9		0.0	160
2016	AA	Chattanooga	2	3	16	38	45	0.71	0.71	4.2	163	23	96	0.81	1.4	10.6	7.5	0.5	171

Side-arming closer who ended season early due to elbow ailment. Extreme groundballer who is tough to hit, but doesn't own dependable breaking ball. Doesn't fit closer profile as velocity a little short. Relies on heavy pitch mix and command. CU may be best pitch as it drops late and has nice separation from FB. Rarely walks hitters.

Hill,David — SP — Colorado

EXP MLB DEBUT: 2018 | H/W: 6-2 195 | FUT: #4 starter | 7D

Thrws R Age 22
2015 (4) San Diego

Velo	Pitch	Grade
90-93	FB	+++
	SL	+++
	CU	++

Year	Lev	Team	W	L	Sv	IP	K	ERA	WHIP	BF/G	OBA	H%	S%	xERA	Ctl	Dom	Cmd	hr/9	BPV
2015	NCAA	San Diego	9	3	0	100	115	2.34	1.01	27.4	190	27	77	1.67	3.1	10.3	3.3	0.3	119
2015	A-	Boise	0	0	0	23	23	3.12	1.26	11.8	235	31	75	2.97	3.5	9.0	2.6	0.4	85
2016	A	Asheville	4	4	0	82	82	4.49	1.33	24.3	291	37	67	4.38	1.5	9.0	5.9	0.9	138

4th round pick continues to put up solid numbers despite pedestrian stuff. FB sits at 90-93 mph with good sink from a low 3/4 arm slot. Gets arm-side run on FB and showed improved command, walking just 14 in 82. IP. SL flashes plus but is inconsistent and split-change also has potential. Worth watching.

Hillman,Juan — SP — Cleveland

EXP MLB DEBUT: 2019 | H/W: 6-2 185 | FUT: #4 starter | 8E

Thrws L Age 19
2015 (2) HS (FL)

Velo	Pitch	Grade
87-91	FB	++
75-78	CB	+++
79-82	CU	++++

Year	Lev	Team	W	L	Sv	IP	K	ERA	WHIP	BF/G	OBA	H%	S%	xERA	Ctl	Dom	Cmd	hr/9	BPV
2015	Rk	AZL Indians	0	2	0	24	20	4.13	1.29	12.3	278	35	65	3.29	1.9	7.5	4.0	0.0	102
2016	A-	Mahoning Vall	3	4	0	63	47	4.43	1.43	17.8	271	32	69	4.22	3.4	6.7	2.0	0.7	46

Athletic, projectable LHP with advanced feel for secondaries. Sells plus fading CU with fast arm and velo separation off straight, high-80s FB. CB flashes above-average 1/7 shape but struggled to locate in NYPL. Frame requires added mass for velocity development. If that happens, potential for three above-average pitches as solid back-end type arm.

Hinsz,Gage — SP — Pittsburgh

EXP MLB DEBUT: 2019 | H/W: 6-4 210 | FUT: #3 starter | 8D

Thrws R Age 20
2014 (11) HS (MT)

Velo	Pitch	Grade
91-94	FB	+++
74-77	CB	+++
	CU	++

Year	Lev	Team	W	L	Sv	IP	K	ERA	WHIP	BF/G	OBA	H%	S%	xERA	Ctl	Dom	Cmd	hr/9	BPV
2014	Rk	GCL Pirates	0	0	0	8	7	3.38	1.50	11.5	262	34	75	3.59	4.5	7.9	1.8	0.0	38
2015	Rk	Bristol	3	4	0	38	24	3.79	1.58	16.7	257	30	75	3.96	5.4	5.7	1.0	0.2	-27
2016	A	West Virginia	6	8	0	93	67	3.67	1.27	22.4	262	30	73	3.74	2.4	6.5	2.7	0.8	69

11th round pick has good size and nice projection. His FB velocity now sits at 92-94 mph, bumping 95 with a mid-70s CB that flashes as plus but needs more consistency. CU is a fringe offering. Has an easy high 3/4 arm slot and throws downhill, keeping the ball low in the zone. Still youhg with a strong, athletic frame.

Hofacket,Adam — RP — Los Angeles (A)

EXP MLB DEBUT: 2018 | H/W: 6-1 195 | FUT: Middle reliever | 6B

Thrws R Age 23
2015 (10) Calif Baptist

Velo	Pitch	Grade
90-94	FB	+++
82-85	SL	+++
	CU	+

Year	Lev	Team	W	L	Sv	IP	K	ERA	WHIP	BF/G	OBA	H%	S%	xERA	Ctl	Dom	Cmd	hr/9	BPV
2015	Rk	Orem	4	0	8	31	23	3.77	1.13	4.7	268	30	73	4.11	0.9	6.7	7.7	1.5	115
2016	A	Burlington	1	1	7	21	24	2.56	1.04	5.4	252	34	80	3.07	0.9	10.2	12.0	0.9	179
2016	A+	Inland Empire	1	2	2	34	37	6.07	1.50	5.7	283	36	60	4.85	3.4	9.8	2.8	1.1	101

Strong-armed RP who uses lots of pitches to keep hitters off guard. Can vary speeds and add cutting action to SL that may be best offering. Some deception in delivery, but throws across body and hinders FB command. Could throw harder if he wanted, but content on moving ball around plate. Has closer experience, but was hit hard in A+.

Hoffman,Jeff — SP — Colorado

EXP MLB DEBUT: 2016 | H/W: 6-5 225 | FUT: #2 starter | 9D

Thrws R Age 24
2014 (1) East Carolina

Velo	Pitch	Grade
91-96	FB	++++
80-82	CB	+++
85-87	CU	+++

Year	Lev	Team	W	L	Sv	IP	K	ERA	WHIP	BF/G	OBA	H%	S%	xERA	Ctl	Dom	Cmd	hr/9	BPV
2015	A+	Dunedin	3	3	0	56	38	3.21	1.32	21.1	272	31	77	3.90	2.4	6.1	2.5	0.6	63
2015	AA	New Britain	2	2	0	36	29	3.24	1.02	19.8	210	25	71	2.43	2.5	7.2	2.9	0.7	81
2015	AA	New Hampshire	0	0	0	11	8	1.61	0.98	21.3	222	28	82	1.77	1.6	6.4	4.0	0.0	90
2016	AAA	Albuquerque	6	9	0	118	124	4.04	1.36	22.5	260	34	72	3.98	3.4	9.4	2.8	0.8	97
2016	MLB	Colorado	0	4	0	31	22	4.92	1.74	17.7	297	31	79	6.60	4.9	6.4	1.3	2.0	0

9th pick in 2014 draft continues to have electric stuff with a dominant 91-96 mph FB, a hard 11/5 CB, and an improved CU. Command comes and goes and he doesn't miss as many bats as he should. Needs to sequence better and develop more consistent mechanics, but has clean delivery and quick arm. Look for a breakout in '17.

Holder,Jonathan — RP — New York (A)

EXP MLB DEBUT: 2016 | H/W: 6-2 235 | FUT: Setup reliever | 6B

Thrws R Age 23
2014 (6) Mississipi State

Velo	Pitch	Grade
90-95	FB	+++
75-79	CB	+++
84-87	SL	+++

Year	Lev	Team	W	L	Sv	IP	K	ERA	WHIP	BF/G	OBA	H%	S%	xERA	Ctl	Dom	Cmd	hr/9	BPV
2015	AAA	Scranton/WB	0	1	0	5	4	6.92	1.54	22.7	214	22	57	4.71	6.9	6.9	1.0	1.7	-44
2016	A+	Tampa	0	0	0	4	7	0.00	0.50	6.6	151	32	100		0.0	15.8		0.0	302
2016	AA	Trenton	3	1	10	41	59	2.20	0.83	5.3	189	31	75	1.35	1.5	13.0	8.4	0.4	210
2016	AAA	Scranton/WB	2	0	6	20	35	0.90	0.35	5.3	110	22	83		0.0	15.7		0.4	300
2016	MLB	NY Yankees	0	0	0	8	5	5.56	1.48	4.4	259	28	64	4.57	4.4	5.6	1.3	1.1	-2

Big, strong RP who saw K rate drastically escalate and reached majors. Effective at locating pitches and sequences well. Throws all pitches for strikes and changes eye level. Induces weak contact when hitters put bat to ball, but ability to get swings and misses gives him value. Does not allow many HR.

Holmes,Clay — SP — Pittsburgh

EXP MLB DEBUT: 2018 | H/W: 6-5 230 | FUT: #3 starter | 7C

Thrws R Age 24
2011 (9) HS (AL)

Velo	Pitch	Grade
90-93	FB	++++
80-83	CB	++
	CU	++

Year	Lev	Team	W	L	Sv	IP	K	ERA	WHIP	BF/G	OBA	H%	S%	xERA	Ctl	Dom	Cmd	hr/9	BPV
2015	Rk	GCL Pirates	1	0	0	13	10	2.06	1.07	17.0	260	33	79	2.49	0.7	6.9	10.0	0.0	123
2015	A+	Bradenton	0	2	0	23	16	2.74	1.09	15.0	217	27	72	1.98	2.7	6.3	2.3	0.0	57
2016	AA	Altoona	10	9	0	136	101	4.23	1.48	22.5	264	31	72	4.22	4.2	6.7	1.6	0.7	24

Tall RHP had Tommy John surgery in 2014 and has been slow to return. Was fully healthy in '16, but the results were mixed in 26 AA starts. Has a good 90-93 mph FB that has good downhill tilt and generates plenty of GB outs. Scrapped his SL in favor of a more effective CB and CU that still needs work. Below-average control remains an issue.

Holmes,Grant — SP — Oakland

EXP MLB DEBUT: 2019 | H/W: 6-1 215 | FUT: #2 starter | 9D

Thrws R Age 21
2014 (1) HS (SC)

Velo	Pitch	Grade
91-95	FB	++++
82-84	CB	+++
83-84	CU	++

Year	Lev	Team	W	L	Sv	IP	K	ERA	WHIP	BF/G	OBA	H%	S%	xERA	Ctl	Dom	Cmd	hr/9	BPV
2014	Rk	Azl Dodgers	1	2	0	30	33	3.00	0.90	15.9	191	26	68	1.73	2.1	9.9	4.7	0.6	140
2014	Rk	Ogden	1	1	0	18	25	4.97	1.38	19.0	271	41	63	3.84	3.0	12.4	4.2	0.5	161
2015	A	Great Lakes	6	4	0	103	117	3.14	1.36	17.9	228	32	78	3.26	4.7	10.2	2.2	0.5	75
2016	A+	Rancho Cuca	8	4	1	105	100	4.02	1.39	22.1	258	33	71	3.73	3.7	8.6	2.3	0.5	73
2016	A+	Stockton	3	3	0	28	24	7.02	1.91	22.3	356	42	64	7.32	3.2	7.7	2.4	1.3	70

Power SP who saw K rate drop, but has repertoire to front rotation. Can notch Ks with FB and hard CB. Has strong frame to hold velocity deep into games and throws with downhill angle to plate. Throws quality strikes, though FB command needs to improve. Mechanics can get out of sync. Has good feel for CU, but can be too firm.

Honeywell,Brent — SP — Tampa Bay

EXP MLB DEBUT: 2017 | H/W: 6-2 180 | FUT: #2 starter | 8B

Thrws R Age 22
2014 (2) Walters State CC

Velo	Pitch	Grade
90-95	FB	+++
81-84	SC	+++
75-79	CB	+++
81-85	CU	+++

Year	Lev	Team	W	L	Sv	IP	K	ERA	WHIP	BF/G	OBA	H%	S%	xERA	Ctl	Dom	Cmd	hr/9	BPV
2014	Rk	Princeton	2	1	0	33	40	1.08	0.75	13.2	169	25	88	0.79	1.6	10.8	6.7	0.3	169
2015	A	Bowling Green	4	4	0	65	76	2.91	1.00	20.7	224	32	71	2.20	1.7	10.5	6.3	0.4	163
2015	A+	Charlotte	5	2	0	65	53	3.46	1.11	21.3	237	30	67	2.53	2.1	7.3	3.5	0.3	94
2016	A+	Charlotte	4	1	0	56	64	2.41	0.96	21.2	214	29	80	2.35	1.8	10.3	5.8	0.8	155
2016	AA	Montgomery	3	2	0	59	53	2.28	1.10	23.2	234	29	82	2.78	2.1	8.1	3.8	0.6	106

Consistently solid SP who generates explosive life with above average FB with easy delivery and clean arm action. Uses 4 pitches, including screwball, to keep hitters off-guard. Repeats athletic delivery and all pitches grade as at least average. Demonstrates touch for CU and misses bats with multiple offerings. Can leave pitches up on occasion.

Howard,Sam — SP — Colorado

EXP MLB DEBUT: 2018 | H/W: 6-3 170 | FUT: #5 SP/swingman | 7D

Thrws L Age 24
2014 (3) Georgia Southern

Velo	Pitch	Grade
90-92	FB	+++
80-83	SL	+++
	CU	+++

Year	Lev	Team	W	L	Sv	IP	K	ERA	WHIP	BF/G	OBA	H%	S%	xERA	Ctl	Dom	Cmd	hr/9	BPV
2014	NCAA	Georgia Southern	7	6	0	95	94	2.36	1.08	23.2	232	30	80	2.57	2.1	8.9	4.3	0.5	122
2014	Rk	Grand Junction	1	3	0	53	42	5.42	1.56	16.6	328	38	66	5.70	1.7	7.1	4.2	1.0	100
2015	A	Asheville	11	9	0	134	122	3.43	1.22	21.6	257	32	72	3.31	2.1	8.2	3.8	0.5	107
2016	A+	Modesto	4	3	0	65	73	2.48	1.03	22.8	190	27	77	1.86	3.3	10.1	3.0	0.4	110
2016	AA	Hartford	5	6	0	90	67	4.00	1.56	24.7	308	35	78	5.47	2.8	6.7	2.4	1.1	63

Tall, slender lefty impressed at A+/AA, going 9-9 w/ 3.35 ERA. FB velocity jumped into the low-90s, topping out at 96 mph with good, late sink. Backs the FB with a SL and an above-average CU. Pounds the strike zone and locates the FB well to both sides of the plate. Bulldog mentality on the mound with simple mechanics.

Hoyt,James — RP — Houston

EXP MLB DEBUT: 2016 | H/W: 6-6 230 | FUT: Setup reliever | 7A

Thrws R Age 30
2012 NDFA (Centenary)

Velo	Pitch	Grade
93-96	FB	++++
82-85	SL	+++
86-89	SP	++

Year	Lev	Team	W	L	Sv	IP	K	ERA	WHIP	BF/G	OBA	H%	S%	xERA	Ctl	Dom	Cmd	hr/9	BPV
2014	AA	Mississippi	2	2	6	31	43	1.15	0.93	4.2	178	29	89	1.34	2.9	12.4	4.3	0.3	163
2014	AAA	Gwinnett	1	1	1	28	34	5.46	1.86	5.5	325	43	73	6.61	4.5	10.9	2.4	1.3	93
2015	AAA	Fresno	0	1	9	49	66	3.49	1.20	4.2	258	39	69	2.92	2.0	12.1	6.0	0.2	182
2016	AAA	Fresno	4	3	29	55	93	1.64	0.87	4.1	158	30	83	0.98	3.1	15.2	4.9	0.3	208
2016	MLB	Houston	1	1	0	22	28	4.50	1.14	4.0	205	24	70	3.83	3.7	11.5	3.1	2.0	125

Big-framed RP who led PCL in saves and showcased plus arm strength in brief trial with HOU. Spent all career in pen and uses plus FB to advantage. FB exhibits lots of movement and throws consistent strikes. SL gives him second solid offering, though has trouble controlling it. Has been tough to hit while registering extremely high K rate.

Hu,Chih-Wei

SP | Tampa Bay | EXP MLB DEBUT: 2017 | H/W: 6-1 230 | FUT: #4 starter | 7B

Thrws R Age 23
2012 FA (TW)

Velo	Pitch	Grade
90-94	FB	+++
82-84	SL	+++
81-85	CU	++++

Year	Lev	Team	W	L	Sv	IP	K	ERA	WHIP	BF/G	OBA	H%	S%	xERA	Ctl	Dom	Cmd	hr/9	BPV
2015	A+	Charlotte	0	3	1	18	20	7.46	1.71	16.4	311	41	53	5.29	4.0	9.9	2.5	0.5	90
2015	A+	Fort Myers	5	3	0	84	73	2.46	1.16	22.4	250	31	81	3.08	2.0	7.8	3.8	0.5	104
2015	AAA	Rochester	1	0	0	6	6	1.50	1.00	22.9	106	15	83	0.55	6.0	9.0	1.5	0.0	18
2016	AA	Montgomery	7	8	0	142	107	2.59	1.15	23.5	242	29	78	2.87	2.3	6.8	3.0	0.4	78
2016	AAA	Durham	0	1	0	4	7	8.57	2.14	20.8	371	55	63	8.92	4.3	15.0	3.5	2.1	172

Durable, strong SP who led SL in ERA in breakout season. Has always thrown quality strikes with advanced command. FB has added a few ticks and uses same arm speed on CU. Sharp SL shows flashes of being plus, but doesn't miss many bats. Sequences pitches well and mixes in palmball on occasion. Big body needs to be monitored.

Huang,Wei-Chieh

SP | Arizona | EXP MLB DEBUT: 2018 | H/W: 6-1 170 | FUT: #5 SP/swingman | 7E

Thrws R Age 23
2014 FA (TW)

Velo	Pitch	Grade
88-92	FB	++
74-77	CB	++
81-83	CU	++++

Year	Lev	Team	W	L	Sv	IP	K	ERA	WHIP	BF/G	OBA	H%	S%	xERA	Ctl	Dom	Cmd	hr/9	BPV
2015	A	Kane County	7	3	0	76	68	2.01	0.97	19.3	213	28	78	1.73	1.9	8.0	4.3	0.1	112
2016	Rk	Azl Dbacks	0	0	0	3	3	6.00	1.00	11.5	262	27	50	5.14	0.0	9.0		3.0	180
2016	A-	Hillsboro	2	2	0	30	42	5.38	1.46	14.3	280	40	65	4.82	3.3	12.6	3.8	1.2	155
2016	A+	Visalia	1	1	0	26	25	6.55	1.72	19.8	310	37	65	6.47	4.1	8.6	2.1	1.7	61

RH control artist struggled in 2nd year in pro ball. FB only effective when command is in tiptop shape. Not much movement to fool hitters. CB is slow and loopy, struggles staying on top of pitch. CU is best pitch with great late fade and solid deception of FB. Package depends on FB command. Undersized, likely a swing man.

Hudson,Bryan

SP | Chicago (N) | EXP MLB DEBUT: 2019 | H/W: 6-8 220 | FUT: #3 starter | 7D

Thrws L Age 19
2015 (3) HS (IL)

Velo	Pitch	Grade
92-94	FB	+++
75-78	CB	++++
80-83	CU	++

Year	Lev	Team	W	L	Sv	IP	K	ERA	WHIP	BF/G	OBA	H%	S%	xERA	Ctl	Dom	Cmd	hr/9	BPV
2015	Rk	Azl Cubs	0	0	0	6	5	2.90	1.29	5.1	255	32	75	2.98	2.9	7.3	2.5	0.0	70
2016	A-	Eugene	5	4	0	58	41	5.10	1.67	20.1	254	30	69	4.50	6.3	6.3	1.0	0.6	-39

Huge lefty struggled in short-season ball. FB sits at 92-94 mph but has room for more as he matures. Best offering is a potentially plus hard CB while CU remains below-average. Arm lags behind in delivery with poor extension on finish resulting in inconsistent release point. Walked 41 in 58.2 IP.

Hudson,Dakota

SP | St. Louis | EXP MLB DEBUT: 2018 | H/W: 6-5 215 | FUT: #3 starter | 8D

Thrws R Age 22
2016 (1) Mississippi State

Velo	Pitch	Grade
93-95	FB	+++
85-87	CT	++++
78-82	CB	++
	CU	++

Year	Lev	Team	W	L	Sv	IP	K	ERA	WHIP	BF/G	OBA	H%	S%	xERA	Ctl	Dom	Cmd	hr/9	BPV
2016	NCAA	Mississippi St	9	5	0	113	115	2.55	1.25	27.0	250	34	78	2.92	2.8	9.2	3.3	0.2	108
2016	Rk	GCL Cardinals	1	0	0	4	9	0.00	1.00	3.8	262	64	100	2.20	0.0	20.3		0.0	383
2016	A+	Palm Beach	1	1	3	9	10	0.99	1.43	4.8	190	28	92	2.48	6.9	9.9	1.4	0.0	9

Tall, strong-armed hurler was one of three 1st round picks in 2016. Has a plus mid-90s FB that hits 97 mph with good late life. Mixes in a plus CT along with a CB and CU. Poor front-side mechanics results in inconsistent release point and below-average command, but showed improvement in debut. Has the stuff to be a power reliever.

Jackson,Luke

RP | Atlanta | EXP MLB DEBUT: 2015 | H/W: 6-2 210 | FUT: Closer | 7B

Thrws R Age 25
2010 (S-1) HS (FL)

Velo	Pitch	Grade
93-98	FB	++++
77-83	CB	+++
81-84	CU	+++

Year	Lev	Team	W	L	Sv	IP	K	ERA	WHIP	BF/G	OBA	H%	S%	xERA	Ctl	Dom	Cmd	hr/9	BPV
2015	AAA	Round Rock	2	3	0	66	79	4.36	1.47	7.3	250	35	69	3.69	4.8	10.8	2.3	0.4	83
2015	MLB	Texas	0	0	0	6	6	4.43	1.15	3.5	225	26	67	3.60	3.0	8.9	3.0	1.5	98
2016	AA	Frisco	0	1	1	24	32	4.85	1.83	5.6	284	39	78	6.09	6.3	12.0	1.9	1.5	62
2016	AAA	Round Rock	1	0	2	22	27	2.45	1.27	5.6	173	24	85	2.66	6.1	11.0	1.8	0.8	51
2016	MLB	Texas	0	0	0	11	3	11.25	2.68	7.7	411	39	62	12.19	6.4	2.4	0.4	3.2	-112

Durable, strong RP who moved to pen in '15 and has found niche. Still struggles to command plate, but has three very good offerings in arsenal. Can blow FB by hitters up in zone. Sharp-breaking CB can be out pitch and CU has late, tumbling action. FB very tough to square up. Problem has been throwing strikes.

Jackson,Zach

RP | Toronto | EXP MLB DEBUT: 2019 | H/W: 6-4 215 | FUT: Closer | 7D

Thrws R Age 22
2016 (3) Arkansas

Velo	Pitch	Grade
91-96	FB	+++
84-87	CB	++++
83-89	CU	++

Year	Lev	Team	W	L	Sv	IP	K	ERA	WHIP	BF/G	OBA	H%	S%	xERA	Ctl	Dom	Cmd	hr/9	BPV
2016	NCAA	Arkansas	3	4	4	53	66	5.09	1.64	13.1	239	35	68	4.09	6.8	11.2	1.7	0.5	36
2016	Rk	GCL Blue Jays	0	0	0	1	0	0.00	1.00	3.8	262	26	100	2.41	0.0	0.0		0.0	18
2016	A-	Vancouver	1	1	0	17	23	3.66	1.45	5.7	211	34	72	2.78	6.3	12.0	1.9	0.0	65

Hard-throwing RP with one of better breaking balls in org. CB thrown with incredible velocity and hard-breaking action. Doesn't control it well, but is true knockout pitch. Generally commands FB, though has tendency to leave ball up. Long arm action leaves him in pen and needs to repeat slot better.

Jacome,Justin

SP | Miami | EXP MLB DEBUT: 2019 | H/W: 6-6 215 | FUT: #5 SP/swingman | 6C

Thrws L Age 23
2015 (5) UC-Santa Barbara

Velo	Pitch	Grade
89-92	FB	++
	SL	++
	CU	++

Year	Lev	Team	W	L	Sv	IP	K	ERA	WHIP	BF/G	OBA	H%	S%	xERA	Ctl	Dom	Cmd	hr/9	BPV
2015	NCAA	UC SantaBarbara	7	5	0	116	96	2.71	1.17	29.0	251	31	77	2.98	2.0	7.4	3.7	0.4	97
2015	A-	Batavia	0	1	0	32	29	2.52	1.37	11.2	290	37	81	3.91	2.0	8.1	4.1	0.3	111
2016	A	Greensboro	1	5	0	72	47	3.74	1.45	14.7	253	29	75	3.96	4.5	5.9	1.3	0.6	2

Tall lefty has fringe stuff, but keeps hitters at bay with pitchability and by creating downhill tilt on his 89-92 mph FB. SL and CU are fringe-average as well. Struggles to repeat mechanics consistently due to size. Low Dom and poor command suggest a move to relief as he moves up, but there is some projection left.

Jax,Griffin

SP | Minnesota | EXP MLB DEBUT: 2019 | H/W: 6-2 195 | FUT: #4 starter | 7C

Thrws R Age 22
2016 (3) Air Force

Velo	Pitch	Grade
90-95	FB	+++
83-85	SL	+++
80-82	CU	+++

Year	Lev	Team	W	L	Sv	IP	K	ERA	WHIP	BF/G	OBA	H%	S%	xERA	Ctl	Dom	Cmd	hr/9	BPV
2016	NCAA	Air Force	9	2	0	105	90	2.06	1.08	27.4	241	30	82	2.58	1.7	7.7	4.5	0.3	110
2016	Rk	Elizabethton	0	1	0	8	8	4.39	1.95	9.8	393	46	86	8.98	1.1	8.8	8.0	2.2	146

Strong-armed pitcher who could be valuable as SP or RP. Exhibits very fast arm which adds velocity and movement to power arsenal. Throws strikes with sinking FB and likes to go to SL when ahead in count. Can slow arm on CU, though has nice separation from FB. Key is hitting spots as may become pitch-to-contact guy as SP.

Jay,Tyler

SP | Minnesota | EXP MLB DEBUT: 2017 | H/W: 6-1 185 | FUT: #3 starter | 8B

Thrws L Age 22
2015 (1) Illinois

Velo	Pitch	Grade
91-94	FB	+++
85-88	SL	++++
75-77	CB	+++
83-87	CU	++

Year	Lev	Team	W	L	Sv	IP	K	ERA	WHIP	BF/G	OBA	H%	S%	xERA	Ctl	Dom	Cmd	hr/9	BPV
2015	NCAA	Illinois	5	2	14	66	76	1.09	0.71	7.8	176	26	87	0.78	1.0	10.3	10.9	0.3	178
2015	A+	Fort Myers	0	1	1	18	22	3.98	1.44	4.1	261	38	69	3.38	4.0	10.9	2.8	0.0	108
2016	A+	Fort Myers	5	5	0	69	68	2.86	1.23	21.5	247	32	79	3.30	2.7	8.8	3.2	0.7	103
2016	AA	Chattanooga	0	0	0	14	9	5.79	1.29	11.5	248	27	56	4.09	3.2	5.8	1.8	1.3	35

Athletic, aggressive hurler who converted to SP in '16. Season ended in July due to neck/shoulder strain. Dominates with plus slider that is tough to hit and misses bats. Fastball is sneaky quick and can spot to both sides. Needs to improve CU and pitch sequencing, but has fast arm and feel for strikes. Durability is big question.

Jaye,Myles

SP | Detroit | EXP MLB DEBUT: 2017 | H/W: 6-3 170 | FUT: #4 starter | 7D

Thrws R Age 25
2010 (17) HS (GA)

Velo	Pitch	Grade
89-94	FB	+++
80-83	SL	+++
	CU	++

Year	Lev	Team	W	L	Sv	IP	K	ERA	WHIP	BF/G	OBA	H%	S%	xERA	Ctl	Dom	Cmd	hr/9	BPV
2014	A+	Winston-Salem	3	0	0	29	15	1.55	0.93	27.2	212	23	88	2.13	1.6	4.7	3.0	0.6	60
2014	AA	Birmingham	4	12	0	132	73	5.32	1.51	23.8	282	31	64	4.56	3.6	5.0	1.4	0.7	10
2015	AA	Birmingham	12	9	0	147	104	3.30	1.24	23.0	245	29	74	3.18	2.9	6.4	2.2	0.5	55
2016	AA	Erie	4	8	0	122	104	4.05	1.28	23.8	269	33	70	3.89	2.1	7.7	3.6	0.8	98
2016	AAA	Toledo	1	4	0	39	31	3.69	1.08	21.7	214	26	65	2.35	2.8	7.2	2.6	0.5	72

Durable SP who spent bulk of 3rd year in AA before promotion to AAA in August. K rate jumped due to better pitch mixing and more consistent SL. Throws consistent strikes and induces high amount of groundballs. Needs pitch to retire LHH and lacks true put away offering. Potential to eat innings.

Jefferies,Daulton

SP | Oakland | EXP MLB DEBUT: 2019 | H/W: 6-0 180 | FUT: #4 starter | 7B

Thrws R Age 21
2016 (S-1) California

Velo	Pitch	Grade
89-94	FB	+++
81-84	SL	++
83-85	CU	++++

Year	Lev	Team	W	L	Sv	IP	K	ERA	WHIP	BF/G	OBA	H%	S%	xERA	Ctl	Dom	Cmd	hr/9	BPV
2016	NCAA	California	7	0	0	50	53	1.08	0.84	22.9	194	25	95	1.73	1.4	9.5	6.6	0.7	151
2016	Rk	Azl Athletics	0	0	0	11	17	2.43	1.17	8.9	260	43	77	2.67	1.6	13.8	8.5	0.0	222

Consistent, short SP who relies on location and pitch movement to retire hitters. Spots FB to all quadrants of strike zone and messes with timing. Plus CU is best pitch and he can use it to set up hard SL. Very quick arm produces movement and delivery can be deceiving. An upgrade in SL would push prospect status upwards.

Jerez,Williams

RP | Boston | EXP MLB DEBUT: 2017 | H/W: 6-4 200 | FUT: Setup reliever | 7D

Thrws L Age 24	Year	Lev	Team	W	L	Sv	IP	K	ERA	WHIP	BF/G	OBA	H%	S%	xERA	Ctl	Dom	Cmd	hr/9	BPV
2011 (2) HS (NY)	2014	A-	Lowell	1	1	0	10	13	4.50	1.90	9.4	316	46	74	5.35	5.4	11.7	2.2	0.0	83
90-94 FB +++	2015	A	Greenville	3	1	3	39	43	2.07	1.36	11.7	281	37	88	4.12	2.3	9.9	4.3	0.7	134
80-82 SL +++	2015	A+	Salem	1	0	0	12	12	0.74	1.24	9.8	244	33	93	2.68	3.0	8.9	3.0	0.0	98
CU +	2015	AA	Portland	1	2	1	37	31	3.65	1.38	7.1	246	30	73	3.53	4.1	7.5	1.8	0.5	42
	2016	AA	Portland	1	6	0	65	65	4.71	1.54	7.1	276	35	70	4.66	4.2	9.0	2.2	0.8	68

Tall, strong RP who converted from OF to P in '14. Repeats simple delivery despite lack of experience and has SL that can miss bats. FB shows sink, but can be too straight at higher velocity. Tends to keep ball down, though doesn't show ability to change speeds. Slows arm on CU and seems relegated to being FB/SL guy, which is OK given short stints.

Jewell,Jake

SP | Los Angeles (A) | EXP MLB DEBUT: 2018 | H/W: 6-3 200 | FUT: #4 starter | 7C

Thrws R Age 23	Year	Lev	Team	W	L	Sv	IP	K	ERA	WHIP	BF/G	OBA	H%	S%	xERA	Ctl	Dom	Cmd	hr/9	BPV
2014 (5) NE Okla A&M																				
90-95 FB +++	2014	Rk	Azl Angels	1	0	0	30	26	1.50	1.16	13.3	213	28	86	2.11	3.6	7.8	2.2	0.0	61
84-86 SL ++	2014	Rk	Orem	0	2	0	12	9	8.93	2.15	20.0	392	46	56	8.10	3.0	6.7	2.3	0.7	58
77-80 CB ++	2015	A	Burlington	6	8	2	111	110	4.78	1.27	14.7	260	33	62	3.58	2.5	8.9	3.5	0.6	111
75-78 CU +++	2016	A+	Inland Empire	2	15	0	137	104	6.31	1.87	22.9	331	39	65	6.19	4.3	6.8	1.6	0.7	26

Strong-framed SP who had poor season after walk rate rose, K rate dropped, and was very hittable. Worked on secondary offerings as FB continues to be best pitch. Heavy action on FB allows for groundballs, but can't find consistency in either SL or CB. Loses velocity late in games and needs to set up hitters better. Needs CB or SL to be out pitch.

Jimenez,Joe

RP | Detroit | EXP MLB DEBUT: 2017 | H/W: 6-3 220 | FUT: Closer | 8C

Thrws R Age 22	Year	Lev	Team	W	L	Sv	IP	K	ERA	WHIP	BF/G	OBA	H%	S%	xERA	Ctl	Dom	Cmd	hr/9	BPV
2013 FA (PR)	2014	A-	Connecticut	3	2	4	26		2.75	1.07	4.4	229	39	74	2.33	2.1	14.1	6.8	0.3	216
94-99 FB ++++	2015	A	West Michigan	5	1	17	43	61	1.47	0.79	3.9	159	26	84	0.91	2.3	12.8	5.5	0.4	186
84-88 SL +++	2016	A+	Lakeland	0	0	10	17	28	0.00	0.58	3.4	94	20	100		2.6	14.7	5.6	0.0	212
85-87 CU +	2016	AA	Erie	3	2	12	20	34	2.23	0.99	3.7	174	34	75	1.15	3.6	15.1	4.3	0.0	194
	2016	AAA	Toledo	0	1	8	15	16	2.37	0.86	3.3	174	23	75	1.42	2.4	9.5	4.0	0.6	125

Max-effort RP who posted 30 saves on 3 levels. Tough to hit with two solid-average to plus pitches and repeats mechanics despite effort and long arm action. Lively FB misses bats and can vary velocity on SL. Can leave balls up in zone, but hitters have difficulty making hard contact. Shows little feel for changing speeds.

Johnson,Brian

SP | Boston | EXP MLB DEBUT: 2015 | H/W: 6-4 235 | FUT: #4 starter | 7B

Thrws L Age 26	Year	Lev	Team	W	L	Sv	IP	K	ERA	WHIP	BF/G	OBA	H%	S%	xERA	Ctl	Dom	Cmd	hr/9	BPV
2012 (1) Florida	2015	AAA	Pawtucket	9	6	0	96	90	2.53	1.10	20.9	215	27	79	2.50	3.0	8.4	2.8	0.6	89
87-92 FB +++	2015	MLB	Boston	0	1	0	4	3	8.78	1.71	18.6	206	26	43	3.41	8.8	6.6	0.8	0.0	-101
80-83 CT ++	2016	Rk	GCL Red Sox	0	1	0	7	9	3.86	1.29	14.4	262	39	67	3.01	2.6	11.6	4.5	0.0	157
73-78 CB +++	2016	A-	Lowell	0	0	0	11	11	0.00	0.82	20.0	184	26	100	0.89	1.6	9.0	5.5	0.0	136
81-83 CU +++	2016	AAA	Pawtucket	5	6	0	77	54	4.09	1.43	21.8	254	28	74	4.31	4.2	6.3	1.5	1.1	18

Big-bodied SP who missed time due to anxiety issues but has savvy to succeed. No pitch is plus, though effectively sequences offerings and changes speeds with aplomb. Induces groundballs with two-seam FB that he locates in bottom half of zone. CU seems to be regressing, but should return with more innings. Can thrive despite lack of velocity.

Johnson,Chase

SP | San Francisco | EXP MLB DEBUT: 2017 | H/W: 6-3 190 | FUT: #4 starter | 7C

Thrws R Age 25	Year	Lev	Team	W	L	Sv	IP	K	ERA	WHIP	BF/G	OBA	H%	S%	xERA	Ctl	Dom	Cmd	hr/9	BPV
2013 (3) Cal Poly	2013	A-	Salem-Kaizer	3	2	0	41	37	4.17	1.17	16.4	237	30	64	3.05	2.6	8.1	3.1	0.7	93
90-95 FB ++++	2014	A	Augusta	4	7	0	110	94	4.58	1.37	20.1	263	33	65	3.67	3.3	7.7	2.4	0.4	68
80-82 SL ++	2015	A+	San Jose	8	3	0	111	111	2.43	1.16	22.1	233	31	80	2.72	2.8	9.0	3.3	0.4	106
81-84 CU +++	2015	AA	Richmond	1	1	0	13	18	6.14	1.82	20.4	301	45	63	4.91	5.5	12.3	2.3	0.0	92
	2016	AA	Richmond	1	4	5	52	37	3.28	1.25	8.8	242	29	73	3.03	3.1	6.4	2.1	0.3	49

Tall, lean SP who was limited after May due to injury. Very strong against RHH (.181 oppBA) and is sinkerballer with easy velocity. Commands FB well and effortless delivery allows for maintaining velocity. K rate has dropped and doesn't have pitch for LHH. Stock would increase with better breaking ball.

Johnson,Jordan

SP | San Francisco | EXP MLB DEBUT: 2018 | H/W: 6-3 200 | FUT: #3 starter | 8D

Thrws R Age 23	Year	Lev	Team	W	L	Sv	IP	K	ERA	WHIP	BF/G	OBA	H%	S%	xERA	Ctl	Dom	Cmd	hr/9	BPV
2014 (23) Cal St Northridge	2014	Rk	Azl Giants	0	0	0	2	3	0.00	0.91	2.7	0	0	100		8.2	12.3	1.5	0.0	18
92-96 FB +++	2015	Rk	Azl Giants	0	1	0	23	32	1.56	0.87	12.2	226	36	80	1.47	0.4	12.5	32.0	0.0	232
78-82 CB +++	2015	A-	Salem-Kaizer	0	1	0	4	6	4.29	1.19	16.8	297	46	60	3.26	0.0	12.9		0.0	249
82-84 CU +++	2015	A+	San Jose	2	3	0	31	33	4.34	1.41	22.0	279	36	71	4.42	2.9	9.5	3.3	0.9	112
	2016	A+	San Jose	8	9	0	120	111	5.33	1.43	23.2	282	32	68	5.39	2.9	8.3	2.8	1.8	89

Strong-armed, projectable SP who pitches to contact with three solid-average offerings. Has sneaky quick FB thrown with plus arm speed, but lacks movement. More of flyball pitcher despite downhill plane to plate. Mixes in average CB and sinking CU. Injury history gives pause, though has quick, clean delivery that looks effortless.

Johnson,Pierce

RP | Chicago (N) | EXP MLB DEBUT: 2017 | H/W: 6-3 200 | FUT: Setup reliever | 8D

Thrws R Age 25	Year	Lev	Team	W	L	Sv	IP	K	ERA	WHIP	BF/G	OBA	H%	S%	xERA	Ctl	Dom	Cmd	hr/9	BPV
2012 (S-1) Missouri State	2013	A+	Daytona	6	1	0	48	50	2.24	1.29	19.8	232	32	82	2.81	3.9	9.3	2.4	0.2	80
92-94 FB ++++	2014	A	Kane County	0	1	0	11	8	2.45	0.64	19.0	114	12	67	0.50	2.5	6.5	2.7	0.8	70
86-88 CT ++	2014	AA	Tennessee	5	4	0	91	91	2.57	1.25	20.6	189	24	83	2.78	5.3	9.0	1.7	0.8	36
82-84 CU ++	2015	AA	Tennessee	6	2	0	95	72	2.08	1.14	23.5	221	27	83	2.51	3.0	6.8	2.3	0.4	59
80-83 CB ++++	2016	AAA	Iowa	4	6	0	63	75	6.14	1.63	12.8	252	34	63	4.85	6.1	10.7	1.7	1.1	45

Tall righty took a step back in '16, posting a 6.14 ERA at AAA. FB still grades as plus and sits at 92-94 mph. Plus hard CB gets swings and misses, but CU remains inconsistent. Mechanics and release point result in below-average control. Was hit by line drive and was limited to 63 IP. Worked in relief in August and that could be his future.

Jones,Connor

SP | St. Louis | EXP MLB DEBUT: 2019 | H/W: 6-3 200 | FUT: #4 starter | 7C

Thrws R Age 22	Year	Lev	Team	W	L	Sv	IP	K	ERA	WHIP	BF/G	OBA	H%	S%	xERA	Ctl	Dom	Cmd	hr/9	BPV
2016 (2) Virginia																				
90-93 SL +++																				
80-83 CB +++	2016	NCAA	Virginia	11	1	0	103	72	2.35	1.19	27.6	226	27	80	2.60	3.3	6.3	1.9	0.3	42
CU ++	2016	Rk	GCL Cardinals	0	0	0	4	3	2.25	1.00	3.8	210	27	75	1.67	2.3	6.8	3.0	0.0	79
SL ++	2016	A-	State College	0	0	1	10	8	4.41	1.67	6.5	343	42	71	5.26	1.8	7.1	4.0	0.0	97

Yet another strong-armed college hurler taken by the Cards in 2016. Has a good low-90s sinking FB, a four-seamer that can hit 96 mph, along with SL, CU, and CB. Simple, repeatable mechanics allows him to pound the strike zone and sinker keeps the ball on the ground. Profiles as a solid back-end workhorse.

Jorge,Felix

SP | Minnesota | EXP MLB DEBUT: 2018 | H/W: 6-2 170 | FUT: #4 starter | 7D

Thrws R Age 23	Year	Lev	Team	W	L	Sv	IP	K	ERA	WHIP	BF/G	OBA	H%	S%	xERA	Ctl	Dom	Cmd	hr/9	BPV
2011 FA (DR)	2014	Rk	Elizabethton	4	2	0	66	61	2.59	1.09	21.5	238	31	76	2.49	1.9	8.3	4.4	0.3	116
88-92 FB +++	2014	A	Cedar Rapids	2	5	0	39	23	9.00	1.97	15.6	341	36	56	7.99	4.6	5.3	1.2	2.1	-11
78-82 SL +++	2015	A	Cedar Rapids	6	7	0	142	114	2.79	1.06	23.9	228	27	76	2.68	2.0	7.2	3.6	0.7	93
81-84 CU +++	2016	A+	Fort Myers	9	3	0	93	77	1.55	0.94	24.9	225	28	85	1.96	1.1	7.5	7.0	0.3	123
	2016	AA	Chattanooga	3	5	0	74	32	4.13	1.28	27.6	284	30	69	4.19	1.5	3.9	2.7	0.9	49

Lean, athletic SP who was brilliant in High-A. Hope that he adds velocity as he owns solid secondary offerings. Throws pinpoint strikes and gets ahead of hitters with commandable FB that exhibits late run and sink. SL shows late break and hard CU flashes plus. Keeps ball on ground, but has posted inconsistent Dom.

Junis,Jake

SP | Kansas City | EXP MLB DEBUT: 2017 | H/W: 6-2 225 | FUT: #4 starter | 7B

Thrws R Age 24	Year	Lev	Team	W	L	Sv	IP	K	ERA	WHIP	BF/G	OBA	H%	S%	xERA	Ctl	Dom	Cmd	hr/9	BPV
2011 (29) HS (IL)	2014	A	Lexington	9	8	0	136	109	4.30	1.28	21.4	262	30	69	4.03	2.5	7.2	2.9	1.1	80
90-95 FB +++	2015	A+	Wilmington	5	11	0	155	123	3.65	1.12	23.5	249	30	68	3.06	1.7	7.1	4.2	0.6	101
78-82 CB +++	2015	AA	NW Arkansas	0	1	0	4	3	9.00	2.00	19.3	383	46	50	6.85	2.3	6.8	3.0	0.0	79
81-86 CU +++	2016	AA	NW Arkansas	9	7	0	119	117	3.25	1.15	22.5	247	31	75	3.35	2.0	8.8	4.3	0.9	122
	2016	AAA	Omaha	1	3	0	30	26	7.20	1.53	21.8	316	36	55	6.16	2.1	7.8	3.7	1.8	102

Emerging SP who was 3rd in TL in ERA. Hit hard in 6 AAA starts, but has good stuff and control. Throws with angle to plate and repeats slot and delivery consistently. Has feel for changing speeds and adds movement to FB at lesser velocities. LHH have given him fits and has given up fair share of HR. Velocity inching up and hard CB can miss bats.

Jurado,Ariel

SP | Texas | EXP MLB DEBUT: 2018 | H/W: 6-1 180 | FUT: #3 starter | 8D

Thrws R Age 21	Year	Lev	Team	W	L	Sv	IP	K	ERA	WHIP	BF/G	OBA	H%	S%	xERA	Ctl	Dom	Cmd	hr/9	BPV
2012 FA (PN)	2013	Rk	DSL Rangers	6	0	0	49	47	2.39	1.04	21.0	258	34	76	2.54	0.6	8.6	15.7	0.2	159
90-95 FB +++	2014	Rk	Azl Rangers	2	1	0	38	35	1.65	1.13	10.8	245	32	86	2.64	1.9	8.2	4.4	0.2	116
79-83 SL +++	2015	A	Hickory	12	1	0	99	95	2.45	1.05	17.4	248	32	78	2.69	1.1	8.6	7.9	0.5	144
81-82 CU ++	2016	A+	High Desert	7	2	0	79	71	3.87	1.35	20.6	271	34	71	3.77	2.7	8.1	3.0	0.5	90
	2016	AA	Frisco	1	4	0	43	35	3.33	1.25	22.0	265	32	75	3.60	2.1	7.3	3.5	0.6	93

Sinkerballer who was promoted to AA in July and has been young for level. Throws consistent strikes with solid two-seam FB that induces high amount of groundballs. Can add velocity to FB at times and go up in zone. Lacks true out pitch, but can throw SL for strikes from low 3/4 slot. Mixes in CU that could become average in time.

Justo,Salvador — RP — Colorado

EXP MLB DEBUT: 2020 | H/W: 6-5 210 | FUT: Setup reliever | 7D

Thrws R Age 22
2013 FA (DR)

Velo	Pitch	Grade
95-97	FB	+ + + +
	SL	+ +
	CU	+ +

Year	Lev	Team	W	L	Sv	IP	K	ERA	WHIP	BF/G	OBA	H%	S%	xERA	Ctl	Dom	Cmd	hr/9	BPV
2015	A-	Boise	2	0	0	22	13	3.26	1.63	3.9	252	29	80	4.19	6.1	5.3	0.9	0.4	-52
2016	A	Asheville	3	1	2	46	34	2.15	1.24	4.9	217	26	85	2.90	4.1	6.6	1.6	0.6	27

Lean, projectable reliever from the D.R. features a plus 95-97 mph FB that tops out at 101 mph. Backs the FB with a hard SL and fringe-average CU. Inconsistent mechanics and release point results in below-average command (4.1 Ctl). Held his own in full-season debut.

Kahaloa,Ian — SP — Cincinnati

EXP MLB DEBUT: 2020 | H/W: 6-1 185 | FUT: #3 starter | 8D

Thrws R Age 19
2015 (5) HS (HI)

Velo	Pitch	Grade
92-95	FB	+ + + +
80-84	SL	+ + + +
	CU	+ +

Year	Lev	Team	W	L	Sv	IP	K	ERA	WHIP	BF/G	OBA	H%	S%	xERA	Ctl	Dom	Cmd	hr/9	BPV
2015	Rk	AZL Reds	0	0	0	24	31	2.25	0.92	11.2	191	29	76	1.55	2.3	11.6	5.2	0.4	167
2016	Rk	AZL Reds	1	0	0	8	10	0.00	0.38	12.8	81	14	100		1.1	11.3	10.0	0.0	190
2016	Rk	Billings	2	2	0	44	42	2.85	1.15	17.6	234	29	79	3.10	2.6	8.6	3.2	0.8	100

Strike-throwing RH out of Hawaii was favorite of scouts in Pioneer League. Sits low-to-mid 90s with 2-seam FB that bores into RHH's wrists. Power CB has great shape and solid break. CU is in infancy of development. Doesn't give in to hitters.

Kaminsky,Rob — SP — Cleveland

EXP MLB DEBUT: 2017 | H/W: 5-11 190 | FUT: #4 starter | 7C

Thrws L Age 22
2013 (1) HS (NJ)

Velo	Pitch	Grade
88-92	FB	+ + +
76-79	CB	+ + + +
80-83	CU	+ + +

Year	Lev	Team	W	L	Sv	IP	K	ERA	WHIP	BF/G	OBA	H%	S%	xERA	Ctl	Dom	Cmd	hr/9	BPV
2013	Rk	GCL Cardinals	0	3	0	22	28	3.68	1.45	11.8	270	39	74	3.94	3.7	11.5	3.1	0.4	125
2014	A	Peoria	8	2	0	100	79	1.89	1.02	21.4	201	25	81	1.77	2.8	7.1	2.5	0.2	71
2015	A+	Lynchburg	0	1	0	9	4	3.91	1.96	22.0	334	37	78	5.87	4.9	3.9	0.8	0.0	-44
2015	A+	Palm Beach	6	5	0	94	79	2.10	1.17	22.1	236	31	80	2.41	2.7	7.5	2.8	0.0	82
2016	AA	Akron	11	7	0	137	92	3.28	1.24	22.3	240	28	74	3.09	3.2	6.0	1.9	0.5	42

Smallish LH witnessed across-the-board setbacks in first taste of the upper minors. Heavy FB the cornerstone to his quality ground-ball profile, but struggled to locate and work ahead. CB still flashes plus 12/6 shape as future out pitch; CU a passable pace-changer. Still young with time to figure everything out, but dwindling Dom is concerning.

Kaprielian,James — SP — New York (A)

EXP MLB DEBUT: 2018 | H/W: 6-4 200 | FUT: #2 starter | 9D

Thrws R Age 23
2015 (1) UCLA

Velo	Pitch	Grade
90-96	FB	+ + + +
75-78	CB	+ + +
81-85	SL	+ + +
84-86	CU	+ + +

Year	Lev	Team	W	L	Sv	IP	K	ERA	WHIP	BF/G	OBA	H%	S%	xERA	Ctl	Dom	Cmd	hr/9	BPV
2015	NCAA	UCLA	10	4	0	106	114	2.03	1.12	24.6	223	30	85	2.66	2.8	9.7	3.5	0.6	116
2015	Rk	GCL Yankees 2	0	0	0	2	2	12.86	1.90	5.0	252	34	25	4.47	8.6	8.6	1.0	0.0	-59
2015	A-	Staten Island	0	1	0	9	12	2.00	1.11	11.8	240	37	80	2.27	2.0	12.0	6.0	0.0	180
2016	A+	Tampa	2	1	0	18	22	1.50	0.61	20.6	136	20	80	0.31	1.5	11.0	7.3	0.5	176

Tall, athletic SP who missed most of season with flexor strain. Returned in AFL and showcased dynamic, heavy FB. Uses two breaking balls that miss bats and has CU with wicked late movement. Needs innings to iron out delivery and arm slot. Locates pitches fairly well and will need more consistent CU to battle hitters from left side.

Kay,Anthony — SP — New York (N)

EXP MLB DEBUT: 2019 | H/W: 6-0 190 | FUT: #3 starter | 8C

Thrws L Age 22
2016 (1) Connecticut

Velo	Pitch	Grade
91-93	FB	+ + +
	SL	+ + +
	CU	+ + +

Year	Lev	Team	W	L	Sv	IP	K	ERA	WHIP	BF/G	OBA	H%	S%	xERA	Ctl	Dom	Cmd	hr/9	BPV
2016		Did not pitch																	

1st Rd pick has yet to make pro debut due to arm injury. When healthy, LH showcases advanced command of three average or better pitches. While none of his pitches are flashy, he keeps hitters off balance by changing eye levels and working each side of the plate. SL is solid and CU features good fade. CU has potential to be lone plus offering.

Keller,Brad — SP — Arizona

EXP MLB DEBUT: 2018 | H/W: 6-5 230 | FUT: #4 starter | 7C

Thrws R Age 21
2013 (8) HS (GA)

Velo	Pitch	Grade
90-94	FB	+ + + +
82-84	SL	+ +
84-86	CU	+ + +

Year	Lev	Team	W	L	Sv	IP	K	ERA	WHIP	BF/G	OBA	H%	S%	xERA	Ctl	Dom	Cmd	hr/9	BPV
2014	Rk	Azl Dbacks	4	0	0	31	20	2.32	1.25	21.1	255	29	84	3.44	2.6	5.8	2.2	0.6	52
2014	Rk	Missoula	1	4	0	33	30	7.05	2.05	20.2	348	41	68	7.84	4.9	8.1	1.7	1.6	33
2014	A-	Hillsboro	1	0	0	6	8	0.00	0.33	18.9	56	10	100		1.5	12.0	8.0	0.0	194
2015	A	Kane County	8	9	0	142	109	2.60	1.16	21.7	242	30	77	2.66	2.3	6.9	2.9	0.2	79
2016	A+	Visalia	9	7	0	135	99	4.47	1.28	23.1	279	32	66	4.10	1.7	6.6	3.8	0.9	90

Big-bodied, strike-throwing RH improved all 3 offerings in '16. Generates natural downward plane by using size and arm angle. FB sits low 90s with advanced command. CU is best secondary offering. Borderline plus with good deception and late fade. SL is 40-grade pitch w/ fleeting two-plane movement.

Keller,Mitch — SP — Pittsburgh

EXP MLB DEBUT: 2018 | H/W: 6-3 195 | FUT: #2 starter | 9D

Thrws R Age 21
2014 (2) HS (IA)

Velo	Pitch	Grade
93-96	FB	+ + + +
75-77	CB	+ + +
	CU	+ +

Year	Lev	Team	W	L	Sv	IP	K	ERA	WHIP	BF/G	OBA	H%	S%	xERA	Ctl	Dom	Cmd	hr/9	BPV
2014	Rk	GCL Pirates	0	0	0	27	29	1.99	1.18	12.0	199	29	81	1.97	4.3	9.6	2.2	0.0	75
2015	Rk	Bristol	0	3	0	19	25	5.63	2.14	15.9	316	45	73	6.39	7.5	11.7	1.6	0.5	26
2016	A	West Virginia	8	5	0	124	131	2.47	0.92	20.2	215	30	73	1.78	1.3	9.5	7.3	0.3	154
2016	A+	Bradenton	1	0	0	6	7	0.00	1.00	22.9	228	34	100	1.86	1.5	10.5	7.0	0.0	167

Breakout season after arm injury limited him in 2015. Mechanical adjustments led to improved Ctl (19 BB/130.1 IP). FB now plus at 93-96 topping at 99 mph with easy arm action and repeatable mechanics. Gets good, late life on the FB and keeps it down in the zone. Mixes in a hard CB that flashes plus, but lacks consistency.

Kilome,Franklyn — SP — Philadelphia

EXP MLB DEBUT: 2019 | H/W: 6-6 175 | FUT: #2 starter | 9C

Thrws R Age 21
2013 FA (DR)

Velo	Pitch	Grade
93-96	FB	+ + + +
81-85	CB	+ + +
79-83	CU	+ +

Year	Lev	Team	W	L	Sv	IP	K	ERA	WHIP	BF/G	OBA	H%	S%	xERA	Ctl	Dom	Cmd	hr/9	BPV
2014	Rk	GCL Phillies	3	1	0	40	25	3.14	1.17	14.6	241	28	73	2.93	2.5	5.6	2.3	0.4	52
2015	A-	Williamsport	3	2	0	49	36	3.30	1.26	18.2	228	28	72	2.74	3.8	6.6	1.7	0.2	33
2016	A	Lakewood	5	8	0	114	130	3.86	1.43	21.1	260	36	73	3.80	3.9	10.2	2.6	0.5	96

Tall and lean, uses height to his advantage with downhill plane on mid-90s FB and a potential plus CB. High leg kick and 3/4s slot adds deception. Adjusted from three disastrous April outings; better control, more Ks and GBs followed. Moves FB in/out well. Has frame to take on good weight, which could add another velo tick.

Kingham,Nick — SP — Pittsburgh

EXP MLB DEBUT: 2017 | H/W: 6-6 225 | FUT: #3 starter | 8D

Thrws R Age 25
2010 (4) HS (NV)

Velo	Pitch	Grade
90-93	FB	+ + + +
83-85	CB	+ + +
	CU	+ + +

Year	Lev	Team	W	L	Sv	IP	K	ERA	WHIP	BF/G	OBA	H%	S%	xERA	Ctl	Dom	Cmd	hr/9	BPV
2016	Rk	GCL Pirates	0	4	0	24	16	3.00	1.00	15.3	254	31	67	2.23	0.4	6.0	16.0	0.0	116
2016	A+	Bradenton	2	0	0	11	10	0.00	0.82	20.0	205	28	100	1.14	0.8	8.2	10.0	0.0	143
2016	AA	Altoona	1	1	0	11	10	5.73	0.91	20.5	162	19	33	1.66	3.3	8.2	2.5	0.8	77

Missed first half of season recovering from TJS, but was solid once he returned. FB velocity is now at 90-94, down a tick from pre-surgery levels with good arm-side run. 11-5 CB and CU are average to above with good command of all three offerings (6 BB in 46 IP).

Kirby,Nathan — SP — Milwaukee

EXP MLB DEBUT: 2019 | H/W: 6-2 200 | FUT: #4 starter | 7C

Thrws L Age 23
2015 (S-1) Virginia

Velo	Pitch	Grade
89-93	FB	+ + +
80-82	CB	+ + +
80-84	CU	+ + +

Year	Lev	Team	W	L	Sv	IP	K	ERA	WHIP	BF/G	OBA	H%	S%	xERA	Ctl	Dom	Cmd	hr/9	BPV
2015	NCAA	Virginia	5	3	1	64	81	2.53	1.36	22.3	234	34	82	3.22	4.5	11.4	2.5	0.4	102
2015	A	Wisconsin	0	1	0	12	7	5.90	1.80	11.3	304	35	64	4.99	5.2	5.2	1.0	0.0	-28
2016		Did not pitch (injury)																	

Former college standout missed all of '16 after undergoing TJS. Athlete who shows solid command of low-90s FB with good arm-side bore. Feel for fading CU that flashes above-avg potential; CB has slurvy action but effective when thrown from same tunnel as FB. Lot of uncertainty coming off injury, but has ceiling of #3/4 SP with average Dom upside.

Kline,Branden — SP — Baltimore

EXP MLB DEBUT: 2017 | H/W: 6-3 210 | FUT: #4 starter | 7D

Thrws R Age 25
2012 (2) Virginia

Velo	Pitch	Grade
90-95	FB	+ + +
81-84	SL	+ + +
80-83	CU	+ +

Year	Lev	Team	W	L	Sv	IP	K	ERA	WHIP	BF/G	OBA	H%	S%	xERA	Ctl	Dom	Cmd	hr/9	BPV
2013	A	Delmarva	1	2	0	35	32	5.90	1.57	22.0	293	36	63	5.16	3.6	8.2	2.3	1.0	69
2014	A+	Frederick	8	6	0	126	95	3.85	1.39	23.1	287	34	73	4.27	2.3	6.8	3.0	0.6	78
2014	AA	Bowie	0	2	0	16	9	6.11	1.79	24.9	283	32	64	5.16	6.1	5.0	0.8	0.6	-57
2015	AA	Bowie	3	3	0	39	27	3.68	1.38	20.5	241	27	76	3.89	4.4	6.2	1.4	0.9	12
2016		Did not pitch (injury)																	

Hard-throwing SP who missed all season after October 2015 Tommy John surgery. Status declining as command issues haven't gone away. Lacks dependable secondary offering, though SL can be average at times. Lacks feel and touch for changing speeds and can fail to repeat delivery and slot.

Koch,Brandon — RP — Tampa Bay

EXP MLB DEBUT: 2018 | H/W: 6-1 205 | FUT: Closer | 8D

Thrws R Age 23 — 2015 (4) Dallas Baptist

- 92-98 FB ++++
- 84-88 SL ++++
- CU +

Year	Lev	Team	W	L	Sv	IP	K	ERA	WHIP	BF/G	OBA	H%	S%	xERA	Ctl	Dom	Cmd	hr/9	BPV
2015	NCAA	Dallas Baptist	3	2	14	43	76	1.26	1.09	6.5	159	32	91	1.64	5.0	15.9	3.2	0.4	169
2015	A-	Hudson Valley	0	1	6	32	47	3.08	0.90	6.6	210	33	69	2.15	1.4	13.2	9.4	0.8	217
2016	A+	Charlotte	0	0	2	7	7	2.57	1.00	5.3	132	19	71	0.80	5.1	9.0	1.8	0.0	41

Hard-throwing RP who did not pitch after April due to arm tenderness. Has closer-type stuff with electric FB and power SL with extreme, late action. Throws with ton of effort, but has decent control. Can overthrow FB and leave ball up, but has velocity to get by. No feel or touch for changing speeds.

Koch,Matt — SP — Arizona

EXP MLB DEBUT: 2016 | H/W: 6-3 215 | FUT: Middle reliever | 6A

Thrws R Age 26 — 2012 (3) Louisville

- 91-93 FB +++
- 77-81 CB +++
- 88-90 CT +++
- 83-86 CU ++

Year	Lev	Team	W	L	Sv	IP	K	ERA	WHIP	BF/G	OBA	H%	S%	xERA	Ctl	Dom	Cmd	hr/9	BPV
2015	AA	Binghamton	4	8	0	88	55	3.47	1.25	10.2	277	32	72	3.66	1.5	5.6	3.7	0.5	78
2015	AA	Mobile	1	0	0	7	6	0.00	0.85	26.0	91	12	100	0.03	5.1	7.6	1.5	0.0	18
2016	AA	Mobile	2	4	0	74	49	4.73	1.35	22.1	294	33	66	4.48	1.6	5.9	3.8	0.8	82
2016	AAA	Reno	4	2	0	46	25	3.12	1.32	27.3	297	33	78	4.22	1.2	4.9	4.2	0.6	74
2016	MLB	Arizona	1	1	1	18	10	2.00	0.72	9.1	151	16	75	0.80	2.0	5.0	2.5	0.5	54

Big, strong RH made MLB debut after spending most of the season as a starter. Throws four pitches. 2-seam FB is average and ordinary, but plays up due to command. Best pitch is CT. Runs in on hands of LHH. 12/6 CB is a change of eye level offering. CU is a below-average pitch with some fade but poor deception.

Kolek,Tyler — SP — Miami

EXP MLB DEBUT: 2019 | H/W: 6-5 260 | FUT: #2 starter | 9D

Thrws R Age 21 — 2014 (1) HS (TX)

- 93-96 FB ++++
- 85-87 SL +++
- CB ++
- CU +

Year	Lev	Team	W	L	Sv	IP	K	ERA	WHIP	BF/G	OBA	H%	S%	xERA	Ctl	Dom	Cmd	hr/9	BPV
2014	Rk	GCL Marlins	0	3	0	22	18	4.50	1.59	10.8	262	33	69	3.82	5.3	7.4	1.4	0.0	7
2015	A	Greensboro	4	10	0	108	81	4.57	1.56	19.0	261	31	70	4.30	5.1	6.7	1.3	0.6	2
2016		Did not pitch (injury)																	

2014 2nd overall pick missed the entire season with Tommy John surgery. FB velocity was down from 98-100 mph when drafted but still sat at 93-96 mph. Mixes in a hard CB and power SL that flash as plus. CU remains below average. Throws across his body, but mechanics are simple and he repeats them well. Control will be an issue going forward.

Kopech,Michael — SP — Chicago (A)

EXP MLB DEBUT: 2018 | H/W: 6-3 205 | FUT: #2 starter | 9D

Thrws R Age 20 — 2014 (1) HS (TX)

- 94-99 FB +++++
- 84-89 SL +++
- 86-90 CU ++

Year	Lev	Team	W	L	Sv	IP	K	ERA	WHIP	BF/G	OBA	H%	S%	xERA	Ctl	Dom	Cmd	hr/9	BPV
																			49
2014	Rk	GCL Red Sox	0	1	0	13	16	4.77	1.52	7.2	228	34	65	3.15	6.1	10.9	1.8	0.0	92
2015	A	Greenville	4	5	0	65	70	2.63	1.23	16.5	224	31	78	2.66	3.7	9.7	2.6	0.3	-61
2016	A-	Lowell	0	0	0	4	4	0.00	1.95	19.6	257	35	100	4.65	8.8	8.8	1.0	0.0	
2016	A+	Salem	4	1	0	52	82	2.25	1.04	18.2	146	27	77	1.14	5.0	14.2	2.8	0.2	138

Tall, aggressive pitcher who routinely reaches triple digits on gun and rack up Ks with high frequency. Began season late after breaking hand, though has premium arm strength. Very tough to make hard contact against due to explosive FB and hard SL. Has some separation between FB and CU, but can aim pitches too often. Needs to clean up control.

Krook,Matt — SP — San Francisco

EXP MLB DEBUT: 2019 | H/W: 6-4 195 | FUT: #3 starter | 8D

Thrws L Age 22 — 2016 (4) Oregon

- 91-95 FB ++++
- 81-82 SL +++
- 79-80 CB ++
- CU ++

Year	Lev	Team	W	L	Sv	IP	K	ERA	WHIP	BF/G	OBA	H%	S%	xERA	Ctl	Dom	Cmd	hr/9	BPV
2016	NCAA	Oregon	4	3	0	53	68	5.08	1.60	15.7	194	31	65	2.94	8.3	11.5	1.4	0.0	1
2016	Rk	Azl Giants	0	1	0	5	2	1.73	1.54	11.3	290	32	88	4.14	3.5	3.5	1.0	0.0	-13
2016	A-	Salem-Keizer	1	3	0	35	39	6.17	1.94	15.2	262	36	67	5.16	8.5	10.0	1.2	0.5	-31

Power-armed SP with upside, but fails to repeat mechanics and throw strikes. Had Tommy John surgery in past, but has explosive FB with plus, late life. Can be tough to control due to movement. Also owns SL that can be plus and CB that may be shelved. Lives in lower half of zone by pitching downhill and has promising, tumbling CU.

Kubitza,Austin — RP — Detroit

EXP MLB DEBUT: 2017 | H/W: 6-5 225 | FUT: Middle reliever | 6B

Thrws R Age 25 — 2013 (4) Rice

- 87-91 FB +++
- 80-82 SL ++
- 83-86 CU +++

Year	Lev	Team	W	L	Sv	IP	K	ERA	WHIP	BF/G	OBA	H%	S%	xERA	Ctl	Dom	Cmd	hr/9	BPV
2013	A+	Lakeland	0	1	0	17	14	5.82	1.53	9.2	250	32	58	3.51	5.3	7.4	1.4	0.0	8
2014	A	West Michigan	10	2	0	131	140	2.34	1.08	22.2	210	29	79	2.16	3.0	9.6	3.3	0.3	111
2015	AA	Erie	9	13	0	133	96	5.81	1.79	22.8	337	40	66	5.87	3.2	6.5	2.0	0.4	47
2016	A+	Lakeland	2	1	1	43	35	4.60	1.67	8.8	275	33	72	4.81	5.4	7.3	1.3	0.6	3
2016	AA	Erie	2	3	0	20	11	5.40	1.90	13.5	281	32	70	5.31	7.2	5.0	0.7	0.5	-87

Sinkerballer who was moved to bullpen in '16 and saw poor K rate climb. More of a pitch-to-contact guy with extreme groundball tendencies. No FB is ever straight and often features cutting action. Lacks out pitch and SL remains below average offering. CU has moments of plus action, but has trouble commanding plate with any pitch.

Labourt,Jairo — RP — Detroit

EXP MLB DEBUT: 2018 | H/W: 6-4 205 | FUT: Setup reliever | 8E

Thrws L Age 23 — 2011 FA (DR)

- 91-96 FB ++++
- 83-86 SL +++
- 81-83 CU +

Year	Lev	Team	W	L	Sv	IP	K	ERA	WHIP	BF/G	OBA	H%	S%	xERA	Ctl	Dom	Cmd	hr/9	BPV
2014	A-	Vancouver	5	3	0	71	82	1.77	1.18	19.0	190	28	83	1.86	4.7	10.4	2.2	0.0	78
2014	A	Lansing	0	0	0	14	11	6.43	2.50	12.4	275	33	74	6.91	12.9	7.1	0.6	0.6	-202
2015	A+	Dunedin	2	7	0	80	70	4.61	1.59	19.6	269	33	71	4.53	4.9	7.9	1.6	0.7	26
2015	A+	Lakeland	1	5	0	35	34	6.39	1.70	22.8	312	39	61	5.55	3.8	8.7	2.3	0.8	71
2016	A+	Lakeland	7	9	1	87	81	5.27	1.55	12.7	209	27	64	3.32	7.2	8.4	1.2	0.3	-27

Tall, erratic pitcher who led FSL in walks. Moved to pen and posted much better results. Possesses horrendous control and lively pitches tough to locate. When on, is very tough to hit. LHH can't square up FB and sharp SL can be potent K offering. Doesn't change speeds well, but brings tough, downhill angle to plate.

Lail,Brady — SP — New York (A)

EXP MLB DEBUT: 2017 | H/W: 6-2 205 | FUT: #4 starter | 7E

Thrws R Age 23 — 2012 (18) HS (UT)

- 89-93 FB +++
- 75-78 CB +++
- CU +++

Year	Lev	Team	W	L	Sv	IP	K	ERA	WHIP	BF/G	OBA	H%	S%	xERA	Ctl	Dom	Cmd	hr/9	BPV
2015	A+	Tampa	1	0	0	5	9	0.00	0.80	18.1	221	44	100	1.21	0.0	16.2		0.0	310
2015	AA	Trenton	6	4	0	106	63	2.46	1.10	20.8	233	27	77	2.39	2.2	5.3	2.4	0.2	55
2015	AAA	Scranton/WB	3	2	0	37	13	4.62	1.70	23.9	306	31	75	5.70	4.1	3.2	0.8	1.0	-37
2016	AA	Trenton	1	2	0	31	17	3.75	1.44	22.2	273	30	74	4.17	3.5	4.9	1.4	0.6	13
2016	AAA	Scranton/WB	7	6	0	92	58	5.08	1.38	22.7	272	30	65	4.45	2.9	5.7	1.9	1.1	41

Durable arm who exhibits good command, but can get into trouble with pitch-to-contact ways. Was dreadful late in season and can be hit hard when FB location is off. When on, FB shows nifty late action and tough to elevate. Can get on side of CB, but shows solid break. CU shows flashes of being best pitch. Needs to keep ball down in zone to succeed.

Lakins,Travis — SP — Boston

EXP MLB DEBUT: 2018 | H/W: 6-1 180 | FUT: #4 starter | 7C

Thrws R Age 22 — 2015 (6) Ohio State

- 88-94 FB +++
- 81-84 SL +++
- CU +++

Year	Lev	Team	W	L	Sv	IP	K	ERA	WHIP	BF/G	OBA	H%	S%	xERA	Ctl	Dom	Cmd	hr/9	BPV
2015	NCAA	Ohio State	4	4	0	96	84	3.75	1.34	26.6	264	33	73	3.84	3.0	7.9	2.6	0.7	79
2015	A-	Lowell	0	0	0	2	3	0.00	0.50	6.6	0	0	100		4.5	13.5	3.0	0.0	140
2016	A+	Salem	6	3	0	91	79	5.93	1.62	21.2	302	37	63	5.20	3.6	7.8	2.2	0.8	63

Athletic SP who got off to great start before ending season in July. Extreme groundball pitcher with heavy sink to solid-average FB. Switched CB to SL and needs to have more power to be effective. Repeats delivery which enhances CU, though doesn't miss many bats. Can succeed by inducing weak contact and CU good enough to battle LHH.

Lambert,Peter — SP — Colorado

EXP MLB DEBUT: 2019 | H/W: 6-2 185 | FUT: #3 starter | 7C

Thrws R Age 19 — 2015 (2) HS (CA)

- 88-92 FB +++
- 73-75 CB ++
- 82-84 CU ++

Year	Lev	Team	W	L	Sv	IP	K	ERA	WHIP	BF/G	OBA	H%	S%	xERA	Ctl	Dom	Cmd	hr/9	BPV
2015	Rk	Grand Junction	0	4	0	31	26	3.47	1.29	16.0	248	30	76	3.69	3.2	7.5	2.4	0.9	67
2016	A	Asheville	5	8	0	126	108	3.93	1.25	19.7	260	32	68	3.42	2.4	7.7	3.3	0.5	93

2015 2nd round pick has good raw stuff. FB sits in the low-90s, topping out at 94 mph. Mixes in a 12/6 CB that shows above-average potential and a solid CU. Not a huge player, but has good athleticism, simple repeatable mechanics, and a live arm. Solid full-season debut in the SAL and has nice mid-rotation potential.

Lamet,Dinelson — SP — San Diego

EXP MLB DEBUT: 2017 | H/W: 6-4 187 | FUT: Setup reliever | 8C

Thrws R Age 24 — 2014 FA (DR)

- 93-95 FB ++++
- 87-90 SL ++++
- 84-85 CU ++

Year	Lev	Team	W	L	Sv	IP	K	ERA	WHIP	BF/G	OBA	H%	S%	xERA	Ctl	Dom	Cmd	hr/9	BPV
2015	A	Fort Wayne	5	8	0	105	120	3.00	1.20	16.2	217	29	78	2.94	3.8	10.3	2.7	0.8	101
2016	A+	Lake Elsinore	7	1	0	65	54	2.35	1.25	22.0	231	28	83	3.06	3.6	7.5	2.1	0.6	55
2016	AA	San Antonio	5	7	0	74	91	3.40	1.19	21.2	214	32	70	2.38	3.8	11.1	2.9	0.2	115
2016	AAA	El Paso	0	2	0	10	13	4.41	1.67	22.9	311	41	80	6.36	3.5	11.5	3.3	1.8	129

Hard-throwing RH with two-plus offerings. Mid-90s FB is best pitch. Traditional 2-seam movement with solid bore. SL became swing-and-miss offering as season progressed. Accounted for uptick in strikeout rate from June on. CU is still developing and used sparingly.

Lauer,Eric
SP | **San Diego** | EXP MLB DEBUT: 2019 | H/W: 6-3 205 | FUT: #3 starter | **8C**

Thrws L Age 21
2016 (1) Kent State

Velo	Pitch	Grade
89-92	FB	++++
74-75	CB	+++
79-82	SL	+++
82-84	CU	+++

Year	Lev	Team	W	L	Sv	IP	K	ERA	WHIP	BF/G	OBA	H%	S%	xERA	Ctl	Dom	Cmd	hr/9	BPV
2016	NCAA	Kent State	10	2	0	104	125	0.69	0.74	24.7	143	21	95	0.56	2.4	10.8	4.5	0.3	147
2016	Rk	Azl Padres	0	1	0	4	7	6.75	2.00	9.6	383	58	71	8.87	2.3	15.8	7.0	2.3	241
2016	A-	Tri-City	1	0	0	25	28	1.44	0.96	13.5	194	29	83	1.35	2.5	10.1	4.0	0.0	131
2016	A	Fort Wayne	0	0	0	2	2	0.00	0.50	6.6	0	0	100		4.5	9.0	2.0	0.0	59

Collegiate 1st rd pick in '16, eased in during pro debut. Features four average or better pitches across the board. FB plays up w/ natural cut and sink, making it doubly difficult to square up. Has loads of pitchability to go with arsenal. A solid out pitch is needed to reach full projection.

Lawson,Reggie
SP | **San Diego** | EXP MLB DEBUT: 2020 | H/W: 6-4 205 | FUT: #3 starter | **8D**

Thrws R Age 19
2016 (S-2) HS (CA)

Velo	Pitch	Grade
94-95	FB	++++
74-78	CB	+++
	CU	+

Year	Lev	Team	W	L	Sv	IP	K	ERA	WHIP	BF/G	OBA	H%	S%	xERA	Ctl	Dom	Cmd	hr/9	BPV
2016	Rk	Azl Padres	0	0	0	8	7	8.78	1.83	7.6	342	43	47	5.65	3.3	7.7	2.3	0.0	67

Athletic RHP with huge upside. Firmed up body pre-draft. FB 94-95, jumps on hitters. CB has improved as pro—was 68-70 w/ good spin as amateur; added depth and velocity and now has makings of potentially plus pitch. CU is a work-in-progress. Has bulldog mentality on mound. Not afraid to pitch inside.

Leclerc,Jose
RP | **Texas** | EXP MLB DEBUT: 2016 | H/W: 6-0 190 | FUT: Setup reliever | **7B**

Thrws R Age 23
2010 FA (DR)

Velo	Pitch	Grade
91-96	FB	+++
78-81	CB	+++
83-86	CU	+++

Year	Lev	Team	W	L	Sv	IP	K	ERA	WHIP	BF/G	OBA	H%	S%	xERA	Ctl	Dom	Cmd	hr/9	BPV
2014	A+	Myrtle Beach	4	1	14	57		3.31	1.33	5.6	195	27	81	3.46	5.8	12.5	2.1	1.3	85
2015	AA	Frisco	6	8	0	103	98	5.77	1.65	17.7	250	32	64	4.46	6.4	8.6	1.3	0.7	0
2016	AA	Frisco	0	5	1	23	28	3.52	1.17	9.2	208	30	69	2.41	3.9	11.0	2.8	0.4	110
2016	AAA	Round Rock	2	2	1	43	50	2.72	1.19	5.9	159	22	79	2.12	5.9	10.5	1.8	0.6	48
2016	MLB	Texas	0	0	0	15	15	1.80	1.60	5.5	206	29	88	3.12	7.8	9.0	1.2	0.0	-31

Short pitcher who reached majors as RP, though has starting experience. Has three pitches that all can miss bats, highlighted by sneaky quick FB. Has crossfire delivery which negatively impacts command and needs to repeat arm slot. Hard CU has blistering, late life and CB is weapon against RHH. Size and effort best in bullpen.

Lee,Chris
SP | **Baltimore** | EXP MLB DEBUT: 2017 | H/W: 6-3 180 | FUT: #3 starter | **8D**

Thrws L Age 24
2011 (4) Santa Fe CC

Velo	Pitch	Grade
89-95	FB	+++
83-86	SL	+++
	CU	+++

Year	Lev	Team	W	L	Sv	IP	K	ERA	WHIP	BF/G	OBA	H%	S%	xERA	Ctl	Dom	Cmd	hr/9	BPV
2015	A	Quad Cities	3	2	0	30	24	4.17	1.52	18.7	297	36	71	4.44	3.0	7.2	2.4	0.3	66
2015	A+	Frederick	3	6	0	76	48	3.07	1.38	22.8	262	31	76	3.41	3.4	5.7	1.7	0.1	28
2015	AA	Bowie	4	2	0	38	26	3.08	1.37	22.7	230	28	75	2.85	4.7	6.2	1.3	0.0	1
2016	AA	Bowie	5	0	0	51	19	2.99	1.06	24.8	221	23	74	2.65	2.3	3.3	1.5	0.7	16

Tall, athletic SP who ended season in May due to lat issue. Extremely stingy against LHH (.155) with ability to repeat deceptive delivery. Works aggressively with FB and likes to use hard SL as put away pitch. CU has movement and is effective against RHH. Throws quality strikes, though prefers to pitch to contact than blow ball by hitters.

Lee,Zach
SP | **San Diego** | EXP MLB DEBUT: 2015 | H/W: 6-4 227 | FUT: #4 starter | **7D**

Thrws R Age 25
2010 (1) HS (TX)

Velo	Pitch	Grade
88-93	FB	+++
81-84	SL	++
78-79	CB	++
	CU	++

Year	Lev	Team	W	L	Sv	IP	K	ERA	WHIP	BF/G	OBA	H%	S%	xERA	Ctl	Dom	Cmd	hr/9	BPV
2015	AAA	Oklahoma City	11	6	0	113	81	2.71	1.11	23.4	251	30	76	2.86	1.5	6.4	4.3	0.4	93
2015	MLB	LA Dodgers	0	1	0	4	3	15.00	2.86	23.8	482	53	45	13.33	2.1	6.4	3.0	2.1	76
2016	AAA	Oklahoma City	7	5	0	73	57	4.92	1.50	24.3	315	36	71	5.66	1.8	7.0	3.8	1.4	94
2016	AAA	Tacoma	0	9	0	74	50	7.41	1.65	23.6	319	35	55	6.09	2.9	6.1	2.1	1.3	49

Tall, athletic SP who was acquired by SEA in June, claimed by SD in December, but was poor all season. Has the feel and touch for craft, but remains too hittable with average stuff. K rate continues to fall, but throws consistent strikes and gets good movement to arsenal. Allows lot of HR. Hope is that he regains confidence and starts to attack with potent FB/SL combo.

Lemoine,Jake
SP | **Texas** | EXP MLB DEBUT: 2019 | H/W: 6-5 220 | FUT: #3 starter | **8E**

Thrws R Age 23
2015 (4) Houston

Velo	Pitch	Grade
90-96	FB	+++
84-85	SL	+++
82-85	CU	+

Year	Lev	Team	W	L	Sv	IP	K	ERA	WHIP	BF/G	OBA	H%	S%	xERA	Ctl	Dom	Cmd	hr/9	BPV
2015		Did not play in minors																	
2016		Did not play in minors																	

Tall pitcher who has yet to pitch as pro due to shoulder problems. Future up in the air, but has outstanding pitches in FB and hard SL. FB is rarely straight and has incredible, late life. Pitches tough to elevate and SL can be thrown for strikes or used as chase pitch. Not much touch on CU. Has very high upside, but needs to pitch.

Lewicki,Artie
SP | **Detroit** | EXP MLB DEBUT: 2018 | H/W: 6-3 195 | FUT: #4 starter | **7D**

Thrws R Age 24
2014 (8) Virginia

Velo	Pitch	Grade
91-95	FB	+++
80-85	SL	+++
78-80	CB	++
82-85	CU	++

Year	Lev	Team	W	L	Sv	IP	K	ERA	WHIP	BF/G	OBA	H%	S%	xERA	Ctl	Dom	Cmd	hr/9	BPV
2014	Rk	GCL Tigers	0	0	0	2	4	0.00	1.50	4.3	262	55	100	3.49	4.5	18.0	4.0	0.0	221
2014	A	West Michigan	2	2	2	25	22	2.50	1.11	9.9	211	26	81	2.62	3.2	7.9	2.4	0.7	73
2015	A	West Michigan	3	4	0	79	77	3.53	1.42	22.3	281	36	75	4.06	2.8	8.8	3.1	0.5	99
2016	A+	Lakeland	2	1	0	21	20	3.40	1.27	17.4	260	35	70	2.98	2.5	8.5	3.3	0.0	102
2016	AA	Erie	1	7	0	67	57	3.49	1.19	22.4	261	32	71	3.31	1.7	7.6	4.4	0.5	109

Tall, lean SP who missed time early with injury, but increased stock when healthy. Has two quality offerings in FB and SL while keeping ball low in zone. Sequences well despite sub-par CB and CU. Downhill plane has been effective, but needs to stay healthy to mute durability concerns.

Leyva,Lazaro
RP | **Baltimore** | EXP MLB DEBUT: 2019 | H/W: 6-2 190 | FUT: Setup reliever | **8E**

Thrws R Age 22
2014 FA (CU)

Velo	Pitch	Grade
91-96	FB	++++
80-83	SL	++
	CU	+

Year	Lev	Team	W	L	Sv	IP	K	ERA	WHIP	BF/G	OBA	H%	S%	xERA	Ctl	Dom	Cmd	hr/9	BPV
2016		Did not pitch																	

Raw, SP who has yet to appear in full-season, but has easy delivery and velocity. Works with smooth arm action to generate plus FB. Secondary offerings lag behind, though show promise. Learning how to consistently throw SL with arm slot while slows arm speed on CU. Both pitches could be average at peak. May move to pen if command doesn't improve.

Light,Pat
RP | **Minnesota** | EXP MLB DEBUT: 2016 | H/W: 6-5 220 | FUT: Setup reliever | **7C**

Thrws R Age 26
2012 (S-1) Monmouth

Velo	Pitch	Grade
94-98	FB	++++
81-85	SP	++++

Year	Lev	Team	W	L	Sv	IP	K	ERA	WHIP	BF/G	OBA	H%	S%	xERA	Ctl	Dom	Cmd	hr/9	BPV
2015	AAA	Pawtucket	2	4	2	33	35	5.18	1.73	5.8	250	33	69	4.49	7.1	9.5	1.3	0.5	-2
2016	AAA	Pawtucket	1	1	7	31	36	2.32	1.23	5.0	194	28	81	2.29	4.9	10.5	2.1	0.3	73
2016	AAA	Rochester	1	0	2	7	6	2.57	1.00	4.5	202	27	71	1.57	2.6	7.7	3.0	0.0	87
2016	MLB	Boston	0	0	0	2	2	28.64	3.64	7.1	530	54	17	22.45	4.1	8.2	2.0	8.2	55
2016	MLB	Minnesota	0	1	0	14	14	9.00	2.14	4.6	275	34	57	6.59	9.6	9.0	0.9	1.3	-80

Tall, hard-throwing RP who has been in pen since '15. Velocity and K rate spiked in conversion and has closer stuff. Lively FB is best pitch, though splitter can be lethal to RHH. Has trouble maintaining mechanics and tends to overthrow FB, which impacts command. Allows too many walks, though is difficult to make hard contact against.

Lilek,Brett
SP | **Miami** | EXP MLB DEBUT: 2019 | H/W: 6-4 220 | FUT: #4 starter | **7D**

Thrws L Age 23
2015 (2) Arizona State

Velo	Pitch	Grade
92-94	FB	+++
77-78	CB	+++
	SL	++
80-83	CU	++

Year	Lev	Team	W	L	Sv	IP	K	ERA	WHIP	BF/G	OBA	H%	S%	xERA	Ctl	Dom	Cmd	hr/9	BPV
2015	NCAA	Arizona State	4	2	0	78	66	3.22	1.27	18.8	208	26	75	2.75	4.7	7.6	1.6	0.5	27
2015	A-	Batavia	1	2	0	35	43	3.34	1.06	12.3	233	34	67	2.30	1.8	11.1	6.1	0.3	168
2016	A	Greensboro	0	1	0	16	13	5.06	2.19	11.4	296	36	76	6.35	9.0	7.3	0.8	0.6	-93

2nd round pick has a four-pitch mix, but a shoulder strain limited him to just 16 IP in 2016. When healthy features a FB that sits a 92-94 mph but without much movement. CB is second offering and has nice, late sink. SL and CU project as average. Struggled with command prior to the injury. If healthy, look for a rebound.

Lindgren,Jacob
RP | **Atlanta** | EXP MLB DEBUT: 2015 | H/W: 5-11 210 | FUT: Closer | **7C**

Thrws L Age 24
2014 (2) Mississippi State

Velo	Pitch	Grade
90-95	FB	++++
82-86	SL	++++
80-83	CU	++

Year	Lev	Team	W	L	Sv	IP	K	ERA	WHIP	BF/G	OBA	H%	S%	xERA	Ctl	Dom	Cmd	hr/9	BPV
2014	A+	Tampa	0	0	0	7	17	0.00	0.99	4.5	130	50	100	0.62	5.1	21.5	4.3	0.0	269
2014	AA	Trenton	1	1	0	11	18	4.02	1.34	5.8	160	31	67	1.88	7.2	14.5	2.0	0.0	83
2015	AAA	Scranton/WB	1	1	3	22	29	1.23	1.18	5.9	205	33	88	2.02	4.1	11.9	2.9	0.0	121
2015	MLB	NY Yankees	0	0	0	7	8	5.14	1.29	4.1	202	15	83	5.89	5.1	10.3	2.0	3.9	64
2016	A+	Tampa	1	0	1	7	8	2.57	1.29	4.8	0	0	78	0.37	11.6	10.3	0.9	0.0	-109

Short, max-effort RP who will miss all '17 after Tommy John surgery in August. Got to majors quickly and has premium stuff, highlighted by FB/SL combo. Has difficulty throwing strikes due to mechanical issues and erratic command. Leaves ball up in zone, but two-pitch combo has high upside. Registers very high K rate, but surgery may set him back a few years.

Littell,Zack — SP — New York (A)
EXP MLB DEBUT: 2018 | H/W: 6-3 190 | FUT: #4 starter | 7C

Thrws R Age 21
2013 (11) HS (NC)

- 90-94 FB + + +
- 77-81 CB + + +
- 82-85 CU + +

Year	Lev	Team	W	L	Sv	IP	K	ERA	WHIP	BF/G	OBA	H%	S%	xERA	Ctl	Dom	Cmd	hr/9	BPV
2013	Rk	Azl Mariners	0	6	1	33	28	5.98	1.57	14.5	295	36	60	4.75	3.5	7.6	2.2	0.5	60
2014	Rk	Pulaski	5	5	0	69	64	4.55	1.26	21.7	278	35	62	3.56	1.6	8.3	5.3	0.4	126
2015	A	Clinton	3	6	0	112	84	3.93	1.35	22.3	277	33	69	3.72	2.4	6.7	2.8	0.3	74
2016	A	Clinton	5	5	0	97	95	2.78	1.18	24.3	255	33	77	3.13	1.9	8.8	4.5	0.5	124
2016	A+	Bakersfield	8	1	0	68	61	2.51	1.13	22.4	250	32	78	2.87	1.7	8.1	4.7	0.4	117

Tall SP who has solid three-pitch mix and ability to sequence to keep hitters guessing. Promoted to A+ in July and has advanced pitchability and feel. Throws strikes with all pitches and lively FB tough to square up. CB shows promise and can miss bats while CU needs some polish. Keeps ball on ground thanks to lively, commandable FB.

Lively,Ben — SP — Philadelphia
EXP MLB DEBUT: 2017 | H/W: 6-4 190 | FUT: #5 SP/swingman | 7A

Thrws R Age 25
2013 (4) Central Florida

- 90-93 FB + + +
- 81-83 SL + +
- 75-77 CB + +
- 83-86 CU + + +

Year	Lev	Team	W	L	Sv	IP	K	ERA	WHIP	BF/G	OBA	H%	S%	xERA	Ctl	Dom	Cmd	hr/9	BPV
2014	A+	Bakersfield	10	1	0	79	95	2.28	0.92	22.8	204	29	79	2.01	1.8	10.8	5.9	0.7	164
2014	AA	Pensacola	3	6	0	72	76	3.88	1.33	23.0	228	29	73	3.53	4.5	9.5	2.1	0.9	68
2015	AA	Reading	8	7	0	143	111	4.15	1.43	24.4	284	33	73	4.56	2.8	7.0	2.5	0.9	67
2016	AA	Reading	7	0	0	53	49	1.87	0.94	22.2	190	25	80	1.44	2.5	8.3	3.3	0.2	99
2016	AAA	Lehigh Valley	11	5	0	117	90	3.07	0.94	23.2	201	23	70	2.13	2.1	6.9	3.3	0.8	86

Overlooked prospect earned first shot at AAA. A deception-over-stuff pitcher, has predictably struggled to maintain K rate as he's moved up the ladder. FB tends to be straight; slow CB is trackable. CU is best secondary pitch. Overall, he's much more effective when he's able to get on top of the ball and work down in the zone. Back-end SP option.

Long,Grayson — SP — Los Angeles (A)
EXP MLB DEBUT: 2018 | H/W: 6-5 230 | FUT: #4 starter | 7B

Thrws R Age 22
2015 (3) Texas A&M

- 89-94 FB + + +
- 81-83 SL + + +
- CU + + +

Year	Lev	Team	W	L	Sv	IP	K	ERA	WHIP	BF/G	OBA	H%	S%	xERA	Ctl	Dom	Cmd	hr/9	BPV
2015	NCAA	Texas A&M	9	1	0	95		2.84	1.30	23.1	240	34	77	2.96	3.7	10.0	2.7	0.2	99
2015	Rk	Orem	0	0	0	19	22	5.16	1.51	6.4	260	36	64	4.00	4.7	10.3	2.2	0.5	77
2016	Rk	Azl Angels	0	1	0	11	10	6.55	1.64	12.3	295	38	56	4.41	4.1	8.2	2.0	0.0	55
2016	A	Burlington	3	3	0	40	45	1.58	1.08	19.5	193	27	88	2.05	3.6	10.1	2.8	0.5	103
2016	A+	Inland Empire	2	1	0	14	15	5.14	1.29	19.2	262	27	77	6.05	2.6	9.6	3.8	3.2	122

Tall, physical SP who missed most of season due to shoulder strain. Combines nice delivery with tough angle to plate to give hitters fits. Repeats slot that allows pitches to play up. No pitches stand out, though throws all for strikes. SL gives him potential above average offering. Sequences well.

Lopez,Jorge — SP — Milwaukee
EXP MLB DEBUT: 2015 | H/W: 6-3 195 | FUT: #4 starter | 7B

Thrws R Age 24
2011 (2) HS (PR)

- 92-95 FB + + + +
- 79-83 CB + + + +
- 84-87 CU + +

Year	Lev	Team	W	L	Sv	IP	K	ERA	WHIP	BF/G	OBA	H%	S%	xERA	Ctl	Dom	Cmd	hr/9	BPV
2014	A+	Brevard County	10	10	0	137	119	4.59	1.38	23.1	271	33	67	4.17	3.0	7.8	2.6	0.8	77
2015	AA	Biloxi	12	5	0	143	137	2.26	1.10	23.4	206	26	82	2.39	3.3	8.6	2.6	0.6	85
2015	MLB	Milwaukee	1	1	0	10	10	5.40	1.90	23.6	332	43	68	5.65	4.5	9.0	2.0	0.0	59
2016	AA	Biloxi	2	4	0	45	47	3.99	1.35	23.5	261	33	73	4.13	3.2	9.4	2.9	1.0	101
2016	AAA	Colorado Springs	1	7	0	79	66	6.83	1.97	22.3	312	36	67	6.80	6.3	7.5	1.2	1.4	-16

Tall, lean SP made solid major-league impression in 2015, but struggled mightily in PCL tour. Will touch 97 mph on occasion but hums 92-95 with FB. Complements with plus 12/6 CB for bulk of whiffs; feel for CU still a project. Command may never be great, but needs to throw more strikes to back up otherwise solid SwK/GB skills for rotation.

Lopez,Reynaldo — SP — Chicago (A)
EXP MLB DEBUT: 2016 | H/W: 6-0 185 | FUT: #2 SP/closer | 9C

Thrws R Age 23
2012 FA (DR)

- 94-98 FB + + + +
- 79-81 CB + + +
- 87-89 CU + +

Year	Lev	Team	W	L	Sv	IP	K	ERA	WHIP	BF/G	OBA	H%	S%	xERA	Ctl	Dom	Cmd	hr/9	BPV
2014	A	Hagerstown	4	1	0	47	39	1.34	0.81	19.0	169	22	84	0.89	2.1	7.5	3.5	0.2	95
2015	A+	Potomac	6	7	0	99	94	4.09	1.22	21.1	250	32	66	3.15	2.5	8.5	3.4	0.5	103
2016	AA	Harrisburg	3	5	0	76	100	3.19	1.24	22.0	243	35	77	3.41	3.0	11.8	4.0	0.8	151
2016	AAA	Syracuse	2	2	0	33	26	3.27	0.94	24.8	184	18	76	2.75	2.7	7.1	2.6	1.6	72
2016	MLB	Washington	5	3	0	44	42	4.91	1.57	17.6	275	34	69	4.70	4.5	8.6	1.9	0.8	51

Small-statured but strong, ridiculous arm speed pumps in mid-90s fastballs with ease. Double-A hitters were overpowered; MLB batters weren't. Command comes and goes, and although CB has depth and CU flashes plus, he'll need to hit his spots. Aggressive demeanor seems well-suited for a late-innings role, but he'll remain in rotation for now.

Lowry,Thad — SP — Chicago (A)
EXP MLB DEBUT: 2017 | H/W: 6-4 215 | FUT: #4 starter | 7D

Thrws R Age 22
2013 (5) HS (TX)

- 90-94 FB + + +
- 81-84 SL + +
- 81-85 CU + + +

Year	Lev	Team	W	L	Sv	IP	K	ERA	WHIP	BF/G	OBA	H%	S%	xERA	Ctl	Dom	Cmd	hr/9	BPV
2013	Rk	Bristol	3	5	0	44	30	5.51	1.75	13.4	307	36	67	5.26	4.5	6.1	1.4	0.4	7
2014	A	Kannapolis	4	6	0	87	43	4.76	1.52	22.2	296	33	68	4.64	3.0	4.4	1.5	0.5	17
2015	A	Kannapolis	12	8	0	150	94	4.49	1.32	23.9	272	31	65	3.74	2.4	5.6	2.4	0.5	55
2016	A+	Winston-Salem	8	8	0	135	90	4.06	1.34	23.4	273	32	69	3.86	2.5	6.0	2.4	0.5	58
2016	AA	Birmingham	0	3	0	24	11	4.13	1.13	23.7	254	29	59	2.57	1.5	4.1	2.8	0.0	52

Tall SP who is advancing quickly and has back-end profile. Uses three pitches effectively, though rarely misses bats. Uses clean, quick delivery to spot FB low in zone and has SL that exhibits depth. CU features splitter action and thrown with impressive arm speed. Throws strikes with all pitches and has durability to pitch deep into games.

Luzardo,Jesus — SP — Washington
EXP MLB DEBUT: 2022 | H/W: 6-1 205 | FUT: #3 starter | 7E

Thrws L Age 19
2016 (3) HS (FL)

- 91-93 FB + + +
- SL + +
- CB + +
- CU + +

Year	Lev	Team	W	L	Sv	IP	K	ERA	WHIP	BF/G	OBA	H%	S%	xERA	Ctl	Dom	Cmd	hr/9	BPV
2016		Did not pitch																	

A likely first-rounder, he had Tommy John surgery in March 2016 and in time-honored Nationals tradition, they scooped him up in the 3rd round. When healthy, uses four pitches and considerable moxie to get through lineups. Plus makeup convinced the team he'll be able to face the road back. Likely will make his pro debut in late 2017.

MacGregor,Travis — SP — Pittsburgh
EXP MLB DEBUT: 2020 | H/W: 6-3 180 | FUT: #4 starter | 7C

Thrws R Age 19
2016 (2) HS (FL)

- 88-92 FB + + +
- CB + +
- CU + +

Year	Lev	Team	W	L	Sv	IP	K	ERA	WHIP	BF/G	OBA	H%	S%	xERA	Ctl	Dom	Cmd	hr/9	BPV
2016	Rk	GCL Pirates	1	1	0	31	19	3.17	1.25	14.1	248	29	74	3.06	2.9	5.5	1.9	0.3	39

Pirates 2nd round pick has a lean projectable frame and already pumps his FB in at 88-92 mph, topping at 94 with room for more. Shows ability to spin a good 12/6 CB with some feel for his CU. Good athlete with simple, repeatable mechanics and solid Cmd for HS arm though his arm does lag at times. Nice upside.

Mader,Michael — SP — Atlanta
EXP MLB DEBUT: 2018 | H/W: 6-2 195 | FUT: #5 SP/swingman | 7D

Thrws L Age 23
2014 (3) Chipola JC

- 90-92 FB + + +
- 75-77 CB + +
- 83-85 CU + + +

Year	Lev	Team	W	L	Sv	IP	K	ERA	WHIP	BF/G	OBA	H%	S%	xERA	Ctl	Dom	Cmd	hr/9	BPV
2014	A-	Batavia	1	0	0	45	28	2.00	1.04	14.5	196	22	84	2.20	3.2	5.6	1.8	0.6	32
2015	A	Greensboro	6	12	0	140	86	4.75	1.41	22.0	263	30	65	3.89	3.7	5.5	1.5	0.5	19
2016	A+	Jupiter	7	6	0	103	81	3.50	1.27	19.2	250	31	72	3.28	3.0	7.1	2.4	0.4	65
2016	AA	Mississippi	0	3	0	30	26	2.40	1.10	23.5	242	32	76	2.31	1.8	7.8	4.3	0.0	110

LHP acquired in Hunter Cervenka deal with MIA. Cross-fire delivery. Poorly commands all three offerings. 2 seam FB has solid arm side run. Needs to tighten up grip on CB; it's currently too loopy. CU has solid fade and deception. Frame is tapped out. Will need to keep hitters off balance to be successful.

Maese,Justin — SP — Toronto
EXP MLB DEBUT: 2019 | H/W: 6-3 190 | FUT: #3 starter | 8D

Thrws R Age 20
2015 (3) HS (TX)

- 88-94 FB + + + +
- 83-87 SL + + +
- 81-82 CU +

Year	Lev	Team	W	L	Sv	IP	K	ERA	WHIP	BF/G	OBA	H%	S%	xERA	Ctl	Dom	Cmd	hr/9	BPV
2015	Rk	GCL Blue Jays	5	0	0	35	19	1.02	1.08	17.2	244	29	89	2.32	1.5	4.9	3.2	0.0	64
2016	A-	Vancouver	2	2	0	26	20	2.07	0.80	18.9	214	26	75	1.55	0.3	6.9	20.0	0.3	133
2016	A	Lansing	2	4	0	56	44	3.37	1.30	23.1	272	33	73	3.53	2.2	7.1	3.1	0.3	84

Live-armed SP who effectively uses low 3/4 slot for pitch movement and inordinate number of groundballs. Has frame to add weight and strength. Velocity is average and could add a few ticks to FB. Hard SL has chance to be wicked offering; CU shows flashes as well. Raw ingredients are here for a mid-rotation SP with potential to miss bats.

Mahle,Tyler — SP — Cincinnati
EXP MLB DEBUT: 2018 | H/W: 6-4 200 | FUT: #3 starter | 8D

Thrws R Age 22
2013 (7) HS (CA)

- 92-94 FB + + + +
- 75-77 CB + + +
- 81-83 SL + +
- 81-84 CU + + +

Year	Lev	Team	W	L	Sv	IP	K	ERA	WHIP	BF/G	OBA	H%	S%	xERA	Ctl	Dom	Cmd	hr/9	BPV
2013	Rk	AZL Reds	1	3	0	34	30	2.38	1.17	11.3	250	33	78	2.60	2.1	7.9	3.8	0.0	104
2014	Rk	Billings	5	4	0	76	71	3.90	1.25	20.7	271	34	69	3.63	1.8	8.4	4.7	0.6	121
2015	A	Dayton	13	8	0	152	135	2.43	1.12	22.2	253	32	79	2.89	1.5	8.0	5.4	0.4	122
2016	A+	Daytona	8	3	0	79	76	2.50	0.95	22.9	206	26	77	2.12	1.9	8.7	4.5	0.7	121
2016	AA	Pensacola	6	3	0	71	65	4.94	1.38	21.3	280	33	69	4.96	2.5	8.2	3.3	1.5	98

Strong, sturdy RH added a few mph to FB in '16. Command/control pitcher who adds and subtracts velocity. Secondary pitches all average offerings. Will likely have trouble maintaining minor league strikeout rate in majors without swing-and-miss secondary pitch.

Manarino,Evan — SP — Oakland

EXP MLB DEBUT: 2018 | H/W: 6-1 195 | FUT: #5 SP/swingman | 6B

Thrws L Age 24
2015 (25) UC-Irvine

Velo	Pitch	Grade
87-92	FB	+ + +
74-77	CB	+ +
79-82	SL	+ +
80-84	CU	+ + +

Year	Lev	Team	W	L	Sv	IP	K	ERA	WHIP	BF/G	OBA	H%	S%	xERA	Ctl	Dom	Cmd	hr/9	BPV
2015	NCAA	UC Irvine	7	3	0	94	76	3.82	1.45	25.2	297	36	72	4.25	2.4	7.3	3.0	0.3	84
2015	A-	Vermont	3	2	1	38	28	5.65	1.36	10.6	299	36	56	4.23	1.4	6.6	4.7	0.5	99
2016	A	Beloit	8	5	0	121	103	2.15	1.09	21.5	247	32	79	2.42	1.5	7.6	5.2	0.1	116
2016	A+	Stockton	2	1	0	28	18	1.28	1.10	18.4	225	27	87	2.13	2.6	5.8	2.3	0.0	53

Sinkerballer who led MWL in ERA in breakout season. Has two quality offerings in lively FB and outstanding CU. Needs to find dependable breaking ball that he can use as chase pitch. Can be around plate too much, though sinking FB tough to elevate. Natural stuff is fringy at best, but plus command gives him chance to succeed.

Manning,Matt — SP — Detroit

EXP MLB DEBUT: 2020 | H/W: 6-6 190 | FUT: #1 starter | 9D

Thrws R Age 19
2016 (1) HS (CA)

Velo	Pitch	Grade
92-96	FB	+ + + +
79-83	CB	+ +
83-85	CU	+ +

Year	Lev	Team	W	L	Sv	IP	K	ERA	WHIP	BF/G	OBA	H%	S%	xERA	Ctl	Dom	Cmd	hr/9	BPV
2016	Rk	GCL Tigers	0	2	0	29	46	4.02	1.17	11.6	248	41	66	3.08	2.2	14.2	6.6	0.6	216

Tall, very athletic SP with mammoth upside predicated on arm speed, projection, and potential plus CB. FB can be unhittable due to velocity and angle to plate. Commands FB well for age. Hard CB could develop into dynamite offering and needs time to polish throwing motion. CU could evolve into third average to plus pitch in time.

Mark,Tyler — SP — Arizona

EXP MLB DEBUT: 2019 | H/W: 6-1 195 | FUT: Setup reliever | 8E

Thrws R Age 22
2015 (6) Concordia

Velo	Pitch	Grade
90-93	FB	+ + +
81-83	SL	+ + +
85-86	SP	+ +

Year	Lev	Team	W	L	Sv	IP	K	ERA	WHIP	BF/G	OBA	H%	S%	xERA	Ctl	Dom	Cmd	hr/9	BPV
2015	Rk	Azl Dbacks	1	0	0	4	5	4.50	1.75	6.1	307	44	71	4.85	4.5	11.3	2.5	0.0	99
2015	A-	Hillsboro	2	2	0	36	24	5.25	1.44	17.1	298	33	65	4.92	2.3	6.0	2.7	1.0	65
2016	A-	Hillsboro	5	5	0	78	75	3.92	1.31	21.5	264	33	72	3.99	2.7	8.6	3.3	0.9	102
2016	A	Kane County	0	5	0	24	25	8.18	1.94	16.5	333	43	56	6.46	4.8	9.3	1.9	0.7	55

Athletic RH converted into starter in pro ball. Worked 90-93 with 2-seam FB as starter. FB lacks command. SL has swing-and-miss potential, solid shape but lacks bite as of now. Throws splitter to change speeds, which has good bite but he telegraphs his delivery.

Marquez,German — SP — Colorado

EXP MLB DEBUT: 2016 | H/W: 6-1 185 | FUT: #3 starter | 8D

Thrws R Age 22
2011 FA (VZ)

Velo	Pitch	Grade
93-96	FB	+ + + +
76-81	CB	+ + + +
82-84	CU	+ +

Year	Lev	Team	W	L	Sv	IP	K	ERA	WHIP	BF/G	OBA	H%	S%	xERA	Ctl	Dom	Cmd	hr/9	BPV
2014	A	Bowling Green	5	7	0	98	95	3.21	1.14	17.7	231	30	72	2.70	2.7	8.7	3.3	0.5	103
2015	A+	Charlotte	7	13	0	139	104	3.56	1.27	21.8	273	33	71	3.53	1.9	6.7	3.6	0.4	89
2016	AA	Hartford	9	6	0	135	126	2.86	1.16	25.6	245	31	77	3.07	2.2	8.4	3.8	0.6	110
2016	AAA	Albuquerque	2	0	0	31	29	4.35	1.16	24.7	255	30	68	4.01	1.7	8.4	4.8	1.5	123
2016	MLB	Colorado	1	1	0	20	15	5.35	1.68	15.2	330	38	69	5.92	2.7	6.7	2.5	0.9	66

Acquired from TAM in the Corey Dickerson deal, Marquez saw FB velocity jump from 88-91 mph when drafted to 93-96 mph now. Backs up the FB with a plus CB and a CU that is tough on lefties and gives him three solid offerings. Throws plenty of strikes, but can be wild in the zone. Has some work to do, but has huge upside.

Martes,Francis — SP — Houston

EXP MLB DEBUT: 2017 | H/W: 6-1 225 | FUT: #2 starter | 9C

Thrws R Age 21
2012 FA (DR)

Velo	Pitch	Grade
93-95	FB	+ + + +
82-84	CB	+ + + +
84-87	CU	+ +

Year	Lev	Team	W	L	Sv	IP	K	ERA	WHIP	BF/G	OBA	H%	S%	xERA	Ctl	Dom	Cmd	hr/9	BPV
2014	Rk	GCL Astros	1	1	0	11	12	0.82	0.73	9.8	139	21	88	0.17	2.5	9.8	4.0	0.0	128
2015	A	Quad Cities	3	2	2	52	45	1.04	0.88	19.3	184	24	89	1.23	2.3	7.8	3.5	0.2	97
2015	A+	Lancaster	4	1	0	35	37	2.31	1.11	23.0	239	33	79	2.54	2.1	9.5	4.6	0.3	134
2015	AA	Corpus Christi	1	0	0	14	16	5.07	1.83	22.0	322	41	75	6.49	4.4	10.1	2.3	1.3	81
2016	AA	Corpus Christi	9	6	0	125	131	3.31	1.21	20.2	228	31	71	2.66	3.4	9.4	2.8	0.3	96

High-ceiling SP who can mess with and dominate hitters with multiple offerings. Adds and subtracts from plus FB that exhibits heavy, late life. Power CB also serves as K pitch. CU can be too firm, but has good arm speed and deception. Needs better FB command, but that is nit-picking. Has frame for durability and maintaining velocity.

Martin,Brett — SP — Texas

EXP MLB DEBUT: 2018 | H/W: 6-4 190 | FUT: #3 starter | 8D

Thrws L Age 21
2014 (4) Walters State CC

Velo	Pitch	Grade
89-93	FB	+ + +
78-82	CB	+ + +
	CU	+ +

Year	Lev	Team	W	L	Sv	IP	K	ERA	WHIP	BF/G	OBA	H%	S%	xERA	Ctl	Dom	Cmd	hr/9	BPV
2014	Rk	Azl Rangers	1	4	1	35	39	5.40	1.37	9.8	267	36	60	4.04	3.1	10.0	3.3	0.8	115
2015	A	Hickory	5	6	0	95	72	3.50	1.24	19.3	255	30	72	3.39	2.5	6.8	2.8	0.6	74
2016	Rk	Azl Rangers	0	0	0	2	6	4.29	1.43	4.5	336	103	67	4.37	0.0	25.7		0.0	481
2016	A	Hickory	2	3	0	43	48	4.58	1.67	21.5	323	43	72	5.48	2.9	10.0	3.4	0.6	119
2016	A+	High Desert	2	1	0	23	16	4.29	1.34	16.0	269	30	71	4.41	2.7	6.2	2.3	1.2	57

Lanky SP who missed part of season due to forearm issue. Has solid-average three pitch mix and can throw all for strikes. Has over the top delivery and tough angle to late that allows FB to play up. Spots FB into zone with precision and uses power CB as out pitch. CU can be too firm, but has flashes of becoming average. Still projection remaining.

Martinez,Jonathan — SP — Chicago (N)

EXP MLB DEBUT: 2019 | H/W: 6-1 205 | FUT: #5 SP/swingman | 6C

Thrws R Age 22
2011 FA (VZ)

Velo	Pitch	Grade
90-94	FB	+ + +
	SL	+ +
	CU	+ + +

Year	Lev	Team	W	L	Sv	IP	K	ERA	WHIP	BF/G	OBA	H%	S%	xERA	Ctl	Dom	Cmd	hr/9	BPV
2014	A	Great Lakes	7	5	0	106	91	3.48	1.22	22.5	269	33	73	3.61	1.6	7.7	4.8	0.7	113
2014	A	Kane County	4	0	0	23	15	2.34	1.04	17.8	252	29	82	3.05	0.8	5.8	7.5	0.8	102
2015	A+	Myrtle Beach	9	2	0	116	66	2.56	0.94	19.0	200	22	77	2.15	2.1	5.1	2.4	0.8	54
2016	A+	Myrtle Beach	12	6	0	131	77	4.19	1.31	23.5	259	28	70	3.94	3.0	5.3	1.8	0.9	33
2016	AA	Tennessee	1	1	0	12	15	5.25	1.17	23.9	278	35	64	5.05	0.8	11.3	15.0	2.3	200

Short Venezuelan righty has a decent three-pitch mix. FB sits at 90-94, but without plus movement. Throws his SL for strikes, but lack of movement makes the pitch avg at best. CU is another solid-average offering. Throws tons of strikes, but lacks Dom needed to thrive in the majors.

Martinez,Luis — SP — Chicago (A)

EXP MLB DEBUT: 2019 | H/W: 6-6 190 | FUT: #3 starter | 8E

Thrws R Age 22
2011 FA (VZ)

Velo	Pitch	Grade
89-94	FB	+ + +
82-83	SL	+ + +
	CU	+

Year	Lev	Team	W	L	Sv	IP	K	ERA	WHIP	BF/G	OBA	H%	S%	xERA	Ctl	Dom	Cmd	hr/9	BPV
2014	Rk	Azl White Sox	3	2	0	33	40	4.09	1.42	20.0	250	35	73	3.97	4.4	10.9	2.5	0.8	97
2014	Rk	Great Falls	2	1	0	25	22	1.43	1.35	21.0	253	31	94	3.78	3.6	7.9	2.2	0.7	63
2015	A	Kannapolis	4	14	0	108	69	5.41	1.43	19.2	251	28	61	3.91	4.4	5.7	1.3	0.7	2
2016	A	Kannapolis	8	9	0	137	141	3.81	1.29	20.1	246	32	71	3.39	3.4	9.3	2.8	0.6	94

Long, lean SP who repeated Low-A to much better results. Improved ERA while walking less and missing more bats as he started to repeat delivery. Loose arm provides ample movement to impressive FB while showing more potent SL. Very raw CU and can telegraph by slowing arm. Has decent upside, but long way away.

Martinez,Nolan — SP — New York (A)

EXP MLB DEBUT: 2021 | H/W: 6-2 165 | FUT: #3 starter | 8D

Thrws R Age 18
2016 (3) HS (CA)

Velo	Pitch	Grade
87-93	FB	+ + +
77-79	CB	+ + +
	CU	+ +

Year	Lev	Team	W	L	Sv	IP	K	ERA	WHIP	BF/G	OBA	H%	S%	xERA	Ctl	Dom	Cmd	hr/9	BPV
2016	Rk	GCL Yankees	0	1	0	7	3	3.86	1.43	9.9	233	26	70	3.07	5.1	3.9	0.8	0.0	-51

Young, projectable SP who is long way from majors, but has tools to be mid-rotation guy. Exhibits extremely fast arm that adds movement to average pitch mix. Can reach back for more velocity, but sits in low 90s to generate more late sink. CB has potential to be wipeout offering while CU needs work. Should add durability as he gains strength.

Martinez,Rodolfo — RP — San Francisco

EXP MLB DEBUT: 2018 | H/W: 6-2 180 | FUT: Closer | 7B

Thrws R Age 23
2013 FA (DR)

Velo	Pitch	Grade
95-99	FB	+ + + +
85-87	SL	+ +
85-86	CU	+

Year	Lev	Team	W	L	Sv	IP	K	ERA	WHIP	BF/G	OBA	H%	S%	xERA	Ctl	Dom	Cmd	hr/9	BPV
2014	Rk	Azl Giants	1	5	0	27	35	8.93	2.24	9.2	370	51	57	7.47	5.3	11.6	2.2	0.3	84
2015	A	Augusta	1	2	0	46	44	2.54	1.20	5.3	240	32	78	2.71	2.7	8.6	3.1	0.2	99
2016	A+	San Jose	1	1	21	30	33	0.89	1.09	3.7	213	30	94	2.19	3.0	9.8	3.3	0.3	115
2016	AA	Richmond	0	3	3	23	17	6.65	1.91	4.4	309	37	63	5.70	5.9	6.7	1.1	0.4	-21

Intimidating, aggressive RP who served as closer and was dominant in A+. Hit hard upon promotion to AA as he tends to overthrow. Everything is hard, especially FB that he works in and out. Needs to find weapon against LHH, though SL has chance to be plus offering with more consistency. FB among best in org and good enough for upper levels.

Maton,Phil — RP — San Diego

EXP MLB DEBUT: 2017 | H/W: 6-3 220 | FUT: Middle reliever | 7C

Thrws R Age 24
2015 (20) Louisiana Tech

Velo	Pitch	Grade
91-93	FB	+ + + +
85-88	SL	+ + +
77-79	CB	+ +

Year	Lev	Team	W	L	Sv	IP	K	ERA	WHIP	BF/G	OBA	H%	S%	xERA	Ctl	Dom	Cmd	hr/9	BPV
2015	NCAA	Louisiana Tech	4	4	0	88	90	3.68	1.31	24.2	279	35	75	4.19	1.9	9.2	4.7	0.9	131
2015	A-	Tri-City	4	2	6	32	58	1.40	0.87	5.2	202	41	82	1.16	1.4	16.2	11.6	0.0	272
2016	A	Fort Wayne	1	1	1	12	19	1.48	1.23	6.2	289	48	87	3.23	0.7	14.0	19.0	0.0	250
2016	A+	Lake Elsinore	3	2	9	33	47	1.91	0.76	4.7	154	25	78	0.89	2.2	12.8	5.9	0.5	190
2016	AAA	El Paso	1	0	1	6	12	1.50	0.50	4.0	56	0	100	0.16	3.0	18.0	6.0	1.5	261

Sleeper RH reliever breezed through 3 levels and pitched well in AFL. Throws 3 pitches. 4-seam FB sits low 90s with late movement. SL has sharp break and could become a plus offering. CB has good shape but below-average break. Good at changing eye levels and avoiding fat part of plate.

Matuella,Michael

SP | Texas | EXP MLB DEBUT: 2019 | H/W: 6-6 220 | FUT: #1 starter | 9E

Thrws R Age 22
2015 (3) Duke

Velo	Pitch	Grade
91-96	FB	++++
80-82	CB	+++
84-85	SL	+++
83-86	CU	++

Year	Lev	Team	W	L	Sv	IP	K	ERA	WHIP	BF/G	OBA	H%	S%	xERA	Ctl	Dom	Cmd	hr/9	BPV
2015		Did not play (injured)																	
2016	A-	Spokane	0	0	0	3	1	0.00	1.00	11.5	106	12	100	0.61	6.0	3.0	0.5	0.0	-90

Injury-prone SP with significant ceiling if he can stay on mound. Only pitched 3 innings in June due to ligament sprain in elbow. Uses four pitches, including plus FB with electric life. Has two power breaking balls that could become plus. CU is distant fourth pitch and lacks feel for changing speeds. Uses great angle to plate.

May,Dustin

SP | Los Angeles (N) | EXP MLB DEBUT: 2021 | H/W: 6-6 180 | FUT: #4 starter | 7D

Thrws R Age 19
2016 (3) HS (TX)

Velo	Pitch	Grade
90-93	FB	+++
78-82	SL	++
	CU	+

Year	Lev	Team	W	L	Sv	IP	K	ERA	WHIP	BF/G	OBA	H%	S%	xERA	Ctl	Dom	Cmd	hr/9	BPV
2016	Rk	Azl Dodgers	0	1	1	30	34	3.89	1.36	12.6	304	42	68	3.82	1.2	10.2	8.5	0.0	169

Tall, projectable 3rd round pick out of TX had a stellar pro debut, posting a 3.86 ERA with 4 BB/34 K in 30.1 IP. FB already sits at 90-93 mph with good sink and room for more. Low-80s SL projects as above-average, but lacks reliable third offering. Should add more bulk as he matures. Lots of work to do, but a good base on which to build.

Mayers,Mike

SP | St. Louis | EXP MLB DEBUT: 2016 | H/W: 6-3 200 | FUT: #4 starter | 7D

Thrws R Age 25
2013 (3) Mississippi

Velo	Pitch	Grade
92-94	FB	+++
83-85	SL	++
84-86	CU	++

Year	Lev	Team	W	L	Sv	IP	K	ERA	WHIP	BF/G	OBA	H%	S%	xERA	Ctl	Dom	Cmd	hr/9	BPV
2015	Rk	GCL Cardinals	1	0	0	7		1.29	0.86	12.9	233	32	83	1.58	0.0	9.0		0.0	180
2015	AA	Springfield	1	4	0	46	36	6.62	1.60	20.4	289	32	61	5.71	4.1	7.0	1.7	1.6	34
2016	AA	Springfield	5	2	0	54	43	2.32	1.18	24.1	235	28	83	3.06	2.8	7.1	2.5	0.7	70
2016	AAA	Memphis	4	8	0	89	84	3.74	1.32	23.1	257	32	74	3.83	3.1	8.5	2.7	0.8	86
2016	MLB	St. Louis	1	1	0	5	2	28.24	3.73	8.3	527	51	19	19.89	5.3	3.5	0.7	5.3	-61

RHP had a breakout campaign, going 9-10 w/ 3.19 ERA between AA/AAA and making his MLB debut. Works off firm 92-94 mph FB that can go as high as 97 mph. Keeps hitters off balance with a solid CU with good fade and sink and a fringy SL. Keeps ball down in the zone and pounds the strike zone. Back-end starter.

McCurry,Brendan

RP | Houston | EXP MLB DEBUT: 2017 | H/W: 5-10 170 | FUT: Setup reliever | 6B

Thrws R Age 25
2014 (22) Oklahoma State

Velo	Pitch	Grade
87-92	FB	++
77-79	CB	+++
80-82	SL	++
	CU	++

Year	Lev	Team	W	L	Sv	IP	K	ERA	WHIP	BF/G	OBA	H%	S%	xERA	Ctl	Dom	Cmd	hr/9	BPV
2014	A+	Stockton	0	0	0	1	1	0.00	0.00	2.8	0	0			0.0	9.0		0.0	180
2015	A+	Stockton	1	2	21	46	56	1.95	0.89	4.8	187	27	82	1.64	2.1	10.9	5.1	0.6	157
2015	AA	Midland	0	1	6	16	26	1.67	0.93	4.3	165	29	86	1.42	3.3	14.4	4.3	0.6	188
2016	AA	Corpus Christi	2	4	13	39	50	2.30	0.92	5.2	202	28	81	2.19	1.8	11.5	6.3	0.9	175
2016	AAA	Fresno	1	1	3	42	44	3.85	1.43	6.4	284	38	72	4.09	2.8	9.4	3.4	0.4	112

Short, yet durable SP who was effective on two levels. No pitch stands out, but throws with deceptive mechanics and has unique ability to throw strikes from multiple arm angles. Spots pitches at will and consistently works ahead in count. Lively FB is OK while CB is best offering. Will serve 50-game drug suspension at start of '17.

McGee,Easton

SP | Tampa Bay | EXP MLB DEBUT: 2021 | H/W: 6-6 205 | FUT: #3 starter | 8D

Thrws R Age 19
2016 (4) HS (KY)

Velo	Pitch	Grade
87-91	FB	+++
75-79	CB	++
	CU	++

Year	Lev	Team	W	L	Sv	IP	K	ERA	WHIP	BF/G	OBA	H%	S%	xERA	Ctl	Dom	Cmd	hr/9	BPV
2016	Rk	GCL Devil Rays	1	1	0	23	14	3.12	1.17	15.4	226	26	73	2.67	3.1	5.5	1.8	0.4	32

Lean, projectable SP with raw secondary offerings. Learning to pitch, but exhibits potential due to easy arm action and clean delivery. Uses height well and throws downhill. Pitch location is average, but tends to aim ball. CB has makings of becoming out pitch, but can get on side of it. Lot of potential here, but need to be patient.

McGowin,Kyle

SP | Washington | EXP MLB DEBUT: 2017 | H/W: 6-3 195 | FUT: #4 starter | 7C

Thrws R Age 25
2013 (5) Savannah State

Velo	Pitch	Grade
89-94	FB	+++
82-84	SL	+++
80-83	CU	++

Year	Lev	Team	W	L	Sv	IP	K	ERA	WHIP	BF/G	OBA	H%	S%	xERA	Ctl	Dom	Cmd	hr/9	BPV
2014	A+	Inland Empire	1	5	0	58	48	2.94	1.15	23.1	237	29	76	2.97	2.5	7.4	3.0	0.6	85
2014	AA	Arkansas	0	1	0	5	3	5.40	1.20	20.1	299	31	60	5.08	0.0	5.4		1.8	115
2015	AA	Arkansas	9	9	0	154	125	4.38	1.29	23.4	254	30	68	3.83	2.9	7.3	2.5	0.9	71
2016	AA	Arkansas	3	2	0	25	32	4.64	1.23	20.4	236	32	67	3.88	3.2	11.4	3.6	1.4	137
2016	AAA	Salt Lake	6	12	0	116	98	6.12	1.64	23.5	305	36	64	5.74	3.6	7.6	2.1	1.2	58

Lean, athletic SP who buries ball with heavy FB, but leaves secondary offerings hanging. Allows lot of HR and needs to find consistency with average SL and fringy CU. Possesses average FB command and can miss bats with SL when exhibiting quality breaking action. Can rely on FB too much and give up too many hits. Seems on verge of breakout.

McKenzie,Triston

SP | Cleveland | EXP MLB DEBUT: 2019 | H/W: 6-5 165 | FUT: #3 starter | 8D

Thrws R Age 19
2015 (S-1) HS (FL)

Velo	Pitch	Grade
88-91	FB	+++
73-77	CB	+++
81-84	CU	+++

Year	Lev	Team	W	L	Sv	IP	K	ERA	WHIP	BF/G	OBA	H%	S%	xERA	Ctl	Dom	Cmd	hr/9	BPV
2015	Rk	AZL Indians	1	1	0	12	17	0.75	0.58	10.2	106	19	86		2.3	12.8	5.7	0.0	187
2016	A-	Mahoning Vall	4	3	0	49	55	0.55	0.96	20.6	183	26	98	1.56	2.9	10.1	3.4	0.4	120
2016	A	Lake County	2	2	0	34	49	3.18	0.97	21.5	220	35	68	2.15	1.6	13.0	8.2	0.5	209

Rail-thin, statuesque right-hander with considerable projection remaining. FB touches 92 mph with minimal movement. Good feel for mid-70s curve with flashes of plus 11/5 bite; CU also advanced for age. More control than command, but knows how to fill the zone. Long levers create deception to plate; repeats delivery well for frame. Lots of upside.

McWilliams,Sam

SP | Arizona | EXP MLB DEBUT: 2019 | H/W: 6-7 190 | FUT: #4 starter | 7C

Thrws R Age 21
2014 (8) HS (TN)

Velo	Pitch	Grade
92-94	FB	++++
75-77	CB	++
	CU	+++

Year	Lev	Team	W	L	Sv	IP	K	ERA	WHIP	BF/G	OBA	H%	S%	xERA	Ctl	Dom	Cmd	hr/9	BPV
2014	Rk	GCL Phillies	2	3	0	25	10	5.40	1.36	11.6	284	31	58	3.93	2.2	3.6	1.7	0.4	24
2015	Rk	GCL Phillies	0	2	0	33	21	3.27	1.03	18.2	238	28	67	2.36	1.4	5.7	4.2	0.3	84
2016	A	Kane County	3	6	0	74	43	4.00	1.40	20.9	291	33	71	4.24	2.2	5.2	2.4	0.5	53

Tall, slim RH made strides during extended spring training to start 15 games in Single-A. Uses size to create downward plane on sinking FB. FB generates tons of ground balls but little swing-and-miss. Ditched SL for CB. CB has solid 12/6 shape and promising dive. Could be swing-and-miss offering needed to start. CU is average offering.

Medeiros,Kodi

SP | Milwaukee | EXP MLB DEBUT: 2018 | H/W: 6-2 180 | FUT: #2 SP/closer | 8E

Thrws L Age 20
2014 (1) HS (HI)

Velo	Pitch	Grade
92-95	FB	++++
78-81	SL	++++
	CU	+++

Year	Lev	Team	W	L	Sv	IP	K	ERA	WHIP	BF/G	OBA	H%	S%	xERA	Ctl	Dom	Cmd	hr/9	BPV
2014	Rk	Azl Brewers	0	2	1	17	26	7.33	2.15	9.5	331	49	66	7.20	6.8	13.6	2.0	1.0	79
2015	A	Wisconsin	4	5	1	93	94	4.45	1.28	15.3	231	32	61	2.61	3.9	9.1	2.4	0.0	77
2016	A+	Brevard County	4	12	0	85	64	5.93	1.94	17.6	299	36	68	5.64	6.7	6.8	1.0	0.4	-40

Young southpaw whose peripheral ability took a step backward in High-A. Low arm slot produces heavy sink on plus FB, but also makes it hard to command. Sweeping SL has violent late break for Ks; has made strides with CU. Struggles to work ahead; must throw more strikes to stay SP. FB/SL combo could have intriguing potential from setup/closer role.

Medina,Adonis

SP | Philadelphia | EXP MLB DEBUT: 2020 | H/W: 6-1 185 | FUT: #2 starter | 9D

Thrws R Age 20
2014 FA (DR)

Velo	Pitch	Grade
92-95	FB	++++
77-79	CB	++
79-83	SL	++++
84-86	CU	+++

Year	Lev	Team	W	L	Sv	IP	K	ERA	WHIP	BF/G	OBA	H%	S%	xERA	Ctl	Dom	Cmd	hr/9	BPV
2015	Rk	GCL Phillies	3	2	0	45	35	2.99	1.20	18.1	248	31	74	2.84	2.4	7.0	2.9	0.2	79
2016	A-	Williamsport	5	3	0	64	34	2.94	1.11	19.4	206	22	76	2.57	3.4	4.8	1.4	0.7	13

Pairs a mid-90s, heavy FB with two breaking pitches: a slower CB and a vicious, late-breaking SL. Also shows a feel for his CU. With a simple, repeatable delivery, an athletic build and advanced approach, his upside is higher than stats might suggest. Should register more strikeouts at higher levels.

Medina,Javier

SP | Colorado | EXP MLB DEBUT: 2020 | H/W: 6-2 190 | FUT: #4 starter | 7D

Thrws R Age 20
2015 (3) HS (AZ)

Velo	Pitch	Grade
88-92	FB	+++
	CB	++
	CU	++

Year	Lev	Team	W	L	Sv	IP	K	ERA	WHIP	BF/G	OBA	H%	S%	xERA	Ctl	Dom	Cmd	hr/9	BPV
2015	Rk	Grand Junction	1	3	0	34	30	6.86	1.79	17.5	347	40	65	7.37	2.6	7.9	3.0	1.8	89
2016	A-	Boise	5	1	0	39	35	5.75	1.69	19.6	308	38	64	5.16	3.9	8.1	2.1	0.5	57

3rd round pick in '15 remains raw and struggled in short season ball. Flashes a good low-90s FB, which he locates well. Also has a decent feel for a CB and CU. Poor front-side mechanics result in inconsistent release point, but does have a good idea of how to change speed and keep hitters off-balance.

Meisner,Casey — SP — Oakland

EXP MLB DEBUT: 2018 | H/W: 6-7 190 | FUT: #3 starter | 8E

Thrws R Age 21 — 2013 (3) HS (TX)

Velo	Pitch	Grade
90-94	FB	+++
78-81	CB	++
83-85	CU	+++

Year	Lev	Team	W	L	Sv	IP	K	ERA	WHIP	BF/G	OBA	H%	S%	xERA	Ctl	Dom	Cmd	hr/9	BPV
2014	A-	Brooklyn	5	3	0	62	67	3.77	1.37	20.0	277	37	73	3.99	2.6	9.7	3.7	0.6	122
2015	A	Savannah	7	2	0	76	66	2.13	1.03	24.4	216	26	83	2.47	2.3	7.8	3.5	0.7	98
2015	A+	St. Lucie	3	2	0	35	23	2.83	1.40	24.6	262	29	84	4.32	3.6	5.9	1.6	1.0	27
2015	A+	Stockton	3	1	0	32	24	2.80	1.06	17.8	230	28	73	2.33	2.0	6.7	3.4	0.3	86
2016	A+	Stockton	1	14	1	117	100	4.85	1.58	18.4	276	33	71	4.86	4.5	7.7	1.7	0.9	34

Tall, lean SP who moved to pen during season to work on erratic mechanics. Walk rate spiked and faded down stretch. Needs to add strength for durability. Mixes two and four-seam FB effecitvely and uses advanced CU to retire LHH. Has big-bending CB, but not reliable. Throws with good angle, but leaves too many balls up in zone.

Mejia,Adalberto — SP — Minnesota

EXP MLB DEBUT: 2016 | H/W: 6-3 195 | FUT: #4 starter | 7B

Thrws L Age 23 — 2011 FA (DR)

Velo	Pitch	Grade
88-94	FB	+++
82-84	SL	+++
77-79	CB	+
83-85	CU	+++

Year	Lev	Team	W	L	Sv	IP	K	ERA	WHIP	BF/G	OBA	H%	S%	xERA	Ctl	Dom	Cmd	hr/9	BPV
2015	AA	Richmond	5	2	0	51	38	2.47	1.10	16.7	209	25	78	2.23	3.2	6.7	2.1	0.4	53
2016	AA	Richmond	3	2	0	65	58	1.94	0.98	22.5	208	26	83	2.11	2.2	8.0	3.6	0.6	103
2016	AAA	Rochester	2	2	0	26	25	3.79	1.19	26.2	276	34	71	3.96	1.0	8.6	8.3	1.0	145
2016	AAA	Sacramento	4	1	0	40	43	4.25	1.32	23.8	270	34	71	4.28	2.5	9.6	3.9	1.1	125
2016	MLB	Minnesota	0	0	0	2	0	8.57	2.86	11.9	458	46	67	10.75	4.3	0.0	0.0	0.0	-98

Thick-framed SP who reached majors and has repertoire to serve as back-end guy or hard-throwing RP. Hits spots with solid-average FB and possesses feel for changing speeds. Uses two breaking balls and SL is far ahead of CB. CU may end up being best offering as he maintains arm speed and slot. Lethal to LHH.

Mella,Keury — SP — Cincinnati

EXP MLB DEBUT: 2018 | H/W: 6-2 200 | FUT: Closer | 8E

Thrws R Age 23 — 2011 FA (DR)

Velo	Pitch	Grade
93-96	FB	++++
78-81	CB	++++
79-81	CU	+++

Year	Lev	Team	W	L	Sv	IP	K	ERA	WHIP	BF/G	OBA	H%	S%	xERA	Ctl	Dom	Cmd	hr/9	BPV
2014	A	Augusta	3	3	0	66		3.95	1.24	22.4	270	36	65	3.17	1.8	8.6	4.8	0.1	125
2015	A+	Daytona	3	1	0	21	23	2.99	1.23	21.4	156	20	79	2.42	6.4	9.8	1.5	0.9	22
2015	A+	San Jose	5	3	0	81	83	3.33	1.13	20.1	224	29	71	2.67	2.9	9.2	3.2	0.6	106
2016	A+	Daytona	8	9	0	131	95	3.91	1.57	23.0	288	34	75	4.61	3.8	6.5	1.7	0.5	32
2016	AAA	Louisville	1	0	0	7	6	1.29	0.57	23.7	132	13	100	0.94	1.3	7.7	6.0	1.3	122

Strong, hard-throwing RH with #3 starter stuff but poor command. Struggles to corral mid-90s FB with plus movement. Cross-fire delivery leads to inconsistent finish. CB is hard, wipeout 12/6 offering with solid sink. Loses luster due to poor command of FB. CU is an effective 3rd option.

Melotakis,Mason — RP — Minnesota

EXP MLB DEBUT: 2017 | H/W: 6-2 220 | FUT: Setup reliever | 6B

Thrws L Age 25 — 2012 (2) NW State

Velo	Pitch	Grade
92-95	FB	+++
82-85	CB	+++
80-83	CU	++

Year	Lev	Team	W	L	Sv	IP	K	ERA	WHIP	BF/G	OBA	H%	S%	xERA	Ctl	Dom	Cmd	hr/9	BPV
2012	A	Beloit	3	1	1	17	24	2.11	1.11	5.2	237	33	94	3.72	2.1	12.6	6.0	1.6	189
2013	A	Cedar Rapids	11	4	1	111	84	3.16	1.31	19.1	253	30	76	3.45	3.2	6.8	2.2	0.5	55
2014	A+	Fort Myers	3	1	1	47	45	3.45	1.57	8.3	274	35	79	4.48	4.6	8.6	1.9	0.6	49
2014	AA	New Britain	1	0	2	16	17	2.25	1.25	5.0	274	38	80	3.11	1.7	9.6	5.7	0.0	145
2016	AA	Chattanooga	1	2	0	33	42	2.99	1.45	3.9	278	39	82	4.42	3.3	11.4	3.5	0.8	135

Big-bodied RP who was healthy all year and shows upside as lefty reliever. DNP in '15 due to Tommy John surgery and velocity returned quicker than expected. Short arm action provides hint of deception and CB is neutralizer against LHH. Posts high K rate in pen and making progress with CU for RHH.

Mendez,Yohander — SP — Texas

EXP MLB DEBUT: 2016 | H/W: 6-5 200 | FUT: #3 starter | 8B

Thrws L Age 22 — 2011 FA (VZ)

Velo	Pitch	Grade
88-94	FB	+++
80-82	SL	++
82-84	CU	++++

Year	Lev	Team	W	L	Sv	IP	K	ERA	WHIP	BF/G	OBA	H%	S%	xERA	Ctl	Dom	Cmd	hr/9	BPV
2015	A	Hickory	3	3	3	66	74	2.45	1.09	12.3	234	33	77	2.42	2.0	10.1	4.9	0.3	144
2016	A+	High Desert	4	1	0	33	45	2.45	0.97	17.9	184	28	77	1.75	3.0	12.3	4.1	0.5	158
2016	AA	Frisco	4	1	0	46	46	3.12	1.15	18.3	230	31	73	2.64	2.7	9.0	3.3	0.4	106
2016	AAA	Round Rock	4	1	0	31	22	0.58	0.90	16.5	120	15	93	0.46	4.6	6.4	1.4	0.0	8
2016	MLB	Texas	0	0	0	3	0	18.00	2.33	7.7	371	37	14	7.54	6.0	0.0	0.0	0.0	-144

Long, projectable SP who pitched on four levels and set career high in IP. Uses height to throw on tough plane to plate and keeps ball low in zone. Throws with clean arm action and adds hint of deception and pitch movement. Plus CU is knockout offering and commands it well. SL needs to be enhanced to give him full arsenal.

Meyer,Alex — SP — Los Angeles (A)

EXP MLB DEBUT: 2015 | H/W: 6-9 225 | FUT: #3 starter | 8E

Thrws R Age 27 — 2011 (1) Kentucky

Velo	Pitch	Grade
94-99	FB	++++
83-87	CB	+++
81-83	CU	++

Year	Lev	Team	W	L	Sv	IP	K	ERA	WHIP	BF/G	OBA	H%	S%	xERA	Ctl	Dom	Cmd	hr/9	BPV
2016	A+	Inland Empire	0	0	0	2	3	12.86	1.90	9.9	336	51	25	5.69	4.3	12.9	3.0	0.0	134
2016	AAA	Rochester	1	1	1	17	19	1.05	0.88	21.1	186	27	87	1.05	2.1	10.0	4.8	0.0	141
2016	AAA	Salt Lake	0	0	0	4	6	0.00	0.50	13.3	151	27	100		0.0	13.5			261
2016	MLB	LA Angels	1	2	0	21	24	4.67	1.42	18.0	221	30	68	3.62	5.5	10.2	1.8	0.8	52
2016	MLB	Minnesota	0	1	0	3	5	14.06	3.75	10.5	470	63	64	15.82	11.3	14.1	1.3	2.8	-33

Large-framed pitcher who was acquired at deadline and will be used as SP. Can't stay healthy as he missed time with shoulder issue. Can fire FB by anybody with electric life, yet can also add sinking action in low 90s. Has hard knuckle curve that can be tough to hit while CU remains erratic. Keys will be to throw strikes and develop offspeed pitch.

Middleton,Keynan — RP — Los Angeles (A)

EXP MLB DEBUT: 2017 | H/W: 6-2 195 | FUT: Setup reliever | 7C

Thrws R Age 23 — 2013 (3) Lane CC

Velo	Pitch	Grade
93-98	FB	++++
84-87	SL	+++
	CU	++

Year	Lev	Team	W	L	Sv	IP	K	ERA	WHIP	BF/G	OBA	H%	S%	xERA	Ctl	Dom	Cmd	hr/9	BPV
2014	Rk	Orem	5	4	0	67	53	6.45	1.48	20.6	268	31	57	4.75	4.0	7.1	1.8	1.2	37
2015	A	Burlington	6	11	0	125	88	5.32	1.56	21.1	295	33	67	5.24	3.4	6.3	1.9	1.1	41
2016	A+	Inland Empire	1	1	0	36	56	3.74	1.16	5.8	178	25	77	3.28	5.0	14.0	2.8	1.7	135
2016	AA	Arkansas	0	0	6	15	18	1.20	1.00	4.4	206	29	93	2.15	2.4	10.8	4.5	0.6	148
2016	AAA	Salt Lake	0	1	2	14	14	5.07	1.27	7.3	259	33	59	3.55	2.5	8.9	3.5	0.6	109

Athletic RP who had career resurrection with move to pen. Features electric FB with vicious late life and has added touch and feel for hard SL. Will add and subtract from velocity at times, but likes to challenge hitters aggressively. Control comes and goes, but is very tough to hit. Doesn't repeat max-effort delivery and rarely uses poor CU.

Miller,Brandon — SP — Seattle

EXP MLB DEBUT: 2019 | H/W: 6-4 210 | FUT: #4 starter | 7D

Thrws R Age 21 — 2016 (6) Millersville

Velo	Pitch	Grade
88-92	FB	+++
80-84	SL	+++
75-77	CB	++
	CU	+

Year	Lev	Team	W	L	Sv	IP	K	ERA	WHIP	BF/G	OBA	H%	S%	xERA	Ctl	Dom	Cmd	hr/9	BPV
2016	NCAA	Millersville	12	2	0	107	115	1.43	0.71	25.2	172	25	80	0.64	1.1	9.7	8.8	0.2	162
2016	A-	Everett	4	2	0	56	51	2.73	0.96	15.2	229	29	73	2.25	1.1	8.2	7.3	0.5	135

Big, physical SP who came from small college, but has stuff to succeed. Has impeccable command for age and throws with clean, loose arm. Has deep pitch mix, though works off FB. Short SL gives him second average pitch, but also mixes in fringy CB and below average CU. Doesn't get great pitch movement and will have to hope for increased velocity.

Miller,Jared — RP — Arizona

EXP MLB DEBUT: 2017 | H/W: 6-7 240 | FUT: Setup reliever | 8C

Thrws L Age 23 — 2014 (11) Vanderbilt

Velo	Pitch	Grade
92-95	FB	++++
84-86	CT	+++
78-80	CB	++

Year	Lev	Team	W	L	Sv	IP	K	ERA	WHIP	BF/G	OBA	H%	S%	xERA	Ctl	Dom	Cmd	hr/9	BPV
2015	A	Kane County	4	5	0	59	42	5.93	1.69	20.5	292	34	64	5.23	4.7	6.4	1.4	0.8	6
2016	A	Kane County	0	0	2	14	21	0.00	0.64	5.4	91	18	100		3.2	13.4	4.2	0.0	173
2016	A+	Visalia	0	1	1	14	20	1.91	0.85	4.3	185	31	75	0.94	1.9	12.8	6.7	0.0	196
2016	AA	Mobile	0	1	2	26	36	3.78	1.18	5.5	196	31	67	2.23	4.5	12.4	2.8	0.3	120
2016	AAA	Reno	0	0	0	6	3	6.00	1.17	4.8	228	18	60	5.16	3.0	4.5	1.5	3.0	18

Strong, tall LH moved to pen in '16, breaking out in the AFL. Added velocity throughout season. Up to 97 in AFL. FB has late, explosive movement. Soft CT, often mistaken for SL, cuts in on hands of RHH. CB has solid shape but lacks sharp break.

Miller,Tyson — SP — Chicago (N)

EXP MLB DEBUT: 2020 | H/W: 6-5 200 | FUT: #4 starter | 6C

Thrws R Age 21 — 2016 (4) California Baptist

Velo	Pitch	Grade
91-94	FB	+++
80-83	SL	++
	CU	++

Year	Lev	Team	W	L	Sv	IP	K	ERA	WHIP	BF/G	OBA	H%	S%	xERA	Ctl	Dom	Cmd	hr/9	BPV
2016	NCAA	Calif Baptist	9	3	1	107	92	2.27	1.05	25.9	228	29	79	2.32	1.9	7.7	4.0	0.3	105
2016	Rk	Azl Cubs	1	0	0	3	2	0.00	0.67	10.5	106	13	100		3.0	6.0	2.0	0.0	45
2016	A-	Eugene	1	1	0	22	14	4.05	1.35	15.4	293	31	77	5.21	1.6	5.7	3.5	1.6	76

4th round pick out of Dallas Baptist is a tall, projectable right-hander. Best pitch is a good 91-94 mph FB that tops at 96 mph with good late sink. Mixes in an average SL and a fringe CU. Pounds the strike zone and generates tons of ground ball outs. Back-end starter.

Mills,Alec — SP — Kansas City

EXP MLB DEBUT: 2016 | H/W: 6-4 190 | FUT: #4 starter | 7C

Thrws R Age 25 — 2012 (22) Tenn-Martin

Velo	Pitch	Grade
90-93	FB	+++
82-83	SL	++
79-82	CB	++
81-85	CU	+++

Year	Lev	Team	W	L	Sv	IP	K	ERA	WHIP	BF/G	OBA	H%	S%	xERA	Ctl	Dom	Cmd	hr/9	BPV
2014	A	Lexington	2	1	0	38	33	1.18	0.92	20.3	189	25	86	1.22	2.4	7.8	3.3	0.0	95
2015	A+	Wilmington	7	7	0	113	111	3.02	1.20	21.7	277	36	74	3.26	1.1	8.8	7.9	0.2	147
2016	AA	NW Arkansas	1	2	0	67	68	2.41	1.03	21.5	231	31	76	2.23	1.6	9.1	5.7	0.3	139
2016	AAA	Omaha	4	3	0	58	54	4.19	1.40	20.4	275	33	74	4.67	2.9	8.4	2.8	1.2	89
2016	MLB	KC Royals	0	0	0	3	4	14.52	2.58	5.6	255	39	38	6.19	14.5	11.6	0.8	0.0	-165

Tall, durable SP who exhibits plus command of deep repertoire. Lacks put-away pitch, but sequences with precision and varies speeds on two breaking balls. Delivery offers hint of deception and does nice job of burying ball low in zone. Maintains velocity deep into games and has enhanced CU to near-plus status. Locates FB and can challenge inside.

Minaya,Juan — RP — Chicago (A)

EXP MLB DEBUT: 2016 | H/W: 6-4 210 | FUT: Setup reliever | 7E

Thrws R Age 26
2008 FA (DR)

Velo	Pitch	Grade
93-97	FB	+++
84-88	SL	+++
	CU	+

Year	Lev	Team	W	L	Sv	IP	K	ERA	WHIP	BF/G	OBA	H%	S%	xERA	Ctl	Dom	Cmd	hr/9	BPV
2015	AA	Corpus Christi	1	0	1	44	48	3.27	1.34	6.3	257	35	75	3.48	3.3	9.8	3.0	0.4	106
2015	AAA	Fresno	0	0	0	10	11	0.89	1.09	6.6	174	26	91	1.45	4.5	9.8	2.2	0.0	74
2016	AAA	Charlotte	4	3	1	26	28	3.44	1.26	6.3	237	31	74	3.28	3.4	9.6	2.8	0.7	98
2016	AAA	Fresno	0	3	0	24	19	4.11	1.45	6.4	269	33	71	3.92	3.7	7.1	1.9	0.4	45
2016	MLB	Chi White Sox	1	0	0	10	6	4.46	1.49	4.0	260	31	67	3.55	4.5	5.3	1.2	0.0	-6

Big, strong RP who was obtained off waivers in June and rewarded with September callup. Has two hard offerings in lively FB and nifty SL. Generates easy velocity due to loose arm action. Command comes and goes and walk rate needs to be watched. Has stuff to miss bats, but can be tentative when going for kill with two strikes.

Minter,AJ — RP — Atlanta

EXP MLB DEBUT: 2017 | H/W: 6-0 205 | FUT: Closer | 8C

Thrws L Age 23
2015 (S-2) Texas A&M

Velo	Pitch	Grade
95-98	FB	++++
90-92	CT	++++
83-85	SL	+++

Year	Lev	Team	W	L	Sv	IP	K	ERA	WHIP	BF/G	OBA	H%	S%	xERA	Ctl	Dom	Cmd	hr/9	BPV
2015	NCAA	Texas A&M	2	0	0	21	29	0.43	1.19	21.1	223	36	96	2.26	3.4	12.4	3.6	0.0	149
2016	A	Rome	0	0	2	6	6	0.00	0.48	4.1	103	15	100		1.5	8.7	6.0	0.0	136
2016	A+	Carolina	0	0	0	9	10	0.00	0.77	4.1	105	16	100		4.0	9.9	2.5	0.0	89
2016	AA	Mississippi	1	0	0	18	31	2.47	1.04	3.9	202	39	74	1.60	3.0	15.3	5.2	0.0	214

Dominant debut between 3 levels, advancing as far as Double-A. Move to pen has increased velocity of FB to high end range. CT is a newer winkle, giving RH hitters fits. SL is an average offering that saw more swing-and-miss potential as the season wore on.

Molina,Marcos — SP — New York (N)

EXP MLB DEBUT: 2018 | H/W: 6-3 188 | FUT: #3 starter | 8D

Thrws R Age 22
2012 FA (DR)

Velo	Pitch	Grade
91-94	FB	+++
85-87	SL	++++
84-86	CU	+++

Year	Lev	Team	W	L	Sv	IP	K	ERA	WHIP	BF/G	OBA	H%	S%	xERA	Ctl	Dom	Cmd	hr/9	BPV
2013	Rk	GCL Mets	4	3	0	53		4.41	1.32	20.0	272	33	66	3.76	2.4	7.3	3.1	0.5	85
2014	A-	Brooklyn	7	3	0	76	91	1.77	0.84	23.2	177	26	79	1.07	2.1	10.8	5.1	0.2	154
2015	Rk	GCL Mets	0	0	0	3	3	0.00	0.00	8.5	0	0			0.0	9.0		0.0	180
2015	A+	St. Lucie	1	5	0	41	36	4.60	1.46	22.0	297	38	66	4.20	2.4	7.9	3.3	0.2	95
2016		did not pitch (injury)																	

Tommy John surgery robbed himof '16 regular season. Did appear in AFL with a degree of success. FB looked to be a bit off, but was able to avoid hard contact due to late arm-side FB run. SL was missing bite too. CU presents as average offering. Not as much effort in delivery as before. Some scouts scream RP profile.

Moll,Sam — RP — Colorado

EXP MLB DEBUT: 2017 | H/W: 5-10 185 | FUT: Setup reliever | 7C

Thrws L Age 25
2013 (3) Memphis

Velo	Pitch	Grade
93-96	FB	++++
83-85	SL	++
	CU	++

Year	Lev	Team	W	L	Sv	IP	K	ERA	WHIP	BF/G	OBA	H%	S%	xERA	Ctl	Dom	Cmd	hr/9	BPV
2014	A-	Tri-City	0	1	0	13	7	4.15	1.62	6.4	317	35	75	5.38	2.8	4.8	1.8	0.7	30
2015	A+	Modesto	0	1	2	53	57	3.05	0.98	8.1	210	26	76	2.71	2.0	9.6	4.8	1.2	137
2015	AA	New Britain	0	0	0	14	17	1.27	0.77	3.9	149	23	82	0.38	2.5	10.8	4.3	0.0	143
2016	Rk	Grand Junction	0	0	0	2	5	0.00	0.00	2.8	0	0			0.0	22.5		0.0	423
2016	AAA	Albuquerque	3	5	2	47	39	4.97	1.57	4.9	293	35	70	5.11	3.6	7.5	2.1	1.0	54

Hard throwing lefty reliever shows good command of his 93-96 mph heater. He mixes in a power SL and a CU that remains below-average. Low 3/4 arm slot and release point need to be more consistent, and control is always going to be an issue. SL and CU could give him tools to be a LOOGY.

Montas,Frankie — SP — Oakland

EXP MLB DEBUT: 2015 | H/W: 6-2 255 | FUT: #2 SP/closer | 8C

Thrws R Age 24
2009 FA (DR)

Velo	Pitch	Grade
94-99	FB	++++
84-88	SL	++++
83-87	CU	+

Year	Lev	Team	W	L	Sv	IP	K	ERA	WHIP	BF/G	OBA	H%	S%	xERA	Ctl	Dom	Cmd	hr/9	BPV
2014	AA	Birmingham	0	0	0	5	1	0.00	0.40	16.1	66	7	100		1.8	1.8	1.0	0.0	2
2015	AA	Birmingham	5	5	0	112	108	2.97	1.22	19.7	220	29	75	2.56	3.9	8.7	2.3	0.2	70
2015	MLB	Chi White Sox	0	2	0	15	20	4.80	1.53	9.3	249	37	68	4.02	5.4	12.0	2.2	0.6	88
2016	AA	Tulsa	0	0	0	4	7	2.14	0.71	4.9	144	17	100	2.16	2.1	15.0	7.0	2.1	230
2016	AAA	Oklahoma City	0	0	0	11	15	2.43	1.26	11.3	277	42	79	3.16	1.6	12.2	7.5	0.0	193

Dynamic, big-bodied pitcher who missed most of season with strained oblique and was lights-out in AFL upon return. Can overpower hitters with plus FB and maintains velocity deep into games. Can miss bats with vicious SL, but has difficulty repeating complicated delivery. Injury history and poor command could lead to explosive late-innings arm.

Montgomery,Jordan — SP — New York (A)

EXP MLB DEBUT: 2017 | H/W: 6-6 225 | FUT: #4 starter | 7D

Thrws L Age 24
2014 (4) South Carolina

Velo	Pitch	Grade
89-93	FB	+++
72-77	CB	++
77-81	CU	+++

Year	Lev	Team	W	L	Sv	IP	K	ERA	WHIP	BF/G	OBA	H%	S%	xERA	Ctl	Dom	Cmd	hr/9	BPV
2014	A-	Staten Island	1	0	0	13	15	3.44	1.15	7.4	229	33	67	2.24	2.7	10.3	3.8	0.0	129
2015	A	Charleston (Sc)	4	3	0	43	55	2.71	1.11	18.9	228	34	74	2.32	2.5	11.5	4.6	0.2	157
2015	A+	Tampa	6	5	0	90	77	3.09	1.18	22.5	244	31	74	2.90	2.4	7.7	3.2	0.4	92
2016	AA	Trenton	9	4	0	102	97	2.56	1.27	22.0	246	32	81	3.21	3.2	8.6	2.7	0.4	86
2016	AAA	Scranton/WB	5	1	0	37	37	0.97	1.00	23.6	212	29	89	1.67	2.2	9.0	4.1	0.0	121

Tall pitcher who flies under radar despite consistent approach and results. Advancing quickly on basis of deceptive, over-the-top delivery and ability to change speeds. FB velocity is fringy, but has impressive arm speed on CU and repeats delivery and slot. CB could become average. Induces groundballs and rarely allows HR.

Moore,Andrew — SP — Seattle

EXP MLB DEBUT: 2018 | H/W: 6-0 185 | FUT: #4 starter | 7B

Thrws R Age 22
2015 (S-2) Oregon State

Velo	Pitch	Grade
89-93	FB	+++
74-75	CB	+++
80-83	SL	++
83-84	CU	+++

Year	Lev	Team	W	L	Sv	IP	K	ERA	WHIP	BF/G	OBA	H%	S%	xERA	Ctl	Dom	Cmd	hr/9	BPV
2015	NCAA	Oregon State	4	1	0	77	70	1.40	0.81	27.9	187	25	82	1.01	1.4	8.2	5.8	0.1	127
2015	A-	Everett	1	1	0	39	43	2.08	1.00	10.6	252	34	81	2.60	0.5	9.9	21.5	0.5	184
2016	A+	Bakersfield	3	1	0	54	47	1.66	0.90	22.4	191	24	83	1.51	2.2	7.8	3.6	0.3	100
2016	AA	Jackson	9	3	0	108	86	3.16	1.20	22.9	269	32	76	3.64	1.5	7.2	4.8	0.7	106

Polished SP who is moving quickly and dominated A+. Lacks a standout offering, but has four pitches at disposal. Adds and subtracts from FB and locates very well. Best pitch is CU that is thrown with deceptive arm speed. Tight CB can be average, but tends to leave up in zone. May not be high K guy, but solid bet to be innings eater.

Morejon,Adrian — SP — San Diego

EXP MLB DEBUT: 2019 | H/W: 6-0 165 | FUT: #2 starter | 9E

Thrws R Age 18
2016 FA (CU)

Velo	Pitch	Grade
91-94	FB	++++
	CB	++++
	CU	+++
	KB	+++

Year	Lev	Team	W	L	Sv	IP	K	ERA	WHIP	BF/G	OBA	H%	S%	xERA	Ctl	Dom	Cmd	hr/9	BPV
2016		did not pitch																	

Cuban LH signed by SD for $11 million. Has been regulated to Dominican camp since signing. Expected to start '16 in Single-A. Throws 2-seam FB in low 90s. Reported to have four above-average or better pitches. Throws two types of CU, a straight CU and unique knuckle-change.

Moreno,Gerson — RP — Detroit

EXP MLB DEBUT: 2019 | H/W: 6-0 175 | FUT: Closer | 8E

Thrws R Age 21
2012 FA (DR)

Velo	Pitch	Grade
93-98	FB	++++
82-85	SL	++
	CU	+

Year	Lev	Team	W	L	Sv	IP	K	ERA	WHIP	BF/G	OBA	H%	S%	xERA	Ctl	Dom	Cmd	hr/9	BPV
2014	Rk	GCL Tigers	1	1	0	28	22	4.47	1.74	9.2	287	36	71	4.55	5.4	7.0	1.3	0.0	-2
2015	A-	Connecticut	2	5	2	28	29	3.86	1.43	7.9	262	36	70	3.39	3.9	9.3	2.4	0.0	82
2015	A	West Michigan	0	0	1	9	9	0.00	0.66	6.3	105	15	100		3.0	8.9	3.0	0.0	98
2016	A	West Michigan	1	1	11	25	27	1.08	1.08	4.2	212	30	89	1.87	2.9	9.7	3.4	0.0	115
2016	A+	Lakeland	0	3	3	24	27	7.07	1.74	5.2	244	30	61	5.32	7.4	10.0	1.4	1.5	-2

Live-armed RP who dominated in Low-A before knocked around in High-A. Inconsistent command has been issue, but electric FB can be blown by any hitter. Inconsistent SL needs to be enhanced and rarely changes speeds. Mechanics aren't smooth, but give hint of deception. Has velocity and power to be closer and needs time to develop secondary pitches.

Morimando,Shawn — SP — Cleveland

EXP MLB DEBUT: 2016 | H/W: 6-0 200 | FUT: #5 SP/swingman | 6B

Thrws L Age 24
2011 (19) HS (VA)

Velo	Pitch	Grade
90-94	FB	+++
75-79	CB	+++
80-82	SL	++
83-85	CU	+++

Year	Lev	Team	W	L	Sv	IP	K	ERA	WHIP	BF/G	OBA	H%	S%	xERA	Ctl	Dom	Cmd	hr/9	BPV
2014	AA	Akron	2	6	0	56	38	3.85	1.43	23.8	285	34	72	4.05	2.7	6.1	2.2	0.3	54
2015	AA	Akron	10	12	0	158	128	3.19	1.29	23.2	238	29	76	3.22	3.7	7.3	2.0	0.5	49
2016	AA	Akron	10	3	0	93	73	3.09	1.21	23.5	227	28	75	2.87	3.5	7.1	2.0	0.5	51
2016	AAA	Columbus	5	2	0	59	46	3.51	1.44	22.9	278	33	78	4.39	3.2	7.0	2.2	0.8	58
2016	MLB	Cleveland	0	0	0	4	5	12.86	3.33	12.9	432	51	67	15.24	10.7	10.7	1.0	4.3	-78

Shorter, even-keeled southpaw who survives off durability and pitchability. Low-effort, online delivery with clean arm action. Command still spotty, but throws strikes with sinking low-90s FB. Gets bulk of whiffs on fading CU; SL and CB are passable pace-changers. Has low Dom ceiling and small margin for error, but will eat innings as back-end SP.

Moronta,Reyes — RP — San Francisco

EXP MLB DEBUT: 2018 | H/W: 6-0 175 | FUT: Closer | 7C

Thrws R Age 24
2010 FA (DR)

Velo	Pitch	Grade
93-96	FB	++++
82-85	SL	++
	CU	+

Year	Lev	Team	W	L	Sv	IP	K	ERA	WHIP	BF/G	OBA	H%	S%	xERA	Ctl	Dom	Cmd	hr/9	BPV
2012	Rk	Azl Giants	3	0	1	17	18	3.14	1.45	4.3	248	31	83	4.25	4.7	9.4	2.0	1.0	60
2013	A-	Salem-Kaizer	2	2	0	21	22	5.09	1.51	15.3	286	37	67	4.74	3.4	9.3	2.8	0.8	94
2014	Rk	Azl Giants	0	1	5	19	30	4.71	1.41	4.0	229	39	65	3.32	5.2	14.1	2.7	0.5	133
2015	A	Augusta	1	7	12	48	64	5.79	1.64	5.1	292	43	62	4.50	4.3	12.0	2.8	0.2	117
2016	A+	San Jose	0	3	14	59	93	2.59	1.07	3.8	205	33	82	2.72	3.1	14.2	4.7	1.1	191

Short, stout RP who has served as closer. Improved control and K rate with deception and pure heat. SL continues to evolve and just needs consistency. Likes to use FB early and often. Tends to flatten and plane to plate isn't effective. Command could get better as he repeats delivery, but will have to watch body. Allows lot of flyballs.

Morris,Akeel — RP — Atlanta

EXP MLB DEBUT: 2015 | H/W: 6-1 195 | FUT: Middle reliever | 7C

Thrws R Age 24 — 2010 (10) HS (VG)

Velo	Pitch	Grade
91-94	FB	++++
78-82	SL	++
81-85	CU	++++

Year	Lev	Team	W	L	Sv	IP	K	ERA	WHIP	BF/G	OBA	H%	S%	xERA	Ctl	Dom	Cmd	hr/9	BPV
2015	A+	St. Lucie	0	1	13	32	46	1.69	0.78	4.8	109	18	79	0.25	3.9	12.9	3.3	0.3	145
2015	AA	Binghamton	0	1	0	29	35	2.47	1.10	5.0	172	25	77	1.73	4.6	10.8	2.3	0.3	88
2015	MLB	NY Mets	0	0	0	0	0		30.00	6.6	842	78	20	154.96		0.0	0.0	45.0	-3627
2016	AA	Binghamton	2	2	6	25	36	4.66	1.39	4.8	212	30	71	3.97	5.7	12.9	2.3	1.4	95
2016	AA	Mississippi	3	1	0	35	50	2.30	1.36	5.9	214	35	81	2.58	5.4	12.8	2.4	0.0	103

Acquired in Kelly Johnson trade with NYM, RHP features arms and legs delivery. Flat FB gets on hitters quicker than radar gun indicates. Best secondary pitch is straight CU. Looks and acts like fastball with much more fade. Lacks two-plane movement with SL, struggling with his slot to throw it. Primarily FB/CU pitcher as big leaguer.

Muller,Kyle — SP — Atlanta

EXP MLB DEBUT: 2021 | H/W: 6-6 225 | FUT: #4 starter | 8D

Thrws L Age 19 — 2016 (2) HS (TX)

Velo	Pitch	Grade
90-93	FB	+++
	CB	+++
	CU	++

Year	Lev	Team	W	L	Sv	IP	K	ERA	WHIP	BF/G	OBA	H%	S%	xERA	Ctl	Dom	Cmd	hr/9	BPV
2016	Rk	GCL Braves	1	0	0	27	38	0.66	0.96	10.3	154	27	92	0.88	4.0	12.6	3.2	0.0	137

Big LH in mold of Sean Newcomb. Can dial it up to 95-96, works best in the low 90s with solid 2-seam run on FB. CB has potential to be a plus pitch. CU lags behind rest of package and may go to determining whether LH is a starter or reliever. Clunky delivery.

Murphy,Patrick — SP — Toronto

EXP MLB DEBUT: 2019 | H/W: 6-4 220 | FUT: #3 starter | 8E

Thrws R Age 21 — 2013 (3) HS (AZ)

Velo	Pitch	Grade
90-95	FB	+++
75-80	CB	+++
	CU	++

Year	Lev	Team	W	L	Sv	IP	K	ERA	WHIP	BF/G	OBA	H%	S%	xERA	Ctl	Dom	Cmd	hr/9	BPV
2014	Rk	GCL Blue Jays	0	1	0	4	4	11.25	2.50	7.1	415	52	50	8.75	4.5	9.0	2.0	0.0	59
2016	A-	Vancouver	4	5	0	69	48	2.86	1.36	22.2	267	33	77	3.31	3.0	6.2	2.1	0.0	50
2016	A	Lansing	0	1	2	21	20	4.29	1.81	12.2	288	35	80	5.95	6.0	8.6	1.4	1.3	10

Big, strong SP who was healthy all year after Tommy John surgery and other ailments in past. Regained velocity and peppers zone with quality FB and power CB. Uses tough angle to plate and pitches tough to elevate. FB can be fairly straight at higher velocities and has trouble repeating arm speed on CU. Has body and demeanor for RP, but will stay in rotation.

Musgrave,Harrison — SP — Colorado

EXP MLB DEBUT: 2018 | H/W: 6-1 205 | FUT: #5 SP/swingman | 7C

Thrws L Age 25 — 2014 (8) West Virginia

Velo	Pitch	Grade
88-91	FB	++
85-87	SL	++
75-78	CB	++
80-83	CU	++

Year	Lev	Team	W	L	Sv	IP	K	ERA	WHIP	BF/G	OBA	H%	S%	xERA	Ctl	Dom	Cmd	hr/9	BPV
2014	Rk	Grand Junction	2	4	0	48	50	5.44	1.54	16.1	307	37	70	6.10	2.6	9.4	3.6	1.9	116
2015	A+	Modesto	10	1	0	90	83	2.89	1.11	22.1	242	30	76	2.98	1.9	8.3	4.4	0.7	116
2015	AA	New Britain	3	4	0	56	53	3.20	1.21	20.6	258	31	79	3.85	2.1	8.5	4.1	1.1	115
2016	AA	Hartford	5	1	0	40	30	1.80	0.70	23.5	150	19	74	0.46	1.8	6.7	3.8	0.2	91
2016	AAA	Albuquerque	8	7	0	113	79	4.30	1.40	25.1	270	30	74	4.74	3.2	6.3	2.0	1.4	45

Short, durable lefty has a chance to develop into a back-end starter. FB sits at 88-91 mph, SL, CB, and CU. Pounds the strike zone, with 4-pitch mix, but control abandoned him when moved up to AAA. Not particularly athletic and delivery is stiff, but he knows how to pitch and held his own between AA/AAA.

Neidert,Nick — SP — Seattle

EXP MLB DEBUT: 2019 | H/W: 6-1 180 | FUT: #3 starter | 8C

Thrws R Age 20 — 2015 (2) HS (GA)

Velo	Pitch	Grade
89-94	FB	+++
82-84	SL	++
77-79	CB	+++
	CU	+++

Year	Lev	Team	W	L	Sv	IP	K	ERA	WHIP	BF/G	OBA	H%	S%	xERA	Ctl	Dom	Cmd	hr/9	BPV
2015	Rk	Azl Mariners	0	2	0	35	23	1.54	0.97	12.1	202	24	85	1.74	2.3	5.9	2.6	0.3	62
2016	A	Clinton	7	3	0	91	69	2.57	0.97	18.1	226	27	77	2.44	1.3	6.8	5.3	0.7	106

Young, advanced SP who found A- much to his liking. Started in mid-May and had success with plus command and control. Needs to add strength to add consistent velocity, but has deep pitch mix and polished mixing ability. Throws from high 3/4 slot and uses FB/CU combo deftly. Deceptive CU is menace to LHH, but needs better SL.

Neverauskas,Dovydas — RP — Pittsburgh

EXP MLB DEBUT: 2017 | H/W: 6-3 175 | FUT: Setup reliever | 7C

Thrws R Age 24 — 2009 FA (LT)

Velo	Pitch	Grade
95-97	FB	++++
90-92	SL	++
87-90	CT	++

Year	Lev	Team	W	L	Sv	IP	K	ERA	WHIP	BF/G	OBA	H%	S%	xERA	Ctl	Dom	Cmd	hr/9	BPV
2014	A	West Virginia	6	12	0	123	88	5.63	1.67	20.5	303	35	66	5.46	4.0	6.4	1.6	0.9	25
2015	A	West Virginia	1	2	2	49	37	3.67	1.18	10.9	220	26	69	2.76	3.5	6.8	1.9	0.5	46
2015	A+	Bradenton	0	0	4	16	10	1.67	1.23	5.5	247	30	85	2.74	2.8	5.6	2.0	0.0	43
2016	AA	Altoona	1	0	1	28	32	2.57	0.82	4.6	132	20	65	0.34	3.5	10.3	2.9	0.0	108
2016	AAA	Indianapolis	3	4	4	30	24	3.60	1.57	5.3	299	37	76	4.57	3.3	7.2	2.2	0.3	59

Hard-throwing RH reliever from Lithuania continues to impress. FB sits at 95-96, topping out at 99 mph and is backed up by a hard SL and a CT. CT has been the difference maker, resulting in fewer Ks but more GB outs. Ctl is below-average and will need to improve. Pitched in '16 Futures Game and was added to the Pirates 40-man roster.

Newcomb,Sean — SP — Atlanta

EXP MLB DEBUT: 2017 | H/W: 6-5 255 | FUT: #2 starter | 9E

Thrws L Age 23 — 2014 (1) Hartford

Velo	Pitch	Grade
92-95	FB	++++
78-81	CB	++++
85-86	CU	+++

Year	Lev	Team	W	L	Sv	IP	K	ERA	WHIP	BF/G	OBA	H%	S%	xERA	Ctl	Dom	Cmd	hr/9	BPV
2014	A	Burlington	0	1	0	11	15	7.23	1.61	12.4	292	42	53	5.00	4.0	12.1	3.0	0.8	126
2015	A	Burlington	1	0	0	34	45	1.85	1.29	20.0	206	32	86	2.56	5.0	11.9	2.4	0.3	96
2015	A+	Inland Empire	6	1	0	65	84	2.48	1.27	20.5	214	32	80	2.62	4.6	11.6	2.5	0.3	104
2015	AA	Arkansas	2	2	0	36	39	2.75	1.28	21.1	178	24	80	2.45	6.0	9.8	1.6	0.5	32
2016	AA	Mississippi	8	7	0	140	152	3.86	1.31	21.4	223	31	69	2.83	4.6	9.8	2.1	0.3	71

Monster LH struggles with command and control despite loud pitching tools. Mid-90s FB is effortless. CB has tremendous depth while CU has solid deception. Stuff screams #1 starter but inconsistencies with delivery and control forces projection downward.

Nielsen,Trey — SP — St. Louis

EXP MLB DEBUT: 2018 | H/W: 6-1 190 | FUT: #4 starter | 6C

Thrws R Age 25 — 2013 (30) Utah

Velo	Pitch	Grade
90-94	FB	+++
	SL	+
	CU	++

Year	Lev	Team	W	L	Sv	IP	K	ERA	WHIP	BF/G	OBA	H%	S%	xERA	Ctl	Dom	Cmd	hr/9	BPV
2013	NCAA	Utah	0	0	0	6	7	6.00	2.83	8.5	394	53	76	9.13	9.0	10.5	1.2	0.0	-36
2014	A-	State College	3	2	1	50	49	2.51	1.00	12.8	203	26	77	2.07	2.5	8.8	3.5	0.5	109
2015	A+	Palm Beach	9	6	0	111	78	2.59	1.22	17.9	244	29	78	2.88	2.8	6.3	2.3	0.2	57
2016	AA	Springfield	8	8	1	122	81	3.84	1.39	22.3	276	31	75	4.41	2.8	6.0	2.1	1.0	50
2016	AAA	Memphis	1	0	0	5	4	1.76	1.18	20.4	122	9	100	2.82	7.1	7.1	1.0	1.8	-46

30th round pick has been surprisingly effective as a pro despite the lack of overpowering stuff. Had TJS in '13 but has been healthy since. Low-90s sinking FB is best offering and consistently gets hitters to beat the ball into the ground. Complements the sinker with a SL and CU, both of which are works in progress. Low Dom limits his upside.

Nikorak,Mike — SP — Colorado

EXP MLB DEBUT: 2021 | H/W: 6-5 205 | FUT: #2 starter | 9E

Thrws R Age 20 — 2015 (1) HS (PA)

Velo	Pitch	Grade
92-95	FB	++++
80-83	CB	++
78-81	CU	+++

Year	Lev	Team	W	L	Sv	IP	K	ERA	WHIP	BF/G	OBA	H%	S%	xERA	Ctl	Dom	Cmd	hr/9	BPV
2015	Rk	Grand Junction	0	4	0	17	14	12.03	3.37	13.3	349	42	61	10.16	16.7	7.3	0.4	0.5	-302
2016	Rk	Grand Junction	1	0	0	29	20	3.71	1.79	19.2	287	33	80	5.26	5.9	6.2	1.1	0.6	-29

1st round pick from '15 has a plus FB that sits at 92-95 mph with good sink and run topping out at 97 mph. Mixes in a potentially plus CB and a solid-average CU. Has an ideal power pitching frame with good athleticism, but an inconsistent release point results in below-average command. Struggled with control in limited action—19 BB/20 K in 29.1 IP.

Nix,Jacob — SP — San Diego

EXP MLB DEBUT: 2019 | H/W: 6-4 220 | FUT: #3 starter | 8E

Thrws R Age 21 — 2015 (3) HS (FL)

Velo	Pitch	Grade
91-94	FB	++++
76-79	CB	+++
	CU	++

Year	Lev	Team	W	L	Sv	IP	K	ERA	WHIP	BF/G	OBA	H%	S%	xERA	Ctl	Dom	Cmd	hr/9	BPV
2015	Rk	Azl Padres	0	2	0	19	19	5.63	1.56	12.0	298	38	62	4.70	3.3	8.9	2.7	0.5	90
2016	A	Fort Wayne	3	7	0	105	90	3.94	1.28	17.3	280	35	68	3.70	1.7	7.7	4.5	0.4	110

Tall, durable RH ironed out mechanical issues to have successful full-season debut. Low 90s FB elicits soft contact with moderate late sink and bore. 12/6 CB has flashed plus potential. Has a feel for CU, uses sparingly. Only walked 20 batters in 105.1 IP.

Oaks,Trevor — SP — Los Angeles (N)

EXP MLB DEBUT: 2017 | H/W: 6-3 220 | FUT: #4 starter | 7C

Thrws R Age 24 — 2014 (7) California Baptist

Velo	Pitch	Grade
92-95	FB	+++
83-85	CU	+++
85-87	SL	++
	CB	+

Year	Lev	Team	W	L	Sv	IP	K	ERA	WHIP	BF/G	OBA	H%	S%	xERA	Ctl	Dom	Cmd	hr/9	BPV
2015	A	Great Lakes	5	5	0	102	58	2.56	0.96	21.4	226	26	73	2.04	1.2	5.1	4.1	0.3	77
2015	A+	Rancho Cuca	3	0	0	23	16	3.10	1.42	19.7	300	34	81	4.69	1.9	6.2	3.2	0.8	77
2016	A+	Rancho Cuca	1	1	0	25	22	3.60	1.16	24.9	269	34	68	3.17	1.1	7.9	7.3	0.4	131
2016	AA	Tulsa	8	1	0	63	38	2.14	1.03	24.3	240	28	78	2.27	1.3	5.4	4.2	0.1	81
2016	AAA	Oklahoma City	5	1	0	63	48	3.00	1.16	25.1	265	31	79	3.72	1.3	6.9	5.3	1.0	107

Strike-throwing RHP from Cal Baptist has some of the best command in the minors. FB sits at 90-93 mph, topping out at 96 mph. CU is second best offering with average to below SL, and CB. Uses four-pitch mix to keep hitters off-balance and went 14-3 with a 2.74 ERA at three levels.

Ogle,Braeden — SP — Pittsburgh

EXP MLB DEBUT: 2020 | H/W: 6-2 170 | FUT: #3 starter | 8D

Thrws L Age 19
2016 (4) HS (FL)

Velo	Pitch	Grade
91-93	FB	++++
85-87	SL	++
	CU	++

Year	Lev	Team	W	L	Sv	IP	K	ERA	WHIP	BF/G	OBA	H%	S%	xERA	Ctl	Dom	Cmd	hr/9	BPV
2016	Rk	GCL Pirates	0	2	0	27	20	2.65	1.07	13.2	190	22	78	2.23	3.6	6.6	1.8	0.7	39

Projectable lefty was 4th round pick. Already features a plus 91-93 mph FB that tops at 96 mph. Scrapped CB in favor of a hard SL and CU that shows potential. Mechanics need refinement and he tends to rush his delivery and fly open on the front-side, resulting in below-average Cmd. Nice upside but lots of work to do.

Okert,Steven — RP — San Francisco

EXP MLB DEBUT: 2016 | H/W: 6-3 210 | FUT: Setup reliever | 6A

Thrws L Age 25
2012 (4) Oklahoma

Velo	Pitch	Grade
91-94	FB	+++
82-86	SL	+++
	CU	++

Year	Lev	Team	W	L	Sv	IP	K	ERA	WHIP	BF/G	OBA	H%	S%	xERA	Ctl	Dom	Cmd	hr/9	BPV
2014	A+	San Jose	1	2	19	35	54	1.54	1.25	4.3	250	41	90	3.23	2.8	13.8	4.9	0.5	191
2014	AA	Richmond	1	0	5	33	38	2.73	1.06	5.3	205	28	78	2.50	3.0	10.4	3.5	0.8	124
2015	AAA	Sacramento	5	3	3	61	69	3.83	1.49	5.1	265	35	77	4.54	4.3	10.2	2.4	1.0	86
2016	AAA	Sacramento	4	3	3	47	60	3.82	1.36	4.8	285	41	71	3.89	2.1	11.5	5.5	0.4	168
2016	MLB	SF Giants	0	0	0	14	14	3.21	1.29	3.6	262	32	81	4.24	2.6	9.0	3.5	1.3	111

Durable RP who repeated AAA and has spent all career in pen. Owns complicated delivery with lots of moving parts, but repeats consistently and doesn't allow many walks. Throws from low 3/4 slot which adds to effectiveness of short SL. Can miss bats with both FB and CU and will cut FB at times.

Orozco,Jio — RP — New York (A)

EXP MLB DEBUT: 2020 | H/W: 6-1 210 | FUT: Setup reliever | 8E

Thrws R Age 19
2015 (14) HS (AZ)

Velo	Pitch	Grade
90-95	FB	++++
77-79	CB	+++
	CU	++

Year	Lev	Team	W	L	Sv	IP	K	ERA	WHIP	BF/G	OBA	H%	S%	xERA	Ctl	Dom	Cmd	hr/9	BPV
2015	Rk	Azl Mariners	3	1	0	21	24	2.99	1.14	10.4	252	36	71	2.51	1.7	10.2	6.0	0.0	156
2016	Rk	Azl Mariners	2	2	0	48	63	4.11	1.29	16.5	253	37	68	3.41	3.0	11.8	3.9	0.6	149

Live-armed pitcher who could start or be late-innings arm. Establishes plate with either sinking FB or power CB. Shows touch and feel for changing speeds and can blow FB by hitters in short stints. Not much projection in sturdy frame and throws with effort. Command comes and goes, but FB/CB combo could give him a solid chance. Needs pitch for LHH.

Ortiz,Luis — SP — Milwaukee

EXP MLB DEBUT: 2018 | H/W: 6-3 230 | FUT: #3 starter | 8B

Thrws R Age 21
2014 (1) HS (CA)

Velo	Pitch	Grade
93-96	FB	++++
81-84	SL	++++
80-84	CU	+++

Year	Lev	Team	W	L	Sv	IP	K	ERA	WHIP	BF/G	OBA	H%	S%	xERA	Ctl	Dom	Cmd	hr/9	BPV
2014	A	Hickory	0	0	1	7	4	1.29	1.00	8.9	168	16	100	2.42	3.9	5.1	1.3	1.3	6
2015	A	Hickory	4	1	0	50	46	1.80	1.08	15.0	242	32	83	2.43	1.6	8.3	5.1	0.2	123
2016	A+	High Desert	3	2	0	27	28	2.65	1.07	15.1	231	28	84	3.31	2.0	9.3	4.7	1.3	131
2016	AA	Biloxi	2	2	0	23	16	1.95	1.56	16.9	285	33	91	4.82	3.9	6.2	1.6	0.8	25
2016	AA	Frisco	1	4	1	39	34	4.13	1.38	18.3	298	37	71	4.45	1.6	7.8	4.9	0.7	115

Thick, durable SP missed time with groin tweak mid-year, but posted 4.9 Cmd as TL's third-youngest arm. Sinking FB touches 97 mph from low-effort, online delivery. Snaps off plus SL for solid SwK profile and has made progress with CU. Pounds zone and has advanced pitchability for his age. #2/3 SP upside with innings-eating ability in near future.

Overton,Dillon — SP — Oakland

EXP MLB DEBUT: 2016 | H/W: 6-2 175 | FUT: #3 starter | 8C

Thrws L Age 25
2013 (2) Oklahoma

Velo	Pitch	Grade
86-92	FB	+++
76-79	CB	+++
81-84	CU	++++

Year	Lev	Team	W	L	Sv	IP	K	ERA	WHIP	BF/G	OBA	H%	S%	xERA	Ctl	Dom	Cmd	hr/9	BPV
2014	A-	Vermont	0	1	0	15	22	2.40	0.80	10.9	206	35	67	1.06	0.6	13.2	22.0	0.0	239
2015	A+	Stockton	2	4	0	61	59	3.83	1.21	17.6	265	33	72	3.86	1.8	8.7	4.9	1.0	127
2015	AA	Midland	5	2	0	64	47	3.08	1.25	20.1	264	31	76	3.52	2.1	6.6	3.1	0.6	80
2016	AAA	Nashville	13	5	0	125	105	3.31	1.30	24.6	272	34	75	3.64	2.2	7.5	3.4	0.4	94
2016	MLB	Oakland	1	3	0	24	17	11.58	2.28	17.6	414	41	56	12.42	2.6	6.3	2.4	4.5	62

Deceptive SP who reached OAK and got knocked around. Has upside due to command and plus pitch location. Can be around plate too much, though has three average pitches in arsenal. Knockout CU is best pitch and can register Ks. CB shows good shape while FB exhibits run and tail. Due to lack of velocity, needs to hit spots. Could regain ticks to FB.

Paddack,Chris — SP — San Diego

EXP MLB DEBUT: 2020 | H/W: 6-4 195 | FUT: #3 starter | 8C

Thrws R Age 21
2015 (8) HS (TX)

Velo	Pitch	Grade
90-93	FB	+++
83-85	CU	++++
74-75	CB	+++

Year	Lev	Team	W	L	Sv	IP	K	ERA	WHIP	BF/G	OBA	H%	S%	xERA	Ctl	Dom	Cmd	hr/9	BPV
2015	Rk	GCL Marlins	4	3	0	45	39	2.20	0.98	15.6	225	29	77	1.98	1.4	7.8	5.6	0.2	120
2016	A	Fort Wayne	0	0	0	14	23	0.64	1.00	17.8	218	40	93	1.69	1.9	14.8	7.7	0.0	232
2016	A	Greensboro	2	0	0	28	48	0.96	0.39	15.0	102	18	89		0.6	15.4	24.0	0.6	277

Tall, lean RHP will miss '17 season recovering from Tommy John surgery. 71:5 K:BB ratio before injury. Didn't allow a hit over 3 starts (15 IP). Command/control guy with 3 average or better pitches. CU potentially plus-plus offering w/ tremendous fade and deception. Tightened up CB, borderline plus pitch. Will add velocity as he grows into body.

Palumbo,Joe — SP — Texas

EXP MLB DEBUT: 2018 | H/W: 6-1 168 | FUT: #4 starter | 7C

Thrws L Age 22
2013 (30) HS (NY)

Velo	Pitch	Grade
90-94	FB	+++
75-79	CB	+++
82-85	CU	++

Year	Lev	Team	W	L	Sv	IP	K	ERA	WHIP	BF/G	OBA	H%	S%	xERA	Ctl	Dom	Cmd	hr/9	BPV
2013	Rk	Azl Rangers	1	1	0	19	22	5.16	1.72	6.7	260	37	67	4.09	6.6	10.3	1.6	0.0	26
2014	Rk	Azl Rangers	4	4	0	42	49	2.35	1.04	11.6	196	29	75	1.58	3.2	10.5	3.3	0.0	120
2015	A-	Spokane	3	3	0	54	42	2.83	1.37	18.9	254	31	80	3.63	3.7	7.0	1.9	0.5	45
2015	A	Hickory	0	0	0	4	1	6.59	1.95	19.6	302	32	63	5.36	6.6	2.2	0.3	0.0	-120
2016	A	Hickory	7	5	8	96	122	2.25	1.11	11.5	208	31	81	2.32	3.4	11.4	3.4	0.5	133

Undersized pitcher who was moved to SP late in first full season. Posted very high K rate and held LHH to .149 BA. Works off clean, repeatable delivery and mixes pitches deftly. Can run FB to mid-90s with lightning arm speed and has slow, big-breaking CB that is lights out to LHH. CU could become average, though lack of size is concern.

Pastrone,Sam — SP — Los Angeles (A)

EXP MLB DEBUT: 2020 | H/W: 6-0 185 | FUT: #4 starter | 7E

Thrws R Age 19
2015 (17) HS (NV)

Velo	Pitch	Grade
86-92	FB	+++
75-78	CB	+++
80-82	CU	++

Year	Lev	Team	W	L	Sv	IP	K	ERA	WHIP	BF/G	OBA	H%	S%	xERA	Ctl	Dom	Cmd	hr/9	BPV
2015	Rk	Azl Angels	0	2	0	30	22	3.29	1.26	12.3	261	32	71	2.99	2.4	6.6	2.8	0.0	72
2016	Rk	Orem	3	4	0	57	45	6.00	1.72	18.5	324	39	64	5.67	3.3	7.1	2.1	0.6	56

Lean, raw SP who needs development time, but could be worth it. Generates lots of pitch movement, though difficult to command. Tends to overthrow at times which makes pitches easy to pick up. Has feel for adding and subtracting from FB and CU has shown improvement. Around plate too much and needs to enhance shape of rudimentary CB.

Paulino,David — SP — Houston

EXP MLB DEBUT: 2016 | H/W: 6-7 215 | FUT: #3 starter | 8B

Thrws R Age 23
2010 FA (DR)

Velo	Pitch	Grade
91-95	FB	++++
77-79	CB	+++
83-84	CU	+++

Year	Lev	Team	W	L	Sv	IP	K	ERA	WHIP	BF/G	OBA	H%	S%	xERA	Ctl	Dom	Cmd	hr/9	BPV
2015	A+	Lancaster	1	1	1	29	30	4.95	1.17	19.3	226	31	55	2.56	3.1	9.3	3.0	0.3	102
2016	Rk	GCL Astros	0	0	0	12	14	0.75	0.92	14.9	210	31	91	1.43	1.5	10.5	7.0	0.0	167
2016	AA	Corpus Christi	5	2	1	64	72	1.83	0.91	17.0	207	29	82	1.76	1.5	10.1	6.5	0.4	158
2016	AAA	Fresno	0	2	0	14	20	3.86	1.57	20.5	288	44	76	4.70	3.9	12.9	3.3	0.6	145
2016	MLB	Houston	0	1	0	7	2	5.14	1.29	9.6	233	25	56	2.72	3.9	2.6	0.7	0.0	-40

Tall, angular SP who set career high in IP despite team suspension and sore shoulder. Quickly made way to HOU and features incredible arm strength and plus FB. Repeats delivery and is adept at sequencing. Injury history is major concern and hope is he improves secondary offerings. CU could become plus pitch with deceptive arm speed.

Paulino,Jose — SP — Chicago (N)

EXP MLB DEBUT: 2020 | H/W: 6-2 165 | FUT: #4 starter | 7D

Thrws L Age 21
2011 FA (DR)

Velo	Pitch	Grade
91-94	FB	++++
83-85	SL	+++
	CU	+

Year	Lev	Team	W	L	Sv	IP	K	ERA	WHIP	BF/G	OBA	H%	S%	xERA	Ctl	Dom	Cmd	hr/9	BPV
2013	Rk	DSL Cubs	5	3	0	58	71	2.33	1.02	17.1	223	33	76	1.98	1.9	11.0	5.9	0.2	166
2014	Rk	Azl Cubs	3	4	0	46	42	6.04	1.62	17.1	297	37	61	4.95	3.9	8.2	2.1	0.6	60
2015	A-	Eugene	4	6	0	55	57	4.42	1.45	19.6	276	36	71	4.42	3.4	9.3	2.7	0.8	93
2016	A-	Eugene	4	0	0	35	37	0.51	0.63	20.1	161	24	91	0.16	0.8	9.5	12.3	0.0	168
2016	A	South Bend	3	1	0	40	32	3.15	1.15	22.7	242	29	74	3.08	2.3	7.2	3.2	0.7	87

Tall, skinny lefty from the D.R. started well in short season ball and then held his own when moved up to Low-A. Pounds the strike zone with a good 91-94 mph FB and a potentially plus hard SL. CU is a work in progress, but showed signs of improvement. Overall numbers were impressive, going 7-1 with a 1.92 ERA and 13 BB/69 K. Interesting potential.

Payano,Pedro — SP — Texas

EXP MLB DEBUT: 2018 | H/W: 6-2 170 | FUT: #4 starter | 7C

Thrws R Age 22
2011 FA (DR)

Velo	Pitch	Grade
89-95	FB	+++
77-79	CB	+++
	CU	+++

Year	Lev	Team	W	L	Sv	IP	K	ERA	WHIP	BF/G	OBA	H%	S%	xERA	Ctl	Dom	Cmd	hr/9	BPV
2015	Rk	Azl Rangers	6	0	0	40	46	1.57	1.04	19.4	225	33	83	1.94	2.0	10.3	5.1	0.0	149
2015	A	Hickory	3	1	0	32	31	1.12	1.15	21.3	229	30	92	2.53	2.8	8.7	3.1	0.3	98
2016	A	Hickory	3	3	0	73	82	2.09	1.20	19.6	222	31	83	2.53	3.6	10.1	2.8	0.2	103

Sturdy SP who got off to hot start, but ended season in July. Generally throws with good control, but walk rate elevated due to focus on throwing harder. Can work FB to both sides of plate and uses advanced CU to keep LHH at bay. All three pitches at least average, though none grade as plus yet. Has confidence to throw any pitch in any count.

Payano,Victor
SP | Miami | EXP MLB DEBUT: 2017 | H/W: 6-5 185 | FUT: #4 starter | 7E

Thrws L Age 24
2010 FA (DR)
90-94 FB + + +
74-77 CB + +
79-82 CU + +

Year	Lev	Team	W	L	Sv	IP	K	ERA	WHIP	BF/G	OBA	H%	S%	xERA	Ctl	Dom	Cmd	hr/9	BPV
2013	A+	Myrtle Beach	5	7	0	87	96	6.30	1.63	17.6	257	33	62	4.90	5.9	9.9	1.7	1.1	38
2014	A+	Myrtle Beach	5	8	0	125	86	4.60	1.70	19.5	258	30	74	4.81	6.5	6.2	1.0	0.8	-45
2015	AA	Frisco	4	4	0	92	78	5.08	1.68	14.3	259	30	73	5.20	6.2	7.6	1.2	1.3	-14
2016	AA	Frisco	7	6	0	100	96	4.05	1.50	22.7	273	34	76	4.75	4.0	8.6	2.2	1.1	67
2016	AAA	Round Rock	2	2	0	27	20	5.63	1.21	18.3	181	19	55	3.12	5.3	6.6	1.3	1.3	-6

Tall, athletic starter who just can't take next step despite having good raw talent. Struggles to hit his spots with a FB that flashes as plus. Generates plenty of movement on his FB and has a clean, fast arm. Slows arm on poor CU that he needs in order to combat RHH. Leaves ball up too often, but misses bats with FB and slow CB.

Pazos,James
RP | Seattle | EXP MLB DEBUT: 2015 | H/W: 6-2 235 | FUT: Setup reliever | 6B

Thrws L Age 25
2012 (13) San Diego
89-95 FB + + +
82-84 SL + + +
84-88 CU +

Year	Lev	Team	W	L	Sv	IP	K	ERA	WHIP	BF/G	OBA	H%	S%	xERA	Ctl	Dom	Cmd	hr/9	BPV
2015	AAA	Scranton/WB	3	1	2	33	37	1.09	1.21	6.3	212	31	90	2.20	4.1	10.1	2.5	0.0	89
2015	MLB	NY Yankees	0	0	0	5	3	0.00	1.20	1.8	175	21	100	1.79	5.4	5.4	1.0	0.0	-31
2016	A-	Staten Island	0	0	0	3	6	0.00	1.25	6.5	250	50	100	2.70	2.8	16.9	6.0	0.0	246
2016	AAA	Scranton/WB	2	2	1	27	41	2.66	1.40	5.0	199	34	81	2.80	6.3	13.6	2.2	0.3	93
2016	MLB	NY Yankees	1	0	0	3	3	14.52	2.58	2.4	445	47	50	15.10	2.9	8.7	3.0	5.8	96

Big-framed, aggressive RP who has spent entire career in pen. Posts high K rate due to intriguing FB/SL combo. Works both sides of plate with hard stuff and uses SL as chase pitch. Walk rate elevated in '16 and needs to throw more strikes to be dependable in late innings. Doesn't change speeds much, but doesn't need to do so.

Pena,Felix
RP | Chicago (N) | EXP MLB DEBUT: 2016 | H/W: 6-2 185 | FUT: #5 SP/swingman | 6C

Thrws R Age 27
2009 FA (DR)
90-93 FB + + +
CU + +
SL + +

Year	Lev	Team	W	L	Sv	IP	K	ERA	WHIP	BF/G	OBA	H%	S%	xERA	Ctl	Dom	Cmd	hr/9	BPV
2014	A+	Daytona	4	6	0	96		3.19	1.27	20.7	245	30	76	3.32	3.2	7.1	2.2	0.6	60
2014	AA	Tennessee	2	4	0	27	26	7.61	1.73	20.6	281	33	57	5.98	5.6	8.6	1.5	1.7	21
2015	AA	Tennessee	7	8	0	129	140	3.76	1.24	21.0	234	31	71	3.19	3.4	9.8	2.9	0.7	101
2016	AAA	Iowa	3	4	3	63	81	3.42	1.09	6.9	205	30	69	2.34	3.3	11.6	3.5	0.6	137
2016	MLB	Chi Cubs	0	0	1	9	13	4.00	0.89	3.0	165	24	57	1.76	3.0	13.0	4.3	1.0	171

Late developing Dominican hurler was moved to relief in '16 with solid results. Dom rate spiked while showing improved Ctl. Pitches off a good low-90s FB and mixes in an average SL and CU. Keeps hitters off-balance and throws plenty of strikes. Got into 11 games with the Cubs and held his own. Solid middle reliever.

Pennington,Josh
SP | Milwaukee | EXP MLB DEBUT: 2019 | H/W: 6-0 175 | FUT: #3 starter | 8E

Thrws R Age 21
2014 (29) HS (NJ)
93-96 FB + + + +
77-79 CB + +
84-86 CU + +

Year	Lev	Team	W	L	Sv	IP	K	ERA	WHIP	BF/G	OBA	H%	S%	xERA	Ctl	Dom	Cmd	hr/9	BPV
2015	Rk	GCL Red Sox	2	1	0	22	22	0.82	1.36	13.1	215	30	93	2.63	5.3	9.0	1.7	0.0	36
2016	A-	Lowell	5	3	0	56	49	2.88	1.17	17.3	197	25	75	2.25	4.3	7.8	1.8	0.3	43

Slight-framed SP who is all the way back from Tommy John surgery with increased velocity. Exhibits flashes of dominance, but lacks consistency in breaking ball or changing speeds. FB can be flat at higher velocities and plane to plate offers little assistance. Could become power reliever where he can let fastball fly in short stints.

Peralta,Freddy
RP | Milwaukee | EXP MLB DEBUT: 2018 | H/W: 5-11 175 | FUT: #4 starter | 8D

Thrws R Age 20
2013 FA (DR)
90-93 FB + + +
80-82 SL + + +
84-86 CU + + +

Year	Lev	Team	W	L	Sv	IP	K	ERA	WHIP	BF/G	OBA	H%	S%	xERA	Ctl	Dom	Cmd	hr/9	BPV
2013	Rk	DSL Mariners	3	3	0	55	49	1.47	0.96	16.0	197	26	83	1.40	2.5	8.0	3.3	0.0	96
2014	Rk	Azl Mariners	1	6	0	51	42	5.29	1.55	18.6	277	34	64	4.42	4.2	7.4	1.8	0.5	37
2015	Rk	Azl Mariners	2	3	0	57	67	4.11	1.05	20.1	244	35	58	2.35	1.3	10.6	8.4	0.2	174
2016	A	Wisconsin	4	1	2	60	77	2.85	1.15	14.9	210	31	76	2.43	3.6	11.6	3.2	0.5	129
2016	A+	Brevard County	0	3	0	22	20	5.73	1.77	12.6	303	35	71	6.41	4.9	8.2	1.7	1.6	33

Young RH with high Dom as pro between rotation and bullpen. Shorter frame produces low-90s FB with slight arm-side bore; slurvy low-80s SL has avg potential and continues to make strides with CU. Control comes and goes, command still needs development and will needs to pitch deeper into starts for rotation. Fallback role of setup relief.

Peralta,Ofelky
SP | Baltimore | EXP MLB DEBUT: 2020 | H/W: 6-5 195 | FUT: #3 starter | 8D

Thrws R Age 19
2013 FA (DR)
91-96 FB + + + +
84-85 SL + +
CU + +

Year	Lev	Team	W	L	Sv	IP	K	ERA	WHIP	BF/G	OBA	H%	S%	xERA	Ctl	Dom	Cmd	hr/9	BPV
2015	Rk	GCL Orioles	0	2	0	25	31	5.71	1.55	10.0	220	33	59	3.13	6.8	11.1	1.6	0.0	34
2016	A	Delmarva	8	5	0	103	101	4.02	1.43	19.0	230	31	70	3.22	5.2	8.8	1.7	0.3	35

Long, raw SP who showed promise in first full season as pro. Uses height and slot to throw downhill, but repeating delivery has been issue. Has projectable frame and could add a few ticks to plus FB. SL flashes plus, but telegraphs pitch along with CU by changing slot and arm speed. Has to work on control to realize potential.

Perdomo,Angel
SP | Toronto | EXP MLB DEBUT: 2018 | H/W: 6-6 200 | FUT: #3 starter | 8D

Thrws L Age 22
2011 FA (DR)
90-94 FB + + +
82-85 SL + +
80-82 CU + +

Year	Lev	Team	W	L	Sv	IP	K	ERA	WHIP	BF/G	OBA	H%	S%	xERA	Ctl	Dom	Cmd	hr/9	BPV
2013	Rk	DSL Blue Jays	0	1	2	26	43	3.09	1.30	9.0	178	33	76	2.30	6.2	14.8	2.4	0.3	117
2014	Rk	GCL Blue Jays	3	2	1	46	57	2.54	1.24	14.4	217	32	79	2.50	4.1	11.2	2.7	0.2	108
2015	Rk	Bluefield	4	1	0	48	36	2.63	1.17	21.3	237	28	79	2.95	2.6	6.8	2.6	0.6	69
2015	A-	Vancouver	2	0	0	21	31	2.56	1.23	17.1	144	24	80	1.86	6.8	13.2	1.9	0.4	72
2016	A	Lansing	5	7	1	127	156	3.19	1.22	19.0	220	32	73	2.57	3.8	11.1	2.9	0.3	114

Tall, lively SP who led MWL in Ks and pitched in Futures Game. Long limbs make it difficult to repeat mechanics, but has three pitches that could become average to plus. Has high Dom potential and dominates LHP. Deceptive delivery adds to arsenal, but can be guilty of overthrowing. Key to future is development of SL.

Perez,Franklin
SP | Houston | EXP MLB DEBUT: 2019 | H/W: 6-3 197 | FUT: #2 starter | 9D

Thrws R Age 19
2014 FA (VZ)
90-94 FB + + + +
75-79 CB + + +
82-84 CU + +

Year	Lev	Team	W	L	Sv	IP	K	ERA	WHIP	BF/G	OBA	H%	S%	xERA	Ctl	Dom	Cmd	hr/9	BPV
2016	A	Quad Cities	3	3	1	66	75	2.85	1.24	17.9	252	36	75	2.90	2.6	10.2	3.9	0.1	132

Athletic SP who started in first full season. Has treasured arm with clean, loose mechanics and advanced ability to mix offerings. Gets ahead of hitters with FB that could add more velocity. Shows touch for CU, but needs to repeat arm speed and slot to become average. Can miss bats with big-breaking CB that he can throw for strikes.

Perez,Freicer
SP | New York (A) | EXP MLB DEBUT: 2019 | H/W: 6-8 190 | FUT: #3 starter | 8E

Thrws R Age 21
2014 FA (DR)
93-97 FB + + + +
76-80 CB + +
CU + +

Year	Lev	Team	W	L	Sv	IP	K	ERA	WHIP	BF/G	OBA	H%	S%	xERA	Ctl	Dom	Cmd	hr/9	BPV
2016	A-	Staten Island	2	4	0	52	49	4.49	1.46	17.1	258	33	68	3.91	4.3	8.5	2.0	0.5	54

Long, lean SP with plus projection. Spent first year in US and shows advanced ability to repeat easy delivery. Can be more thrower than pitcher and tends to telegraph pitches. Throws downhill and FB could become double-plus in time. Features some feel for CU, though has trouble finding consistent break on CB. Long ways away from ceiling.

Perez,Sam
SP | Miami | EXP MLB DEBUT: 2019 | H/W: 6-3 210 | FUT: #4 starter | 7D

Thrws R Age 22
2016 (5) Missouri State
92-94 FB + + +
CB + +
CU + +

Year	Lev	Team	W	L	Sv	IP	K	ERA	WHIP	BF/G	OBA	H%	S%	xERA	Ctl	Dom	Cmd	hr/9	BPV
2016	NCAA	Missouri State	8	0	1	91	112	2.86	1.10	9.9	202	30	73	2.06	3.5	11.1	3.2	0.3	124
2016	A-	Batavia	1	1	0	48	36	3.56	1.16	12.0	232	27	71	3.06	2.8	6.7	2.4	0.7	63

Strong, physically mature collegiate reliever was used in both roles after being drafted. For now, the Marlins view him as a starter and his best offering is a an above-average FB that sits at 92-94, topping out at 95 mph. His CB and CU are average at best and will need to improve for him to remain a starter.

Peters,Dillon
SP | Miami | EXP MLB DEBUT: 2018 | H/W: 5-9 195 | FUT: #5 SP/swingman | 7C

Thrws L Age 24
2014 (10) Texas
88-92 FB + + +
CB + + +
CU + +

Year	Lev	Team	W	L	Sv	IP	K	ERA	WHIP	BF/G	OBA	H%	S%	xERA	Ctl	Dom	Cmd	hr/9	BPV
2015	Rk	GCL Marlins	1	1	0	13	13	0.69	0.99	12.5	213	29	92	1.67	2.1	8.9	4.3	0.0	123
2015	A-	Batavia	0	3	0	31	27	4.90	1.60	19.7	313	38	69	5.14	2.9	7.8	2.7	0.6	80
2016	A+	Jupiter	11	6	0	106	89	2.46	1.11	20.8	254	32	77	2.67	1.4	7.6	5.6	0.2	117
2016	AA	Jacksonville	3	0	0	22	16	2.03	0.95	20.9	214	24	84	2.34	1.6	6.5	4.0	0.8	91

Short, stocky lefty thrives despite having less than overpowering stuff. FB sits at 88-92 mph but is located well to both sides of the plate. He mixes in an above-average CB, and a usable CU, but best tool is his command. He walked just 20 in 128.2 IP in route to posting a 2.38 ERA between AA and AAA, and he repeats mechanics well.

Pfeifer, Phil — RP — Atlanta

EXP MLB DEBUT: 2017 H/W: 6-0 190 FUT: Setup reliever 8D

Thrws L Age 24 2015 (3) Vanderbilt
94-98 FB ++++
77-80 CB ++++

Year	Lev	Team	W	L	Sv	IP	K	ERA	WHIP	BF/G	OBA	H%	S%	xERA	Ctl	Dom	Cmd	hr/9	BPV
2015	Rk	Ogden	0	0	0	1	2	0.00	3.33	7.4	228	42	100	7.69	22.5	15.0	0.7	0.0	-320
2016	A	Great Lakes	1	0	0	6	9	0.00	0.00	6.6	106	20	100		1.5	13.5	9.0	0.0	221
2016	A+	Carolina	0	0	2	7	10	2.57	1.00	4.5	132	24	71	0.76	5.1	12.9	2.5	0.0	111
2016	A+	Rancho Cuca	2	1	0	24	33	3.36	1.58	7.6	236	36	78	3.74	6.3	12.3	1.9	0.4	68
2016	AA	Mississippi	1	0	0	10	8	4.46	1.49	4.0	240	31	67	3.27	5.3	7.1	1.3	0.0	2

Hard throwing LHP acquired from LAD. Impressed with bulldog mentality. Struggles commanding stuff due to wayward max-effort delivery. Touches 99 with FB. FB command paramount to establishing effectiveness of CB. Power CB untouchable at times with sharp, devastating drop. Future 8th inning man.

Phillips, Evan — RP — Atlanta

EXP MLB DEBUT: 2017 H/W: 6-2 215 FUT: Middle reliever 7C

Thrws R Age 22 2015 (17) UNC-Wilmington
94-96 FB ++++
82-83 SL +++
87-88 CU +

Year	Lev	Team	W	L	Sv	IP	K	ERA	WHIP	BF/G	OBA	H%	S%	xERA	Ctl	Dom	Cmd	hr/9	BPV
2015	Rk	Danville	1	1	0	13	17	0.69	0.92	8.2	178	26	100	1.69	2.7	11.7	4.3	0.7	154
2015	A	Rome	1	2	2	16	20	4.47	1.30	5.5	223	32	65	3.07	4.5	11.2	2.5	0.6	98
2016	A+	Carolina	2	1	8	28	19	1.28	0.93	5.0	185	23	85	1.20	2.6	6.1	2.4	0.0	58
2016	AA	Mississippi	6	3	2	34	43	4.49	1.44	6.6	255	37	68	3.80	4.2	11.3	2.7	0.5	108

Hard-throwing RHP has quickly moved through system since '15 draft. FB sits 94-96 with explosive late movement. Struggles commanding FB. Not afraid to use SL in any count. Solid two-plane movement. CU used infrequently. Mimics 2-seam FB with movement.

Phillips, Tyler — SP — Texas

EXP MLB DEBUT: 2020 H/W: 6-5 200 FUT: #3 starter 8E

Thrws R Age 19 2015 (16) HS (NJ)
88-93 FB +++
74-76 CB ++
CU +

Year	Lev	Team	W	L	Sv	IP	K	ERA	WHIP	BF/G	OBA	H%	S%	xERA	Ctl	Dom	Cmd	hr/9	BPV
2015	Rk	Azl Rangers	0	1	1	15	10	3.60	0.93	4.3	235	25	67	2.95	0.6	6.0	10.0	1.2	110
2016	A-	Spokane	4	7	0	58	57	6.49	1.68	20.2	322	42	58	5.23	3.1	8.8	2.9	0.3	93

Athletic, tall SP with high ceiling predicated on projection and smooth arm action. Lacks velocity now, but should grow into frame and develop cleaner delivery. Angle to plate is tough on hitters and keeps walks to minimum. Telegraphs poor CU while CB can be too loose and loopy. Lot of development in front of him.

Pint, Riley — SP — Colorado

EXP MLB DEBUT: 2021 H/W: 6-4 195 FUT: #1 starter 9D

Thrws R Age 19 2016 (1) HS (KS)
95-99 FB +++++
80-83 CB +++
86-88 CU +++

Year	Lev	Team	W	L	Sv	IP	K	ERA	WHIP	BF/G	OBA	H%	S%	xERA	Ctl	Dom	Cmd	hr/9	BPV
2016	Rk	Grand Junction	1	5	0	37	36	5.35	1.78	15.5	292	37	69	5.18	5.6	8.8	1.6	0.5	25

4th overall pick had the best raw stuff of any pitcher in the draft. Already features three plus offerings including a 95-99 mph FB that hits 102, a low-80s power CB, and a seldom used CU that has plus fade. Delivery is max-effort leading to inconsistent release point, below-average command, and concerns about injury. Walked 23 in 37 IP in debut.

Pinto, Ricardo — SP — Philadelphia

EXP MLB DEBUT: 2018 H/W: 6-0 165 FUT: #5 SP/swingman 7C

Thrws R Age 23 2011 FA (VZ)
91-93 FB +++
80-83 CU +++
76-79 SL ++

Year	Lev	Team	W	L	Sv	IP	K	ERA	WHIP	BF/G	OBA	H%	S%	xERA	Ctl	Dom	Cmd	hr/9	BPV
2014	A-	Williamsport	1	5	0	47	48	2.11	1.09	20.4	214	27	85	2.63	2.9	9.2	3.2	0.8	106
2015	A	Lakewood	6	2	0	67	60	3.09	1.24	24.7	256	32	76	3.35	2.4	8.1	3.3	0.5	98
2015	A+	Clearwater	9	2	0	78	45	2.88	1.06	23.3	225	25	75	2.68	2.2	5.2	2.4	0.7	52
2016	AA	Reading	7	6	0	156	101	4.10	1.29	23.7	254	28	72	4.06	2.9	5.8	2.0	1.2	43

Survived, but didn't dominate, his first crack at the high minors. Attacks with FB and can spot it, but only average velocity and lack of plane works against. CU flashes plus with depth and drop, but mistakes get hit hard. Below-average SL not a weapon. Simple 3/4s delivery, but can struggle with release point and is inconsistent start-to-start.

Pivetta, Nick — SP — Philadelphia

EXP MLB DEBUT: 2017 H/W: 6-5 220 FUT: #4 starter 7C

Thrws R Age 24 2013 (4) New Mexico JC
92-94 FB +++
78-82 CB +++
85-86 SL ++
85-87 CU ++

Year	Lev	Team	W	L	Sv	IP	K	ERA	WHIP	BF/G	OBA	H%	S%	xERA	Ctl	Dom	Cmd	hr/9	BPV
2015	A+	Potomac	7	4	0	86	72	2.30	1.15	22.8	224	28	81	2.60	3.0	7.5	2.5	0.4	72
2015	AA	Harrisburg	0	2	0	15	6	7.20	1.87	23.4	310	29	67	7.52	5.4	3.6	0.7	2.4	-63
2015	AA	Reading	2	2	0	28	25	7.37	1.81	18.6	288	34	60	5.95	6.1	8.0	1.3	1.3	-2
2016	AA	Reading	11	6	0	124	111	3.41	1.20	22.7	236	29	73	3.17	3.0	8.1	2.7	0.7	83
2016	AAA	Lehigh Valley	1	2	0	24	27	2.60	1.24	19.6	227	30	82	3.15	3.7	10.0	2.7	0.7	98

Intriguing under-the-radar arm with power pitcher's build and velocity. FB is low-to-mid-90s with some life, but with loose command. Best secondary is low-80s CB that added a few ticks in 2016. Uses CU and SL as below average change-of-pace offerings. Gets GBs, and some wonder if stuff would play up in relief, though remains a starter for now.

Plutko, Adam — SP — Cleveland

EXP MLB DEBUT: 2016 H/W: 6-3 200 FUT: #4 starter 7B

Thrws R Age 25 2013 (11) UCLA
89-93 FB +++
74-77 CB +++
81-84 SL +++
81-83 CU +++

Year	Lev	Team	W	L	Sv	IP	K	ERA	WHIP	BF/G	OBA	H%	S%	xERA	Ctl	Dom	Cmd	hr/9	BPV
2015	A+	Lynchburg	4	2	0	49	47	1.28	0.71	21.7	178	23	88	1.07	0.9	8.6	9.4	0.5	148
2015	AA	Akron	9	5	0	116	90	2.87	1.02	23.5	227	27	75	2.59	1.8	7.0	3.9	0.7	95
2016	AA	Akron	3	3	0	71	63	3.29	1.07	21.3	242	30	70	2.82	1.5	8.0	5.3	0.6	120
2016	AAA	Columbus	6	5	0	90	67	4.10	1.34	25.0	255	30	71	3.87	3.4	6.7	2.0	0.8	47
2016	MLB	Cleveland	0	0	0	3	3	8.44	2.19	8.0	357	40	67	9.45	5.6	8.4	1.5	2.8	18

Mature righty led EL in Cmd (min. 70 IP) and earned MLB cup of coffee in September. Fills zone and hits mitt with low-effort, online delivery and clean arm swing. FB hums in low-90s with slight arm-side bore; mixes in SL/CB combo with avg potential; CU is out pitch. Fly-ball profile; fringy SwK ability; innings-eater surviving on pitchability.

Ponce, Cody — SP — Milwaukee

EXP MLB DEBUT: 2018 H/W: 6-6 240 FUT: #3 starter 8D

Thrws R Age 22 2015 (2) Cal Poly Pomona
92-94 FB ++++
85-88 CT +++
77-79 CB +++
83-85 CU ++

Year	Lev	Team	W	L	Sv	IP	K	ERA	WHIP	BF/G	OBA	H%	S%	xERA	Ctl	Dom	Cmd	hr/9	BPV
2015	Rk	Helena	0	0	0	5	4	3.60	0.80	9.1	221	28	50	1.30	0.0	7.2		0.0	148
2015	A	Wisconsin	2	1	3	46	36	2.15	1.13	15.1	249	31	80	2.67	1.8	7.0	4.0	0.2	97
2016	A+	Brevard County	2	8	0	72	69	5.25	1.40	17.9	293	37	62	4.48	2.1	8.6	4.1	0.8	116

Big, muscular RH started season on DL with arm fatigue; posted excellent peripheral skills upon return. Creates angle to plate with 92-94 mph FB and mixes in CT for weak contact; CU remains raw and CB projects to be an average fourth pitch. Pounds zone, but can be too over the plate. Will need to pitch deeper into starts, but has solid SP profile.

Poteet, Cody — SP — Miami

EXP MLB DEBUT: 2019 H/W: 6-1 190 FUT: #5 SP/swingman 7D

Thrws R Age 22 2015 (4) UCLA
90-92 FB +++
84-86 SL +++
75-77 CB ++
CU

Year	Lev	Team	W	L	Sv	IP	K	ERA	WHIP	BF/G	OBA	H%	S%	xERA	Ctl	Dom	Cmd	hr/9	BPV
2015	NCAA	UCLA	7	1	0	73	68	2.46	1.26	11.0	231	30	81	2.92	3.7	8.4	2.3	0.4	69
2015	A-	Batavia	0	1	0	12	12	2.21	0.90	9.1	207	26	80	2.07	1.5	8.9	6.0	0.7	138
2016	A	Greensboro	4	9	0	117	106	2.92	1.30	20.1	246	31	78	3.23	3.4	8.1	2.4	0.4	73

Thrived against younger competition in the SAL. Isn't overpowering, but knows how to pitch and keeps hitters off-balance with nice four-pitch mix. FB sits 90-92 mph with an above-average SL, CB, and below-average CU. None of his peripherals support this level of effectiveness going forward and High-A could be challenge.

Povse, Max — SP — Seattle

EXP MLB DEBUT: 2018 H/W: 6-8 185 FUT: #4 starter 7B

Thrws R Age 23 2014 (3) UNC/Greensboro
92-95 FB ++++
73-75 CB ++
83-85 SL ++++

Year	Lev	Team	W	L	Sv	IP	K	ERA	WHIP	BF/G	OBA	H%	S%	xERA	Ctl	Dom	Cmd	hr/9	BPV
2014	Rk	Danville	4	2	0	47	37	3.44	1.13	15.5	240	30	67	2.54	2.1	7.1	3.4	0.2	89
2015	A	Rome	4	2	0	59	50	2.58	1.11	19.4	230	29	77	2.49	2.4	7.6	3.1	0.3	89
2015	A+	Carolina	1	3	0	18	10	9.45	1.71	16.4	320	37	39	5.02	3.5	5.0	1.4	0.0	14
2016	A+	Carolina	5	5	0	87	91	3.72	1.22	23.4	266	35	69	3.40	1.8	9.4	5.4	0.5	140
2016	AA	Mississippi	4	1	0	70	48	2.95	1.04	24.6	236	28	72	2.58	1.5	6.2	4.0	0.6	87

Tall, projectable RHP. Throws from over the top, naturally creating solid downward plane. Uses leverage to create illusion of sink on 4-seam FB. In reality, FB is flat. True 12/6 CB sputters and is ineffective. CU best secondary offering with great deception and terrific fade. Despite size, repeats delivery consistently.

Puckett, A.J. — SP — Kansas City

EXP MLB DEBUT: 2018 H/W: 6-4 200 FUT: #4 starter 7C

Thrws R Age 21 2016 (2) Pepperdine
90-94 FB +++
77-79 CB ++
80-84 CU +++

Year	Lev	Team	W	L	Sv	IP	K	ERA	WHIP	BF/G	OBA	H%	S%	xERA	Ctl	Dom	Cmd	hr/9	BPV
2016	NCAA	Pepperdine	9	3	0	99	95	1.27	0.92	26.5	189	25	87	1.37	2.4	8.6	3.7	0.2	110
2016	Rk	Azl Royals	0	1	0	7	8	3.86	1.14	13.9	288	37	71	4.25	0.0	10.3		1.3	203
2016	A	Lexington	2	3	0	51	37	3.69	1.11	18.3	225	26	68	2.81	2.6	6.5	2.5	0.7	64

Big, strong SP who has elements of finesse pitcher, but can rear back and fire hard FB into zone. Changes speeds impeccably and locates FB and CU well. CB can be too loose and easy to hit. Needs to add velocity to CB to have better breaking ball for RHH. Keeps ball on ground and has frame for durability. CU may be best offering.

Puk,A.J. — SP — Oakland — EXP MLB DEBUT: 2018 — H/W: 6-7 220 — FUT: #2 starter — 9D

Thrws L Age 21
2016 (1) Florida

Velo	Pitch	Grade
92-96	FB	++++
84-86	SL	+++
83-85	CU	++

Year	Lev	Team	W	L	Sv	IP	K	ERA	WHIP	BF/G	OBA	H%	S%	xERA	Ctl	Dom	Cmd	hr/9	BPV
2016	NCAA	Florida	2	3	0	73	101	3.07	1.20	17.3	198	30	77	2.68	4.5	12.4	2.7	0.7	119
2016	A-	Vermont	0	4	0	32	40	3.07	1.09	12.6	202	31	69	1.75	3.4	11.2	3.3	0.0	129

Tall, projectable SP with plus stuff and effective angle to plate. Can be high K pitcher with electric FB thrown downhill. Counters with hard SL that he can use as chase pitch and CU that flashes plus. Still relatively raw with mixing, though tough to hit when on. Will need to prove he can pitch deep into games.

Quantrill,Cal — SP — San Diego — EXP MLB DEBUT: 2018 — H/W: 6-2 170 — FUT: #2 starter — 8B

Thrws R Age 22
2016 (1) Stanford

Velo	Pitch	Grade
92-96	FB	++++
78-79	CB	+++
83-85	SL	+++
83-85	CU	++++

Year	Lev	Team	W	L	Sv	IP	K	ERA	WHIP	BF/G	OBA	H%	S%	xERA	Ctl	Dom	Cmd	hr/9	BPV
2016	Rk	Azl Padres	0	2	0	13	16	5.45	1.06	10.2	244	36	43	2.21	1.4	10.9	8.0	0.0	178
2016	A-	Tri-City	0	2	0	18	28	1.98	0.93	13.7	226	39	76	1.63	1.0	13.8	14.0	0.0	241
2016	A	Fort Wayne	0	1	0	4	2	19.29	3.81	13.9	503	53	47	16.39	8.6	4.3	0.5	2.1	-136

Eased into pro ball after Tommy John surgery in 2015, and consistently hit the low-to-mid 90s with 2-seam FB. It will take time to regain top form. Throws four average or better pitches. Feel for CU separates him from other starters. Son a former major leaguer, his pitchability is off the charts.

Ragans,Cole — SP — Texas — EXP MLB DEBUT: 2020 — H/W: 6-4 190 — FUT: #3 starter — 8C

Thrws L Age 19
2016 (1) HS (FL)

Velo	Pitch	Grade
90-94	FB	+++
75-77	CB	++
82-85	CU	++

Year	Lev	Team	W	L	Sv	IP	K	ERA	WHIP	BF/G	OBA	H%	S%	xERA	Ctl	Dom	Cmd	hr/9	BPV
2016	Rk	Azl Rangers	0	0	0	7	9	5.00	2.36	9.3	351	49	76	7.12	7.5	11.3	1.5	0.0	18

Young, advanced SP with athletic delivery and polished approach to pitching. Has solid understanding of sequencing and setting up hitters. Uses FB early in count to get ahead and mixes in CB and CU that show plus potential. Works in lower half of strike zone and should be able to get Ks and groundballs.

Rainey,Tanner — RP — Cincinnati — EXP MLB DEBUT: 2018 — H/W: 6-2 235 — FUT: Setup reliever — 8E

Thrws R Age 24
2015 (S-2) West Alabama

Velo	Pitch	Grade
92-95	FB	++++
83-86	SL	+++
	CU	++

Year	Lev	Team	W	L	Sv	IP	K	ERA	WHIP	BF/G	OBA	H%	S%	xERA	Ctl	Dom	Cmd	hr/9	BPV
2015	Rk	Billings	2	2	0	59	57	4.27	1.46	16.8	258	34	69	3.71	4.3	8.7	2.0	0.3	59
2016	A	Dayton	5	10	0	103	113	5.59	1.70	16.1	273	36	67	4.95	5.8	9.9	1.7	0.8	40

Converted RH reliever struggled with high walk rate in '16. Lost a tick or two on FB as a starter, still featured explosive late-movement. Struggles corralling movement due to inconsistent release point. SL is more slurvy than a true slider. It flashes plus but is widely inconsistent. Used CU as a starter with minimal results.

Raudes,Roniel — SP — Boston — EXP MLB DEBUT: 2019 — H/W: 6-1 160 — FUT: #3 starter — 8D

Thrws R Age 19
2014 FA (NI)

Velo	Pitch	Grade
86-90	FB	+++
78-80	CB	+++
81-82	CU	++

Year	Lev	Team	W	L	Sv	IP	K	ERA	WHIP	BF/G	OBA	H%	S%	xERA	Ctl	Dom	Cmd	hr/9	BPV
2016	A	Greenville	11	6	0	113	104	3.66	1.19	18.9	260	33	70	3.38	1.8	8.3	4.5	0.6	118

Advanced, lean SP with exceptional control and command for age. Uses whip-like arm action to get movement to all pitches. Should add a few ticks to FB as he gains strength and could use better sequencing. CU needs work, but shows promise with late tumbling action. CB is best secondary and can use as chase pitch. Doesn't beat himself with walks.

Ravenelle,Adam — RP — Detroit — EXP MLB DEBUT: 2017 — H/W: 6-3 185 — FUT: Setup reliever — 7D

Thrws R Age 24
2014 (4) Vanderbilt

Velo	Pitch	Grade
91-96	FB	+++
80-85	SL	+++
	CU	+

Year	Lev	Team	W	L	Sv	IP	K	ERA	WHIP	BF/G	OBA	H%	S%	xERA	Ctl	Dom	Cmd	hr/9	BPV
2014	A	West Michigan	0	0	1	3	5	0.00	0.00	4.2	0	0			0.0	15.0		0.0	288
2015	Rk	GCL Tigers	0	0	0	4	1	0.00	0.75	7.1	0	0	100		6.8	2.3	0.3	0.0	-124
2015	A	West Michigan	2	0	0	34	40	3.96	1.47	7.7	244	34	73	3.73	5.0	10.6	2.1	0.5	73
2016	A+	Lakeland	2	1	3	28	34	2.88	1.21	4.9	177	24	81	2.68	5.4	10.9	2.0	1.0	67
2016	AA	Erie	1	1	1	29	23	4.93	1.58	4.8	267	30	71	5.02	4.9	7.1	1.4	1.2	12

Tall, athletic RP who was successful in A+ before getting knocked around in AA. Best pitch is heavy FB that features velocity and movement. Can be tough to square up and often buried into ground. SL shows flashes of becoming 2nd reliable offering and has chance of being out pitch. Has stuff to be dynamic, but lack of control plagues reliability.

Ray,Corey — SP — Kansas City — EXP MLB DEBUT: 2018 — H/W: 6-4 175 — FUT: #4 starter — 7D

Thrws L Age 24
2014 (5) Texas A&M

Velo	Pitch	Grade
90-95	FB	+++
79-82	CB	++
80-83	CU	+++

Year	Lev	Team	W	L	Sv	IP	K	ERA	WHIP	BF/G	OBA	H%	S%	xERA	Ctl	Dom	Cmd	hr/9	BPV
2014	NCAA	Texas A&M	6	1	0	37	25	1.94	1.29	9.0	245	29	85	3.08	3.4	6.0	1.8	0.2	35
2014	Rk	Burlington	1	2	0	44	36	3.06	1.32	16.6	278	35	75	3.55	2.0	7.3	3.6	0.2	95
2015	A	Lexington	5	7	0	107	88	6.06	1.68	19.3	314	38	62	5.29	3.5	7.4	2.1	0.5	56
2016	A	Lexington	2	1	0	39	32	3.92	1.44	20.7	295	36	74	4.56	2.3	7.4	3.2	0.7	89
2016	A+	Wilmington	8	6	0	100	87	4.14	1.32	21.8	256	31	70	3.81	3.1	7.8	2.5	0.8	74

Lean, angular SP who has added velocity and more could be in the offing. Started to put everything together with upgraded offerings and better command. CB lacks consistency, but has solid-average potential and could miss more bats down road. Likes to use CU early in count and then blow FB by hitters upstairs. Deep sleeper who should be watched.

Reed,Chris — RP — Miami — EXP MLB DEBUT: 2015 — H/W: 6-3 225 — FUT: Setup reliever — 7D

Thrws L Age 26
2011 (1) Stanford

Velo	Pitch	Grade
88-93	FB	+++
77-81	SL	+++
79-83	CU	++

Year	Lev	Team	W	L	Sv	IP	K	ERA	WHIP	BF/G	OBA	H%	S%	xERA	Ctl	Dom	Cmd	hr/9	BPV
2015	AAA	New Orleans	1	0	0	20	23	4.01	1.53	6.3	240	31	79	4.62	5.8	10.2	1.8	1.3	46
2015	AAA	Oklahoma City	0	0	0	11	5	3.27	1.36	5.8	262	30	73	3.28	3.3	4.1	1.3	0.0	3
2015	MLB	Miami	0	0	0	4	1	4.50	1.75	9.1	347	37	71	5.60	2.3	2.3	1.0	0.0	-2
2016	AA	Jacksonville	1	0	0	14	11	3.17	1.20	14.3	231	29	71	2.42	3.2	7.0	2.2	0.0	58
2016	AAA	New Orleans	3	4	0	66	54	3.81	1.22	13.4	224	25	74	3.56	3.7	7.3	2.0	1.2	51

Hard-throwing LHP was 16th overall pick, but has been slow to develop and was traded to the Marlins. Has some funk in his delivery that creates deception, but also inconsistency in mechanics, which results in below-average control. FB sits in the low-90s with good, late sink. Complements it with a plus SL and a below average CU.

Reed,Cody — SP — Arizona — EXP MLB DEBUT: 2019 — H/W: 6-3 245 — FUT: #4 starter — 7D

Thrws L Age 20
2014 (2) HS (AL)

Velo	Pitch	Grade
89-91	FB	+++
82-84	SL	+++
85-87	CU	++

Year	Lev	Team	W	L	Sv	IP	K	ERA	WHIP	BF/G	OBA	H%	S%	xERA	Ctl	Dom	Cmd	hr/9	BPV
2014	Rk	Azl Dbacks	0	1	0	20	26	2.23	1.09	7.9	230	35	77	2.09	2.2	11.6	5.2	0.0	166
2014	Rk	Missoula	0	1	0	12	14	2.25	0.83	11.0	81	9	78	0.59	5.3	10.5	2.0	0.8	65
2015	A-	Hillsboro	5	4	0	63	72	3.28	1.14	16.7	223	30	73	2.82	3.0	10.3	3.4	0.7	122
2016	A	Kane County	5	2	0	39	55	1.84	0.89	20.8	224	36	79	1.74	0.7	12.6	18.3	0.2	227
2016	A+	Visalia	0	5	0	35	29	6.14	1.62	19.5	287	34	62	5.21	4.3	7.4	1.7	1.0	34

Big-bodied LH has lost velocity and sharpness on FB as pro. FB in low 90s with fringe-average 2-seam movement. SL flashes more swing-and-miss potential. CU is a below-average offering. Control artist struggled with command in CAL debut.

Reed,Jake — RP — Minnesota — EXP MLB DEBUT: 2017 — H/W: 6-2 190 — FUT: Setup reliever — 7C

Thrws R Age 24
2014 (5) Oregon

Velo	Pitch	Grade
91-96	FB	++++
81-83	SL	+++
	CU	++

Year	Lev	Team	W	L	Sv	IP	K	ERA	WHIP	BF/G	OBA	H%	S%	xERA	Ctl	Dom	Cmd	hr/9	BPV
2014	A	Cedar Rapids	3	0	5	25	31	0.36	0.52	5.2	124	20	92		1.1	11.2	10.3	0.0	190
2015	A+	Fort Myers	1	0	1	12	7	0.00	0.74	4.8	190	23	100	0.81	0.7	5.2	7.0	0.0	92
2015	AA	Chattanooga	4	4	1	47	39	6.32	1.62	6.0	293	36	59	4.88	4.0	7.5	1.9	0.6	44
2016	AA	Chattanooga	3	3	3	60	64	3.90	1.22	5.9	232	32	66	2.74	3.3	9.6	2.9	0.3	102
2016	AAA	Rochester	1	1	0	10	8	1.76	0.98	4.3	218	28	80	1.71	1.8	7.1	4.0	0.0	97

Durable RP who pitches aggressively and was very good after midseason. Has some deception in delivery that allows quick FB to play up. Uses SL as out pitch and very effective from low 3/4 slot. Has strength in lean frame and shows some feel for CU. SL remains inconsistent, but throws good strikes.

Reid-Foley,Sean — SP — Toronto — EXP MLB DEBUT: 2018 — H/W: 6-3 220 — FUT: #2 starter — 9D

Thrws R Age 21
2014 (2) HS (FL)

Velo	Pitch	Grade
91-96	FB	++++
82-86	SL	+++
77-79	CB	+++
84-87	CU	++

Year	Lev	Team	W	L	Sv	IP	K	ERA	WHIP	BF/G	OBA	H%	S%	xERA	Ctl	Dom	Cmd	hr/9	BPV
2014	Rk	GCL Blue Jays	1	2	0	22	25	4.86	1.40	10.4	251	36	61	3.16	4.1	10.1	2.5	0.0	91
2015	A	Lansing	3	5	0	63	90	3.71	1.58	16.3	243	38	76	3.90	6.1	12.8	2.1	0.4	83
2015	A+	Dunedin	1	5	0	32	35	5.31	1.52	17.5	216	30	63	3.29	6.7	9.8	1.5	0.3	13
2016	A	Lansing	4	3	0	58	59	2.95	1.12	20.8	208	28	73	2.22	3.4	9.2	2.7	0.3	91
2016	A+	Dunedin	6	2	0	57	71	2.68	0.89	21.2	179	27	69	1.29	2.5	11.2	4.4	0.3	151

Power pitcher who was cruising along before minor elbow injury shelved him in August. Posts low oppBA thanks to arsenal that features power and movement. Locates plus FB to both sides, and can miss bats with hard SL and big-breaking CB. Has worked hard to repeat delivery and throw more strikes. CU has improved, but still not average.

Reyes,Alex — SP — St. Louis
EXP MLB DEBUT: 2016 | H/W: 6-3 175 | FUT: #1 starter | **10D**

Thrws R Age 22 — 2012 FA (NJ)

Velo	Pitch	Grade
95-98	FB	+++++
75-78	CB	++++
88-90	CU	+++

Year	Lev	Team	W	L	Sv	IP	K	ERA	WHIP	BF/G	OBA	H%	S%	xERA	Ctl	Dom	Cmd	hr/9	BPV
2015	Rk	GCL Cardinals	0	0	0	3	3	0.00	0.00	8.5	0	0			0.0	9.0		0.0	180
2015	A+	Palm Beach	2	5	0	63	96	2.28	1.27	19.9	216	37	80	2.34	4.4	13.7	3.1	0.0	145
2015	AA	Springfield	3	2	0	34	52	3.16	1.14	16.9	179	31	71	1.84	4.7	13.7	2.9	0.3	136
2016	AAA	Memphis	2	3	0	65	93	4.98	1.46	19.9	255	39	66	4.13	4.4	12.9	2.9	0.8	130
2016	MLB	St. Louis	4	1	1	46	52	1.57	1.22	15.5	203	29	87	2.28	4.5	10.2	2.3	0.2	80

Proved he has one of the best arms in baseball with a good three-pitch mix that is highlighted by a plus-plus 96-97 mph FB that tops at 102 mph with good arm-side run. Plus 12/6 power CB and improved 90 mph CU allow him to dominate when he's on. Mechanics have been smoothed out and now draws on the plus velocity with ease.

Rios,Francisco — SP — Toronto
EXP MLB DEBUT: 2019 | H/W: 6-1 180 | FUT: #4 starter | **7C**

Thrws R Age 21 — 2012 FA (MX)

Velo	Pitch	Grade
89-93	FB	+++
80-82	SL	+++
74-76	CB	++
	CU	+

Year	Lev	Team	W	L	Sv	IP	K	ERA	WHIP	BF/G	OBA	H%	S%	xERA	Ctl	Dom	Cmd	hr/9	BPV
2013	Rk	DSL Blue Jays	4	6	1	52	48	4.49	1.34	14.5	258	34	64	3.29	3.3	8.3	2.5	0.2	79
2014	Rk	Bluefield	3	2	0	53	38	5.93	1.83	19.0	345	40	67	6.52	3.1	6.4	2.1	0.8	52
2015	A-	Vancouver	3	6	0	65	59	4.29	1.49	18.7	282	36	69	3.97	3.5	8.2	2.4	0.1	72
2016	A	Lansing	2	0	0	30	43	1.20	0.97	18.9	199	34	86	1.40	2.4	12.9	5.4	0.0	185
2016	A+	Dunedin	5	6	0	90	65	3.49	1.21	19.1	257	30	71	3.27	2.1	6.5	3.1	0.5	78

Deceptive SP who dominated Low-A and pitched in Futures Game. Faded down stretch and could use additional stamina and strength. Pops FB consistently into zone and keeps ball down. Allows very few HR and hitters have difficulty making hard contact due to delivery. Possesses good SL, but CB and CU need attention. Pitches inside effectively.

Rodgers,Brady — SP — Houston
EXP MLB DEBUT: 2016 | H/W: 6-2 210 | FUT: #4 starter | **7E**

Thrws R Age 26 — 2012 (3) Arizona State

Velo	Pitch	Grade
88-93	FB	++
80-83	SL	+++
74-77	CB	++
81-84	CU	++

Year	Lev	Team	W	L	Sv	IP	K	ERA	WHIP	BF/G	OBA	H%	S%	xERA	Ctl	Dom	Cmd	hr/9	BPV
2014	AA	Corpus Christi	5	12	2	120		4.79	1.28	19.0	285	32	65	4.43	1.4	6.5	4.6	1.1	97
2014	AAA	Oklahoma City	1	0	0	6	4	0.00	0.50	19.9	106	13	100		1.5	6.0	4.0	0.0	86
2015	AAA	Fresno	9	7	0	115	89	4.53	1.40	23.1	295	34	70	4.77	2.0	7.0	3.6	1.0	90
2016	AAA	Fresno	12	4	0	132	116	2.86	1.15	23.8	257	32	76	3.10	1.6	7.9	5.0	0.5	118
2016	MLB	Houston	0	1	0	8	3	15.56	2.72	9.0	396	43	36	8.96	7.8	3.3	0.4	0.0	-132

Command/control pitcher who led PCL in ERA. Spent 2nd season in AAA and was much better in '16. Establishes plate with FB, though is rather pedestrian. Can be too flat, but sequences well with two breaking balls that he can drop low in zone for strikes. Improved K rate, but more on mixing than natural action. Has been tougher on LHH.

Rodriguez,Chris — SP — Los Angeles (A)
EXP MLB DEBUT: 2021 | H/W: 6-2 185 | FUT: #3 starter | **8E**

Thrws R Age 18 — 2016 (4) HS (FL)

Velo	Pitch	Grade
90-94	FB	+++
83-87	SL	+++
	CU	++

Year	Lev	Team	W	L	Sv	IP	K	ERA	WHIP	BF/G	OBA	H%	S%	xERA	Ctl	Dom	Cmd	hr/9	BPV
2016	Rk	Azl Angels	0	0	0	11	17	1.62	0.81	5.8	161	30	78	0.57	2.4	13.8	5.7	0.0	200

Raw, athletic pitcher who could develop vicious, sinking FB once he fills out frame. Throws with surprising control despite lots of effort in delivery that he repeats. SL also could grow into plus pitch, but needs refinement. Maintains velocity deep into games. Long way from ceiling, but very intriguing.

Rodriguez,Hansel — SP — San Diego
EXP MLB DEBUT: 2020 | H/W: 6-2 170 | FUT: #4 starter | **8E**

Thrws R Age 20 — 2014 FA (DR)

Velo	Pitch	Grade
93-95	FB	++++
	SL	++
	CU	++

Year	Lev	Team	W	L	Sv	IP	K	ERA	WHIP	BF/G	OBA	H%	S%	xERA	Ctl	Dom	Cmd	hr/9	BPV
2014	Rk	GCL Blue Jays	0	3	0	19	13	7.11	1.58	9.3	251	31	50	3.66	5.7	6.2	1.1	0.0	-25
2015	Rk	GCL Blue Jays	1	2	0	42	37	4.70	1.38	17.7	288	37	63	3.85	2.1	7.9	3.7	0.2	103
2016	Rk	Bluefield	2	1	0	32	26	3.08	1.12	21.1	216	27	71	2.31	3.1	7.3	2.4	0.3	66
2016	A-	Tri-City	0	2	0	20	13	7.13	1.83	15.7	305	34	60	5.91	5.3	5.8	1.1	0.9	-22

Hard-throwing, slim RH acquired in Melvin Upton Jr. trade. FB sits mid-90s with explosive late movement. Loses velocity as game pushes on. Will need to add strength. Reports on his secondary pitches vary. Has incredible arm strength. Will be given plenty of time to develop.

Rodriguez,Helmis — SP — Colorado
EXP MLB DEBUT: 2019 | H/W: 5-11 155 | FUT: #4 starter | **7D**

Thrws L Age 22 — 2010 FA (VZ)

Velo	Pitch	Grade
87-91	FB	+++
80-83	CU	++
	CB	+

Year	Lev	Team	W	L	Sv	IP	K	ERA	WHIP	BF/G	OBA	H%	S%	xERA	Ctl	Dom	Cmd	hr/9	BPV
2013	Rk	Grand Junction	2	4	0	54	36	5.15	1.40	15.3	282	32	63	4.42	2.7	6.0	2.3	0.8	54
2014	A-	Tri-City	4	7	0	91	41	1.98	1.10	23.8	242	27	82	2.53	1.8	4.1	2.3	0.2	43
2015	A	Asheville	9	8	0	147	101	3.37	1.36	22.8	248	29	76	3.58	3.9	6.2	1.6	0.6	25
2016	A+	Modesto	5	9	0	131	94	3.36	1.12	17.2	234	28	70	2.73	2.3	6.5	2.8	0.5	71

Short lefty worked in relief and as starter. Best offering is a 87-91 mph sinking FB that he pounds down in the zone, getting tons of GB outs. CU has above-average potential with good late sink, but breaking ball remains inconsistent. Pitches to contact and needs to throw strikes to be successful. Funky delivery adds deception, but doesn't miss bats.

Romano,Sal — SP — Cincinnati
EXP MLB DEBUT: 2017 | H/W: 6-5 260 | FUT: Setup reliever | **8E**

Thrws R Age 23 — 2011 (23) HS (CT)

Velo	Pitch	Grade
94-96	FB	++++
83-86	CB	++
88-90	CU	+

Year	Lev	Team	W	L	Sv	IP	K	ERA	WHIP	BF/G	OBA	H%	S%	xERA	Ctl	Dom	Cmd	hr/9	BPV
2013	A	Dayton	7	11	0	120	89	4.87	1.59	21.2	283	33	70	4.84	4.3	6.7	1.6	0.7	23
2014	A	Dayton	8	11	0	148	128	4.13	1.42	22.5	288	36	71	4.28	2.6	7.8	3.0	0.5	89
2015	A+	Daytona	6	5	0	104	79	3.46	1.31	22.6	260	32	72	3.25	2.9	6.8	2.4	0.2	64
2015	AA	Pensacola	0	4	0	23	9	10.96	2.04	16.0	350	36	44	7.86	4.7	3.5	0.8	1.6	-45
2016	AA	Pensacola	6	11	0	156	144	3.52	1.22	23.4	263	33	72	3.45	2.0	8.3	4.2	0.6	115

Big-bodied RH lives and dies off FB. Struggles commanding sinking FB in zone, resulting in hard contact. Missed more bats in '16. Throws CB too hard. Has better movement and shape in the low 80s. Lacks feel for CU. Likely two-pitch reliever long term.

Romero,Fernando — SP — Minnesota
EXP MLB DEBUT: 2018 | H/W: 6-0 215 | FUT: #3 starter | **8C**

Thrws R Age 22 — 2011 FA (DR)

Velo	Pitch	Grade
91-97	FB	++++
84-88	SL	+++
84-87	CU	+++

Year	Lev	Team	W	L	Sv	IP	K	ERA	WHIP	BF/G	OBA	H%	S%	xERA	Ctl	Dom	Cmd	hr/9	BPV
2013	Rk	GCL Twins	2	0	0	45	47	1.60	1.00	14.3	201	29	82	1.54	2.6	9.4	3.6	0.0	117
2014	A	Cedar Rapids	0	0	0	12	9	3.00	1.50	17.3	278	33	82	4.52	3.8	6.8	1.8	0.8	38
2015		did not pitch (injury)																	
2016	A	Cedar Rapids	4	1	0	28	25	1.93	0.82	20.4	186	25	74	0.93	1.6	8.0	5.0	0.0	119
2016	A+	Fort Myers	5	2	0	62	65	1.88	0.93	21.2	215	30	79	1.68	1.4	9.4	6.5	0.1	148

Loose-armed SP who is realizing potential. Was dominant all year on two levels and uses velocity and hard SL effectively. Did not pitch in '15 due to Tommy John surgery, but showed no rust. Lives in lower half of strike zone with plus FB and sinking CU. Strong frame and loose arm should lead to innings-eating SP. Has been under radar for years.

Romero,JoJo — SP — Philadelphia
EXP MLB DEBUT: 2020 | H/W: 6-0 190 | FUT: #4 starter | **7D**

Thrws L Age 20 — 2016 (4) Yavapai JC

Velo	Pitch	Grade
91-93	FB	+++
80-81	SL	++
	CU	+++
	CB	++

Year	Lev	Team	W	L	Sv	IP	K	ERA	WHIP	BF/G	OBA	H%	S%	xERA	Ctl	Dom	Cmd	hr/9	BPV
2016	A-	Williamsport	2	2	0	45	31	2.59	1.22	18.2	257	30	79	3.19	2.2	6.2	2.8	0.4	70

A bit undersized, has a four-pitch mix and compact delivery. Can sink his fastball to get grounders with a chance for three average secondary pitches; change-up the most advanced currently. Showed good control in NYPL, but not a huge strikeout guy. Back end of rotation upside.

Rosario,Jose — RP — Chicago (N)
EXP MLB DEBUT: 2017 | H/W: 6-1 170 | FUT: Setup reliever | **7C**

Thrws R Age 26 — 2008 FA (DR)

Velo	Pitch	Grade
96-98	FB	++++
83-85	SL	+++
	CU	+

Year	Lev	Team	W	L	Sv	IP	K	ERA	WHIP	BF/G	OBA	H%	S%	xERA	Ctl	Dom	Cmd	hr/9	BPV
2014	A+	Daytona	5	8	0	101	92	5.44	1.75	17.8	308	37	70	5.91	4.5	8.2	1.8	1.1	45
2016	A+	Myrtle Beach	1	0	5	16	14	1.68	1.43	5.7	248	32	87	3.23	4.5	7.8	1.8	0.0	38
2016	AA	Tennessee	0	0	4	16	15	2.80	0.87	5.4	195	25	69	1.68	1.7	8.4	5.0	0.6	124
2016	AAA	Iowa	1	1	5	21	18	2.99	1.52	4.2	304	39	78	4.25	2.6	7.7	3.0	0.0	87

Small, wiry Dominican reliever has surprising velocity. Features a double-plus FB that sits at 96-98 mph, topping out at 100 mph. Backs up the FB with a good power SL and a below-average CU. Cubs added him to their 40-man roster in November and could be in the majors by mid-season.

Russell,Ashe — SP — Kansas City
EXP MLB DEBUT: 2020 | H/W: 6-4 205 | FUT: #2 starter | **8E**

Thrws R Age 20 — 2015 (1) HS (IN)

Velo	Pitch	Grade
91-95	FB	+++
80-84	SL	+++
75-78	CB	++
	CU	++

Year	Lev	Team	W	L	Sv	IP	K	ERA	WHIP	BF/G	OBA	H%	S%	xERA	Ctl	Dom	Cmd	hr/9	BPV
2015	Rk	Burlington	0	3	0	36	24	4.24	1.25	13.3	239	24	76	4.54	3.2	6.0	1.8	2.0	38
2016	Rk	Azl Royals	0	1	0	2	1	9.00	1.50	4.3	151	18	33	2.29	9.0	4.5	0.5	0.0	-144

Tall, quick-armed SP who barely pitched in '16 as he worked on cleaning up mechanics. Velocity decreased substantially; he will need to regain. Throws from low 3/4 slot, though pitches tend to be flat. SL flashes plus while CB has potential to be average. Focus will be on honing delivery and throwing strikes. Still has healthy upside.

Sadzeck, Connor — SP — Texas

EXP MLB DEBUT: 2017 H/W: 6-7 240 FUT: #3 starter **8D**

Thrws R Age 25
2011 (11) Howard JC

93-98	FB	++++
83-85	SL	+++
84-88	CU	++

Year	Lev	Team	W	L	Sv	IP	K	ERA	WHIP	BF/G	OBA	H%	S%	xERA	Ctl	Dom	Cmd	hr/9	BPV
2015	A+	High Desert	2	1	0	40	48	4.03	1.39	15.4	220	30	73	3.59	5.4	10.7	2.0	0.9	66
2015	AA	Frisco	1	1	0	19	16	9.84	2.03	13.3	289	36	47	5.76	8.0	7.5	0.9	0.5	-62
2016	AA	Frisco	10	8	0	140	133	4.17	1.28	23.0	243	29	71	3.85	3.3	8.5	2.6	1.2	82

Tall, hard-throwing SP who ended season on sour note, but has naturally plus stuff. Showed much improved control after ironing out mechanical issues and posts high K rate with two solid offerings. Works electric FB to both sides and complements with hard SL. Needs better CU for LHH. Has injury history, but healthy all year.

Sanchez, Ricardo — SP — Atlanta

EXP MLB DEBUT: 2020 H/W: 5-11 170 FUT: #3 starter **8E**

Thrws L Age 19
2013 FA (VZ)

91-93	FB	+++
76-79	CB	+++
84-85	CU	+++

Year	Lev	Team	W	L	Sv	IP	K	ERA	WHIP	BF/G	OBA	H%	S%	xERA	Ctl	Dom	Cmd	hr/9	BPV
2014	Rk	Azl Angels	2	2	0	38	43	3.53	1.62	14.1	271	38	76	4.00	5.2	10.1	2.0	0.0	60
2015	A	Rome	1	6	0	39	31	5.51	1.48	16.9	251	30	62	4.04	4.8	7.1	1.5	0.7	16
2016	A	Rome	7	10	0	119	103	4.76	1.45	21.2	262	31	69	4.46	4.1	7.8	1.9	1.1	48

Forgotten LHP on staff with Allard, Toussaint, Soroka, Fried and Weigel. Struggles commanding 2-seam FB despite above-average arm-side run and sink. Tightened up CB and has made strides with CU. CU has potential to be plus offering when all is said and done. Will take time to develop. Solid #3 starter upside.

Sanchez, Sixto — SP — Philadelphia

EXP MLB DEBUT: 2021 H/W: 6-0 185 FUT: #2 starter **9D**

Thrws R Age 18
2015 FA (DR)

93-97	FB	++++
79-83	CB	+++
81-84	CU	+++
88-90	SL	+++

Year	Lev	Team	W	L	Sv	IP	K	ERA	WHIP	BF/G	OBA	H%	S%	xERA	Ctl	Dom	Cmd	hr/9	BPV
2016	Rk	GCL Phillies	5	0	0	54	44	0.50	0.76	17.6	178	23	93	0.69	1.3	7.3	5.5	0.0	114

A pop-up guy dominated the GCL (just 3 ER in 11 starts). Generates an explosive mid-90s FB with life and sink; secondaries include promising CB and CU, along with a hard SL that he added late in the season. All garner both strikeouts and weak contact. Repeats simple, athletic delivery, which fuels uncanny command. It's a very high ceiling.

Sands, Carson — SP — Chicago (N)

EXP MLB DEBUT: 2019 H/W: 6-3 205 FUT: #4 starter **7D**

Thrws L Age 22
2014 (4) HS (FL)

90-93	FB	+++
73-75	CB	+++
76-78	CU	++

Year	Lev	Team	W	L	Sv	IP	K	ERA	WHIP	BF/G	OBA	H%	S%	xERA	Ctl	Dom	Cmd	hr/9	BPV
2014	Rk	Azl Cubs	3	1	0	19	20	1.89	1.16	8.4	219	31	82	2.15	3.3	9.5	2.9	0.0	99
2015	A-	Eugene	3	4	0	57	41	3.94	1.45	17.4	278	34	70	3.71	3.3	6.5	2.0	0.0	45
2016	A	South Bend	7	4	1	74	51	5.94	1.63	15.7	274	32	62	4.56	5.1	6.2	1.2	0.5	-8

Strong lefty has been slow to develop. FB velocity was down after sitting in the mid-90s in HS. Mixes in an average CU and an inconsistent CB. Cross-fire action results in good movement, but poor mechanics and inconsistent release point results in below-average command, and he walked 42 in 74.2 IP. Next step might be in relief.

Santana, Edgar — RP — Pittsburgh

EXP MLB DEBUT: 2017 H/W: 6-2 180 FUT: Setup reliever **7C**

Thrws R Age 25
2013 FA (DR)

93-97	FB	++++
85-87	SL	+++

Year	Lev	Team	W	L	Sv	IP	K	ERA	WHIP	BF/G	OBA	H%	S%	xERA	Ctl	Dom	Cmd	hr/9	BPV
2015	A-	West Virginia	1	0	3	30	32	2.70	1.00	8.2	228	31	72	2.15	1.5	9.6	6.4	0.3	150
2015	A	West Virginia	0	0	1	12	16	4.46	1.32	6.3	260	33	77	5.17	3.0	11.9	4.0	2.2	152
2016	A+	Bradenton	2	0	0	22	20	0.81	0.68	8.6	173	23	87	0.42	0.8	8.1	10.0	0.0	143
2016	AA	Altoona	2	1	2	41	39	2.85	1.05	7.6	216	27	77	2.67	2.4	8.5	3.5	0.9	107
2016	AAA	Indianapolis	0	0	1	16	12	5.06	1.75	5.6	328	39	70	5.75	3.4	6.8	2.0	0.6	48

Hard-throwing Dominican reliever had a breakout season, going 4-1 with a 2.71 ERA across three levels. Plus FB sits at 93-97 mph and is backed up by a swing-and-miss SL. Pounds the strike zone, keeping the ball down and gave up just 5 HR in 79.2 IP. Pitched well in the AFL - 0.00 ERA, 2 BB/18 K in 13.2 IP and is a nice bullpen sleeper.

Santillan, Tony — SP — Cincinnati

EXP MLB DEBUT: 2019 H/W: 6-3 240 FUT: #4 starter **8E**

Thrws R Age 19
2015 (2) HS (TX)

93-96	FB	++++
82-85	CB	++++
84-85	CU	+

Year	Lev	Team	W	L	Sv	IP	K	ERA	WHIP	BF/G	OBA	H%	S%	xERA	Ctl	Dom	Cmd	hr/9	BPV
2015	Rk	AZL Reds	0	2	0	19	19	5.16	1.35	10.0	217	28	60	3.07	5.2	8.9	1.7	0.5	39
2016	Rk	Billings	1	0	0	39	46	3.92	1.42	19.7	225	30	70	3.27	3.7	10.6	2.9	0.9	109
2016	A	Dayton	2	3	0	30	38	6.88	1.69	19.4	241	34	58	4.61	7.2	11.4	1.6	0.9	29

Raw, athletic RH with dynamite FB/SL combo. Mid-90s FB explodes late. Struggles corralling movement. Power CB is a wipeout 12/6, but has zero feel for a CU. Struggles repeating delivery, especially zeroing in on target.

Sborz, Josh — RP — Los Angeles (N)

EXP MLB DEBUT: 2018 H/W: 6-3 225 FUT: Setup reliever **7B**

Thrws R Age 23
2015 (S-2) Virginia

91-95	FB	++++
	SL	+++
	CU	+

Year	Lev	Team	W	L	Sv	IP	K	ERA	WHIP	BF/G	OBA	H%	S%	xERA	Ctl	Dom	Cmd	hr/9	BPV
2015	Rk	Ogden	0	1	0	4	4	2.25	1.25	8.1	81	12	80	0.95	9.0	9.0	1.0	0.0	-63
2015	A	Great Lakes	0	1	0	6	9	2.95	1.15	12.1	225	27	100	4.94	3.0	13.3	4.5	3.0	177
2015	A+	Rancho Cuca	0	0	2	12	12	1.50	1.25	5.4	262	33	93	3.65	2.3	9.0	4.0	0.8	119
2016	A+	Rancho Cuca	8	4	0	108	108	2.66	1.04	20.8	212	27	77	2.39	2.5	9.0	3.6	0.7	112
2016	AA	Tulsa	0	1	1	16	17	3.89	1.42	6.9	271	34	76	4.54	3.3	9.4	2.8	1.1	98

Was used both as RP and SP and was effective in both roles. Plus 91-95 mph FB that hits 98 mph and has good late life. Backs it up with an above-average SL that has swing-and-miss action. Mixes in an occasional CU to keep hitters off-balance. Has effort to delivery, but also some nice deception. Dodgers will likely keep him in a mixed role for now.

Schultz, Jaime — SP — Tampa Bay

EXP MLB DEBUT: 2017 H/W: 5-10 200 FUT: #4 starter **7B**

Thrws R Age 25
2013 (14) High Point

92-97	FB	++++
77-81	CB	+++
83-87	CU	++

Year	Lev	Team	W	L	Sv	IP	K	ERA	WHIP	BF/G	OBA	H%	S%	xERA	Ctl	Dom	Cmd	hr/9	BPV
2013	A-	Hudson Valley	1	2	0	44	55	3.06	1.38	10.9	205	29	79	3.11	5.9	11.2	1.9	0.6	60
2014	A	Bowling Green	2	1	0	37	58	1.95	1.11	16.1	206	35	85	2.28	3.4	14.1	4.1	0.5	180
2014	A+	Charlotte	2	0	0	23	21	3.13	1.48	19.8	227	30	76	3.07	5.9	8.2	1.4	0.0	7
2015	AA	Montgomery	9	5	0	135	168	3.67	1.44	21.3	216	31	76	3.51	6.0	11.2	1.9	0.7	58
2016	AAA	Durham	5	7	0	130	163	3.59	1.39	20.3	235	33	76	3.70	4.7	11.3	2.4	0.8	94

Short, compact SP who continues to register Ks with exemplary arm speed. Delivery difficult to repeat and has effort, but provides deception. Can fire FB up in zone and use CB as out pitch. Doesn't show much feel for changing speeds and needs to improve CU to combat LHH. Could make for a late-innings arm if starting doesn't work. Led the IL in Ks.

Scott, Tanner — RP — Baltimore

EXP MLB DEBUT: 2017 H/W: 6-2 220 FUT: Setup reliever **8D**

Thrws L Age 22
2014 (6) Howard JC

94-99	FB	++++
84-88	SL	++

Year	Lev	Team	W	L	Sv	IP	K	ERA	WHIP	BF/G	OBA	H%	S%	xERA	Ctl	Dom	Cmd	hr/9	BPV
2014	Rk	GCL Orioles	1	5	0	23	23	6.26	1.78	10.6	245	33	61	4.06	7.8	9.0	1.2	0.0	-31
2015	A-	Aberdeen	4	0	0	21	31	3.41	1.33	9.7	212	36	71	2.46	5.1	13.2	2.6	0.0	118
2015	A	Delmarva	0	3	2	11	29	4.29	1.38	9.8	243	39	66	2.99	4.3	12.4	2.9	0.0	126
2016	A+	Frederick	4	2	5	48	63	4.49	1.33	6.9	140	22	63	1.86	7.9	11.8	1.5	0.2	18
2016	AA	Bowie	1	2	0	16	18	5.63	2.06	5.6	285	40	70	5.31	8.4	10.1	1.2	0.0	-28

Flamethrowing RP who dominates with Ks and weak groundballs. Continues to post very high Dom, though erratic control has always been major issue. Fails to repeat delivery, but can be effectively wild and intimidating. Arm strength is best in org and can reach 100 mph. Mixes in wipeout SL, but rarely for strikes. Hitters rarely put ball in air.

Sedlock, Cory — SP — Baltimore

EXP MLB DEBUT: 2018 H/W: 6-3 190 FUT: #2 starter **8B**

Thrws R Age 21
2016 (1) Illinois

90-97	FB	++++
80-84	SL	+++
78-80	CB	+++
	CU	++

Year	Lev	Team	W	L	Sv	IP	K	ERA	WHIP	BF/G	OBA	H%	S%	xERA	Ctl	Dom	Cmd	hr/9	BPV
2016	NCAA	Illinois	5	3	0	101	116	2.49	1.10	28.3	219	31	78	2.33	2.8	10.3	3.7	0.4	129
2016	A-	Aberdeen	0	1	0	27	25	3.00	1.07	11.7	174	23	71	1.74	4.3	8.3	1.9	0.3	51

Strong, durable SP with potential for four average-to-plus offerings in repertoire. Establishes plate with heavy FB that induces high amount of groundballs. Offers two breaking balls that flash plus and mixes in below average CU. Can slow arm speed on CU, but exhibits late sink and tumble. Better sequencing would get him to ceiling quickly.

Senzatlea, Antonio — SP — Colorado

EXP MLB DEBUT: 2018 H/W: 6-1 180 FUT: #3 starter **8D**

Thrws R Age 22
2011 FA (VZ)

92-95	FB	++++
78-80	CB	+++
82-85	CU	++

Year	Lev	Team	W	L	Sv	IP	K	ERA	WHIP	BF/G	OBA	H%	S%	xERA	Ctl	Dom	Cmd	hr/9	BPV
2013	Rk	DSL Rockies	6	1	0	51	46	1.76	0.69	22.4	182	24	74	0.71	0.5	8.1	15.3	0.2	150
2013	A-	Tri-City	2	4	0	42	20	3.85	1.45	22.5	288	32	72	4.07	2.8	4.3	1.5	0.2	20
2014	A	Asheville	15	3	0	144	89	3.12	1.18	22.2	248	28	75	3.26	2.2	5.6	2.5	0.7	57
2015	A+	Modesto	9	9	0	154	143	2.51	1.06	23.0	232	29	79	2.64	1.9	8.4	4.3	0.6	116
2016	AA	Hartford	4	1	0	34	27	1.84	1.05	18.9	219	27	83	2.16	2.4	7.1	3.0	0.3	82

Venezuelan hurler was sidelined with shoulder inflammation that limited him to 34.2 IP. When healthy uses a high 3/4 arm slot to get late life on his 92-95 mph FB. Backs FB up with a quality SL and average CU. Attacks the strike zone with some of the best control in the system that gives him the potential to be a #3 starter.

Shawaryn, Mike — SP — Boston
EXP MLB DEBUT: 2019 | H/W: 6-2 200 | FUT: #4 starter | 7C

Thrws R Age 22 — 2016 (5) Maryland

89-94	FB	+++	Year	Lev	Team	W	L	Sv	IP	K	ERA	WHIP	BF/G	OBA	H%	S%	xERA	Ctl	Dom	Cmd	hr/9	BPV
82-85	SL	++
	CU	+++	2016	NCAA	Maryland	6	4	0	99	97	3.18	0.96	24.9	198	27	65	1.58	2.4	8.8	3.7	0.2	113
			2016	A-	Lowell	0	1	0	15	22	2.96	1.45	10.8	259	42	77	3.37	4.1	13.0	3.1	0.0	141

Durable, strong starter who relies on pitch movement and command to thrive. Lacks frontline stuff, but no pitch is straight and sequences effectively. CU may be best pitch and thrown with same arm speed as FB. Throws from low 3/4 slot and holds velocity deep into games. Improvement to SL is needed in order to miss more bats.

Sheffield, Jordan — SP — Los Angeles (N)
EXP MLB DEBUT: 2020 | H/W: 6-0 185 | FUT: #2 SP/closer | 9D

Thrws R Age 21 — 2016 (S-1) Vanderbilt

94-96	FB	++++	2016	NCAA	Vanderbilt	8	6	0	101	113	3.02	1.21	25.5	223	31	74	2.57	3.6	10.0	2.8	0.3	103
80-83	SL	+++	2016	Rk	Azl Dodgers	0	0	0	1	0	0.00	0.00	2.8	0	0			0.0	0.0		0.0	18
85-87	CU	++	2016	A	Great Lakes	0	1	0	11	13	4.09	1.55	6.9	262	33	80	5.21	4.9	10.6	2.2	1.6	77

1st round comp pick out of Vanderbilt has a plus FB that sits at 94-96, topping at 99 mph. Throws the heater with average SL and circle change that has good fade and sink. Plus athlete with good raw stuff, but small frame and max-effort, violent delivery are red flags. Had Tommy John surgery in 2013.

Sheffield, Justus — SP — New York (A)
EXP MLB DEBUT: 2017 | H/W: 5-10 195 | FUT: #3 starter | 8B

Thrws L Age 20 — 2014 (1) HS (TN)

			2014	Rk	AZL Indians	3	1	0	20		4.90	1.63	11.2	296	46	67	4.37	4.0	12.9	3.2	0.0	142
91-95	FB	++++	2015	A	Lake County	9	4	0	127	138	3.33	1.36	20.5	273	37	76	3.91	2.7	9.8	3.6	0.6	121
80-84	SL	+++	2016	A+	Lynchburg	7	5	0	95	93	3.60	1.38	21.0	253	33	74	3.69	3.8	8.8	2.3	0.6	74
81-82	CU	++	2016	A+	Tampa	3	1	0	26	27	1.73	0.92	19.5	160	23	79	0.89	3.5	9.3	2.7	0.0	93
			2016	AA	Trenton	0	0	0	4	9	0.00	1.25	16.3	151	47	100	1.51	6.8	20.3	3.0	0.0	200

Short SP who was acquired at deadline and has upside despite frame. Owns very athletic delivery that he repeats consistently and maintains velocity deep in games. Mixes three offerings that should play to above average or plus in time. Keeps ball down with lively FB and SL serves as legitimate out pitch. Needs better CU to combat RHH.

Shepherd, Chandler — RP — Boston
EXP MLB DEBUT: 2017 | H/W: 6-3 185 | FUT: Setup reliever | 7D

Thrws R Age 24 — 2014 (13) Kentucky

			2014	A-	Lowell	4	3	0	33	35	4.08	1.24	8.4	261	34	68	3.67	2.2	9.5	4.4	0.8	131
90-93	FB	+++	2015	A	Greenville	3	0	1	14	16	1.27	1.34	8.4	285	38	94	4.09	1.9	10.1	5.3	0.6	149
82-84	SL	+++	2015	A+	Salem	0	2	6	52	46	3.63	1.06	7.2	246	31	65	2.74	1.2	7.9	6.6	0.5	128
	CU	++	2016	AA	Portland	1	1	6	30	39	1.80	0.80	4.9	142	19	86	1.21	3.0	11.7	3.9	0.9	148
			2016	AAA	Pawtucket	1	2	1	34	23	3.71	1.06	7.3	226	26	67	2.77	2.1	6.1	2.9	0.8	70

Deep sleeper who dominated AA en route to AAA. Advancing quickly based on ability to command plate with three pitches. Has deceptive delivery due to quick arm and ability to hide ball. Adds pitch movement with easy arm action and hits spots with solid-average FB. May not miss enough bats in BOS and is flyball guy.

Sherfy, Jimmie — RP — Arizona
EXP MLB DEBUT: 2017 | H/W: 6-0 175 | FUT: Setup reliever | 8E

Thrws R Age 25 — 2013 (10) Oregon

			2014	AA	Mobile	3	1	1	38	45	4.97	1.37	4.3	241	33	65	3.84	4.3	10.7	2.5	0.9	95
94-97	FB	++++	2015	AA	Mobile	1	6	2	49	50	6.59	1.59	4.9	265	35	56	4.35	5.1	9.1	1.8	0.5	44
83-86	SL	++++	2016	A+	Visalia	0	0	8	12	21	0.00	0.91	3.8	128	28	100	0.46	4.5	15.6	3.5	0.0	179
	CU	+	2016	AA	Mobile	2	0	10	19	31	0.47	0.57	4.1	100	18	100		2.3	14.5	6.2	0.5	216
			2016	AAA	Reno	1	4	12	23	27	6.23	1.43	4.1	235	28	61	4.85	5.1	10.5	2.1	1.9	71

Max-effort RH reliever improved command of FB in '16. 2-seam FB touches 97-98, best in mid-90s. Bores in on hands of RHH. Is a ground ball inducer when firing low in the zone. SL took step forward and is now swing-and-miss offering with consistent two-plane movement. Struggled in 24 PCL appearances walking a batter every two innings.

Shore, Logan — SP — Oakland
EXP MLB DEBUT: 2018 | H/W: 6-2 215 | FUT: #4 starter | 7C

Thrws R Age 22 — 2016 (2) Florida

89-92	FB	+++
80-82	SL	++
81-82	CU	+++	2016	NCAA	Florida	12	1	0	105	96	2.31	0.96	22.1	217	28	76	1.96	1.6	8.2	5.1	0.3	122
			2016	A-	Vermont	0	2	0	21	21	2.57	1.14	11.9	223	30	78	2.57	3.0	9.0	3.0	0.4	99

Strong, advanced SP who can use three pitches in any count. More of a command/control pitcher than natural stuff at present, though could get better with cleaner mechanics. Lively FB is quality offering and CU has been effective against LHH. Development of SL is paramount to success. Needs to throw it for more strikes to keep hitters guessing.

Sims, Lucas — SP — Atlanta
EXP MLB DEBUT: 2017 | H/W: 6-2 220 | FUT: Closer | 8C

Thrws R Age 22 — 2012 (1) HS (GA)

			2015	Rk	GCL Braves	0	0	0	5	7	9.00	1.80	11.6	332	50	44	5.36	3.6	12.6	3.5	0.0	148
93-96	FB	++++	2015	A+	Carolina	3	4	0	40	37	5.18	1.55	19.4	257	33	65	4.06	5.2	8.3	1.6	0.5	28
76-78	CB	+++	2016	AA	Mississippi	4	2	0	47	56	3.24	1.23	21.2	179	27	72	2.03	5.5	10.7	1.9	0.2	61
84-85	CU	++	2016	AA	Mississippi	5	5	0	91	101	2.67	1.31	22.1	200	28	79	2.57	5.4	10.0	1.8	0.3	51
			2016	AAA	Gwinnett	2	6	0	50	58	7.56	1.86	21.3	284	35	63	6.82	6.7	10.4	1.6	2.2	26

Hard throwing RHP with FB command issues best suited for late inning relief role. Struggles throwing FB inside and will leave up. Victimized by advanced Triple-A competition. CB is best pitch. Classic 12/6 drop is among the best in the organization. CU suffers from same command issues as FB. CU has great fade when it is on.

Skoglund, Eric — SP — Kansas City
EXP MLB DEBUT: 2017 | H/W: 6-7 200 | FUT: #4 starter | 7B

Thrws L Age 24 — 2014 (3) Central Florida

			2013	NCAA	Central Florida	1	4	0	56	26	5.12	1.55	17.5	268	29	66	4.43	4.6	4.2	0.9	0.6	-32
88-92	FB	+++	2014	NCAA	Central Florida	9	3	0	110	94	2.54	1.03	28.2	217	28	73	1.89	2.2	7.7	3.5	0.1	97
75-78	CB	+++	2014	Rk	Idaho Falls	0	2	0	23	25	5.09	1.70	11.5	316	41	70	5.60	3.5	9.8	2.8	0.8	99
77-81	CU	+++	2015	A+	Wilmington	6	3	0	84	66	3.53	1.12	22.1	259	32	66	2.80	1.2	7.1	6.0	0.2	113
			2016	AA	NW Arkansas	7	10	0	156	134	3.46	1.11	22.7	235	27	73	3.27	2.2	7.7	3.5	1.1	98

Angular SP who led TL in Ks in breakout campaign. Tall and thin frame, yet repeats delivery and arm slot. Deception allows average pitch mix to play up, but won't miss many bats in majors. Posts low oppBA as he mixes well. Could add a few ticks to FB as he matures and has CB that he can use as chase pitch or drop in zone for strikes.

Slegers, Aaron — SP — Minnesota
EXP MLB DEBUT: 2017 | H/W: 6-10 245 | FUT: #5 SP/swingman | 6B

Thrws R Age 24 — 2013 (5) Indiana

			2014	A	Cedar Rapids	7	7	0	113	90	4.54	1.22	22.8	270	33	62	3.53	1.6	7.2	4.5	0.6	104
86-92	FB	+++	2014	A+	Fort Myers	2	1	0	19	12	3.32	0.95	23.9	207	22	69	2.41	1.9	5.7	3.0	0.9	69
80-82	SL	++	2015	A+	Fort Myers	8	6	0	119	80	2.87	1.04	24.2	235	28	72	2.37	1.6	6.0	3.8	0.3	84
81-84	CU	++	2015	AA	Chattanooga	1	4	0	36	24	4.97	1.44	25.7	282	32	65	4.43	3.0	6.0	2.0	0.7	45
			2016	AA	Chattanooga	10	7	0	145	104	3.41	1.26	23.7	251	29	74	3.49	2.9	6.5	2.3	0.7	57

Tall, angular SP with lots of durability and polish. Doesn't throw hard and lack of velocity limits ceiling. Commands and controls plate with three pitches and does nice job of sequencing. Doesn't own out pitch in arsenal, though likes to use SL as chase pitch. Could have value in providing length in bullpen.

Smith, Austin — SP — San Diego
EXP MLB DEBUT: 2020 | H/W: 6-4 220 | FUT: #4 starter | 8D

Thrws R Age 20 — 2015 (2) HS (FL)

93-95	FB	++++
74-78	CB	+++
83-84	CU	+	2015	Rk	Azl Padres	0	3	0	17	11	7.94	2.12	9.3	360	42	58	6.73	4.8	5.8	1.2	0.0	-6
			2016	A	Fort Wayne	4	6	1	90	63	5.29	1.66	16.2	290	34	67	4.98	4.6	6.3	1.4	0.6	7

Tall, athletic RHP struggled with release points throughout '16, though added a few ticks to his fastball. Sat 93-95 with easy arm action. CB has plus potential but struggles corralling pitch. CU is sub-par on its best days. Athletic pitcher capable of repeating delivery. May only have pen upside.

Smith, Drew — RP — Detroit
EXP MLB DEBUT: 2018 | H/W: 6-2 190 | FUT: Setup reliever | 7C

Thrws R Age 23 — 2015 (3) Dallas Baptist

			2015	NCAA	Dallas Baptist	3	2	4	45	38	3.99	1.40	7.6	266	33	72	3.95	3.4	7.6	2.2	0.6	63
92-97	FB	++++	2015	Rk	GCL Tigers	0	0	0	1	3	0.00	0.83	4.4	228	72	100	1.32	0.0	22.5		0.0	423
80-83	CB	+++	2015	A-	Connecticut	2	0	2	27	33	0.33	0.70	8.7	164	26	95	0.35	1.3	10.9	8.3	0.0	179
	CU	+	2015	A	West Michigan	1	0	0	1	0	0.00	1.67	5.4	228	42	100	3.49	7.5	0.0	0.0	0.0	86
			2016	A	West Michigan	1	2	4	48	62	2.99	1.18	5.5	200	32	72	1.97	4.3	11.6	2.7	0.0	110

Athletic RP who mows down hitters with plus FB and improving CB. Generates quality velocity from quick arm action and provides hint of deception. Has yet to allow HR in career, though inconsistent control has hindered reliability. Misses bats with FB and CB gives him second average offering. Has been lights out against RHH (.155 oppBA).

Smith,Nate — SP — Los Angeles (A)

EXP MLB DEBUT: 2017 | H/W: 6-3 210 | FUT: #4 starter | 7B

Thrws L Age 25 — 2013 (8) Furman

Pitches	Year	Lev	Team	W	L	Sv	IP	K	ERA	WHIP	BF/G	OBA	H%	S%	xERA	Ctl	Dom	Cmd	hr/9	BPV
87-91 FB ++	2014	A+	Inland Empire	6	3	0	55	51	3.10	1.00	21.1	208	27	69	2.09	2.3	8.3	3.6	0.5	106
80-82 SL ++	2014	AA	Arkansas	5	3	0	62	67	2.90	1.26	23.0	215	29	77	2.76	4.3	9.7	2.2	0.4	75
74-77 CB +++	2015	AA	Arkansas	8	4	0	101	81	2.49	1.09	23.3	223	26	82	2.88	2.5	7.2	2.9	0.9	80
75-78 CU +++	2015	AAA	Salt Lake	2	4	0	36	23	7.75	1.75	23.5	321	34	57	6.77	3.8	5.8	1.5	1.8	20
	2016	AAA	Salt Lake	8	9	0	150	122	4.62	1.40	24.4	282	33	69	4.63	2.6	7.3	2.8	1.1	78

Durable SP who pitched in Futures Game and possesses deep arsenal of average offerings. Dom likely to remain low, but throws all pitches for strikes. CU may be best pitch with sink and fade and high arm slot provide some deception. Lacks ideal velocity for frontline SP, but has mixing ability to become #4 guy.

Smoker,Josh — RP — New York (N)

EXP MLB DEBUT: 2016 | H/W: 6-2 250 | FUT: Setup reliever | 7C

Thrws L Age 28 — 2007 (S-1) HS (GA)

Pitches	Year	Lev	Team	W	L	Sv	IP	K	ERA	WHIP	BF/G	OBA	H%	S%	xERA	Ctl	Dom	Cmd	hr/9	BPV
	2015	A	Savannah	1	0	0	6	8	8.71	2.10	5.1	386	54	54	7.11	2.9	11.6	4.0	0.0	149
94-97 FB ++++	2015	A+	St. Lucie	1	0	6	21	26	1.71	0.85	5.5	168	25	82	1.18	2.6	11.1	4.3	0.4	149
79-82 SL ++	2015	AA	Binghamton	1	0	0	21	26	3.00	1.29	4.1	213	33	74	2.38	4.7	11.1	2.4	0.0	91
82-84 SP +++	2016	AAA	Las Vegas	3	2	3	57	81	4.11	1.47	4.7	291	43	73	4.63	2.8	12.8	4.5	0.8	171
	2016	MLB	NY Mets	3	0	0	15	25	4.77	1.32	3.1	273	41	75	5.47	2.4	14.9	6.3	2.4	222

Older LHP bounced around minors and Indy lg before making 2016 MLB debut. FB up to 99 in 2016; explodes on hitters. SL not enough against LHH, as it struggles to achieve two-plane break. Split very effective against RHH during MLB stint and could develop into plus pitch.

Sobotka,Chad — RP — Atlanta

EXP MLB DEBUT: 2018 | H/W: 6-7 200 | FUT: Middle reliever | 6C

Thrws R Age 23 — 2014 (4) SC-Upstate

Pitches	Year	Lev	Team	W	L	Sv	IP	K	ERA	WHIP	BF/G	OBA	H%	S%	xERA	Ctl	Dom	Cmd	hr/9	BPV
	2015	Rk	Danville	0	0	0	2		0.00	0.00	5.6	0	0			0.0	9.0		0.0	180
91-94 FB ++++	2015	A	Rome	1	6	0	32	18	7.31	2.06	13.0	333	36	66	7.43	5.9	5.1	0.9	1.4	-50
78-82 SL ++	2016	A	Rome	1	2	0	19	19	4.26	1.84	5.9	300	39	76	5.44	5.7	9.0	1.6	0.5	27
83-84 CU ++	2016	A+	Carolina	1	1	3	17	24	2.09	0.87	4.9	198	33	73	1.15	1.6	12.6	8.0	0.0	202
	2016	AA	Mississippi	0	0	0	2	2	0.00	0.00	2.8	0	0			0.0	9.0		0.0	180

Tall RH found consistency within delivery to break away from control issues that plagued '15 season. Over-the-top thrower, gets natural sink on FB. Throws 2-seam and 4-seam FB, both with little movement. Is hurt leaving ball up. SL only works on one plane. Needs to add depth. CU is non-existent as reliever. Lacks durability.

Soroka,Mike — SP — Atlanta

EXP MLB DEBUT: 2019 | H/W: 6-4 195 | FUT: #3 starter | 8D

Thrws R Age 19 — 2015 (1) HS (AB)

Pitches	Year	Lev	Team	W	L	Sv	IP	K	ERA	WHIP	BF/G	OBA	H%	S%	xERA	Ctl	Dom	Cmd	hr/9	BPV
89-92 FB +++																				
77-79 CB +++	2015	Rk	Danville	0	2	0	24	26	3.75	1.33	16.6	293	40	69	3.59	1.5	9.8	6.5	0.0	153
81-83 CU +++	2015	Rk	GCL Braves	0	0	0	10	11	1.80	0.60	8.6	151	23	67		0.9	9.9	11.0	0.0	172
	2016	A	Rome	9	9	0	143	125	3.02	1.13	22.6	244	31	72	2.60	2.0	7.9	3.9	0.2	105

Canadian RHP drew comparisons to Michael Fulmer in early stages of career. Command was off the charts for level. Could throw all three pitches for strikes. FB has true two-seam run and fade. Velocity should increase as he gets older. Features two solid secondary offerings. CB is gritty with plus potential. CU has above-average run and late sink.

Speas,Alex — SP — Texas

EXP MLB DEBUT: 2021 | H/W: 6-4 180 | FUT: #2 starter | 9E

Thrws R Age 19 — 2016 (2) HS (GA)

Pitches	Year	Lev	Team	W	L	Sv	IP	K	ERA	WHIP	BF/G	OBA	H%	S%	xERA	Ctl	Dom	Cmd	hr/9	BPV
92-96 FB +++																				
83-86 SL +++																				
CU ++																				
	2016	Rk	Azl Rangers	0	0	0	8	11	0.00	1.36	8.5	149	25	100	1.84	7.8	12.2	1.6	0.0	28

Lanky, athletic SP with electric arm and high ceiling. Has incredible arm speed to add both velocity and life to pitches. FB could evolve to double-plus with more consistency and power, while hard SL can miss bats easily. Has trouble repeating delivery and varying arm slot hinders control. With polish and time, could front starting rotation.

Stanek,Ryne — RP — Tampa Bay

EXP MLB DEBUT: 2017 | H/W: 6-4 180 | FUT: Closer | 8D

Thrws R Age 25 — 2013 (1) Arkansas

Pitches	Year	Lev	Team	W	L	Sv	IP	K	ERA	WHIP	BF/G	OBA	H%	S%	xERA	Ctl	Dom	Cmd	hr/9	BPV
	2014	A+	Charlotte	1	1	0	13	4	5.54	1.38	18.2	262	28	56	3.35	3.5	2.8	0.8	0.0	-26
91-99 FB ++++	2015	A+	Charlotte	4	2	0	50	38	1.79	0.96	21.1	189	23	83	1.65	2.7	6.8	2.5	0.4	68
82-86 SL +++	2015	AA	Montgomery	4	3	1	61	41	4.12	1.36	16.0	232	25	72	3.81	4.6	6.0	1.3	1.0	3
75-78 CB +++	2016	AA	Montgomery	2	6	2	78	91	3.80	1.27	17.7	225	31	71	3.15	4.0	10.5	2.6	0.7	98
CU ++	2016	AAA	Durham	2	4	1	24	22	5.98	1.45	6.4	245	29	59	4.28	4.9	8.2	1.7	1.1	35

Tall, strong pitcher who converted to RP in AAA. Pitched in Futures Game and showed plus arm strength. Added velocity as RP and may have found niche. FB and SL play up in short stints and mixes in CB and sub-par CU. May struggle with FB location at times as he tends to overthrow. Has demeanor and pitch mix to be dynamic late-innings guy.

Staumont,Josh — SP — Kansas City

EXP MLB DEBUT: 2018 | H/W: 6-3 200 | FUT: #2 SP/closer | 9E

Thrws R Age 23 — 2015 (2) Azusa Pacific

Pitches	Year	Lev	Team	W	L	Sv	IP	K	ERA	WHIP	BF/G	OBA	H%	S%	xERA	Ctl	Dom	Cmd	hr/9	BPV
95-99 FB ++++																				
82-84 CB ++++	2015	Rk	Idaho Falls	3	1	1	31	51	3.18	1.35	9.3	170	33	74	2.02	6.9	14.8	2.1	0.0	96
CU +	2016	A+	Wilmington	2	10	0	73	94	5.05	1.77	18.6	231	35	70	4.17	8.3	11.6	1.4	0.4	4
	2016	AA	NW Arkansas	2	1	0	50	73	3.05	1.58	20.0	229	37	81	3.64	6.6	13.1	2.0	0.4	75

Electric-armed pitcher who led minors in K/9. Dominates with double-plus FB and throws with little effort. Plus CB gives him 2nd swing-and-miss pitch and features incredible break. Maintains velocity, but has severe trouble locating pitches. Delivery gets out of sync and can overthrow. Command needs significant work. When on, is nearly unhittable.

Steele,Justin — SP — Chicago (N)

EXP MLB DEBUT: 2019 | H/W: 6-2 195 | FUT: #3 starter | 7D

Thrws L Age 21 — 2014 (5) HS (MS)

Pitches	Year	Lev	Team	W	L	Sv	IP	K	ERA	WHIP	BF/G	OBA	H%	S%	xERA	Ctl	Dom	Cmd	hr/9	BPV
90-93 FB +++																				
75-78 CB +++	2014	Rk	Azl Cubs	0	0	0	18	25	2.97	1.26	8.3	226	36	74	2.48	4.0	12.4	3.1	0.0	134
CU ++	2015	A-	Eugene	3	1	0	40	38	2.69	1.32	16.6	251	34	77	2.98	3.4	8.5	2.5	0.0	80
	2016	A	South Bend	5	7	0	77	76	5.02	1.71	18.4	300	39	69	4.99	4.6	8.9	1.9	0.4	55

LHP who struggles with control. Attacks hitters with a good 90-93 sinkng FB that hits 95 mph. Flashes a potentially plus CB that needs to be more consistent, and an average CU. Keeps hitters off balance with good deception, but cannot find the strike zone on a consistent basis and when he did in 2016, he got hammered.

Stephens,Jordan — SP — Chicago (A)

EXP MLB DEBUT: 2018 | H/W: 6-1 190 | FUT: #3 starter | 8D

Thrws R Age 24 — 2015 (5) Rice

Pitches	Year	Lev	Team	W	L	Sv	IP	K	ERA	WHIP	BF/G	OBA	H%	S%	xERA	Ctl	Dom	Cmd	hr/9	BPV
90-95 FB +++	2015	NCAA	Rice	6	5	1	59	75	3.19	1.15	13.8	234	35	70	2.44	2.6	11.4	4.4	0.2	153
82-86 SL ++	2015	Rk	Azl White Sox	0	0	0	14	18	0.63	0.63	5.4	149	24	89	0.02	1.3	11.4	9.0	0.0	189
75-79 CB +++	2015	Rk	Great Falls	0	0	0	3	3	0.00	1.00	5.7	191	27	100	1.43	3.0	9.0	3.0	0.0	99
CU ++	2016	A+	Winston-Salem	7	10	0	141	155	3.45	1.26	21.3	245	33	75	3.44	3.1	9.9	3.2	0.8	113

Athletic pitcher who led CAR in Ks. Was outstanding in August and uses four pitches to keep hitters off guard. Keeps ball low with sinking FB and uses two breaking balls with CB being best one. SL and CU are below average, which could lead to a bullpen role. Maintains velocity deep into games and misses bats.

Stephenson,Robert — SP — Cincinnati

EXP MLB DEBUT: 2016 | H/W: 6-2 200 | FUT: #2 SP/Closer | 8D

Thrws R Age 24 — 2011 (1) HS (CA)

Pitches	Year	Lev	Team	W	L	Sv	IP	K	ERA	WHIP	BF/G	OBA	H%	S%	xERA	Ctl	Dom	Cmd	hr/9	BPV
	2014	AA	Pensacola	7	10	0	136	140	4.76	1.38	21.2	229	28	68	3.96	4.9	9.3	1.9	1.2	52
91-95 FB ++++	2015	AA	Pensacola	4	7	0	78	89	3.69	1.23	22.6	194	26	73	2.89	5.0	10.3	2.1	0.9	69
78-82 CB ++++	2015	AAA	Louisville	4	4	0	55	51	4.08	1.41	21.2	247	32	70	3.47	4.4	8.3	1.9	0.3	49
84-87 CU ++	2016	AAA	Louisville	8	9	0	136	120	4.43	1.37	23.8	230	27	70	3.89	4.7	7.9	1.7	1.1	34
	2016	MLB	Cincinnati	2	3	0	37	31	6.08	1.62	20.5	282	30	69	6.24	4.6	7.5	1.6	2.2	29

Power pitcher made his MLB debut in '16. Struggled to command FB in zone, an issue that has plagued him throughout the minor leagues. Plus FB/CB combination still has mid-rotation starting capability, though lack of command and control lends itself to back end of the bullpen. Could dominate in closer role.

Stewart,Brock — SP — Los Angeles (N)

EXP MLB DEBUT: 2016 | H/W: 6-3 210 | FUT: #4 starter | 7C

Thrws R Age 25 — 2014 (6) Illinois State

Pitches	Year	Lev	Team	W	L	Sv	IP	K	ERA	WHIP	BF/G	OBA	H%	S%	xERA	Ctl	Dom	Cmd	hr/9	BPV
	2015	A+	Rancho Cuca	2	4	0	63	65	5.43	1.48	15.0	297	38	63	4.82	2.6	9.3	3.6	0.9	116
92-96 FB +++	2016	A+	Rancho Cuca	2	0	0	11	10	0.82	0.64	19.0	139	19	86		1.6	8.2	5.0	0.0	121
83-88 SL +	2016	AA	Tulsa	3	4	0	59	65	1.37	0.88	21.9	197	29	83	1.19	1.7	9.9	5.9	0.0	151
CU +++	2016	AAA	Oklahoma City	4	0	0	50	54	2.51	0.94	21.0	225	30	77	2.34	1.1	9.7	9.0	0.7	163
	2016	MLB	LA Dodgers	2	2	0	28	25	5.79	1.61	17.7	295	33	71	6.44	3.9	8.0	2.1	2.3	59

Played 3B in college but was moved to mound when drafted. Now features a plus 92-96 mph two- and four-seam FB. His SL has cutter action but lacks late movement. CU flashes as plus with late fade and sink and gives him the tools to neutralize LHH. Has good size and a fresh arm. Held his own in 5 MLB starts.

Stewart,Kohl — SP — Minnesota

EXP MLB DEBUT: 2017 | H/W: 6-3 195 | FUT: #3 starter | 8D

Thrws R Age 22
2013 (1) HS (TX)

Velo	Pitch	Grade
91-95	FB	+++
82-85	SL	+++
75-79	CB	++
	CU	+++

Year	Lev	Team	W	L	Sv	IP	K	ERA	WHIP	BF/G	OBA	H%	S%	xERA	Ctl	Dom	Cmd	hr/9	BPV
2013	Rk	Elizabethton	0	0	0	4	8	0.00	0.50	13.3	81	23	100		2.3	18.0	8.0	0.0	281
2014	A	Cedar Rapids	3	5	0	87	62	2.59	1.14	18.1	234	28	78	2.71	2.5	6.4	2.6	0.4	66
2015	A+	Fort Myers	7	8	0	129	71	3.21	1.39	24.7	269	31	75	3.56	3.1	4.9	1.6	0.1	22
2016	A+	Fort Myers	3	2	0	51	44	2.64	1.13	22.5	213	27	77	2.36	3.3	7.7	2.3	0.4	67
2016	AA	Chattanooga	9	6	0	92	47	3.03	1.47	24.7	260	29	79	3.88	4.3	4.6	1.1	0.4	-15

Athletic, loose-armed SP who posted nice results despite middling K rate. Likes to establish pitch with hard sinker and is extreme groundballer. Has put-away pitches in SL and CB, but prefers to pitch to contact. Dom could increase with better sequencing. Spike in walk rate not a concern as he can throw any pitch in any count. Rarely allows HR.

Stinnett,Jake — SP — Chicago (N)

EXP MLB DEBUT: 2018 | H/W: 6-4 200 | FUT: #3 starter | 7C

Thrws R Age 24
2014 (2) Maryland

Velo	Pitch	Grade
92-95	FB	++++
75-78	SL	+++
	CU	++

Year	Lev	Team	W	L	Sv	IP	K	ERA	WHIP	BF/G	OBA	H%	S%	xERA	Ctl	Dom	Cmd	hr/9	BPV
2014	NCAA	Maryland	8	6	1	118	132	2.67	0.97	26.3	203	28	75	2.07	2.3	10.1	4.4	0.6	137
2014	Rk	Azl Cubs	0	1	0	4	3	8.57	2.14	6.9	432	50	56	8.26	0.0	6.4		0.0	134
2014	A-	Boise	0	0	0	6	7	2.95	0.82	11.1	149	16	75	1.88	3.0	10.3	3.5	1.5	124
2015	A	South Bend	7	6	0	117	91	4.46	1.43	22.6	262	32	68	3.85	3.8	7.0	1.8	0.5	40
2016	A+	Myrtle Beach	9	4	0	116	97	4.27	1.33	24.1	258	32	67	3.62	3.1	7.5	2.4	0.5	70

2nd rounder put up pedestrian numbers at High-A. Best pitch is a good 92-95 mph sinking FB. Mixes in SL with good late break that shows potential and a below-average CU. Fringy control continues to be an issue and can leave pitches up in the zone. Has good size and durability and still profiles as a potential #3 starter.

Strahm,Matthew — SP — Kansas City

EXP MLB DEBUT: 2016 | H/W: 6-3 185 | FUT: #4 starter | 7A

Thrws L Age 25
2012 (21) Neosho Co CC

Velo	Pitch	Grade
89-94	FB	+++
79-82	CB	+++
82-84	SL	++
81-84	CU	+++

Year	Lev	Team	W	L	Sv	IP	K	ERA	WHIP	BF/G	OBA	H%	S%	xERA	Ctl	Dom	Cmd	hr/9	BPV
2014	Rk	Idaho Falls	1	0	1	19		2.34	1.04	7.4	156	25	79	1.55	4.7	12.7	2.7	0.5	119
2015	A	Lexington	2	1	4	26	38	2.08	0.92	7.0	141	24	78	0.98	4.2	13.2	3.2	0.3	143
2015	A+	Wilmington	1	6	1	68	83	2.78	0.99	17.3	200	27	77	2.35	2.5	11.0	4.4	0.9	148
2016	AA	NW Arkansas	3	8	0	102	107	3.44	1.22	18.8	262	33	77	4.03	2.0	9.4	4.7	1.2	133
2016	MLB	KC Royals	2	2	0	22	30	1.23	1.09	4.1	173	29	88	1.43	4.5	12.3	2.7	0.0	117

Tall, angular SP who set career high in IP and posted high Dom. Has deceptive delivery that allows FB to play up and exhibits solid control with all pitches. Improving CB and CU give him chance to miss bats and lives down in zone consistently. Has injury history, but maintained velocity all season. Could pitch in rotation or in bullpen.

Stratton,Chris — SP — San Francisco

EXP MLB DEBUT: 2016 | H/W: 6-3 190 | FUT: #4 starter | 7D

Thrws R Age 26
2012 (1) Mississippi State

Velo	Pitch	Grade
89-92	FB	+++
78-82	SL	+++
74-77	CB	++
80-81	CU	++

Year	Lev	Team	W	L	Sv	IP	K	ERA	WHIP	BF/G	OBA	H%	S%	xERA	Ctl	Dom	Cmd	hr/9	BPV
2014	AA	Richmond	1	1	0	23	18	3.52	1.78	21.2	309	37	82	5.74	4.7	7.0	1.5	0.8	18
2015	AA	Richmond	1	5	0	50	39	4.14	1.24	22.6	221	27	66	2.92	4.0	7.0	1.8	0.5	37
2015	AAA	Sacramento	4	5	0	98	72	3.86	1.31	23.8	242	29	70	3.36	3.7	6.6	1.8	0.6	38
2016	AAA	Sacramento	12	6	0	125	103	3.88	1.27	24.4	254	31	69	3.31	2.8	7.4	2.6	0.4	76
2016	MLB	SF Giants	1	0	0	10	6	3.60	1.60	6.3	281	31	80	4.97	4.5	5.4	1.2	0.9	-6

Tall, durable SP who got off to slow start, but finished strong. Uses effortless delivery to generate decent FB/SL combo. Gets good movement to FB while throwing consistent strikes to all quadrants. Lacks power in offerings and will be pitch-to-contact guy. Needs to improve CU in order to keep LHH off balance.

Suarez,Andrew — SP — San Francisco

EXP MLB DEBUT: 2017 | H/W: 6-2 205 | FUT: #4 starter | 7C

Thrws L Age 24
2015 (2) Miami

Velo	Pitch	Grade
88-93	FB	+++
81-82	SL	+++
78-80	CB	++
81-84	CU	++

Year	Lev	Team	W	L	Sv	IP	K	ERA	WHIP	BF/G	OBA	H%	S%	xERA	Ctl	Dom	Cmd	hr/9	BPV
2015	Rk	Azl Giants	0	0	0	5	6	1.80	0.60	5.7	124	20	67		1.8	10.8	6.0	0.0	164
2015	A-	Salem-Kaizer	1	0	0	19	15	1.41	0.99	14.6	240	28	94	2.92	0.9	7.1	7.5	0.9	120
2015	A+	San Jose	1	0	0	15	16	1.80	1.00	19.1	235	29	92	3.08	1.2	9.6	8.0	1.2	158
2016	A+	San Jose	2	1	0	29	34	2.47	1.03	22.5	233	32	79	2.57	1.5	10.5	6.8	0.6	165
2016	AA	Richmond	7	7	0	114	90	3.95	1.34	25.0	286	34	73	4.36	1.9	7.1	3.8	0.9	95

Advanced SP who is moving quickly on basis of improving repertoire and deft sequencing. Establishes plate with solid FB that he locates low in zone. Hard SL flashes plus and can mix in slower CB for different look. Changes eye levels well and has fluid delivery for deception. Can be too hittable, but doesn't beat himself.

Suarez,Jose — SP — Los Angeles (A)

EXP MLB DEBUT: 2020 | H/W: 5-10 170 | FUT: #4 starter | 7E

Thrws L Age 19
2014 FA (VZ)

Velo	Pitch	Grade
88-92	FB	++
74-77	CB	+++
77-79	CU	+++

Year	Lev	Team	W	L	Sv	IP	K	ERA	WHIP	BF/G	OBA	H%	S%	xERA	Ctl	Dom	Cmd	hr/9	BPV
2016	Rk	Azl Angels	1	3	0	40	46	5.39	1.52	15.8	298	41	62	4.35	2.9	10.3	3.5	0.2	125
2016	Rk	Orem	0	1	0	4	7	0.00	1.71	18.6	342	57	100	5.26	2.2	15.4	7.0	0.0	235

Small, advanced SP with pitchability and solid control. Repeats smooth, simple delivery and is menace to LHH with solid-average CB. Can pitch backwards, but will need to continue to add velocity to FB. Has feel and touch for CU that exhibits depth and fade. More innings guy than dominant SP.

Supak,Trey — SP — Milwaukee

EXP MLB DEBUT: 2019 | H/W: 6-5 210 | FUT: #3 starter | 7C

Thrws R Age 20
2014 (S-2) HS (TX)

Velo	Pitch	Grade
90-93	FB	+++
73-75	CB	+++
	CU	++

Year	Lev	Team	W	L	Sv	IP	K	ERA	WHIP	BF/G	OBA	H%	S%	xERA	Ctl	Dom	Cmd	hr/9	BPV
2014	Rk	GCL Pirates	1	3	0	24	21	4.88	1.58	13.2	285	33	74	5.54	4.1	7.9	1.9	1.5	48
2015	Rk	Bristol	1	2	0	28	23	6.73	1.42	14.9	306	37	50	4.65	1.6	7.4	4.6	0.6	107
2016	Rk	Helena	1	1	0	14	11	1.29	0.79	12.6	202	26	82	1.04	0.6	7.1	11.0	0.0	128
2016	A	Wisconsin	2	3	1	44	40	3.88	1.47	17.2	278	35	74	4.33	3.5	8.2	2.4	0.6	71

Big, tall RH who split time as starter and reliever in full-season debut. Clean arm action, low-effort delivery produce low-90s FB with minimal arm-side bore. Aptitude for spinning 12/6 CB with good depth to miss some bats; CU is raw with fringe-avg fading action. Slight crossfire toward home could limit his command as #3 SP with some Dom ability.

Szapucki,Thomas — SP — New York (N)

EXP MLB DEBUT: 2020 | H/W: 6-2 205 | FUT: #3 starter | 8D

Thrws L Age 20
2015 (5) HS (FL)

Velo	Pitch	Grade
93-96	FB	++++
82-85	CB	++++
83-85	CU	++

Year	Lev	Team	W	L	Sv	IP	K	ERA	WHIP	BF/G	OBA	H%	S%	xERA	Ctl	Dom	Cmd	hr/9	BPV
2015	Rk	GCL Mets	0	0	0	2	3	17.14	2.38	3.6	458	63	20	9.42	0.0	12.9		0.0	249
2016	Rk	Kingsport	2	1	0	29	47	0.62	0.86	21.4	164	29	100	1.30	2.8	14.6	5.2	0.6	205
2016	A-	Brooklyn	2	2	0	23	39	2.35	0.91	21.5	134	28	71	0.53	4.3	15.3	3.5	0.0	176

LH was breakout performer in NYM system. FB up to 97 after sitting in the low 90s in '15. Late arm-side movement makes it difficult to square up. Power CB is dynamic and a true swing-and-miss offering. CU has made strides but still lacks the fade needed to compete against advanced competition.

Szynski,Skylar — SP — Oakland

EXP MLB DEBUT: 2021 | H/W: 6-2 195 | FUT: #3 starter | 8E

Thrws R Age 19
2016 (4) HS (IN)

Velo	Pitch	Grade
89-94	FB	+++
77-80	SL	+++
84-85	CU	+

Year	Lev	Team	W	L	Sv	IP	K	ERA	WHIP	BF/G	OBA	H%	S%	xERA	Ctl	Dom	Cmd	hr/9	BPV
2016	Rk	Azl Athletics	0	3	0	13	8	8.24	1.53	8.1	302	34	42	4.91	2.7	5.5	2.0	0.7	43

Quick-armed SP with significant potential, but will take time to develop. Not much projection unless works for smoother delivery. Generates velocity and movement with nice FB while ability to hide ball gives hint of deception. SL a bit slow, but can drop off table and tough to make hard contact against. Rarely uses CU and will need against LHH.

Tate,Dillon — SP — New York (A)

EXP MLB DEBUT: 2018 | H/W: 6-2 175 | FUT: #3 starter | 8D

Thrws R Age 22
2015 (1) UC-Santa Barbara

Velo	Pitch	Grade
90-96	FB	+++
83-86	SL	+++
81-84	CU	++

Year	Lev	Team	W	L	Sv	IP	K	ERA	WHIP	BF/G	OBA	H%	S%	xERA	Ctl	Dom	Cmd	hr/9	BPV
2015	NCAA	UC SantaBarbara	8	5	0	103	111	2.27	0.91	27.5	185	26	75	1.38	2.4	9.7	4.0	0.3	126
2015	A-	Spokane	0	0	0	2	3	0.00	1.50	4.3	0	0	100	0.88	13.5	13.5	1.0		-104
2015	A	Hickory	0	0	0	7	5	1.29	0.43	5.7	132	12	100	0.59	0.0	6.4		1.3	134
2016	A	Charleston (Sc)	1	0	0	17	15	3.16	1.58	10.7	303	38	81	4.89	3.2	7.9	2.5	0.5	75
2016	A	Hickory	3	3	0	65	55	5.12	1.62	17.0	299	36	68	5.06	3.7	7.6	2.0	0.7	54

Lean, athletic pitcher who had disappointing season, but hopes to resurrect in new organization. Pitched in pen upon acquisition, but still has starter upside. Has two pitches that miss bats in FB and SL, though drop in velocity is concern. FB can be too straight, but seemed to be on track in a short stint in AFL.

Taylor,Blake — SP — New York (N)

EXP MLB DEBUT: 2020 | H/W: 6-3 220 | FUT: #4 starter | 7E

Thrws L Age 21
2013 (2) HS (CA)

Velo	Pitch	Grade
88-90	FB	+++
75-77	CB	+++
86-87	SL	+
81-82	CU	++

Year	Lev	Team	W	L	Sv	IP	K	ERA	WHIP	BF/G	OBA	H%	S%	xERA	Ctl	Dom	Cmd	hr/9	BPV
2014	Rk	GCL Mets	2	0	0	10	10	0.00	0.78	12.3	34	5	100		6.2	8.8	1.4	0.0	10
2014	Rk	Kingsport	2	1	0	30	20	5.38	2.13	18.6	326	38	73	6.43	6.9	6.0	0.9	0.3	-60
2015	Rk	GCL Mets	0	0	0	3	3	6.00	1.33	6.2	321	42	50	4.04	0.0	9.0		0.0	180
2015	A-	Brooklyn	0	0	0	9	5	1.00	1.00	11.5	191	23	89	1.47	3.0	5.0	1.7	0.0	27
2016	Rk	Kingsport	0	0	1	8	12	4.39	1.59	7.2	178	31	69	2.71	8.8	13.2	1.5	0.0	18

Tall, projectable LH close to physical projection. Missed most of 2016 due to Tommy John surgery. Fastball and curveball flashed plus when healthy, and has a feel for the change-up. Slider is easily fourth-best pitch and in dire need of improvement.

Taylor,Cory

SP | San Francisco | EXP MLB DEBUT: 2018 | H/W: 6-2 255 | FUT: #4 starter | 7D

Thrws R Age 23
2015 (8) Dallas Baptist

Velo	Pitch	Grade
90-95	FB	+ + +
82-87	SL	+ + +
	CU	+

Year	Lev	Team	W	L	Sv	IP	K	ERA	WHIP	BF/G	OBA	H%	S%	xERA	Ctl	Dom	Cmd	hr/9	BPV
2015	NCAA	Dallas Baptist	7	1	0	80	71	3.60	1.45	21.4	274	34	75	4.05	3.5	8.0	2.3	0.5	68
2015	A-	Salem-Kaizer	2	0	1	33	50	2.45	1.45	7.8	279	45	83	3.91	3.3	13.6	4.2	0.3	175
2016	A	Augusta	9	5	0	97	100	2.59	1.28	22.1	265	35	80	3.40	2.3	9.3	4.0	0.4	122
2016	A+	San Jose	1	1	0	9	11	6.92	1.76	13.9	319	45	56	5.05	4.0	10.9	2.8	0.0	107
2016	AA	Richmond	1	0	0	12	10	0.75	1.25	24.4	228	30	93	2.52	3.8	7.5	2.0	0.0	52

Huge-framed SP was very good in Low-A, but appeared to tire late in season. Body needs to be watched and has lots of moving parts in delivery. Throws very heavy FB that induces high amount of groundballs, and complements with solid-average SL. Mostly focuses on two pitches and will mix in CU. Likely to move to pen without improved offspeed offering.

Taylor,Jacob

SP | Pittsburgh | EXP MLB DEBUT: 2021 | H/W: 6-3 205 | FUT: #3 starter | 8D

Thrws R Age 21
2015 (4) Pearl River CC

Velo	Pitch	Grade
92-95	FB	+ + + +
	SL	+ + +
	CU	+ +

Year	Lev	Team	W	L	Sv	IP	K	ERA	WHIP	BF/G	OBA	H%	S%	xERA	Ctl	Dom	Cmd	hr/9	BPV
2015	Rk	GCL Pirates	0	0	0	2	2	0.00	1.50	8.6	0	0	100	0.92	13.5	9.0	0.7	0.0	-185
2016	Rk	GCL Pirates	0	2	0	9	9	5.93	1.32	9.4	190	15	67	5.00	5.9	8.9	1.5	3.0	18
2016	A-	West Virginia	0	1	0	1	1	37.50	6.67	11.4	639	72	38	27.23	15.0	7.5	0.5	0.0	-252

4th round pick was limited to just 13 IP as he recovered from TJS. Prior to the injury he showed a good FB that topped out at 97 mph. FB was at 92-95 in his return. Backs up the FB with a slurvy SL and a below-average CU. Taylor is still relatively new to pitching and was drafted more for his athleticism and potential than his polish.

Taylor,Josh

SP | Arizona | EXP MLB DEBUT: 2018 | H/W: 6-5 225 | FUT: Setup reliever | 8E

Thrws L Age 24
2014 NDFA (Georga College)

Velo	Pitch	Grade
91-95	FB	+ + + +
80-83	CB	+ +
	CU	+ +

Year	Lev	Team	W	L	Sv	IP	K	ERA	WHIP	BF/G	OBA	H%	S%	xERA	Ctl	Dom	Cmd	hr/9	BPV
2014	Rk	GCL Phillies	2	0	0	9		0.00	0.99	11.6	163	28	100	1.05	4.0	12.9	3.3	0.0	143
2015	A	Kane County	4	3	0	59	53	3.20	1.58	23.6	305	39	79	4.69	3.1	8.1	2.7	0.3	81
2015	A	Lakewood	4	5	0	68	70	4.63	1.40	22.1	270	35	67	4.17	3.2	9.3	2.9	0.8	99
2016	A+	Visalia	2	7	0	78	77	5.65	1.65	23.3	323	41	66	5.64	2.8	8.9	3.2	0.8	103
2016	AA	Mobile	3	4	0	54	46	4.98	1.49	21.3	292	36	66	4.63	3.0	7.6	2.6	0.7	75

Hard throwing, big-bodied LH improved FB control in '16. FB sits 91-95 with moderate late action and some sink. Struggles hitting catcher's mitt consistently. Would play up in pen. Made improvements with slurvy CB and CU, though both are still below-average offerings. Will be given every chance to start because of durable frame.

Thompson,Dylan

SP | Tampa Bay | EXP MLB DEBUT: 2020 | H/W: 6-2 180 | FUT: #3 starter | 8E

Thrws R Age 20
2015 (4) HS (SC)

Velo	Pitch	Grade
88-93	FB	+ + +
80-82	SL	+ +
80-83	CU	+ +

Year	Lev	Team	W	L	Sv	IP	K	ERA	WHIP	BF/G	OBA	H%	S%	xERA	Ctl	Dom	Cmd	hr/9	BPV
2015	Rk	Azl Mariners	2	1	0	26	25	2.40	0.99	11.1	196	27	73	1.47	2.7	8.6	3.1	0.0	98
2016	Rk	Azl Mariners	0	1	0	4	6	6.43	2.38	7.3	336	51	70	6.89	8.6	12.9	1.5	0.0	18

Athletic and projectable, but with current average stuff. Uses quick arm to add movement to FB, though could throw harder with added strength. Delivery is smooth and repeatble, and he shows makings of average slider. CU is distant third pitch and may struggle with LHH. Focuses on keeping hitters off balance.

Thompson,Mason

SP | San Diego | EXP MLB DEBUT: 2020 | H/W: 6-7 186 | FUT: #2 starter | 9D

Thrws R Age 19
2016 (3) HS (TX)

Velo	Pitch	Grade
93-96	FB	+ + + +
76-78	CB	+ + + +
85-87	CU	+ +

Year	Lev	Team	W	L	Sv	IP	K	ERA	WHIP	BF/G	OBA	H%	S%	xERA	Ctl	Dom	Cmd	hr/9	BPV
2016	Rk	Azl Padres	0	0	0	12	12	2.25	1.08	9.4	191	27	77	1.64	3.8	9.0	2.4	0.0	79

Tall, athletic and projectable RHP, missed senior season due to Tommy John surgery. Leverages body in delivery, and controls it throughout. FB explodes; power 12/6 CB devastates hitters. CU projects as average offering. Stood out on loaded instructional league team. Potential front line starter.

Thompson,Zach

SP | Chicago (A) | EXP MLB DEBUT: 2019 | H/W: 6-7 230 | FUT: #3 starter | 8E

Thrws R Age 23
2014 (5) Texas-Arlington

Velo	Pitch	Grade
90-94	FB	+ + +
77-79	CB	+ + +
	CU	+

Year	Lev	Team	W	L	Sv	IP	K	ERA	WHIP	BF/G	OBA	H%	S%	xERA	Ctl	Dom	Cmd	hr/9	BPV
2014	NCAA	Texas-Arlington	5	4	0	87	62	4.65	1.48	23.4	283	34	66	4.05	3.3	6.4	1.9	0.2	44
2014	Rk	Great Falls	2	3	0	44	26	3.27	1.30	16.5	257	27	80	4.19	2.9	5.3	1.9	1.2	36
2015	A	Kannapolis	3	8	0	75	64	4.44	1.52	20.3	267	34	69	3.94	4.4	7.7	1.7	0.2	36
2016	A	Kannapolis	6	3	0	86	88	2.62	1.13	21.2	193	26	78	2.26	4.1	9.2	2.3	0.5	74
2016	A+	Winston-Salem	3	5	0	54	40	5.65	1.49	23.4	302	34	64	5.26	2.5	6.6	2.7	1.2	70

Big-framed SP who was dynamite in Low-A, but knocked around in High-A. Uses height very effectively by throwing downhill and giving hitters tough angle. FB has promise, but can flatten out when he overthrows. Mechanics tough to keep in sync, though doing better job of staying on top of CB. Gets Ks with CB, though CU is far from average.

Thorpe,Lewis

SP | Minnesota | EXP MLB DEBUT: 2019 | H/W: 6-1 160 | FUT: #3 starter | 8D

Thrws L Age 21
2012 FA (AU)

Velo	Pitch	Grade
89-94	FB	+ + +
78-80	CB	+ + +
81-83	SL	+ +
80-83	CU	+ + +

Year	Lev	Team	W	L	Sv	IP	K	ERA	WHIP	BF/G	OBA	H%	S%	xERA	Ctl	Dom	Cmd	hr/9	BPV
2013	Rk	GCL Twins	4	1	0	44	64	2.05	0.86	13.5	205	33	78	1.59	1.2	13.1	10.7	0.4	221
2014	A	Cedar Rapids	3	2	0	71	80	3.54	1.38	18.7	236	31	77	3.74	4.6	10.1	2.2	0.9	77
2015	A	Did not pitch (injury)																	
2016	A	Did not pitch (injury)																	

High-ceiling SP who hasn't pitched since '14 due to Tommy John surgery and Twins cautious approach. Offers unique upside despite lean frame. Advanced pitchability with use of four pitches and ability to add and subtract. CU can be plus pitch at times and hard FB can be used up in zone. Pitch movement is paramount.

Tinoco,Jesus

SP | Colorado | EXP MLB DEBUT: 2019 | H/W: 6-4 190 | FUT: #4 starter | 7D

Thrws R Age 21
2011 FA (VZ)

Velo	Pitch	Grade
92-95	FB	+ + + +
83-85	SL	+ + +
88-90	CU	+ +

Year	Lev	Team	W	L	Sv	IP	K	ERA	WHIP	BF/G	OBA	H%	S%	xERA	Ctl	Dom	Cmd	hr/9	BPV
2014	Rk	Bluefield	1	9	1	56	47	4.97	1.46	18.5	282	34	65	4.38	3.2	7.5	2.4	0.6	67
2015	A	Asheville	5	0	0	40	37	1.80	1.10	22.4	242	31	86	2.73	1.8	8.3	4.6	0.5	119
2015	A	Lansing	2	6	0	81	68	3.55	1.36	22.6	278	35	72	3.56	2.4	7.5	3.1	0.1	88
2016	A	Asheville	3	8	0	86	53	5.64	1.66	24.1	327	36	67	5.98	2.6	5.5	2.1	1.0	47
2016	A+	Modesto	0	3	0	13	8	15.11	3.05	19.2	500	54	49	14.31	2.1	5.5	2.7	2.1	61

Projectable RHP from Valenzuela struggled all season, going 3-11 with a 6.86 ERA. FB sits at 92-95 mph, topping out at 97 mph with good late sink. Mixes in a SL that shows some potential and a serviceable CU, both of which need refinement. Throws all three offerings for strikes, but didn't miss many bats.

Tirado,Alberto

RP | Philadelphia | EXP MLB DEBUT: 2018 | H/W: 6-0 180 | FUT: Setup reliever | 9D

Thrws R Age 22
2011 FA (DR)

Velo	Pitch	Grade
95-98	FB	+ + + + +
83-86	SL	+ + + +
86-87	CU	+ +

Year	Lev	Team	W	L	Sv	IP	K	ERA	WHIP	BF/G	OBA	H%	S%	xERA	Ctl	Dom	Cmd	hr/9	BPV
2014	A	Lansing	1	2	1	40	40	6.30	2.10	15.1	285	37	69	6.05	8.8	9.0	1.0	0.7	-57
2015	A+	Clearwater	1	0	0	15	16	0.60	1.60	7.4	124	19	96	2.23	10.8	9.6	0.9	0.0	-101
2015	A+	Dunedin	4	3	3	61	61	3.24	1.31	8.1	207	27	76	2.95	5.2	9.0	1.7	0.6	41
2016	A	Lakewood	7	1	0	61	96	3.24	1.37	12.8	218	37	77	3.05	5.3	14.1	2.7	0.4	129
2016	A+	Clearwater	0	0	0	3	6	17.42	2.90	8.9	255	52	33	6.94	17.4	17.4	1.0	0.0	-139

Found his control after mid-season move into the rotation (83 K/25 BB in 53.1 IP as a SP). Explosive FB, late-breaking two-plane SL both get swings and misses. Not tall, but strong lower half pumps out easy high-90s velocity and lets him live up in zone. Lack of usable CU likely pushes him to the bullpen long-term, where elements in place for impact RP.

Torrez,Daury

RP | Chicago (N) | EXP MLB DEBUT: 2018 | H/W: 6-3 210 | FUT: Setup reliever | 6C

Thrws R Age 23
2010 FA (DR)

Velo	Pitch	Grade
90-92	FB	+ + +
83-85	SL	+ + +
	CU	+

Year	Lev	Team	W	L	Sv	IP	K	ERA	WHIP	BF/G	OBA	H%	S%	xERA	Ctl	Dom	Cmd	hr/9	BPV
2013	Rk	Azl Cubs	4	2	1	49	49	3.31	1.10	16.0	262	35	69	2.92	0.9	9.0	9.8	0.4	155
2013	A	Kane County	0	1	0	5	2	5.40	1.20	20.1	262	25	60	4.57	1.8	3.6	2.0	1.8	34
2014	A	Kane County	11	7	0	131	81	2.75	1.00	21.8	229	26	74	2.44	1.4	5.6	3.9	0.5	79
2015	A+	Myrtle Beach	10	6	0	134	86	3.76	1.18	22.3	266	30	69	3.55	1.4	5.8	4.1	0.7	84
2016	A+	Myrtle Beach	2	2	2	68	69	3.57	1.37	6.8	278	36	76	4.21	2.5	9.1	3.6	0.8	114

23-year-old Dominican hurler was moved from starting to relief in '16 and showed improved Dom. FB sits at 89-92 mph with good sink. Mixes in a decent SL and a below-average CU. Pounds the strike zone, inducing weak contact and tons of GB outs. Profiles as a set-up reliever.

Toussaint,Touki

SP | Atlanta | EXP MLB DEBUT: 2019 | H/W: 6-3 185 | FUT: #3 starter | 8C

Thrws R Age 20
2014 (1) HS (FL)

Velo	Pitch	Grade
90-94	FB	+ + +
77-78	CB	+ + + + +
83-85	CU	+ + +

Year	Lev	Team	W	L	Sv	IP	K	ERA	WHIP	BF/G	OBA	H%	S%	xERA	Ctl	Dom	Cmd	hr/9	BPV
2014	Rk	Azl Dbacks	1	1	0	15	17	4.80	1.73	9.8	249	36	69	3.97	7.2	10.2	1.4	0.0	7
2014	Rk	Missoula	1	3	0	13	15	12.95	2.27	13.4	392	46	44	10.89	4.1	10.2	2.5	3.4	92
2015	A	Kane County	2	2	0	39	29	3.69	1.18	22.3	220	25	71	3.11	3.5	6.7	1.9	0.9	45
2015	A	Rome	3	5	0	48	38	5.79	1.51	20.9	227	26	63	4.23	6.2	7.1	1.2	1.1	-21
2016	A	Rome	4	8	0	132	128	3.88	1.33	20.3	220	27	73	3.44	4.8	8.7	1.8	0.9	44

ATL rebuilt raw RH from the bottom up. Reworking his delivery, turned this thrower into pitcher, and dominance appeared. By regaining velocity and learning to command FB, plus-plus 12/6 CB was able to rack up 12 K/9 in 2nd half. CU took leap forward as well. Upside.

Travieso,Nicholas

SP | Cincinnati | EXP MLB DEBUT: 2017 | H/W: 6-2 225 | FUT: #4 starter | 7C

Thrws R Age 23
2012 (1) HS (FL)

Velo	Pitch	Grade
93-95	FB	++++
85-87	SL	+++
84-85	CU	++

Year	Lev	Team	W	L	Sv	IP	K	ERA	WHIP	BF/G	OBA	H%	S%	xERA	Ctl	Dom	Cmd	hr/9	BPV
2012	Rk	AZL Reds	0	2	0	21	14	4.71	1.19	10.5	252	27	64	3.91	2.1	6.0	2.8	1.3	68
2013	A	Dayton	7	4	0	81	61	4.66	1.35	19.9	266	31	66	4.02	3.0	6.8	2.3	0.8	59
2014	A	Dayton	14	5	0	142	114	3.04	1.17	21.8	235	28	76	3.01	2.8	7.2	2.6	0.6	73
2015	A+	Daytona	6	6	0	93	76	2.71	1.20	19.7	238	29	78	2.89	2.9	7.3	2.5	0.4	72
2016	AA	Pensacola	5	7	0	117	91	3.84	1.38	21.4	248	29	74	3.91	4.1	7.0	1.7	0.8	34

Another CIN RH pitcher struggling with FB command. FB is clearly best pitch, sitting mid-90s with dynamite sink. SL added extra bite in '16, becoming a swing-and-miss offering. Fringe-average CU continues to make strides. Innings-eating physique.

Tseng,Jen-Ho

SP | Chicago (N) | EXP MLB DEBUT: 2018 | H/W: 6-1 195 | FUT: #5 SP/swingman | 7D

Thrws R Age 22
2013 FA (TW)

Velo	Pitch	Grade
88-91	FB	++
75-78	CB	+++
80-82	CU	++

Year	Lev	Team	W	L	Sv	IP	K	ERA	WHIP	BF/G	OBA	H%	S%	xERA	Ctl	Dom	Cmd	hr/9	BPV
2014	A	Kane County	6	1	0	105	85	2.40	0.87	20.4	204	25	75	1.83	1.3	7.3	5.7	0.6	114
2015	A+	Myrtle Beach	7	7	0	119	87	3.55	1.22	21.8	255	31	70	3.16	2.3	6.6	2.9	0.4	75
2016	AA	Tennessee	6	8	0	113	69	4.30	1.50	22.2	302	34	73	5.10	2.5	5.5	2.2	1.0	48

Taiwanese hurler has fringy 88-91 mph FB and backs it up with a mid-70s CB, and a plus CU. Tseng hides the ball well and locates all three offerings. Raw stuff took a step back at Double-A and his 32 BB/69 K leaves plenty to be desired. Double-A hitters roasted him; a move to relief seems likely.

Tuivailala,Sam

RP | St. Louis | EXP MLB DEBUT: 2014 | H/W: 6-3 225 | FUT: Closer | 7C

Thrws R Age 24
2010 (3) HS (CA)

Velo	Pitch	Grade
95-97	FB	++++
81-83	CB	++
87-89	CT	+++

Year	Lev	Team	W	L	Sv	IP	K	ERA	WHIP	BF/G	OBA	H%	S%	xERA	Ctl	Dom	Cmd	hr/9	BPV
2014	MLB	St. Louis	0	0	0	1		36.00	7.00	4.9	639	62	60	44.98	18.0	9.0	0.5	18.0	-306
2015	AAA	Memphis	3	1	17	45	43	1.60	1.20	4.2	181	24	88	2.20	5.2	8.6	1.7	0.4	32
2015	MLB	St. Louis	0	1	0	14	20	3.17	1.48	4.4	245	35	84	4.45	5.1	12.7	2.5	1.3	109
2016	AAA	Memphis	3	2	17	46	72	5.26	1.49	4.7	265	43	64	4.10	4.3	14.0	3.3	0.6	155
2016	MLB	St. Louis	0	0	0	9	7	6.00	2.00	3.6	321	39	67	5.74	6.0	7.0	1.2	0.0	-18

Dominates with a blazing upper-90s fastball that has good late life and tops out at 100 mph. Struggled all year with control, but still dominated striking out 72 in 46.2 IP at AAA. Potentially plus, but inconsistent CB and CT to fend off lefty bats. Strong body with thick legs gives him an ideal pitching frame so durability shouldn't be an issue.

Turnbull,Spencer

SP | Detroit | EXP MLB DEBUT: 2018 | H/W: 6-3 215 | FUT: #3 starter | 8D

Thrws R Age 24
2014 (2) Alabama

Velo	Pitch	Grade
91-97	FB	++++
83-87	SL	++
81-85	CU	++

Year	Lev	Team	W	L	Sv	IP	K	ERA	WHIP	BF/G	OBA	H%	S%	xERA	Ctl	Dom	Cmd	hr/9	BPV
2014	A-	Connecticut	0	2	0	28	19	4.48	1.60	11.3	281	33	70	4.43	4.5	6.1	1.4	0.3	6
2015	A	West Michigan	11	3	0	116	106	3.02	1.36	22.1	244	32	75	3.00	4.0	8.2	2.0	0.0	57
2016	Rk	GCL Tigers	0	1	0	14	12	4.47	0.92	8.8	150	15	55	1.99	3.8	7.7	2.0	1.3	52
2016	A+	Lakeland	1	1	0	30	27	3.00	1.13	19.8	221	29	73	2.41	3.0	8.1	2.7	0.3	83

Big, strong SP who missed most of season with shoulder impingement. When healthy, establishes plate with very heavy FB and is groundballer. Long arm action and effort in delivery could move him to bullpen down line, but DET interested in FB/SL combo. CU well below average now, but shows ample movement.

Tyler,Robert

SP | Colorado | EXP MLB DEBUT: 2018 | H/W: 6-4 226 | FUT: Closer | 8D

Thrws R Age 21
2016 (S-1) Georgia

Velo	Pitch	Grade
93-96	FB	++++
	CB	++
	CU	+++

Year	Lev	Team	W	L	Sv	IP	K	ERA	WHIP	BF/G	OBA	H%	S%	xERA	Ctl	Dom	Cmd	hr/9	BPV
2016	NCAA	Georgia	3	5	0	74	89	4.12	1.33	22.0	202	29	69	2.95	5.6	10.8	1.9	0.6	62
2016	A-	Boise	0	2	0	7	5	6.43	2.57	7.5	92	12	72	4.40	20.6	6.4	0.3	0.0	-422

1st round compensation pick out of Georgia has a plus mid-90s FB that has good late sink and tops out at 99 mph. CU with good fade is second best offering, but CB is inconsistent and below-average. That could mean a move to relief where he has the stuff to get to the majors quickly and be an impact arm out of the pen.

Underwood,Duane

SP | Chicago (N) | EXP MLB DEBUT: 2018 | H/W: 6-2 210 | FUT: #3 starter | 8D

Thrws R Age 22
2012 (2) HS (GA)

Velo	Pitch	Grade
91-95	FB	++++
86-88	CT	++
82-84	CU	++
80-83	CB	++

Year	Lev	Team	W	L	Sv	IP	K	ERA	WHIP	BF/G	OBA	H%	S%	xERA	Ctl	Dom	Cmd	hr/9	BPV
2015	A+	Myrtle Beach	6	3	0	73	48	2.59	1.04	20.2	201	23	79	2.37	3.0	5.9	2.0	0.7	45
2016	Rk	Azl Cubs	0	0	0	1	2	0.00	1.00	3.8	262	55	100	2.23	0.0	18.0		0.0	342
2016	A	South Bend	0	1	0	8	12	2.20	1.10	10.7	178	31	78	1.48	4.4	13.2	3.0	0.0	137
2016	A+	Myrtle Beach	0	0	0	4	2	2.14	0.71	14.8	202	23	67	0.88	0.0	4.3		0.0	95
2016	AA	Tennessee	0	5	0	58	46	4.95	1.67	20.1	287	33	72	5.39	4.8	7.1	1.5	1.1	17

Attacks hitters with a good 91-95 mph fastball that tops out at 99 mph. He missed action with forearm inflammation in '15 and was limited to 73 IP in'16. Raw stuff has not progressed as quickly as the Cubs would have liked. Backs up the FB with a good, hard CB and an inconsistent CU. Below-average control and command remain his biggest weakness.

Unsworth,Dylan

SP | Seattle | EXP MLB DEBUT: 2017 | H/W: 6-1 175 | FUT: #5 SP/swingman | 6B

Thrws R Age 24
2009 FA (SA)

Velo	Pitch	Grade
86-90	FB	+++
75-78	CB	++
79-82	SL	++
	CU	+++

Year	Lev	Team	W	L	Sv	IP	K	ERA	WHIP	BF/G	OBA	H%	S%	xERA	Ctl	Dom	Cmd	hr/9	BPV
2013	A	Clinton	4	1	0	66	46	2.32	0.91	22.4	238	29	74	2.05	0.3	6.3	23.0	0.3	124
2014	A+	High Desert	6	9	0	119	119	5.89	1.44	19.5	313	39	61	5.40	1.4	9.0	6.3	1.3	141
2015	A+	Bakersfield	1	3	0	40	44	3.36	1.09	14.3	261	34	73	3.37	0.9	9.9	11.0	0.9	171
2015	AA	Jackson	4	7	0	66	51	4.36	1.38	21.3	295	35	69	4.53	1.8	6.9	3.9	0.8	95
2016	AA	Jackson	3	1	0	46	35	1.17	1.06	19.9	244	30	91	2.61	1.4	6.8	5.0	0.4	104

Control-oriented SP who ended season in early June after leg injury. Mixes pitches with precision and locates offerings at will. Repeats simple delivery and rarely walks hitters. Lacks frontline stuff and velocity and doesn't project well with K rate. Could upgrade CB or SL to give him third average pitch. Good CU gives him chance against LHH.

Vargas,Emilio

SP | Arizona | EXP MLB DEBUT: 2019 | H/W: 6-3 200 | FUT: #4 starter | 8E

Thrws R Age 20
2013 FA (DR)

Velo	Pitch	Grade
92-94	FB	++++
82-84	SL	++
	CU	++

Year	Lev	Team	W	L	Sv	IP	K	ERA	WHIP	BF/G	OBA	H%	S%	xERA	Ctl	Dom	Cmd	hr/9	BPV
2015	Rk	Azl Dbacks	5	1	1	53	49	2.54	1.11	16.1	235	31	75	2.25	2.2	8.3	3.8	0.0	108
2015	Rk	Missoula	1	0	0	4	3	0.00	1.00	7.6	210	27	100	1.67	2.3	6.8	3.0	0.0	79
2015	A+	Visalia	0	0	0	2	3	12.27	2.73	12.2	446	61	50	10.01	4.1	12.3	3.0	0.0	128
2016	A	Kane County	5	6	0	70	69	3.33	1.15	21.5	241	30	74	3.28	2.3	8.8	3.8	0.9	115
2016	A+	Visalia	0	0	0	15	15	7.80	1.80	17.3	321	40	56	6.34	4.2	9.0	2.1	1.2	67

Hard throwing RH enjoyed mid-season dominance after scrapping CB. FB up to 95 with late movement. Secondary pitches lag behind FB. SL has inconsistent 2-plane movement. Has feel for CU, needs to use it more often. Struck out 17 batters in one MWL game.

Voelker,Paul

RP | Detroit | EXP MLB DEBUT: 2017 | H/W: 5-10 185 | FUT: Setup reliever | 6B

Thrws R Age 24
2014 (10) Dallas Baptist

Velo	Pitch	Grade
91-95	FB	+++
83-87	SL	++
	CU	+

Year	Lev	Team	W	L	Sv	IP	K	ERA	WHIP	BF/G	OBA	H%	S%	xERA	Ctl	Dom	Cmd	hr/9	BPV
2014	A-	Connecticut	0	1	1	25	31	2.52	1.08	6.1	203	30	77	2.09	3.2	11.2	3.4	0.4	131
2015	A	West Michigan	2	0	2	16	20	2.25	0.81	5.8	166	26	69	0.66	2.3	11.3	5.0	0.0	160
2015	A+	Lakeland	3	0	7	22	26	1.64	1.05	6.1	215	31	86	2.19	2.5	10.6	4.3	0.4	143
2015	AA	Erie	1	1	9	17	17	2.63	1.40	4.5	225	29	83	3.35	5.3	8.9	1.7	0.5	37
2016	AA	Erie	3	4	13	54	79	4.17	1.44	4.4	262	39	75	4.49	4.0	13.2	3.3	1.2	147

Short RP with surprising Dom. Lacks the look of late innings arm, but retires hitters with two pitches and max-effort delivery. Plane to plate is flat and can be victimized by HR. Hasn't found success against LHH, though RHH have trouble squaring up moving FB. Size will always work against him, but has chance to be big league RP.

Voth,Austin

SP | Washington | EXP MLB DEBUT: 2017 | H/W: 6-2 215 | FUT: #5 SP/swingman | 7C

Thrws R Age 24
2013 (5) Washington

Velo	Pitch	Grade
87-89	FB	+++
82-83	SL	+++
79-81	CU	++
74-77	CB	++

Year	Lev	Team	W	L	Sv	IP	K	ERA	WHIP	BF/G	OBA	H%	S%	xERA	Ctl	Dom	Cmd	hr/9	BPV
2014	A	Hagerstown	4	3	0	69	74	2.47	1.05	20.6	207	29	75	1.87	2.9	9.6	3.4	0.1	114
2014	A+	Potomac	2	1	0	37	40	1.45	0.62	21.3	132	18	81	0.29	1.7	9.7	5.7	0.5	146
2014	AA	Harrisburg	1	3	0	19	19	6.60	1.62	17.0	290	34	63	6.06	4.2	9.0	2.1	1.9	65
2015	AA	Harrisburg	6	7	0	157	148	2.92	1.11	22.0	232	30	75	2.74	2.3	8.5	3.7	0.6	109
2016	AAA	Syracuse	7	9	0	157	133	3.15	1.24	23.6	238	29	76	3.21	3.3	7.6	2.3	0.6	67

Control-and-command pitcher who will only survive on plus location. FB/SL combination will be his bread and butter, but keeping hitters off balance will be key, and doesn't have one outstanding pitch. Has some good outings, but some skepticism stuff will play at highest level.

Waddell,Brandon

SP | Pittsburgh | EXP MLB DEBUT: 2018 | H/W: 6-3 180 | FUT: #5 SP/swingman | 6C

Thrws L Age 22
2015 (5) Virginia

Velo	Pitch	Grade
89-93	FB	++
	CB	++
	CU	++

Year	Lev	Team	W	L	Sv	IP	K	ERA	WHIP	BF/G	OBA	H%	S%	xERA	Ctl	Dom	Cmd	hr/9	BPV
2015	NCAA	Virginia	5	5	0	110	89	3.93	1.48	24.9	269	33	72	3.95	4.0	7.3	1.8	0.3	41
2015	A-	West Virginia	1	1	0	20	18	5.82	1.54	14.6	297	38	58	4.21	3.1	8.1	2.6	0.0	78
2016	A+	Bradenton	4	0	0	29	26	0.93	0.52	19.4	137	18	86		0.6	8.1	13.0	0.3	146
2016	AA	Altoona	7	9	0	118	94	4.12	1.55	23.4	268	32	74	4.46	4.7	7.2	1.5	0.7	21

Projectable lefty remains inconsistent, but has a potential three-pitch mix. FB sits at 88-93 mph and is backed by a solid 11/5 CB and an avg CU. Showed an ability to change speeds and keep hitters off-balance, but struggles with control, walking 63 in 147 IP. Could develop into a decent back-end starter.

Wagner,Tyler — SP — Texas

EXP MLB DEBUT: 2015 | H/W: 6-3 205 | FUT: #4 starter | 7C

Thrws R Age 26
2012 (4) Utah
89-93 FB +++
82-85 SL +++
81-85 CU ++

Year	Lev	Team	W	L	Sv	IP	K	ERA	WHIP	BF/G	OBA	H%	S%	xERA	Ctl	Dom	Cmd	hr/9	BPV
2014	A+	Brevard County	13	6	0	150	118	1.86	1.11	23.6	218	26	87	2.60	2.9	7.1	2.5	0.6	68
2015	AA	Biloxi	11	5	0	152	120	2.25	1.15	24.2	233	28	82	2.72	2.7	7.1	2.7	0.4	74
2015	MLB	Milwaukee	0	2	0	13	5	7.50	2.20	22.1	371	39	64	7.80	4.8	3.4	0.7	0.7	-50
2016	AAA	Reno	1	4	0	26	15	3.09	1.53	22.8	282	32	79	4.29	3.8	5.2	1.4	0.3	9
2016	MLB	Arizona	1	0	0	10	7	2.70	1.10	13.1	242	30	73	2.33	1.8	6.3	3.5	0.0	83

Sinkerballer who ended season in early May due to injury. Claimed off waivers from ARI and is now in 3rd org. Uses low 3/4 slot and repeats delivery consistently, allowing for solid command of 3 pitch mix. Thrives with sinker low in zone to induce high amount of groundballs. CU needs polish, but SL serves as out pitch.

Wahl,Bobby — RP — Oakland

EXP MLB DEBUT: 2017 | H/W: 6-2 210 | FUT: Setup reliever | 8E

Thrws R Age 25
2013 (5) Mississippi
92-97 FB ++++
82-84 CB +++
80-82 CU ++

Year	Lev	Team	W	L	Sv	IP	K	ERA	WHIP	BF/G	OBA	H%	S%	xERA	Ctl	Dom	Cmd	hr/9	BPV
2014	A+	Stockton	0	0	0	10	19	4.41	1.37	4.8	218	38	75	4.26	5.3	16.8	3.2	1.8	177
2015	AA	Midland	2	0	4	32	36	4.21	1.56	5.9	285	38	73	4.56	3.9	10.1	2.6	0.6	94
2016	A+	Stockton	0	0	0	4	3	6.75	2.00	6.4	210	27	63	4.19	11.3	6.8	0.6	0.0	-164
2016	AA	Midland	0	1	10	40	48	2.24	1.07	4.7	187	26	83	2.17	3.8	10.7	2.8	0.7	109
2016	AAA	Nashville	1	0	4	9	14	2.93	1.41	4.3	212	37	77	2.67	5.9	13.7	2.3	0.0	106

Big-framed RP who found niche in pen. Posts high K rate in short stints while upping quality of FB and hard CB. Works quickly and likes to challenge hitters inside. FB can be straight at times and has difficulty keeping delivery intact. Walks too many hitters, but has fast arm and should get better with more time on mound. Minor injuries in past.

Walsh,Connor — RP — Chicago (A)

EXP MLB DEBUT: 2017 | H/W: 6-2 180 | FUT: Setup reliever | 6B

Thrws R Age 24
2014 (12) Cincinnati
92-96 FB +++
80-83 CB +++

Year	Lev	Team	W	L	Sv	IP	K	ERA	WHIP	BF/G	OBA	H%	S%	xERA	Ctl	Dom	Cmd	hr/9	BPV
2015	A	Kannapolis	2	3	0	53		4.92	1.57	8.0	207	34	68	3.47	7.5	13.4	1.8	0.5	58
2016	Rk	Azl White Sox	0	0	0	1	3	0.00	0.00	2.8	0	0			0.0	27.0		0.0	504
2016	A+	Winston-Salem	2	2	5	39	41	3.44	1.20	6.3	202	28	70	2.27	4.4	9.4	2.2	0.2	70
2016	AA	Birmingham	0	0	0	7	7	5.00	1.67	5.4	256	34	67	3.92	6.3	8.8	1.4	0.0	7

Career RP who exhibited much better control, but still struggles with command. FB inching up in velocity and could evolve to plus offering. Violent delivery creates deception and can retire hitters with hard CB. Doesn't allow many HR, and lives in lower half of zone. Needs to continue to focus on FB location to succeed.

Warren,Art — SP — Seattle

EXP MLB DEBUT: 2018 | H/W: 6-3 230 | FUT: #4 starter | 7D

Thrws R Age 24
2015 (23) Ashland
88-94 FB +++
75-79 CB +++
80-84 CU ++

Year	Lev	Team	W	L	Sv	IP	K	ERA	WHIP	BF/G	OBA	H%	S%	xERA	Ctl	Dom	Cmd	hr/9	BPV
2015	Rk	Azl Mariners	1	0	0	7	10	3.86	1.43	5.0	262	42	70	3.36	3.9	12.9	3.3	0.0	145
2016	A	Clinton	9	1	0	74	55	2.19	1.20	21.3	254	31	81	2.86	2.2	6.7	3.1	0.1	79
2016	A+	Bakersfield	2	1	0	36	38	5.22	1.93	13.2	291	39	71	5.32	7.0	9.4	1.4	0.2	0

Sleeper prospect who was knocked around in A+ upon promotion and moved to pen, but showed signs of recovery. Establishes plate with solid-average FB that he commands well. Can be straight at times, but has good velocity. Mixes in very good CB that he throws for strikes and promising CU. Missed most of '15 after TJS and could throw harder.

Watson,Nolan — SP — Kansas City

EXP MLB DEBUT: 2019 | H/W: 6-2 195 | FUT: #3 starter | 8E

Thrws R Age 20
2015 (1) HS (IN)
90-93 FB +++
81-84 CB ++
CU ++

Year	Lev	Team	W	L	Sv	IP	K	ERA	WHIP	BF/G	OBA	H%	S%	xERA	Ctl	Dom	Cmd	hr/9	BPV
2015	Rk	Burlington	0	3	0	29	16	4.95	1.72	12.0	322	36	71	5.65	3.4	4.9	1.5	0.6	15
2016	A	Lexington	3	11	0	96	60	7.59	1.76	18.3	316	33	59	6.73	4.1	5.6	1.4	1.8	8

Projectable SP who struggled all season and didn't have one positive month. Can be very hittable as pitches lack movement, though FB has shown plus sinking action in past. Had trouble missing bats with CB and was behind in count far too often. Has natural stuff to improve drastically and has athletic, repeatable delivery to upgrade command.

Watson,Tyler — SP — Washington

EXP MLB DEBUT: 2021 | H/W: 6-5 200 | FUT: #4 starter | 7D

Thrws L Age 19
2015 (34) HS (AZ)
89-92 FB +++
75-76 CB ++
80-84 CU ++

Year	Lev	Team	W	L	Sv	IP	K	ERA	WHIP	BF/G	OBA	H%	S%	xERA	Ctl	Dom	Cmd	hr/9	BPV
2015	Rk	GCL Nationals	1	1	0	13	16	0.00	0.84	9.6	159	25	100	0.65	2.7	11.0	4.0	0.0	142
2016	A-	Auburn	1	2	0	43	48	1.88	0.91	17.8	198	28	79	1.46	1.9	10.0	5.3	0.2	148
2016	A	Hagerstown	1	1	0	15	16	4.80	1.47	21.4	274	38	64	3.66	3.6	9.6	2.7	0.0	94

A tall and projectable lefty, he has some effort and funk to his delivery that could be smoothed out. Creates deception now, but also affects command as he attempts to coordinate his long levers. Best when spotting his low-90s FB and downer CB low in the zone. CU still developing, and a chance that he add some velocity as he fills out.

Weaver,Luke — SP — St. Louis

EXP MLB DEBUT: 2016 | H/W: 6-2 170 | FUT: #3 starter | 8C

Thrws R Age 23
2014 (1) Florida State
90-94 FB +++
79-81 CB ++
78-81 CU ++++

Year	Lev	Team	W	L	Sv	IP	K	ERA	WHIP	BF/G	OBA	H%	S%	xERA	Ctl	Dom	Cmd	hr/9	BPV
2014	A+	Palm Beach	0	1	0	3	3	23.23	4.84	11.9	557	64	50	21.49	11.6	8.7	0.8	2.9	-139
2015	A+	Palm Beach	8	5	0	105	88	1.63	1.11	21.8	248	32	85	2.60	1.6	7.5	4.6	0.2	110
2016	AA	Springfield	6	3	0	77	88	1.40	0.95	24.2	225	31	88	2.13	1.2	10.3	8.8	0.5	172
2016	AAA	Memphis	1	0	0	6	4	0.00	0.67	20.9	106	13	100		3.0	6.0	2.0	0.0	45
2016	MLB	St. Louis	1	4	0	36	45	5.73	1.61	17.8	311	41	69	6.19	3.0	11.2	3.8	1.7	139

Comes after hitters with a good 90-94 mph FB that hits 98 mph. Keeps the ball down in the zone and gets nice late action. Improved mechanics results in plus Cmd and walked just 12 in 83 IP. Mixes in a decent SL and a plus CU that has good late fade and sink. Held his own in MLB debut. Breakout candidate in 2017.

Weigel,Patrick — SP — Atlanta

EXP MLB DEBUT: 2018 | H/W: 6-6 220 | FUT: Setup reliever | 8E

Thrws R Age 22
2015 (7) Houston
92-95 FB ++++
75-77 CB +++
83-86 SL ++
82-84 CU ++

Year	Lev	Team	W	L	Sv	IP	K	ERA	WHIP	BF/G	OBA	H%	S%	xERA	Ctl	Dom	Cmd	hr/9	BPV
2015	NCAA	Houston	4	1	2	50	45	3.41	1.08	8.5	194	25	67	2.00	3.6	8.1	2.3	0.4	66
2015	Rk	Danville	0	3	0	51	49	4.57	1.54	16.0	269	35	69	4.11	4.6	8.6	1.9	0.4	50
2016	A	Rome	10	4	0	129	135	2.51	1.08	22.9	202	27	78	2.20	3.3	9.4	2.9	0.5	99
2016	AA	Mississippi	1	2	0	20	17	2.23	0.84	24.7	136	15	80	1.30	3.6	7.6	2.1	0.9	58

College reliever made Single-A starter was revelation of farm system in '16. Featuring four solid pitches, only his FB and CB has potential to be MLB quality pitches. Loads of pitchability in package, can command FB and CB to catcher's glove. SL is flat and CU lacks solid fade. Likely a RP as a MLB pitcher.

Wells,Alex — SP — Baltimore

EXP MLB DEBUT: 2020 | H/W: 6-1 190 | FUT: #4 starter | 7D

Thrws R Age 20
2015 FA (AU)
86-91 FB +++
74-77 CB ++
80-83 CU +++

Year	Lev	Team	W	L	Sv	IP	K	ERA	WHIP	BF/G	OBA	H%	S%	xERA	Ctl	Dom	Cmd	hr/9	BPV
2016	A-	Aberdeen	4	5	0	62	50	2.17	0.92	17.9	215	27	75	1.65	1.3	7.2	5.6	0.1	113

Young, savvy SP who may not stand out for pitch mix, but has polish for age. Works with three offerings that he throws for strikes at any count. Can pitch backwards and use CU early in count. Spots FB anywhere he wants and could add velocity with strength. Tends to leave CB up in zone and is generally flyball pitcher. Not much upside.

Wells,Lachlan — SP — Minnesota

EXP MLB DEBUT: 2020 | H/W: 5-8 165 | FUT: #4 starter | 7D

Thrws R Age 20
2014 FA (AU)
87-92 FB +++
74-77 CB ++
79-84 CU +++

Year	Lev	Team	W	L	Sv	IP	K	ERA	WHIP	BF/G	OBA	H%	S%	xERA	Ctl	Dom	Cmd	hr/9	BPV
2016	A	Cedar Rapids	6	4	0	71	63	1.77	1.03	22.8	221	28	86	2.34	2.0	8.0	3.9	0.5	107

Short, wiry SP who thrives with deception and quick arm. Lacks strength and doesn't project to much with velocity. Commands plate with precision and throws quality strikes to all quadrants of zone. Can leave CB up in zone, but generally messes with hitters timing. Needs to add significant weight and strength to provide durability.

Wendelken,J.B. — RP — Oakland

EXP MLB DEBUT: 2016 | H/W: 6-0 220 | FUT: Middle reliever | 6B

Thrws R Age 24
2012 (13) Mid Georgia JC
89-93 FB ++
81-82 SL ++
77-79 CU ++++

Year	Lev	Team	W	L	Sv	IP	K	ERA	WHIP	BF/G	OBA	H%	S%	xERA	Ctl	Dom	Cmd	hr/9	BPV
2014	A+	Winston-Salem	7	10	0	145	129	5.27	1.47	23.1	307	37	65	5.05	2.0	8.0	3.9	0.9	107
2015	AA	Birmingham	6	2	5	43	56	2.72	1.09	6.2	229	33	79	2.88	2.3	11.7	5.1	0.8	167
2015	AAA	Charlotte	0	0	0	16	13	4.50	1.19	5.3	237	27	65	3.53	2.8	7.3	2.6	1.1	74
2016	AAA	Nashville	1	4	5	46	65	4.11	1.61	5.2	270	40	77	4.85	5.1	12.7	2.5	1.0	110
2016	MLB	Oakland	0	0	0	12	12	10.33	2.21	7.7	343	40	54	8.72	6.6	8.9	1.3	2.2	-2

Short, thick RP who has spent most of career in pen. Unusual repertoire for RP as he uses CU a lot. Has deceptive arm action and speed and effectively pitches backwards. Has little stamina and had elbow injury at end of season. Upgrade of SL would give him chance to miss bats with true out pitch. Lot of effort in delivery and has fringy velocity.

Wentz,Joey — SP — Atlanta

EXP MLB DEBUT: 2020 | H/W: 6-5 210 | FUT: #2 starter | 8D

Thrws L Age 19
2016 (S-1) HS (KS)

- 89-93 FB ++++
- 75-77 CB +++
- CU +++

Year	Lev	Team	W	L	Sv	IP	K	ERA	WHIP	BF/G	OBA	H%	S%	xERA	Ctl	Dom	Cmd	hr/9	BPV
2016	Rk	GCL Braves	0	0	0	12	18	0.00	0.67	10.5	81	16	100		3.8	13.5	3.6	0.0	160
2016	Rk	Danville	1	4	0	32	35	5.06	1.59	17.7	256	36	65	3.72	5.6	9.8	1.8	0.0	43

LH pitcher propelled himself high on draft boards after a spring awakening. FB up to mid 90s, sitting 89-93. A big kid, velocity should continue to increase. 12/6 hammer curve very promising. Secondary pitches have potential to be average or better offerings when developed. Can command all pitches in zone. Pro struggles likely due to arm fatigue.

Whalen,Rob — SP — Seattle

EXP MLB DEBUT: 2016 | H/W: 6-2 220 | FUT: #4 starter | 7C

Thrws R Age 23
2012 (12) HS (PA)

- 88-91 FB +++
- 79-82 SL +++
- 73-75 CB ++
- 81-83 CU +++

Year	Lev	Team	W	L	Sv	IP	K	ERA	WHIP	BF/G	OBA	H%	S%	xERA	Ctl	Dom	Cmd	hr/9	BPV
2015	A+	Carolina	1	2	0	13	7	3.41	1.14	17.4	228	23	77	3.54	2.7	4.8	1.8	1.4	30
2015	A+	St. Lucie	4	5	0	83	61	3.36	1.28	22.7	235	28	74	3.09	3.7	6.6	1.8	0.4	38
2016	AA	Mississippi	7	5	0	101	94	2.49	1.23	22.7	234	30	80	2.86	3.3	8.4	2.5	0.4	80
2016	AAA	Gwinnett	0	1	0	18	18	1.98	1.04	23.4	190	26	79	1.52	3.5	8.9	2.6	0.0	85
2016	MLB	Atlanta	1	2	0	24	25	6.69	1.32	20.0	227	27	50	4.06	4.5	9.3	2.1	1.5	65

Acquired in Alex Jackson trade, RHP advanced 3 levels to make MLB debut. Throws kitchen sink. Struggles to command 2-seam FB, has high BB rate as result. SL has taken step forward; is the secondary pitch he relies on. CB used exclusively to change eye levels. CU was his best pitch in minors but was used scarcely in big league debut. Struggles with health.

White,Mitchell — SP — Los Angeles (N)

EXP MLB DEBUT: 2019 | H/W: 6-4 205 | FUT: #3 starter | 8D

Thrws R Age 22
2016 (2) Santa Clara

- 92-95 FB +++
- 86-88 CT ++++
- 75-78 CB ++
- CU +++

Year	Lev	Team	W	L	Sv	IP	K	ERA	WHIP	BF/G	OBA	H%	S%	xERA	Ctl	Dom	Cmd	hr/9	BPV
2016	NCAA	Santa Clara	3	6	0	92	118	3.72	1.27	25.1	258	38	71	3.38	2.6	11.5	4.4	0.5	154
2016	Rk	Azl Dodgers	0	0	0	4	8	0.00	0.75	7.1	210	48	100	0.93	0.0	18.0		0.0	342
2016	A	Great Lakes	0	0	0	16	20	0.00	0.56	6.8	62	11	100		3.4	11.3	3.3	0.0	129
2016	A+	Rancho Cuca	1	0	0	2	2	0.00	0.50	6.6	151	22	100		0.0	9.0		0.0	180

2nd round pick had TJS after Sr. year in HS before a standout career at Santa Clara. Has a nice four-pitch mix. FB sits at 92-95 mph with late life and is backed up by a plus CT, CB, and CU. Features solid FB command and pounds the zone, walking just 6 in 22 IP in his debut.

Whitley,Forrest — SP — Houston

EXP MLB DEBUT: 2020 | H/W: 6-7 240 | FUT: #2 starter | 9D

Thrws R Age 19
2016 (1) HS (TX)

- 91-94 FB +++
- 83-85 SL +++
- 79-83 CB ++
- CU ++

Year	Lev	Team	W	L	Sv	IP	K	ERA	WHIP	BF/G	OBA	H%	S%	xERA	Ctl	Dom	Cmd	hr/9	BPV
2016	Rk	GCL Astros	0	1	0	4	6	10.98	1.71	6.2	302	47	29	4.64	4.4	13.2	3.0	0.0	137
2016	Rk	Greeneville	0	1	0	11	13	3.24	1.26	11.3	260	38	71	2.93	2.4	10.5	4.3	0.0	142

Big-framed SP with very high upside, yet has shown feel for pitching and clean delivery. Arm strength is among best in org and can fire plus FB into strike zone. Can miss bats with both FB and hard SL as both exhibit plus movement. Slows arm speed on CU and needs to enhance, but has shown aptitude. Some effort in delivery.

Wieck,Brad — RP — San Diego

EXP MLB DEBUT: 2018 | H/W: 6-9 255 | FUT: Middle reliever | 7C

Thrws L Age 25
2014 (7) Oklahoma City

- 90-93 FB ++++
- 73-75 CB ++
- 82-84 CU +++

Year	Lev	Team	W	L	Sv	IP	K	ERA	WHIP	BF/G	OBA	H%	S%	xERA	Ctl	Dom	Cmd	hr/9	BPV
2015	A	Fort Wayne	2	0	0	10	12	2.67	1.09	19.7	219	33	73	1.97	2.7	10.7	4.0	0.0	138
2015	A	Savannah	3	5	0	56	74	3.21	1.34	23.3	255	38	75	3.35	3.4	11.9	3.5	0.3	141
2015	A+	Lake Elsinore	2	6	0	57	53	5.21	1.53	22.5	275	34	67	4.72	4.1	8.4	2.0	0.9	58
2016	A+	Lake Elsinore	3	1	1	41	62	1.54	1.22	6.4	227	39	86	2.37	3.5	13.6	3.9	0.0	168
2016	AA	San Antonio	1	0	0	20	31	0.45	0.90	5.0	150	28	94	0.67	3.6	13.9	3.9	0.0	171

Tall, sturdy LH became full-time reliever in '15. Excelled in High-A & Double-A but struggled in AFL. Uses 6'9" frame to create downward plane in delivery. 2-seam FB has little movement and must rely on good command. 12/6 CB is slow and loopy. Has an above-average CU he uses against RHH. Could be a reverse-split pitcher.

Wilcox,Kyle — RP — Seattle

EXP MLB DEBUT: 2018 | H/W: 6-3 195 | FUT: Setup reliever | 8E

Thrws R Age 22
2015 (6) Bryant

- 90-97 FB +++
- 79-83 CB ++
- CU ++

Year	Lev	Team	W	L	Sv	IP	K	ERA	WHIP	BF/G	OBA	H%	S%	xERA	Ctl	Dom	Cmd	hr/9	BPV
2015	NCAA	Bryant	7	3	0	80	50	3.25	1.23	21.7	212	26	71	2.30	4.3	5.6	1.3	0.0	4
2015	A-	Everett	2	3	9	23	24	3.51	1.17	4.8	187	25	69	2.17	4.7	9.4	2.0	0.4	60
2016	A	Clinton	4	5	0	76	80	7.11	1.86	9.9	254	35	58	4.58	8.1	9.5	1.2	0.2	-29

Live-armed pitcher who converted to RP in May due to mechanical difficulties and poor control. Has upside as reliever with potential plus FB and knockout CB. Tends to get on side of CB and lacks feel for changing speeds. If he can iron out delivery, has a chance to be high Dom pitcher in short stints.

Williams,Devin — SP — Milwaukee

EXP MLB DEBUT: 2018 | H/W: 6-3 165 | FUT: #3 starter | 8D

Thrws R Age 22
2013 (2) HS (MO)

- 91-94 FB ++++
- 82-85 SL +++
- CU +++

Year	Lev	Team	W	L	Sv	IP	K	ERA	WHIP	BF/G	OBA	H%	S%	xERA	Ctl	Dom	Cmd	hr/9	BPV
2013	Rk	Azl Brewers	1	3	1	34	39	3.42	1.46	11.3	225	33	74	2.99	5.8	10.3	1.8	0.0	46
2014	Rk	Helena	4	7	0	66	66	4.49	1.42	18.7	284	36	69	4.34	2.7	9.0	3.3	0.7	106
2015	A	Wisconsin	3	9	0	89	89	3.44	1.25	16.5	230	31	71	2.81	3.6	9.0	2.5	0.3	82
2016	A	Wisconsin	6	3	2	72	74	3.62	1.36	17.7	239	32	73	3.39	4.2	9.2	2.2	0.5	70
2016	A+	Brevard County	1	2	0	25	20	4.32	1.56	21.9	277	33	73	4.63	4.3	7.2	1.7	0.7	31

Long, lean RH who has split time as SP/RP as pro. Free and easy arm action produces 91-94 mph FB; chance to add tick of velo with added mass. Flashes feel for late-fading CU and complements with solid-average SL. Command needs work, but is good athlete and should develop it. Mid-rotation upside, but production as late-inning RP has been impressive.

Williams,Ronnie — SP — St. Louis

EXP MLB DEBUT: 2019 | H/W: 6-0 170 | FUT: #4 starter | 7C

Thrws R Age 21
2014 (2) HS (FL)

- 92-95 FB +++
- CB ++
- CU ++

Year	Lev	Team	W	L	Sv	IP	K	ERA	WHIP	BF/G	OBA	H%	S%	xERA	Ctl	Dom	Cmd	hr/9	BPV
2014	Rk	GCL Cardinals	0	5	1	36	30	4.74	1.33	15.0	277	35	62	3.61	2.2	7.5	3.3	0.2	92
2015	Rk	Johnson City	3	3	0	56	43	3.70	1.25	19.0	222	26	72	3.20	4.0	6.9	1.7	0.8	34
2016	A-	State College	4	2	0	46	33	2.73	0.95	24.9	222	27	70	1.89	1.4	6.4	4.7	0.2	97
2016	A	Peoria	1	3	0	35	36	4.35	1.36	24.5	238	28	76	4.59	4.3	9.2	2.1	1.8	66

Small, athletic righty pounds the strike zone with a plus 92-95 mph FB. Throws a CT and a CB though both are below average. Shows some feel for a CU and this will be key to his development with only an average breaking ball. There is some effort to his high ¾ delivery, but he has good front-side mechanics and a nice compact motion.

Williams,Ryan — SP — Chicago (N)

EXP MLB DEBUT: 2018 | H/W: 6-4 220 | FUT: #4 starter | 7C

Thrws R Age 25
2014 (10) East Carolina

- 90-92 FB +++
- 82-84 SL ++
- 78-80 CB ++

Year	Lev	Team	W	L	Sv	IP	K	ERA	WHIP	BF/G	OBA	H%	S%	xERA	Ctl	Dom	Cmd	hr/9	BPV
2014	Rk	Azl Cubs	1	0	0	2	3	0.00	0.50	3.3	151	27	100		0.0	13.5		0.0	261
2014	A-	Boise	1	1	1	24	26	1.49	0.95	10.1	227	30	90	2.42	1.1	9.7	8.7	0.7	162
2015	A	South Bend	4	1	0	53	37	1.18	0.71	20.9	194	24	82	0.76	0.3	6.3	18.5	0.0	122
2015	AA	Tennessee	10	2	0	88	61	2.76	1.01	19.8	227	28	71	2.11	1.6	6.2	3.8	0.2	86
2016	AAA	Iowa	4	1	0	44	30	3.27	1.25	19.9	257	29	76	3.68	2.5	6.1	2.5	0.8	62

Strong, physically mature righty competes well despite not being overpowering. Was limited to 44 IP before being shut down with a sore shoulder. Best pitch is an 88-91 mph sinking FB that he keeps down in the zone and induces tons of GB out. Lacks a quality secondary offering, but has a 2.20 career ERA.

Williams,Trevor — SP — Pittsburgh

EXP MLB DEBUT: 2016 | H/W: 6-3 230 | FUT: #5 SP/swingman | 6B

Thrws R Age 24
2013 (2) Arizona State

- 90-93 FB +++
- 77-80 CU +++
- 83-85 SL ++
- CB ++

Year	Lev	Team	W	L	Sv	IP	K	ERA	WHIP	BF/G	OBA	H%	S%	xERA	Ctl	Dom	Cmd	hr/9	BPV
2015	AA	Jacksonville	7	8	0	117	88	4.00	1.38	22.4	276	33	72	4.16	2.8	6.8	2.4	0.7	65
2015	AAA	New Orleans	0	2	0	14	13	2.57	1.57	20.5	275	36	82	3.95	4.5	8.4	1.9	0.0	47
2016	A+	Bradenton	1	0	0	5	4	0.00	0.80	18.1	221	28	100	1.30	0.0	7.2		0.0	148
2016	AAA	Indianapolis	9	6	0	110	74	2.53	1.21	22.2	249	29	80	3.08	2.5	6.0	2.5	0.4	61
2016	MLB	Pittsburgh	1	1	0	12	11	8.11	1.97	8.3	356	39	65	9.01	3.7	8.1	2.2	3.0	64

Big, durable righty has an avg FB that sits in the low-90s and he complements with an above-average CU that has good fade. Also mixes in a SL and a get-me-over CB. None of his offerings are plus. Has a good idea of how to set up hitters and throws tons of strikes. Was roughed up in MLB debut. Back-end starter at best.

Wood,Hunter — SP — Tampa Bay

EXP MLB DEBUT: 2017 | H/W: 6-1 175 | FUT: #4 starter | 7D

Thrws R Age 23
2013 (29) Howard JC

- 89-94 FB +++
- 77-80 CB +++
- 81-82 SL ++
- CU ++

Year	Lev	Team	W	L	Sv	IP	K	ERA	WHIP	BF/G	OBA	H%	S%	xERA	Ctl	Dom	Cmd	hr/9	BPV
2014	A	Bowling Green	1	0	0	24	21	4.11	1.41	17.0	245	28	77	4.53	4.5	7.8	1.8	1.5	38
2015	A	Bowling Green	1	4	4	64	81	1.83	0.81	11.6	166	25	80	1.05	2.2	11.4	5.1	0.4	162
2015	A+	Charlotte	1	3	0	42	32	2.79	0.98	17.7	213	26	70	1.85	1.9	6.9	3.6	0.2	89
2016	A+	Charlotte	3	3	0	63	56	1.71	0.92	21.5	160	21	82	1.16	3.4	8.0	2.3	0.3	69
2016	AA	Montgomery	6	2	0	49	49	3.30	1.14	19.4	206	26	75	2.82	3.7	9.0	2.5	0.9	81

Intriguing SP with no plus pitches, but hitters have trouble squaring him up. Can rear back and add ticks to FB, but effective low in zone. Works with plus arm speed which adds deception to improving CU. Uses two breaking balls in arsenal with varying shapes, but needs to throw more quality strikes to win big league role.

Woodford,Jake — SP — St. Louis

EXP MLB DEBUT: 2019 | H/W: 6-4 210 | FUT: #3 starter | 8D

Thrws R Age 20
2015 (S-1) HS (FL)

Velo	Pitch	Grade
90-93	FB	+ + +
	SL	+ + +
	CU	+ +

Year	Lev	Team	W	L	Sv	IP	K	ERA	WHIP	BF/G	OBA	H%	S%	xERA	Ctl	Dom	Cmd	hr/9	BPV
2015	Rk	GCL Cardinals	1	0	1	26	21	2.41	1.26	13.3	261	32	81	3.31	2.4	7.2	3.0	0.3	83
2016	A	Peoria	5	5	0	108	82	3.33	1.30	21.2	254	30	75	3.54	3.1	6.8	2.2	0.6	58

39th pick in the 2015 draft was signed to an over-slot $1.8 million. Features a good 90-93 mph sinking FB that hits 95 mph. Also has a SL and CU, both of which flash at least average. Tall, strong-bodied has added velocity and has room for more and had a solid full-season debut in the MWL.

Woodruff,Brandon — SP — Milwaukee

EXP MLB DEBUT: 2017 | H/W: 6-4 215 | FUT: #4 starter | 7B

Thrws R Age 24
2014 (11) Mississippi State

Velo	Pitch	Grade
90-93	FB	+ + +
	SL	+ + +
	CU	+ + +

Year	Lev	Team	W	L	Sv	IP	K	ERA	WHIP	BF/G	OBA	H%	S%	xERA	Ctl	Dom	Cmd	hr/9	BPV
2014	NCAA	Mississippi St	1	3	0	37	29	6.79	1.94	11.8	310	38	61	5.41	6.1	7.0	1.2	0.0	-19
2014	Rk	Helena	1	2	0	46	37	3.31	1.39	13.9	269	33	76	3.77	3.1	7.2	2.3	0.4	64
2015	A+	Brevard County	4	7	0	109	71	3.46	1.33	21.6	267	32	72	3.40	2.7	5.9	2.2	0.2	50
2016	A+	Brevard County	4	1	0	44	49	1.84	0.98	20.9	210	29	83	1.96	2.0	10.0	4.9	0.4	143
2016	AA	Biloxi	10	8	0	113	124	3.02	1.04	21.9	216	30	70	2.12	2.4	9.9	4.1	0.3	131

Matured, durable SP who led SL starters in FIP, Dom, and WHIP. Works ahead and spots heavy, low-90s FB effectively for tons of weak contact. Lacks plus secondary pitch, but sequences average SL/CU combo well enough and keeps hitters off balance. Dom production a bit misleading given stuff, but floor remains high as a low-risk #4/5 SP type arm.

Yarbrough,Ryan — SP — Seattle

EXP MLB DEBUT: 2017 | H/W: 6-5 205 | FUT: #4 starter | 7B

Thrws L Age 25
2014 (4) Old Dominion

Velo	Pitch	Grade
89-93	FB	+ + +
81-83	SL	+ +
80-82	CU	+ + +

Year	Lev	Team	W	L	Sv	IP	K	ERA	WHIP	BF/G	OBA	H%	S%	xERA	Ctl	Dom	Cmd	hr/9	BPV
2014	A-	Everett	0	1	0	38		1.41	0.76	11.4	188	30	82	0.98	0.9	12.5	13.3	0.2	217
2015	Rk	Azl Mariners	0	0	0	10	13	1.80	1.20	10.1	281	42	83	3.06	0.9	11.7	13.0	0.0	204
2015	A	Clinton	0	1	0	5	1	14.12	3.14	15.2	455	47	50	11.37	7.1	1.8	0.3	0.0	-141
2015	A+	Bakersfield	4	7	0	81	74	3.77	1.28	20.8	273	34	72	3.93	2.0	8.2	4.1	0.8	112
2016	AA	Jackson	12	4	0	128	99	2.95	1.12	20.2	237	29	74	2.76	2.2	7.0	3.2	0.5	84

Angular SP who finished 2nd in SL in ERA. Emerging prospect who dominates LHH and keeps ball low in zone due to downhill plane. Lacks plus pitch, but mixes and sets up hitters well. Gets ton of groundballs from natural sinking FB and uses above average CU to keep hitters off guard. Won't be high K guy, but maintains velocity and has good command.

Ynoa,Gabriel — SP — New York (N)

EXP MLB DEBUT: 2016 | H/W: 6-2 205 | FUT: Middle reliever | 7C

Thrws R Age 23
2009 FA (DR)

Velo	Pitch	Grade
92-95	FB	+ + +
84-86	SL	+ + +
81-83	CB	+ +
84-87	CU	+ + +

Year	Lev	Team	W	L	Sv	IP	K	ERA	WHIP	BF/G	OBA	H%	S%	xERA	Ctl	Dom	Cmd	hr/9	BPV
2014	A+	St. Lucie	8	2	0	82	64	3.95	1.32	24.2	291	34	71	4.28	1.4	7.0	4.9	0.8	106
2014	AA	Binghamton	3	2	0	66	42	4.22	1.30	24.8	284	31	71	4.58	1.6	5.7	3.5	1.2	77
2015	AA	Binghamton	9	9	0	152	82	3.91	1.24	24.7	268	29	70	3.82	1.8	4.9	2.6	0.8	56
2016	AAA	Las Vegas	12	5	0	154	78	3.97	1.36	25.8	281	30	73	4.37	2.3	4.6	2.0	0.9	37
2016	MLB	NY Mets	1	0	0	18	17	6.46	1.82	8.4	337	43	61	5.55	3.5	8.5	2.4	0.0	76

Command/control RHP made MLB debut in '16. FB velocity was up but movement was gone. Secondary pitches are all fairly average, no swing-and-miss offerings. Must rely on pinpoint command to be successful. Better in shorter appearances. Could develop into solid RP.

Young,Alex — SP — Arizona

EXP MLB DEBUT: 2018 | H/W: 6-2 205 | FUT: #4 starter | 8D

Thrws L Age 23
2015 (2) Texas Christian

Velo	Pitch	Grade
90-93	FB	+ + +
82-84	SL	+ + + +
82-85	CU	+ +

Year	Lev	Team	W	L	Sv	IP	K	ERA	WHIP	BF/G	OBA	H%	S%	xERA	Ctl	Dom	Cmd	hr/9	BPV
2015	NCAA	Texas Christian	9	3	0	97	103	2.22	1.00	21.8	215	28	84	2.57	2.0	9.5	4.7	0.9	135
2015	Rk	Azl Dbacks	0	0	0	1	1	0.00	0.00	2.8	0	0			0.0	9.0		0.0	180
2015	A-	Hillsboro	0	0	1	6	5	1.50	1.00	3.8	228	30	83	1.89	1.5	7.5	5.0	0.0	113
2016	A	Kane County	3	1	0	50	37	2.16	1.10	21.8	217	27	80	2.18	2.9	6.7	2.3	0.2	60
2016	A+	Visalia	2	7	0	68	56	4.62	1.47	24.4	291	34	72	5.17	2.8	7.4	2.7	1.3	76

Former college RP, struggled with High-A assignment in hitters league. Relies on plus downward movement of 90-93 mph FB to elict ground balls. Did not happen in Cal league. SL is best pitch. A wipe out offering with plus two-plane movements, hitters on both sides of plate struggle with it. CU is a work in progress.

Ysla,Luis — RP — Boston

EXP MLB DEBUT: 2017 | H/W: 6-1 185 | FUT: Setup reliever | 7C

Thrws L Age 24
2012 FA (VZ)

Velo	Pitch	Grade
92-97	FB	+ + +
80-83	SL	+ + +
82-84	CU	+ +

Year	Lev	Team	W	L	Sv	IP	K	ERA	WHIP	BF/G	OBA	H%	S%	xERA	Ctl	Dom	Cmd	hr/9	BPV
2014	A	Augusta	6	7	0	121	115	2.45	1.23	20.4	233	30	82	3.08	3.3	8.5	2.6	0.6	82
2015	A+	Salem	0	0	0	5	6	0.00	0.40	8.1	0	0	100		3.6	10.8	3.0	0.0	115
2015	A+	San Jose	3	6	0	79	95	6.25	1.89	11.3	328	44	67	6.51	4.7	10.8	2.3	1.0	87
2016	AA	Portland	2	5	3	55	60	4.08	1.47	6.1	258	34	73	4.05	4.4	9.8	2.2	0.7	75
2016	AAA	Pawtucket	0	0	1	1	2	0.00	1.00	3.8	262	55	100	2.23	0.0	18.0		0.0	342

Power RP who was moved to pen in '15 and throwing harder. Uses low slot to add to effectiveness of SL, which he uses as K pitch. Tough on RHH despite lack of CU and throws with lot of effort. Command comes and goes and will need to locate FB better in order to use SL when ahead in count. Delivery a bit funky, but effective.

Zastryzny,Rob — RP — Chicago (N)

EXP MLB DEBUT: 2016 | H/W: 6-3 205 | FUT: Setup reliever | 7C

Thrws L Age 25
2013 (2) Missouri

Velo	Pitch	Grade
90-93	FB	+ + +
83-85	CT	+ +
	CB	+
	CU	+ + +

Year	Lev	Team	W	L	Sv	IP	K	ERA	WHIP	BF/G	OBA	H%	S%	xERA	Ctl	Dom	Cmd	hr/9	BPV
2015	Rk	Azl Cubs	0	0	0	4	4	2.25	1.25	16.3	210	29	80	2.28	4.5	9.0	2.0	0.0	59
2015	AA	Tennessee	2	5	0	60	48	6.28	1.74	19.6	312	36	66	6.21	4.2	7.2	1.7	1.3	34
2016	AA	Tennessee	3	2	0	54	42	4.32	1.29	24.8	246	28	69	3.80	3.3	7.0	2.1	1.0	54
2016	AAA	Iowa	7	3	0	81	77	4.33	1.21	21.8	227	28	65	3.12	3.4	8.6	2.5	0.8	79
2016	MLB	Chi Cubs	1	0	0	16	17	1.13	1.06	7.8	210	30	88	1.80	2.8	9.6	3.4	0.0	114

Bounce-back season after disastrous '15. Held his own at AA/AAA and made 8 appearances with the Cubs. FB sits at 90-92 maxing out at 94 mph, Replaced below-average SL with an improved CT, but CU remains 2nd best offering. Lack of a plus second offering means future is likely to remain in relief.

Zeuch,T.J. — SP — Toronto

EXP MLB DEBUT: 2019 | H/W: 6-7 225 | FUT: #3 starter | 8D

Thrws R Age 21
2016 (1) Pittsburgh

Velo	Pitch	Grade
90-95	FB	+ + + +
78-80	CB	+ + +
82-85	SL	+ +
	CU	+

Year	Lev	Team	W	L	Sv	IP	K	ERA	WHIP	BF/G	OBA	H%	S%	xERA	Ctl	Dom	Cmd	hr/9	BPV
2016	NCAA	Pittsburgh	6	1	0	69	74	3.12	1.16	27.5	238	32	73	2.75	2.5	9.6	3.9	0.4	125
2016	Rk	GCL Blue Jays	0	0	0	3	2	0.00	0.00	8.5	0	0			0.0	6.0		0.0	126
2016	A-	Vancouver	0	1	0	23	22	3.52	1.13	15.1	245	32	68	2.78	2.0	8.6	4.4	0.4	120
2016	A	Lansing	0	1	0	8	14	9.00	1.50	17.3	307	51	36	5.23	2.3	15.8	7.0	1.1	241

Tall, angular SP who has body type to withstand innings and high pitch counts. Has proven tough to hit with plus FB that exhibits sink. Downhill angle to plate is deceptive and adds to effectiveness of CB. Can get on side of SL and needs to enhance CU. Commands plate well for size and next step is to upgrade sequencing.

Zimmer,Kyle — SP — Kansas City

EXP MLB DEBUT: 2017 | H/W: 6-3 225 | FUT: #2 starter | 9E

Thrws R Age 25
2012 (1) San Francisco

Velo	Pitch	Grade
92-96	FB	+ + + +
80-81	CB	+ + + +
82-84	SL	+ +
83-85	CU	+ + +

Year	Lev	Team	W	L	Sv	IP	K	ERA	WHIP	BF/G	OBA	H%	S%	xERA	Ctl	Dom	Cmd	hr/9	BPV
2015	A	Lexington	1	0	0	16	21	1.13	1.06	6.9	196	29	94	2.14	3.4	11.8	3.5	0.6	140
2015	AA	NW Arkansas	2	5	3	48	51	2.81	1.17	12.8	237	31	79	3.10	2.6	9.6	3.6	0.8	119
2016	A+	Wilmington	0	1	0	4	9	2.14	1.67	9.4	202	51	86	3.13	8.6	19.3	2.3	0.0	134
2016	AA	NW Arkansas	0	1	0	1	2	0.00	3.00	5.8	262	55	100	7.27	18.0	18.0	1.0	0.0	-144

Injury-prone SP who cannot stay on mound, but tantalizes with plus stuff when healthy. Plus FB features vicious, late life and can miss bats up and down in zone. Best secondary is plus CB with incredible break. SL gives him second breaker and CU should be average at best. Injury history is major concern and '17 will be huge.

Ziomek,Kevin — SP — Detroit

EXP MLB DEBUT: 2018 | H/W: 6-3 200 | FUT: #4 starter | 7C

Thrws L Age 25
2013 (2) Vanderbilt

Velo	Pitch	Grade
89-94	FB	+ + +
80-82	SL	+ +
75-78	CB	+ +
	CU	+ + +

Year	Lev	Team	W	L	Sv	IP	K	ERA	WHIP	BF/G	OBA	H%	S%	xERA	Ctl	Dom	Cmd	hr/9	BPV
2013	A-	Connecticut	0	1	0	8	3	4.50	1.25	8.1	181	20	60	2.01	5.6	3.4	0.6	0.0	-73
2014	A	West Michigan	10	6	0	123	152	2.27	1.15	21.3	204	30	81	2.29	3.9	11.1	2.9	0.4	113
2015	A+	Lakeland	9	11	0	154	143	3.44	1.14	22.6	246	32	68	2.63	2.0	8.3	4.2	0.2	115
2016	A+	Lakeland	0	1	0	4	1	10.98	2.44	21.6	438	43	56	11.25	2.2	2.2	1.0	2.2	-2

Tall, polished SP who missed most of season after shoulder surgery. Uses deep arsenal to keep hitters guessing and throws downhill to induce groundballs. Repeats athletic delivery, but no pitch grades as plus. Heavy FB is best offering, though no reliable breaking ball. CU provides deceptive look.

Zych,Tony — RP — Seattle

EXP MLB DEBUT: 2015 | H/W: 6-3 190 | FUT: Setup reliever | 6A

Thrws R Age 26
2011 (4) Louisville

Velo	Pitch	Grade
91-96	FB	+ + + +
82-84	SL	+ + +

Year	Lev	Team	W	L	Sv	IP	K	ERA	WHIP	BF/G	OBA	H%	S%	xERA	Ctl	Dom	Cmd	hr/9	BPV
2015	MLB	Seattle	0	0	0	18	24	2.49	1.10	5.5	250	37	79	2.86	1.5	11.9	8.0	0.5	193
2016	Rk	Azl Mariners	0	0	0	1	0	0.00	1.00	3.8	0	0	100		9.0	0.0	0.0	0.0	-225
2016	AA	Jackson	0	0	0	1	2	0.00	1.00	3.8	0	0	100		9.0	18.0	2.0	0.0	99
2016	AAA	Tacoma	0	0	0	3	6	0.00	0.00	2.8	0	0			0.0	18.0		0.0	342
2016	MLB	Seattle	1	0	0	13	21	3.41	1.52	4.8	212	38	75	2.92	6.8	14.3	2.1	0.0	92

Dominant RP who missed time with shoulder tendinitis, but has success in limited time in majors. Works off dynamic FB with electric, late life and mixes in sharp SL with big break. Has cleaned up delivery last two years and has enhanced command. Doesn't have go-to pitch against LHH and control still needs work.

In his 1985 *Baseball Abstract,* Bill James introduced the concept of major league equivalencies. His assertion was that, with the proper adjustments, a minor leaguer's statistics could be converted to an equivalent major league level performance with a great deal of accuracy.

Because of wide variations in the level of play among different minor leagues, it is difficult to get a true reading on a player's potential. For instance, a .300 batting average achieved in the high-offense Pacific Coast League is not nearly as much of an accomplishment as a similar level in the Eastern League. MLEs normalize these types of variances, for all statistical categories.

The actual MLEs are not projections. They represent how a player's previous performance might look at the major league level. However, the MLE stat line can be used in forecasting future performance in just the same way as a major league stat line would.

The model we use contains a few variations to James' version and updates all of the minor league and ballpark factors. In addition, we designed a module to convert pitching statistics, which is something James did not originally do.

Do MLEs really work?

Used correctly, MLEs are excellent indicators of potential. But just like we cannot take traditional major league statistics at face value, the same goes for MLEs. The underlying measures of base skill—batting eye ratios, pitching command ratios, etc.—are far more accurate in evaluating future talent than raw home runs, batting averages or ERAs.

The charts we present here also provide the unique perspective of looking at up to five years' worth of data. Ironically, the longer the history, the less likely the player is a legitimate prospect—he should have made it to the majors before compiling a long history in AA and/or AAA ball. Of course, the shorter trends

are more difficult to read despite them often belonging to players with higher ceilings. But even here we can find small indications of players improving their skills, or struggling, as they rise through more difficult levels of competition. Since players—especially those with any talent—are promoted rapidly through major league systems, a two or three-year scan is often all we get to spot any trends.

Here are some things to look for as you scan these charts:

Target players who...

- spent a full year in AA and then a full year in AAA
- had consistent playing time from one year to the next
- improved their base skills as they were promoted

Raise the warning flag for players who...

- were stuck at a level for multiple seasons, or regressed
- displayed marked changes in playing time from one year to the next
- showed large drops in BPIs from one year to the next

Players are listed on the charts if they spent at least part of 2012-2016 in Triple-A or Double-A and had at least 100 AB or 30 IP within those two levels. Each is listed with the organization with which they finished the season.

Only statistics accumulated in Triple-A and Double-A ball are included (players who split a season are indicated as a/a); Single-A stats are excluded.

Each player's actual AB and IP totals are used as the base for the conversion. However, it is more useful to compare performances using common levels, so rely on the ratios and sabermetric gauges. Complete explanations of these formulas appear in the Glossary.

BATTER	B	Yr	Age	Pos	Lvl	Tm	AB	R	H	D	T	HR	RBI	BB	K	SB	CS	BA	OB	Slg	OPS	bb%	ct%	Eye	PX	SX	RC/G	BPV
Adames, Willy	R	16	21	SS	aa	TAM	486	75	120	27	5	9	48	63	135	11	7	247	333	380	713	11%	72%	0.46	92	114	3.37	21
Adams, Caleb	R	16	23	LF	aa	LAA	246	26	52	5	2	3	22	16	92	8	4	211	261	292	553	6%	63%	0.18	57	123	2.10	-53
Albies, Ozhaino	B	16	19	2B	a/a	ATL	552	81	159	32	9	6	52	52	104	29	13	287	349	410	758	9%	81%	0.50	77	142	3.92	48
Alfaro, Jorge	R	15	22	C	aa	TEX	190	17	43	13	2	4	16	7	66	2	1	225	253	374	628	4%	65%	0.11	126	89	2.36	-2
		16	23	C	aa	PHI	404	55	102	20	1	14	54	18	122	2	2	253	285	410	696	4%	70%	0.15	106	75	3.40	-3
Anderson, Brian	R	16	23	3B	aa	MIA	301	34	67	9	1	6	35	32	63	0	0	222	297	318	615	10%	79%	0.51	57	43	2.75	-4
Andujar, Miguel	R	16	21	3B	aa	NYY	282	28	74	15	2	2	42	21	45	2	1	262	313	352	666	7%	84%	0.47	59	67	3.09	19
Aplin, Andrew	L	14	23	CF	a/a	HOU	452	46	102	12	2	5	48	59	82	19	12	226	316	290	606	12%	82%	0.72	46	87	2.61	15
		15	24	CF	a/a	HOU	338	46	84	8	5	2	29	50	64	23	12	248	345	314	660	13%	81%	0.78	41	135	3.06	25
		16	25	CF	aaa	HOU	399	43	73	12	3	4	22	29	117	15	10	182	238	258	497	7%	71%	0.25	53	123	1.50	-23
Arroyo, Christian	R	16	21	SS	aa	SF	474	55	125	35	1	2	47	29	78	1	1	263	305	358	663	6%	84%	0.37	68	55	2.93	18
Asuaje, Carlos	L	15	24	2B	aa	BOS	495	47	112	24	5	6	48	44	97	7	7	226	290	331	620	8%	80%	0.46	71	92	2.42	24
		16	25	2B	aaa	SD	535	66	138	26	7	6	46	33	102	7	6	257	301	366	667	6%	81%	0.32	67	100	2.94	21
Austin, Tyler	R	13	22	RF	aa	NYY	319	36	75	15	1	6	34	35	85	3	0	236	312	342	655	10%	73%	0.41	84	70	3.09	3
		14	23	RF	aa	NYY	396	44	97	17	3	8	37	29	89	2	2	244	296	366	662	7%	78%	0.33	89	78	3.01	20
		15	24	RF	a/a	NYY	341	35	74	11	1	6	30	30	110	10	3	218	281	310	591	8%	68%	0.27	72	99	2.48	-24
		16	25	1B	a/a	NYY	378	55	102	30	1	18	71	57	121	5	1	270	366	494	860	13%	68%	0.47	161	72	5.29	51
Bader, Harrison	R	16	22	CF	a/a	STL	465	56	109	17	4	15	47	30	151	10	14	235	281	381	662	6%	68%	0.20	98	98	2.76	-8
Barnes, Austin	R	13	24	C	aa	MIA	62	8	19	2	2	1	6	10	11	0	0	307	404	431	835	14%	82%	0.90	73	75	5.05	39
		14	25	2B	aa	MIA	284	41	70	17	2	7	32	37	42	6	0	245	333	397	730	12%	85%	0.90	104	99	3.77	79
		15	26	C	aaa	LA	292	29	75	14	1	7	31	24	44	9	2	257	314	385	699	8%	85%	0.55	80	87	3.60	47
		16	27	C	aaa	LA	336	45	80	19	3	5	30	30	65	14	4	239	301	353	655	8%	81%	0.46	74	123	2.92	37

BATTER	B	Yr	Age	Pos	Lvl	Tm	AB	R	H	D	T	HR	RBI	BB	K	SB	CS	BA	OB	Slg	OPS	bb%	ct%	Eye	PX	SX	RC/G	BPV
Barnes,Barrett	R	15	24	LF	aa	PIT	126	13	26	5	0	2	13	12	27	3	5	210	279	301	579	9%	78%	0.44	65	66	2.07	5
		16	25	LF	aa	PIT	405	49	107	24	5	7	38	33	117	8	5	263	318	397	716	7%	71%	0.28	95	110	3.39	10
Barreto,Franklin	R	16	20	SS	a/a	OAK	479	58	130	25	4	9	47	32	97	27	18	271	317	396	712	6%	80%	0.33	78	119	3.35	32
Bauers,Jake	L	15	20	1B	aa	TAM	257	30	64	16	0	4	30	18	45	5	3	249	297	357	654	6%	83%	0.39	78	70	2.90	29
		16	21	RF	aa	TAM	493	67	121	25	1	12	66	62	99	8	7	246	330	371	701	11%	80%	0.62	78	69	3.45	27
Bautista,Rafael	R	16	23	CF	aa	WAS	543	67	143	12	2	3	34	40	101	49	11	263	313	310	623	7%	81%	0.40	29	129	3.27	3
Bell,Josh	B	15	23	1B	a/a	PIT	489	57	140	22	7	5	66	52	70	8	4	285	354	389	744	10%	86%	0.75	65	101	3.97	47
		16	24	1B	aaa	PIT	421	52	113	21	3	12	55	51	80	3	8	268	347	416	763	11%	81%	0.64	87	59	3.97	35
Bellinger,Cody	L	16	21	1B	a/a	LA	410	59	104	17	1	24	63	49	102	7	2	253	333	474	807	11%	75%	0.48	129	70	4.90	48
Benintendi,Andrew	L	16	22	CF	aa	BOS	237	34	67	19	4	6	37	20	32	7	7	285	341	481	822	8%	86%	0.63	112	117	4.03	88
Blandino,Alex	R	15	23	SS	aa	CIN	115	13	25	6	0	3	15	16	24	2	2	214	307	349	656	12%	79%	0.64	92	50	2.78	30
		16	24	2B	aa	CIN	401	49	88	17	0	9	35	54	133	13	6	219	311	326	637	12%	67%	0.40	80	79	2.89	-19
Bonifacio,Jorge	R	13	20	RF	aa	KC	93	13	26	7	0	2	16	9	23	2	1	283	348	405	753	9%	75%	0.39	102	59	4.05	19
		14	21	RF	aa	KC	505	40	108	19	4	3	42	41	130	7	3	213	272	285	557	7%	74%	0.31	59	87	2.04	-13
		15	22	RF	aa	KC	483	49	105	28	2	13	52	34	131	2	2	218	269	365	634	7%	73%	0.26	108	62	2.59	11
		16	23	RF	aaa	KC	495	62	120	20	5	13	65	38	141	5	2	243	297	387	684	7%	72%	0.27	93	98	3.22	6
Brett,Ryan	R	13	22	2B	aa	TAM	105	16	22	5	1	2	13	7	16	3	0	211	257	347	603	6%	85%	0.42	87	132	2.45	64
		14	23	2B	aa	TAM	422	51	112	22	5	6	30	19	85	22	8	265	297	385	682	4%	80%	0.22	88	140	3.17	43
		15	24	2B	aaa	TAM	328	39	70	15	1	4	25	12	74	3	2	212	241	300	541	4%	77%	0.17	65	86	1.87	-3
Brinson,Lewis	R	15	21	CF	a/a	TEX	140	19	41	8	1	6	22	11	37	4	1	295	345	489	834	7%	74%	0.29	133	95	5.25	46
		16	22	CF	a/a	MIL	393	50	98	21	5	13	50	16	92	12	6	249	278	423	701	4%	77%	0.17	106	131	3.16	40
Brito,Socrates	L	15	23	RF	aa	ARI	490	58	138	15	15	8	47	24	92	17	7	283	315	425	741	5%	81%	0.26	81	138	3.70	42
		16	24	RF	aaa	ARI	303	32	77	9	8	4	27	9	69	5	7	253	275	374	649	3%	77%	0.13	68	114	2.55	6
Brown,Aaron	L	16	24	CF	aa	PHI	228	31	44	12	3	3	21	17	74	2	5	193	250	306	556	7%	68%	0.24	85	115	1.65	-11
Brugman,Jaycob	L	15	23	LF	aa	OAK	500	45	111	24	7	4	46	47	98	8	8	222	289	320	609	9%	80%	0.48	67	98	2.25	24
		16	24	CF	a/a	OAK	543	64	138	31	6	9	72	43	132	6	7	255	310	385	695	7%	76%	0.33	86	95	3.12	17
Burns,Andy	R	13	23	3B	aa	TOR	265	30	59	18	2	6	24	17	62	9	6	223	270	365	635	6%	76%	0.27	108	106	2.44	38
		14	24	3B	aa	TOR	495	56	113	30	4	13	50	32	113	14	9	228	275	383	658	6%	77%	0.28	117	111	2.67	50
		15	25	3B	a/a	TOR	499	55	131	26	0	5	39	34	85	5	10	263	310	342	652	6%	83%	0.40	59	48	2.90	8
		16	26	2B	aaa	TOR	418	35	86	24	1	7	32	28	97	11	6	205	255	320	575	6%	77%	0.29	79	83	2.08	9
Calhoun,Willie	L	16	22	2B	aa	LA	503	70	121	25	1	26	82	39	70	0	0	241	296	449	745	7%	86%	0.56	110	36	3.95	59
Camargo,Johan	B	16	23	2B	aa	ATL	446	45	112	25	5	4	42	24	94	1	2	252	290	357	647	5%	79%	0.25	69	74	2.69	6
Candelario,Jeimer	B	15	22	3B	aa	CHC	158	17	42	9	1	4	20	18	23	0	0	264	340	410	750	10%	85%	0.77	92	40	4.01	49
		16	23	3B	a/a	CHC	474	57	118	35	3	11	60	55	113	0	2	250	328	403	732	10%	76%	0.49	104	51	3.47	26
Caratini,Victor	B	16	23	C	aa	CHC	412	45	107	22	2	5	37	43	91	2	1	259	330	358	687	10%	78%	0.48	68	56	3.34	4
Cave,Jake	L	15	23	CF	a/a	NYY	529	64	135	23	4	2	35	42	119	15	3	256	310	325	635	7%	78%	0.35	53	117	2.92	4
		16	24	LF	a/a	NYY	426	55	106	24	7	8	51	34	120	6	8	249	305	397	701	7%	72%	0.28	99	111	3.02	17
Cecchini,Gavin	R	15	22	SS	aa	NYM	439	55	125	23	3	6	44	36	62	3	4	286	340	395	735	8%	86%	0.58	72	65	3.87	38
		16	23	SS	aaa	NYM	446	49	118	23	1	6	38	33	65	3	1	264	316	359	674	7%	85%	0.51	59	61	3.30	23
Chapman,Matt	R	16	23	3B	a/a	OAK	514	78	109	26	5	28	81	57	185	6	4	212	292	443	734	10%	64%	0.31	160	102	3.46	37
Cole,Hunter	R	15	23	RF	aa	SF	192	22	53	15	4	2	20	13	51	1	1	276	323	437	760	7%	74%	0.27	120	97	3.50	35
		16	24	RF	aa	SF	469	52	116	23	4	10	57	29	131	2	4	247	291	377	667	6%	72%	0.22	88	71	2.95	-6
Cordell,Ryan	R	15	23	CF	aa	TEX	221	20	42	4	2	4	14	9	80	8	1	191	223	285	508	4%	64%	0.12	69	134	1.79	-39
		16	24	CF	aa	TEX	405	57	95	19	4	16	58	28	107	10	5	234	283	419	703	6%	74%	0.26	114	123	3.26	37
Cordero,Franchy	L	16	22	CF	a/a	SD	258	25	68	7	6	5	15	16	81	9	7	262	305	391	696	6%	68%	0.20	81	121	3.18	-11
Cozens,Dylan	L	15	21	RF	aa	PHI	40	5	13	2	0	3	7	2	8	2	1	318	358	564	922	6%	80%	0.31	146	54	6.45	67
		16	22	RF	aa	PHI	521	87	132	34	2	37	103	51	210	17	1	254	320	541	862	9%	60%	0.24	217	126	5.27	70
Crawford,J.P.	L	15	20	SS	aa	PHI	351	43	84	19	5	4	27	40	50	6	2	241	319	364	683	10%	86%	0.81	78	110	3.00	61
		16	21	SS	a/a	PHI	472	57	111	18	1	7	39	66	89	11	7	235	329	322	650	12%	81%	0.74	55	70	3.01	16
Daal,Calten	R	16	23	SS	aa	CIN	116	15	35	3	1	1	6	9	30	5	1	299	349	366	715	7%	74%	0.30	44	102	4.27	-21
Davidson,Matt	R	12	21	3B	aa	ARI	486	65	119	28	2	19	62	54	133	2	4	245	320	428	748	10%	73%	0.40	129	59	3.81	33
		13	22	3B	aaa	ARI	443	35	104	28	2	11	47	29	148	1	0	235	282	385	667	6%	67%	0.19	128	51	2.93	-2
		14	23	3B	aaa	CHW	478	39	78	15	0	15	37	36	189	0	0	164	222	290	512	7%	61%	0.19	112	21	1.76	-46
		15	24	3B	aaa	CHW	528	51	95	19	0	20	60	54	218	1	0	179	255	332	587	9%	59%	0.25	128	33	2.35	-32
		16	25	3B	aaa	CHW	284	27	64	16	0	8	36	27	104	0	0	224	291	369	660	9%	63%	0.26	115	20	2.98	-29
Davis,J.D.	R	16	23	3B	aa	HOU	485	48	115	30	1	20	63	35	164	1	3	236	288	422	710	7%	66%	0.21	135	34	3.34	-2
Dean,Austin	R	16	23	LF	aa	MIA	480	53	105	22	5	8	59	43	118	1	2	220	283	340	623	8%	75%	0.36	77	74	2.47	4
DeJong,Paul	R	16	23	3B	aa	STL	496	51	113	26	2	17	60	34	168	2	2	228	277	391	668	6%	66%	0.20	117	58	3.01	-10
Diaz,Elias	R	14	24	C	a/a	PIT	359	33	94	18	0	4	39	23	63	2	3	261	307	345	651	6%	83%	0.37	66	38	3.02	8
		15	25	C	aaa	PIT	325	28	77	14	3	3	40	23	52	1	5	237	288	326	614	7%	84%	0.45	59	61	2.39	17
		16	26	C	a/a	PIT	101	3	23	3	0	0	9	3	20	1	0	229	253	255	508	3%	80%	0.16	21	26	1.96	-47
Diaz,Yandy	R	15	24	3B	a/a	CLE	495	55	138	14	3	6	50	67	80	8	8	279	365	359	724	12%	84%	0.83	49	75	3.95	23
		16	25	3B	a/a	CLE	444	55	127	21	3	8	49	58	95	9	3	285	368	397	765	12%	79%	0.61	72	90	4.45	24

BATTER	B	Yr	Age	Pos	Lvl	Tm	AB	R	H	D	T	HR	RBI	BB	K	SB	CS	BA	OB	Slg	OPS	bb%	ct%	Eye	PX	SX	RC/G	BPV
Difo,Wilmer	R	15	23	SS	aa	WAS	359	40	92	20	4	2	32	10	84	22	1	256	276	346	621	3%	77%	0.12	69	157	2.80	16
		16	24	SS	a/a	WAS	415	52	98	14	2	5	36	30	66	25	12	237	289	315	604	7%	84%	0.46	47	116	2.57	24
Dozier,Hunter	R	14	23	3B	aa	KC	234	26	43	11	0	3	17	25	74	2	2	186	263	270	533	9%	68%	0.33	79	60	1.80	-24
		15	24	3B	aa	KC	475	50	87	24	1	9	41	34	163	5	2	182	238	293	531	7%	66%	0.21	94	81	1.77	-22
		16	25	3B	a/a	KC	486	61	125	41	1	17	58	41	138	5	1	256	314	446	760	8%	72%	0.30	135	76	3.89	35
Dubon,Mauricio	R	16	22	SS	aa	BOS	251	40	82	21	5	5	34	9	39	5	3	327	351	510	861	4%	85%	0.24	109	130	4.97	74
Duggar,Steven	L	16	23	CF	aa	SF	243	33	74	15	5	1	22	27	57	8	8	306	374	420	794	10%	77%	0.47	77	120	4.06	26
Engel,Adam	R	16	25	CF	a/a	CHW	455	58	95	20	8	6	32	41	145	30	16	209	274	324	598	8%	68%	0.28	80	160	2.12	3
Escalera,Alfredo	R	16	21	CF	aa	KC	202	22	54	14	0	2	21	5	53	4	1	266	285	361	645	3%	74%	0.10	77	79	2.92	-12
Evans,Phillip	R	16	24	SS	aa	NYM	361	41	104	27	0	7	32	16	71	1	1	289	319	418	737	4%	80%	0.22	88	39	3.89	14
Farmer,Kyle	R	15	25	C	aa	LA	283	21	67	23	1	2	33	11	64	0	1	238	267	343	610	4%	77%	0.18	89	38	2.25	1
		16	26	C	aa	LA	266	27	59	16	1	4	27	20	52	2	0	221	275	342	617	7%	80%	0.38	79	72	2.47	23
Fields,Roemon	L	15	25	CF	a/a	TOR	225	24	51	3	1	1	10	18	45	21	6	227	283	260	543	7%	80%	0.39	22	128	2.41	-7
		16	26	CF	aa	TOR	497	53	98	11	4	4	26	36	118	36	19	197	252	257	509	7%	76%	0.31	38	133	1.69	-9
Fisher,Derek	L	16	23	CF	a/a	HOU	478	54	107	18	4	17	57	63	177	21	8	223	313	384	697	12%	63%	0.35	115	110	3.41	2
Fletcher,David	R	16	22	SS	aa	LAA	80	9	23	6	0	0	6	3	14	1	0	285	309	356	666	3%	82%	0.20	58	60	3.21	1
Fowler,Dustin	L	16	22	CF	aa	NYY	541	66	149	29	12	13	87	22	93	25	12	275	303	447	750	4%	83%	0.24	96	145	3.62	61
Frazier,Clint	R	16	22	LF	a/a	NYY	463	73	119	26	4	18	53	47	132	13	4	258	326	444	770	9%	71%	0.36	122	117	4.17	39
Garcia,Willy	R	14	22	RF	aa	PIT	439	44	102	24	3	12	47	17	153	6	4	232	262	385	647	4%	65%	0.11	133	93	2.66	5
		15	23	RF	a/a	PIT	480	52	117	17	4	11	56	18	131	3	7	245	273	365	638	4%	73%	0.14	83	86	2.72	-8
		16	24	RF	aaa	PIT	462	48	103	27	3	5	39	27	140	5	10	222	266	327	593	6%	70%	0.20	82	79	2.03	-19
Garver,Mitch	R	16	25	C	a/a	MIN	434	41	103	27	0	9	60	40	118	1	3	237	301	365	666	8%	73%	0.34	92	25	2.95	-9
Gillaspie,Casey	B	16	23	1B	a/a	TAM	472	66	120	30	2	15	54	68	134	4	2	253	347	418	765	13%	72%	0.51	114	70	4.11	25
Gonzalez,Erik	R	14	23	SS	aa	CLE	129	17	41	6	2	1	13	6	27	5	1	315	343	406	749	4%	79%	0.21	68	127	4.35	20
		15	24	SS	a/a	CLE	549	62	127	23	5	8	61	22	118	16	8	231	261	332	593	4%	79%	0.19	69	123	2.33	16
		16	25	SS	aaa	CLE	429	52	115	30	1	9	45	16	97	10	11	267	293	406	699	4%	77%	0.16	95	78	3.12	18
Goodwin,Brian	L	12	22	OF	aa	WAS	166	14	34	7	1	4	12	14	52	2	3	203	265	332	597	8%	68%	0.27	98	65	2.21	-11
		13	23	CF	aa	WAS	457	66	104	17	8	8	32	51	129	15	12	227	305	354	659	10%	72%	0.40	91	136	2.67	22
		14	24	CF	aaa	WAS	275	23	51	9	3	3	24	35	104	4	5	186	279	269	547	11%	62%	0.34	76	90	1.83	-39
		15	25	CF	aa	WAS	429	46	85	15	3	6	36	30	103	12	8	197	250	286	535	6%	76%	0.29	62	111	1.83	2
		16	26	CF	aaa	WAS	436	44	108	23	1	11	58	41	120	13	3	248	312	380	692	9%	72%	0.34	92	79	3.48	6
Granite,Zach	L	16	24	CF	aa	MIN	525	68	138	16	6	3	41	32	46	44	16	263	306	336	642	6%	91%	0.71	39	149	3.00	55
Greiner,Grayson	R	16	24	C	a/a	DET	212	17	54	8	3	6	25	9	61	1	0	256	285	405	689	4%	71%	0.14	94	76	3.30	-7
Guerrero,Gabriel	R	15	22	RF	aa	ARI	460	43	95	24	4	6	39	19	115	9	2	207	239	320	559	4%	75%	0.16	83	117	1.95	11
		16	23	RF	a/a	ARI	418	38	89	22	6	7	42	22	111	5	3	214	254	347	601	5%	74%	0.20	88	105	2.15	8
Gurriel,Yulieski	R	16	32	3B	a/a	HOU	35	2	4	1	0	1	3	1	13	0	0	127	158	208	367	4%	63%	0.10	60	21	0.87	-86
Guzman,Ronald	L	16	22	1B	a/a	TEX	463	51	116	19	5	13	57	34	112	2	2	251	303	402	705	7%	76%	0.31	91	79	3.43	16
Haniger,Mitch	R	14	24	RF	aa	ARI	267	36	62	9	1	8	30	17	50	3	0	233	278	365	642	6%	81%	0.33	88	88	3.03	35
		15	25	CF	aa	ARI	153	18	38	9	1	1	15	13	37	3	5	249	306	339	645	8%	76%	0.34	72	93	2.52	7
		16	26	CF	a/a	ARI	458	59	125	30	5	19	70	51	117	9	5	273	345	484	829	10%	74%	0.43	133	97	4.73	55
Hanson,Alen	B	13	21	SS	aa	PIT	137	11	32	4	4	1	8	6	27	5	2	231	264	327	592	4%	81%	0.24	59	123	2.15	17
		14	22	SS	aa	PIT	482	48	117	19	8	7	43	22	93	19	12	242	276	360	636	4%	81%	0.24	80	128	2.53	36
		15	23	2B	aaa	PIT	475	58	114	16	9	4	38	31	96	31	13	240	286	341	627	6%	80%	0.32	63	160	2.56	32
		16	24	2B	aaa	PIT	432	52	105	14	6	7	29	28	84	33	17	243	289	346	636	6%	81%	0.34	59	146	2.68	28
Happ,Ian	B	16	22	2B	aa	CHC	248	28	59	13	0	7	26	16	67	5	2	237	284	370	655	6%	73%	0.25	91	69	3.01	0
Hawkins,Courtney	R	15	22	LF	aa	CHW	300	34	68	18	2	9	36	19	110	1	4	227	273	383	656	6%	63%	0.17	130	68	2.65	-8
		16	23	LF	aa	CHW	418	28	73	21	0	10	48	24	157	0	3	175	220	299	519	5%	63%	0.15	100	18	1.62	-52
Hernandez,Marco	L	15	23	SS	a/a	BOS	463	48	134	32	5	7	45	14	95	4	2	290	311	426	738	3%	80%	0.15	97	93	3.73	32
		16	24	SS	aaa	BOS	223	25	68	8	4	4	28	11	55	4	2	303	337	432	769	5%	75%	0.21	77	108	4.39	6
Hernandez,Teoscar	R	15	23	CF	aa	HOU	470	70	89	10	2	14	37	25	144	25	8	189	230	305	535	5%	69%	0.18	79	151	2.02	-2
		16	24	RF	a/a	HOU	423	55	111	24	3	8	40	34	95	25	17	263	317	389	707	7%	78%	0.36	83	118	3.23	29
Herrera,Rosell	B	16	24	LF	aa	COL	425	50	119	15	3	5	55	46	79	30	9	280	350	363	713	10%	81%	0.58	51	119	3.99	24
Hinojosa,C.J.	R	16	22	SS	aa	SF	226	26	54	7	3	2	18	19	47	1	0	238	298	323	621	8%	79%	0.42	51	83	2.71	1
Hinshaw,Chad	R	15	25	CF	aa	LAA	263	41	66	15	0	1	22	30	88	23	6	252	328	318	647	10%	66%	0.34	68	119	3.16	-22
		16	26	CF	aa	LAA	205	22	34	5	1	4	20	17	82	12	6	164	229	257	486	8%	60%	0.21	72	126	1.53	-48
Hood,Destin	R	12	22	OF	aa	WAS	355	37	79	19	2	3	37	19	93	5	1	223	263	310	573	5%	74%	0.20	70	96	2.14	-8
		13	23	RF	aa	WAS	392	36	79	16	4	3	32	21	124	4	8	201	242	287	529	5%	68%	0.17	72	91	1.61	-29
		14	24	LF	a/a	WAS	382	37	97	22	1	8	30	17	93	7	3	255	286	379	665	4%	76%	0.18	99	81	3.06	17
		15	25	LF	a/a	PHI	366	32	83	22	4	8	44	16	120	5	2	228	260	380	641	4%	67%	0.13	120	100	2.53	6
		16	26	LF	aaa	MIA	476	51	110	26	3	11	66	31	130	9	7	230	277	365	642	6%	73%	0.24	92	93	2.63	7
Hoskins,Rhys	R	16	23	1B	aa	PHI	498	77	126	23	1	34	93	58	144	6	3	253	331	510	841	10%	71%	0.40	159	65	5.15	54
Ibanez,Andy	R	16	23	2B	aa	TEX	307	33	72	16	2	5	26	22	51	4	2	235	286	348	635	7%	83%	0.43	69	83	2.70	29
Jagielo,Eric	L	15	23	3B	aa	NYY	222	32	59	15	1	9	31	16	65	0	0	265	315	465	781	7%	71%	0.25	145	61	4.24	33
		16	24	3B	aa	CIN	365	25	71	14	1	7	25	43	149	0	0	194	279	299	578	11%	59%	0.29	87	21	2.26	-65

BATTER	B	Yr	Age	Pos	Lvl	Tm	AB	R	H	D	T	HR	RBI	BB	K	SB	CS	BA	OB	Slg	OPS	bb%	ct%	Eye	PX	SX	RC/G	BPV
Jhang,Jin-De	L	16	23	C	a/a	PIT	208	19	55	13	0	1	20	10	15	1	0	263	298	337	635	5%	93%	0.70	49	43	2.86	35
Jones,JaCoby	R	15	23	SS	aa	DET	146	22	35	6	2	5	18	15	55	9	3	242	311	414	726	9%	63%	0.27	133	153	3.57	23
		16	24	CF	a/a	DET	369	36	86	18	7	6	35	30	127	11	6	234	291	369	660	7%	66%	0.23	97	124	2.68	-6
Judge,Aaron	R	15	23	RF	a/a	NYY	478	56	113	23	2	20	63	48	161	6	2	237	306	419	726	9%	66%	0.30	137	81	3.71	20
		16	24	RF	aaa	NYY	352	57	89	16	1	20	59	43	110	5	0	254	336	472	808	11%	69%	0.39	142	80	4.92	36
Kelly,Carson	R	16	22	C	a/a	STL	329	35	84	15	0	5	26	21	73	0	1	255	299	343	642	6%	78%	0.28	60	31	3.00	-18
Kemmer,Jon	L	15	25	RF	aa	HOU	364	50	100	23	3	14	48	34	108	7	1	275	336	473	809	8%	70%	0.31	144	109	4.68	48
		16	26	RF	aaa	HOU	407	36	87	19	3	13	47	26	157	6	12	215	262	377	639	6%	61%	0.17	123	81	2.36	-18
Kingery,Scott	R	16	22	2B	aa	PHI	156	13	35	6	0	2	15	4	41	3	2	224	244	300	545	3%	74%	0.10	56	67	2.02	-32
Knapp,Andrew	B	15	24	C	aa	PHI	214	30	66	18	1	9	43	17	52	1	0	311	362	540	902	7%	76%	0.33	160	66	5.93	68
		16	25	C	aaa	PHI	403	51	98	22	1	8	42	34	126	2	2	242	302	363	664	8%	69%	0.27	90	59	3.04	-18
Laureano,Ramon	R	16	22	CF	aa	HOU	124	16	37	8	2	4	10	16	37	8	3	294	375	496	872	11%	70%	0.43	136	129	5.34	52
Leyba,Domingo	B	16	21	SS	aa	ARI	156	19	46	7	1	4	18	15	23	4	2	295	359	429	788	9%	85%	0.67	75	84	4.67	46
Lien,Connor	R	16	22	CF	aa	ATL	223	29	50	7	6	6	17	23	95	12	6	226	299	390	689	9%	57%	0.25	121	142	2.88	-10
Machado,Dixon	R	14	22	SS	aa	DET	292	33	78	20	1	4	24	29	38	6	6	267	333	380	713	9%	87%	0.76	85	68	3.37	56
		15	23	SS	aaa	DET	509	47	117	19	1	3	37	28	90	12	3	230	271	290	560	5%	82%	0.32	44	91	2.26	4
		16	24	SS	aaa	DET	492	51	120	26	2	3	42	52	79	15	6	244	316	326	642	10%	84%	0.66	55	92	2.85	28
Mancini,Trey	R	15	23	1B	aa	BAL	326	52	108	27	2	12	49	19	64	2	1	332	369	540	909	6%	80%	0.30	138	79	6.23	69
		16	24	1B	a/a	BAL	546	65	139	23	4	19	57	48	154	2	2	255	315	412	727	8%	72%	0.31	100	63	3.81	4
Margot,Manuel	R	15	21	CF	aa	BOS	258	31	68	23	3	2	27	17	38	16	8	263	310	402	713	6%	85%	0.46	98	137	3.00	76
		16	22	CF	aaa	SD	517	69	133	18	8	4	39	26	75	21	12	258	293	348	641	5%	86%	0.35	51	138	2.75	36
Marlette,Tyler	R	15	22	C	aa	SEA	178	13	41	12	1	2	10	8	35	0	0	232	266	348	614	4%	80%	0.23	85	33	2.42	10
		16	23	C	aa	SEA	50	4	14	2	0	1	6	3	13	1	0	281	319	375	693	5%	75%	0.22	63	39	3.93	-26
Marmolejos,Jose	L	16	23	1B	aa	WAS	127	13	36	9	0	2	13	4	31	0	0	280	305	387	692	3%	76%	0.14	80	28	3.43	-17
Marrero,Deven	R	13	23	SS	aa	BOS	72	5	15	0	0	0	4	8	17	5	0	211	285	211	496	9%	76%	0.43	0	76	2.27	-53
		14	24	SS	a/a	BOS	454	51	107	30	2	5	46	35	104	13	9	235	291	339	629	7%	77%	0.34	89	92	2.48	24
		15	25	SS	aaa	BOS	375	42	89	14	1	5	25	28	97	10	6	236	290	315	605	7%	74%	0.29	59	88	2.61	-14
		16	26	SS	aaa	BOS	363	27	68	12	1	1	25	20	102	9	3	188	230	232	462	5%	72%	0.20	36	88	1.43	-45
May,Jacob	B	15	23	CF	aa	CHW	389	41	98	14	1	2	28	27	82	32	19	251	299	305	604	6%	79%	0.33	42	110	2.52	-3
		16	24	CF	aaa	CHW	301	30	68	16	1	1	19	13	85	15	9	226	258	297	555	4%	72%	0.15	58	118	1.90	-22
McGuire,Reese	L	16	21	C	aa	TOR	319	30	78	19	2	1	37	32	37	5	6	243	312	322	635	9%	88%	0.86	53	73	2.53	38
McKinney,Billy	L	15	21	RF	aa	CHC	274	23	72	25	1	2	31	22	52	0	0	262	318	384	702	8%	81%	0.43	97	30	3.16	28
		16	22	RF	aa	NYY	426	51	103	18	3	4	43	59	105	4	6	241	333	330	663	12%	75%	0.56	61	70	2.92	-3
McMahon,Ryan	L	16	22	3B	aa	COL	466	42	113	27	6	11	65	47	154	9	6	243	312	399	711	9%	67%	0.30	112	101	3.25	8
Meadows,Austin	L	15	20	CF	aa	PIT	25	4	9	2	2	0	1	2	5	1	0	340	380	596	976	6%	79%	0.32	151	131	5.27	92
		16	21	CF	a/a	PIT	293	45	74	22	9	10	43	28	68	15	5	252	317	489	806	9%	77%	0.41	143	155	3.82	88
Michalczewski,Trey	B	16	21	3B	aa	CHW	487	51	98	21	4	10	49	50	171	3	0	202	276	320	595	9%	65%	0.29	88	90	2.33	-23
Moncada,Yoan	B	16	21	2B	aa	BOS	177	32	47	7	3	9	24	23	68	8	4	264	348	477	826	12%	61%	0.34	149	137	4.77	31
Moran,Colin	L	14	22	3B	aa	HOU	112	9	30	5	0	2	17	7	26	0	1	268	312	359	671	6%	77%	0.27	75	25	3.25	-12
		15	23	3B	aa	HOU	366	36	97	22	2	7	52	34	92	1	0	266	328	395	723	8%	75%	0.37	95	53	3.73	10
		16	24	3B	aaa	HOU	459	36	99	15	1	8	50	34	146	2	2	216	270	304	574	7%	68%	0.23	63	46	2.32	-48
Moroff,Max	B	15	22	2B	aa	PIT	523	65	138	26	4	6	42	55	117	14	14	264	334	358	692	10%	78%	0.47	69	99	3.16	17
		16	23	2B	aaa	PIT	421	56	90	17	3	7	42	81	135	8	8	213	341	317	658	16%	68%	0.60	74	89	2.81	-8
Munoz,Yairo	R	16	21	SS	aa	OAK	387	36	84	15	3	7	32	19	79	5	8	217	253	322	576	5%	79%	0.24	64	80	2.06	4
Murphy,Tom	R	15	24	C	a/a	COL	394	39	91	23	3	16	45	20	132	4	3	231	268	429	697	5%	66%	0.15	150	80	3.07	21
		16	25	C	aaa	COL	303	38	90	23	7	15	43	11	81	1	1	296	322	567	889	4%	73%	0.14	169	87	5.12	64
Newman,Kevin	R	16	23	SS	aa	PIT	233	35	60	10	2	2	24	21	26	5	3	258	321	333	654	8%	89%	0.84	45	98	3.00	40
Ngoepe,Gift	B	13	23	SS	aa	PIT	220	23	34	9	1	2	12	21	86	8	3	152	227	234	461	9%	61%	0.25	78	124	1.26	-37
		14	24	2B	aa	PIT	437	41	86	14	6	6	37	35	147	9	9	196	256	295	550	7%	66%	0.24	82	111	1.80	-19
		15	25	SS	a/a	PIT	307	29	68	14	1	2	21	23	90	3	9	221	275	296	571	7%	71%	0.26	63	69	1.92	-30
		16	26	SS	aaa	PIT	332	35	62	17	1	6	23	26	145	2	4	187	247	302	549	7%	56%	0.18	105	83	1.89	-49
Nicholas,Brett	L	13	25	1B	aa	TEX	506	57	131	23	3	18	73	38	137	2	1	259	311	424	734	7%	73%	0.27	117	58	3.93	18
		14	26	C	aaa	TEX	452	26	99	16	1	7	37	18	132	3	1	219	248	304	553	4%	71%	0.13	71	40	2.15	-38
		15	27	C	aaa	TEX	403	36	88	18	0	9	46	20	95	1	2	219	256	329	585	5%	77%	0.21	78	39	2.33	-8
		16	28	C	aaa	TEX	400	41	91	21	1	9	42	29	107	1	2	228	280	355	634	7%	73%	0.27	87	50	2.69	-7
Nimmo,Brandon	L	14	21	CF	aa	NYM	240	28	47	10	2	5	19	27	62	4	1	198	278	317	595	10%	74%	0.43	90	103	2.29	22
		15	22	CF	a/a	NYM	360	35	85	13	3	4	19	34	86	4	7	237	303	321	624	9%	76%	0.40	59	71	2.58	-7
		16	23	CF	aaa	NYM	392	50	113	21	5	8	42	32	87	5	9	290	343	429	773	8%	78%	0.37	87	89	3.97	25
Nottingham,Jacob	R	16	21	C	aa	MIL	415	43	95	14	0	11	35	28	145	9	2	228	277	337	614	6%	65%	0.19	79	77	2.82	-39
Nunez,Renato	R	15	21	3B	aa	OAK	381	47	92	21	0	13	47	22	71	0	0	242	283	397	680	5%	81%	0.31	100	47	3.27	32
		16	22	3B	aaa	OAK	505	56	108	20	2	19	68	29	124	2	0	214	256	378	634	5%	76%	0.23	98	67	2.76	13
Ohlman,Mike	R	16	26	C	a/a	STL	251	32	59	10	1	5	33	19	91	1	2	233	287	343	630	7%	64%	0.21	83	73	2.69	-40
Olson,Matt	L	15	21	1B	aa	OAK	466	62	101	33	0	12	57	82	149	4	1	216	333	364	697	15%	68%	0.55	123	57	3.19	20
		16	22	RF	aaa	OAK	464	64	103	34	1	14	55	66	137	1	0	222	319	393	711	12%	70%	0.48	123	54	3.30	23

BATTER	B	Yr	Age	Pos	Lvl	Tm	AB	R	H	D	T	HR	RBI	BB	K	SB	CS	BA	OB	Slg	OPS	bb%	ct%	Eye	PX	SX	RC/G	BPV
Osuna,Jose	R	15	23	LF	aa	PIT	323	37	82	18	1	6	42	13	66	5	3	253	282	370	652	4%	80%	0.20	82	86	2.86	20
		16	24	1B	a/a	PIT	473	53	117	33	3	10	60	31	87	3	5	248	294	397	690	6%	82%	0.35	94	71	3.02	37
Palka,Daniel	L	16	25	RF	a/a	MIN	503	60	112	22	3	27	73	44	205	7	6	223	286	439	725	8%	59%	0.22	161	87	3.48	10
Papi,Mike	L	16	24	LF	aa	CLE	259	28	54	15	1	7	34	34	78	3	0	208	300	359	658	12%	70%	0.44	107	79	2.85	14
Patterson,Jordan	L	15	23	RF	aa	COL	185	21	50	18	0	6	26	9	44	7	4	271	304	473	777	5%	76%	0.20	149	81	3.79	60
		16	24	RF	aaa	COL	427	55	115	22	7	11	46	34	120	7	0	270	324	434	758	7%	72%	0.29	106	130	4.06	29
Peter,Jake	L	16	23	2B	a/a	CHW	481	46	119	23	0	5	43	42	112	7	2	246	307	327	634	8%	77%	0.37	58	60	2.91	-11
Peterson,D.J.	R	14	22	3B	aa	SEA	222	25	51	8	0	9	30	17	58	1	1	229	282	390	672	7%	74%	0.29	115	37	3.26	15
		15	23	1B	a/a	SEA	372	29	70	17	1	5	33	22	107	4	1	187	234	281	515	6%	71%	0.21	74	75	1.69	-20
		16	24	1B	a/a	SEA	455	47	103	24	1	15	65	30	143	1	2	226	274	383	657	6%	69%	0.21	110	38	2.89	-12
Peterson,Dustin	R	16	22	LF	aa	ATL	524	65	142	37	2	11	88	46	112	4	1	271	330	414	744	8%	79%	0.41	95	73	3.90	30
Phillips,Brett	L	15	21	CF	aa	MIL	214	33	61	14	6	1	22	21	61	8	3	285	348	425	773	9%	72%	0.34	105	143	3.75	33
		16	22	CF	aa	MIL	441	56	98	13	5	15	58	64	164	11	7	222	320	380	700	13%	63%	0.39	109	111	3.32	-1
Pinder,Chad	R	15	23	SS	aa	OAK	477	53	129	28	2	10	64	21	115	5	6	270	302	402	704	4%	76%	0.19	96	71	3.41	12
		16	24	SS	aaa	OAK	426	64	100	22	3	11	45	22	117	4	1	236	273	381	655	7%	73%	0.19	97	110	2.89	13
Powell,Boog	L	15	22	CF	a/a	TAM	444	55	118	14	8	2	33	51	88	15	15	266	342	351	693	10%	80%	0.58	53	121	3.11	22
		16	23	CF	aaa	SEA	248	31	58	8	1	2	21	17	49	8	7	232	281	301	582	6%	80%	0.34	44	103	2.27	2
Quinn,Roman	B	15	22	CF	aa	PHI	232	35	63	5	4	4	12	14	48	23	11	272	314	379	693	6%	79%	0.30	63	171	3.28	32
		16	23	CF	aa	PHI	286	47	73	12	4	5	20	25	79	25	9	255	314	386	700	8%	72%	0.31	85	168	3.37	26
Ramirez,Harold	R	16	22	CF	aa	TOR	383	53	113	18	6	2	44	19	73	6	11	295	329	387	716	5%	81%	0.27	58	110	3.35	15
Ramos,Henry	B	14	22	RF	aa	BOS	181	21	56	10	2	2	19	9	41	2	4	310	342	408	750	5%	78%	0.22	78	77	3.90	7
		15	23	RF	aa	BOS	131	6	30	12	1	0	6	11	28	0	0	231	292	342	634	8%	79%	0.40	91	46	2.24	19
		16	24	RF	a/a	BOS	361	33	90	15	5	6	35	19	76	6	6	249	287	374	662	5%	79%	0.25	74	102	2.84	18
Ramsey,James	L	13	24	CF	a/a	STL	350	45	72	9	1	10	32	39	124	6	5	205	286	327	612	10%	65%	0.32	95	87	2.61	-17
		14	25	CF	a/a	CLE	352	49	87	20	1	12	40	33	119	4	2	247	311	411	722	9%	66%	0.27	141	77	3.62	19
		15	26	LF	aaa	CLE	440	38	92	19	1	10	35	43	153	3	5	209	279	326	605	9%	65%	0.28	94	50	2.40	-29
		16	27	RF	aaa	SEA	351	32	73	14	2	6	32	25	144	4	6	209	262	317	578	7%	59%	0.18	89	79	2.07	-53
Ravelo,Rangel	R	14	22	1B	aa	CHW	476	55	129	32	3	10	50	47	88	8	7	272	337	411	748	9%	82%	0.53	105	75	3.80	53
		15	23	1B	a/a	OAK	189	18	49	10	2	2	27	13	43	0	1	260	307	365	673	6%	77%	0.30	76	60	3.03	3
		16	24	1B	aaa	OAK	367	53	88	22	1	6	48	30	68	1	1	239	297	357	654	8%	81%	0.44	77	65	2.87	24
Reed,Michael	R	15	23	RF	a/a	MIL	439	49	105	29	5	5	55	60	126	20	8	239	330	361	691	12%	71%	0.47	97	126	3.05	27
		16	24	CF	aaa	MIL	411	49	86	17	1	6	32	54	141	14	9	209	301	299	600	12%	66%	0.38	70	93	2.39	-29
Reinheimer,Jack	R	15	23	SS	aa	ARI	485	53	121	23	3	4	35	42	102	17	7	249	309	337	646	8%	79%	0.41	64	111	2.93	18
		16	24	SS	aaa	ARI	500	44	123	25	7	1	33	33	107	14	13	246	293	330	623	6%	79%	0.31	57	107	2.37	7
Renfroe,Hunter	R	14	22	LF	aa	SD	224	14	45	10	0	4	19	21	61	2	1	201	269	302	570	8%	73%	0.34	83	32	2.19	-14
		15	23	RF	a/a	SD	511	48	115	22	4	14	58	28	154	4	1	226	266	367	633	5%	70%	0.18	102	85	2.72	-1
		16	24	RF	aaa	SD	533	65	132	28	3	21	71	15	140	3	2	248	269	433	702	3%	74%	0.11	116	84	3.33	21
Riddle,J.T.	L	15	24	SS	a/a	MIA	176	23	46	6	1	3	16	8	27	0	0	260	293	363	656	4%	85%	0.31	61	61	3.24	17
		16	25	SS	a/a	MIA	445	45	111	18	4	3	45	29	91	5	1	249	295	328	623	6%	80%	0.32	52	95	2.71	3
Rios,Edwin	L	16	22	3B	aa	LA	122	13	29	7	0	5	16	7	34	0	0	240	281	416	697	5%	72%	0.20	116	23	3.39	2
Robertson,Daniel	R	15	21	SS	aa	TAM	299	40	73	18	4	3	33	27	64	2	3	245	308	364	672	8%	78%	0.42	84	100	2.76	30
		16	22	SS	aaa	TAM	436	45	104	19	3	4	38	52	112	2	1	237	318	323	641	11%	74%	0.46	60	66	2.84	-11
Rodriguez,Nellie	R	16	22	1B	aa	CLE	492	58	117	28	1	23	75	65	193	1	0	238	326	444	771	12%	61%	0.33	158	46	4.17	9
Romero,Avery	R	16	23	2B	aa	MIA	100	11	18	3	2	1	9	13	18	2	0	179	275	273	548	12%	82%	0.73	51	116	1.80	29
Rondon,Jose	R	15	21	SS	aa	SD	100	5	17	2	1	0	7	3	17	1	3	168	196	203	398	3%	83%	0.20	22	74	0.84	-18
		16	22	SS	a/a	SD	456	42	114	22	1	5	42	13	89	10	6	250	270	338	608	3%	80%	0.14	59	88	2.55	3
Rosario,Amed	R	16	21	SS	aa	NYM	214	32	67	13	4	2	27	16	57	5	2	311	360	435	795	7%	73%	0.29	86	127	4.47	17
Ruiz,Rio	L	15	21	3B	aa	ATL	420	42	92	20	1	4	41	56	105	2	2	218	310	301	611	12%	75%	0.53	65	49	2.49	-8
		16	22	3B	aaa	ATL	465	45	114	22	2	8	54	54	133	1	4	246	325	357	682	10%	71%	0.41	78	43	3.18	-16
Scavuzzo,Jacob	R	16	22	LF	aa	LA	421	55	104	21	1	10	36	24	109	4	2	248	288	373	661	5%	74%	0.22	84	81	3.08	1
Schrock,Max	L	16	22	2B	aa	OAK	23	2	8	1	0	0	2	0	0	0	0	357	357	399	756	0%	100%	0.00	28	51	4.06	40
Shaffer,Richie	R	14	23	3B	aa	TAM	427	46	82	24	4	14	51	44	135	3	0	191	266	365	632	9%	68%	0.32	142	88	2.49	34
		15	24	3B	a/a	TAM	393	51	89	23	1	19	58	44	144	3	1	226	303	435	738	10%	63%	0.30	166	65	3.71	28
		16	25	3B	aaa	TAM	428	41	83	23	0	9	40	54	160	3	1	193	284	310	594	11%	63%	0.34	96	49	2.31	-33
Shaw,Chris	L	16	23	1B	aa	SF	232	24	54	15	5	4	28	19	61	0	4	233	291	393	684	8%	74%	0.31	105	78	2.74	20
Sisco,Chance	L	15	20	C	aa	BAL	74	8	18	4	0	2	7	8	14	0	1	248	322	379	702	10%	80%	0.56	88	33	3.38	24
		16	21	C	a/a	BAL	426	51	128	26	1	6	45	54	92	2	2	300	378	406	784	11%	78%	0.58	74	40	4.66	9
Slater,Austin	R	15	23	2B	aa	SF	199	20	55	10	1	0	12	14	53	1	1	278	324	342	666	6%	73%	0.26	57	62	3.14	-28
		16	24	LF	a/a	SF	390	48	103	18	1	13	58	50	103	7	8	265	349	417	766	11%	74%	0.48	98	65	4.18	17
Smith,Dominic	L	16	21	1B	aa	NYM	484	54	132	27	2	12	77	43	82	2	1	273	332	410	743	8%	83%	0.52	83	54	4.04	33
Smith,Dwight	L	15	23	LF	aa	TOR	460	62	113	26	2	6	37	39	73	3	3	246	305	352	657	8%	84%	0.53	73	76	2.92	35
		16	24	LF	aa	TOR	471	47	115	24	4	14	63	38	104	10	8	243	300	399	699	7%	78%	0.36	95	90	3.22	31
Sparks,Taylor	R	16	23	3B	aa	CIN	224	22	39	4	1	9	27	17	96	2	0	174	232	315	547	7%	57%	0.18	103	74	2.11	-50

BATTER	B	Yr	Age	Pos	Lvl	Tm	AB	R	H	D	T	HR	RBI	BB	K	SB	CS	BA	OB	Slg	OPS	bb%	ct%	Eye	PX	SX	RC/G	BPV
Starling,Bubba	R	15	23	CF	aa	KC	331	40	75	17	4	8	25	24	97	3	6	227	279	370	649	7%	71%	0.24	105	100	2.56	13
		16	24	CF	a/a	KC	399	33	64	21	1	5	31	17	157	9	1	161	195	257	452	4%	61%	0.11	86	110	1.22	-46
Stassi,Max	R	13	22	C	aa	HOU	289	32	72	18	1	14	48	15	77	1	1	248	286	463	748	5%	73%	0.20	154	50	3.78	44
		14	23	C	aaa	HOU	392	35	81	17	1	7	32	16	119	1	0	208	239	309	548	4%	70%	0.13	86	57	2.00	-26
		15	24	C	aaa	HOU	294	25	50	6	1	9	29	18	109	1	1	171	218	298	516	6%	63%	0.16	94	63	1.76	-41
		16	25	C	aaa	HOU	243	15	46	10	1	5	22	14	78	1	0	188	232	301	533	5%	68%	0.18	80	42	1.86	-39
Staton,Allen	R	16	24	2B	aa	STL	180	19	43	7	2	2	16	13	42	2	0	240	292	334	627	7%	77%	0.32	60	83	2.79	-4
Stevenson,Andrew	L	16	22	CF	aa	WAS	256	34	60	11	1	2	14	18	53	11	5	233	284	304	588	7%	79%	0.34	49	112	2.36	4
Stewart,Christin	L	16	23	LF	aa	DET	87	14	17	2	0	5	15	10	27	0	0	192	275	375	650	10%	69%	0.36	112	42	3.08	-1
Stuart,Champ	R	16	24	CF	aa	NYM	184	18	31	3	1	2	8	11	84	12	3	170	218	219	437	6%	54%	0.13	42	133	1.40	-96
Stubbs,Garrett	L	16	23	C	aa	HOU	120	18	35	8	1	3	13	11	13	4	0	289	349	457	805	8%	89%	0.87	93	105	4.91	82
Swanson,Dansby	R	16	22	SS	aa	ATL	333	54	84	13	5	8	45	36	79	7	2	252	324	386	710	10%	76%	0.45	80	125	3.57	27
Tapia,Raimel	L	16	22	CF	a/a	COL	528	76	170	24	11	7	39	22	59	19	18	322	349	451	800	4%	89%	0.37	68	130	4.33	59
Taylor,Tyrone	R	15	21	CF	aa	MIL	454	44	113	19	3	3	39	29	59	9	6	250	295	325	620	6%	87%	0.49	50	86	2.66	28
		16	22	RF	aa	MIL	465	48	104	14	1	9	32	36	78	8	5	225	280	314	595	7%	83%	0.47	52	75	2.53	14
Telis,Tomas	B	13	22	C	aa	TEX	348	27	87	18	0	4	37	9	48	7	2	251	269	336	605	2%	86%	0.18	62	67	2.61	21
		14	23	C	a/a	TEX	406	36	114	21	3	4	37	17	45	6	2	281	310	377	687	4%	89%	0.38	67	83	3.42	44
		15	24	C	aaa	MIA	330	39	87	14	1	4	24	16	41	3	2	265	299	346	645	5%	88%	0.39	53	67	3.03	24
		16	25	C	aaa	MIA	336	39	93	15	3	4	38	23	47	3	2	276	322	377	699	6%	86%	0.49	59	86	3.52	32
Tellez,Rowdy	L	16	21	1B	aa	TOR	438	63	126	30	2	22	72	56	100	4	3	288	369	518	887	11%	77%	0.56	141	59	5.72	63
Tilson,Charlie	L	14	22	CF	aa	STL	139	15	29	4	1	1	13	5	30	2	3	208	235	276	510	3%	78%	0.16	49	89	1.63	-13
		15	23	CF	aa	STL	539	63	137	18	6	3	24	33	80	34	21	255	298	328	626	6%	85%	0.42	46	135	2.58	32
		16	24	CF	aaa	STL	351	39	83	13	6	3	25	25	62	11	3	236	287	329	616	7%	82%	0.40	55	133	2.54	29
Torres,Nick	R	16	23	LF	a/a	SD	503	42	126	32	1	10	45	16	153	8	7	250	274	377	650	3%	70%	0.11	96	71	2.75	-15
Toups,Corey	R	16	23	2B	aa	KC	338	53	87	25	2	8	33	31	102	14	3	256	318	413	731	8%	70%	0.30	115	128	3.66	28
Travis,Sam	R	15	22	1B	aa	BOS	243	29	70	18	2	3	31	27	36	7	6	287	359	413	772	10%	85%	0.76	88	85	3.94	59
		16	23	1B	aaa	BOS	173	25	47	11	0	5	28	15	43	1	0	272	328	431	759	8%	75%	0.34	106	53	4.23	20
Urena,Richard	B	16	20	SS	aa	TOR	124	13	32	6	4	0	16	4	20	0	2	262	283	383	666	3%	84%	0.18	69	96	2.35	26
Valentin,Jesmuel	B	16	22	2B	a/a	PHI	446	68	112	18	4	9	47	45	90	4	4	252	321	371	692	9%	80%	0.50	71	90	3.33	24
Valera,Breyvic	B	14	22	2B	aa	STL	227	25	58	7	1	0	16	12	24	3	6	254	292	298	590	5%	89%	0.51	33	79	2.33	20
		15	23	2B	aa	STL	360	27	72	8	1	2	23	24	30	1	4	201	252	249	501	6%	92%	0.83	29	51	1.67	20
		16	24	2B	a/a	STL	395	37	102	16	1	0	33	32	48	9	6	259	314	307	621	7%	88%	0.66	34	78	2.75	19
Vielma,Engelb	B	16	22	SS	aa	MIN	314	39	79	7	3	0	17	27	64	8	9	251	310	293	603	8%	79%	0.42	27	107	2.48	-10
Vincej,Zach	R	16	25	SS	aa	CIN	399	42	103	23	2	3	44	24	102	7	7	259	301	351	651	6%	75%	0.24	68	86	2.79	-8
Wade,Tyler	L	15	21	SS	aa	NYY	113	6	22	4	0	1	3	2	26	2	1	194	207	254	461	2%	77%	0.07	46	50	1.42	-35
		16	22	SS	aa	NYY	505	89	128	15	6	6	27	66	111	27	8	254	340	340	679	12%	78%	0.59	52	143	3.43	21
Walker,Christian	R	13	22	1B	aa	BAL	62	5	13	4	0	0	1	5	11	0	0	214	269	285	554	7%	83%	0.43	65	28	1.87	7
		14	23	1B	a/a	BAL	532	54	134	21	1	21	71	41	146	1	1	252	306	417	723	7%	72%	0.28	123	41	3.85	17
		15	24	1B	aaa	BAL	534	64	130	31	1	19	70	47	148	1	3	243	304	410	714	8%	72%	0.32	120	38	3.49	14
		16	25	LF	aaa	BAL	504	56	121	25	1	18	56	35	153	1	3	240	290	402	692	6%	70%	0.23	110	46	3.27	-5
Wallach,Chad	R	16	25	C	aa	CIN	200	25	45	9	0	8	28	35	55	0	1	224	340	395	736	15%	73%	0.64	110	23	3.82	17
Ward,Drew	L	16	22	3B	aa	WAS	178	17	37	7	0	2	21	20	53	0	1	208	287	288	575	10%	70%	0.37	60	29	2.24	-41
Westbrook,Jamie	R	16	21	2B	aa	ARI	435	46	111	22	1	5	33	24	63	9	5	256	294	343	637	5%	85%	0.37	56	81	2.85	23
Williams,Justin	L	16	21	RF	aa	TAM	148	17	32	5	2	5	23	4	33	0	1	219	241	377	618	3%	77%	0.13	91	82	2.41	15
Williams,Mason	L	13	22	CF	aa	NYY	72	6	10	3	1	1	3	1	19	0	0	139	149	234	382	1%	73%	0.04	72	88	0.78	-19
		14	23	CF	aa	NYY	507	53	99	16	3	4	32	38	75	17	9	196	252	263	515	7%	85%	0.50	47	108	1.76	27
		15	24	CF	a/a	NYY	201	23	58	12	1	0	19	24	26	11	8	288	364	356	720	11%	87%	0.91	54	87	3.55	40
		16	25	CF	aaa	NYY	125	17	33	7	1	0	21	5	24	1	1	267	293	336	629	4%	80%	0.19	52	87	2.65	-1
Williams,Nick	L	15	22	CF	aa	PHI	475	61	128	23	4	15	43	28	111	10	9	270	310	432	742	6%	77%	0.25	107	101	3.75	35
		16	23	LF	aaa	PHI	497	75	122	31	5	14	61	18	153	6	4	246	273	415	688	4%	69%	0.12	119	124	2.98	18
Winker,Jesse	L	15	22	LF	aa	CIN	443	60	117	22	2	14	48	65	95	7	4	264	359	414	773	13%	79%	0.69	99	73	4.37	43
		16	23	RF	aaa	CIN	380	35	108	21	0	3	41	55	68	0	0	284	375	363	738	13%	82%	0.81	56	16	4.10	5
Yastrzemski,Mike	L	14	24	CF	aa	BAL	184	17	39	11	3	2	9	10	38	1	2	213	254	340	594	5%	79%	0.27	96	85	1.97	32
		15	25	LF	aa	BAL	476	52	102	26	4	5	48	36	113	7	8	215	269	321	590	7%	76%	0.31	79	95	2.07	12
		16	26	RF	a/a	BAL	466	54	94	22	3	12	47	48	135	11	4	201	276	334	610	9%	71%	0.36	90	107	2.46	9
Young,Chesny	R	16	24	2B	aa	CHC	491	47	130	23	2	3	28	24	74	12	16	265	326	337	664	8%	85%	0.61	48	65	2.94	16
Yrizarri,Yeyson	R	15	18	SS	aaa	TEX	33	2	9	1	1	0	4	1	5	0	1	278	297	366	663	3%	85%	0.18	50	85	2.53	14
Zagunis,Mark	R	16	23	LF	a/a	CHC	358	47	91	22	4	8	38	41	89	4	2	255	332	407	739	10%	75%	0.46	100	93	3.65	31
Zimmer,Bradley	L	15	23	CF	aa	CLE	187	22	38	9	1	5	22	16	60	11	2	202	265	344	608	8%	68%	0.26	107	119	2.58	10
		16	24	CF	a/a	CLE	468	65	107	24	4	13	53	64	185	32	16	229	322	382	704	12%	61%	0.35	121	133	3.25	5

PITCHER	Th	Yr	Age	LvL	Org	W	L	G	Sv	IP	H	ER	HR	BB	K	ERA	WHIP	BF/G	OBA	bb/9	k/9	Cmd	hr/9	H%	S%	BPV
Adams,Austin	R	15	24	a/a	LAA	1	1	29	1	40	25	17	0	37	42	3.90	1.54	6.1	183	8.2	9.4	1.1	0.0	26%	72%	99
		16	25	aa	LAA	0	1	32	4	41	37	20	2	26	51	4.26	1.53	5.6	240	5.7	11.1	1.9	0.5	34%	72%	99
Adams,Chance	R	16	22	aa	NYY	8	1	13	0	70	44	23	8	27	63	3.01	1.01	20.5	182	3.4	8.1	2.4	1.0	21%	75%	87
Adams,Spencer	R	16	20	aa	CHW	2	5	9	0	55	64	27	2	10	24	4.39	1.34	25.6	291	1.7	3.9	2.4	0.4	32%	66%	59
Alcantara,Raul	R	16	24	a/a	OAK	9	6	25	0	136	164	68	13	31	84	4.52	1.44	23.1	300	2.1	5.6	2.7	0.8	34%	70%	60
Alcantara,Victor	R	16	23	aa	LAA	3	7	29	0	111	129	71	10	60	69	5.76	1.70	17.3	291	4.9	5.6	1.1	0.8	33%	66%	29
Alexander,Tyler	L	16	22	aa	DET	2	1	6	0	34	41	14	4	4	19	3.73	1.30	23.6	296	1.1	4.9	4.6	1.1	32%	75%	89
Almonte,Miguel	R	15	22	a/a	KC	6	6	28	0	104	112	62	7	41	80	5.42	1.48	15.9	276	3.6	6.9	1.9	0.6	33%	62%	62
		16	23	a/a	KC	5	8	32	0	76	101	60	9	46	59	7.14	1.94	11.3	321	5.4	7.0	1.3	1.1	37%	63%	27
Almonte,Yency	R	16	22	aa	COL	3	1	5	0	30	28	15	6	18	17	4.58	1.53	26.1	250	5.3	5.2	1.0	1.8	25%	77%	2
Altavilla,Dan	R	16	24	aa	SEA	7	3	43	16	57	49	16	4	23	56	2.53	1.26	5.4	234	3.6	8.9	2.5	0.6	30%	82%	96
Anderson,Chris	R	15	23	a/a	LA	9	10	26	0	133	154	81	16	64	86	5.46	1.64	22.8	291	4.3	5.8	1.4	1.1	32%	68%	28
		16	24	aa	LA	3	6	18	0	40	45	35	4	34	21	7.86	2.01	10.6	288	7.8	4.7	0.6	0.9	31%	59%	13
Appel,Mark	R	14	23	aa	HOU	1	2	7	0	39	39	18	2	13	33	4.07	1.31	23.0	260	2.9	7.6	2.6	0.5	32%	68%	89
		15	24	a/a	HOU	10	3	25	0	132	150	71	14	50	94	4.84	1.52	22.9	288	3.4	6.4	1.9	0.9	33%	69%	47
		16	25	aaa	PHI	3	3	8	0	38	53	29	5	23	29	6.85	2.00	23.1	329	5.5	6.7	1.2	1.1	38%	66%	22
Arano,Victor	R	16	21	PHI	1	1	11	1	17	12	5	2	4	22	2.54	0.98	5.8	208	2.1	11.8	5.5	1.3	28%	83%	160
Armenteros,Rogelio	R	16	22	aa	HOU	2	0	3	0	18	19	5	1	4	12	2.23	1.24	24.8	267	1.9	5.7	3.0	0.6	31%	84%	82
Armstrong,Shawn	R	13	23	aa	CLE	2	3	30	0	33	35	16	2	19	37	4.33	1.64	4.9	271	5.3	10.0	1.9	0.5	37%	73%	85
		14	24	a/a	CLE	6	2	49	15	56	49	17	4	21	61	2.75	1.25	4.7	236	3.4	9.8	2.8	0.6	32%	80%	107
		15	25	aaa	CLE	1	2	46	16	50	46	18	0	27	66	3.18	1.48	4.6	247	5.0	12.0	2.4	0.0	38%	76%	128
		16	26	aaa	CLE	3	1	47	9	49	35	14	0	32	55	2.61	1.37	4.4	202	5.9	10.2	1.7	0.0	30%	79%	112
Aro,Jonathan	R	15	25	a/a	BOS	3	3	34	2	74	73	35	2	20	58	4.21	1.26	8.9	259	2.4	7.0	2.9	0.3	32%	65%	97
		16	26	aaa	SEA	3	2	24	1	36	33	11	2	10	21	2.74	1.18	6.0	244	2.4	5.1	2.1	0.5	28%	78%	67
Banda,Anthony	L	16	23	a/a	ARI	10	6	26	0	150	165	58	11	55	129	3.49	1.47	24.7	281	3.3	7.7	2.3	0.7	34%	77%	74
Banuelos,Manny	L	14	23	a/a	NYY	2	3	21	0	64	62	37	12	30	48	5.16	1.43	12.9	255	4.2	6.8	1.6	1.7	27%	69%	28
Barlow,Scott	R	16	24	aa	LA	4	7	24	0	124	153	73	11	51	85	5.30	1.64	23.1	304	3.7	6.2	1.7	0.8	35%	68%	42
Beck,Chris	R	14	24	a/a	CHW	6	11	27	0	150	169	65	9	47	73	3.92	1.44	23.7	286	2.8	4.4	1.5	0.6	31%	73%	40
		15	25	aaa	CHW	3	2	10	0	54	62	26	4	16	33	4.28	1.45	23.2	290	2.7	5.5	2.0	0.7	33%	71%	52
		16	26	aaa	CHW	5	4	22	0	66	94	39	6	29	41	5.33	1.84	14.1	334	3.9	5.6	1.4	0.8	38%	71%	27
Beede,Tyler	R	15	22	aa	SF	3	8	13	0	72	73	54	4	37	43	6.67	1.52	24.1	263	4.6	5.3	1.2	0.5	30%	53%	44
		16	23	aa	SF	8	7	24	0	147	165	63	9	57	117	3.82	1.51	26.6	284	3.5	7.1	2.0	0.6	34%	75%	67
Blach,Ty	L	14	24	aa	SF	8	8	25	0	141	161	56	7	39	75	3.56	1.41	23.9	288	2.5	4.8	2.0	0.5	32%	75%	53
		15	25	aaa	SF	11	12	27	0	165	208	87	13	31	76	4.72	1.45	26.1	309	1.7	4.2	2.5	0.7	33%	67%	49
		16	26	aaa	SF	14	7	26	0	163	175	75	8	40	92	4.13	1.32	25.9	276	2.2	5.1	2.3	0.5	31%	68%	64
Black,Corey	R	14	23	aa	CHC	6	7	26	0	124	112	55	14	72	101	3.99	1.48	20.6	243	5.2	7.3	1.4	1.0	28%	76%	50
		15	24	aa	CHC	3	5	37	0	86	86	57	8	49	85	5.94	1.58	10.2	262	5.2	8.9	1.7	0.8	33%	62%	68
		16	25	a/a	CHC	0	6	48	14	53	56	30	1	38	51	5.12	1.78	5.1	274	6.4	8.7	1.4	0.2	36%	69%	75
Black,Ray	R	16	26	aa	SF	1	4	35	6	31	22	24	1	37	43	6.92	1.87	4.2	199	10.6	12.3	1.2	0.3	31%	60%	104
Blackburn,Clayton	R	14	21	aa	SF	5	6	18	0	93	101	37	1	19	74	3.56	1.29	21.2	278	1.8	7.2	3.9	0.1	35%	70%	123
		15	22	aaa	SF	10	4	23	0	123	130	37	5	30	85	2.69	1.30	22.1	273	2.2	6.3	2.9	0.3	33%	79%	88
		16	23	aaa	SF	7	10	25	0	136	158	75	16	35	87	4.92	1.42	23.1	292	2.3	5.8	2.5	1.0	32%	67%	53
Blackburn,Paul	R	16	23	aa	SEA	9	5	26	0	143	165	68	9	36	87	4.25	1.40	23.2	290	2.2	5.5	2.5	0.6	33%	70%	64
Brault,Steven	L	15	23	aa	PIT	9	3	15	0	90	80	22	1	18	65	2.25	1.08	23.4	240	1.8	6.5	3.7	0.1	30%	78%	121
		16	24	aaa	PIT	2	7	16	0	71	82	43	7	37	64	5.40	1.68	20.0	290	4.7	8.1	1.7	0.9	36%	68%	56
Brice,Austin	R	15	23	aa	MIA	6	9	25	0	125	132	80	10	70	105	5.72	1.62	22.2	273	5.0	7.6	1.5	0.7	33%	64%	55
		16	24	a/a	MIA	4	7	32	4	102	101	42	6	33	72	3.71	1.31	13.2	260	2.9	6.4	2.2	0.6	31%	72%	71
Bridwell,Parker	R	15	24	aa	BAL	4	5	18	0	97	118	58	9	41	76	5.38	1.64	24.1	302	3.8	7.1	1.8	0.9	36%	68%	50
		16	25	a/a	BAL	2	1	22	1	66	76	42	11	32	41	5.73	1.64	13.3	291	4.4	5.7	1.3	1.5	31%	68%	12
Burdi,Nick	R	15	22	aa	MIN	3	4	30	2	44	44	25	3	30	45	5.06	1.70	6.6	263	6.3	9.3	1.5	0.6	34%	70%	72
Burdi,Zack	R	16	21	a/a	CHW	2	0	42	2	64	35	25	4	42	83	3.56	1.20	6.1	164	5.8	11.7	2.0	0.6	24%	71%	116
Cash,Ralston	R	15	24	a/a	LA	2	6	50	3	58	51	26	8	27	49	4.01	1.33	4.8	236	4.2	7.6	1.8	1.2	27%	74%	55
		16	25	a/a	LA	9	3	46	2	69	62	28	2	32	69	3.67	1.36	6.3	241	4.2	9.0	2.1	0.3	32%	72%	96
Chacin,Alejandro	R	16	23	aa	CIN	5	2	52	30	61	65	18	3	30	67	2.65	1.57	5.1	276	4.5	10.0	2.2	0.5	37%	84%	93
Chargois,J.T.	R	15	25	a/a	MIN	1	1	32	11	33	30	12	1	20	27	3.24	1.53	4.5	246	5.5	7.3	1.3	0.3	31%	78%	69
		16	26	a/a	MIN	2	1	39	16	47	45	10	2	14	42	1.87	1.26	4.9	253	2.7	8.1	3.0	0.5	32%	87%	101
Clark,Brian	L	16	23	a/a	CHW	0	5	37	4	57	70	20	1	13	42	3.20	1.46	6.5	304	2.0	6.7	3.3	0.2	37%	77%	98
Clarke,Taylor	R	16	23	aa	ARI	8	6	17	0	98	123	54	12	23	61	5.00	1.49	24.7	308	2.1	5.6	2.7	1.1	34%	68%	52
Cole,A.J.	R	13	21	aa	WAS	4	2	7	0	45	35	13	3	9	41	2.54	0.96	24.5	213	1.8	8.2	4.5	0.6	27%	76%	138
		14	22	a/a	WAS	13	3	25	0	134	158	49	9	29	93	3.32	1.39	22.6	294	1.9	6.2	3.2	0.6	34%	77%	83
		15	23	aaa	WAS	5	6	21	0	106	110	49	10	35	62	4.16	1.37	21.1	269	3.0	5.3	1.8	0.8	30%	71%	45
		16	24	aaa	WAS	8	8	22	0	125	167	85	19	40	89	6.15	1.66	25.4	322	2.9	6.4	2.2	1.4	36%	65%	34

PITCHER	Th	Yr	Age	LvL	Org	W	L	G	Sv	IP	H	ER	HR	BB	K	ERA	WHIP	BF/G	OBA	bb/9	k/9	Cmd	hr/9	H%	S%	BPV
Cooney,Tim	L	13	23	aa	STL	7	10	20	0	118	142	53	7	17	105	4.02	1.35	24.7	299	1.3	8.0	6.0	0.5	37%	70%	153
		14	24	aaa	STL	14	6	26	0	158	170	63	18	45	98	3.57	1.36	25.4	276	2.5	5.6	2.2	1.0	30%	77%	48
		15	25	aaa	STL	6	4	14	0	89	70	31	9	16	50	3.10	0.96	23.9	218	1.6	5.1	3.2	0.9	23%	72%	82
Coonrod,Sam	R	16	24	aa	SF	4	3	13	0	77	73	35	7	42	44	4.11	1.48	25.6	251	4.9	5.1	1.0	0.8	27%	74%	32
Cotton,Jharel	R	15	23	a/a	LA	5	2	16	0	70	65	23	4	22	69	2.96	1.24	17.8	249	2.8	8.9	3.2	0.6	32%	77%	109
		16	24	aaa	OAK	11	6	28	0	136	134	89	23	42	125	5.90	1.30	20.0	259	2.8	8.3	2.9	1.5	30%	57%	69
Covey,Dylan	R	16	25	aa	OAK	2	1	6	0	29	25	7	2	17	20	2.20	1.43	20.8	229	5.3	6.3	1.2	0.6	27%	87%	53
Crick,Kyle	R	14	22	aa	SF	6	7	23	0	90	85	42	6	58	96	4.14	1.58	17.3	250	5.8	9.6	1.7	0.6	33%	74%	79
		15	23	aa	SF	3	4	36	0	63	56	30	2	71	62	4.28	2.02	8.5	241	10.2	8.9	0.9	0.3	32%	78%	70
		16	24	aa	SF	4	11	23	0	109	136	83	8	74	73	6.84	1.92	22.5	307	6.1	6.0	1.0	0.7	35%	63%	30
Danish,Tyler	R	15	21	aa	CHW	8	12	26	0	142	207	93	17	67	80	5.91	1.93	25.9	341	4.2	5.1	1.2	1.1	37%	70%	10
		16	22	a/a	CHW	4	10	19	0	105	123	65	3	27	61	5.59	1.44	23.5	294	2.3	5.3	2.2	0.3	34%	58%	66
Davis,Rookie	R	15	22	aa	NYY	2	1	6	0	33	45	21	1	9	21	5.71	1.62	24.6	325	2.3	5.7	2.5	0.4	38%	62%	65
		16	23	a/a	CIN	10	5	24	0	125	158	76	19	42	69	5.48	1.60	23.0	310	3.0	5.0	1.6	1.4	33%	69%	16
Drake,Oliver	R	13	26	aa	BAL	3	0	19	8	31	23	8	1	14	30	2.18	1.19	6.5	208	4.0	8.7	2.1	0.4	27%	83%	99
		14	27	aa	BAL	2	4	50	31	53	50	22	3	18	55	3.84	1.30	4.3	252	3.1	9.3	3.0	0.1	34%	70%	111
		15	28	aaa	BAL	1	2	42	23	44	33	7	2	20	50	1.38	1.22	4.2	211	4.2	10.2	2.4	0.3	30%	90%	115
		16	29	aaa	BAL	1	4	47	10	56	63	28	8	31	58	4.49	1.68	5.4	285	5.0	9.2	1.8	1.3	35%	77%	52
Edwards,Andrew	R	16	25	a/a	KC	0	1	42	7	61	70	35	8	34	58	5.08	1.71	6.6	289	5.0	8.6	1.7	1.1	35%	72%	51
Enns,Dietrich	L	16	25	a/a	NYY	14	4	26	1	135	135	40	9	65	103	2.64	1.48	22.3	261	4.4	6.8	1.6	0.6	31%	84%	58
Faulkner,Andrew	L	15	23	a/a	TEX	7	4	34	1	100	99	52	10	49	86	4.65	1.47	12.7	259	4.4	7.7	1.8	0.9	31%	70%	60
		16	24	aaa	TEX	5	3	41	4	45	46	25	3	22	32	4.99	1.50	4.8	266	4.3	6.3	1.5	0.7	31%	66%	50
Fernandez,Pedro	R	16	22	aa	KC	1	2	8	0	29	34	17	2	10	16	5.27	1.54	15.8	296	3.2	4.9	1.6	0.7	33%	65%	38
Fillmyer,Heath	R	16	22	aa	OAK	2	0	8	0	39	34	12	3	8	24	2.85	1.07	19.0	237	1.8	5.6	3.1	0.6	27%	76%	88
Flores,Kendry	R	15	24	a/a	MIA	6	5	19	0	115	98	39	6	30	68	3.00	1.12	23.9	232	2.4	5.3	2.2	0.5	26%	74%	74
		16	25	a/a	MIA	3	6	19	0	97	139	65	9	43	62	6.04	1.88	24.0	336	4.0	5.8	1.4	0.8	38%	67%	28
Freeland,Kyle	L	16	23	a/a	COL	11	10	26	0	162	209	102	23	48	83	5.66	1.59	27.5	314	2.7	4.6	1.7	1.3	33%	66%	18
Fry,Paul	L	15	23	aa	SEA	0	2	22	7	25	25	6	0	10	37	2.11	1.39	4.8	262	3.5	13.5	3.9	0.0	43%	83%	165
		16	24	aaa	SEA	3	1	48	0	55	52	18	1	29	56	2.95	1.48	4.9	253	4.7	9.2	2.0	0.2	34%	79%	96
Fulmer,Carson	R	16	23	a/a	CHW	6	10	21	0	103	110	63	9	60	92	5.49	1.65	21.9	274	5.2	8.0	1.5	0.8	34%	67%	56
Gant,John	R	15	23	aa	ATL	8	5	18	0	100	113	48	3	41	76	4.36	1.54	24.2	285	3.7	6.9	1.8	0.3	35%	70%	69
		16	24	aaa	ATL	3	3	12	0	56	69	33	5	23	50	5.25	1.65	20.8	304	3.8	8.0	2.1	0.9	37%	69%	60
Garcia,Jarlin	L	15	22	aa	MIA	1	3	7	0	37	43	24	4	17	30	5.90	1.64	23.4	295	4.2	7.3	1.7	0.9	35%	64%	49
		16	23	aa	MIA	1	3	9	0	40	46	27	4	12	22	6.04	1.46	18.8	291	2.7	5.1	1.9	0.9	32%	58%	39
Garcia,Jason	R	16	24	aa	BAL	6	10	24	0	124	163	82	6	56	58	5.97	1.77	23.7	319	4.1	4.2	1.0	0.5	35%	64%	24
Garrett,Amir	L	16	24	a/a	CIN	7	8	25	0	145	127	60	9	68	116	3.74	1.35	24.1	237	4.2	7.2	1.7	0.6	29%	73%	70
Gibson,Daniel	L	15	24	aa	ARI	1	0	26	2	24	22	5	0	15	17	2.01	1.53	4.0	246	5.5	6.2	1.1	0.0	30%	85%	67
		16	25	a/a	ARI	6	1	45	0	44	57	21	5	23	28	4.43	1.82	4.5	315	4.7	5.7	1.2	1.0	35%	78%	23
Giolito,Lucas	R	15	21	aa	WAS	4	2	8	0	47	55	25	2	17	38	4.68	1.52	25.7	292	3.2	7.2	2.3	0.4	36%	68%	76
		16	22	a/a	WAS	6	5	21	0	108	118	46	6	47	95	3.79	1.53	22.4	279	3.9	7.9	2.0	0.5	35%	75%	75
Glasnow,Tyler	R	15	22	a/a	PIT	7	4	20	0	104	83	31	3	38	108	2.69	1.16	20.7	220	3.3	9.3	2.8	0.2	30%	76%	120
		16	23	a/a	PIT	8	3	22	0	117	82	32	5	69	117	2.47	1.30	21.8	199	5.3	9.0	1.7	0.4	27%	82%	92
Glover,Koda	R	16	23	a/a	WAS	3	1	33	6	46	44	19	3	11	42	3.73	1.19	5.6	253	2.1	8.2	3.9	0.7	32%	70%	115
Gomber,Austin	L	16	23	aa	STL	1	0	4	0	19	13	4	0	9	13	1.69	1.14	19.1	189	4.3	6.2	1.4	0.0	24%	83%	85
Gonsalves,Stephen	L	16	22	aa	MIN	8	1	13	0	74	49	18	1	36	74	2.19	1.14	22.7	190	4.3	8.9	2.1	0.1	26%	80%	110
Gonzales,Marco	L	14	22	a/a	STL	7	3	15	0	84	80	28	8	18	73	2.97	1.16	22.4	252	1.9	7.8	4.1	0.8	30%	78%	112
		15	23	aa	STL	1	5	16	0	76	105	45	9	22	47	5.34	1.68	21.4	330	2.6	5.6	2.1	1.1	37%	70%	34
Gossett,Daniel	R	16	24	a/a	OAK	6	5	18	0	108	102	37	4	29	79	3.06	1.22	24.2	252	2.4	6.6	2.7	0.4	30%	75%	90
Green,Chad	R	15	24	aa	DET	5	14	27	0	149	203	82	11	46	108	4.99	1.67	24.7	326	2.8	6.5	2.4	0.6	38%	70%	59
		16	25	aaa	NYY	7	6	16	0	95	89	24	5	24	83	2.27	1.20	23.8	250	2.3	7.9	3.4	0.4	31%	82%	111
Greene,Conner	R	15	20	aa	TOR	3	1	5	0	25	28	16	1	12	14	5.78	1.61	22.2	287	4.3	5.0	1.2	0.4	32%	62%	39
		16	21	aa	TOR	6	5	12	0	69	66	40	6	34	43	5.31	1.45	24.5	255	4.4	5.7	1.3	0.8	28%	63%	40
Gregorio,Joan	R	15	23	aa	SF	3	2	37	1	79	77	35	6	35	62	4.02	1.41	9.0	257	4.0	7.0	1.8	0.7	31%	72%	63
		16	24	a/a	SF	6	10	26	0	134	150	87	13	52	129	5.85	1.50	22.3	284	3.5	8.6	2.5	0.9	35%	61%	75
Grimes,Matthew	R	16	25	aa	BAL	3	5	11	0	58	73	39	7	24	29	6.04	1.69	23.6	310	3.8	4.6	1.2	1.0	33%	65%	15
Gsellman,Robert	R	15	22	aa	NYM	7	7	16	0	92	99	42	4	25	44	4.05	1.35	24.1	276	2.5	4.2	1.7	0.4	30%	69%	48
		16	23	a/a	NYM	4	9	20	0	115	120	52	9	29	76	4.06	1.29	23.6	269	2.3	5.9	2.6	0.7	31%	69%	70
Guduan,Reymin	L	15	23	aa	HOU	1	3	16	0	16	22	24	3	19	17	13.20	2.52	5.5	327	10.4	9.1	0.9	1.8	39%	45%	9
		16	24	a/a	HOU	3	3	43	2	56	57	30	3	37	54	4.77	1.67	5.8	264	5.9	8.6	1.5	0.5	34%	71%	69
Guerrero,Jordan	L	16	22	aa	CHW	7	8	25	0	136	149	85	15	76	97	5.60	1.66	24.3	279	5.1	6.4	1.3	1.0	32%	67%	35
Guerrero,Tayron	R	15	24	a/a	SD	1	5	48	14	56	44	19	2	30	52	3.11	1.31	4.8	217	4.8	8.4	1.8	0.4	28%	76%	86
		16	25	a/a	MIA	1	4	44	4	50	54	33	4	25	41	6.02	1.59	5.0	279	4.4	7.4	1.7	0.8	33%	61%	55
Guerrieri,Taylor	R	15	23	aa	TAM	3	1	8	0	36	31	7	2	8	24	1.69	1.09	17.6	235	2.0	6.0	3.1	0.5	27%	87%	94
		16	24	aa	TAM	12	6	28	1	146	152	74	12	47	77	4.55	1.36	21.8	269	2.9	4.7	1.6	0.7	29%	67%	42

PITCHER	Th	Yr	Age	LvL	Org	W	L	G	Sv	IP	H	ER	HR	BB	K	ERA	WHIP	BF/G	OBA	bb/9	k/9	Cmd	hr/9	H%	S%	BPV
Gustave,Jandel	R	15	23	aa	HOU	5	2	46	20	59	57	16	2	25	43	2.45	1.40	5.4	257	3.8	6.6	1.7	0.3	31%	83%	69
		16	24	aaa	HOU	3	3	47	3	57	51	26	1	22	47	4.17	1.29	5.0	241	3.5	7.4	2.1	0.2	31%	65%	90
Heller,Ben	R	16	25	a/a	NYY	3	3	49	13	48	34	14	3	16	46	2.57	1.06	3.8	202	3.1	8.5	2.8	0.6	26%	78%	107
Hildenberger,Trevor	R	16	26	aa	MIN	2	3	32	16	39	26	4	2	6	34	0.92	0.84	4.4	193	1.5	8.0	5.4	0.5	24%	95%	162
Hoffman,Jeff	R	15	22	aa	COL	2	2	9	0	48	45	22	5	13	31	4.12	1.21	21.5	250	2.5	5.8	2.3	0.9	28%	68%	63
		16	23	aaa	COL	6	9	22	0	119	143	72	15	47	96	5.49	1.60	23.9	300	3.5	7.2	2.0	1.1	35%	67%	47
Holder,Jonathan	R	16	23	a/a	NYY	5	1	40	16	61	43	18	5	8	81	2.57	0.83	5.6	199	1.2	11.9	10.3	0.7	30%	72%	284
Holmes,Clay	R	16	23	aa	PIT	10	9	26	0	136	160	78	10	63	82	5.13	1.64	23.4	293	4.2	5.4	1.3	0.7	33%	68%	36
Honeywell,Brent	R	16	21	aa	TAM	3	2	10	0	59	57	17	4	14	48	2.62	1.18	23.7	253	2.1	7.2	3.5	0.6	30%	80%	103
Howard,Sam	L	16	23	aa	COL	5	6	16	0	90	148	62	17	32	52	6.20	1.99	27.1	367	3.2	5.1	1.6	1.7	39%	72%	-4
Hoyt,James	R	13	27	aa	ATL	0	1	22	1	33	22	13	1	15	26	3.48	1.13	5.9	193	4.1	7.3	1.8	0.3	24%	68%	87
		14	28	a/a	ATL	3	3	52	7	60	70	26	6	26	60	3.95	1.62	5.1	295	4.0	9.1	2.3	0.8	38%	77%	74
		15	29	aaa	HOU	0	1	47	9	49	58	22	1	12	50	4.10	1.43	4.4	297	2.2	9.3	4.3	0.2	39%	69%	135
		16	30	aaa	HOU	4	3	49	29	55	36	12	2	21	70	2.04	1.04	4.3	190	3.4	11.5	3.4	0.4	29%	82%	145
Hu,Chih-Wei	R	16	23	a/a	TAM	7	9	25	0	147	157	57	9	39	99	3.46	1.33	24.5	274	2.4	6.1	2.6	0.5	32%	74%	74
Jackson,Luke	R	14	23	a/a	TEX	9	5	26	1	123	129	86	16	53	105	6.29	1.47	20.4	271	3.8	7.6	2.0	1.2	32%	58%	53
		15	24	aaa	TEX	2	3	39	0	66	74	40	3	37	65	5.47	1.67	7.6	283	5.0	8.8	1.8	0.5	37%	66%	74
		16	25	a/a	TEX	1	1	36	3	46	49	25	7	36	47	4.88	1.84	6.0	274	7.0	9.1	1.3	1.4	33%	77%	41
Jaye,Myles	R	15	24	aa	CHW	12	9	26	0	148	168	75	11	55	88	4.55	1.51	24.6	288	3.3	5.4	1.6	0.7	32%	70%	43
		16	25	a/a	DET	5	12	28	0	162	194	95	15	46	104	5.27	1.48	24.9	299	2.5	5.8	2.3	0.9	34%	65%	52
Jerez,Williams	L	15	23	aa	BOS	1	2	22	1	37	40	19	2	18	26	4.59	1.56	7.4	277	4.3	6.3	1.5	0.5	33%	70%	53
		16	24	aa	BOS	1	6	40	0	65	85	45	7	32	54	6.21	1.80	7.5	317	4.4	7.5	1.7	0.9	38%	65%	44
Jimenez,Joe	R	16	21	a/a	DET	3	3	38	20	36	24	11	1	12	41	2.77	1.01	3.7	191	3.1	10.3	3.3	0.3	27%	72%	140
Johnson,Brian	L	14	24	aa	BOS	10	2	20	0	118	94	30	7	33	81	2.29	1.08	23.0	221	2.5	6.2	2.4	0.5	26%	81%	84
		15	25	aaa	BOS	9	6	18	0	96	96	40	8	37	72	3.71	1.38	22.4	262	3.4	6.8	2.0	0.7	31%	74%	64
		16	26	aaa	BOS	5	6	15	0	77	104	58	13	44	43	6.83	1.92	24.3	323	5.2	5.0	1.0	1.5	34%	66%	-3
Johnson,Chase	R	16	24	aa	SF	1	4	24	5	52	58	26	2	20	31	4.44	1.49	9.4	282	3.4	5.4	1.6	0.4	32%	69%	53
Johnson,Pierce	R	14	23	aa	CHC	5	4	18	0	92	67	30	8	55	77	2.93	1.33	21.2	207	5.4	7.6	1.4	0.8	25%	81%	64
		15	24	aa	CHC	6	2	16	0	95	89	27	4	34	61	2.52	1.29	24.4	248	3.2	5.8	1.8	0.4	29%	81%	66
		16	25	aaa	CHC	4	6	22	0	63	70	51	9	45	62	7.27	1.82	13.3	282	6.4	8.9	1.4	1.3	34%	60%	42
Jorge,Felix	R	16	22	aa	MIN	3	5	11	0	74	95	41	7	12	27	4.96	1.43	28.7	311	1.4	3.2	2.3	0.9	32%	66%	33
Jurado,Ariel	R	16	20	aa	TEX	1	4	8	0	44	50	20	3	10	31	4.10	1.39	23.0	290	2.1	6.3	2.9	0.7	34%	71%	76
Kaminsky,Rob	L	16	22	aa	CLE	11	7	25	0	137	144	64	8	49	77	4.23	1.40	23.1	271	3.2	5.1	1.6	0.6	30%	70%	48
Kingham,Nick	R	14	23	a/a	PIT	6	11	26	0	159	152	62	8	47	96	3.51	1.25	24.9	253	2.7	5.4	2.0	0.4	29%	72%	66
		15	24	aaa	PIT	1	2	6	0	31	40	19	3	7	25	5.43	1.51	22.6	314	2.0	7.3	3.7	0.8	37%	64%	88
Kline,Branden	R	15	24	aa	BAL	3	3	8	0	39	43	22	5	21	22	4.93	1.62	21.8	280	4.7	5.1	1.1	1.2	30%	72%	15
Koch,Matt	R	15	25	aa	ARI	5	8	36	0	96	122	47	7	20	50	4.38	1.48	11.4	311	1.9	4.7	2.4	0.6	34%	71%	53
		16	26	a/a	ARI	6	6	21	0	121	175	71	12	20	59	5.27	1.61	25.6	338	1.5	4.4	2.9	0.9	36%	68%	48
Kubitza,Austin	R	15	24	aa	DET	9	13	27	0	134	228	109	7	51	76	7.34	2.09	24.3	377	3.4	5.1	1.5	0.5	42%	63%	27
		16	25	aa	DET	2	3	7	0	20	26	15	1	17	8	6.81	2.19	14.3	319	7.8	3.8	0.5	0.5	35%	67%	9
Lail,Brady	R	15	22	a/a	NYY	9	6	27	0	143	162	63	8	46	67	3.93	1.45	22.7	287	2.9	4.2	1.5	0.5	31%	73%	39
		16	23	a/a	NYY	8	8	23	0	124	165	95	20	47	65	6.88	1.71	24.4	320	3.4	4.7	1.4	1.4	34%	61%	5
Lamet,Dinelson	R	16	24	a/a	SD	5	9	16	0	85	79	37	4	35	90	3.92	1.33	22.1	247	3.7	9.5	2.6	0.5	33%	70%	103
Leclerc,Jose	R	15	22	aa	TEX	6	8	26	0	103	108	76	9	72	84	6.65	1.75	18.1	271	6.3	7.3	1.2	0.7	33%	61%	47
		16	23	a/a	TEX	2	7	39	2	66	47	28	5	41	65	3.80	1.34	7.0	202	5.6	8.8	1.6	0.6	26%	72%	82
Lee,Chris	L	15	23	aa	BAL	4	2	7	0	38	39	17	0	21	22	4.06	1.58	23.9	265	5.0	5.2	1.0	0.0	31%	71%	54
		16	24	aa	BAL	5	0	8	0	51	49	21	5	13	15	3.76	1.21	25.9	252	2.4	2.7	1.2	0.9	25%	71%	18
Lee,Zach	R	12	21	aa	LA	4	3	13	0	66	75	35	6	20	44	4.74	1.46	21.6	289	2.8	6.1	2.2	0.8	33%	68%	55
		13	22	aa	LA	10	10	28	0	143	152	62	15	36	114	3.94	1.31	21.1	274	2.2	7.2	3.2	0.9	32%	72%	83
		14	23	aaa	LA	7	13	28	0	151	169	75	14	44	83	4.45	1.41	22.8	285	2.6	5.0	1.9	0.8	31%	69%	43
		15	24	aaa	LA	11	6	19	0	113	119	37	5	18	68	2.95	1.20	24.0	271	1.4	5.4	3.9	0.4	31%	76%	103
		16	25	aaa	SEA	7	14	27	0	148	215	109	21	37	90	6.65	1.70	24.8	340	2.2	5.5	2.4	1.3	37%	62%	33
Lewicki,Artie	R	16	24	aa	DET	1	7	12	0	67	79	32	4	14	45	4.29	1.38	23.6	294	1.8	6.0	3.3	0.6	34%	69%	83
Light,Pat	R	15	24	a/a	BOS	5	3	47	5	63	60	37	6	40	55	5.25	1.61	5.9	255	5.8	7.9	1.4	0.8	31%	68%	55
		16	25	aaa	MIN	2	1	31	9	38	33	14	1	21	33	3.41	1.43	5.2	238	4.9	7.8	1.6	0.3	30%	75%	78
Lindgren,Jacob	L	15	22	aaa	NYY	1	1	15	3	22	19	4	0	11	26	1.58	1.33	6.1	233	4.3	10.5	2.4	0.0	34%	87%	122
Lively,Ben	R	14	22	aa	CIN	3	6	13	0	72	66	35	8	35	68	4.37	1.40	23.4	246	4.3	8.5	1.9	1.0	30%	71%	66
		15	23	aa	PHI	8	7	25	0	144	178	75	16	45	98	4.67	1.55	25.1	306	2.8	6.1	2.2	1.0	35%	72%	46
		16	24	a/a	PHI	18	5	28	0	171	146	69	15	46	120	3.65	1.12	24.0	232	2.4	6.3	2.6	0.8	27%	69%	77
Lopez,Jorge	R	15	22	aa	MIL	12	5	24	0	143	128	49	13	58	121	3.10	1.29	24.6	240	3.6	7.6	2.1	0.8	29%	79%	71
		16	23	a/a	MIL	3	11	25	0	125	172	101	20	75	96	7.30	1.98	23.9	329	5.4	6.9	1.3	1.4	37%	64%	15
Lopez,Reynaldo	R	16	22	a/a	WAS	5	7	19	0	109	108	52	15	38	107	4.31	1.33	23.9	260	3.1	8.8	2.8	1.2	32%	71%	79
Mader,Michael	L	16	22	aa	ATL	0	3	5	0	30	33	11	0	7	24	3.37	1.33	24.9	282	2.0	7.1	3.6	0.0	35%	72%	116
Mahle,Tyler	R	16	22	aa	CIN	6	3	14	0	71	98	56	18	23	60	7.00	1.69	23.0	327	2.9	7.5	2.6	2.3	36%	63%	22

PITCHER	Th	Yr	Age	LvL	Org	W	L	G	Sv	IP	H	ER	HR	BB	K	ERA	WHIP	BF/G	OBA	bb/9	k/9	Cmd	hr/9	H%	S%	BPV
Marquez,German	R	16	21	a/a	COL	11	6	26	0	167	189	82	20	42	123	4.42	1.38	26.9	287	2.2	6.6	3.0	1.1	33%	71%	68
Martes,Francis	R	16	21	aa	HOU	9	6	25	0	125	114	52	4	45	118	3.72	1.27	20.5	244	3.2	8.5	2.6	0.3	32%	69%	102
Martinez,Rodolfo	R	16	22	aa	SF	0	3	25	3	23	34	22	1	16	15	8.67	2.19	4.6	347	6.2	5.9	0.9	0.4	40%	57%	29
Mayers,Mike	R	14	23	a/a	STL	6	5	14	0	81	97	29	4	23	47	3.26	1.47	24.9	297	2.5	5.2	2.1	0.4	34%	78%	58
		15	24	aa	STL	1	4	10	0	47	58	37	8	20	29	7.10	1.68	21.0	308	3.8	5.6	1.5	1.5	33%	59%	15
		16	25	a/a	STL	9	10	25	0	144	157	61	13	50	108	3.83	1.44	24.5	279	3.1	6.8	2.2	0.8	33%	75%	62
McCurry,Brendan	R	15	23	aa	OAK	0	1	14	6	17	10	3	1	6	22	1.69	0.93	4.5	170	3.1	11.6	3.7	0.5	26%	85%	155
		16	24	a/a	HOU	3	5	56	16	82	85	32	7	21	80	3.51	1.29	6.0	269	2.3	8.8	3.9	0.7	34%	75%	113
McGowin,Kyle	R	15	24	aa	LAA	9	9	27	0	154	176	96	17	50	106	5.58	1.46	24.4	288	2.9	6.2	2.1	1.0	33%	62%	49
		16	25	a/a	LAA	9	14	27	0	142	194	110	20	56	109	6.96	1.76	24.1	327	3.5	6.9	1.9	1.3	37%	61%	33
Mejia,Adalberto	L	14	21	aa	SF	7	9	22	0	108	128	61	8	29	72	5.05	1.46	21.0	296	2.4	6.0	2.5	0.6	34%	65%	64
		15	22	aa	SF	5	2	12	0	51	45	18	2	19	33	3.13	1.24	17.4	235	3.3	5.8	1.7	0.3	28%	74%	69
		16	23	aa	MIN	9	5	22	0	132	141	57	14	30	102	3.90	1.30	24.7	275	2.1	7.0	3.4	0.9	32%	72%	84
Melotakis,Mason	L	16	25	aa	MIN	1	2	36	0	33	44	14	3	12	33	3.81	1.68	4.2	317	3.3	8.8	2.6	0.9	40%	80%	73
Mendez,Yohander	L	16	21	aa	TEX	8	2	17	0	78	58	22	2	31	58	2.55	1.15	18.2	210	3.6	6.7	1.9	0.3	26%	77%	85
Meyer,Alex	R	13	23	aa	MIN	4	3	13	0	70	66	28	3	29	70	3.58	1.36	22.5	252	3.7	9.0	2.5	0.4	33%	73%	100
		14	24	aaa	MIN	7	7	27	0	130	138	64	10	66	124	4.42	1.56	21.2	273	4.5	8.6	1.9	0.7	34%	72%	70
		15	25	aaa	MIN	4	5	38	0	92	128	69	5	53	79	6.76	1.97	11.6	331	5.2	7.7	1.5	0.5	41%	64%	52
		16	26	aaa	LAA	1	1	4	1	21	15	2	0	4	20	0.90	0.86	19.6	194	1.6	8.6	5.3	0.0	27%	88%	179
Middleton,Keynan	R	16	23	a/a	LAA	0	1	21	8	30	28	11	2	8	28	3.47	1.21	5.7	251	2.4	8.5	3.6	0.6	32%	72%	113
Miller,Jared	L	16	23	a/a	ARI	0	1	24	2	33	27	18	3	15	33	5.01	1.27	5.6	224	4.1	9.1	2.2	0.9	28%	61%	83
Mills,Alec	R	16	25	a/a	KC	5	5	24	0	126	144	58	11	32	96	4.13	1.41	22.1	289	2.3	6.9	3.0	0.8	34%	72%	78
Minaya,Juan	R	15	25	a/a	HOU	1	0	35	1	55	56	19	2	21	49	3.16	1.41	6.6	266	3.5	8.1	2.3	0.4	34%	77%	89
		16	26	aaa	CHW	5	6	34	1	52	58	27	4	23	39	4.60	1.56	6.7	285	4.0	6.7	1.7	0.6	34%	70%	55
Moll,Sam	L	16	24	aaa	COL	3	5	42	2	47	69	36	7	21	29	6.90	1.89	5.3	340	3.9	5.6	1.4	1.3	37%	64%	11
Montas,Frankie	R	15	22	aa	CHW	5	5	23	0	112	106	49	4	54	95	3.95	1.43	20.7	252	4.3	7.6	1.8	0.3	32%	71%	78
		16	23	a/a	LA	0	0	7	0	16	16	5	1	3	19	2.76	1.19	9.2	265	1.6	10.6	6.7	0.7	36%	79%	186
Montgomery,Jordan	L	16	24	a/a	NYY	14	5	25	0	139	158	49	8	51	113	3.17	1.50	24.1	287	3.3	7.3	2.2	0.5	35%	79%	73
Moore,Andrew	R	16	22	aa	SEA	9	3	19	0	108	131	48	10	18	77	4.02	1.38	23.9	301	1.5	6.4	4.3	0.8	35%	72%	99
Morimando,Shawn	L	14	22	aa	CLE	2	6	10	0	56	69	27	2	16	33	4.24	1.50	24.4	302	2.5	5.3	2.1	0.3	35%	70%	61
		15	23	aa	CLE	10	12	28	0	159	168	75	11	67	111	4.23	1.48	24.4	273	3.8	6.3	1.7	0.6	32%	72%	54
		16	24	a/a	CLE	15	5	27	0	152	174	74	13	60	96	4.40	1.54	24.6	288	3.6	5.7	1.6	0.7	33%	72%	42
Morris,Akeel	R	15	23	aa	NYM	0	1	23	0	29	19	9	1	15	31	2.89	1.17	5.1	190	4.6	9.4	2.0	0.3	26%	75%	106
		16	24	aa	ATL	5	3	47	6	61	59	32	5	42	75	4.75	1.66	5.8	255	6.3	11.0	1.8	0.7	36%	72%	85
Musgrave,Harrison	L	15	23	aa	COL	3	4	11	0	57	71	30	11	14	43	4.75	1.50	22.3	306	2.3	6.8	3.0	1.7	34%	74%	46
		16	24	a/a	COL	13	8	25	0	153	178	91	27	54	82	5.32	1.51	26.6	292	3.2	4.8	1.5	1.6	30%	69%	11
Neverauskas,Dovydas	R	16	23	a/a	PIT	4	4	47	5	58	57	26	1	22	46	3.97	1.37	5.2	258	3.5	7.1	2.0	0.2	32%	69%	83
Newcomb,Sean	L	15	22	aa	LAA	2	2	7	0	36	25	13	2	23	34	3.36	1.34	21.4	199	5.7	8.6	1.5	0.5	26%	75%	83
		16	23	aa	ATL	8	7	27	0	140	142	86	5	80	135	5.53	1.58	22.8	264	5.1	8.7	1.7	0.3	35%	63%	80
Oaks,Trevor	R	16	23	a/a	LA	13	2	20	0	126	139	44	9	17	74	3.16	1.24	25.6	282	1.2	5.3	4.4	0.7	32%	76%	102
Okert,Steven	L	14	23	aa	SF	1	0	24	5	33	27	11	3	11	32	3.04	1.13	5.4	222	2.9	8.8	3.0	0.7	28%	75%	105
		15	24	aaa	SF	4	3	52	3	61	67	27	6	28	58	3.95	1.55	5.2	279	4.1	8.5	2.0	0.8	35%	76%	69
		16	25	aaa	SF	4	3	41	3	47	60	24	2	11	50	4.48	1.52	5.0	312	2.2	9.4	4.4	0.3	41%	69%	131
Ortiz,Luis	R	16	21	aa	MIL	3	6	15	1	63	89	32	6	19	44	4.61	1.71	19.0	335	2.7	6.2	2.3	0.9	38%	75%	47
Overton,Dillon	L	15	24	aa	OAK	5	2	13	0	65	71	23	4	15	38	3.27	1.33	20.6	281	2.1	5.3	2.6	0.5	32%	76%	70
		16	25	aaa	OAK	13	5	21	0	126	167	64	7	34	83	4.60	1.60	26.5	320	2.5	5.9	2.4	0.5	37%	71%	62
Payano,Victor	L	15	23	aa	TEX	4	4	29	0	93	104	61	14	64	65	5.95	1.81	14.8	284	6.3	6.3	1.0	1.4	31%	69%	16
		16	24	a/a	TEX	9	8	25	0	128	148	80	19	66	94	5.66	1.68	23.0	292	4.6	6.6	1.4	1.3	33%	68%	27
Pazos,James	L	15	24	a/a	NYY	3	1	27	3	43	36	8	1	17	41	1.72	1.23	6.4	229	3.5	8.7	2.5	0.3	30%	87%	105
		16	25	aaa	NYY	2	2	23	1	27	25	12	2	22	34	3.94	1.71	5.4	244	7.2	11.2	1.5	0.5	35%	77%	90
Pena,Felix	R	15	25	aa	CHC	7	8	25	0	130	132	67	11	53	116	4.63	1.42	22.0	265	3.6	8.0	2.2	0.8	33%	68%	73
		16	26	aaa	CHC	3	4	36	3	63	55	29	5	24	66	4.13	1.25	7.2	235	3.5	9.3	2.7	0.7	31%	67%	101
Peters,Dillon	L	16	24	aa	MIA	3	0	4	0	23	21	7	2	4	13	2.70	1.12	22.3	247	1.7	5.2	3.0	0.8	27%	80%	74
Phillips,Evan	R	16	22	aa	ATL	6	3	22	2	34	41	24	2	18	39	6.26	1.70	7.0	296	4.6	10.2	2.2	0.6	40%	62%	85
Pinto,Ricardo	R	16	22	aa	PHI	7	6	27	0	156	170	84	24	51	91	4.86	1.42	24.5	278	2.9	5.2	1.8	1.4	29%	69%	26
Pivetta,Nick	R	15	22	aa	PHI	2	4	10	0	43	56	39	9	27	28	8.05	1.92	20.5	313	5.7	5.8	1.0	1.9	33%	60%	-7
		16	23	a/a	PHI	12	8	27	0	149	155	72	16	55	121	4.35	1.41	23.3	270	3.3	7.4	2.2	1.0	32%	71%	62
Plutko,Adam	R	15	24	aa	CLE	9	5	19	0	116	119	50	11	24	76	3.89	1.23	24.8	265	1.9	5.9	3.2	0.9	30%	70%	78
		16	25	a/a	CLE	9	8	28	0	162	190	93	17	50	102	5.15	1.48	24.8	294	2.8	5.7	2.1	0.9	33%	66%	46
Povse,Max	R	16	23	aa	ATL	4	1	11	0	71	77	33	5	13	43	4.20	1.27	26.3	278	1.7	5.4	3.2	0.6	31%	67%	80
Ravenelle,Adam	R	16	24	aa	DET	1	1	27	1	30	35	20	4	17	18	6.00	1.76	5.0	297	5.2	5.5	1.1	1.3	32%	68%	11

PITCHER	Th	Yr	Age	LvL	Org	W	L	G	Sv	IP	H	ER	HR	BB	K	ERA	WHIP	BF/G	OBA	bb/9	k/9	Cmd	hr/9	H%	S%	BPV
Reed,Chris	L	12	22	aa	LA	0	4	12	0	35	34	21	2	19	25	5.46	1.50	12.7	255	4.8	6.4	1.3	0.5	30%	62%	55
		13	23	aa	LA	4	11	29	0	138	150	74	10	65	91	4.82	1.57	20.8	279	4.3	5.9	1.4	0.7	32%	69%	43
		14	24	a/a	LA	4	11	28	0	158	153	69	13	57	112	3.91	1.33	23.5	256	3.2	6.4	2.0	0.7	30%	72%	62
		15	25	a/a	MIA	3	2	38	1	55	63	42	5	38	35	6.82	1.81	6.7	286	6.1	5.7	0.9	0.8	32%	61%	27
		16	26	a/a	MIA	4	4	24	0	81	85	47	10	36	51	5.17	1.49	14.6	270	4.0	5.6	1.4	1.1	30%	67%	31
Reed,Cody	L	16	23	aaa	CIN	6	4	13	0	73	88	35	8	22	58	4.27	1.51	24.3	299	2.7	7.2	2.6	1.0	35%	74%	62
Reed,Jake	R	15	23	aa	MIN	4	4	35	1	47	62	38	3	20	32	7.19	1.74	6.1	317	3.9	6.1	1.6	0.6	37%	56%	44
		16	24	a/a	MIN	4	4	50	3	71	72	37	2	25	57	4.74	1.37	5.9	266	3.2	7.2	2.3	0.3	33%	63%	84
Reyes,Alex	R	16	22	aaa	STL	2	3	14	0	65	68	39	6	31	84	5.33	1.51	20.2	269	4.2	11.6	2.7	0.8	38%	64%	105
Rodgers,Brady	R	15	25	aaa	HOU	9	7	21	0	116	151	62	13	25	74	4.85	1.52	23.9	316	1.9	5.8	3.0	1.0	35%	70%	59
		16	26	aaa	HOU	12	4	22	0	132	150	48	8	23	95	3.29	1.31	24.8	287	1.6	6.5	4.1	0.5	34%	76%	106
Romano,Sal	R	16	23	aa	CIN	6	11	27	0	156	201	91	15	39	129	5.25	1.54	25.2	314	2.3	7.5	3.3	0.9	37%	66%	80
Rosario,Jose	R	16	25	a/a	CHC	1	1	33	9	38	44	14	1	9	27	3.46	1.41	4.8	291	2.3	6.5	2.9	0.3	35%	74%	88
Sadzeck,Connor	R	15	24	aa	TEX	1	1	7	0	20	26	25	1	17	13	11.55	2.19	14.1	316	8.0	6.0	0.8	0.5	37%	42%	29
		16	25	aa	TEX	10	8	25	0	141	159	89	22	59	106	5.67	1.55	24.6	286	3.8	6.8	1.8	1.4	32%	66%	34
Santana,Edgar	R	16	25	a/a	PIT	2	1	34	3	57	67	29	6	18	40	4.61	1.48	7.3	292	2.8	6.2	2.2	0.9	33%	70%	54
Schultz,Jaime	R	15	24	aa	TAM	9	5	27	0	135	119	63	11	91	142	4.22	1.56	21.9	239	6.0	9.5	1.6	0.7	31%	74%	76
		16	25	aaa	TAM	5	7	27	0	131	140	69	14	74	136	4.77	1.63	21.5	275	5.1	9.4	1.9	1.0	35%	72%	66
Scott,Tanner	L	16	22	aa	BAL	1	2	14	0	16	21	12	0	15	15	6.82	2.22	5.8	313	8.4	8.6	1.0	0.0	41%	66%	65
Shepherd,Chandler	R	16	24	a/a	BOS	2	3	40	7	64	54	29	7	20	51	4.07	1.15	6.4	229	2.8	7.2	2.6	1.0	26%	67%	76
Sherfy,Jimmie	R	14	23	aa	ARI	3	1	37	1	38	40	26	5	18	38	6.16	1.52	4.5	270	4.3	8.9	2.1	1.1	34%	60%	65
		15	24	aa	ARI	1	6	44	2	50	61	48	4	29	41	8.75	1.83	5.2	305	5.3	7.5	1.4	0.7	37%	49%	47
		16	25	aa	ARI	3	4	40	22	43	31	21	7	19	47	4.50	1.16	4.3	205	3.9	9.9	2.5	1.5	25%	66%	82
Sims,Lucas	R	15	21	aa	ATL	4	2	9	0	48	33	21	1	29	51	3.97	1.31	21.9	199	5.5	9.7	1.8	0.2	28%	68%	104
		16	22	a/a	ATL	7	11	28	0	141	142	90	17	97	144	5.72	1.70	22.7	263	6.2	9.2	1.5	1.1	33%	67%	56
Skoglund,Eric	L	16	24	aa	KC	7	10	27	0	156	167	82	22	40	108	4.70	1.33	24.0	275	2.3	6.2	2.7	1.3	30%	68%	56
Slegers,Aaron	R	15	23	aa	MIN	1	4	6	0	37	45	23	3	12	20	5.59	1.54	26.6	302	2.9	4.8	1.7	0.7	33%	63%	37
		16	24	aa	MIN	10	7	25	0	145	163	69	12	46	83	4.28	1.44	24.8	284	2.9	5.1	1.8	0.8	32%	71%	44
Smith,Nate	L	14	23	aa	LAA	5	3	11	0	62	56	25	3	30	57	3.57	1.38	23.8	242	4.3	8.3	1.9	0.5	31%	74%	83
		15	24	a/a	LAA	10	8	24	0	138	144	64	15	40	88	4.21	1.33	23.8	270	2.6	5.7	2.2	1.0	30%	71%	52
		16	25	aaa	LAA	8	9	26	0	150	181	80	16	42	102	4.80	1.48	24.9	300	2.5	6.1	2.4	1.0	34%	69%	54
Smoker,Josh	L	15	27	aa	NYM	1	0	21	0	21	20	9	0	12	21	3.85	1.51	4.3	251	5.1	8.9	1.7	0.0	34%	72%	95
		16	28	aaa	NYM	3	2	52	3	57	74	27	5	18	63	4.20	1.61	4.9	315	2.8	9.9	3.5	0.7	41%	75%	103
Stanek,Ryne	R	15	24	aa	TAM	4	3	16	1	62	59	32	7	31	35	4.71	1.46	16.5	254	4.5	5.1	1.1	1.0	27%	70%	28
		16	25	a/a	TAM	4	10	34	3	103	104	63	10	51	94	5.51	1.51	13.1	265	4.5	8.3	1.9	0.9	33%	64%	64
Staumont,Josh	R	16	23	aa	KC	2	1	11	0	50	51	23	2	38	60	4.05	1.77	21.0	264	6.9	10.7	1.6	0.4	37%	77%	87
Stephenson,Robert	R	14	21	aa	CIN	7	10	27	0	137	124	80	21	71	126	5.29	1.43	21.5	244	4.7	8.3	1.8	1.4	28%	66%	52
		15	22	a/a	CIN	8	11	25	0	134	121	72	14	73	127	4.84	1.45	22.9	243	4.9	8.5	1.7	0.9	30%	68%	66
		16	23	aaa	CIN	8	9	24	0	137	142	93	24	79	108	6.11	1.62	25.3	269	5.2	7.1	1.4	1.6	30%	65%	25
Stewart,Brock	R	16	25	a/a	LA	7	4	19	0	110	99	29	5	17	98	2.41	1.05	22.4	243	1.4	8.0	5.9	0.4	31%	78%	166
Stewart,Kohl	R	16	22	aa	MIN	9	6	16	0	92	104	37	4	43	39	3.66	1.59	25.4	286	4.2	3.8	0.9	0.4	31%	77%	28
Stratton,Chris	R	15	25	a/a	SF	5	10	26	0	148	149	77	8	65	91	4.70	1.45	24.3	264	4.0	5.5	1.4	0.5	30%	67%	50
		16	26	aaa	SF	12	6	21	0	126	142	65	6	41	83	4.65	1.46	25.6	287	3.0	6.0	2.0	0.4	34%	67%	64
Suarez,Andrew	L	16	24	aa	SF	7	7	19	0	114	159	68	11	26	76	5.36	1.63	26.7	331	2.1	6.0	2.9	0.9	38%	68%	58
Taylor,Josh	L	16	23	aa	ARI	3	4	11	0	55	78	42	5	19	39	6.87	1.78	22.9	336	3.2	6.4	2.0	0.8	39%	60%	43
Tseng,Jen-Ho	R	16	22	aa	CHC	6	8	22	0	113	154	62	13	32	61	4.96	1.64	23.0	325	2.5	4.8	1.9	1.1	35%	72%	27
Tuivailala,Sam	R	15	23	aaa	STL	3	1	43	17	45	31	9	2	24	36	1.74	1.22	4.2	194	4.9	7.1	1.5	0.4	24%	87%	78
		16	24	aaa	STL	3	2	42	17	47	53	30	3	22	63	5.83	1.60	4.9	286	4.2	12.1	2.8	0.6	42%	62%	113
Unsworth,Dylan	R	15	23	aa	SEA	4	7	13	0	66	89	38	6	13	44	5.09	1.52	22.2	321	1.7	6.0	3.5	0.9	37%	67%	76
		16	24	aa	SEA	3	1	9	0	47	51	8	2	7	30	1.54	1.25	21.1	280	1.4	5.8	4.2	0.5	33%	90%	108
Voelker,Paul	R	15	23	aa	DET	1	1	16	9	17	16	6	1	10	14	3.22	1.55	4.7	251	5.4	7.1	1.3	0.6	30%	80%	57
		16	24	aa	DET	3	4	52	13	54	64	31	8	25	62	5.15	1.65	4.6	295	4.2	10.4	2.4	1.3	38%	72%	71
Voth,Austin	R	15	23	aa	WAS	6	7	28	0	157	158	65	11	41	122	3.70	1.27	23.0	263	2.3	7.0	3.0	0.6	31%	71%	88
		16	24	aaa	WAS	7	9	27	0	157	176	79	13	65	108	4.55	1.53	25.3	284	3.7	6.2	1.7	0.8	33%	71%	48
Waddell,Brandon	L	16	22	aa	PIT	7	9	22	0	118	138	64	9	59	78	4.90	1.67	24.1	294	4.5	5.9	1.3	0.7	34%	71%	39
Wagner,Tyler	R	15	24	aa	MIL	11	5	25	0	152	165	54	11	52	101	3.20	1.42	25.8	277	3.1	6.0	2.0	0.6	32%	79%	58
		16	25	aaa	ARI	1	4	5	0	27	33	10	1	11	12	3.40	1.64	23.8	304	3.6	4.1	1.1	0.3	34%	79%	32
Wahl,Bobby	R	15	23	aa	OAK	2	0	24	4	32	39	16	2	14	30	4.37	1.61	6.0	298	3.8	8.3	2.2	0.5	38%	72%	77
		16	24	a/a	OAK	1	1	42	14	50	39	16	3	24	50	2.93	1.26	4.9	217	4.3	8.9	2.1	0.6	28%	78%	92
Weigel,Patrick	R	16	22	aa	ATL	1	2	3	0	21	11	7	2	9	15	3.06	0.96	26.1	160	3.8	6.7	1.8	1.1	17%	74%	68
Whalen,Rob	R	16	22	a/a	ATL	7	6	21	0	120	117	42	5	46	102	3.12	1.36	23.9	257	3.5	7.6	2.2	0.3	32%	77%	85
Wieck,Brad	L	16	25	aa	SD	1	0	15	0	20	12	1	0	9	26	0.58	1.03	5.2	177	3.8	11.6	3.0	0.0	28%	94%	152
Williams,Ryan	R	15	24	aa	CHC	10	2	17	0	88	85	33	2	17	52	3.34	1.16	20.6	255	1.7	5.3	3.1	0.2	30%	69%	93
		16	25	aaa	CHC	4	1	9	0	44	50	19	5	12	25	3.88	1.42	20.7	288	2.6	5.1	2.0	0.9	31%	75%	42

PITCHER	Th	Yr	Age	LvL	Org	W	L	G	Sv	IP	H	ER	HR	BB	K	ERA	WHIP	BF/G	OBA	bb/9	k/9	Cmd	hr/9	H%	S%	BPV
Williams,Trevor	R	15	23	a/a	MIA	7	10	25	0	131	166	70	9	44	84	4.84	1.60	23.2	310	3.0	5.8	1.9	0.6	35%	69%	49
		16	24	aaa	PIT	9	6	20	0	110	128	43	6	32	59	3.49	1.45	23.6	292	2.6	4.8	1.8	0.5	33%	76%	50
Wood,Hunter	R	16	23	aa	TAM	6	2	10	0	49	41	21	5	20	43	3.89	1.24	20.0	228	3.6	7.8	2.1	1.0	27%	71%	72
Woodruff,Brandon	R	16	23	aa	MIL	10	8	20	0	114	111	55	5	34	105	4.35	1.27	23.3	257	2.7	8.3	3.1	0.4	33%	64%	106
Yarbrough,Ryan	L	16	25	aa	SEA	12	4	25	0	128	138	57	8	33	84	3.99	1.33	21.3	277	2.3	5.9	2.5	0.6	32%	70%	71
Ynoa,Gabriel	R	14	21	aa	NYM	3	2	11	0	66	75	29	8	11	38	4.00	1.28	24.7	285	1.4	5.2	3.6	1.1	31%	72%	71
		15	22	aa	NYM	9	9	25	0	152	175	76	15	30	73	4.50	1.35	25.4	290	1.8	4.3	2.4	0.9	31%	68%	46
		16	23	aaa	NYM	12	5	25	0	154	171	62	13	36	67	3.64	1.34	25.7	282	2.1	3.9	1.9	0.7	30%	74%	40
Ysla,Luis	L	16	24	a/a	BOS	2	5	40	4	56	70	36	5	30	51	5.78	1.78	6.5	306	4.8	8.2	1.7	0.8	38%	67%	56
Zastryzny,Rob	L	15	23	aa	CHC	2	5	14	0	61	88	50	10	29	41	7.38	1.92	20.6	339	4.3	6.1	1.4	1.4	38%	63%	11
		16	24	a/a	CHC	10	5	24	0	136	135	77	15	52	101	5.10	1.38	23.7	261	3.5	6.7	1.9	1.0	30%	64%	54
Zimmer,Kyle	R	15	24	aa	KC	2	5	15	3	48	49	18	4	14	41	3.46	1.33	13.3	267	2.7	7.6	2.8	0.8	32%	76%	83
Zych,Tony	R	13	23	aa	CHC	5	5	47	3	56	58	22	2	22	34	3.58	1.42	5.1	268	3.5	5.5	1.6	0.3	31%	74%	57
		14	24	aa	CHC	4	5	45	2	58	86	39	3	19	29	5.97	1.80	6.0	344	2.9	4.5	1.6	0.5	38%	65%	31
		15	25	a/a	SEA	1	2	40	9	48	51	18	2	9	46	3.28	1.22	4.9	271	1.6	8.6	5.4	0.4	35%	73%	154

ORGANIZATION RATINGS/RANKINGS

Each organization is graded on a standard A-F scale in four separate categories, and then after weighing the categories and adding some subjectivity, a final grade and ranking are determined. The four categories are the following:

Hitting: The quality and quantity of hitting prospects, the balance between athleticism, power, speed, and defense, and the quality of player development.

Pitching: The quality and quantity of pitching prospects and the quality of player development.

Top-End Talent: The quality of the top players within the organization. Successful teams are ones that have the most star-quality players. These are the players who are a teams' above average regulars, front-end starters, and closers.

Depth: The depth of both hitting and pitching prospects within the organization.

Overall Grade: The four categories are weighted, with top-end talent being the most important and depth being the least.

TEAM	Hitting	Pitching	Top-End Talent	Depth	Overall
New York (A)	A-	B+	A	A-	A-
San Diego	B	A	A	A-	A-
Atlanta	B+	A	A-	A	A-
Milwaukee	A-	B+	A-	A	A-
Pittsburgh	A-	B	A-	A-	A-
Chicago (A)	C-	A-	A	B+	B+
Oakland	B+	B	A-	B+	B+
Colorado	B+	B+	B+	A-	B+
Los Angeles (N)	B+	B+	B+	A-	B+
Philadelphia	B+	B+	B	A	B+
Boston	B-	B-	B+	B	B
Houston	B	B	B	B+	B
St. Louis	B	A-	B-	B	B
Toronto	B-	B	B	C+	B
Tampa Bay	B-	C	B	B-	B-
Chicago (N)	B	B-	B-	B	B-
Cincinnati	B	B-	B-	C+	B-
Minnesota	C+	B-	B-	B-	B-
New York (N)	B	B-	C+	B-	B-
Cleveland	B-	C	B	B-	C+
San Francisco	C+	C	B-	C	C+
Washington	B+	C	C	D	C
Texas	C+	C	C-	C-	C
Kansas City	C-	C	C-	C	C
Seattle	B-	D	C	C	C-
Miami	D	C	D+	D	D
Baltimore	D+	C-	D	D	D
Detroit	D	C-	D	D+	D
Los Angeles (A)	D-	D-	D-	D	D-
Arizona	D	D+	F	C-	D-

This section of the book may be the smallest as far as word count is concerned, but may be the most important, as this is where players' skills and potential are tied together and ranked against their peers. The rankings that follow are divided into long-term potential in the major leagues and shorter-term fantasy value.

ORGANIZATIONAL: Lists the top 15 minor league prospects within each organization in terms of long-range potential in the major leagues.

POSITIONAL: Lists the top 15 prospects, by position, in terms of long-range potential in the major leagues.

TOP POWER: Lists the top 25 prospects that have the potential to hit for power in the major leagues, combining raw power, plate discipline, and at the ability to make their power game-usable.

TOP BA: Lists the top 25 prospects that have the potential to hit for high batting average in the major leagues, combining contact ability, plate discipline, hitting mechanics and strength.

TOP SPEED: Lists the top 25 prospects that have the potential to steal bases in the major leagues, combining raw speed and base-running instincts.

TOP FASTBALL: Lists the top 25 pitchers that have the best fastball, combining velocity and pitch movement.

TOP BREAKING BALL: Lists the top 25 pitchers that have the best breaking ball, combining pitch movement, strikeout potential, and consistency.

2017 TOP FANTASY PROSPECTS: Lists the top 75 minor league prospects that will have the most value to their respective fantasy teams in 2017. This list is ranked in terms of short-term value only.

TOP 100 ARCHIVE: Takes a look back at the top 100 lists from the past eight years.

The rankings in this book are the creation of the minor league department at BaseballHQ.com. While several baseball personnel contributed player information to the book, no opinions were solicited or received in comparing players.

TOP PROSPECTS BY ORGANIZATION

AL EAST

BALTIMORE ORIOLES
1. Cory Sedlock, RHP
2. Hunter Harvey, RHP
3. Chance Sisco, C
4. Jomar Reyes, 3B
5. Trey Mancini, 1B
6. Ryan Mountcastle, SS
7. Tanner Scott, LHP
8. Keegan Akin, LHP
9. Austin Hays, OF
10. Matthias Dietz, RHP
11. Chris Lee, LHP
12. D.J. Stewart, OF
13. Ofelky Peralta, RHP
14. Alex Murphy, C/1B
15. Garrett Cleavinger, LHP

BOSTON RED SOX
1. Andrew Benintendi, OF
2. Rafael Devers, 3B
3. Jason Groome, LHP
4. Sam Travis, 1B
5. Brian Johnson, LHP
6. Roniel Raudes, RHP
7. C.J. Chatham, SS
8. Bobby Dalbec, 3B
9. Jake Cosart, RHP
10. Travis Lakins, RHP
11. Michael Chavis, 3B
12. Josh Ockimey, 1B
13. Trey Ball, LHP
14. Shaun Anderson, RHP
15. Mike Shawaryn, RHP

NEW YORK YANKEES
1. Clint Frazier, OF
2. Gleyber Torres, SS
3. Jorge Mateo, SS
4. Aaron Judge, OF
5. James Kaprielian, RHP
6. Blake Rutherford, OF
7. Justus Sheffield, LHP
8. Domingo Acevedo, RHP
9. Chance Adams, RHP
10. Albert Abreu, RHP
11. Miguel Andujar, 3B
12. Dustin Fowler, OF
13. Dillon Tate, RHP
14. Ian Clarkin, LHP
15. Wilkerman Garcia, SS

TAMPA BAY RAYS
1. Willy Adames, SS
2. Brent Honeywell, RHP
3. Jake Bauers, 1B/OF
4. Joshua Lowe, 3B
5. Garrett Whitley, OF
6. Casey Gillaspie, 1B
7. Jacob Faria, RHP
8. Justin Williams, OF
9. Jesus Sanchez, OF
10. Chih-Wei Hu, RHP
11. Jaime Schultz, RHP
12. Taylor Guerrieri, RHP
13. Jake Fraley, OF
14. Daniel Robertson, SS
15. Ryne Stanek, RHP

TORONTO BLUE JAYS
1. Sean Reid-Foley, RHP
2. Vladimir Guerrero, 3B
3. Anthony Alford, OF
4. Rowdy Tellez, 1B
5. Richard Urena, SS
6. Jon Harris, RHP
7. Conner Greene, RHP
8. Reese McGuire, C
9. Harold Ramirez, OF
10. Bo Bichette, SS
11. T.J. Zeuch, RHP
12. Justin Maese, RHP
13. Angel Perdomo, LHP
14. J.B. Woodman, OF
15. Max Pentecost, C

AL CENTRAL

CHICAGO WHITE SOX
1. Lucas Giolito, RHP
2. Yoan Moncada, 2B
3. Reynaldo Lopez, RHP
4. Michael Kopech, RHP
5. Carson Fulmer, RHP
6. Zack Collins, C
7. Alec Hansen, RHP
8. Zack Burdi, RHP
9. Dane Dunning, RHP
10. Luis Alex Basabe, OF
11. Charlie Tilson, OF
12. Trey Michalczewski, 3B
13. Spencer Adams, RHP
14. Adam Engel, OF
15. Jordan Stephens, RHP

CLEVELAND INDIANS
1. Bradley Zimmer, OF
2. Francisco Mejia, C
3. Brady Aiken, LHP
4. Bobby Bradley, 1B
5. Greg Allen, OF
6. Triston McKenzie, RHP
7. Will Benson, OF
8. Nolan Jones, 3B
9. Yu-Cheng Chang, SS
10. Gabriel Mejia, OF
11. Yandy Diaz, 3B
12. Adam Plutko, RHP
13. Erik Gonzalez, 2B/SS
14. Tyler Krieger, SS
15. Juan Hillman, LHP

DETROIT TIGERS
1. Matt Manning, RHP
2. Christin Stewart, OF
3. Beau Burrows, RHP
4. Joe Jimenez, RHP
5. Michael Gerber, OF
6. Kyle Funkhouser, RHP
7. Tyler Alexander, LHP
8. Sandy Baez, RHP
9. JaCoby Jones, OF
10. Spencer Turnbull, RHP
11. Derek Hill, OF
12. A.J. Simcox, SS
13. Kevin Ziomek, LHP
14. Matt Hall, LHP
15. Zac Shepherd, 3B

KANSAS CITY ROYALS
1. Hunter Dozier, 3B/OF
2. Matthew Strahm, LHP
3. Josh Staumont, RHP
4. Ryan O'Hearn, 1B
5. Jorge Bonifacio, OF
6. Kyle Zimmer, RHP
7. Khalil Lee, OF
8. Miguel Almonte, RHP
9. Chase Vallot, C
10. Jake Junis, RHP
11. Scott Blewett, RHP
12. Seuly Matias, OF
13. Eric Skoglund, LHP
14. A.J. Puckett, RHP
15. Marten Gasparini, SS

MINNESOTA TWINS
1. Tyler Jay, LHP
2. Nick Gordon, SS
3. Alex Kirilloff, OF
4. Stephen Gonsalves, LHP
5. Fernando Romero, RHP
6. Travis Blankenhorn, 3B
7. J.T. Chargois, RHP
8. Kohl Stewart, RHP
9. Adalberto Mejia, LHP
10. Wander Javier, SS
11. Nick Burdi, RHP
12. Ben Rortvedt, C
13. Daniel Palka, OF
14. Zach Granite, OF
15. Lewin Diaz, 1B

AL WEST

HOUSTON ASTROS
1. Francis Martes, RHP
2. Kyle Tucker, OF
3. Yulieski Gurriel, 1B/3B/OF
4. Derek Fisher, OF
5. David Paulino, RHP
6. Forrest Whitley, RHP
7. Franklin Perez, RHP
8. Teoscar Hernandez, OF
9. James Hoyt, RHP
10. Colin Moran, 3B
11. J.D. Davis, 3B
12. Daz Cameron, OF
13. Lupe Chavez, RHP
14. Jandel Gustave, RHP
15. Miguelangel Sierra, SS

LOS ANGELES ANGELS
1. Matt Thaiss, 1B
2. Jahmai Jones, OF
3. Taylor Ward, C
4. Nate Smith, LHP
5. Nonie Williams, SS
6. Grayson Long, RHP
7. Brandon Marsh, OF
8. Keynan Middleton, RHP
9. Alex Meyer, RHP
10. Vicente Campos, RHP
11. David Fletcher, 2B/SS
12. Jared Foster, OF
13. Jaime Barria, RHP
14. Manny Banuelos, LHP
15. Troy Montgomery, OF

OAKLAND ATHLETICS
1. Franklin Barreto, SS
2. Matt Chapman, 3B
3. A.J. Puk, LHP
4. Grant Holmes, RHP
5. Jharel Cotton, RHP
6. Renato Nunez, 3B
7. Chad Pinder, 2B
8. Matt Olson, 1B
9. Frankie Montas, RHP
10. Lazaro Armenteros, OF
11. Richie Martin, SS
12. Yairo Munoz, SS
13. Dillon Overton, LHP
14. Dakota Chalmers, RHP
15. Daniel Gossett, RHP

SEATTLE MARINERS
1. Kyle Lewis, OF
2. Tyler O'Neill, OF
3. Nick Neidert, RHP
4. Luiz Gohara, LHP
5. Drew Jackson, SS
6. Mitch Haniger, OF
7. Max Povse, RHP
8. Brayan Hernandez, OF
9. Andrew Moore, RHP
10. D.J. Peterson, 1B
11. Dan Vogelbach, 1B
12. Ryan Yarbrough, LHP
13. Dan Altavilla, RHP
14. Christopher Torres, SS
15. Braden Bishop, OF

TEXAS RANGERS
1. Yohander Mendez, LHP
2. Leody Taveras, OF
3. Andy Ibanez, 2B
4. Cole Ragans, LHP
5. Josh Morgan, 3B
6. Eric Jenkins, OF
7. Brett Martin, LHP
8. Ronald Guzman, 1B
9. Jairo Beras, OF
10. Ariel Jurado, RHP
11. Michael De Leon, SS
12. Jose Leclerc, RHP
13. Alex Speas, RHP
14. Yanio Perez, 3B/OF
15. Anderson Tejeda, SS

Top Prospects by Organization

NL EAST

ATLANTA BRAVES
1. Dansby Swanson, SS
2. Ozhaino Albies, 2B
3. Kolby Allard, LHP
4. Kevin Maitan, SS
5. Ian Anderson, RHP
6. Sean Newcomb, LHP
7. Ronald Acuna, OF
8. Joey Wentz, LHP
9. Touki Toussaint, RHP
10. Mike Soroka, RHP
11. Max Fried, LHP
12. Travis Demeritte, 2B
13. Austin Riley, 3B
14. AJ Minter, LHP
15. Alex Jackson, OF

MIAMI MARLINS
1. Braxton Garrett, LHP
2. Luis Castillo, RHP
3. Tyler Kolek, RHP
4. Brian Anderson, 3B
5. Stone Garrett, OF
6. Jarlin Garcia, LHP
7. Thomas Jones, OF
8. Austin Dean, OF
9. Austin Brice, RHP
10. Garvis Lara, SS
11. Isael Soto, OF
12. Dillon Peters, LHP
13. Tayron Guerrero, RHP
14. J.T. Riddle, 2B/3B/SS
15. Tomas Telis, C

NEW YORK METS
1. Amed Rosario, SS
2. Desmond Lindsay, OF
3. Dominic Smith, 1B
4. Justin Dunn, RHP
5. Robert Gsellman, RHP
6. Thomas Szapucki, LHP
7. Gavin Cecchini, SS
8. Brandon Nimmo, OF
9. Peter Alonso, 1B
10. Tomas Nido, C
11. Andres Gimenez, SS
12. Marcos Molina, RHP
13. Anthony Kay, LHP
14. Wuilmer Becerra, OF
15. Luis Carpio, SS

PHILADELPHIA PHILLIES
1. J.P. Crawford, SS
2. Jorge Alfaro, C
3. Mickey Moniak, OF
4. Franklyn Kilome, RHP
5. Adonis Medina, RHP
6. Sixto Sanchez, RHP
7. Nick Williams, OF
8. Roman Quinn, OF
9. Dylan Cozens, OF
10. Corneilus Randolph, OF
11. Jhailyn Ortiz, OF
12. Mark Appel, RHP
13. Scott Kingery, 2B
14. Rhys Hoskins, 1B
15. Jose Pujols, OF

WASHINGTON NATIONALS
1. Victor Robles, OF
2. Juan Soto, OF
3. Erick Fedde, RHP
4. Carter Kieboom, SS
5. Andrew Stevenson, OF
6. Rafael Bautista, OF
7. A.J. Cole, RHP
8. Sheldon Neuse, 3B
9. Anderson Franco, 3B
10. Drew Ward, 3B
11. Nick Banks, OF
12. Austin Voth, RHP
13. Koda Glover, RHP
14. Wilmer Difo, SS
15. Raudy Read, C

NL CENTRAL

CHICAGO CUBS
1. Eloy Jimenez, OF
2. Ian Happ, OF
3. Dylan Cease, RHP
4. Jeimer Candelario, 3B
5. Mark Zagunis, OF
6. Oscar De La Cruz, RHP
7. Donnie Dewees, OF
8. Trevor Clifton, RHP
9. Eddy Martinez, OF
10. Jose Albertos, RHP
11. Duane Underwood, RHP
12. Thomas Hatch, RHP
13. Victor Caratini, C
14. Darryl Wilson, OF
15. Pierce Johnson, RHP

CINCINNATI REDS
1. Nick Senzel, 3B
2. Amir Garrett, LHP
3. Vladimir Gutierrez, RHP
4. Jesse Winker, OF
5. Robert Stephenson, RHP
6. Taylor Trammell, OF
7. Aristides Aquino, OF
8. Tyler Mahle, RHP
9. Ian Kahaloa, RHP
10. Antonio Santillan, RHP
11. Keury Mella, RHP
12. Nicholas Travieso, RHP
13. Rookie Davis, RHP
14. Tyler Stephenson, C
15. Chris Okey, C

MILWAUKEE BREWERS
1. Lewis Brinson, OF
2. Corey Ray, OF
3. Josh Hader, LHP
4. Luis Ortiz, RHP
5. Trent Clark, OF
6. Phil Bickford, RHP
7. Isan Diaz, SS
8. Brett Phillips, OF
9. Mauricio Dubon, 2B
10. Ryan Cordell, OF
11. Gilbert Lara, 3B/SS
12. Cody Ponce, RHP
13. Jorge Lopez, RHP
14. Lucas Erceg, 3B
15. Marcos Diplan, RHP

PITTSBURGH PIRATES
1. Tyler Glasnow, RHP
2. Josh Bell, 1B
3. Austin Meadows, OF
4. Kevin Newman, SS
5. Mitch Keller, RHP
6. Ke'Bryan Hayes, 3B
7. Alen Hanson, 2B
8. Will Craig, 3B
9. Cole Tucker, SS
10. Elias Diaz, C
11. Nick Kingham, RHP
12. Clay Holmes, RHP
13. Yeudy Garcia, RHP
14. Steven Brault, LHP
15. Gage Hinsz, RHP

ST. LOUIS CARDINALS
1. Alex Reyes, RHP
2. Delvin Perez, SS
3. Luke Weaver, RHP
4. Jack Flaherty, RHP
5. Magneuris Sierra, OF
6. Harrison Bader, OF
7. Edmundo Sosa, SS
8. Dakota Hudson, RHP
9. Sandy Alcantara, RHP
10. Junior Fernandez, RHP
11. Carson Kelly, C
12. Nick Plummer, OF
13. Jake Woodford, RHP
14. Dylan Carlson, OF
15. Randy Arozarena, 2B

NL WEST

ARIZONA DIAMONDBACKS
1. Anthony Banda, LHP
2. Domingo Leyba, 2B/SS
3. Socrates Brito, OF
4. Anfernee Grier, OF
5. Taylor Clarke, RHP
6. Alex Young, LHP
7. Jon Duplantier, RHP
8. Jasrado Chisholm, SS
9. Jared Miller, LHP
10. Dawel Lugo, 3B/SS
11. Emilio Vargas, RHP
12. Josh Taylor, LHP
13. Sam McWilliams, RHP
14. Brad Keller, RHP
15. Tyler Mark, RHP

COLORADO ROCKIES
1. Brendan Rodgers, SS
2. Jeff Hoffman, RHP
3. Raimel Tapia, OF
4. Riley Pint, RHP
5. Ryan McMahon, 1B
6. Tom Murphy, C
7. German Marquez, RHP
8. Kyle Freeland, LHP
9. Forrest Wall, 2B
10. Antonio Senzatela, RHP
11. Ryan Castellani, RHP
12. Tyler Nevin, 3B
13. Mike Nikorak, RHP
14. Ben Bowden, LHP
15. Dom Nunez, C

LOS ANGELES DODGERS
1. Cody Bellinger, 1B
2. Jose De Leon , RHP
3. Alex Verdugo, OF
4. Yadier Alvarez, RHP
5. Willie Calhoun, 2B
6. Gavin Lux, SS
7. Yusniel Diaz, OF
8. Walker Buehler, RHP
9. Austin Barnes, C
10. Will Smith, C
11. Jordan Sheffield, RHP
12. Mitch Hansen, OF
13. Brock Stewart, RHP
14. Starling Heredia, OF
15. Omar Estevez, 2B

SAN DIEGO PADRES
1. Anderson Espinoza, RHP
2. Manuel Margot, OF
3. Hunter Renfroe, OF
4. Cal Quantrill, RHP
5. Eric Lauer, LHP
6. Adrian Morejon, RHP
7. Mason Thompson, RHP
8. Chris Paddack, RHP
9. Josh Naylor, 1B
10. Javier Guerra, SS
11. Luis Urias, 2B/3B/SS
12. Jose Rondon, SS
13. Jorge Ona, OF
14. Fernando Tatis Jr., 3B/SS
15. Michael Gettys, OF

SAN FRANCISCO GIANTS
1. Chris Shaw, 1B
2. Tyler Beede, RHP
3. Christian Arroyo, 2B
4. Sam Coonrod, RHP
5. Bryan Reynolds, OF
6. Steven Duggar, OF
7. Ty Blach, LHP
8. Aramis Garcia, C
9. Heath Quinn, OF
10. Matt Krook, LHP
11. Rodolfo Martinez, RHP
12. Joan Gregorio, RHP
13. Andrew Suarez, LHP
14. Dylan Davis, OF
15. Hunter Cole, 2B/OF

TOP PROSPECTS BY POSITION

CATCHER

1   Jorge Alfaro, PHI
2   Francisco Mejia, CLE
3   Zack Collins, CHW
4   Tom Murphy, COL
5   Chance Sisco, BAL
6   Will Smith, LA
7   Andrew Knapp, PHI
8   Luis Torrens, SD
9   Elias Diaz, PIT
10. Taylor Ward, LAA
11. Reese McGuire, TOR
12. Aramis Garcia, SF
13. Chase Vallot, KC
14. Carson Kelly, STL
15. Austin Barnes, LA

FIRST BASEMEN

1. Cody Bellinger, LA
2. Josh Bell, PIT
3. Dominic Smith, NYM
4   Bobby Bradley, CLE
5. Chris Shaw, SF
6   Rowdy Tellez, TOR
7   Josh Naylor, SD
8   Casey Gillaspie, TAM
9   Matt Thaiss, LAA
10 Ryan O'Hearn, KC
11. Dan Vogelbach, SEA
12. Ronald Guzman, TEX
13 Matt Olson, OAK
14 Rhys Hoskins, PHI
15 Sam Travis, BOS

SECOND BASEMEN

1. Yoan Moncada, CHW
2   Ozzie Albies, ATL
3   Ian Happ, CHC
4   Willie Calhoun, LA
5   Travis Demeritte, ATL
6   Forrest Wall, COL
7   Andy Ibanez, TEX
8   Luis Urias, SD
9   Alen Hanson, PIT
10 Randy Arozarena, STL
11 Travis Blankenhorn, MIN
12 Omar Estevez, LA
13 Chad Pinder, OAK
14 Josh Morgan, TEX
15 Scott Kingery, PHI

SHORTSTOP

1   Dansby Swanson, ATL
2   J.P. Crawford, PHI
3   Brendan Rodgers, COL
4   Gleyber Torres, NYY
5   Amed Rosario, NYM
6   Willy Adames, TAM
7   Franklin Barreto, OAK
8   Jorge Mateo, NYY
9   Nick Gordon, MIN
10 Kevin Newman, PIT
11 Kevin Maitan, ATL
12 Isan Diaz, MIL
13 Richard Urena, TOR
14 Christian Arroyo, SF
15 Delvin Perez, STL

THIRD BASEMEN

1   Rafael Devers, BOS
2   Nick Senzel, CIN
3   Vladimir Guerrero, Jr., TOR
4   Yulieski Gurriel, HOU
5   Matt Chapman, OAK
6   Ryan McMahon, COL
7   Joshua Lowe, TAM
8   Ke'Bryan Hayes, PIT
9   Miguel Andujar, NYY
10 Jeimer Candelario, CHC
11 Hunter Dozier, KC
12 Brian Anderson, MIA
13 Renato Nunez, OAK
14 Will Craig, PIT
15 Colin Moran, HOU

OUTFIELDERS

1   Andrew Benintendi, BOS
2   Victor Robles, WAS
3   Austin Meadows, PIT
4   Lewis Brinson, MIL
5   Eloy Jimenez, CHC
6   Manuel Margot, SD
7   Clint Frazier, NYY
8   Bradley Zimmer, CLE
9   Mickey Moniak, PHI
10 Kyle Tucker, HOU
11 Aaron Judge, NYY
12 Kyle Lewis, SEA
13 Hunter Renfroe, SD
14 Corey Ray, MIL
15 Tyler O'Neill, SEA
16 Nick Williams, PHI
17 Alex Verdugo, LA
18 Blake Rutherford, NYY
19 Anthony Alford, TOR
20 Jesse Winker, CIN
21 Raimel Tapia, COL
22 Jake Bauers, TAM
23 Ronald Acuna, ATL
24 Derek Fisher, HOU
25 Brett Phillips, MIL
26 Leody Taveras, TEX
27 Trent Clark, MIL
28 Alex Kirilloff, MIN
29 Harrison Bader, STL
30 Juan Soto, WAS
31 Desmond Lindsay, NYM
32 Yusniel Diaz, LA
33 Roman Quinn, PHI
34 Garrett Whitley, TAM
35 Cornelius Randolph, PHI
36 Magneuris Sierra, STL
37 Christin Stewart, DET
38 Andrew Stevenson, WAS
39 Teoscar Hernandez, HOU
40 Jahmai Jones, LAA
41 Dylan Cozens, PHI
42 Bryan Reynolds, SF
43 Luis Alex Basabe, CHW
44 Aristides Aquino, CIN
45 Justin Williams, TAM

STARTING PITCHERS

1   Alex Reyes, STL
2   Lucas Giolito, CHW
3   Tyler Glasnow, PIT
4   Anderson Espinoza, SD
5   Brent Honeywell, TAM
6   Francis Martes, HOU
7   Reynaldo Lopez, CHW
8   Jose De Leon, LA
9   Michael Kopech, CHW
10 Amir Garrett, CIN
11 Jeff Hoffman, COL
12 Josh Hader, MIL
13 Kolby Allard, ATL
14 Jason Groome, BOS
15 Sean Newcomb, ATL

16 Carson Fulmer, CHW
17 David Paulino, HOU
18 Mitch Keller, PIT
19 Riley Pint, COL
20 Brady Aiken, CLE
21 Braxton Garrett, MIA
22 Tyler Jay, MIN
23 A.J. Puk, OAK
24 Robert Stephenson, CIN
25 Sean Reid-Foley, TOR
26 Matt Manning, DET
27 James Kaprielian, NYY
28 Erick Fedde, WAS
29 Luis Ortiz, MIL
30 Phil Bickford, MIL

31 Justus Sheffield, NYY
32 Luke Weaver, STL
33 Grant Holmes, OAK
34 Yadier Alvarez, LA
35 Yohander Mendez, TEX
36 Triston McKenzie, CLE
37 Ian Anderson, ATL
38 Tyler Beede, SF
39 Mike Soroka, ATL
40 Dylan Cease, CHC
41 Stephen Gonsalves, MIN
42 Franklyn Kilome, PHI
43 Forrest Whitley, HOU
44 German Marquez, COL
45 Touki Toussaint, ATL

46 Sixto Sanchez, PHI
47 Cory Sedlock, BAL
48 Cal Quantrill, SD
49 Jharel Cotton, OAK
50 Conner Greene, TOR
51 Domingo Acevedo, NYY
52 Jacob Faria, TAM
53 Adonis Medina, PHI
54 Walker Buehler, LA
55 Jack Flaherty, STL
56 Thomas Szapucki, NYM
57 Joey Wentz, ATL
58 Adalberto Mejia, MIN
59 Kyle Freeland, COL
60 Luis Castillo, MIA

61 Marcos Diplan, MIL
62 Franklin Perez, HOU
63 Luiz Gohara, SEA
64 Frankie Montas, OAK
65 Anthony Banda, ARI
66 A.J. Cole, WAS
67 Alec Hansen, CHW
68 Justin Dunn, NYM
69 Cole Ragans, TEX
70 Matt Strahm, KC
71 Josh Staumont, KC
72 Sam Coonrod, SF
73 Jon Harris, TOR
74 Kyle Zimmer, KC
75 Robert Gsellman, NYM

RELIEF PITCHERS

1   Zack Burdi, CHW
2   James Hoyt, HOU
3   Joe Jimenez, DET
4   A.J. Minter, ATL
5   Josh Smoker, NYM
6   Rodolfo Martinez, SF
7   J.T. Chargois, MIN
8   Ryne Stanek, TAM
9   Luke Jackson, ATL
10 Koda Glover, WAS
11 Nick Burdi, MIN
12 Tanner Scott, BAL
13 Josh Sborz, LA
14 Jake Cosart, BOS
15 Tayron Guerrero, MIA

TOP PROSPECTS BY SKILLS

2017 TOP FANTASY IMPACT

TOP POWER

Dylan Cozens, OF, PHI
Matt Chapman, 3B, OAK
Adam Brett Walker, OF, BAL
Aaron Judge, OF, NYY
Hunter Renfroe, OF, SD
Cody Bellinger, 1B, LA
Rhys Hoskins, 1B, PHI
Bobby Bradley, 1B, CLE
Travis Demeritte, 2B, ATL
Brendan Rodgers, SS, COL
Daniel Palka, OF, MIN
Christin Stewart, OF, DET
Eloy Jimenez, OF, CHC
Jose Pujols, OF, PHI
Rowdy Tellez, 1B, TOR
Josh Bell, 1B, PIT
Ryan O'Hearn, 1B, KC
Chris Shaw, 1B, SF
Renato Nunez, 3B, OAK
Kyle Lewis, OF, SEA
Tyler O'Neill, OF, SEA
Derek Fisher, OF, HOU
Clint Frazier, OF, NYY
Aristides Aquino, OF, CIN
Ryan McMahon, 3B, COL

TOP BA

Andrew Benintendi, OF, BOS
Ozzie Albies, 2B, ATL
Yoan Moncada, 2B, BOS
Dansby Swanson, SS, ATL
Victor Robles, OF, WAS
Amed Rosario, SS, NYM
Mickey Moniak, OF, PHI
Franklin Barreto, SS, OAK
Austin Meadows, OF, PIT
J.P. Crawford, SS, PHI
Brendan Rodgers, SS, COL
Nick Gordon, SS, MIN
Nick Senzel, 3B, CIN
Kevin Newman, SS, PIT
Manuel Margot, OF, SD
Dominic Smith, 1B, NYM
Kyle Lewis, OF, SEA
Trey Mancini, 1B, BAL
Alex Kirilloff, OF, MIN
Blake Rutherford, OF, NYY
Chance Sisco, C, BAL
Eloy Jimenez, OF, CHC
Jesse Winker, OF, CIN
Francisco Mejia, C, CLE
Josh Bell, 1B, PIT

TOP SPEED

Yoan Moncada, 2B, CHW
Rafael Bautista, OF, WAS
Jorge Mateo, SS, NYY
Roman Quinn, OF, PHI
Gabriel Mejia, OF, CLE
Eric Jenkins, SS, TEX
Manuel Margot, OF, SD
Derek Hill, OF, DET
Anfernee Seymour, SS, ATL
Victor Robles, OF, WAS
Greg Allen, OF, CLE
Andrew Stevenson, OF, WAS
Teoscar Hernandez, OF, HOU
Ozzie Albies, 2B, ATL
Raimel Tapia, OF, COL
Jahmai Jones, OF, LAA
Garrett Whitley, OF, TAM
Bradley Zimmer, OF, CLE
Mickey Moniak, OF, PHI
Michael Gettys, OF, SD
Delvin Perez, SS, STL
Dustin Fowler, OF, NYY
Mauricio Dubon, SS, MIL
Derek Fisher, OF, HOU
Lucius Fox, SS, TAM

TOP FASTBALL

Alex Reyes, RHP, STL
Lucas Giolito, RHP, CHW
Domingo Acevedo, RHP, NYY
Tyler Glasnow, RHP, PIT
Riley Pint, RHP, COL
Sandy Alcantara, RHP, STL
Yadier Alvarez, RHP, LA
Dylan Cease, RHP, CHC
Junior Fernandez, RHP, STL
Alberto Tirado, RHP, PHI
Michael Kopech, RHP, CHW
Luis Castillo, RHP, MIA
Frankie Montas, RHP, OAK
Josh Staumont, RHP, KC
Francis Martes, RHP, HOU
Sean Newcomb, LHP, ATL
Jose De Leon, RHP, LA
Braxton Garrett, LHP, MIA
A.J. Puk, LHP, OAK
Luis Ortiz, RHP, MIL
Anderson Espinoza, RHP, SD
Erick Fedde, RHP, WAS
Matt Manning, RHP, DET
Mitch Keller, RHP, PIT
David Paulino, RHP, HOU

TOP BREAKING BALL

Touki Toussaint, RHP, ATL
Sean Newcomb, LHP, ATL
Josh Staumont, RHP, KC
Jason Groome, LHP, BOS
Anderson Espinoza, RHP, SD
Alex Reyes, RHP, STL
Max Fried, LHP, ATL
Tyler Jay, LHP, MIN
Frankie Montas, RHP, OAK
Luis Ortiz, RHP, MIL
Robert Gsellman, RHP, NYM
Francis Martes, RHP, HOU
Kyle Zimmer, RHP, KC

Kolby Allard, LHP, ATL
Josh Hader, LHP, MIL
Grant Holmes, RHP, OAK
James Kaprielian, RHP, NYY
Carson Fulmer, RHP, CHW
Erick Fedde, RHP, WAS
Brady Aiken, LHP, CLE
Marcos Diplan, RHP, MIL
Thomas Szapucki, LHP, NYM
Alec Hansen, RH, CHW
Justin Dunn, RHP, NYM
Dakota Hudson, RHP, STL

1   Andrew Benintendi (OF, BOS)
2   Dansby Swanson (SS, ATL)
3   Alex Reyes (RHP, STL)
4   Yoan Moncada (2B, CHW)
5   Lucas Giolito (LHP, CHW)
6   Josh Bell (1B, PIT)
7   Manny Margot (OF, SD)
8   J.P. Crawford (SS, PHI)
9   Hunter Renfroe (OF, SD)
10 Andrew Toles (OF, LA)
11 Tyler Glasnow (RHP, PIT)
12 Jose De Leon (RHP, LA)
13 Raimel Tapia (OF, COL)
14 Roman Quinn (OF, PHI)
15 Ozzie Albies (SS, ATL)

16 Reynaldo Lopez (RHP, CHW)
17 Tom Murphy (C, COL)
18 Aaron Judge (OF, NYY)
19 Franklin Barreto (2B, OAK)
20 Austin Meadows (OF, PIT)
21 Jeff Hoffman (RHP, COL)
22 Clint Frazier (OF, NYY)
23 Tyler O'Neill (OF, SEA)
24 Lewis Brinson (OF, MIL)
25 Robert Stephenson (RHP, CIN)
26 Bradley Zimmer (OF, CLE)
27 Nick Williams (OF, PHI)
28 Jorge Alfaro (C, PHI)
29 Willy Adames (SS, TAM)
30 Luke Weaver (RHP, STL)

31 Robert Gsellman (RHP, NYM)
32 Carson Fulmer (RHP, CHW)
33 Brent Honeywell (RHP, TAM)
34 Jharel Cotton (RHP, OAK)
35 Francis Martes (RHP, HOU)
36 Brett Phillips (OF, MIL)
37 Frankie Montas (RHP, OAK)
38 Joe Jimenez (RHP, DET)

39 Teoscar Hernandez (OF, HOU)
40 Amir Garrett (LHP, CIN)
41 Sean Newcomb (LHP, ATL)
42 Ryan Merritt (LHP, CLE)
43 Derek Fisher (OF, HOU)
44 David Paulino (RHP, HOU)
45 Zack Burdi (RHP, CHW)

46 Josh Hader (LHP, MIL)
47 Dan Vogelbach (1B/DH, SEA)
48 Yulieski Gurriel (3B, HOU)
49 Ty Blach (LHP, SF)
50 Amed Rosario (SS, NYM)
51 Matt Strahm (LHP, KC)
52 Stephen Gonsalves (LHP, MIN)
53 Yohander Mendez (LHP, TEX)
54 Dominic Smith (1B, NYM)
55 Anthony Banda (LHP, ARI)
56 Tyler Beede (RHP, SF)
57 Cody Bellinger (1B, LA)
58 Gavin Cecchini (SS, NYM)
59 Nick Senzel (3B, CIN)
60 Willie Calhoun (2B, LA)

61 Ryan McMahon (3B, COL)
62 Zack Collins (C, CHW)
63 JaCoby Jones (2B/OF, DET)
64 Jesse Winker (OF, CIN)
65 Mitch Garver (C, MIN)
66 Dylan Cozens (OF, PHI)
67 Rhys Hoskins (1B, PHI)
68 Erick Fedde (RHP, WAS)
69 Adam Engel (OF, CHW)
70 Ian Happ (2B, CHC)
71 Joey Wendle (2B, OAK)
72 Kyle Freeland (LHP, COL)
73 Jake Bauers (OF, TAM)
74 Steven Duggar (OF, SF)
75 Alex Verdugo (OF, LA)

TOP 100 PROSPECTS ARCHIVE

2016

1. Byron Buxton (OF, MIN)
2. Corey Seager (SS, LAD)
3. Lucas Giolito (RHP, WAS)
4. J.P. Crawford (SS, PHI)
5. Alex Reyes (RHP, STL)
6. Julio Urias (LHP, LAD)
7. Yoan Moncada (2B, BOS)
8. Tyler Glasnow (RHP, PIT)
9. Joey Gallo (3B, TEX)
10. Steven Matz (LHP, NYM)

11. Rafael Devers (3B, BOS)
12. Jose Berrios (RHP, MIN)
13. Orlando Arcia (SS, MIL)
14. Blake Snell (LHP, TAM)
15. Trea Turner (SS, WAS)
16. Bradley Zimmer (OF, CLE)
17. Jose De Leon (RHP, LAD)
18. Brendan Rodgers (SS, COL)
19. Dansby Swanson (SS, ATL)
20. Robert Stephenson (RHP, CIN)

21. Nomar Mazara (OF, TEX)
22. Victor Robles (OF, WAS)
23. Aaron Judge (OF, NYY)
24. Manuel Margot (OF, SD)
25. Clint Frazier (OF, CLE)
26. Lewis Brinson (OF, TEX)
27. Alex Bregman (SS, HOU)
28. Jon Gray (RHP, COL)
29. Ryan McMahon (3B, COL)
30. Austin Meadows (OF, PIT)

31. Nick Williams (OF, PHI)
32. Franklin Barreto (SS, OAK)
33. David Dahl (OF, COL)
34. Brett Phillips (OF, MIL)
35. Gleyber Torres (SS, CHC)
36. Sean Newcomb (LHP, ATL)
37. Carson Fulmer (RHP, CHW)
38. Ozhaino Albies (SS, ATL)
39. Dillon Tate (RHP, TEX)
40. Andrew Benintendi (OF, BOS)

41. Jameson Taillon (RHP, PIT)
42. Raul Mondesi (SS, KC)
43. Archie Bradley (RHP, ARI)
44. Tim Anderson (SS, CHW)
45. Kolby Allard (LHP, ATL)
46. Jake Thompson (RHP, PHI)
47. Dylan Bundy (RHP, BAL)
48. Willy Adames (SS, TAM)
49. Anderson Espinoza (RHP, BOS)
50. Aaron Blair (RHP, ATL)

51. A.J. Reed (1B, HOU)
52. Jeff Hoffman (RHP, COL)
53. Jesse Winker (OF, CIN)
54. Brent Honeywell (RHP, TAM)
55. Josh Bell (1B, PIT)
56. Anthony Alford (OF, TOR)
57. Tyler Kolek (RHP, MIA)
58. Max Kepler (OF, MIN)
59. Hunter Renfroe (OF, SD)
60. Mark Appel (RHP, PHI)

61. Kyle Zimmer (RHP, KC)
62. Jose Peraza (2B, CIN)
63. Kyle Tucker (OF, HOU)
64. Cody Reed (LHP, CIN)
65. Billy McKinney (OF, CHC)
66. Nick Gordon (SS, MIN)
67. Braden Shipley (RHP, ARI)
68. Jorge Lopez (RHP, MIL)
69. Touki Toussaint (RHP, ATL)
70. Hector Olivera (3B, ATL)

71. Derek Fisher (OF, HOU)
72. Jorge Alfaro (C, PHI)
73. Raimel Tapia (OF, COL)
74. Grant Holmes (RHP, LAD)
75. Dominic Smith (1B, NYM)
76. Daz Cameron (OF, HOU)
77. Alex Jackson (OF, SEA)
78. Sean Manaea (LHP, OAK)
79. Amed Rosario (SS, NYM)
80. Reynaldo Lopez (RHP, WAS)

81. Javier Guerra (SS, SD)
82. Hunter Harvey (RHP, BAL)
83. Luis Ortiz (RHP, TEX)
84. Brady Aiken (LHP, CLE)
85. Matt Olson (1B, OAK)
86. Jorge Mateo (SS, NYY)
87. Daniel Robertson (SS, TAM)
88. Taylor Guerrieri (RHP, TAM)
89. Amir Garrett (LHP, CIN)
90. Willson Contreras (C, CHC)

91. Renato Nunez (3B, OAK)
92. Tyler Jay (LHP, MIN)
93. Tyler Stephenson (C, CIN)
94. Christian Arroyo (SS, SF)
95. Josh Naylor (1B, MIA)
96. Brian Johnson (LHP, BOS)
97. Tyler Beede (RHP, SF)
98. Garrett Whitley (OF, TAM)
99. Cody Bellinger (1B, LAD)
100. Michael Fulmer (RHP, DET)

2015

1. Kris Bryant (3B, CHC)
2. Byron Buxton (OF, MIN)
3. Carlos Correa (SS, HOU)
4. Addison Russell (SS, CHC)
5. Corey Seager (SS, LAD)
6. Francisco Lindor (SS, CLE)
7. Joc Pederson (OF, LAD)
8. Miguel Sano (3B, MIN)
9. Lucas Giolito (P, WAS)
10. Joey Gallo (3B, TEX)

11. Dylan Bundy (P, BAL)
12. Jorge Soler (OF, CHC)
13. Archie Bradley (P, ARI)
14. Julio Urias (P, LAD)
15. Jon Gray (P, COL)
16. Daniel Norris (P, TOR)
17. Carlos Rodon (P, CHW)
18. Tyler Glasnow (P, PIT)
19. Noah Syndergaard (P, NYM)
20. Blake Swihart (C, BOS)

21. Aaron Sanchez (P, TOR)
22. Henry Owens (P, BOS)
23. Jameson Taillon (P, PIT)
24. Robert Stephenson (P, CIN)
25. Andrew Heaney (P, LAA)
26. David Dahl (OF, COL)
27. Jose Berrios (P, MIN)
28. Jorge Alfaro (C, TEX)
29. Hunter Harvey (P, BAL)
30. Alex Meyer (P, MIN)

31. Kohl Stewart (P, MIN)
32. J.P. Crawford (SS, PHI)
33. Alex Jackson (OF, SEA)
34. Jesse Winker (OF, CIN)
35. Raul Mondesi (SS, KC)
36. D.J. Peterson (3B, SEA)
37. Austin Meadows (OF, PIT)
38. Josh Bell (OF, PIT)
39. Kyle Crick (P, SF)
40. Luis Severino (P, NYY)

41. Nick Gordon (SS, MIN)
42. Kyle Schwarber (OF, CHC)
43. Aaron Nola (P, PHI)
44. Kyle Zimmer (P, KC)
45. Alex Reyes (P, STL)
46. Braden Shipley (P, ARI)
47. Albert Almora (OF, CHC)
48. Clint Frazier (OF, CLE)
49. Tyler Kolek (P, MIA)
50. Mark Appel (P, HOU)

51. Rusney Castillo (OF, BOS)
52. Sean Manaea (P, KC)
53. A.J. Cole (P, WAS)
54. Matt Wisler (P, SD)
55. Raimel Tapia (OF, COL)
56. C.J. Edwards (P, CHC)
57. Dalton Pompey (OF, TOR)
58. Hunter Renfroe (OF, SD)
59. Hunter Dozier (3B, KC)
60. Brandon Nimmo (OF, NYM)

61. Tim Anderson (SS, CHW)
62. Maikel Franco (3B, PHI)
63. Mike Foltynewicz (P, HOU)
64. Nick Kingham (P, PIT)
65. Eddie Butler (P, COL)
66. Steven Matz (P, NYM)
67. Domingo Santana (OF, HOU)
68. Aaron Judge (OF, NYY)
69. Daniel Robertson (SS, OAK)
70. Stephen Piscotty (OF, STL)

71. Kyle Freeland (P, COL)
72. Kevin Plawecki (C, NYM)
73. Lucas Sims (P, ATL)
74. Yasmany Tomas (OF, ARI)
75. Jose Peraza (2B, ATL)
76. Eduardo Rodriguez (P, BOS)
77. Max Fried (P, ATL)
78. Manuel Margot (OF, BOS)
79. Matt Olson (1B, OAK)
80. Ryan McMahon (3B, COL)

81. Alex Gonzalez (P, TEX)
82. Tyler Beede (P, SF)
83. Alen Hanson (SS, PIT)
84. Grant Holmes (P, LAD)
85. Aaron Blair (P, ARI)
86. Michael Taylor (OF, WAS)
87. Trea Turner (SS, SD/WAS)
88. Christian Bethancourt (C, ATL)
89. Marco Gonzales (P, STL)
90. Michael Conforto (OF, NYM)

91. Sean Newcomb (P, LAA)
92. Alex Colome (P, TAM)
93. Jeff Hoffman (P, TOR)
94. Luke Jackson (P, TEX)
95. Lewis Brinson (OF, TEX)
96. Willy Adames (SS, TAM)
97. Jake Thompson (P, TEX)
98. Nick Williams (OF, TEX)
99. Colin Moran (3B, HOU)
100. Bradley Zimmer (OF, CLE)

TOP 100 PROSPECTS ARCHIVE

2014

1. Byron Buxton (OF, MIN)
2. Oscar Taveras (OF, STL)
3. Xander Bogaerts (SS, BOS)
4. Taijuan Walker (RHP, SEA)
5. Miguel Sano (3B, MIN)
6. Francisco Lindor (SS, CLE)
7. Javier Baez (SS, CHC)
8. Archie Bradley (RHP, ARI)
9. Carlos Correa (SS, HOU)
10. Gregory Polanco (OF, PIT)

11. Addison Russell (SS, OAK)
12. Jameson Taillon (RHP, PIT)
13. Kris Bryant (3B, CHC)
14. Dylan Bundy (RHP, BAL)
15. George Springer (OF, HOU)
16. Nick Castellanos (3B, DET)
17. Noah Syndergaard (RHP, NYM)
18. Kevin Gausman (RHP, BAL)
19. Carlos Martinez (RHP, STL)
20. Robert Stephenson (RHP, CIN)

21. Yordano Ventura (RHP, KC)
22. Jonathan Gray (RHP, COL)
23. Kyle Zimmer (RHP, KC)
24. Albert Almora (OF, CHC)
25. Mark Appel (RHP, HOU)
26. Aaron Sanchez (RHP, TOR)
27. Travis d'Arnaud (C, NYM)
28. Kyle Crick (RHP, SF)
29. Joc Pederson (OF, LA)
30. Alex Meyer (RHP, MIN)

31. Garin Cecchini (3B, BOS)
32. Jorge Soler (OF, CHC)
33. Jonathan Singleton (1B, HOU)
34. Maikel Franco (3B, PHI)
35. Lucas Giolito (RHP, WAS)
36. Eddie Butler (RHP, COL)
37. Andrew Heaney (LHP, MIA)
38. Jackie Bradley (OF, BOS)
39. Taylor Guerrieri (RHP, TAM)
40. Corey Seager (SS, LA)

41. Adalberto Mondesi (SS, KC)
42. Billy Hamilton (OF, CIN)
43. Clint Frazier (OF, CLE)
44. Tyler Glasnow (RHP, PIT)
45. Kolten Wong (2B, STL)
46. Henry Owens (LHP, BOS)
47. Gary Sanchez (C, NYY)
48. Jorge Alfaro (C, TEX)
49. Austin Meadows (OF, PIT)
50. Austin Hedges (C, SD)

51. Alen Hanson (SS, PIT)
52. Marcus Stroman (RHP, TOR)
53. Kohl Stewart (RHP, MIN)
54. Max Fried (LHP, SD)
55. Jake Odorizzi (RHP, TAM)
56. Michael Choice (OF, TEX)
57. C.J. Edwards (RHP, CHC)
58. Trevor Bauer (RHP, CLE)
59. Julio Urias (LHP, LA)
60. Jake Marisnick (OF, MIA)

61. Jesse Biddle (LHP, PHI)
62. Eddie Rosario (2B, MIN)
63. Lucas Sims (RHP, ATL)
64. Lance McCullers (RHP, HOU)
65. A.J. Cole (RHP, WAS)
66. Rougned Odor (2B, TEX)
67. Colin Moran (3B, MIA)
68. Mike Foltynewicz (RHP, HOU)
69. Allen Webster (RHP, BOS)
70. Chris Owings (SS, ARI)

71. Eduardo Rodriguez (LHP, BAL)
72. Miguel Almonte (RHP, KC)
73. Blake Swihart (C, BOS)
74. Jose Abreu (1B, CHW)
75. Zach Lee (RHP, LA)
76. Danny Hultzen (LHP, SEA)
77. Matt Wisler (RHP, SD)
78. Matt Barnes (RHP, BOS)
79. James Paxton (LHP, SEA)
80. Rosell Herrera (SS, COL)

81. Erik Johnson (RHP, CHW)
82. David Dahl (OF, COL)
83. Hak-Ju Lee (SS, TAM)
84. D.J. Peterson (3B, SEA)
85. Luke Jackson (RHP, TEX)
86. Delino DeShields (OF, HOU)
87. Brian Goodwin (OF, WAS)
88. Hunter Dozier (SS, KC)
89. Matt Davidson (3B, CHW)
90. Anthony Ranaudo (RHP, BOS)

91. Jimmy Nelson (RHP, MIL)
92. Bubba Starling (OF, KC)
93. Christian Bethancourt (C, ATL)
94. Courtney Hawkins (OF, CHW)
95. Domingo Santana (OF, HOU)
96. Kaleb Cowart (3B, LAA)
97. Jose Berrios (RHP, MIN)
98. Braden Shipley (RHP, ARI)
99. Justin Nicolino (LHP, MIA)
100. Alex Colome (RHP, TAM)

2013

1. Jurickson Profar (SS, TEX)
2. Dylan Bundy (RHP, BAL)
3. Wil Myers (OF, TAM)
4. Gerrit Cole (RHP, PIT)
5. Oscar Taveras (OF, STL)
6. Taijuan Walker (RHP, SEA)
7. Trevor Bauer (RHP, CLE)
8. Jose Fernandez (RHP, MIA)
9. Travis d'Arnaud (C, NYM)
10. Miguel Sano (3B, MIN)

11. Zack Wheeler (RHP, NYM)
12. Christian Yelich (OF, MIA)
13. Tyler Skaggs (LHP, ARI)
14. Francisco Lindor (SS, CLE)
15. Javier Baez (SS, CHC)
16. Shelby Miller (RHP, STL)
17. Nick Castellanos (OF, DET)
18. Xander Bogaerts (SS, BOS)
19. Jameson Taillon (RHP, PIT)
20. Danny Hultzen (LHP, SEA)

21. Jonathan Singleton (1B, HOU)
22. Mike Zunino (C, SEA)
23. Billy Hamilton (OF, CIN)
24. Anthony Rendon (3B, WAS)
25. Mike Olt (3B, TEX)
26. Byron Buxton (OF, MIN)
27. Nolan Arenado (3B, COL)
28. Carlos Correa (SS, HOU)
29. Archie Bradley (RHP, ARI)
30. Julio Teheran (RHP, ATL)

31. Matt Barnes (RHP, BOS)
32. Gary Sanchez (C, NYY)
33. Jackie Bradley (OF, BOS)
34. Carlos Martinez (RHP, STL)
35. Bubba Starling (OF, KC)
36. Jake Odorizzi (RHP, TAM)
37. Jedd Gyorko (3B, SD)
38. Alen Hanson (SS, PIT)
39. George Springer (OF, HOU)
40. Nick Franklin (2B, SEA)

41. Aaron Sanchez (RHP, TOR)
42. Albert Almora (OF, CHC)
43. Kaleb Cowart (3B, LAA)
44. Taylor Guerrieri (RHP, TAM)
45. Kyle Zimmer (RHP, KC)
46. Noah Syndergaard (RHP, NYM)
47. Kolten Wong (2B, STL)
48. Tyler Austin (OF, NYY)
49. James Paxton (LHP, SEA)
50. Rymer Liriano (OF, SD)

51. Jake Marisnick (OF, MIA)
52. Trevor Story (SS, COL)
53. Kevin Gausman (RHP, BAL)
54. Trevor Rosenthal (RHP, STL)
55. Alex Meyer (RHP, MIN)
56. Jorge Soler (OF, CHC)
57. Matt Davidson (3B, ARI)
58. Brett Jackson (OF, CHC)
59. Michael Choice (OF, OAK)
60. David Dahl (OF, COL)

61. Mason Williams (OF, NYY)
62. Robert Stephenson (RHP, CIN)
63. Chris Archer (RHP, TAM)
64. Oswaldo Arcia (OF, MIN)
65. Zach Lee (RHP, LA)
66. Tony Cingrani (LHP, CIN)
67. Jesse Biddle (LHP, PHI)
68. Gregory Polanco (OF, PIT)
69. Addison Russell (SS, OAK)
70. Robbie Erlin (RHP, SD)

71. Courtney Hawkins (OF, CHW)
72. Brian Goodwin (OF, WAS)
73. Martin Perez (LHP, TEX)
74. Luis Heredia (RHP, PIT)
75. Yasiel Puig (OF, LA)
76. Wilmer Flores (3B, NYM)
77. Justin Nicolino (LHP, MIA)
78. Max Fried (LHP, SD)
79. Adam Eaton (OF, ARI)
80. Gary Brown (OF, SF)

81. Casey Kelly (RHP, SD)
82. Lucas Giolito (RHP, WAS)
83. Wily Peralta (RHP, MIL)
84. Michael Wacha (RHP, STL)
85. Austin Hedges (C, SD)
86. Kyle Gibson (RHP, MIN)
87. Hak-Ju Lee (SS, TAM)
88. Dan Straily (RHP, OAK)
89. Kyle Crick (RHP, SF)
90. Avisail Garcia (OF, DET)

91. Cody Buckel (RHP, TEX)
92. Tyler Thornburg (RHP, MIL)
93. Allen Webster (RHP, BOS)
94. Jarred Cosart (RHP, HOU)
95. Bruce Rondon (RHP, DET)
96. Delino DeShields (2B, HOU)
97. A.J. Cole (RHP, OAK)
98. Manny Banuelos (LHP, NYY)
99. Yordano Ventura (RHP, KC)
100. Trevor May (RHP, MIN)

TOP 100 PROSPECTS ARCHIVE

2012

1. Bryce Harper (OF, WAS)
2. Matt Moore (LHP, TAM)
3. Mike Trout (OF, LAA)
4. Julio Teheran (RHP, ATL)
5. Jesus Montero (C, NYY)
6. Jurickson Profar (SS, TEX)
7. Manny Machado (SS, BAL)
8. Gerrit Cole (RHP, PIT)
9. Devin Mesoraco (C, CIN)
10. Wil Myers (OF, KC)

11. Miguel Sano (3B, MIN)
12. Jacob Turner (RHP, DET)
13. Anthony Rendon (3B, WAS)
14. Trevor Bauer (RHP, ARI)
15. Nolan Arenado (3B , COL)
16. Jameson Taillon (RHP, PIT)
17. Shelby Miller (RHP, STL)
18. Dylan Bundy (RHP, BAL)
19. Brett Jackson (OF, CHC)
20. Drew Pomeranz (LHP, COL)

21. Martin Perez (LHP, TEX)
22. Yonder Alonso (1B, SD)
23. Taijuan Walker (RHP, SEA)
24. Danny Hultzen (LHP, SEA)
25. Gary Brown (OF, SF)
26. Anthony Rizzo (1B, CHC)
27. Bubba Starling (OF, KC)
28. Travis d'Arnaud (C, TOR)
29. Mike Montgomery (LHP, KC)
30. Jake Odorizzi (RHP, KC)

31. Hak-Ju Lee (SS, TAM)
32. Jonathan Singleton (1B, HOU)
33. Garrett Richards (RHP, LAA)
34. Manny Banuelos (LHP, NYY)
35. James Paxton (LHP, SEA)
36. Jarrod Parker (RHP, OAK)
37. Carlos Martinez (RHP, STL)
38. Jake Marisnick (OF, TOR)
39. Yasmani Grandal (C, SD)
40. Trevor May (RHP, PHI)

41. Gary Sanchez (C, NYY)
42. Mike Olt (3B, TEX)
43. Wilin Rosario (C, COL)
44. John Lamb (LHP, KC)
45. Francisco Lindor (SS, CLE)
46. Dellin Betances (RHP, NYY)
47. Michael Choice (OF, OAK)
48. Arodys Vizcaino (RHP, ATL)
49. Trayvon Robinson (OF, SEA)
50. Matt Harvey (RHP, NYM)

51. Will Middlebrooks (3B, BOS)
52. Jedd Gyorko (3B, SD)
53. Randall Delgado (RHP, ATL)
54. Zack Wheeler (RHP, NYM)
55. Zach Lee (RHP, LA)
56. Tyler Skaggs (LHP, ARI)
57. Nick Castellanos (3B, DET)
58. Robbie Erlin (LHP, SD)
59. Christian Yelich (OF, MIA)
60. Anthony Gose (OF, TOR)

61. Addison Reed (RHP, CHW)
62. Javier Baez (SS, CHC)
63. Starling Marte (OF, PIT)
64. Kaleb Cowart (3B, LAA)
65. George Springer (OF, HOU)
66. Jarred Cosart (RHP, HOU)
67. Jean Segura (2B, LAA)
68. Kolten Wong (2B, STL)
69. Nick Franklin (SS, SEA)
70. Alex Torres (RHP, TAM)

71. Rymer Liriano (OF, SD)
72. Josh Bell (OF, PIT)
73. Leonys Martin (OF, TEX)
74. Joe Wieland (RHP, SD)
75. Joe Benson (OF, MIN)
76. Wily Peralta (RHP, MIL)
77. Tim Wheeler (OF, COL)
78. Oscar Taveras (OF, STL)
79. Xander Bogaerts (SS, BOS)
80. Archie Bradley (RHP, ARI)

81. Kyle Gibson (RHP, MIN)
82. Allen Webster (RHP, LA)
83. C.J. Cron (1B, LAA)
84. Grant Green (OF, OAK)
85. Brad Peacock (RHP, OAK)
86. Chris Dwyer (LHP, KC)
87. Billy Hamilton (SS, CIN)
88. A.J. Cole (RHP, OAK)
89. Aaron Hicks (OF, MIN)
90. Noah Syndergaard (RHP, TOR)

91. Tyrell Jenkins (RHP, STL)
92. Anthony Ranaudo (RHP, BOS)
93. Jed Bradley (LHP, MIL)
94. Nathan Eovaldi (RHP, LA)
95. Andrelton Simmons (SS, ATL)
96. Taylor Guerrieri (RHP, TAM)
97. Cheslor Cuthbert (3B, KC)
98. Edward Salcedo (3B, ATL)
99. Domingo Santana, OF, HOU)
100. Jesse Biddle (LHP, PHI)

2011

1. Bryce Harper (OF, WAS)
2. Domonic Brown (OF, PHI)
3. Jesus Montero (C, NYY)
4. Mike Trout (OF, LAA)
5. Jeremy Hellickson (RHP, TAM)
6. Aroldis Chapman (LHP, CIN)
7. Eric Hosmer (1B, KC)
8. Dustin Ackley (2B, SEA)
9. Desmond Jennings (OF, TAM)
10. Julio Teheran (RHP, ATL)

11. Mike Moustakas (3B, KC)
12. Brandon Belt (1B, SF)
13. Freddie Freeman (1B, ATL)
14. Michael Pineda (RHP, SEA)
15. Matt Moore (LHP, TAM)
16. Mike Montgomery (LHP, KC)
17. Brett Jackson (OF, CHC)
18. Nick Franklin (SS, SEA)
19. Jameson Taillon (RHP, PIT)
20. Jacob Turner (RHP, DET)

21. Shelby Miller (RHP, STL)
22. Martin Perez (LHP, TEX)
23. Wil Myers (C, KC)
24. Kyle Gibson (RHP, MIN)
25. Lonnie Chisenhall (3B, CLE)
26. Tyler Matzek (LHP, COL)
27. Brett Lawrie (2B, TOR)
28. Yonder Alonso (1B, CIN)
29. Jarrod Parker (RHP, ARI)
30. Jonathan Singleton (1B, PHI)

31. Tanner Scheppers (RHP,TEX)
32. Kyle Drabek (RHP, TOR)
33. Jason Knapp (RHP, CLE)
34. Manny Banuelos (LHP, NYY)
35. Alex White (RHP, CLE)
36. Jason Kipnis (2B, CLE)
37. Wilin Rosario (C, COL)
38. Manny Machado (SS, BAL)
39. Chris Sale (LHP, CHW)
40. Devin Mesoraco (C, CIN)

41. Tyler Chatwood (RHP, LAA)
42. John Lamb (LHP, KC)
43. Danny Duffy (LHP, KC)
44. Trevor May (RHP, PHI)
45. Mike Minor (LHP, ATL)
46. Jarred Cosart (RHP, PHI)
47. Tony Sanchez (C, PIT)
48. Brody Colvin (RHP, PHI)
49. Zach Britton (LHP, BAL)
50. Dee Gordon (SS, LA)

51. Miguel Sano (3B, MIN)
52. Grant Green (SS, OAK)
53. Danny Espinosa (SS, WAS)
54. Simon Castro (RHP, SD)
55. Derek Norris (C, WAS)
56. Chris Archer (RHP, CHC)
57. Jurickson Profar (SS, TEX)
58. Zack Cox (3B, STL)
59. Billy Hamilton (2B, CIN)
60. Gary Sanchez (C, NYY)

61. Zach Lee (RHP, LA)
62. Drew Pomeranz (LHP, CLE)
63. Randall Delgado (RHP, ATL)
64. Michael Choice (OF, OAK)
65. Nick Weglarz (OF, CLE)
66. Nolan Arenado (3B, COL)
67. Chris Carter (1B/OF, OAK)
68. Arodys Vizcaino (RHP, ATL)
69. Trey McNutt (RHP, CHC)
70. Dellin Betances (RHP, NYY)

71. Aaron Hicks (OF, MIN)
72. Aaron Crow (RHP, KC)
73. Jake McGee (LHP, TAM)
74. Lars Anderson (1B, BOS)
75. Fabio Martinez (RHP, LAA)
76. Ben Revere (OF, MIN)
77. Jordan Lyles (RHP, HOU)
78. Casey Kelly (RHP, SD)
79. Trayvon Robinson (OF, LA)
80. Craig Kimbrel (RHP, ATL)

81. Jose Iglesias (SS, BOS)
82. Garrett Richards (RHP, LAA)
83. Allen Webster (RHP, LA)
84. Chris Dwyer (LHP, KC)
85. Alex Colome (RHP, TAM)
86. Zack Wheeler (RHP, SF)
87. Andy Oliver (LHP, DET)
88. Andrew Brackman (RHP,NYY)
89. Wilmer Flores (SS, NYM)
90. Christian Friedrich (LHP, COL)

91. Anthony Ranaudo (RHP, BOS)
92. Aaron Miller (LHP, LA)
93. Matt Harvey (RHP, NYM)
94. Mark Rogers (RHP, MIL)
95. Jean Segura (2B, LAA)
96. Hank Conger (C, LAA)
97. J.P. Arencibia (C, TOR)
98. Matt Dominguez (3B, FLA)
99. Jerry Sands (1B, LA)
100. Nick Castellanos (3B, DET)

Top 100 Prospects Archive

2010

1. Stephen Strasburg (RHP, WAS)
2. Jason Heyward (OF, ATL)
3. Jesus Montero (C, NYY)
4. Buster Posey (C, SF)
5. Justin Smoak (1B, TEX)
6. Pedro Alvarez (3B, PIT)
7. Carlos Santana (C, CLE)
8. Desmond Jennings (OF, TAM)
9. Brian Matusz (LHP, BAL)
10. Neftali Feliz (RHP, TEX)

11. Brett Wallace (3B, TOR)
12. Mike Stanton (OF. FLA)
13. M. Bumgarner (LHP, SF)
14. J. Hellickson (RHP, TAM)
15. Dustin Ackley (1B/OF, SEA)
16. Aroldis Chapman (LHP, CIN)
17. Yonder Alonso (1B, CIN)
18. Alcides Escobar (SS, MIL)
19. Brett Lawrie (2B, MIL)
20. Starlin Castro (SS, CHC)

21. Logan Morrison (1B, FLA)
22. Mike Montgomery (LHP, KC)
23. Domonic Brown (OF, PHI)
24. Josh Vitters (3B, CHC)
25. R. Westmoreland (OF, BOS)
26. Todd Frazier (3B/OF, CIN)
27. Eric Hosmer (1B, KC)
28. Freddie Freeman (1B, ATL)
29. Derek Norris (C, WAS)
30. Martin Perez (LHP, TEX)

31. Wade Davis (RHP, TAM)
32. Trevor Reckling (LHP, LAA)
33. Jordan Walden (RHP, LAA)
34. Mat Gamel (3B, MIL)
35. Tyler Flowers (C, CHW)
36. T. Scheppers (RHP, TEX)
37. Casey Crosby (LHP, DET)
38. Austin Jackson (OF, DET)
39. Devaris Gordon (SS, LA)
40. Kyle Drabek (RHP, TOR)

41. Ben Revere (OF, MIN)
42. Michael Taylor (OF, OAK)
43. Jacob Turner (RHP, DET)
44. Tim Beckham (SS, TAM)
45. Carlos Triunfel (SS, SEA)
46. Aaron Crow (RHP, KC)
47. Matt Moore (LHP, TAM)
48. Jarrod Parker (RHP, ARI)
49. F. Martinez (OF, NYM)
50. C. Friedrich (LHP, COL)

51. Jenrry Mejia (RHP, NYM)
52. Tyler Matzek (LHP, COL)
53. Brett Jackson (OF, CHC)
54. Aaron Hicks (OF, MIN)
55. Jhoulys Chacin (RHP, COL)
56. Josh Bell (3B, BAL)
57. Brandon Allen (1B, ARI)
58. Chris Carter (1B, OAK)
59. Jason Knapp (RHP, CLE)
60. Danny Duffy (LHP, KC)

61. Tim Alderson (RHP, PIT)
62. Matt Dominguez (3B, FLA)
63. Mike Moustakas (3B, KC)
64. Jake Arrieta (RHP, BAL)
65. Carlos Carrasco (RHP, CLE)
66. Wilmer Flores (SS, NYM)
67. Drew Storen (RHP, WAS)
68. Lonnie Chisenhall (3B, CLE)
69. Aaron Poreda (LHP, SD)
70. A. Cashner (RHP, CHC)

71. Tony Sanchez (C, PIT)
72. Julio Teheran (RHP, ATL)
73. Jose Tabata (OF, PIT)
74. Jason Castro (C, HOU)
75. Casey Kelly (RHP, BOS)
76. Alex White (RHP, CLE)
77. Jay Jackson (RHP, CHC)
78. Dan Hudson (RHP, CHW)
79. Brandon Erbe (RHP, BAL)
80. Zack Wheeler (RHP, SF)

81. Shelby Miller (RHP, STL)
82. Jordan Lyles (RHP, HOU)
83. Simon Castro (RHP, SD)
84. Aaron Miller (LHP, LA)
85. Michael Ynoa (RHP, OAK)
86. Ethan Martin (RHP, LA)
87. Scott Elbert (LHP, LA)
88. Nick Weglarz (OF, CLE)
89. Donavan Tate (OF, SD)
90. Jordan Danks (OF, CHW)

91. Hector Rondon (RHP, CLE)
92. Chris Heisey (OF, CIN)
93. Kyle Gibson (RHP, MIN)
94. Mike Leake (RHP, CIN)
95. Mike Trout (OF, LAA)
96. Jake McGee (LHP, TAM)
97. Chad James (LHP, FLA)
98. C. Bethancourt (C, NYY)
99. Miguel Sano (SS, MIN)
100. Noel Arguelles (LHP, KC)

2009

1. Matt Wieters (C, BAL)
2. David Price (LHP, TAM)
3. Rick Porcello (RHP, DET)
4. Colby Rasmus (OF, STL)
5. Madison Bumgarner (LHP, SF)
6. Neftali Feliz (RHP, TEX)
7. Jason Heyward (OF, ATL)
8. Andrew McCutchen (OF, PIT)
9. Pedro Alvarez (3B, PIT)
10. Cameron Maybin (OF, FLA)

11. Trevor Cahill (RHP, OAK)
12. Mike Moustakas (3B/SS, KC)
13. Jordan Zimmermann (RHP, WAS)
14. Travis Snider (OF, TOR)
15. Tim Beckham (SS, TAM)
16. Eric Hosmer (1B, KC)
17. Tommy Hanson (RHP, ATL)
18. Dexter Fowler (OF, COL)
19. Brett Anderson (LHP, OAK)
20. Carlos Triunfel (SS/2B, SEA)

21. Buster Posey (C, SF)
22. Chris Tillman (RHP, BAL)
23. Brian Matusz (LHP, BAL)
24. Justin Smoak (1B, TEX)
25. Jarrod Parker (RHP, ARI)
26. Derek Holland (LHP, TEX)
27. Lars Anderson (1B, BOS)
28. Michael Inoa (RHP, OAK)
29. Mike Stanton (OF, FLA)
30. Taylor Teagarden (C, TEX)

31. Gordon Beckham (SS, CHW)
32. Brett Wallace (3B, STL)
33. Matt LaPorta (OF, CLE)
34. Jordan Schafer (OF, ATL)
35. Carlos Santana (C, CLE)
36. Aaron Hicks (OF, MIN)
37. Adam Miller (RHP, CLE)
38. Elvis Andrus (SS, TEX)
39. Alcides Escobar (SS, MIL)
40. Wade Davis (RHP, TAM)

41. Austin Jackson (OF, NYY)
42. Jesus Montero (C, NYY)
43. Tim Alderson (RHP, SF)
44. Jhoulys Chacin (RHP, COL)
45. Phillippe Aumont (RHP, SEA)
46. James McDonald (RHP, LA)
47. Reid Brignac (SS, TAM)
48. Desmond Jennings (OF, TAM)
49. Fernando Martinez (OF, NYM)
50. JP Arencibia (C, TOR)

51. Wilmer Flores (SS, NYM)
52. Brett Cecil (LHP, TOR)
53. Aaron Poreda (LHP, CHW)
54. Jeremy Jeffress (RHP, MIL)
55. Michael Main (RHP, TEX)
56. Josh Vitters (3B, CHC)
57. Mat Gamel (3B, MIL)
58. Yonder Alonso (1B, CIN)
59. Gio Gonzalez (LHP, OAK)
60. Michael Bowden (RHP, BOS)

61. Angel Villalona (1B, SF)
62. Carlos Carrasco (RHP, PHI)
63. Jake Arrieta (RHP, BAL)
64. Jordan Walden (RHP, LAA)
65. Freddie Freeman (1B, ATL)
66. Logan Morrison (1B, FLA)
67. Shooter Hunt (RHP, MIN)
68. Junichi Tazawa (RHP, BOS)
69. Nick Adenhart (RHP, LAA)
70. Jose Tabata (OF, PIT)

71. Adrian Cardenas (SS/2B, OAK)
72. Chris Carter (3B/OF, OAK)
73. Ben Revere (OF, MIN)
74. Josh Reddick (OF, BOS)
75. Jeremy Hellickson (RHP, TAM)
76. Justin Jackson (SS, TOR)
77. Wilson Ramos (C, MIN)
78. Jason Castro (C, HOU)
79. Julio Borbon (OF, TEX)
80. Tyler Flowers (C, CHW)

81. Gorkys Hernandez (OF, ATL)
82. Neftali Soto (3B, CIN)
83. Henry Rodriguez (RHP, OAK)
84. Dan Duffy (LHP, KC)
85. Daniel Cortes (RHP, KC)
86. Dayan Viciedo (3B, CHW)
87. Matt Dominguez (3B, FLA)
88. Jordan Danks (OF, CHW)
89. Chris Coghlan (2B, FLA)
90. Brian Bogusevic (OF, HOU)

91. Ryan Tucker (RHP, FLA)
92. Jonathon Niese (LHP, NYM)
93. Martin Perez (LHP, TEX)
94. James Simmons (RHP, OAK)
95. Nick Weglarz (OF/1B, CLE)
96. Daniel Bard (RHP, BOS)
97. Yamaico Navarro (SS, BOS)
98. Jose Ceda (RHP, FLA)
99. Jeff Samardzija (RHP, CHC)
100. Jason Donald (SS, PHI)

AVG: Batting Average (see also BA)

BA: Batting Average (see also AVG)

Base Performance Indicator (BPI): A statistical formula that measures an isolated aspect of a player's situation-independent raw skill or a gauge that helps capture the effects of random chance has on a skill. Although there are many such formulas, there are only a few that we are referring to when the term is used in this book. For pitchers, our BPI's are control (bb%), dominance (k/9), command (k/bb), opposition on base average (OOB), ground/line/fly ratios (G/L/F), and expected ERA (xERA). Random chance is measured witih the hit rate (H%) and strand rate (S%).

*Base Performance Value (BPV): A single value that describes a pitcher's overall raw skill level. This is more useful than any traditional statistical gauge to track performance trends and project future statistical output. The BPV formula combines and weights several BPIs:

(Dominance Rate x 6) + (Command ratio x 21) – Opposition HR Rate x 30) – ((Opp. Batting Average - .275) x 200)

The formula combines the individual raw skills of power, command, the ability to keep batters from reaching base, and the ability to prevent long hits, all characteristics that are unaffected by most external team factors. In tandem with a pitcher's strand rate, it provides a complete picture of the elements that contribute to a pitcher's ERA, and therefore serves as an accurate tool to project likely changes in ERA. **BENCHMARKS:** We generally consider a BPV of 50 to be the minimum level required for long-term success. The elite of bullpen aces will have BPV's in the excess of 100 and it is rare for these stoppers to enjoy long-term success with consistent levels under 75.

Batters Faced per Game *(Craig Wright)*

((IP x 2.82) + H + BB) / G

A measure of pitcher usage and one of the leading indicators for potential pitcher burnout.

Batting Average (BA, or AVG)

(H/AB)

Ratio of hits to at-bats, though it is a poor evaluative measure of hitting performance. It neglects the offensive value of the base on balls and assumes that all hits are created equal.

Batting Eye (Eye)

(Walks / Strikeouts)

A measure of a player's strike zone judgment, the raw ability to distinguish between balls and strikes. **BENCHMARKS:** The best hitters have eye ratios over 1.00 (indicating more walks than strikeouts) and are the most likely to be among a league's .300 hitters. At the other end of the scale are ratios

less than 0.50, which represent batters who likely also have lower BAs.

bb%: Walk rate (hitters)

bb/9: Opposition Walks per 9 IP

BF/Gm: Batters Faced Per Game

BPI: Base Performance Indicator

*BPV: Base Performance Value

Cmd: Command ratio

Command Ratio (Cmd)

(Strikeouts / Walks)

This is a measure of a pitcher's raw ability to get the ball over the plate. There is no more fundamental a skill than this, and so it is accurately used as a leading indicator to project future rises and falls in other gauges, such as ERA. Command is one of the best gauges to use to evaluate minor league performance. It is a prime component of a pitcher's base performance value. **BENCHMARKS:** Baseball's upper echelon of command pitchers will have ratios in excess of 3.0. Pitchers with ratios under 1.0 — indicating that they walk more batters than they strike out — have virtually no potential for long term success. If you make no other changes in your approach to drafting a pitching staff, limiting your focus to only pitchers with a command ratio of 2.0 or better will substantially improve your odds of success.

Contact Rate (ct%)

((AB - K) / AB)

Measures a batter's ability to get wood on the ball and hit it into the field of play. **BENCHMARK:** Those batters with the best contact skill will have levels of 90% or better. The hackers of society will have levels of 75% or less.

Control Rate (bb/9), or Opposition Walks per Game

BB Allowed x 9 / IP

Measures how many walks a pitcher allows per game equivalent. **BENCHMARK:** The best pitchers will have bb/9 levels of 3.0 or less.

ct%: Contact rate

Ctl: Control Rate

Dom: Dominance Rate

Dominance Rate (k/9), or Opposition Strikeouts per Game

(K Allowed x 9 / IP)

Measures how many strikeouts a pitcher allows per game equivalent. **BENCHMARK:** The best pitchers will have k/9 levels of 6.0 or higher.

Expected Earned Run Average (Gill and Reeve)

(.575 x H [per 9 IP]) + (.94 x HR [per 9 IP]) + (.28 x BB [per 9 IP]) - (.01 x K [per 9 IP]) - Normalizing Factor

"xERA represents the expected ERA of the pitcher based on a normal distribution of his statistics. It is not influenced by situation-dependent factors." xERA erases the inequity between starters' and relievers' ERA's, eliminating the effect that a pitcher's success or failure has on another pitcher's ERA.

Similar to other gauges, the accuracy of this formula changes with the level of competition from one season to the next. The normalizing factor allows us to better approximate a pitcher's actual ERA. This value is usually somewhere around 2.77 and varies by league and year. BENCHMARKS: In general, xERA's should approximate a pitcher's ERA fairly closely. However, those pitchers who have large variances between the two gauges are candidates for further analysis.

Extra-Base Hit Rate (X/H)

(2B + 3B + HR) / Hits

X/H is a measure of power and can be used along with a player's slugging percentage and isolated power to gauge a player's ability to drive the ball. BENCHMARKS: Players with above average power will post X/H of greater than 38% and players with moderate power will post X/H of 30% or greater. Weak hitters with below average power will have a X/H level of less than 20%.

Eye: Batting Eye

h%: Hit rate (batters)

H%: Hits Allowed per Balls in Play (pitchers)

Hit Rate (h% or H%)

(H—HR) / (AB – HR - K)

The percent of balls hit into the field of play that fall for hits.

hr/9: Opposition Home Runs per 9 IP

ISO: Isolated Power

Isolated Power (ISO)

(Slugging Percentage - Batting Average)

Isolated Power is a measurement of power skill. Subtracting a player's BA from his SLG, we are essentially pulling out all the singles and single bases from the formula. What remains are the extra-base hits. ISO is not an absolute measurement as it assumes that two doubles is worth one home run, which certainly is not the case, but is another statistic that is a good measurement of raw power. BENCHMARKS: The game's top sluggers will tend to have ISO levels over .200. Weak hitters will be under .100.

k/9: Dominance rate (opposition strikeouts per 9 IP)

Major League Equivalency (Bill James)

A formula that converts a player's minor or foreign league statistics into a comparable performance in the major leagues. These are not projections, but conversions of current performance.

Contains adjustments for the level of play in individual leagues and teams. Works best with Triple-A stats, not quite as well with Double-A stats, and hardly at all with the lower levels. Foreign conversions are still a work in process. James' original formula only addressed batting. Our research has devised conversion formulas for pitchers, however, their best use comes when looking at BPI's, not traditional stats.

MLE: Major League Equivalency

OBP: On Base Percentage (batters)

OBA: Opposition Batting Average (pitchers)

On Base Percentage (OBP)

(H + BB) / (AB + BB)

Addressing one of the two deficiencies in BA, OBP gives value to those events that get batters on base, but are not hits. By adding walks (and often, hit batsmen) into the basic batting average formula, we have a better gauge of a batter's ability to reach base safely. An OBP of .350 can be read as "this batter gets on base 35% of the time."

Why this is a more important gauge than batting average? When a run is scored, there is no distinction made as to how that runner reached base. So, two thirds of the time—about how often a batter comes to the plate with the bases empty—a walk really is as good as a hit. BENCHMARKS: We all know what a .300 hitter is, but what represents "good" for OBP? That comparable level would likely be .400, with .275 representing the level of futility.

On Base Plus Slugging Percentage (OPS)

A simple sum of the two gauges, it is considered as one of the better evaluators of overall performance. OPS combines the two basic elements of offensive production — the ability to get on base (OBP) and the ability to advance baserunners (SLG). BENCHMARKS: The game's top batters will have OPS levels over .900. The worst batters will have levels under .600.

Opposition Batting Average (OBA)

(Hits Allowed / ((IP x 2.82) + Hits Allowed))

A close approximation of the batting average achieved by opposing batters against a particular pitcher. BENCHMARKS: The converse of the benchmark for batters, the best pitchers will have levels under .250; the worst pitchers levels over .300.

Opposition Home Runs per Game (hr/9)

(HR Allowed x 9 / IP)

Measures how many home runs a pitcher allows per game equivalent. BENCHMARK: The best pitchers will have hr/9 levels of under 1.0.

Opposition On Base Average (OOB)

(Hits Allowed + BB) / ((IP x 2.82) + H + BB)

A close approximation of the on base average achieved by opposing batters against a particular pitcher. BENCHMARK: The best pitchers will have levels under .300; the worst pitchers levels over .375.

Opposition Strikeouts per Game: See Dominance Rate.

Opposition Walks per Game: See Control Rate.

OPS: On Base Plus Slugging Percentage

RC: Runs Created

RC/G: Runs Created Per Game

Runs Created *(Bill James)*

(H + BB - CS) x (Total bases + (.55 x SB)) / (AB + BB)

A formula that converts all offensive events into a total of runs scored. As calculated for individual teams, the result approximates a club's actual run total with great accuracy.

Runs Created Per Game *(Bill James)*

Runs Created / ((AB - H + CS) / 25.5)

RC expressed on a per-game basis might be considered the hypothetical ERA compiled against a particular batter. **BENCHMARKS:** Few players surpass the level of a 10.00 RC/G in any given season, but any level over 7.50 can still be considered very good. At the bottom are levels below 3.00.

S%: Strand Rate

Save: There are six events that need to occur in order for a pitcher to post a single save...

1. The starting pitcher and middle relievers must pitch well.
2. The offense must score enough runs.
3. It must be a reasonably close game.
4. The manager must choose to put the pitcher in for a save opportunity.
5. The pitcher must pitch well and hold the lead.
6. The manager must let him finish the game.

Of these six events, only one is within the control of the relief pitcher. As such, projecting saves for a reliever has little to do with skill and a lot to do with opportunity. However, pitchers with excellent skills sets may create opportunity for themselves.

Situation Independent: Describing a statistical gauge that measures performance apart from the context of team, ballpark, or other outside variables. Strikeouts and Walks, inasmuch as they are unaffected by the performance of a batter's surrounding team, are considered situation independent stats.

Conversely, RBIs are situation dependent because individual performance varies greatly by the performance of other batters on the team (you can't drive in runs if there is nobody on base). Similarly, pitching wins are as much a measure of the success of a pitcher as they are a measure of the success of the offense and defense performing behind that pitcher, and are therefore a poor measure of pitching performance alone.

Situation independent gauges are important for us to be able to separate a player's contribution to his team and isolate his performance so that we may judge it on its own merits.

Slg: Slugging Percentage

Slugging Percentage (Slg)

(Singles + (2 x Doubles) + (3 x Triples) + (4 x HR)) / AB

A measure of the total number of bases accumulated per at bat. It is a misnomer; it is not a true measure of a batter's slugging ability because it includes singles. SLG also assumes that each type of hit has proportionally increasing value (i.e. a double is twice as valuable as a single, etc.) which is not true. **BENCHMARKS:** The top batters will have levels over .500. The bottom batters will have levels under .300.

Strand Rate (S%)

(H + BB - ER) / (H + BB - HR)

Measures the percentage of allowed runners a pitcher strands, which incorporates both individual pitcher skill and bullpen effectiveness. **BENCHMARKS:** The most adept at stranding runners will have S% levels over 75%. Once a pitcher's S% starts dropping down below 65%, he's going to have problems with his ERA. Those pitchers with strand rates over 80% will have artificially low ERAs, which will be prone to relapse.

Strikeouts per Game: See Opposition Strikeouts per game.

Walks + Hits per Innings Pitched (WHIP): The number of baserunners a pitcher allows per inning. **BENCHMARKS:** Usually, a WHIP of under 1.20 is considered top level and over 1.50 is indicative of poor performance. Levels under 1.00 — allowing fewer runners than IP — represent extraordinary performance and are rarely maintained over time.

Walk rate (bb%)

(BB / (AB + BB))

A measure of a batter's eye and plate patience. BENCHMARKS: The best batters will have levels of over 10%. Those with the least plate patience will have levels of 5% or less.

Walks per Game: See Opposition Walks per Game.

WHIP: Walks + Hits per Innings Pitched

Wins: There are five events that need to occur in order for a pitcher to post a single win...

1. He must pitch well, allowing few runs.
2. The offense must score enough runs.
3. The defense must successfully field all batted balls.
4. The bullpen must hold the lead.
5. The manager must leave the pitcher in for 5 innings, and not remove him if the team is still behind.

X/H: Extra-base Hit Rate

*xERA: Expected ERA

* Asterisked formulas have updated versions in the Baseball Forecaster. *However, those updates include statistics like Ground Ball Rate, Fly Ball Rate or Line Drive Rate, for which we do not have reliable data for minor leaguers. So we use the previous version of those formulas, as listed here, for the players in this book.*

TEAM AFFILIATIONS

TEAM	ORG	LEAGUE	LEV	TEAM	ORG	LEAGUE	LEV
Aberdeen	BAL	New York-Penn League	SS	Columbia	NYM	South Atlantic League	A-
Akron	CLE	Eastern League	AA	Columbus	CLE	International League	AAA
Albuquerque	COL	Pacific Coast League	AAA	Connecticut	DET	New York-Penn League	SS
Altoona	PIT	Eastern League	AA	Corpus Christi	HOU	Texas League	AA
Arkansas	SEA	Texas League	AA	Danville	ATL	Appalachian League	Rk
Asheville	COL	South Atlantic League	A-	Dayton	CIN	Midwest League	A-
Auburn	WAS	New York-Penn League	SS	Daytona	CIN	Florida State League	A+
Augusta	SF	South Atlantic League	A-	Delmarva	BAL	South Atlantic League	A-
AZL Angels	LAA	Arizona League	Rk	Down East	TEX	Carolina League	A+
AZL Athletics	OAK	Arizona League	Rk	Dunedin	TOR	Florida State League	A+
AZL Brewers	MIL	Arizona League	Rk	Durham	TAM	International League	AAA
AZL Cubs	CHC	Arizona League	Rk	El Paso	SD	Pacific Coast League	AAA
AZL Diamondbacks	ARI	Arizona League	Rk	Elizabethton	MIN	Appalachian League	Rk
AZL Dodgers	LAD	Arizona League	Rk	Erie	DET	Eastern League	AA
AZL Giants	SF	Arizona League	Rk	Eugene	CHC	Northwest League	SS
AZL Indians	CLE	Arizona League	Rk	Everett	SEA	Northwest League	SS
AZL Mariners	SEA	Arizona League	Rk	Florida	ATL	Florida State League	A+
AZL Padres	SD	Arizona League	Rk	Fort Myers	MIN	Florida State League	A+
AZL Rangers	TEX	Arizona League	Rk	Fort Wayne	SD	Midwest League	A-
AZL Reds	CIN	Arizona League	Rk	Frederick	BAL	Carolina League	A+
AZL Royals	KC	Arizona League	Rk	Fresno	HOU	Pacific Coast League	AAA
AZL White Sox	CHW	Arizona League	Rk	Frisco	TEX	Texas League	AA
Batavia	MIA	New York-Penn League	SS	GCL Astros	HOU	Gulf Coast League	Rk
Beloit	OAK	Midwest League	A-	GCL Blue Jays	TOR	Gulf Coast League	Rk
Billings	CIN	Pioneer League	Rk	GCL Braves	ATL	Gulf Coast League	Rk
Biloxi	MIL	Southern League	AA	GCL Cardinals	STL	Gulf Coast League	Rk
Binghamton	NYM	Eastern League	AA	GCL Marlins	MIA	Gulf Coast League	Rk
Birmingham	CHW	Southern League	AA	GCL Mets	NYM	Gulf Coast League	Rk
Bluefield	TOR	Appalachian League	Rk	GCL Nationals	WAS	Gulf Coast League	Rk
Boise	COL	Northwest League	SS	GCL Orioles	BAL	Gulf Coast League	Rk
Bowie	BAL	Eastern League	AA	GCL Phillies	PHI	Gulf Coast League	Rk
Bowling Green	TAM	Midwest League	A-	GCL Pirates	PIT	Gulf Coast League	Rk
Bradenton	PIT	Florida State League	A+	GCL Rays	TAM	Gulf Coast League	Rk
Bristol	PIT	Appalachian League	Rk	GCL Red Sox	BOS	Gulf Coast League	Rk
Brooklyn	NYM	New York-Penn League	SS	GCL Tigers East	DET	Gulf Coast League	Rk
Buffalo	TOR	International League	AAA	GCL Tigers West	DET	Gulf Coast League	Rk
Buies Creek	HOU	Carolina League	A+	GCL Twins	MIN	Gulf Coast League	Rk
Burlington	KC	Appalachian League	Rk	GCL Yankees East	NYY	Gulf Coast League	Rk
Burlington	LAA	Midwest League	A-	GCL Yankees West	NYY	Gulf Coast League	Rk
Carolina	MIL	Carolina League	A+	Grand Junction	COL	Pioneer League	Rk
Cedar Rapids	MIN	Midwest League	A-	Great Falls	CHW	Pioneer League	Rk
Charleston	NYY	South Atlantic League	A-	Great Lakes	LAD	Midwest League	A-
Charlotte	CHW	International League	AAA	Greeneville	HOU	Appalachian League	Rk
Charlotte	TAM	Florida State League	A+	Greensboro	MIA	South Atlantic League	A-
Chattanooga	MIN	Southern League	AA	Greenville	BOS	South Atlantic League	A-
Clearwater	PHI	Florida State League	A+	Gwinnett	ATL	International League	AAA
Clinton	SEA	Midwest League	A-	Hagerstown	WAS	South Atlantic League	A-
Colorado Springs	MIL	Pacific Coast League	AAA	Harrisburg	WAS	Eastern League	AA

TEAM	ORG	LEAGUE	LEV	TEAM	ORG	LEAGUE	LEV
Hartford	COL	Eastern League	AA	Pensacola	CIN	Southern League	AA
Helena	MIL	Pioneer League	Rk	Peoria	STL	Midwest League	A-
Hickory	TEX	South Atlantic League	A-	Portland	BOS	Eastern League	AA
Hillsboro	ARI	Northwest League	SS	Potomac	WAS	Carolina League	A+
Hudson Valley	TAM	New York-Penn League	SS	Princeton	TAM	Appalachian League	Rk
Idaho Falls	KC	Pioneer League	Rk	Pulaski	NYY	Appalachian League	Rk
Indianapolis	PIT	International League	AAA	Quad Cities	HOU	Midwest League	A-
Inland Empire	LAA	California League	A+	Rancho Cucamonga	LAD	California League	A+
Iowa	CHC	Pacific Coast League	AAA	Reading	PHI	Eastern League	AA
Jackson	ARI	Southern League	AA	Reno	ARI	Pacific Coast League	AAA
Jacksonville	MIA	Southern League	AA	Richmond	SF	Eastern League	AA
Johnson City	STL	Appalachian League	Rk	Rochester	MIN	International League	AAA
Jupiter	MIA	Florida State League	A+	Rome	ATL	South Atlantic League	A-
Kane County	ARI	Midwest League	A-	Round Rock	TEX	Pacific Coast League	AAA
Kannapolis	CHW	South Atlantic League	A-	Sacramento	SF	Pacific Coast League	AAA
Kingsport	NYM	Appalachian League	Rk	Salem	BOS	Carolina League	A+
Lake County	CLE	Midwest League	A-	Salem-Keizer	SF	Northwest League	SS
Lake Elsinore	SD	California League	A+	Salt Lake	LAA	Pacific Coast League	AAA
Lakeland	DET	Florida State League	A+	San Antonio	SD	Texas League	AA
Lakewood	PHi	South Atlantic League	A-	San Jose	SF	California League	A+
Lancaster	COL	California League	A+	Scranton/Wilkes-Barre	NYY	International League	AAA
Lansing	TOR	Midwest League	A-	South Bend	CHC	Midwest League	A-
Las Vegas	NYM	Pacific Coast League	AAA	Spokane	TEX	Northwest League	SS
Lehigh Valley	PHI	International League	AAA	Springfield	STL	Texas League	AA
Lexington	KC	South Atlantic League	A-	St. Lucie	NYM	Florida State League	A+
Louisville	CIN	International League	AAA	State College	STL	New York-Penn League	SS
Lowell	BOS	New York-Penn League	SS	Staten Island	NYY	New York-Penn League	SS
Lynchburg	CLE	Carolina League	A+	Stockton	OAK	California League	A+
Mahoning Valley	CLE	New York-Penn League	SS	Syracuse	WAS	International League	AAA
Memphis	STL	Pacific Coast League	AAA	Tacoma	SEA	Pacific Coast League	AAA
Midland	OAK	Texas League	AA	Tampa	NYY	Florida State League	A+
Mississippi	ATL	Southern League	AA	Tennessee	CHC	Southern League	AA
Missoula	ARI	Pioneer League	Rk	Toledo	DET	International League	AAA
Mobile	LAA	Southern League	AA	Trenton	NYY	Eastern League	AA
Modesto	SEA	California League	A+	Tri-City	HOU	New York-Penn League	SS
Montgomery	TAM	Southern League	AA	Tri-City	SD	Northwest League	SS
Myrtle Beach	CHC	Carolina League	A+	Tulsa	LAD	Texas League	AA
Nashville	OAK	Pacific Coast League	AAA	Vancouver	TOR	Northwest League	SS
New Hampshire	TOR	Eastern League	AA	Vermont	OAK	New York-Penn League	SS
New Orleans	MIA	Pacific Coast League	AAA	Visalia	ARI	California League	A+
Norfolk	BAL	International League	AAA	West Michigan	DET	Midwest League	A-
Northwest Arkansas	KC	Texas League	AA	West Virginia	PIT	New York-Penn League	SS
Ogden	LAD	Pioneer League	Rk	West Virginia	PIT	South Atlantic League	A-
Oklahoma City	LAD	Pacific Coast League	AAA	Williamsport	PHI	New York-Penn League	SS
Omaha	KC	Pacific Coast League	AAA	Wilmington	KC	Carolina League	A+
Orem	LAA	Pioneer League	Rk	Winston-Salem	CHW	Carolina League	A+
Palm Beach	STL	Florida State League	A+	Wisconsin	MIL	Midwest League	A-
Pawtucket	BOS	International League	AAA				

In-person answers to all your fantasy baseball questions.

Just in time for Draft Day.

Get ready for an unforgettable experience—BaseballHQ.com's **First Pitch Forums**. These 3+ hour events—with a new format in 2017—will be packed full of fantasy baseball talk, interactive activities and fun! The forums will come to seven cities in 2017 and help you prepare for your championship season. Top national baseball analysts disclose competitive secrets unique to 2017: Players to watch, trends to monitor, new strategies to employ and more! Plus, they answer YOUR questions as you look for the edge that will lead to a 2017 championship.

BaseballHQ.com founder Ron Shandler, along with current co-GMs Brent Hershey and Ray Murphy chair the sessions and bring a dynamic energy to every event. They are joined by experts from BaseballHQ.com as well as other sports media sources, such as ESPN.com, MLB.com, RotoWire, FanGraphs, Baseball Prospectus, Mastersball, Sirius/XM Radio and more.

PRELIMINARY* 2017
FIRST PITCH FORUMS DATES & SITES

Sat, February 25	CHICAGO
Sun, February 26	ST. LOUIS
Fri, March 3	WASHINGTON DC
Sat, March 4	NEW YORK
Sun, March 5	BOSTON
Sat, March 11	LOS ANGELES
Sun, March 12	SAN FRANCISCO

Dates are subject to change, but will be confirmed soon. PLUS—check out the link below during March for more info about our NEW online version of the program. Find complete description and details at:

www.firstpitchforums.com
Registration:
$39 per person in advance // $49 per person at the door

Plus, don't forget First Pitch Arizona: November 3-5, 2017 in Phoenix, AZ, at the Arizona Fall League!!